MARKETING STRATEGY

SECOND EDITION

MARKETING STRATEGY

SECOND EDITION

O. C. Ferrell
Colorado State University

Michael D. Hartline
Florida State University

George H. Lucas, Jr.
U.S. Learning, Inc.

HARCOURT COLLEGE PUBLISHERS

FORT WORTH   PHILADELPHIA   SAN DIEGO   NEW YORK   ORLANDO   AUSTIN
SAN ANTONIO   TORONTO   MONTREAL   LONDON   SYDNEY   TOKYO

Publisher	Mike Roche
Acquisitions Editor	Mark Orr
Developmental Editor	Jana Pitts
Marketing Strategist	Beverly Dunn
Project Manager	Elaine Hellmund

Cover image provided by PhotoDisc © 2002.

ISBN: 0-03-032103-4
Library of Congress Catalog Card Number: 2001089968

Address for Domestic Orders
Harcourt, Inc., 6277 Sea Harbor Drive, Orlando, FL 32887-6777
800-782-4479

Address for International Orders
International Customer Service
Harcourt, Inc., 6277 Sea Harbor Drive, Orlando, FL 32887-6777
407-345-3800
(fax) 407-345-4060
(e-mail) hbintl@harcourt.com

Address for Editorial Correspondence
Harcourt College Publishers, 301 Commerce Street, Suite 3700, Fort Worth, TX 76102

Web Site Address
http://www.harcourtcollege.com

Harcourt College Publishers will provide complimentary supplements or supplement packages to those adopters qualified under our adoption policy. Please contact your sales representative to learn how you qualify. If as an adopter or potential user you receive supplements you do not need, please return them to your sales representative or send them to:
Attn: Returns Department, Troy Warehouse, 465 South Lincoln Drive, Troy, MO 63379.

Printed in the United States of America

1 2 3 4 5 6 7 8 9 0   0 4 8   9 8 7 6 5 4 3 2 1

Harcourt College Publishers

To my wife, Linda
—O. C. Ferrell

To my wife, Marsha, and my daughters, Meghan, Madison, and Mallory
—Michael Hartline

To my wife, Linda, and my sons, Taylor and Austin
—George Lucas

The Harcourt Series in Marketing

Assael
Marketing

Bateson and Hoffman
Managing Services Marketing:
Text and Readings
Fourth Edition

Blackwell, Blackwell, and Talarzyk
Contemporary Cases in Consumer
Behavior
Fourth Edition

Blackwell, Miniard, and Engel
Consumer Behavior
Ninth Edition

Boone and Kurtz
Contemporary Marketing
Tenth Edition

Churchill
Basic Marketing Research
Fourth Edition

Churchill
Marketing Research: Methodological
Foundations
Eighth Edition

Clark and Allen
Marketing: Hits on the Web

Czinkota and Ronkainen
International Marketing
Sixth Edition

Czinkota and Ronkainen
International Marketing Strategy:
Environmental Assessment and
Entry Strategies

Dickson
Marketing Management
Second Edition

Dunne and Lusch
Retailing
Fourth Edition

Ferrell, Hartline, and Lucas
Marketing Strategy
Second Edition

Futrell
Sales Management: Teamwork,
Leadership, and Technology
Sixth Edition

Hoffman
Marketing: Best Practices

Hoffman and Bateson
Essentials of Services Marketing
Second Edition

Hutt and Speh
Business Marketing Management:
A Strategic View of Industrial and
Organizational Markets
Seventh Edition

Ingram, LaForge, Avila,
Schwepker, and Williams
Professional Selling: A Trust-Based
Approach

Ingram, LaForge, Avila,
Schwepker, and Williams
Sales Management: Analysis and
Decision Making
Fourth Edition

Ingram, LaForge, Avila,
Schwepker, and Williams
Selling

Lindgren and Shimp
Marketing: An Interactive
Learning System
Second Edition

Parente
Advertising Campaign Strategy:
A Guide to Marketing
Communication Plans
Second Edition

Reedy
Electronic Marketing

Rosenbloom
Marketing Channels: A Management
View
Sixth Edition

Sandburg
Discovering Your Marketing Career
CD-ROM

Schaffer
The Marketing Game

Schnaars
MICROSIM

Sheth, Mittal, and Newman
Customer Behavior: Consumer
Behavior and Beyond
Second Edition

Shimp
Advertising, Promotions, and
Supplemental Aspects of Integrated
Marketing Communications
Fifth Edition

Stauble
Marketing Strategy: A Global
Perspective

Terpstra and Sarathy
International Marketing
Eighth Edition

Watson
Electronic Commerce

Weitz and Wensley
Readings in Strategic Marketing
Analysis, Planning, and
Implementation
Second Edition

Zikmund
Essentials of Marketing Research

Zikmund
Exploring Marketing Research
Seventh Edition

Harcourt College Outline Series

Peterson
Principles of Marketing

Dr. David J. Luck is a highly respected scholar who has played an important role in the development of marketing thought. He has been our coauthor and mentor in the development of this textbook.

Dr. Luck received his Ph.D. from the University of Texas, his M.S. from the University of Pennsylvania, and a bachelor's degree from Dartmouth College in 1934. He has achieved a highly successful and visible career in marketing.

He has taught in marketing faculties at several universities—most notably Michigan State University, University of Illinois, and Southern Illinois University—and has published several books on marketing strategy and marketing research. He was a coauthor on one of the pioneering marketing research texts. His chief focus has been strategies for product development. He also has conducted marketing research for Ford Motor Company and has held consulting positions at many business firms.

His leadership in providing insight on the role of product decisions in marketing strategy contributed to the establishment of product management as an important area for research and teaching. His 1969 *Journal of Marketing* article, "Interfaces of a Product Manager," was viewed as a significant contribution to both academic research and marketing management. Dr. Luck played a critical role in the debate over broadening the concept of marketing in society. His classic reply to Philip Kotler, "Broadening the Concept of Marketing—Too Far," also published in 1969 in the *Journal of Marketing*, is still read by many marketing students who are examining the definition of marketing and the role of marketing in society. His close association with Wroe Alderson and other pioneers of the field of marketing gave him many insights into the evolution of current marketing thought. His contributions have helped shape marketing theory and practice over the past 55 years.

Dr. Luck inspired the development of this text and was a significant contributor to the first edition. His coauthors sincerely appreciate his leadership, guidance, and insights about marketing strategy. Dr. Luck is now retired and continues to have an active interest in marketing thought and continues to provide encouragement.

Marketing Strategy, second edition, provides a practical, straightforward approach to analyzing, planning, and implementing marketing strategies. Our focus is on the creative process involved in applying the knowledge and concepts of marketing to the development and implementation of marketing strategy. Integration of marketing's many decisions and coordination with other functional business areas is important to the success of both for-profit and nonprofit organizations.

Marketing Strategy provides a comprehensive framework for the development of competitive marketing strategies that achieve organizational goals and objectives and build competitive advantage. The core of our strategic market planning framework is the organization's analysis of internal strengths and weaknesses and external opportunities and threats (SWOT analysis). Our framework describes all of the activities and processes necessary to develop a marketing plan, including the implementation, evaluation, and control of a firm's marketing activities. We stress that effective marketing strategies and plans are developed in concert with the organization's mission and goals as well as plans from other functional areas. The end result of the strategic planning process is an overall strategic marketing plan that outlines the activities and resources required to fulfill the organization's mission and achieve its goals and objectives. We offer many examples of successful planning and implementation to illustrate how to capitalize on an organization's strengths and gain competitive advantage.

Purpose

We view strategic marketing planning not only as a process for achieving organizational goals, but also as a means to build long-term relationships with customers. Creating a customer orientation takes imagination, vision, and courage, especially in today's rapidly changing economic and technological environments. To help meet these challenges, this text approaches marketing strategy from both traditional and cutting-edge practices. Topics such as segmentation, creating a competitive advantage, marketing mix issues, and the implementation process are covered with a solid grounding in traditional marketing, but with an eye toward emerging practices. We also cover social, ethical, and global considerations throughout the text, as well as more specific coverage on our Web site. Recent lessons from the world of electronic commerce illustrate the importance of a balance between the traditional and emerging practices of marketing strategy. Our text never loses sight of this balance.

While our approach allows for the use of sophisticated research and decision-making processes, we have employed a practical perspective that permits marketing managers in organizations of any size to develop and implement a marketing strategy. We have avoided esoteric, abstract, and highly academic material that does not relate to typical marketing strategy decisions in most organizations. The marketing plan framework that we utilize throughout the text has been used by a number of organizations to successfully plan their marketing strategies. Many companies report great success in using our approach, partially due to the ease of communicating the plan to all functional areas of the business.

Target Audience

This text is relevant for a number of educational environments, including undergraduate, graduate, and corporate training courses. At the undergraduate level, the text is appropriate for the capstone course or any upper-level integrating course, often called "Marketing Management," "Marketing Strategy," or "Marketing Policy." At this level, this text provides an excellent framework to use with text-based cases, live-client cases, or computer simulations. At the graduate level, the text is appropriate for courses addressing strategic marketing planning or competitive marketing strategies, or as a supplement for any case- or simulation-based course. A growing segment of the market, corporate training, can utilize this text when educating business professionals who are interested in developing marketing plans of their own, or interpreting and implementing the plans of others.

Nineteen of the cases in the text were written specifically for this book and, with few exceptions, describe the strategic situations of real-world, identifiable organizations. Because these cases feature real companies, students have an opportunity to update them by conducting research to find the latest information. In addition to the cases provided in the text, instructors can customize a casebook from the available cases in the Harcourt Digital Marketing Case Library at http://www.harcourtcollege.com/marketing/mkgcase/. Many additional resources for students and instructors can be found at our text's Web site, http://www.harcourtcollege.com/marketing/ferrell/.

Key Features of the Second Edition

The key features of *Marketing Strategy*, second edition, include:

- A continued emphasis on the development of the marketing plan, including the how and why of each of its component parts. The SWOT analysis approach to marketing planning used in the text is both powerful and easy to use.

- A completely updated text, including six new chapters:

  Chapter 4: Market Segmentation, Target Marketing, and Positioning

  Chapter 5: Developing Customer Relationships Through Quality, Value, and Satisfaction

  Chapter 6: Product Strategy

  Chapter 7: Developing a Pricing Strategy

  Chapter 8: Distribution and Supply Chain Management

  Chapter 9: Integrated Marketing Communications

- A continued focus on writing a user-friendly text. Though the text has been completely revised to include six new chapters, it remains a manageable 10 chapters in length.

- A completely revised set of cases, including nine that are new to the second edition. The new cases, such as Napster, Microsoft, Papa John's Pizza, Bridgestone-Firestone, and DoubleClick, bring recent events into the classroom to increase student involvement and interest. Many cases focus on the ethical, legal, and global dimensions of marketing strategy.

- A revised set of marketing plan worksheets, provided in Appendix A. The worksheets have been updated to reflect a more concise approach to marketing plan development. However, the worksheets remain comprehensive in scope to help ensure that students and managers do not omit important issues in developing strategic marketing plans.

- New example marketing plans, provided in Appendix B. These examples illustrate the format and writing style used in creating an actual marketing plan document.

- An expanded PowerPoint package, available on CD-ROM and our Web site.

- An updated, state-of-the-art Web site to support the text and cases.

For students, the Web site provides the following:

- Online exercises for each chapter in the text

- Links to important sources of research data and information

- Online exams to help students prepare for actual course exams

- A tutorial on how to perform a case analysis

- A downloadable, electronic version of the marketing plan worksheets found in Appendix A

- Links to additional reading material not found in the text

- An online resource center containing links and information on ethical and social issues, electronic commerce, and global marketing

- Helpful information on choosing a marketing career, developing a personal marketing plan, and finding a good job

For instructors, the Web site provides the following:

- Password-protected site

- Downloadable, electronic versions of the lecture outlines, case notes, and PowerPoint slides from the Instructor's Resource Manual

- Links to additional reading material not found in the text

- An online resource center containing links and information on ethical and social issues, electronic commerce, and global marketing

Instructor's Resource Manual

The Instructor's Resource Manual for *Marketing Strategy*, second edition, is designed to assist the instructor who teaches from our text. The following teaching aids are provided in the manual:

- Chapter outlines to guide class lectures. These outlines may be used to quickly review chapter content before class or to gain an overview of the entire book. These outlines also can be downloaded from our Web site. Instructors can download the outlines and add their own personal notes and examples before class.

- Case teaching notes that provide a uniform format to help instructors evaluate the cases before use, or to assist instructors in leading case analysis and class discussion. These case notes are also available on our Web site. While there are many different approaches to using cases, the notes are designed to help instructors identify key issues and alternatives as they relate to the content of the cases and corresponding text chapters.

- Examination materials, including a test bank of twenty multiple-choice and five discussion questions per chapter.

- For those instructors who choose not to use PowerPoint, the Instructor's Resource Manual contains transparency masters taken from the PowerPoint package.

Acknowledgments

Throughout the development of this text, several extraordinary individuals provided their talent and expertise to make important contributions to the book. A number of individuals have made many useful comments and recommendations as reviewers of this text. We appreciate the generous help of these reviewers:

Linda Ferrell, *University of Northern Colorado*

Rolf Hackmann, *Western Illinois University*

Keith C. Jones, *Lynchburg College*

Ajay Menon, *Colorado State University*

Donald P. Roy, *Middle Tennessee State University*

Victoria Seitz, *California State University—San Bernardino*

Tracy A. Suter, *Oklahoma State University*

Debbie M. Thorne, *Southwest Texas State University*

Elizabeth Wilson Woodside, *Boston College*

We deeply appreciate the assistance of Jan Morgan, Colorado State University, who played a major role in organizing and refining the chapters, cases, and Instructor's Resource Manual. For their assistance in developing cases for the second edition, we thank the following individuals:

David J. Arnold, *Global Research Group*

John Fraedrich, *Southern Illinois University—Carbondale*

Nikole Haiar, *Colorado State University*

Neil Herndon, *Hofstra University*

Keith C. Jones, *Lynchburg College*

Carin-Isbael Knoop, *Global Research Group*

Jeffrey A. Krug, *University of Illinois at Urbana—Champaign*

Geoffrey Lantos, *Stonehill College*

James G. Maxham, *University of Virginia*

Donald P. Roy, *Middle Tennessee State University*

Carol A. and Linda E. Rustad, *Colorado State University*

Donald and Mike Sapit, *Sigma Press*

Dana Schubert, *Colorado State University*

Rachel Smith, *University of Memphis*

Robyn Smith, *Colorado State University*

Tracy A. Suter, *Oklahoma State University*

Jane Swoboda, *Southern Illinois University—Carbondale*

Debbie M. Thorne, *Southwest Texas State University*

Brent Wren, *University of Alabama—Huntsville*

The editorial and production staff at Harcourt cannot be thanked enough. With a deep sense of appreciation, we thank Mark Orr, acquisitions editor; Jana Pitts, developmental editor; Elaine Hellmund, project manager; Beverly Dunn, marketing manager; and Gretchen Otto from G&S Typesetters. We also would like to thank Bill Schoof on Harcourt's BRiDGe team, who was our editor on the first edition of this text and continues to provide insight and encouragement.

Finally, we express appreciation for the support and encouragement of our families and our colleagues at Colorado State University, Florida State University, Samford University, and U.S. Learning, Inc.

O. C. Ferrell, Ph.D.
Colorado State University

O. C. Ferrell (Ph.D., Louisiana State University) is chair and professor of marketing at Colorado State University. He is a past president of the Academic Council of the American Marketing Association (AMA). He chaired the American Marketing Association Ethics Committees that developed the AMA Code of Ethics and the AMA Code of Ethics for Marketing on the Internet. Dr. Ferrell is a member of the AMA advisory group for the Professional Marketers certification program. He also is a Society for Marketing Advances Fellow and an Association of Collegiate Marketing Educators Fellow. He is a member of the Board of Governors of the Academy of Marketing Science.

Dr. Ferrell has served in faculty and administrative roles at a number of universities. He was a distinguished professor of marketing and business ethics and interim dean at the University of Memphis. He was a professor of marketing at Texas A&M University, Illinois State University, and Southern Illinois University. He has been a visiting professor at the University of Michigan and University of Tampa.

Dr. Ferrell teaches marketing strategy courses at the graduate and undergraduate levels, including the capstone marketing course. He regularly teaches a course on competitive marketing strategies at Thammasat University in Bangkok, Thailand, using this text. In addition, he is the author or coauthor of fifteen books and approximately seventy academic articles. His principles of marketing and business ethics texts are the leading books in their areas.

Dr. Ferrell has extensive experience speaking for and assisting business and professional associations. He has been a major event speaker for organizations such as General Motors, Society of American Florists, Water Quality Association, and the National Bank of Commerce of Mississippi. He has served as a marketing and business ethics expert witness for a number of leading law firms throughout the United States.

Dr. Ferrell and his wife Linda live in Ft. Collins, Colorado, and they enjoy skiing, golfing, fishing, and international travel.

Michael D. Hartline, Ph.D.
Florida State University

Michael D. Hartline (Ph.D., University of Memphis) is a senior assistant professor of marketing in the College of Business at Florida State University. Prior to joining the faculty at FSU, Dr. Hartline taught at the University of Arkansas at Little Rock, Louisiana State University, and Samford University. His M.B.A. and B.S. degrees are from Jacksonville State University in Alabama.

Dr. Hartline has taught a wide variety of courses, including marketing strategy, retailing management, services marketing, electronic commerce, sports marketing, and international marketing. He has won numerous awards for teaching and research excellence and has made many presentations to industry and academic audiences. He has served as a consultant to several for-profit and nonprofit organizations in the areas of marketing plan development, market feasibility analysis, customer satisfaction measurement, employee training, and pricing policy.

Dr. Hartline's research focuses on implementation issues in service firms, especially issues related to managing customer-contact employees. His research has appeared in the *Journal of Marketing*, the *Journal of Business Research*, the *Journal of Strategic Marketing*, the *Journal of Business Ethics*, the *Journal of Services Marketing*, and the *Marketing Science Institute Working Paper Series*.

A native of Alabama, Dr. Hartline and his wife Marsha live in Tallahassee with their daughters, Meghan, Madison, and Mallory. He enjoys golfing, personal computing, college athletics, reading, and playing with his children.

George H. Lucas, Jr., Ph.D.
President, U.S. Learning, Inc.

George Lucas has spent his entire career in the customer relationship development business. After receiving his bachelor's degree from the University of Missouri, Columbia, Lucas served in field sales positions with American Hospital Supply Corporation and Pitney Bowes. He then returned to the University of Missouri to complete his M.B.A. and later his Ph.D.

Following graduate school he accepted a position on the graduate faculty of Texas A&M University's marketing department, where he served as one of the founding faculty committee members for the now internationally recognized Center for Retailing Studies. While there he also was a research fellow for the Institute for Ventures in New Technology (INVENT).

In 1987 he joined the faculty at the University of Memphis, where he served as a full professor on the graduate faculty of the Fogelman College of Business and Economics until January 1998. He now serves as president and COO of U.S. Learning, Inc., a corporate training and consulting firm with headquarters in Memphis.

Dr. Lucas is highly regarded in the fields of marketing strategy, international marketing, retailing, and personal selling. He is a business negotiations speaker, trainer, and researcher, and has published numerous articles in leading marketing and business journals. He is frequently quoted in the business sections of magazines, newspapers, and trade publications, and is a featured presenter in one of the most frequently aired cable television programs on personal selling.

Dr. Lucas lives in Memphis with his wife Linda and sons, Taylor and Austin. He enjoys golfing, fishing, and travel.

1

Strategic Marketing Planning

Introduction

To be successful, every organization requires effective planning and a marketing strategy focused on achieving its goals and objectives and satisfying customers' needs and wants. Without effective strategic marketing planning, it is unlikely that Intel will be able to develop a new processor that boosts your PC's performance, that Kellogg will be able to offer new and improved versions of its cereals, or that your school will be able to offer the courses you need to complete your education. These organizations engage in the process of strategic marketing planning to capitalize on their strengths in order to provide goods or services that satisfy your needs and wants. Every organization—from your favorite restaurant to giant global food corporations, from city, state, and federal governments to charities such as Habitat for Humanity and the American Red Cross—is involved in developing and implementing marketing strategies.

This book is about strategic marketing management, including the process of planning, organizing, implementing, and controlling marketing activities. In this book, we provide an orderly process for developing customer-oriented strategic marketing plans and strategies that match an organization with its internal and external environments. Our approach uses practical methods that reflect how this process actually occurs. We focus on real-world applications of marketing planning and the development of the marketing plan. We assume that the reader has at least some basic knowledge of marketing principles.

In this first chapter, we introduce the strategic marketing planning process. We begin by examining the overall process and defining the terms and concepts used throughout the book. Then we discuss each step in the process by considering the hierarchy of decisions that must be made in strategic marketing planning. Next we introduce the marketing plan and discuss its role and importance. Finally, we explore how customer-oriented organizations use strategic marketing planning for success. Our discussion of marketing planning continues in the appendix to this chapter, which discusses the marketing plan framework used throughout the text.

An Overview of Strategic Marketing Planning

The process of strategic marketing planning includes identifying or establishing an organizational mission, corporate strategy, marketing goals and objectives, marketing strategy, and, finally, a marketing plan. The process begins with an in-depth analysis of the organization's internal and external environments—sometimes referred to as a *situation analysis*. This analysis aids the manager in determining the organization's internal strengths and weaknesses and identifying external opportunities and threats. Based on an exhaustive examination of these relevant environmental issues, the firm next establishes its organizational mission, goals, and objectives; the corporate or business-unit strategy; functional goals and objectives; functional strategies; implementation; and evaluation and control. This process is depicted in Exhibit 1.1.

Although our emphasis in this book is on the processes and concerns necessary to develop a customer-oriented marketing strategy and marketing plan, we should stress that effective marketing strategies and plans are developed in concert with the organization's mission and goals, as well as the plans from other functional areas. Developing a marketing strategy is impossible without organizational goals/objectives and marketing goals/objectives that establish specific, intended outcomes to be attained when the strategy is executed through the marketing plan. Not having goals and objectives is similar to driving a car without knowing your destination.

To fulfill its mission and achieve its goals and objectives, an organization needs a *strategy*, a term derived from an ancient Greek word that means "art of the general." Although the term is based on the art of directing military campaigns, marketing strategies involve the selection and analysis of target markets (the group of people the organization wants to reach) and the creation and maintenance of an appropriate marketing mix (product, distribution, promotion, and price) that satisfies the needs of customers in those target markets. General Motors' Cadillac division, for example, has moved aggressively to combat the erosion of its once-dominant share of the luxury car market. Over the past 20 years, Cadillac sales dropped 48 percent as affluent car buyers migrated toward imports—BMW, Mercedes, Lexus, and Infiniti. Cadillac has countered by targeting a younger target consumer segment (the typical Cadillac owner is 65 years old) and greatly enhancing the technological sophistication of its products (with features such as satellite communication and navigation). The company also plans to change body styles dramatically from the 2000 to the 2003 model years. In the end, Cadillac hopes that these changes to their marketing strategy will woo customers away from imports.[1]

As indicated in Exhibit 1.1, planning efforts within each functional area will result in the creation of a strategic plan for each area. At the organizational level, each of these plans must be coordinated by senior management in a manner that will achieve the organization's mission, goals, and objectives. Because this text is concerned with marketing, we are interested in a particular type of functional plan— the marketing plan. A *marketing plan* is a written document that provides the blueprint or outline of the organization's marketing activities, including the implementation, evaluation, and control of marketing activities. The marketing plan serves a number of purposes, including its role as a "roadmap" for implementing the marketing strategy and achieving its objectives. It instructs employees as to their role and function in fulfilling the plan. It specifies how resources are to be allocated and

EXHIBIT 1.1   STRATEGIC MARKETING PLANNING PROCESS

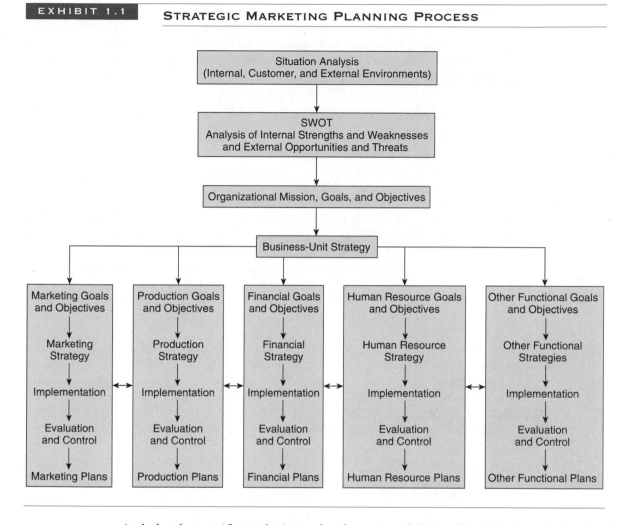

includes the specific marketing tasks, the responsibilities of individuals, and the timing of all marketing activities.

The Strategic Planning Process

As shown in Exhibit 1.1, the strategic planning process begins with an analysis of the firm's internal (organizational), customer, and external environments. This situation analysis plays a key role in strategic marketing management. As we shall see in Chapter 2, situation analysis requires a comprehensive approach toward collecting and analyzing relevant data and information. Further, the evaluation of internal strengths and weaknesses and external opportunities and threats (SWOT Analysis) is an excellent framework that is often used to structure the output of the situation analysis. We explore SWOT analysis in detail in Chapter 3.

While our focus is on marketing planning and strategy, we cannot emphasize enough that marketing decisions must be made within the boundaries of the organization's overall mission, goals, and objectives. The sequencing of decision stages outlined in this section begins with broad decisions regarding the organizational mission, followed by a discussion of the corporate or business-unit strategy. It is within these contexts that marketing goals/objectives and marketing strategies must be developed and implemented.

Organizational Mission vs. Organizational Vision

To adequately address the role of the organizational mission in strategic planning, we must first understand the subtle differences between the organization's mission and its vision. An organizational *mission*, or *mission statement*, seeks to answer the question "What business are we in?" A mission statement is a clear and concise statement (a paragraph or two at most) that explains the organization's reason for being. By contrast, an organizational *vision*, or *vision statement*, seeks to answer the question "What do we want to become?" For example, the mission of Federal Express is "to produce superior financial returns for its shareowners by providing high value-added logistics, transportation, and related information services through focused operating companies." Compare this to the company's vision: "to change the way we all connect with each other in the new Network Economy."[2] Note that an organization's vision tends to be future oriented, in that it represents where the organization is headed and where it wants to go.

If you ask many businesspeople "What is your reason for being?" their response is likely to be: "to make money." Although that may be what they are trying to accomplish, it is not their raison d'être. Profit has a role in this process, of course, but it is a goal or objective of the firm, not its mission or vision. The mission statement identifies what the firm stands for and its basic operating philosophy. Profit and other performance outcomes are "ends," and thus are out of place in, and tend to confuse, the mission statement.

All organizations, no matter how large or small, need mission statements. Sigma Marketing, for example, has only ten employees but has developed a mission statement to communicate its purpose to customers and employees:

> Sigma Marketing is a provider of custom printing and related services focused on meeting customer needs through creativity, flexibility, and on-time performance. Sigma values its partnerships with customers, suppliers, and employees, emphasizing long-term relationships and mutual trust.[3]

Large or small, short or long, all mission and value statements have one thing in common: To be successful, the mission and value statements must be supported by the organization's employees. When IBM divested its printer division to form Lexmark, the new company's senior managers understood the need to develop a strong mission and vision. However, rather than developing the mission themselves, they turned the responsibility over to Lexmark's employees. Their vision, "Customers for Life," has been the driving force behind Lexmark's growth into a $3.5 billion company.[4]

Elements of the Mission Statement   A well-devised mission statement for any organization, unit within an organization, or single-owner business should answer the same five basic questions. These questions should clarify the following for the firm's employees and for anyone else who reads the statement:

1. Who are we?

2. Who are our customers?

3. What is our operating philosophy (basic beliefs, values, ethics, etc.)?

4. What are our core competencies or competitive advantages?

5. What are our concerns and interests related to our employees, our community, social issues, and our environment?

A mission statement that delivers a clear answer to each of these questions installs the cornerstone for the rest of the marketing plan. If the cornerstone is weak, or not in line with the foundation laid in the preliminary steps, the entire plan will have no real chance of long-term success. Exhibit 1.2 outlines several mission statements considered to be among the best. As you read these statements, consider how well they answer these five questions.

The mission statement is the one portion of the strategic plan that should not be kept confidential. It should tell everyone—customers, employees, investors, competitors, regulators, and society in general—what the firm stands for and why it exists. Mission statements facilitate public relations activities and communicate to customers and others important information that can be used to build trust and long-term relationships. The mission statement should be included in annual reports and major press releases, framed on the wall in the personnel office, and possessed by every employee of the organization. Goals, objectives, strategies, budgets, tactics, and implementation plans are not for public viewing. A mission statement kept secret, however, is of little value to the firm.

Mission Width and Stability   In devising a mission statement, management should be concerned about the statement's width. If the mission is too broad, it will be meaningless to those who read and build on it. A mission to "make all people happy around the world by providing them with entertaining products" sounds splendid but provides no useful information. Overly broad missions can lead companies to establish plans and strategies in areas where their strengths are limited. Such endeavors almost always result in failure. Exxon's foray into office products, Sears' expansion into real estate and financial services, and Federal Express' problems with ZapMail all serve as reminders of the problems associated with poorly designed mission statements. While a well-designed mission statement should not stifle an organization's creativity, it must help keep the firm from moving too far from its core competencies.

Overly narrow mission statements that constrain the vision of the organization can prove just as costly. Early in the twentieth century, the railroads defined their businesses as owning and operating trains. Consequently, the railroad industry was not concerned about the invention of the airplane. After all, they thought, the ability to fly had nothing to do with trains or the railroad business. Today we know that the passenger-transportation and time-sensitive-freight businesses are dominated by firms such as American Airlines, Southwest Airlines, and Federal Express, rather than by Burlington, Union Pacific, or Santa Fe. The railroads missed this major opportunity

EXHIBIT 1.2	THE BEST MISSION STATEMENTS

In their 1995 book, Patricia Jones and Larry Kahaner identified fifty companies as possessing the very best mission statements. Several of those companies are listed here, along with their 1995 and 2000 mission statements. Remember that these mission statements were customized to fit the needs and goals of specific organizations, not to match the criteria established in this chapter.

Boeing

1995   To be the number one aerospace company in the world and among the premier industrial concerns in terms of quality, profitability, and growth.

2000   Our mission is bigger and broader than ever. It is to push not just the envelope of flight, but the entire envelope of value relating to our customers and shareholders.

Boston Beer Company

1995   We are the Boston Beer Company. We make the Best Beer in America.
We treat others as we would like to be treated ourselves.
We sell our beer with enthusiasm, energy for our jobs, and respect for our customers. As a company, we seek to add value to our customers, by providing them with a superior product at a favorable price; to our employees, by providing them with employment which encourages personal growth and pride at favorable compensations; to our investors, by providing a superior return on their investment; and to our communities, by providing taxes, charitable contributions, and community support.
Because we represent the Company at all times, we act in a manner which increases the respect of others for the Boston Beer Company and its people.
We constantly seek ways to improve our own skills and how we do our jobs.
We are committed to making Samuel Adams the largest and most respected craft or imported beer in the United States before 2006.

2000   The Company's business goal is to become the leading brewer in the Better Beer category by creating and offering high-quality full-flavored beers. With the support of a large, well-trained sales organization, the Company strives to achieve this goal by increasing brand awareness through point-of-sale, advertising, and promotional programs.

Leo Burnett

1995   The mission of the Leo Burnett Company is to create superior advertising. In Leo's words: "Our primary function in life is to produce the best advertising in the world, bar none. This is to be advertising so interrupting, so daring, so fresh, so engaging, so human, so believable, and so well focused as to themes and ideas that, at one and the same time, it builds a quality reputation for the long haul as it produces sales for the immediate present."

2000   Our Vision: To be an indispensable source of our clients' competitive advantage.
Our Mission: We will work with our clients as a community of star-reachers whose ideas build leadership brands through imagination and a sensitive and deeper understanding of human behavior.

Celestial Seasonings

1995   Our mission is to grow and dominate the U.S. specialty tea market by exceeding consumer expectations with the best-tasting, 100 percent natural hot and iced teas, packaged with Celestial art and philosophy, creating the most valued tea experience.
Through leadership, innovation, focus, and teamwork we are dedicated to continually improving value to our consumers, customers, employees, and stakeholders with a quality-first organization.

2000   We believe in creating and selling healthful, naturally oriented products that nurture people's bodies and uplift their souls. Our products must be
• superior in quality,
• of good value,
• beautifully artistic, and
• philosophically inspiring.

| EXHIBIT 1.2 | **THE BEST MISSION STATEMENTS** (*continued*) |

Our role is to play an active part in making this world a better place by unselfishly serving the public. We believe we can have a significant impact on making people's lives happier and healthier through their use of our products.

Intel Corporation

1995   Do a great job for our customers, employees, and stockholders by being the preeminent building block supplier to the computing industry.

2000   Intel's mission is to be the preeminent building block supplier to the worldwide Internet economy.

Saturn

1995   Market vehicles developed and manufactured in the United States that are world leaders in quality, cost, and customer satisfaction through the interaction of people, technology, and business systems and to transfer knowledge, technology, and experience through General Motors.

2000   Earn the loyalty of Saturn owners and grow our family by developing and marketing U.S. manufactured vehicles that are world leaders in quality, cost, and customer enthusiasm through the integration of people, technology, and business systems.

Source: Patricia Jones and Larry Kahaner, *Say It and Live It: The 50 Corporate Mission Statements That Hit the Mark* (New York: Doubleday, 1995); and the Web sites of these companies.

because their missions were too narrowly tied to railroads, as opposed to a more appropriate definition encompassing the transportation business.

Mission stability refers to the frequency of modifications in an organization's mission statement. Of all the components of the strategic plan, the mission should change least frequently. It is the one element that will likely remain constant through multiple rounds of strategic planning. Goals, objectives, and other planning elements will typically change with each new plan, usually an annual or quarterly event. When the mission changes, the cornerstone has been moved and everything else must change as well. The mission should change only when it is no longer in sync with the firm's capabilities, when competitors drive the firm from certain markets, when new technology changes the way customer benefits are delivered, or when the firm identifies a new opportunity that matches its strengths and expertise. Technological changes, for example, can substantially alter or even destroy a company's reason for being, as was the case with the railroads. In such cases, a total revision of the mission may be necessary to ensure survival. As the Internet and electronic commerce have gained increasing acceptance, many industries have been affected. For example, the importance and role of travel agents, stockbrokers, and car dealers have changed dramatically as consumers became able to compare prices and gather information much faster. Organizations in these industries, and others, have been forced to refocus their efforts by redefining their mission statements.

Customer-Focused Mission Statements   In recent years, organizations have come to realize that, in line with the marketing concept, mission statements should be customer oriented. Peoples' lives and businesses should be enriched because they have had dealings with the firm. A focus on profit in the mission statement displaces this customer orientation. A profit orientation means that something positive happens for the owners and managers of the organization, not necessarily for the customers.

Highly successful firms typically name customers as the top priority in their mission statements. For example, Amazon.com's mission is to:

"build Earth's most customer-centric company, a place where people can come to find and discover anything and everything they might want to buy online. We won't do so alone—we'll do so together with what will be thousands of partners of all sizes. We'll listen to customers, invent on their behalf, and personalize the store for each of them, all while working hard to continue to earn their trust."[5]

One of the leading reasons for the success of Southwest Airlines is its focus on customers:

The mission of Southwest Airlines is dedication to the highest quality of Customer Service delivered with a sense of warmth, friendliness, individual pride, and Company Spirit.[6]

The need for a customer-oriented mission statement was illustrated by the infamous 1982 Tylenol cyanide tragedy. After several deaths resulted from outside tampering with Tylenol capsules, the public expressed concern about the safety of the popular pain reliever. McNeilab, the subsidiary of Johnson & Johnson that markets Tylenol, made the decision to remove all Tylenol capsules from store shelves at a direct cost of $100 million. When asked about the difficulty of this decision, managers declared that the choice was obvious given Johnson & Johnson's mission statement. That statement, developed decades earlier by the firm's founders, establishes that Johnson & Johnson's primary responsibility is to the doctors, nurses, patients, parents, and children who prescribe or use the company's products. Given this responsibility, the choice for management was an easy one: Destroy any products that might harm people. If J&J's mission had been focused on profit maximization, the managers might have chosen to base their decision on probabilities and prior damage settlements. Because the mission dictated the firm's response to the crisis, Tylenol became an even more dominant player in the pain-reliever market after the tragedy. In a time of crisis, the public got a clear picture of where the firm's priorities stood. The firm received a clear reminder in the form of its mission statement, a very useful tool in such difficult times.[7]

Corporate or Business-Unit Strategy

All organizations need a corporate strategy, the central scheme or means for utilizing and integrating resources in the areas of production, finance, research and development, human resources, and marketing to carry out the organization's mission and achieve the desired goals and objectives. In the strategic planning process, issues such as competition, differentiation, diversification, coordination of business units, and environmental issues tend to emerge as corporate strategy concerns. For example, Enron, a large energy network, has led the drive for global deregulation in the electricity and natural gas industries in the hope that it can generate more competition that allows energy consumers to shop around to find the best value. If Enron's strategy is effective, and legislators seem to be moving toward deregulation, the company will have positioned itself to be able to sell energy around the globe.[8]

Larger firms often find it beneficial to devise separate strategies for each strategic business unit (SBU), or subsidiary, division, product line, or other profit center within the parent firm. Business-unit strategy determines the nature and future direction of each business unit, including its competitive advantages, the allocation of its resources, and the coordination of the functional business areas (marketing, production, finance, human resources, etc.). Sony, for example, has a number of SBUs, including Sony Music, Sony Electronics, Sony Movies, Sony Television, Sony Games, Sony Theatres, Sony Gear, and Sony Worldwide. Each of these units has its own goals, objectives, and strategies. In small businesses, corporate strategy blurs with business-unit strategy. Although we use both terms, corporate and business-unit strategy apply to all organizations, from large corporations to small businesses and nonprofit organizations.

An important consideration in selecting a corporate or business-unit strategy is the firm's capabilities. When a firm possesses capabilities that allow it to serve customers' needs better than the competition does, it is said to have a *competitive*, or *differential, advantage.* Although a number of advantages are based on functions other than marketing—such as human resources, research and development, and production—these functions often create important competitive advantages that can be exploited through marketing activities. For example, Wal-Mart's strategic investments in logistics allow the retailer to operate with lower inventory costs than its competitors—an advantage that translates into lower prices at retail.

Competitive advantages cannot be fully realized unless targeted customers see them as valuable. The key issue is the organization's ability to have customers believe that its advantages are superior to those of the competition. Wal-Mart has been able to convey effectively their low-price advantage to customers by adhering to an everyday low-price policy. The company's advertising plays on this fact by using a happy face to "roll back" prices. From logistics to happy faces, Wal-Mart provides a good example of why customer perceptions are everything when it comes to creating and maintaining competitive advantages.

Marketing Goals and Objectives

Marketing and all other business functions must support the organization's mission and goals, translating these into objectives with specific quantitative measurements. For example, a firm's goal to increase return on investment might translate into a marketing objective of a 15 percent increase in sales in the next fiscal year. Therefore, marketing objectives must be consistent with organizational goals. Marketing objectives should be expressed in clear, simple terms so that all marketing personnel understand what type and level of performance is desired. In other words, a marketing objective should be written so that its accomplishment can be measured accurately. In addition, marketing objectives should be expressed in terms of a unit of measurement, such as sales volume (in dollars or units), profitability per unit, percentage gain in market share, sales per square foot, average customer purchase, percentage of customers in the firm's target market who prefer its products, or some other measurable achievement.

Marketing objectives should be reconsidered for each planning period. Perhaps no strategy was found in the previous planning period to meet the stated objectives. Or perhaps some brilliant inspiration was found that propelled the firm beyond those objectives. In either case, realism demands that marketing objectives be revised to remain consistent with the next edition of the marketing plan. In Chapter 3, we discuss the importance and establishment of marketing goals and objectives.

Marketing Strategy

An organization's marketing strategy is designed to provide a total integration of efforts that focus on achieving the marketing objectives. The marketing strategy involves selecting one or more target markets and then developing a marketing mix (product, price, promotion, distribution) that satisfies the needs and wants of members of that target market. AutoZone, for example, targets do-it-yourself "shade tree mechanics" by offering an extensive selection of automotive replacement parts, maintenance items, and accessories at low prices. Although the marketing strategy involves selection of a target market and development of a marketing mix, these decisions are not made in a vacuum. The marketing strategy must (1) fit the needs and purposes of the selected target market, (2) be realistic given the organization's available resources and environment, and (3) be consistent with the organization's mission, goals, and objectives. Within the context of the overall strategic planning process, the marketing strategy must be evaluated to determine its effect on the organization's sales, costs, image, and profitability. In Chapters 4 through 9, we will explore specific marketing strategy decisions, including market segmentation and target marketing, developing customer relationships through quality, satisfaction, and value, and marketing mix issues.

Marketing Implementation and Control

Marketing implementation involves activities that actually execute the marketing strategy. One of the more interesting aspects of marketing strategy is that all organizations have at least two target markets: an external market (customers) and an internal market (employees). The more traditional definition of a target market refers to the external customer market. However, in order for any marketing strategy to be implemented successfully, the organization must rely on the commitment and knowledge of its employees—its internal target market. For this reason, organizations often execute internal marketing activities that are designed to ensure the implementation of external marketing activities. We discuss marketing implementation and internal marketing, as well as marketing control, in depth in Chapter 10.

Maintaining a customer focus is extremely important throughout the market planning process and particularly during implementation. The marketing concept is a widely accepted business philosophy that states that an organization should try to provide products that satisfy customers' needs through a coordinated set of activities that allow the organization to achieve its goals. One of the key aspects of the marketing concept is the coordination of activities. As a result, it is important for the marketing manager to maintain contact and to interact with other functional managers who are involved in executing the overall strategic market plan. For example, accurate and timely distribution almost always depends on accurate and timely production. By maintaining contact with the production manager, the marketing manager helps to ensure effective marketing strategy implementation (by ensuring timely production) and, in the long run, customer satisfaction. One reason that marketing implementation is often difficult to achieve is that executing a marketing strategy depends on the coordinated execution of other functional strategies (i.e., production, research, human resources, etc.).

In some ways, the evaluation-and-control phase of the planning process is an end and a beginning. On one hand, evaluation and control occur after the marketing strategy has been implemented. In fact, the implementation of any marketing strategy would be incomplete without an assessment of its success and the creation of control mechanisms to provide and revise the strategy, its implementation, or both if necessary. On the other hand, evaluation and control serve as the beginning point for the planning process in the next planning cycle. Because strategic market planning is a never-ending process, managers should have a system for monitoring and evaluating implementation outcomes on an ongoing basis. Managers use a variety of financial and planning tools to aid in the evaluation of implementation success. Likewise, managers set performance standards based on marketing objectives to control marketing activities. We discuss these issues in Chapter 10.

The Marketing Plan

The result of the strategic marketing planning process described in the first portion of this chapter is a series of plans for each functional area of the organization. For the marketing department, the marketing plan provides a detailed formulation of the actions necessary to carry out the marketing program. Think of the marketing plan as an action document—it is the handbook for marketing implementation, evaluation, and control.

A great deal of effort and organizational commitment are required to create and implement a marketing plan. In the appendix to this chapter, we discuss the structure of the typical marketing plan document (two example marketing plans are also provided in Appendix B, at the end of the book, and on the text Web site). However, there are potentially many different types of marketing plans. Marketing plans can be developed for specific products, brands, target markets, or industries. Likewise, a plan can focus on a specific element of the marketing mix, such as a product development plan, a promotional plan, a distribution plan, or a pricing plan. It is also important to realize that no matter what type of marketing plan one is developing, a marketing plan is not the same as a business plan. Business plans, while they typically contain a marketing plan, also encompass other issues, such as business organization and ownership, operations, financial strategy, human resources, and risk management. While business plans and marketing plans are not synonymous, many small businesses will consolidate their corporate, business-unit, and marketing plans into a single document.

A critical aspect of the marketing plan is its ability to communicate to other colleagues, particularly top managers. Top managers look to the marketing plan for an explanation of the elements of the marketing strategy and for a justification of needed resources, like the marketing budget.[9] The marketing plan also communicates to line managers and other employees by giving them points of reference to chart the progress of marketing implementation. A survey of marketing executives on the importance of the marketing plan revealed the following:

> The *process* of preparing the plan is more important than the document itself. . . . A marketing plan does compel attention, though. It makes the marketing team concentrate on the market, on the company's objectives, and on the strategies and tactics appropriate to those objectives. It's a mechanism for synchronizing action.[10]

Research has shown that organizations that develop formal, written strategic marketing plans tend to be more tightly integrated across functional areas, more specialized, and more decentralized in decision making. The end result of these marketing planning efforts is improved financial and market performance.[11]

Purposes and Significance of the Marketing Plan

The purposes of a marketing plan must be understood to appreciate its significance. A good marketing plan fulfills these five purposes in detail:

1. It explains both the present and future situations of the organization. This includes the environmental and SWOT analyses and the firm's past performance.

2. It specifies the outcomes that are expected (goals and objectives) so that the organization can anticipate its situation at the end of the planning period.

3. It describes the specific actions that are to take place so that the responsibility for each action can be assigned and implemented.

4. It identifies the resources that will be needed to carry out the planned actions.

5. It permits the monitoring of each action and its results so that controls may be implemented. Feedback from monitoring and control provides information to start the planning cycle again in the next timeframe.

These five purposes are very important to various persons in the firm. Line managers are particularly interested in the third purpose because they are responsible for ensuring that marketing actions are implemented. Middle-level managers have a special interest in the fifth purpose because they want to ensure that tactical changes can be made if needed. These managers must also be able to evaluate why the marketing strategy does or does not succeed.

The most pressing concern for success may lie in the fourth purpose. The marketing plan is the means of communicating the strategy to top executives who make the critical decisions regarding the productive and efficient allocation of resources. Very sound marketing plans can prove unsuccessful if implementation of the plan is not adequately funded. It is important to remember that marketing is not the only business function to compete for scarce resources. Other functions, such as finance, research and development, and human resources, have strategic plans of their own. It is in this vein that the marketing plan must sell itself to top management.

Organizational Aspects of the Marketing Plan

Who writes the marketing plan? In many organizations, the marketing plan is written by the marketing manager, brand manager, or product manager. Some organizations develop marketing plans through committees. Others will hire professional marketing consultants to write the marketing plan. However, most firms assign the responsibility for planning at the level of a marketing vice president or marketing director.[12]

The fact that most marketing plans are developed by top managers does not necessarily refute the logic of having the brand or product manager prepare the plan. However, except in small organizations where one person both develops and approves

| EXHIBIT 1.3 | MAJOR PROBLEMS IN DEVELOPING MARKETING PLANS |

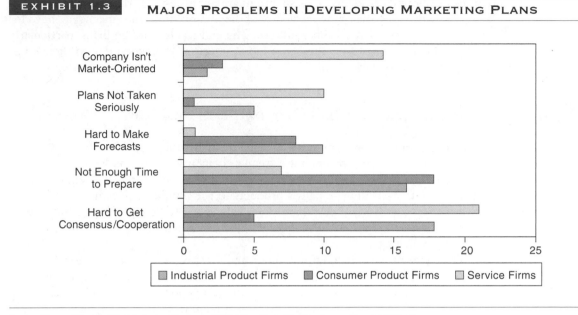

Source: Howard Sutton, *The Marketing Plan in the 1990s* (New York: The Conference Board, 1990), 61.

the plan, the authority to approve the marketing plan is typically vested with upper-level executives. At this stage, top managers usually ask two important questions:

1. Will the proposed marketing plan achieve the desired marketing, business-unit, and corporate goals and objectives?

2. Are there alternative uses of resources that would better meet corporate or business-unit objectives than the marketing plan that has been submitted?

In most cases, *final* approval actually lies with the president, chairman, or CEO of the organization.[13] Many organizations also have executive committees that evaluate and screen marketing plans before they are submitted to the approving executive. In the end, regardless of who writes the marketing plan, the plan must be clear and persuasive to win the approval of the decision makers through which it is routed. It is also critical that these individuals make efficient and timely decisions with respect to the marketing plan. To give the plan every chance for success, very little time should elapse between the completion of the plan and its implementation.

Once a marketing plan has been approved, it still faces many obstacles before its marketing programs can come to fruition. Some of these obstacles are outlined in Exhibit 1.3. One major obstacle involves the relative time horizon of the organization's key stakeholders, particularly its managers and investors. It is quite common for American firms to ignore long-range strategy and focus on short-term results, such as profit, market capitalization, or stock price. Unfortunately, many marketing activities—such as advertising to build brand awareness—produce results only in the mid- to long-term range. When the marketing plan does not produce immediate results, many firms will shift strategies "in midstream" rather than wait for results to emerge. Apple Computer, for example, has shifted its strategic focus numerous times, leading to consumer confusion about its products. Such situations are not necessarily the result of bad planning. In many cases, the reward structure of the organization leads management to focus on short-term financial consequences. The end result: Foreign firms, particularly Japanese firms, pose serious threats to most American businesses due to their long-term planning horizons.

Strategic Planning in the Market-Oriented Organization

In the past decade, many firms have changed the focus and content of their marketing plans. Of these changes, the one most frequently mentioned by marketing planners is an increased emphasis on the customer. For most firms, this change has required shifting their focus from the company's products to the unique requirements of specific target market segments. Other important changes in marketing plans include better analysis of the competition, more specific objectives and measurement, and more reasoned and realistic planning.

The cornerstone of marketing thought and practice over the last 50 years has been the marketing concept, which focuses on customer satisfaction and the achievement of the firm's objectives. Although some firms are quite good at following the marketing concept, others pay only lip service to it. Unfortunately, the marketing plan cannot realize its full potential unless the entire firm is focused on meeting customer needs. Because the emphasis in this book is on the processes and concerns necessary to develop a customer-oriented marketing strategy and marketing plan, it is important to understand this concept and how it fits into the strategic planning process.

Market-oriented firms are those that successfully generate, disseminate, and respond to market information. These firms focus on customer analysis, competitor analysis, and integrating the firm's resources to provide customer value and satisfaction as well as long-term profits.[14] To be successful, the firm must be able to focus its efforts and resources on understanding its customers in ways that enhance the firm's ability to generate sustainable competitive advantages.[15] By creating organizational cultures that put customers first, market-oriented firms tend to perform at higher levels and reap the benefits of more highly satisfied customers.

For an organization to be truly market oriented, it must take a completely different perspective on the organization and structure of the marketing function. This difference is depicted in Exhibit 1.4. A traditional marketing firm is often very authoritative, with decision-making authority emanating from the top. Frontline employees must "answer" to frontline managers, who answer to mid-level managers, who answer to top managers, etc. The market-oriented approach, however, turns this approach on its head to decentralize decision making. In this type of organization, every level of the firm is focused on serving customer needs.

In the market-oriented organization, each level "answers" to the levels above it by taking any actions necessary to ensure that it performs its job well. In this case, the role of the CEO is to ensure that his or her employees have everything they need to perform their jobs well. This "helping mentality" includes removing obstacles, providing resources, and becoming a teacher, cheerleader, and coach.[16] This same approach is carried upward through all levels of the organization, including customers. Thus, the job of a frontline manager is to ensure that frontline employees are capable and efficient. The end result of the market-oriented design is a complete focus on customer needs.

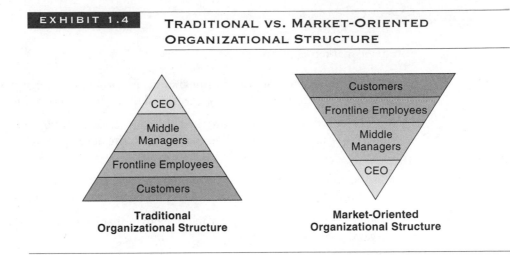

EXHIBIT 1.4 **TRADITIONAL VS. MARKET-ORIENTED ORGANIZATIONAL STRUCTURE**

Creating a market-oriented organization takes an imaginative, visionary, and courageous leader, one who is capable of relinquishing control over the organization. A market-oriented firm gives its employees the resources they need to perform their jobs, trains them well, and then trusts them to serve customers effectively. Although some managers may see the risks as being too great, the rewards can be enormous.

Moving Ahead

Now that you have a basic understanding of the strategic marketing planning process, we turn our attention to developing the marketing plan. The chapters that follow are presented in a sequence that matches the marketing plan framework discussed in the appendix to this chapter. In Chapter 2 we continue our discussion of market orientation by focusing on the generation and dissemination of market information. This includes a thorough analysis of the external environment, the customer environment, and the environment inside the organization. In Chapter 3, we discuss SWOT Analysis, a very useful framework for organizing the information obtained in the situation analysis. Our discussion of marketing strategy begins in Chapter 4, where we address market segmentation, target marketing, and positioning. While this discussion includes traditional topics, we also examine emerging segmentation approaches such as one-to-one marketing, mass customization, and permission marketing. Chapter 5 takes a closer look at managing customer relationships and includes topics such as relationship marketing, quality, satisfaction, and customer value.

The core of our discussion of the marketing mix begins in Chapter 6. There we address issues in product strategy such as core vs. supplemental products, building brand value, and services marketing. Chapter 7 discusses the role of pricing in marketing strategy, price elasticity, and legal/ethical issues in pricing. Distribution and supply chain management is the topic of Chapter 8. Here we examine issues related to customer convenience, trends in marketing channels, and order fulfillment. Chapter 9 looks at several issues related to integrated marketing communication (IMC) strategy, marketing communication, and personal selling. Finally, we discuss the critically important issues of marketing implementation and control in Chapter 10.

Lessons from Chapter 1

Strategic marketing planning:

• involves establishing an organizational mission, corporate strategy, marketing goals and objectives, marketing strategy, and ultimately, a marketing plan.

• must be coordinated with all functional business areas to ensure that the organization's goals and objectives will be considered in the development of each functional plan, one of which is the marketing plan.

• must be consistent with the organization's mission and, if appropriate to the size and complexity of the firm, with the corporate/business-unit strategy.

• establishes marketing-level goals and objectives that support the organization's mission, goals, and objectives.

• develops a marketing strategy, which includes selecting and analyzing target markets and creating and maintaining an appropriate marketing mix to satisfy the needs of customers in those target markets.

• creates a marketing plan, the written document or blueprint governing all the firm's marketing activities, including the implementation, evaluation, and control of marketing activities.

• ultimately results in a strategic market plan that outlines the activities and resources required to fulfill the organization's mission and achieve its goals and objectives.

The organizational mission:

• seeks to answer the broad question "What business are we in?"

• identifies what the firm stands for and its basic operating philosophy by answering five basic questions:

1. Who are we?

2. Who are our customers?

3. What is our operating philosophy (basic beliefs, values, ethics, etc.)?

4. What are our core competencies or competitive advantages?

5. What are our concerns and interests related to our employees, our community, social issues, and our environment?

• is not the same as the organization's vision, which seeks to answer the question "What do we want to become?"

• should not be too broad or too narrow, thereby rendering it useless for planning purposes.

• should be customer oriented. Peoples' lives and businesses should be enriched because they have had dealings with the firm.

• should never focus on profit. A profit orientation means that something positive happens for the owners and managers of the organization, not necessarily for the customers.

- must be owned and supported by employees if the organization has any chance of success.

- should not be kept secret but instead communicated to everyone—customers, employees, investors, competitors, regulators, and society in general.

- should be the least changed part of the strategic plan.

The marketing plan:

- provides a detailed formulation of the actions necessary to execute the marketing program and thus requires a great deal of effort and organizational commitment to create and implement.

- serves as an important communication vehicle to top management and to line managers and employees.

- is an important document, but not nearly as important as the knowledge gained from going through the planning process itself.

- fulfills five purposes:

  1. explains both the present and future situations of the organization.

  2. specifies the expected outcomes.

  3. describes the specific actions that are to take place and assigns responsibility for each action.

  4. identifies the resources needed to carry out the planned actions.

  5. permits the monitoring of each action and its results so that controls may be implemented.

- is most often prepared by the director or vice president of marketing, but is ultimately approved by the organization's president, chairman, or CEO.

A market-oriented organization:

- concentrates on discovering what customers want and providing it in such a way that the firm achieves its own objectives as well.

- uses relationship marketing to build long-term, mutually beneficial arrangements in which both the organization and its customers focus on value enhancement through the creation of more satisfying exchanges.

- develops an organizational culture that values the generation of and response to market intelligence.

- is typically designed so that all efforts point toward customers.

Questions for Discussion

1. In many organizations, marketing is not given a place of importance in the organizational structure or hierarchy. Why do you think this happens? What other business functions get more importance?

2. Though it can be debated, many people believe that marketing is the most important function of any organization. Other than marketing, what do you think is the most important function of an organization? Why?

3. What role should customers play in the strategic marketing planning process? Should they have a voice in developing the mission, marketing goals, or the marketing strategy?

Exercises

1. Find the mission statement of your school or place of business. Does it follow the guidelines discussed in this chapter? Are the mission and value statements separate, or are they combined? How well does the mission statement answer the five basic questions?

2. Talk with a small business owner about the planning process he or she uses. Does the business have a mission statement? Marketing goals and objectives? A marketing plan? What are the major issues he or she faces in implementing the marketing program?

3. Palo Alto Software maintains a Web site devoted to business and marketing plans. Surf to http://www.bplans.com/dp/mp/ and take a look at a few of the many sample marketing plans available.

The Marketing Plan Framework

A good marketing plan requires a great deal of information from many different sources. Your job in developing the marketing plan is to pull all of this information together in an efficient and timely manner. As you do so, it is important to constantly keep in mind "the big picture," to avoid getting caught up in the details. This requires looking at the marketing plan holistically rather than as a collection of related elements. Unfortunately, adopting a holistic perspective is rather difficult in practice. It is easy to get deeply involved in developing marketing strategy, only to discover later that the strategy is inappropriate for the organization's marketing environment. The hallmark of a well-developed marketing plan is its ability to achieve its stated goals and objectives. In this appendix, we explore the marketing plan in detail. We begin by examining the structure of a typical marketing plan.

The Structure of the Marketing Plan

Every marketing plan should be well organized to ensure that all relevant information is considered and included. The structure, or outline, of a typical marketing plan is illustrated in Appendix Exhibit 1.1. We say this outline is "typical" because there are many other ways to organize a marketing plan. In fact, marketers use many different planning approaches, with plans written for strategic business units (SBUs), product lines, individual products/brands, or specific markets. Although the actual outline used is not that important, most plans will share common elements described here. Regardless of the specific outline you use to develop a marketing plan, you should keep three goals in mind. A good marketing plan outline is:

Comprehensive: Having a comprehensive outline is essential to ensure that important information is not omitted. Of course, every element of the outline may not be pertinent to your situation. But at the least, every element is considered during the planning phase.

Flexible: While having a comprehensive outline is essential, flexibility should not be forgotten. Any outline you choose must be flexible enough to be modified to fit the unique needs of your situation. Because all situations and organizations are different, using an overly rigid outline is detrimental to the planning process.

Logical: Because the marketing plan must ultimately sell itself to top managers, the plan's outline must flow in a logical manner. An illogical outline could force top managers to reject or underfund the marketing plan.

The marketing plan structure that we examine in the remaining sections meets all three of these goals. While the structure is comprehensive, you should freely adapt the outline to match the unique requirements of your situation.

APPENDIX EXHIBIT 1.1   THE MARKETING PLAN FRAMEWORK

    I. Executive Summary
       A. Synopsis
       B. Major aspects of the marketing plan

    II. Situation and Environmental Analysis
       A. Analysis of the internal (organizational) environment
       B. Analysis of the customer environment
       C. Analysis of the external environment

    III. SWOT Analysis (strengths, weaknesses, opportunities, and threats)
       A. Strengths
       B. Weaknesses
       C. Opportunities
       D. Threats
       E. SWOT matrix analysis
       F. Matching, converting, minimizing, and avoiding strategies

    IV. Marketing Goals and Objectives
       A. Marketing goals
       B. Marketing objectives

    V. Marketing Strategies
       A. Primary target market and marketing mix
       B. Secondary target market and marketing mix

    VI. Marketing Implementation
       A. Structural issues
       B. Tactical marketing activities

    VII. Evaluation and Control
       A. Formal marketing control
       B. Informal marketing control
       C. Financial assessments

Executive Summary

The executive summary is a synopsis of the overall marketing plan, with an outline that conveys the main thrust of the marketing strategy and its execution. The purpose of the executive summary is to provide an overview of the plan so the reader can quickly identify key issues or concerns related to his or her role in the planning process. Therefore, the executive summary does not provide detailed information found in the situation or SWOT analyses or any other detailed information that supports the final plan. Instead, this synopsis introduces the major aspects of the marketing plan, including sales projections, costs, and performance evaluation measures. Along with the overall thrust of the marketing strategy, the executive summary should also identify the scope and timeframe for the plan. The idea is to give the reader a quick understanding of the breadth of the plan and its timeframe for execution.

Individuals both within and outside of the organization may read the executive summary for reasons other than marketing planning or implementation. Ultimately, many users of a marketing plan ignore some of the details because of the role they play.

The CEO, for example, may be more concerned with the overall cost and expected return of the plan and less interested in how the plan is to be implemented. Financial institutions or investment bankers may want to read the marketing plan before approving any necessary financing. Likewise, suppliers, investors, or others who have a stake in the success of the organization are sometimes given access to the marketing plan. In these cases, the executive summary is critical, for it must convey a concise overview of the plan and its objectives, costs, and returns.

Though the executive summary is the first element of a marketing plan, it should always be the last element to be prepared because it is easier (and more meaningful) to write after the entire marketing plan has been developed. There is another good reason to write the executive summary last: It may be the only element of the marketing plan that is read by a large number of people. As a result, the executive summary must accurately condense the entire marketing plan.

Situation and Environmental Analysis

The next section of the marketing plan is the situation analysis, which summarizes all pertinent information obtained about three key environments: the external environment, the customer environment, and the firm's internal (organizational) environment. Analysis of the external environment includes relevant external factors—economic, competitive, social, political/legal, and technological—that can exert considerable direct and indirect pressures on the firm's marketing activities. The analysis of the customer environment examines the current situation with respect to the needs of the target market (consumer or business-to-business), anticipated changes in these needs, and how well the firm's products are presently meeting these needs. The analysis of the firm's internal environment considers issues such as the availability and deployment of human resources, the age and capacity of equipment or technology, the availability of financial resources, and the power and political struggles within the firm's structure. In addition, this section summarizes the firm's current marketing objectives and performance.

A clear and comprehensive situation analysis is one of the most difficult parts of developing a marketing plan. This difficulty arises because the analysis must be both comprehensive and focused on key issues in order to prevent information overload—a task actually made more complicated by advances in information technology. The information for a situation analysis may be obtained internally through the firm's marketing information system or intranet, or it may have to be obtained externally through primary or secondary marketing research. Either way, the challenge is often having too much data and information to analyze rather than having too little. We will take a closer look at the process of situation analysis in Chapter 2.

SWOT Analysis (Strengths, Weaknesses, Opportunities, and Threats)

SWOT analysis focuses on the internal factors (strengths and weaknesses) and external factors (opportunities and threats)—derived from the environmental analysis in the preceding section—that give the firm certain advantages and disadvantages in satisfying the needs of its target market(s). These strengths, weaknesses, opportunities, and threats should be analyzed relative to market needs and competition. This analysis helps the company determine what it does well and where it needs to make improvements.

While SWOT analysis is not inherently difficult, it is quite common for practitioners and students to make mistakes in separating internal issues from external issues. Strengths and weaknesses are internal issues that are *unique to the firm* conducting the analysis. Opportunities and threats are external issues that *exist independent of the firm* conducting the analysis. A common mistake is to list the firm's strategic alternatives as opportunities. However, alternatives belong in the discussion of marketing strategy, not in the SWOT analysis.

SWOT analysis has gained widespread acceptance because it is a simple framework for organizing and evaluating a company's strategic position when developing a marketing plan. It provides the best framework we have been able to identify for planning. Like any straightforward framework, SWOT analysis can be misused, unless the appropriate research is conducted to identify key variables that will affect the performance of the firm. We will take a closer look at SWOT analysis in Chapter 3.

Marketing Goals and Objectives

Marketing goals and objectives are formal statements of the desired and expected outcomes resulting from the marketing plan. Goals are broad, simple statements of what is to be accomplished through the marketing strategy. The major function of goals is to guide the development of objectives and to provide direction for resource allocation decisions. Marketing objectives are more specific and are essential to planning. Marketing objectives should be stated in quantitative terms to permit reasonably precise measurement. The quantitative nature of marketing objectives makes them easier to implement after the strategy has been developed.

This section of the marketing plan is based on a careful study of the SWOT analysis and should contain objectives related to matching strengths to opportunities and/or the conversion of weaknesses or threats. It is important to remember that neither goals nor objectives can be developed without a clearly defined mission statement. Marketing goals should be consistent with the firm's mission. Likewise, marketing objectives should flow from marketing goals. We discuss marketing goals and objectives at the conclusion of SWOT analysis in Chapter 3.

Marketing Strategies

The strategy section of the marketing plan outlines how the firm will achieve its marketing objectives. In Chapter 1, we said that marketing strategies involve selecting and analyzing target markets and creating and maintaining an appropriate marketing mix (product, distribution, promotion, and price) to satisfy the needs of those target markets. It is at this level where the firm will detail how it will gain a competitive advantage by doing something better than the competition: Its products must be of higher quality than competitive offerings, its prices must be consistent with the level of quality (value), its distribution methods must be as efficient as possible, and its promotions must be more effective in communicating with target customers. It is also important that the firm attempt to make these advantages sustainable. Thus, in its broadest sense, marketing strategy refers to how the firm will manage its relationships with customers in a manner that gives it an advantage over the competition.

Developing the marketing strategy is arguably the most important part of a marketing plan. We devote over half of this text, Chapters 4–9, to discussions of target marketing, managing customer relationships, and developing the marketing mix.

Marketing Implementation

The implementation section of the marketing plan describes how the marketing strategies will be executed. Marketing implementation is the process of executing the marketing strategy by creating specific actions that will ensure that the marketing objectives are achieved. This section of the marketing plan answers several questions with respect to the marketing strategies outlined in the preceding section.

1. What specific marketing activities will be undertaken?
2. How will these activities be performed?
3. When will these activities be performed?
4. Who is responsible for the completion of these activities?
5. How will the completion of planned activities be monitored?
6. How much will these activities cost?

Without a good plan for implementation, the success of the marketing strategy is seriously jeopardized. For this reason, the implementation phase of the marketing plan is just as important as the marketing strategy phase.

Though a well-developed plan for implementation involves several considerations, the most important consideration is gaining the support of employees. It is vitally important to remember that employees, not organizations, implement marketing strategies. As a result, issues such as leadership, employee motivation, communication, and employee training are critical to implementation success. The significance of employees in marketing implementation has led many experts to label "people" as the "5th P" of marketing along with the other "4 Ps" of product, price, promotion, and place. We will explore these and many other key implementation issues in Chapter 10.

Evaluation and Control

The final section of the marketing plan details how the results of the plan will be evaluated and controlled. Marketing control involves establishing performance standards, assessing actual performance by comparing it with these standards, and, if necessary, taking corrective action to reduce discrepancies between desired and actual performance. Performance standards can be based on increases in sales volume, market share, or profitability or even advertising standards, such as brand name recognition or recall. Regardless of the standard selected, all measures of performance must be agreed upon before the results of the plan can be assessed. Internal performance data and external environmental relationships must be identified and monitored to ensure an appropriate evaluation and diagnosis before corrective actions can be taken.

The financial assessment of the marketing plan is also an important component of evaluation and control. Financial projections are based on estimates of costs, sales, and revenues. In reality, budgetary considerations play a key role in the identification of alternative strategies. The financial realities of the firm must be monitored at all times. For example, proposing to expand into new geographic areas or alter products without financial resources is a waste of time, energy, and opportunity. Even if funds are available, the strategy must be a "good value" and provide an acceptable return on investment to be a part of the final plan.

Finally, should it be determined that the marketing plan is not living up to expectations, the firm can use a number of tools to pinpoint potential causes for the discrepancies. One such tool is the *marketing audit*, a systematic examination of the firm's marketing objectives, strategy, and performance. The marketing audit can help isolate weaknesses in the marketing plan and recommend actions to help improve performance. The control phase of the planning process also outlines the actions that can be taken to reduce the differences between planned and actual performance. Because implementation and control are closely linked, we will take a closer look at the evaluation and control process in Chapter 10.

Using the Marketing Plan Framework

The marketing plan structure discussed in this chapter and illustrated in Appendix Exhibit 1.1 is also used as the outline of this text. You will note that the remaining chapters follow the logical order of the marketing plan outline. In addition, Appendix A to the text contains a set of marketing plan worksheets that enlarge the outline into a comprehensive framework for developing a marketing plan. These worksheets are designed to be *comprehensive*, *flexible*, and *logical*. While you may not use every single portion of the worksheets, at the least you should go through them in their entirety to ensure that important information is not omitted.

Appendix B to the text contains two example marketing plans. These plans were developed using the worksheets in Appendix A; hence they follow our marketing plan framework. However, you will note that these plans do not match the framework *exactly*. This is because the framework has been adapted to match the unique planning situation. You will also find additional marketing plan examples on our text's Web site.

Before we move ahead, we offer the following tips to help you in developing a marketing plan:

Plan ahead: Writing a comprehensive marketing plan is very time consuming, especially if the plan is being developed for the first time. Initially, most of your time will be spent on the situation analysis. Though this analysis is very demanding, without it the marketing plan has little chance for success.

Revise, revise, revise: After the situation analysis, you will spend most of your time revising the remaining elements of the marketing plan to ensure that they mesh with each other. Once you have written a first draft of the plan, put it away for a day or so. Then review the plan with a fresh perspective and fine-tune sections that need changing. Because the revision process always takes more time than expected, it is wise to begin the planning process far in advance of when the plan is due.

Be creative: A marketing plan is only as good as the information it contains and the effort and creativity that go into its creation. A plan that is developed half-heartedly will collect dust on the shelf.

Use common sense and judgment: Writing a marketing plan is an art. Common sense and good judgment are necessary to sort through all of the information, weed out poor strategies, and develop a sound marketing plan. Managers must always weigh any information against its accuracy, and their own intuition, when making marketing decisions.

Point toward implementation: As you develop the plan, you should always be mindful of how the plan will be implemented. Great marketing strategies that never see the light of day do little to help the organization meet its goals. Good marketing plans are those that are realistic and doable, given the organization's resources.

Update regularly: Once the marketing plan has been developed and implemented, it should be updated regularly as new data and information are collected. A good strategy is to update the marketing plan on a quarterly basis to ensure that the marketing strategy remains consistent with changes in the external, customer, and internal environments. With this approach, you will always have a working plan that covers 12 months into the future.

2

Situation and Environmental Analysis

Introduction

In this chapter, we begin the process of developing the marketing plan by examining the major elements of situation analysis and illustrating how market data can be structured to assist in the formulation of marketing strategies. Managers in all organizations, large and small, devote a major portion of their time and energy to developing plans and making decisions. Good planning and decision making require access to and analysis of data to generate usable information in a timely manner. Although situation analysis is but one of several tasks performed by marketing managers, it is perhaps the most important task, because practically all decision making and planning depend on how well the analysis is conducted.

There are many issues to be considered in a situation analysis, as outlined in Exhibit 2.1. It is important that any effort at situation analysis be well organized, systematic, and supported by sufficient resources (e.g., people, equipment, information). However, the most important aspect of the analysis is that it be an ongoing effort. Rather than taking place only in the days and weeks immediately preceding the formation of strategies and plans, the collection, creation, analysis, and dissemination of pertinent market data must be ingrained in the culture of the organization. This ongoing effort ensures that the organization is always able to assess its strengths and weaknesses accurately while simultaneously monitoring the environment to uncover any opportunities and threats. This effort drives the development of the SWOT analysis addressed in the next chapter.

In the discussion that follows, we examine several issues related to conducting a situation analysis, the components of a situation analysis, and the collection of market data and information to facilitate strategic marketing planning. Although situation analysis has traditionally been one of the most difficult aspects of market planning, recent advances in technology have made the collection of market data and information much easier and more efficient. A wealth of market data is free for the asking. This chapter examines the different types of market data that are needed for planning, as well as many sources where such data may be obtained.

EXHIBIT 2.1 **COMPONENTS OF A SITUATION ANALYSIS**

The Internal Environment

Review of current objectives, strategy, and performance
Availability of resources
Organizational culture and structure

The Customer Environment

Who are our current and potential customers?
What do customers do with our products?
Where do customers purchase our products?
When do customers purchase our products?
Why (and how) do customers select our products?
Why do potential customers not purchase our products?

The External Environment

Competitive pressures
Economic growth and stability
Political trends
Legal and regulatory issues
Changing technology
Cultural trends

Important Advice in Conducting a Situation Analysis

Before we move forward in our discussion, we offer three important pieces of advice regarding situation analysis. Our advice is aimed at helping you overcome potential problems throughout the situation analysis.

Analysis Is Not a Panacea

While it is true that a comprehensive situation analysis can lead to better planning and decision making, analysis itself is not enough. Put another way, situation analysis is a necessary, but insufficient, prerequisite for effective strategic planning. The analysis must be combined with the manager's intuition and judgment to make the results of the analysis useful for planning purposes. Situation analysis is not intended to replace the manager in the decision-making process. Its purpose is to empower the manager with information for decision making.

A thorough situation analysis empowers the marketing manager because it encourages both analysis and synthesis of information. From this perspective, situation analysis involves taking things apart—be it a customer segment, to study the heavy users; a product, to understand the relationship between its features and customers' needs; or competitors, to weigh their strengths and weaknesses against your own. The purpose of taking things apart is to understand why people, products, or organizations perform the way they do. After this dissection is complete, the manager can then synthesize the information to gain an overall "big picture" understanding of the complex decisions to be made. The result of this synthesis of information is a marketing strategy that integrates complex decisions regarding target markets and the marketing mix.

Data and Information Are Not the Same

Throughout the planning process, managers regularly face the question "How much data and information do I need?" The answer sounds simple, but in practice it is not. Today, there is no shortage of data. In fact, it is virtually impossible to know everything about a specific topic. Thankfully, the cost of collecting and storing vast amounts of data has dropped dramatically over the past decade. Computer-based marketing information systems are commonplace. Online systems, such as intranets and extranets, allow managers to retrieve data in a matter of seconds. The growth of wireless technology now gives managers access to vital data while in the field. The bottom line is that managers are more likely to be overwhelmed with data rather than face a shortage.

Now the challenge: Though data is easy to collect and store, good information is not. In simple terms, data is a collection of numbers or facts that have the potential to provide information. Data, however, does not become informative until a person or computer program transforms it or combines it with other data in a manner that makes it useful to decision makers. For example, the fact that your sales are up 10 percent is not informative until it is compared with the industry's growth rate of 40 percent. It is also important to remember that information is only as good as the data from which it comes. As the saying goes, "Garbage in, garbage out." It is a good idea to be curious about, perhaps even suspicious of, the quality of data being used for planning and decision making. We discuss issues related to data collection later in this chapter.

The Benefits Must Outweigh the Costs

Situation analysis is valuable only to the extent that it improves the quality of the resulting marketing plan. For example, data that costs $4,000 to acquire, but improves the quality of the decision by only $3,999, should not be part of the analysis process. Though the costs of acquiring data are easy to determine, the benefits of improved decisions are quite difficult to estimate. Managers must constantly ask questions such as: "Where do I have knowledge gaps?" "How can these gaps be filled?" "What are the costs of filling these gaps?" and "How much improvement in decision making will be gained by acquiring this information?" By answering such questions, managers can find a happy medium between jumping to conclusions and "paralysis by analysis," or constantly postponing a decision due to a lack of information. Perpetually analyzing data without making any decisions is usually not worth the added expense.

Components of a Situation Analysis

Situation analysis is one of the most difficult parts of developing the marketing plan. Although an organization should maintain an ongoing effort to collect and organize data about the marketing environment, managers are often faced with something less than a well-ordered flow of information. As mentioned earlier, managers have the responsibility of assessing the quality, adequacy, and timeliness of the data and information used for analysis and synthesis. The dynamic nature of internal and external environments often creates breakdowns in the effort to develop effective information flows. This dynamism can be especially troubling when the firm attempts to collect and analyze data in international environments.

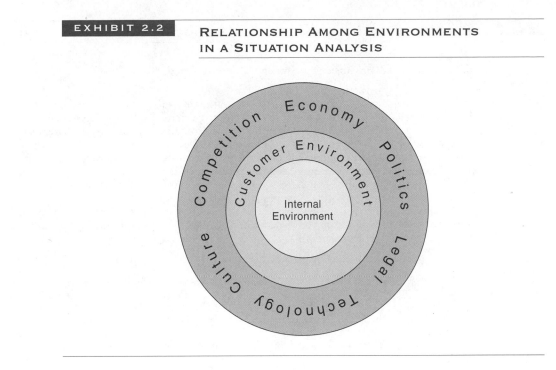

EXHIBIT 2.2 RELATIONSHIP AMONG ENVIRONMENTS IN A SITUATION ANALYSIS

The situation analysis should provide the manager with a complete picture of the organization's current and future situations with respect to three key environments: the internal environment, the customer environment, and the external environment. The relationship among these environments is shown in Exhibit 2.2. The external environment is portrayed as the outer ring because it has an effect on both the organization and its customers. To examine these three environments properly, the manager should look at both internal and external sources of data and information. As we discuss later, a great deal of this information is available through secondary sources. However, if the required data or information is not available, it may have to be collected through primary marketing research. Whatever the source, having data and information readily available makes for an easier and more comprehensive situation analysis.

The Internal Environment

The first aspect of a situation analysis involves the critical evaluation of the organization's internal environment with respect to its objectives, strategy, performance, allocation of resources, structural characteristics, and political and power struggles. A framework for analyzing the internal environment is shown in Exhibit 2.3.

Review of Current Objectives, Strategy, and Performance   First, the marketing manager must assess the organization's current marketing objectives, strategy, and performance. A periodic assessment of marketing objectives is necessary to ensure that they remain consistent with the organization's mission and the changing customer environment and external environment. It may also be necessary to reassess the organization's

EXHIBIT 2.3   A FRAMEWORK FOR ANALYZING THE INTERNAL ENVIRONMENT

1. Review of Current Marketing Objectives, Strategy, and Performance

   a. What are our current marketing goals and objectives?
   b. Are our marketing goals and objectives consistent with the mission, goals, and objectives of the firm? Are they consistent with recent changes in the customer or external environments? Why or why not?
   c. How are current marketing strategies performing in terms of sales volume, market share, profitability, and communication (e.g., awareness and preference) objectives?
   d. How does our current performance compare to that of other firms in the industry? Is the performance of the industry as a whole improving, or is it declining? Why?
   e. If our performance is declining, what is the most likely cause? Are our marketing objectives inconsistent? Is the strategy flawed? Was the strategy poorly implemented?
   f. If our performance is improving, what actions can we take to ensure that our performance continues to improve? Is the improvement in performance due to a better-than-anticipated environment or to superior planning and implementation?

2. Review of Current and Anticipated Organizational Resources

   a. What is the state of our current organizational resources (e.g., financial, human, experience, relationships with key suppliers or customers)?
   b. Are these resources likely to change for the better or for the worse in the near future?
   c. If the changes are for the better, how can we utilize these added resources to our advantage in meeting customer needs better than competitors?
   d. If the changes are for the worse, what can be done to compensate for these new constraints on our resources?

3. Review of Current and Anticipated Cultural and Structural Issues

   a. What are the positive and negative aspects of the current and anticipated culture of the firm?
   b. What issues related to internal politics and power struggles might affect our marketing activities?
   c. What is the overall position and importance of the marketing function as seen by other functional areas? Are key executive positions expected to change in the future?
   d. How will the overall market orientation of the firm (or lack thereof) affect our marketing activities?
   e. Does the firm emphasize a long-term, or a short-term planning horizon? How will this emphasis affect our marketing activities?
   f. Currently, are there any positive or negative issues with respect to motivating our employees, especially those in customer-contact positions (i.e., sales, customer service)?

marketing goals if the objectives are found to be out of date or ineffective. This analysis serves as an important input to later stages of the marketing planning process.

The marketing manager should also evaluate the performance of the current marketing strategy with respect to sales volume, market share, profitability, or other relevant measures. This analysis can take place at many levels: brand, product line, market, business unit, division, etc. It is also important to analyze the marketing strategy relative to overall industry performance. Poor or declining performance may be the result of (1) holding on to marketing goals or objectives that are inconsistent with the current realities of the customer environment or external environment, (2) a flawed marketing strategy, (3) poor implementation, or (4) changes in the customer environment or external environment that are beyond the control of the firm. The causes for poor or declining performance must be pinpointed before marketing strategies can be developed to correct the situation.

Availability of Resources   Second, the marketing manager must review the current and anticipated levels of organizational resources that can be used for marketing purposes. This review includes an analysis of financial, human, and experience resources as well as any resources the organization might hold in key relationships with supply chain partners, strategic alliance partners, or customer groups. An important element of this analysis is to gauge whether the availability or level of these resources is likely to change in the near future. Additional resources might be used to create competitive advantages in meeting customer needs. If resource levels are expected to decline, the marketing manager must find ways to compensate as he or she establishes marketing goals, objectives, and strategies for the next planning period.

Organizational Culture and Structure   Finally, the marketing manager should review current and anticipated cultural and structural issues that could affect marketing activities. One of the most important issues in this review is the internal culture of the firm. In some organizations, marketing does not hold a prominent position in the political hierarchy. This situation can create challenges for the marketing manager in acquiring resources and gaining approval of the marketing plan. The internal culture also includes any anticipated changes in key executive positions within the firm. The marketing manager, for example, could have difficulty in dealing with a new production manager who fails to see the benefits of marketing. Other structural issues to be considered include the overall market orientation of the firm (or lack thereof), employee motivation and commitment to the organization (particularly unionized employees), and the relative emphasis on long- vs. short-term planning. Top managers who are concerned only with short-term profits are unlikely to see the importance of a marketing plan that attempts to create long-term customer relationships.

For most organizations, culture and structure are relatively stable issues that do not change dramatically from one year to the next. In fact, changing or reorienting an organization's culture is a difficult and time-consuming process. In some cases, however, the culture and structure can change swiftly, causing political and power struggles within the organization. Consider the effects when two organizations combine their separate cultures and structures during a merger.

For example, the merger of Chrysler Corporation and Daimler Benz AG in a deal of so-called equals resulted in culture conflicts with the German component of the merged firms taking over most management positions. This resulted in lawsuits, open conflict, and unfairness related to ownership and management decisions. During this struggle, Chrysler sales declined as a part of the new DaimlerChrysler.[1]

The Customer Environment

In the second part of environmental analysis, the marketing manager must examine the current and future situations with respect to customers in the firm's target markets. During this analysis, information should be collected that identifies (1) the firm's current and potential customers, (2) the prevailing needs of current and potential customers, (3) the basic features of the firm's and competitors' products that are perceived as meeting customers' needs, and (4) anticipated changes in customers' needs.

In assessing the firm's target markets, the marketing manager must attempt to understand all relevant buyer behavior and product usage statistics. One method that the manager can use to collect this information is the 5W model: who, what, where, when,

| EXHIBIT 2.4 | THE EXPANDED 5W MODEL FOR CUSTOMER (TARGET MARKET) ANALYSIS |

1. Who Are Our Current and Potential Customers?

   a. What are the demographic, geographic, and psychographic characteristics of our customers?
   b. Who actually purchases our products?
   c. Do these purchasers differ from the users of our products?
   d. Who are the major influencers of the purchase decision?
   e. Who is financially responsible for making the purchase?

2. What Do Customers Do with Our Products?

   a. In what quantities and in what combinations are our products purchased?
   b. How do heavy users of our products differ from light users?
   c. Are complementary products used during the consumption of our products?
   d. What do customers do with our products after consumption?
   e. Are customers recycling our products or our packaging?

3. Where Do Customers Purchase Our Products?

   a. From what types of intermediaries are our products purchased?
   b. Does electronic commerce have an effect on the purchase of our products?
   c. Are customers increasing their purchasing from nonstore outlets, such as catalogs, home shopping networks, and the Internet?

4. When Do Customers Purchase Our Products?

   a. Are the purchase and consumption of our products seasonal?
   b. To what extent do promotional events affect the purchase and consumption of our products?
   c. Do the purchase and consumption of our products vary based on changes in physical/social surroundings, time perceptions, or the purchase task?

5. Why (and How) Do Customers Select Our Products?

   a. What are the basic features provided by our products and competitors' products?
   b. What customer needs are fulfilled by the benefits provided by our products and competitors' products?
   c. How well do our products and competitors' products meet the comprehensive set of customer needs?
   d. How are the needs of customers expected to change in the future?
   e. What methods of payment do customers use when making a purchase?
   f. Are customers prone to developing close, long-term relationships with us and our competitors, or do they buy in a transactional fashion (based primarily on price)?

6. Why Do Potential Customers Not Purchase Our Products?

   a. What are the basic needs of noncustomers that are not being met by our products?
   b. What are the features, benefits, or advantages of competing products that cause noncustomers to choose them over our products?
   c. Are there issues related to distribution, promotion, and pricing that cause customers not to purchase our products?
   d. What is the potential for converting these noncustomers to our products?

Source: Adapted from Donald R. Lehmann and Russell S. Winer, *Analysis for Market Planning* (Plano, TX: Business Publications, Inc., 1988), 89–96.

and why. We have adapted and applied this model to target market analysis, as shown in Exhibit 2.4. Organizations that are truly market oriented should know their customers well enough that they have easy access to the types of information that answer these questions. If not, the firm may have to conduct marketing research to understand fully the current situation of its target markets.

Who Are Our Current and Potential Customers?   Answering the "who" question requires an examination of the relevant characteristics that define target markets. This includes demographic characteristics (gender, age, income, occupation, education, ethnic background, family life cycle, etc.), geographic characteristics (where customers live, density of the target market, etc.), and psychographic characteristics (attitudes, opinions, interests, motives, lifestyles, etc.). Depending on the type of products sold by the firm, purchase influencers, rather than actual customers, may be important as well. In consumer markets, the influence of a spouse or children is critical for products such as cars, homes, meals, toys, and vacations. In business-to-business markets, the analysis typically focuses on the decision-making unit (DMU). Is the buying decision made by an individual or by a committee? Who has the greatest influence on the purchase decision?

The analysis must also assess the viability of potential customers or markets that may be acquired in the future. This involves looking ahead to situations that may increase the ability of the organization to gain new customers. For example, firms around the world have been anxiously awaiting the opening of the Chinese market to gain access to its 1.3 billion potential consumers. United States firms such as Procter & Gamble and 3M have established operations in China to create a presence that can be leveraged for future growth. Likewise, as Internet usage continues to grow, firms such as AOL, Amazon.com, and EarthLink are poised to convert millions of potential customers into active customers.

What Do Customers Do with Our Products?   The "what" question entails an assessment of how customers consume and dispose of the firm's products. Here the marketing manager might be interested in identifying how often products are consumed (sometimes called the *usage rate*), differences between heavy and light users of products, whether complementary products are used during consumption, and what customers do with the firm's products after consumption. In business-to-business markets, customers typically use the firm's products in the creation of their own products. As a result, business customers tend to pay very close attention to product specifications and quality.

Before customers and marketers became more concerned about the natural environment, many firms looked only at how their customers used products. Today, marketers are increasingly interested in how customers dispose of products, such as whether customers recycle the product or its packaging. Another postconsumption issue deals with the need for reverse channels of distribution to handle product repairs. Car manufacturers, for example, must maintain an elaborate network of certified repair facilities (typically their dealers) to handle maintenance and repairs under warranty. Sometimes the recycling and repair issues come into conflict. The relatively low cost of today's home electronics leads many customers to buy new VCRs and televisions rather than have old ones repaired. This causes a problem: What do consumers do with broken or obsolete electronic devices? In 2000, the state of Massachusetts implemented the first-in-the-nation ban on dumping of electronic equipment in landfills and incinerators. As a result, schools, churches, and other charities have been inundated with donations of obsolete electronics.[2]

Where Do Customers Purchase Our Products?   The "where" question is mainly one of distribution. Until recently, most firms looked solely at traditional channels of distribution, such as brokers, wholesalers, and retailers. Thus, the marketing manager would have been concerned with the intensity of the distribution effort and the types of retailers that the firm's customers patronized. Today, however, many other forms of distribution are available. The fastest-growing form of distribution today is nonstore retailing, which includes vending machines, door-to-door selling, direct marketing through catalogs or infomercials, and electronic merchandising through the Internet, interactive television, and video kiosks.[3] Business-to-business markets have also begun to capitalize on the lower costs of procurement via the Internet. Likewise, many manufacturers are bypassing traditional distribution channels in favor of selling through their own outlet stores or Web sites. Major computer manufacturers such as Dell and Gateway sell their products directly to customers via the telephone and the Internet. In the near future, most computer software will be sold over the Internet rather than through retail outlets.

When Do Customers Purchase Our Products?   The "when" question refers to any situational influences that may cause customer purchasing activity to vary over time. This includes broad issues, such as the seasonality of the firm's products and the variability in purchasing activity caused by promotional events or budgetary constraints. Everyone knows that consumer purchasing activity increases just after payday. In business markets, the "when" question is often dictated by budgetary constraints and the timing of a firm's fiscal year. For example, many schools and universities buy large quantities of supplies just before the end of their fiscal years.

The "when" question also includes more subtle influences that can affect purchasing behavior, such as physical and social surroundings, time perceptions, and the purchase task. For example, a consumer may purchase domestic beer for regular home consumption, but purchase an import or microbrew when visiting a bar (physical surroundings), going out with friends (social surroundings), or throwing a party. Customers can also vary their purchasing behavior based on the time of day or how much time they have to search for alternatives. Variation by purchase task depends on what the purchase is intended to accomplish. For example, a customer may purchase brand A for her own use, brand B for her children, and brand C when the purchase is intended as a gift.

Why (and How) Do Customers Select Our Products?   The "why" question involves identifying the basic need-satisfying benefits provided by the firm's products. The potential benefits provided by the features of competing products should also be analyzed. This question is important because customers may purchase the firm's products to fulfill needs that the firm never considered. The answer to the "why" question can also aid in identifying unsatisfied or undersatisfied customer needs. During the analysis, it is also important to identify potential changes in customers' current needs and the needs that customers may have in the future.

The "how" part of this question refers to the means of payment that customers use when making a purchase. While cash (cash, checks, and debit cards) is used for most transactions, the availability of credit makes it possible for customers to take possession of high-priced products like cars and homes. The same is true in business markets, where credit is essential to the exchange of goods and services in both domestic and international transactions. Recently, a very old form of payment has reemerged in business markets: barter. Barter involves the exchange of goods and services for other goods or services—no money changes hands. Barter arrangements are very good for small businesses that are short on cash. According to the International Reciprocal

Trade Association, over $1.5 billion in goods and services is bartered in the United States every year. This amount is expected to grow with the advent of barter networks on the Internet.[4]

Why Do Potential Customers Not Purchase Our Products?   Part of understanding why customers choose a firm's products is the realization that many potential customers choose not to purchase them. Although there are many potential reasons why customers might not purchase a firm's products, some reasons might include:

- Customers have a basic need that the product does not fulfill.
- The product does not match noncustomers' lifestyle or image.
- Competing products have better features or benefits.
- The product is too expensive for some customers.
- Noncustomers may have high switching costs.
- Noncustomers are simply unaware of the product's existence.
- Noncustomers have misconceptions about the product (poor image).
- Poor distribution makes the product hard to find.

Once the reasons for nonpurchase have been identified, the manager should make a realistic assessment of the potential for converting noncustomers into customers. For example, the introduction of low-cost computers in the late 1990s greatly increased the adoption of computers among consumers and small business owners who could not afford the latest technology. The same is true today of low-cost or free Internet access. Firms like NetZero and BlueLight have been able to convert millions of noncustomers into Internet users by providing free dial-up service in exchange for nonremovable banner ads in the browser window. Today, over 1.6 million U.S. households use a free Internet service.[5]

Once the marketing manager has analyzed the firm's current and potential customer groups, the information can be used to identify and select specific target markets for the revised marketing strategy. The firm should target those customer segments where it can create and maintain a sustainable advantage over its competition. We will discuss these aspects of marketing strategy development in Chapter 4.

The External Environment

The final and broadest issue in a situation analysis is an assessment of the external environment, which includes all the external factors—competitive, economic, political, legal/regulatory, technological, and sociocultural—that can exert considerable direct and indirect pressures on both domestic and international marketing activities. Exhibit 2.5 provides a framework for analyzing factors in the external environment. As this framework suggests, the issues involved in examining the external environment can be divided neatly into separate categories (i.e., competitive, economic, legal, etc.). However, some environmental issues fall into multiple categories.

For example, a strike by UPS employees in the 1990s created a situation that led to changes in several environmental sectors. From a competitive perspective, the strike

| EXHIBIT 2.5 | A FRAMEWORK FOR ANALYZING THE EXTERNAL ENVIRONMENT |

1. Competitive Pressures

   a. Who are our major brand, product, generic, and total budget competitors? What are their characteristics in terms of size, growth, profitability, strategies, and target markets?
   b. What are our competitors' key strengths and weaknesses?
   c. What are our competitors' key marketing capabilities in terms of products, distribution, promotion, and pricing?
   d. What response can we expect from our competitors if environmental conditions change or if we change our marketing strategy?
   e. Is this competitive set likely to change in the future? If so, how? Who are our new competitors likely to be?

2. Economic Growth and Stability

   a. What are the general economic conditions of the country, region, state, and local area in which our firm operates?
   b. Overall, are customers optimistic or pessimistic about the economy?
   c. What is the buying power of customers in our target market(s)?
   d. What are the current spending patterns of customers in our target market(s)? Are customers buying less or buying more of our product, and why?

3. Political Trends

   a. Have recent elections changed the political landscape within our domestic or international markets? What type of industry regulations do newly elected officials favor?
   b. What are we doing currently to maintain good relations with elected political officials? Have these activities been effective? Why or why not?

4. Legal and Regulatory Issues

   a. What changes in international, federal, state, or local laws and regulations are being proposed that would affect our marketing activities?
   b. Do recent court decisions suggest that we should modify our marketing activities?
   c. Do the recent rulings of federal, state, local, or self-regulatory agencies suggest that we should modify our marketing activities?
   d. What effect will changes in global trade agreements (e.g., NAFTA and WTO) have on our international marketing opportunities?

5. Changing Technology

   a. What impact has changing technology had on customers?
   b. What technological changes will affect the way we operate or manufacture our products?
   c. What technological changes will affect the way we conduct marketing activities, such as distribution and promotion?
   d. Are there any current technologies that we are not using to their fullest potential in making our marketing activities more effective and efficient?
   e. Do any technological advances threaten to make our product(s) obsolete? Does new technology have the potential to satisfy previously unmet or unknown customer needs?

6. Cultural Trends

   a. How are society's demographics and values changing? What effect will these changes have on our product(s)? pricing? distribution? promotion? people?
   b. What problems or opportunities are being created by changes in the diversity of customers and employees?
   c. What is the general attitude of society about our industry, company, and product(s)? Could we take actions to improve this attitude?
   d. What consumer or environmental groups could intervene in the operations of our industry or company?
   e. What ethical issues should we address?

handed other package delivery firms (FedEx, Airborne Express, U.S. Postal Service) a golden opportunity to increase sales and market share. However, companies that depend on UPS to deliver shipments to their customers faced a tremendous threat to their livelihood. On the economic front, the strike not only put UPS employees out of work, it also led to an economic slowdown in UPS hub cities. And it brought to a head the debate over part-time vs. full-time employment and benefits. The strike became a political issue as President Bill Clinton was continually pressured to invoke the Taft-Hartley Act to force striking UPS employees back to work. Finally, on a cultural level, many people began to debate the wisdom of being so dependent on overnight delivery services such as UPS. Although situations like the UPS strike are rare, they do illustrate how seemingly isolated events can affect many different aspects of the external marketing environment.

Competitive Pressures   In most industries, customers have choices and preferences in terms of the goods and services they can purchase. Thus, when an organization defines the target markets it will serve, it simultaneously selects a set of competing firms. The current and future actions of these competitors must be constantly monitored and hopefully even anticipated. The major problem in analyzing competing firms is one of identification. That is, how does the manager answer the question "Who are our current and future competitors?" To arrive at an answer, the manager must look beyond the obvious examples of competition. Most firms face four basic types of competition:

1. *Brand competitors*, which market products that are similar in features and benefits to the same customers at similar prices.

2. *Product competitors*, which compete in the same product class, but with products that are different in features, benefits, and price.

3. *Generic competitors*, which market very different products that solve the same problem or satisfy the same basic customer need.

4. *Total budget competitors*, which compete for the limited financial resources of the same customers.

Examples of each type of competition for selected product markets are presented in Exhibit 2.6. In the fast-growing sport utility vehicle (SUV) segment of the automobile industry, for example, Ford Explorer, Chevrolet Blazer, Toyota 4Runner, and Honda Passport are all brand competitors. However, each faces competition from other types of automobile products, such as minivans, passenger cars, and trucks. Some of this product competition even comes from within each company's own product line (e.g., Ford's Explorer, Taurus, Windstar, and F-150 pickup). And SUVs also face generic competition from Honda motorcycles, Schwinn bicycles, Hertz car rental, and public transportation—all of which offer products that satisfy the same basic customer need for transportation. Finally, customers have many alternative uses for their available dollars rather than purchasing an SUV: They can take a vacation, install a pool in the backyard, buy a boat, start an investment fund, or pay off their debt.

Though all types of competition are important, brand competitors rightfully receive the greatest attention because consumers typically see the different brands as direct substitutes for each other. For this reason, strategies aimed at getting consumers to switch brands are a major focus in any effort to beat brand competitors. For example,

| EXHIBIT 2.6 | MAJOR TYPES OF COMPETITION | | | |

	Brand Competitors	Product Competitors	Generic Competitors	Total Budget Competitors
Sport utility vehicles (need = transportation)	Ford Expedition Ford Explorer GMC Yukon	Minivans Passenger cars Trucks	Rental cars Motorcycles Bicycles	Vacations Debt reduction Remodeling
Soft drinks (need = thirst)	Coca-Cola Classic Pepsi Cola Dr. Pepper	Tea Orange juice Bottled water	Tap water	Candy Gum Potato chips
Movies (need = entertainment)	*Titanic* *American Beauty* *Star Wars*	Cable TV Pay-per-view Video rental	Athletic event Video arcade Concerts	Shopping Reading Internet
Colleges (Need = education)	Colorado State Samford Notre Dame	Trade school Community college	Correspondence school CD-ROM	New car Vacation Investments

Gatorade, far and away the dominant sports drink, has taken steps to convince Coke and Pepsi drinkers to switch. The company has introduced many new flavors, including Frost and Fierce, as well as developed a low-calorie fitness water called Propel. These changes, along with the introduction of new bottles and multipacks, have placed Gatorade squarely alongside other drink choices in supermarkets and convenience stores. Coke and Pepsi no longer thought of Gatorade as a product competitor—it was now a major player among branded competition in the soft drink market.[6] Gatorade's success resulted in Pepsi's decision to acquire Quaker Oats (owner of Gatorade) for $13.4 billion in stock.[7]

Competitive analysis has received greater attention recently, for several reasons: more intense competition from sophisticated competitors, increased competition from foreign firms, shorter product life cycles, and dynamic environments, particularly in the area of technological innovation. Growing numbers of companies are adopting formalized methods of identifying competitors, tracking their activities, and assessing their strengths and weaknesses. The core of competitive analysis involves observing, tracking, and analyzing the total range of competitive activity, including competitors' sources of supply, technological capabilities, financial strength, manufacturing capacities and qualities, marketing abilities, and target markets. Competitive analysis should progress through the following stages:

1. Identify all current and potential brand, product, generic, and total budget competitors.

2. Assess each key competitor by ascertaining its size, growth, profitability, objectives, strategies, and target markets.

3. Assess each competitor's strengths and weaknesses, including the major competencies that each possesses within its functional areas (marketing, research and development, production, human resources, etc.).

4. Focus the analysis on each competitor's marketing capabilities in terms of its products, distribution, promotion, and pricing.

5. Estimate each competitor's most likely strategies and responses under different environmental situations, as well as its reactions to the firm's own marketing efforts.

Many sources are available for gathering information on current or potential competitors. Company annual reports are useful for determining a firm's current performance and future direction. An examination of a competitor's mission statement can also provide information, particularly with respect to how the company defines itself. A thorough scan of a competitor's Web site can also uncover information—such as the mission statement, product specifications, and prices—that can greatly improve the competitive analysis. Other valuable information sources include business periodicals and trade publications that provide newsworthy tidbits about companies. There are also numerous commercial databases, such as ABI/INFORM, InfoTrac, EBSCO, Hoover's, and Moody's, that provide a wealth of information on companies and their marketing activities. The information contained in these databases can be purchased in print form, on CD-ROM, or through an online connection with a data provider such as a school or public library. We discuss data collection in more detail later in this chapter.

Economic Growth and Stability   If there is one truism about any economy, it is that it will inevitably change. Therefore, current and expected conditions in the economy can have a profound impact on marketing strategy. A thorough examination of economic factors requires marketing managers to gauge and anticipate the general economic conditions of the nation, region, state, and local area in which they operate. These general economic conditions include inflation, employment and income levels, interest rates, taxes, trade restrictions, tariffs, and the current and future stages of the business cycle (prosperity, stagnation, recession, depression, and recovery).

Equally important economic factors include consumers' overall impressions of the economy and their ability and willingness to spend. Consumer confidence (or lack thereof) can greatly affect what the firm can or cannot do in the marketplace. In times of low confidence, consumers may not be willing to pay higher prices for premium products, even if they are able to do so. In other cases, consumers may not have the ability to spend, regardless of the state of the economy. Another important factor is the current and anticipated spending patterns of consumers in the firm's target market. If consumers are buying less (or more) of the firm's products, there could be important economic reasons for the change.

One of the most important economic realities in the United States in the last 30 years is that the middle class is shrinking.[8] Upper-income consumers continue to see their wealth grow, while lower-income consumers continue to fall behind. This reality has forced many firms to seek their fortunes among upper- or lower-income families but not both.

The Gap, Inc., however, does very well by targeting all three consumer groups. The company uses a three-tiered structure to reach customers: Banana Republic competing on the upper end, the flagship Gap stores in the middle position, and Old Navy on the lower end. Other than the obvious benefits of reaching more consumers, Gap's strategy also pays off with higher sales, increased traffic, more leverage with suppliers, and a profit structure that can adapt to changing economic conditions.[9]

Political Trends   Although the importance will vary from firm to firm, most organizations should attempt to maintain good relations with elected political officials. Organizations that do business with government entities, such as defense contractors, must be especially attuned to political trends. Elected officials who are negatively disposed toward a firm or its industry are more likely to create or enforce regulations that are unfavorable for the firm. For example, the antitobacco trend in the United States made its way into politics in 1997 when the White House and Congress began to debate a proposed settlement between the tobacco companies and the attorneys general of several states. The tobacco industry faces continued legal battles today. In 2000 alone, the U.S. Justice Department won its antitrust case against Microsoft, then immediately began an antitrust trial against Visa and MasterCard.[10] The rash of high gas prices prompted Congress and the FTC to begin an investigation into possible price fixing in the Midwest.[11] As these examples show, political discussions can have serious, lasting consequences for any firm or industry.

Many managers view political factors as being beyond their control and do little more than adjust the firm's strategies to accommodate changes in those factors. Other firms, however, take a more proactive stance by seeking to influence elected officials. For example, some organizations publicly protest legislative actions, while others seek influence more discreetly by routing funds to political parties or lobbying groups. Whatever the approach, managers should always stay in touch with the political landscape.

Legal and Regulatory Issues   As you might suspect, legal and regulatory issues are closely related to events in the political environment. Numerous laws and regulations have the potential to influence marketing decisions and activities. The simple existence of these laws and regulations causes many firms to accept this influence as a predetermined aspect of market planning. For example, most organizations comply with procompetitive legislation rather than face the penalties of noncompliance. In reality, most laws and regulations are fairly vague (for instance, the Americans with Disabilities Act), often forcing firms to test the limits of certain laws by operating in a legally questionable manner. Vagueness of the law is particularly troubling for e-commerce firms, who face a number of ambiguous legal issues, such as copyright, liability, taxation, and legal jurisdiction. For reasons such as these, the marketing manager should carefully examine recent court decisions to better understand the law or regulation in question. New court interpretations can point to future changes in existing laws and regulations. The marketing manager should also examine the recent rulings of federal, state, local, and self-regulatory trade agencies to determine their effects on marketing activities.

Companies that engage in international marketing activities should also consider changes in the trade agreements between nations. The implementation of the North American Free Trade Agreement (NAFTA), for example, essentially created an open market of roughly 374 million consumers. Since NAFTA went into effect, many U.S. firms have begun, or expanded, operations in Canada and Mexico. Conversely, the emergence of the World Trade Organization (WTO) as the successor of GATT has met with some resistance. The 1999 WTO meeting in Seattle collapsed in dissension and protest in the midst of a bitter trade dispute between America and the European Union.[12]

Changing Technology   When most people think about technology, they tend to think about new high-tech products such as cellular telephones, broadband Internet access, medical breakthroughs, or interactive television. However, *technology* actually refers to the way we accomplish specific tasks or the processes we use to create the "things" we consider to be new. Of all the new technologies created in the past 30 years, none has had a greater impact on marketing than advances in computer technology and digital electronics. These technologies have changed the way consumers and employees live their daily lives and the way that marketers operate in fulfilling their needs. In some cases, changes in technology can be so profound that they make a firm's products obsolete. Vinyl long-playing (LP) records and typewriters are good examples.

Many changes in technology assume a frontstage presence in creating new marketing opportunities. By frontstage technology, we mean those advances that are most noticeable to customers. For example, products such as digital telephones, DVD, microwave ovens, and genetic engineering have spawned entirely new industries aimed at fulfilling previously unrecognized customer needs. Many frontstage technologies, such as personal digital assistants and satellite navigation systems, are aimed at increasing customer convenience. Likewise, interactive marketing via computers and digital television is poised to make substantial changes in the ways that marketers reach customers.

These and other technological changes can also assume a backstage presence when their advantages are not necessarily apparent to consumers. Advances in backstage technology can affect marketing activities by making them more efficient and effective. For example, advances in computer technology have made warehouse storage and inventory control more efficient and less expensive. Similar changes in communication technology have made field sales representatives more efficient and effective in their dealings with managers and customers. Though most customers are not aware of a firm's intranet or extranet, the combination of these technologies with the Internet is the backbone of today's e-commerce systems.

Cultural Trends   Sociocultural factors are those social and cultural influences that cause changes in attitudes, beliefs, norms, customs, and lifestyles. These forces profoundly affect the way people live and help determine what, where, how, and when customers buy a firm's products. The list of potentially important sociocultural trends is far too long to examine each one here. Examples of some of these trends are shown in Exhibit 2.7. Two of the more important trends, changes in demographics and customer values, are briefly discussed next.

There are many changes taking place in the demographic makeup of the U.S. population. For example, most of us know that the population as a whole is growing older as a result of advances in medicine and healthier lifestyles. The number of Americans age 65 and older will increase 127 percent between 2000 and 2050, from 12.6 percent of the population to 20 percent of the population.[13] As a result, marketers of health care, recreation, tourism, and retirement housing can expect large increases in demand over the next several decades. Other important changes include a decline in the teenage population, an increasing number of singles, and still greater participation of

EXHIBIT 2.7	TRENDS IN THE SOCIOCULTURAL ENVIRONMENT

Demographic Trends

Aging of the American population
Decline in the teen population (as a percentage of the total population)
Increasing number of single-member/individual households
Increasing participation of women in the workforce
Increasing number of single-parent families
Increasing population diversity, especially in the number of Hispanic Americans
Increasing legal immigration
Polarization of income levels (decline of the middle class)

Lifestyle Trends

Clothing has become more casual, especially at work
Americans have less time for leisure activities
Spending time at home is more common
Less shopping in malls, more shopping from home
Growing focus on health and nutrition
Time spent watching television has declined
Time spent using computers has increased
Still growing popularity of sport utility vehicles

Changes in Cultural Values

Less focus on "me-oriented" values
More value-oriented consumption (good quality, good price)
Importance of maintaining close, personal relationships with others
Increasing importance of family and children
Increasing concerns about the natural environment
Giving back to the community
Less tolerance of smoking in public places
More tolerance of individual lifestyle choices

women in the workforce. The increase in the number of two-income and single-parent families has, for example, led to a massive increase in demand and retail shelf space for convenient frozen entrees and meals. Our growing focus on health and nutrition has led many of the marketers of these meals to modify their products and advertising messages to get more consumers to try them.

One of the most important demographic changes taking place is the increasing diversity of the U.S. population. The number of legal immigrants coming to the United States has risen steadily during the past 30 years. By 2050, non-Hispanic whites will still be a majority, at 53 percent of the population. Shortly after 2050, however, the United States will have no true majority group.[14] These changes will create both threats and opportunities for most firms. A diverse population means a diverse customer base. Firms must alter their marketing practices, including the way they recruit and select employees, to match these changing customer segments. For example, women of color, ignored by cosmetics companies for a long time, used to have a very difficult time finding makeup in shades appropriate for their skin tones. Now virtually all cosmetics companies offer product lines designed specifically for these previously unserved markets.

Changes in our cultural values—guiding principles of everyday life—can also create problems and opportunities for marketers. Values influence our views of how to live, the decisions we make, the jobs we do, and the brands we buy.[15] In a major study of American values, researchers found that the three most important values regardless of age, gender, race, income, or region are (1) having close relationships with other people, (2) being secure and stable, and (3) having fun. In fact, despite what we often see depicted on television and in advertising, few Americans are concerned with "me-oriented" values such as power, influence, and developing themselves personally.[16] Astute marketers can use this information to reflect our prevailing values in the products they design and the advertising they create.

As you can see, the external environment encompasses a wide array of important factors that must be analyzed carefully before developing the marketing plan. Although the external environment is the largest of the three environments we have discussed, it is not necessarily the most important. Depending on the firm, its industry, and the timing, the internal and/or customer environments can be much more important in developing marketing strategy. The important point is that all three environments must be analyzed prior to developing a marketing strategy and marketing plan. Good analysis requires the collection of relevant data and information, our next topic in this chapter.

Collecting Environmental Data and Information

To perform a complete situation analysis, the marketing manager must invest time and money to collect data that is pertinent to the development of the marketing plan. This effort will always involve the collection of secondary data, which is compiled inside or outside the organization for some purpose other than the current analysis. However, if the required data or information is not available, primary data may have to be collected through marketing research. Accessing secondary data sources is usually preferable as a first option because they can be obtained more quickly and at less cost than collecting primary data. In this section, we examine the different sources of environmental data and challenges in collecting this data.

Sources of Environmental Data

There are four basic sources of secondary data: internal, government, periodicals/books, and commercial data sources. Examples of each type of data source are illustrated in Exhibit 2.8. Note that many of these data sources are available in both print and electronic forms. Let's look at the major strengths and weaknesses of these sources.

Internal Data Sources (Intranets) The organization's own records are the best source of data on current objectives, strategy, performance, and available resources. Internal sources may also be a good source of data on customer needs, attitudes, and behavior. Internal data also has the advantage of being relevant and believable, because the organization itself is responsible for its collection and organization.

One of the biggest problems with internal data is that it is often not in a form that is readily accessible to the marketing manager. Box after box of printed company

EXHIBIT 2.8   **SOURCES OF SECONDARY DATA**

The following is only a partial list of the many different sources that are available. It is not meant to be exhaustive. Because the Internet is dynamic, some of the Web addresses shown here may have changed. Visit our Web site for up-to-date links to these and other sites.

Internal Sources
Company annual reports, balance sheets, income statements, invoices, inventory records, databases on the intranet, previous research studies. While all internal sources are proprietary, some information is available on company Web sites. Some good examples include:

- *FedEx* (http://www.fedex.com/us/about/)
- *Saturn* (http://www.saturnbp.com)
- *AutoZone* (http://www.autozone.com/aboutUs/Investors/Investors.html)
- *Nissan* (http://global.nissan.co.jp/index_e.html)
- *Napster* (http://www.napster.com/company)
- *Papa John's* (http://www.papajohns.com/investor/index.htm)
- *DoubleClick* (http://ir.doubleclick.net)

Government Sources
U.S. government data sources are too numerous to provide a complete listing. Some of the best sources include:

Bureau of the Census (http://www.census.gov) provides raw data on practically every imaginable demographic, economic, or social aspect of U.S. business and society in general. Some of the best Census Bureau sources include:

- *Statistical Abstract of the United States* (http://www.census.gov/statab/www/)
- *Economic Census* (http://www.census.gov/epcd/www/econ97.html), including the Census of Retail Trade, and the Census of Wholesale Trade

U.S. Industry and Trade Outlook (http://www.ita.doc.gov/td/industry/otea/outlook/index.html) provides projections on production, sales, employment, shipments, etc., all by industry.

Federal Trade Commission (http://www.ftc.gov) provides reports, speeches, and other facts about competitive, antitrust, and consumer protection issues.

FedWorld (http://www.fedworld.gov) offers links to various federal government sources of industry and market statistics.

Edgar Database (http://www.sec.gov/edgarhp.htm) provides comprehensive financial data (10K reports) on public corporations in the United States.

Small Business Administration (http://www.sba.gov) offers numerous resources for small businesses, including industry reports, maps, market analyses (national, regional, or local), library resources, and checklists.

Chambers of Commerce (http://chamber-of-commerce.com) supplies demographic information on consumers and businesses within selected geographical areas.

U.S. International Trade Commission (http://www.usitc.gov) investigates and publishes reports on U.S. industries and the global trends that affect them. The agency also updates and publishes the Harmonized Tariff Schedule of the United States.

International Trade Administration (http://www.ita.doc.gov), a branch of the Department of Commerce, provides information to help U.S. businesses participate fully in the global marketplace.

Periodicals and Books
The examples listed below are excellent sources of business and marketing information. Many sources are available in both print and electronic formats. Although some sources are free and available on the Internet, most require paid subscriptions. Many local libraries, particularly university libraries, subscribe to these information services.

Business Periodicals Index maintains a listing of business-related articles that appear in a vast array of publications. Online versions found in libraries often contain short abstracts of each article. The index is updated monthly.

Moody's Manuals (http://www.moodys.com) and *Hoover's Manuals* (http://www.hoovers.com) both provide basic information about major corporations, including industry and company overviews and analyses.

Standard and Poor's Industry Surveys (http://www.compustat.com) offers in-depth analyses and current statistics about major industries and corporations.

Trade associations, trade magazines, and trade journals offer information on their membership and readers, as well as articles on competing products and companies. Some of the better examples include:

EXHIBIT 2.8 **SOURCES OF SECONDARY DATA** *(continued)*

- *American Marketing Association* (http://www.ama.org)
- *Sales and Marketing Executives* (http://www.smei.org)
- *Advertising Age* (http://www.adage.com)
- *Adweek* (http://www.adweek.com)
- *Chain Store Age* (http://www.chainstoreage.com)
- *Progressive Grocer* (http://www.progressivegrocer.com)
- *Sales and Marketing Management* (http://www.salesandmarketing.com)

Encyclopedia of Associations, available on CD-ROM, provides information on 140,000 major professional and trade organizations around the world.

American Demographics (http://www.demographics.com) provides articles, links to other databases, and tips for finding marketing information.

Fast Company (http://www.fastcompany.com) provides information on state-of-the-art business concepts, business trends, executive profiles, and cases studies.

Business 2.0 (http://www.business2.com) provides in-depth coverage on e-commerce, high-tech firms, and other items of interest related to the "new economy."

Academic journals, such as the *Journal of Marketing* (http://www.ama.org/pubs) and the *Harvard Business Review* (http://www.hbsp.harvard.edu/groups/hbr/index.html).

General business magazines offer a wealth of information on a wide variety of industries and companies. The information tends to focus on newsworthy items about specific industries and companies. Some widely read examples include:

- *The Wall Street Journal* (http://www.wsj.com)
- *Fortune* (http://www.fortune.com)
- *Inc. Magazine* (http://www.inc.com)
- *Business Week* (http://www.businessweek.com)
- *Forbes* (http://www.forbes.com)

Business news sources provide the latest information related to business and financial news. Some examples include:

- *Bloomberg* (http://www.bloomberg.com) provides business trends, financial news, regional business reports, and business briefs in many different languages.
- *Yahoo! Events* (http://www.broadcast.com/Business_and_Finance) offers real-time audio and video events on a wide variety of topics. Also offers online chat sessions.
- *NewsDirectory.com* (http://www.newsdirectory.com) is a great way to browse local, national, and international newspapers and magazines.
- *BizJournals.com* (http://bizjournals.com) offers news from a variety of local and regional business journals.

Commercial (Fee-Based) Sources

Commercial sources generally charge a fee for their services. However, much of their data and information is invaluable to many companies, particularly packaged goods firms. Some commercial sources provide limited information on their Web sites.

- *A. C. Nielsen Company* (http://www.acnielsen.com) supplies data and reports on retail sales of products and brands through the use of scanner technology. The company also provides data on television and magazine audiences.
- *Information Resources, Inc.* (http://www.infores.com) is second only to Nielsen as a marketing research firm. IRI specializes in supermarket scanner data and the impact of promotions on sales of brands and products in supermarkets.
- *Mediamark Research, Inc.* (http://www.mediamark.com/) provides a wealth of data on television markets and selected industries through annual reports that focus on customer demographics and brand preferences.

Other subscription-based services sell a variety of data to interested companies. Common examples include:

- *Arbitron* (http://www.arbitron.com)
- *Dun and Bradstreet* (http://www.dnb.com)
- *Audit Bureau of Circulation* (http://www.accessabc.com)
- *Audits and Surveys* (http://www.surveys.com)

records that sit in a warehouse are hardly useful for marketing planning. To overcome this problem, many organizations maintain corporate intranets that make data easily accessible and interactive. Intranets enable employees to access internal data such as customer profiles and product inventory and to share details of their activities and projects with other company employees across the hall or around the world. Many organizations also maintain virtual private networks (VPNs) to give this same access to managers and employees in the field.[17] Intranets and VPNs provide an opportunity for companywide marketing intelligence that permits coordination and integration of efforts to achieve a true market orientation. Today, over 25 percent of all Web spending is actually for intranets—a $10.9 billion industry in and of itself.[18]

Government Sources   If it exists, the U.S. government has collected data about it. The sheer volume of available information on the economy, our population, and business activities is the major strength of most government data sources. Government sources also have the added advantages of being easily accessed and low in cost—most are free. The major drawback to government data is lack of timeliness. Although many government sources are updated annually, some are updated much less frequently (e.g., the census). As a result, some government sources may be out of date and not particularly useful for market planning purposes.

Periodicals/Book Sources   The articles and research reports that are available in periodicals and books provide a gamut of information about many organizations, industries, and nations. Forget any notion about periodicals and books appearing only in print. Today, many good sources are available only in electronic format. Timeliness is a major strength of these sources, for most are written about current environmental trends and business practices. Some sources, such as academic journals, provide detailed results of research studies that may be pertinent to the manager's planning efforts. Others, such as trade publications, focus on specific industries and the issues that characterize them. The two biggest drawbacks to periodical and book sources are information overload and lack of relevance to the specific problem at hand. That is, despite the sheer volume of information that is available, finding data or information that pertains to the manager's specific and unique situation is often like looking for that proverbial needle in a haystack.

Commercial (Fee-Based) Sources   Commercial sources are almost always relevant to a specific issue because they deal with the actual behaviors of customers in the marketplace. Firms such as Nielsen and Simmons monitor a variety of behaviors, from food purchases in grocery stores to media usage characteristics. Data can also be analyzed by specific customer segments, product category, or geography. The most obvious drawback to commercial sources is cost. Although this is not a problem for large organizations, small companies often cannot afford the expense. However, some commercial sources provide limited access to some data and information for free. Additionally, companies often find "off-the-shelf" studies less costly than conducting primary research.

A Blend of Sources   The situation analysis should always begin with an examination of secondary data sources due to their availability and low cost. Each type of secondary data has its advantages and disadvantages. For that reason, the best approach to secondary data collection is one that blends data and information from a variety of sources. However, if the needed secondary data is unavailable, out of date, inaccurate or unreliable, or irrelevant to the specific problem at hand, the manager may have little choice but to collect primary data through marketing research. Primary marketing research has the major advantages of being both relevant to the specific problem as well as trustworthy due to the control the manager has over data collection. However, primary research is extremely expensive and time consuming.

Overcoming Problems in Data Collection

Despite the best intentions, problems usually arise in collecting data and information. One of the most common problems is an incomplete or inaccurate assessment of the situation for which data is being gathered to address. After expending a great amount of effort on collecting data, the manager may be unsure of the usefulness or relevance of what has been collected. In some cases, the manager might even suffer from severe information overload. To prevent these problems from occurring, the marketing problem must be accurately and specifically defined *before* any data is collected. The problem is often caused by top managers who do not adequately explain their needs and expectations to the marketing researcher.

Another common difficulty is the expense of collecting environmental data. Although data collection does have associated costs (even if the data is free), it need not be prohibitively expensive. The key is to find alternative data collection methods or sources. For example, an excellent way for some businesses to collect data is to engage the cooperation of a local college or university. Many professors seek out marketing projects for their students as a part of course requirements. Likewise, to help overcome data collection costs, many researchers are turning to the Internet as a means of collecting both quantitative and qualitative data on customer opinions and behaviors. Online research has many unresolved challenges; however, the potential time and cost savings are attractive to most researchers.

A third issue is the time it takes to collect environmental data. Although this is certainly true with respect to primary data collection, the collection of secondary data can be quite easy and fast. Online data sources, such as those listed in Exhibit 2.8 are quite accessible. Even if the manager has no idea where to begin the search, the powerful search engines and indexes available on the Internet make it easy to find data. Online data sources have become so good at data retrieval that the real problem involves the time needed to sort through all of the available information to find something that is truly relevant.

A final challenge is finding a way to organize the vast amounts of data and information that are collected during the situation analysis. Clearly defining the marketing problem and blending different data sources are the first steps toward finding all of the pieces to the puzzle. The next step is to convert the data and information into a form that will facilitate strategy development. One method of organizing this information into a catalyst for strategy formulation is the development of a SWOT analysis, which involves classifying data and information into categories labeled strengths, weaknesses, opportunities, and threats (SWOT). This SWOT framework is the focus of our next chapter.

Lessons from Chapter 2

Situation analysis:

- is perhaps the most important task of the marketing manager because practically all decision making and planning depend on how well the analysis is conducted.

- should be an ongoing effort that is well organized, systematic, and supported by sufficient resources.

- involves analysis and synthesis to understand why people, products, and organizations perform the way they do.

- is not intended to replace the marketing manager in the decision-making process, but to empower him or her with information for decision making.

- forces managers to ask continually, "How much data and information do I need?"

- is valuable only to the extent that it improves the quality of the resulting decisions. Marketing managers must avoid "paralysis by analysis."

- should provide as complete a picture as possible about the organization's current and future situations with respect to the internal, customer, and external environments.

Analysis of the internal environment:

- includes an assessment of the firm's current goals, objectives, and performance and how well the current marketing strategy is working.

- includes a review of the current and anticipated levels of organizational resources.

- includes a review of current and anticipated cultural and structural issues that could affect marketing activities.

Analysis of the customer environment:

- examines the firm's customers in its target markets.

- can be conducted by using the expanded 5W model: Who are our current and potential customers? What do customers do with our products? Where do customers purchase our products? When do customers purchase our products? Why (and how) do customers select our products? Why do potential customers not purchase our products?

Analysis of the external environment:

- is the broadest, but necessarily the most important, issue in a situation analysis.

- surveys the competitive, economic, political, legal and regulatory, technological, and cultural factors in the firm's external environment.

Environmental data and information:

- can be collected from a wide array of internal, government, periodical, book, and commercial sources as well as primary marketing research.

- are increasingly being collected and organized through the firm's intranet or virtual private network (VPN).

- must be blended from many different sources to be the most useful for planning purposes.

Problems that can occur during data collection include:

- an incomplete or inaccurate definition of the marketing problem.

- ambiguity about the usefulness or relevance of the data that is collected.

- severe information overload.

- the expense and time associated with data collection.

- finding ways to organize the vast amount of data and information that is collected.

Questions for Discussion

1. Do you think the Internet has made it easier or more difficult to collect data and information? Why? What are the major data collection issues today as compared to the issues in the pre-Internet era?

2. Of the three major environments in a situation analysis (internal, customer, external), which do you think is the most important in a general sense? Why? What might be some situations that would make one environment more important than the others?

3. Do you think that brand competitors are always the most important type of competition? Under what circumstances would product, generic, or total budget competitors be more important?

Exercises

1. Choose a specific product that you use on a weekly basis and apply to yourself the 5W model in Exhibit 2.4: (a) Who are you? (b) What do you do with the product (consumption, storage, disposal, etc.)? (c) Where do you purchase the product? Why? (d) When do you purchase the product? Why? (e) Why and how do you select the product? (f) Why do you not purchase competing products?

2. For each factor in the external environment, identify one issue, situation, or trend that has affected your purchase or consumption behavior.

3. Review the sociocultural trends in Exhibit 2.7. What other trends could be added to the list? What trends are specific to your generation that do not apply universally to all Americans?

3

SWOT Analysis: A Framework for Developing Marketing Strategy

Introduction

The situation analysis, as discussed in Chapter 2, can generate a great deal of data and information for marketing planning. But information, in and of itself, provides little direction to managers preparing to enter the strategic planning process. If information is not structured in a meaningful way that clarifies both present and anticipated situations and provides some direction for action, analysis can become a sterile, "academic" process. This absence of structure and direction is frequently the cause of information overload. People afflicted with this planning malady have massive amounts of data and information about how things are, but they lack direction.

A widely used framework for organizing and utilizing the bits and pieces of information gained from the situation analysis is SWOT analysis (strengths and weaknesses, opportunities and threats), the focus of this chapter. A SWOT analysis encompasses both the internal and external environments of the firm. Internally, the framework addresses a firm's strengths and weaknesses on key dimensions such as financial performance and resources, human resources, production facilities and capacity, market share, customer perceptions, product quality, product availability, and organizational communication. The assessment of the external environment organizes information on the market (customers and competition), economic conditions, social trends, technology, and government regulation. When performed correctly, a SWOT analysis can drive the process of creating a sound marketing plan. SWOT analysis can be especially useful in discovering strategic advantages that can be exploited in the firm's marketing strategy. Before we look at the SWOT analysis, we first need to consider some important issues.

Important Issues in SWOT Analysis

SWOT analysis is a simple, straightforward model that provides direction and serves as a catalyst for the development of viable marketing plans. It fulfills this role by structuring the assessment of the fit between what an organization can and cannot do (strengths and weaknesses) and the environmental conditions working for and against

EXHIBIT 3.1	MAJOR BENEFITS OF SWOT ANALYSIS

Simplicity

Specialized training and technical skills are not required. The analyst needs only a comprehensive understanding of the firm and the industry within which it operates.

Lower Costs

Expensive training and, in some cases, whole planning departments can be reduced or eliminated due to SWOT's simplicity

Flexibility

An extensive marketing information system or intranet is not required to be used successfully. However, SWOT is capable of incorporating the output of any information system into its planning structure.

Integration

SWOT has the ability to integrate and synthesize diverse sources of information.

Collaboration

SWOT analysis fosters collaboration and open information exchange among the managers of different functional areas. This collaboration helps to uncover and eliminate potentially harmful disagreements and fills voids in the analysis before reaching the actual planning stage.

the firm (opportunities and threats). In fact, SWOT analysis is so simple, useful, and logical that its value in planning is often underestimated. However, this simplicity often leads to SWOT analyses that are unfocused and performed rather poorly.[1] In this section, we will explore the benefits of a SWOT analysis and discuss directives for conducting a productive analysis. As a planning tool, SWOT is not inherently productive or unproductive. Rather, the way that SWOT is used will determine whether it yields benefits for the market planning process or wastes management time.

Benefits of SWOT Analysis

The effective use of SWOT analysis delivers several key benefits to a manager as he or she creates the marketing plan, and these are outlined in Exhibit 3.1. The first benefit is simplicity. SWOT analysis requires no extensive training or technical skills to be used successfully, only an understanding of the nature of the company and the industry in which it operates. Because specialized training and skills are not necessary, the use of SWOT analysis can actually reduce the costs associated with strategic planning. As firms begin to recognize this benefit of SWOT analysis, many opt to downsize or eliminate their costly strategic planning departments. These departments are often filled with highly trained employees who have great analytical skills but little understanding of the business or industry for which they are planning.

Closely related to its simplicity is the flexibility of SWOT. It can enhance the quality of an organization's strategic planning even without extensive marketing information systems. However, when comprehensive systems are present, they can be structured to feed information directly into the SWOT framework. In addition, the presence of a comprehensive marketing information system (MIS) or intranet, though not needed, can make repeated SWOT analyses run more smoothly and efficiently.

EXHIBIT 3.2 **DIRECTIVES FOR A PRODUCTIVE SWOT ANALYSIS**

Stay Focused

A single, broad analysis leads to meaningless generalizations. Separate analyses for each product/market combination are recommended.

Search Extensively for Competitors

While major brand competitors are the most important, the analyst must not overlook product, generic, and total budget competitors.

Collaborate with Other Functional Areas

SWOT analysis promotes the sharing of information and perspective across departments. This cross-pollination of ideas allows for more creative and innovative solutions to marketing problems.

Examine Issues from the Customers' Perspective

Customers' beliefs about the firm, its products, and marketing activities are critically important in SWOT analysis. The term "customers" is broadly defined to include customers, employees, stockholders, and other relevant stakeholders.

Separate Internal Issues from External Issues

If an issue would exist even if the firm did not exist, the issue should be classified as external. Marketing options, strategies, or tactics are not the same as opportunities in SWOT analysis.

SWOT analysis allows the marketing manager to integrate and synthesize diverse information, of both a quantitative and a qualitative nature. It organizes information that is widely known as well as information that has only recently been acquired or discovered. SWOT analysis can also deal with a wide diversity of information sources. SWOT can help push the planning team toward agreement as it uncovers and flushes out potentially harmful disagreements. All of these different forms of information are inherent to, and sometimes problematic for, the strategic planning process. SWOT helps transform this information diversity from a weakness of the planning process into one of its major strengths.

A final major benefit of SWOT is its ability to foster collaboration among managers of different functional areas. By learning what their counterparts do, what they know, what they think, and how they feel, marketing managers can solve problems and fill voids in the analysis before the marketing plan is finalized. The SWOT framework provides a process that generates open information exchange in advance of the actual marketing strategy development process.

Directives for a Productive SWOT Analysis

The degree to which a firm receives the full benefits of SWOT analysis will depend on the way the framework is used. If done correctly, SWOT can be a strong catalyst for the planning process. If done haphazardly or incorrectly, it can be a great waste of time and other valuable resources. Following the simple directives listed next will help ensure that the former and not the latter takes place. These directives are outlined in Exhibit 3.2.

Stay Focused A major mistake planners often make in conducting a SWOT analysis is to complete one generic analysis for the entire organization or SBU. Such an approach tends to produce stale, meaningless generalizations that come from the tops of managers' heads or from press release files. Although this type of effort may make managers feel good and provide a quick sense of accomplishment, it does little to add to the creativity and vision of the planning process.

When we say SWOT analysis, we really mean SWOT *analyses*. In most firms, there should be a series of analyses, each focusing on a specific product/market combination. For example, a single SWOT analysis for the Chevrolet division of General Motors would not be focused enough to be meaningful. Instead, separate analyses for each brand in the division would be more appropriate (Prizm, Corvette, Malibu, Tahoe, Suburban, Venture, etc.). Such a focus enables the marketing manager to look at the specific mix of product, price, promotion, and distribution presently being used in a given market. This focus also allows the manager to analyze the specific environmental issues that are relevant to the particular product/market. Chevrolet's Suburban, for example, competes in the SUV market, where competitors continue to release new models at a staggering pace. Consequently, market planning for the Suburban should differ substantially from market planning for Chevrolet's Corvette and Prizm brands. If needed, separate product/market analyses can be combined to examine the issues that are relevant for the entire strategic business unit, and business unit analyses can be combined to create a complete SWOT for the entire organization. The only time a single SWOT would be appropriate is when an organization has only one product/market combination.

Search Extensively for Competitors Information on competitors and their activities is an important aspect of a well-focused SWOT analysis. The key is not to overlook any competitor, whether a current rival or one on the horizon. As we discussed in Chapter 2, the firm will focus most of it efforts on brand competition. As the SWOT analysis is conducted, however, the firm must watch for any current or potential direct substitutes for its products. Product, generic, and total budget competitors are important as well. Looking for all four types of competition is important because many firms and managers never look past brand competitors. While it is important for the SWOT analysis to be focused, it must not be myopic.

Even industry giants can lose sight of their potential competitors by focusing exclusively on brand competition. Kodak, for example, had always taken steps to maintain its market dominance over rivals Fuji, Konica, and Polaroid in the film industry. However, the advent of digital cameras signaled the end of the print film business and completely changed Kodak's set of competing firms. Kodak now competes with giants like Sony, Nikon, and Canon in the highly competitive digital photography market.

Collaborate with Other Functional Areas A major benefit of SWOT analysis is that it generates information and perspective that can be shared across a variety of functional areas in the organization. The SWOT process should be a powerful stimulus for communication outside normal channels. The final outcome of a properly conducted SWOT analysis should be a fusion of information from many areas. Managers in sales, advertising, production, research and development, finance, customer service, inventory control, quality control, and other areas should learn what other managers see as the firm's strengths, weaknesses, opportunities, and threats. This allows the marketing manager to come to terms with multiple perspectives before actually creating the marketing plan.

As the SWOT analyses from individual areas are combined, the marketing manager can identify opportunities for joint projects and cross-selling of the firm's products. In a large organization, the first time a SWOT is undertaken may be the initial point at which managers from some areas have ever formally communicated with each other. Such "cross-pollination" can generate a very conducive environment for creativity and innovation. Moreover, research has shown that the success of introducing a new product, especially a radically new product, is extremely dependent on the ability of different functional areas to collaborate and integrate their differing perspectives. This collaboration must occur horizontally across divisions and vertically between different levels of management.[2]

Examine Issues from the Customers' Perspective   Beyond internal performance and the resources of the firm, which are addressed in the early phases of the strength/weakness assessment, every issue in a SWOT analysis must be examined from the customers' perspective. To do this, the analyst must constantly ask questions such as:

- What do customers (and noncustomers) believe about us as a company?

- What do customers (and noncustomers) think of our product quality, customer service, price and overall value, convenience, and promotional messages in comparison to our competitors'?

- What is the relative importance of these issues, not as we see them, but as customers see them?

Marketing planners must also gauge the perceptions of each customer segment that the firm is attempting to target. For example, older banking customers, due to their reluctance to use automatic teller machines and online banking services, may have vastly different perceptions of a bank's convenience than younger customers. Each customer segment's perceptions of external issues, such as the economy and the environment, are also important. It matters little, for example, that managers think the economy is improving if customers have slowed their spending because they think the economy is weak.

Examining every issue from the customers' perspective also includes the firm's internal customers: its employees. The fact that management perceives the firm as offering competitive compensation and benefits is unimportant. The real issue is what the employees think. Employees are also a valuable source of information on strengths, weaknesses, opportunities, and threats that management may have never considered. Some employees, especially frontline employees, are closer to the customer and can offer a different perspective on what customers think and believe. For example, research indicates that employees are a valuable source of information regarding the effectiveness of a firm's advertising.[3] Other types of customers, such as brokers and investors who are involved in providing capital for the firm, should also be considered. The key is to examine every issue from the most relevant perspective. Exhibit 3.3 shows how taking the customers' perspective can help managers interpret the clichés they might develop and break them down into meaningful customer-oriented strengths and weaknesses.

Taking the customers' perspective is the centerpiece of a well-done SWOT analysis. Prior to SWOT, managers tend to see issues the way they think they are (e.g., "We offer a high-quality product"). The SWOT analysis process forces managers to change

EXHIBIT 3.3	BREAKING DOWN COMMON MANAGERIAL CLICHÉS INTO POTENTIAL STRENGTHS AND WEAKNESSES

Cliché	Potential Strengths	Potential Weaknesses
"We are an old, established firm"	Stable after-sales service Experienced Trustworthy	Old-fashioned Inflexible No innovation
"We are a large supplier"	Comprehensive product line Technical expertise Stable supplier High status	Bureaucratic Deals only with large accounts Impersonal
"We have a comprehensive product line"	Wide variety Single-source supplier Convenient	Shallow assortment Limited expertise in specific products
"We are the industry standard"	Wide product adoption High status and image Good marketing leverage	Vulnerable to changes in technology Limited view of potential competition

Source: Adapted from Nigel Piercy, *Market-Led Strategic Change* (Oxford, UK: Butterworth-Heineman, Ltd., 1992), 261.

their perceptions to the way customers and other important groups see things (e.g., "The product is really overpriced, given the features and benefits it offers, in comparison to the strongest brand competitor"). The contrast between these two perspectives often leads to the identification of a gap between management's version of reality and customers' perceptions. Managers must determine if it is realistic for the firm to be seen as they see it.

Separate Internal Issues from External Issues   In any SWOT analysis, it is important to keep the internal issues separate from the external issues. Internal issues are the firm's strengths and weaknesses, while external issues refer to opportunities and threats in the firm's external environments. The key test to differentiate a strength or weakness from an opportunity or threat is to ask, "Would this issue exist if the firm did not exist?" If the answer is yes, the issue should be classified as external.

At first glance, the distinction between internal and external issues seems simplistic and immaterial. However, failure to understand the difference between internal and external issues is one of the major reasons for a poorly conducted SWOT analysis. This happens because managers tend to get ahead of themselves and list their marketing options as opportunities. However, options are not the same as opportunities in the SWOT framework. Opportunities (and threats) exist independent of the firm and are associated with characteristics or situations present in the economic, customer, cultural, technological, political, or legal environments. A manager's options, strategies, or tactics should be based on what the firm intends to do about its opportunities and threats relative to its own strengths and weaknesses.

In summary, the SWOT analysis should be directed by Socrates' advice: "Know thyself." This knowledge should be realistic, and it must be as customers (external and internal) and other key groups see the company. If managers find it difficult to make an honest and realistic assessment of these issues, they should recognize the need to bring in outside experts/consultants to oversee the process. As you have seen from this discussion, we would expand Socrates' advice to include "Know thy customer," "Know thy competitors," and in general, "Know thy environment." We will look further at these issues in the next section as we explore the elements of the SWOT framework.

The Elements of SWOT Analysis

The situation analysis discussed in Chapter 2 serves the important role of identifying the key factors that should be tracked by the firm and organizing them within a system that will monitor and distribute information on these factors on an ongoing basis. This process feeds into and helps define the boundaries of the SWOT analysis that will be used as a catalyst for the development of the firm's marketing plan. The role of SWOT analysis is to take the information from the situation analysis and separate it into internal issues (strengths and weaknesses) and external issues (opportunities and threats). Once this is done, SWOT analysis determines if the information indicates something that will assist the firm in accomplishing its objectives (a strength or opportunity) or if it is indicative of an obstacle that must be overcome or minimized to achieve desired outcomes (weakness or threat).

The issues that can be considered in a SWOT analysis are numerous and will vary depending on the particular firm or industry being analyzed. To aid your search for relevant issues, we have provided a list of potential strengths, weaknesses, opportunities, and threats in Exhibit 3.4. The items in this list are meant to illustrate some potential issues to be considered in a SWOT analysis. Our role here is not to reiterate issues from the situation analysis, but instead to cast them in a new light. In the next few sections, we will look at how the information from the situation analysis can be structured in the SWOT framework.

Strengths and Weaknesses

Relative to market needs and competitors' characteristics, the marketing manager must begin to think in terms of what the firm can do well and where it may have deficiencies. Strengths and weaknesses exist inside the firm or in key relationships between the firm and its customers or other organizations (supply chain partners, suppliers, alliances, etc.). Given that SWOT analysis must be customer focused to gain maximum benefit, a strength is really meaningful only when it is useful in satisfying a customer need. When this is the case, that strength becomes a capability.[4] The marketing manager can then develop marketing strategies that leverage these capabilities in the form of strategic competitive advantages. At the same time, the manager can develop strategies to overcome the firm's weaknesses or find ways to minimize the negative effects of these weaknesses. In the sections that follow, we look at examples of how firms develop marketing strategy around their strengths and weaknesses.

Size and Financial Resources   When it comes to size, General Motors is the undisputed king of the automotive world. The company sells billions of dollars worth of cars, trucks, and vans every year—almost 9 million vehicles worldwide.[5] Plus, its network of over 8,000 dealerships means that customers can find a GM product in their own backyard. Unfortunately, the sheer size of GM creates a number of problems. First, the automaker is not known for keeping up with customer preferences or being

EXHIBIT 3.4   **POTENTIAL ISSUES TO CONSIDER IN A SWOT ANALYSIS**

Potential Internal Strengths

- Abundant financial resources
- Well-known brand name
- #1 ranking in the industry
- Economies of scale
- Proprietary technology
- Patented processes
- Lower costs (raw materials or <u>processes</u>) *DIST*
- Respected company/product/brand image
- Superior management talent
- Better marketing skills
- Superior product quality
- Alliances with other firms
- Good distribution skills
- Committed employees

Potential Internal Weaknesses

- Lack of strategic direction
- Limited financial resources
- Weak spending on R&D
- Very narrow product line
- Limited distribution *One way*
- Higher costs (raw materials or processes) *Mkts.*
- Out-of-date products or technology
- Internal operating problems
- Internal political problems
- Weak market image
- Poor marketing skills
- Alliances with weak firms
- Limited management skills
- Undertrained employees

· One offering

Potential External Opportunities

- Rapid market growth
- Rival firms are complacent
- Changing customer needs/tastes *health con.*
- Opening of foreign markets
- Mishap of a rival firm
- New uses for product discovered
- Economic boom
- Government deregulation
- New technology
- Demographic shifts
- Other firms seek alliances
- High brand switching *create preference*
- Sales decline for a substitute product
- New distribution methods *Culligan*

Potential External Threats

- Entry of foreign competitors
- Introduction of new substitute products
- Product life cycle in decline
- Changing customer needs/tastes
- Rival firms adopt new strategies *Evian*
- Increased government regulation
- Economic downturn
- New technology
- Demographic shifts
- Foreign trade barriers
- Poor performance of ally firm

- Late entry

on the cutting edge of car design. When four-door trucks became hot sellers for other automakers, GM continued to produce only three-door models. In fact, many GM car and truck designs are considered to be "ugly" by consumers and industry experts.[6] Second, GM suffers from lower productivity and higher expenses than its competitors.[7] In the end, despite its size and financial resources, GM has seen its market share erode from 50 percent to roughly 28 percent and its profitability remain below average.[8]

Scale and Cost Economies   Wal-Mart did not surge ahead of Kmart and Sears in the 1990s because its products were better or different. It did so through its major strengths in information processing/communications, transportation, and distribution systems to build supplier relationships that were more effective (getting the right merchandise on the sales floor in a timely fashion and keeping the proper level of inventory in stock) and efficient (reducing waste and shifting marketing activities to the partner most efficient in carrying them out). Wal-Mart's strengths are meaningful because they give the retailer a competitive advantage in terms of scale and cost economies, thereby allowing them to satisfy customers' needs for lower prices, good variety and assortment, and product availability.[9] When strengths like these are matched to specific customer needs, they become the firm's capabilities. Wal-Mart was able to move ahead of Kmart and Sears because it leveraged its capabilities into unique competitive advantages.

Customer Perceptions A customer-focused SWOT analysis can also uncover a firm's potential weaknesses. Although some weaknesses may be harmless, those that relate to specific customer needs should be minimized if possible. In the crowded minivan market, for example, no one product possesses all three important features that customers look for in a minivan—performance/features, reliability, and safety. As a result, "Which minivan to buy?" remains a difficult question for consumers to answer. The top-selling Dodge Caravan is rated highest in performance and features; however, it rates much lower in reliability and safety. Over the last 5 years, Chrysler has recalled millions of its Caravan, Voyager, and Town & Country minivans.[10] Customers looking for the safest minivan might opt for the Ford Windstar, which consistently receives top ratings in government crash testing. However, the Windstar has a history of reliability concerns.[11] Customers looking for the most reliable minivan are likely to choose the Honda Odyssey, though it suffers from minimal features and a premium price. In fact, the Odyssey was in such demand during the 1999–2001 model years that it often sold at several thousand dollars above MSRP.[12] To overcome its weaknesses, each product is pitched to consumers relative to its major strength.

Opportunities and Threats

In leveraging strengths to create capabilities and competitive advantages, the marketing manager must be mindful of trends and situations in the external environment. Stressing internal strengths while ignoring external issues can lead to an efficient organization that cannot adapt when changes in the external environment either enhance or impede the firm's ability to deliver to its customers. Opportunities and threats exist outside the firm, independent of any internal strengths, weaknesses, or marketing options. Opportunities and threats typically occur within the competitive, economic, political/legal, technological, and/or sociocultural environments. After identifying opportunities and threats, the manager can develop strategies to take advantage of opportunities and minimize or overcome the firm's weaknesses. This section will look at examples of how changes in the external environment can create opportunities or threats for a firm.

Trends in the Competitive Environment One of the most prevalent trends in the U.S. economy in recent years has been the rapid decline in the number of small, independently owned retail businesses. Small mom-and-pop supermarkets and locally owned bookstores are already extinct or severely endangered. Likewise, many locally owned restaurants around the country are struggling due to the growth of large, national restaurant chains. The latest businesses to face extinction are neighborhood hardware stores, which have watched their customers move to hardware giants such as Home Depot and Lowe's. Retail cooperatives Ace Hardware and True Value took bold steps in the late 1990s to shield themselves from this competitive threat: Ace ended its relationship with several other cooperatives, while True Value merged with ServiStar to form the TruServ Corp. However, the fate of both coops is questionable. In early 2000, the CEO of Ace Hardware announced that the coop must improve or fail. Similarly, TruServ lost $131 million in 1999 and saw its stock price fall 65 percent.[13] The reason is that neither coop can gain a foothold in the market. Home Depot and Lowe's continue to grow and are expected to serve over 50 percent of the market by 2004.

Trends in the Technological Environment   Electronic commerce via the Internet is poised to dramatically change the way we do business. In some cases, it may even shatter our accepted ways of buying and selling merchandise. The automotive market is a good example. Sales of U.S. cars over the Internet totaled $2.1 billion in 1999 and are expected to reach $27.3 billion in 2004. The largest car-buying site, Autobytel.com, sells over 50,000 cars per month online. Though these numbers represent only 4 percent of all car sales, there are compelling reasons suggesting the online segment will grow. First, since customers hate to haggle over car prices, the no-haggle pricing of virtually all Web sites appeals to most buyers. Second, buying a car online may actually save money. Automotive Web sites do not incur the standard overhead and advertising fees that traditional dealerships must absorb. Finally, online auto retailing is becoming seamless. Buyers can compare vehicles, place orders, arrange for financing, and buy insurance, all at the same time. Traditional dealerships cannot match the Internet for one-stop-shopping convenience.

Trends in the Sociocultural Environment   Dress-down fashion is a popular clothing trend that began in the early 1990s as "dress-down Fridays." Many believe that the trend began when Levi-Strauss introduced its Dockers line of casual pants for men. It was a natural line extension for Levi's as its core baby-boomer customers put on weight as they aged. The Dockers line grew rapidly, expanding into casual clothing for women as well. In 1992, only 24 percent of American companies offered a dress-down casual day. Today, it is over 95 percent.[14] However, as Levi's capitalized on the dress-down opportunity, it lost sight of its core strength in denim jeans. The Levi's brand began to lose sales as baby boomers moved to more comfortable, casual clothing. Likewise, Levi's was slow to embrace newer fashion trends favored by younger consumers, such as cargo and carpenter pants, flair legs, and stretch fabrics.[15] As a result, younger consumers opted for labels like Gap, Old Navy, and Tommy Hilfiger rather than Levi's. The lesson has been painful. Levi's market share fell from 31 percent to 17 percent in only five years. The company closed 30 of 51 factories, laid off 40 percent of its employees, and lost $1.3 billion. In 2000, Levi's began introducing new styles in an aggressive attempt to broaden its appeal to both boomers and younger consumers.

SWOT-Driven Strategic Planning

The preceding examples illustrate how issues gleaned from a situation analysis can be coordinated in a SWOT analysis. We now consider how a firm can use its strengths, weaknesses, opportunities, and threats to drive the development of strategic plans that will allow the firm to achieve its goals and objectives. Remember that SWOT analysis should not be an academic exercise to classify information correctly. Rather, it should serve as a catalyst to facilitate and guide the creation of marketing strategies that will produce desired results. The process of organizing information within the SWOT analysis can help the firm see the differences between where it thinks it is, where others see it as being, and where it hopes to be. To utilize SWOT analysis successfully as a catalyst for strategic planning, the manager must recognize four issues:[16]

1. The assessment of strengths and weaknesses must look beyond the firm's products to the business processes that are key to meeting customers' needs.

EXHIBIT 3.5   THE SWOT MATRIX

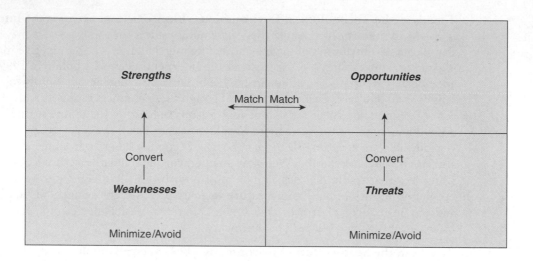

Source: Adapted from Nigel Piercy, *Market-Led Strategic Change* (Oxford, UK: Butterworth-Heineman, Ltd., 1992): 260.

This often entails offering "solutions" to customers' problems rather than specific products.

2. The achievement of the firm's goals and objectives depends on its ability to transform strengths into capabilities by matching them with opportunities in the environment. Capabilities can become competitive advantages if they provide better value to customers than do competitors' offerings.

3. Firms can convert weaknesses into strengths, or even capabilities, by investing strategically in key areas (e.g., customer support, R&D, promotion, HRM) or by linking these areas more effectively. Likewise, threats can often be converted into opportunities if the right resources are available.

4. Weaknesses that cannot be converted become limitations. Any limitation that is obvious and meaningful to customers or other stakeholders must be minimized.

To address these issues properly, the marketing manager should appraise every strength, weakness, opportunity, and threat to determine its total impact on the firm's marketing efforts. This assessment will also give the manager an idea of the basic strategic options that might be available to emphasize the firm's capabilities or convert/minimize its weaknesses and threats. One method of conducting this assessment is to create and analyze a SWOT matrix. Let's look at how a marketing manager might conduct this assessment.

Analysis of the SWOT Matrix

Exhibit 3.5 shows a SWOT matrix, a four-cell array that can be used to categorize information at the conclusion of the SWOT analysis. At this point, the manager must

EXHIBIT 3.6   **QUANTITATIVE ASSESSMENT OF ELEMENTS WITHIN THE SWOT MATRIX**

This analysis was conducted for the AMA Certification Program (see Appendix B for the complete marketing plan). The ratings in each cell are based on customer perceptions.

Strengths	M	•	I	=	R
Size and capacity	3		3		9
Experience	3		3		9
Individual benefits	2		2		4

Opportunities	M	•	I	=	R
A currently untapped market	3		3		9
Growth and popularity of the marketing discipline	3		2		6
Field innovation	2		2		4
Increased competition	2		2		4

Weaknesses	M	•	I	=	R
Getting away from core values	−3		3		−9
Adding value to the customer	−3		3		−9
Maintaining a long-term focus	−3		2		−6
Certification program awareness and value	−2		2		−4

Threats	M	•	I	=	R
Business colleges	−3		3		−9
Businesses might not care about the program	−3		3		−9
Other certification programs	−3		2		−6

M = magnitude of element, *I* = importance of element, *R* = final rating of the element.
Magnitude scale: ranges from +3 (most favorable) to −3 (most unfavorable).
Importance scale: ranges from 3 (highest importance) to 1 (lowest importance).

evaluate each cell of the matrix in order to match strengths to opportunities, convert weaknesses to strengths, and convert threats to opportunities. Weaknesses and threats that cannot be converted should be minimized or avoided. To begin this evaluation, the manager should assess the magnitude and importance of each element in the SWOT matrix. These ratings should ideally be based on customers' perceptions rather than on those of the analyst. Customers' perceptions can be collected through focus group research. If customers' perceptions cannot be gathered, the manager's rating should be based on intuition and expertise.

It is not mandatory that the cells of the SWOT matrix be assessed quantitatively, but it can be quite informative to do so. Exhibit 3.6 illustrates how this assessment might be conducted using information from the sample marketing plan in Appendix B. The first step is to quantify the magnitude of each element within the matrix. A simple method is to use a scale of 1 (low), 2 (medium), 3 (high) for each strength or opportunity, and −1 (low), −2 (medium), and −3 (high) for each weakness or threat. The second step is to rate the importance of each element in the matrix using a scale of 1 (weak importance), 2 (average importance), and 3 (major importance) for all elements. The final step is to multiply the magnitude ratings by the importance ratings. Remember that the magnitude and importance ratings should be heavily influenced by customer perceptions, not just by the perceptions of the manager.

Those elements with the highest numerical rankings (positive or negative) should have the greatest influence in developing the marketing strategy. A sizable strength in an important area must certainly be emphasized in order to convert it to a capability or competitive advantage. On the other hand, a fairly small and insignificant opportunity

EXHIBIT 3.7	SOURCES OF COMPETITIVE ADVANTAGE

Relationships
  Brand-loyal customers
  High customer switching costs
  Long-term relationships with supply
    chain partners
  Strategic alliance agreements
  Co-marketing or co-branding
    agreements

Legal
  Patents and trademarks
  Tax advantages
  Zoning laws
  Global trade restrictions

Product-related advantages
  Brand equity
  Exclusive products
  Superior quality or features
  Guarantees and warranties
  Outstanding customer service
  Research and development

Price-related advantages
  Lower production costs
  Economies of scale
  Large-volume buying
  Low-cost distribution

Promotion-related advantages
  Company image
  Large promotion budget
  Superior sales force
  Creativity

Distribution-related advantages
  Efficient distribution system
  Just-in-time inventory control
  Superior information systems
  Exclusive distribution outlets
  Convenient locations

People-related advantages
  Superior management talent
  Strong organizational culture
  Committed employees

would not play a central role in the planning process. The magnitude and importance of opportunities and threats will depend on the particular product or market. For example, a dramatic increase in new housing starts would be very important for the lumber industry but inconsequential for an industry such as semiconductors. Although the magnitude of the opportunity is the same, the importance ratings are different.

After the magnitude and importance of each element in the SWOT matrix have been assessed, the manager should focus on finding competitive advantages by matching strengths to opportunities. The manager should also attempt to develop strategies that convert weaknesses and threats as well as minimize/avoid those weaknesses or threats that cannot be converted. We examine this stage of SWOT-driven strategic planning in the next few sections.

Identifying and Maintaining a Sustainable Competitive Advantage

The most important, natural, and often most effective strategic option is to match the firm's strengths with the opportunities that the SWOT analysis identified in the environment. Key strengths that are compatible with important and sizable opportunities are most likely to be converted into capabilities. Remember that capabilities that allow a firm to serve customers' needs better than the competition give it a competitive advantage. Although competitive advantages can arise from many internal or external sources, some of the most common sources are listed in Exhibit 3.7.

When we refer to competitive advantages, we usually speak in terms of real differences between competing firms. After all, competitive advantages stem from real strengths possessed by the firm. However, competitive advantages can also be based more on perception than on reality. Most customers make purchase decisions based on their perceptions of how well a firm's capabilities pertain to its unique needs, wants, or problems. How customers see a company is how that firm is, regardless of the facts about a company. If customers perceive the company as slow to react, impersonal, or having excessively high priced or out-of-date products, that is quite simply the way that firm is. Customer perceptions, not market realities, drive customers' attitudes, intentions, and purchase and repurchase behaviors.

Effectively managing customer's perceptions has been a challenge for marketers for generations. The problem lies in developing and maintaining capabilities and competitive advantages that customers can easily understand and that solve specific customer's needs. Capabilities or competitive advantages that do not translate into specific benefits for customers are of little use to a firm. In recent years, many successful firms have developed capabilities and competitive advantages based on one of three strategies: operational excellence, product leadership, and customer intimacy.[17]

Operational excellence: Firms employing a strategy of operational excellence focus on efficiency of operations and processes. These firms operate at lower costs than their competitors, allowing them to deliver goods and services to their customers at lower prices or a better value. Southwest Airlines, for example, offers a no-frills service—no meals or advanced seating—and uses nearly identical Boeing 737 aircraft in order to keep costs down and maintain some of the lowest fares in the industry.

Product leadership: Firms that focus on product leadership excel at technology and product development. As a result, these firms offer customers the most advanced, highest-quality goods and services in the industry. For example, Microsoft, which dominates the market for personal computer operating systems with its Windows program, continues to upgrade and stretch the technology underlying its operating systems while creating complementary software that solves customers' needs, like the Microsoft Office suite of products.

Customer intimacy: Organizations that practice customer intimacy work very hard to know their customers and understand their needs better than the competition does. These firms get very close to their customers by seeking their input on how to make the firm's goods and services better or how to solve specific customer problems. These firms also attempt to create long-term relationships between themselves and their customers. Airborne Express, for example, focuses on distribution solutions that competitors cannot match. The company excels in ultra-early delivery, same-day courier service, special handling of difficult products, warehouse and inventory management, ocean transport, and customs clearance.[18]

To be successful, firms should be able to execute all three strategies. However, the most successful firms choose one area at which to excel and then actively manage customer perceptions so that customers believe that the firm does indeed excel in that area. To implement any one of these strategies successfully, a firm must possess certain core competencies, as outlined in Exhibit 3.8. Organizations that boast such competencies are more likely to create a competitive advantage than those that do not. However, before a competitive advantage can be translated into specific customer benefits, the firm's target market(s) must recognize that its competencies give it an advantage

EXHIBIT 3.8	CORE COMPETENCIES FOR COMPETITIVE ADVANTAGE STRATEGIES

Operational Excellence

Example Firms
- Wal-Mart
- Southwest Airlines
- Dell Computer

Core Competencies
- Totally dependable product supply
- Expedient customer service
- Effective demand management
- Low-cost operations

Common Attributes of Operationally Excellent Firms
- Deliver a combination of acceptable price, consistent quality, and convenient exchange processes
- Target a broad, heterogeneous market of price-sensitive buyers
- Focus their marketing plans on price leadership
- Provide several standardized product options that meet a variety of customer needs
- Make frequent, minor product modifications, but keep products in the acceptable range of cost and quality
- Pass scale economies on to customers in the form of lower prices
- Plan operations to find the most efficient means for carrying out all business processes
- Invest to achieve efficiency-driven production systems
- Develop information systems geared toward capturing and distributing information on inventories, shipments, customer transactions, and costs
- Let customers reap the benefits of lower prices by adapting customers' needs to standardized product offerings
- Assess most managerial decisions on a profit-margin basis
- Maintain a system where waste equals death and efficiency improvement is highly rewarded

Product Leadership

Example Firms
- Microsoft
- IBM
- 3M
- Sony

Core Competencies
- Basic research/rapid research interpretation
- Applied research geared toward product development
- Rapid exploitation of market opportunities
- Excellent marketing skills

Common Attributes of Product-Leading Firms
- Frequently introduce products that push the envelope of new technology
- Target narrow, homogeneous market segment(s)
- Expect some product failures and try to learn from them
- Focus their marketing plans on the rapid introduction of high-quality, technologically sophisticated products in order to create customer loyalty
- Move ideas rapidly from concept to commercialization
- Make products and solutions obsolete with their own innovations
- Scan the environment constantly in search of new opportunities
- Focus on an attitude of "How can we make this work?" rather than "Why can't we make it work?"
- Support flexibility and adaptability in all aspects of business
- View success and failure differently than other organizations (both are fairly fleeting and part of the game)

EXHIBIT 3.8　　**CORE COMPETENCIES FOR**
COMPETITIVE ADVANTAGE STRATEGIES (*continued*)

- Protect their decentralized entrepreneurial environment above all else
- Maintain a system where complacency equals death and creativity is highly rewarded

Customer Intimacy

Example Firms
- Nordstrom
- Federal Express
- Saturn

Core Competencies
- Exceptional skills in discovering customer needs
- Problem solving proficiency
- Flexible product/solution customization
- A customer relationship management mindset
- A wide presence of collaborative (win–win) negotiation skills

Common Attributes of Customer-Intimate Firms
- Emphasize providing customized products (both goods and services) that meet a variety of unique customer needs
- Carefully select customer prospects with whom to pursue a relationship
- Focus their marketing plans on developing and maintaining an intimate knowledge of customer requirements
- Deliver comprehensive solutions that are a good value, without fear of or apology for charging a higher price
- Consistently "reinvent" solutions as their customers' problems and needs change
- See customer loyalty as the firm's greatest asset
- Decentralize most decision-making authority to the customer-contact level
- Assess relationships on a long-term, even lifetime basis
- Avoid one-time sales transactions in order to pursue long-term customer relationships
- Exceed customer expectations consistently
- Seek to solve customers' problems proactively, rather than taking a reactionary approach
- Regularly form strategic alliances with other companies to address customers' needs in a comprehensive fashion
- Have advanced levels of problem/opportunity identification and solution development
- Have a system where customer loss equals death and where accomplishments that generate customer loyalty are highly and visibly rewarded

Source: Michael Treacy and Fred Wiersema, *The Discipline of Market Leaders* (Reading, MA: Addison-Wesley Publishing Co., 1995).

over the competition. Exhibit 3.8 includes a list of attributes that customers might use to describe a company that possesses each particular competitive advantage. The core competencies are internal (strength) issues, while specific attributes refer to activities that customers will notice as they interact with the firm.

Moving Beyond SWOT: Developing Marketing Goals and Objectives

At the conclusion of the SWOT analysis, the marketing manager should have a rough outline of potential marketing activities that can be used to take advantage of capabilities and convert weaknesses and threats. At this stage, however, there are likely to be many potential directions for the manager to pursue. Because most firms have limited resources, it is difficult to accomplish everything at once. Now the manager must prioritize all potential marketing activities and develop specific goals and objectives for the marketing plan.

Once the firm has carefully developed a mission statement that clearly delineates what it is, what it stands for, and what it does for others, it can then begin to lay out what it hopes to achieve. These statements of desired accomplishments are goals and objectives. The terms *goals* and *objectives* are sometimes used interchangeably. However, failure to understand the key differences between them can severely limit the effectiveness of the strategic plan. Goals are general accomplishments that are desired, while objectives provide specific, quantitative benchmarks that can be used to gauge progress toward the achievement of the marketing goals.

Developing Marketing Goals

As statements of desired general accomplishments, goals are expressed in general terms and do not contain specific information about where the organization stands now or where it hopes to be in the future. Home Depot, for example, has a goal of having lower prices on all its products than the local competition. To achieve this goal, the company asks customers who find a lower price to let Home Depot know and then gives them an even larger discount. Because of their nature, goals are sometimes referred to as *qualitative* objectives. We will use the term *goals* here for clarity in developing and evaluating marketing plans.

Goals are important because they indicate the direction the firm is attempting to move and the set of priorities it will use in evaluating alternatives and making decisions. For example, a firm might have a goal to improve service quality by providing more training for customer-contact employees. As with all stages of planning, it is important that all functional areas of the organization be considered in the goal-setting process. In developing goals for the marketing plan, it is important to keep in mind several key issues at all times: All marketing goals should be attainable, consistent, and comprehensive and should involve some degree of intangibility. Failure to consider these attributes will result in goals that are less effective and perhaps even dysfunctional.

Attainability Setting realistic goals is important because the key parties involved in reaching them must see each goal as reasonable. Determining whether a goal is realistic requires an assessment of both the internal and external environments. For example, it would not be unrealistic for a firm in second place in market share, trailing the leading brand by just 2 percent, to set a goal of becoming the industry leader. Other things being equal, such a goal could help motivate employees toward becoming "number one." In contrast, a firm in sixth place, trailing the fifth-place firm by 5 percent and the leader by 30 percent, could set the same goal, but it would not be realistic. Unrealistic goals tend to be demotivational, because they show employees that management is out of touch with reality. Since one of the primary benefits of having goals is to motivate employees toward better performance, having unrealistic goals can cause major problems.

Consistency In addition to setting realistic goals, management must work to set goals that are consistent with one another. Enhancing market share and working to have the highest profit margins in the industry are both reasonable goals by themselves, but together they are inconsistent. Goals to increase sales and market share would be consistent, as would goals to enhance customer service and customer satisfaction. However, reducing inventory levels and increasing the level of customer service are usually incompatible goals. Goals across and within functional areas should also mesh together. Failure to do so causes some concern that "the left hand does not know what the right hand is doing." This is a major concern in large organizations, and it highlights the need for a great deal of information sharing during the goal-formulation process.

Comprehensiveness The goal-setting process should also be comprehensive. This means that each functional area should be able to develop its own goals that relate to the organization's goals. If goals are set only in terms of advancing the technology associated with a firm's products, members of the marketing department may wonder what role they will play in this accomplishment. The goal should be stated so that both marketing and research and development can work together to help advance the organizational goal of offering the most technologically advanced products. Marketing will need to work on the demand side of this effort (measuring customer needs and staying in tune with trends in customers' lives and businesses), while research and development will focus on the supply side (keeping up with basic research breakthroughs and working on applied research related to the development of specific products). Goals should help clarify the roles of all parties in the organization. Functional areas that do not match any of the organization's goals should question their need for future resources and their ability to acquire them.

Intangibility Finally, goals should involve some degree of intangibility. Some planners have been known to confuse strategies, and even tactics, with goals. A goal is not some action the firm can take; it is an outcome the organization hopes to accomplish. "Hiring 100 new salespeople" and "Doubling the advertising budget" are not goals. Any firm with adequate resources can accomplish both tasks. However, "Having the best-trained sales force in the industry" and "Having the best-recognized and most effective advertising campaign in the industry" are suitable goals. Note the intangibility associated with the use of terms such as "best-trained," "best-recognized," and "most effective" to indicate comparison with other firms.

Developing Marketing Objectives

Objectives provide specific and quantitative benchmarks that can be used to gauge progress toward the achievement of the marketing goals. In some cases, a particular goal may require several objectives to monitor its progress, usually across multiple business functions. For example, a goal of "Creating a high-quality image for the firm" cannot be accomplished by better inventory control if mistakes are made in accounts receivable and customer complaints about the firm's salespeople are on the rise. Similarly, Home Depot's objective of operating 1,900 stores by the end of 2003 cannot be accomplished by the marketing department alone.[19] Such an endeavor requires a carefully coordinated effort from many departments.

Goals without objectives are essentially meaningless, because progress is impossible to measure. A typical marketing objective might be "For the sales department to decrease unfilled customer orders from 3 percent to 2 percent between January and June of this fiscal year." Note that this objective contains a high degree of specificity. It is this specificity that sets goals and objectives apart. Objectives involve measurable, quantitative outcomes, with specific assigned responsibility for their accomplishment and a definite time period for their attainment. Let's look at the specific characteristics of marketing objectives.

Attainability As with goals, marketing objectives should be realistic, given the internal and external environments identified during the situation and SWOT analyses. A good objective is one that is attainable with a reasonable amount of effort. Easily achieved objectives will not motivate employees to higher levels of productivity. Likewise, good objectives are not based on false assumptions that everything will go as planned or that every employee will give 150 percent effort. In some cases, competitors will establish objectives that include taking customers and sales away from the firm. Setting objectives that assume inanimate or inept competitors, when history has shown this not to be the case, creates objectives that quickly lose their value as employees recognize them as being unreasonable.

Continuity The need for realism brings up a second consideration: continuity. Desired marketing outcomes can be of two types: continuous objectives or discontinuous objectives. A firm uses continuous objectives when its current objectives are similar to those set in the previous planning period. For example, the objective "To increase market share from 20 percent to 22 percent (a 10 percent increase) between January 1 and June 30" could be carried forward to the subsequent period (July 1 to December 31). This would be a continuous objective, because the factor in question and the magnitude of change are similar, or even identical, from period to period.

Marketing objectives should lead people to perform at higher levels than would otherwise have been the case. However, continuous objectives that are identical, or only slightly modified, from period to period often do not need new strategies, increased effort, or better implementation to be achieved. People naturally tend to be objective oriented. Once the objective is met, the level of creativity and effort tends to fall off. There are internal and external circumstances where continuous objectives are appropriate, but they should not be set simply as a matter of habit.

Discontinuous objectives significantly elevate the level of performance on a given outcome factor, or bring new factors into the set of objectives. If sales growth has been averaging 10 percent, and the SWOT analysis suggests that this is an easily obtainable level, an example of a discontinuous objective might be "To increase sales 18 percent during the next period." This would require new strategies to sell additional products to existing customers, to expand the customer base, or at the very least to develop new tactics and/or enhance the implementation of existing strategies. Discontinuous objectives require more analysis and linkage to strategic planning than do continuous objectives.

Developing discontinuous objectives is one of the major benefits a company can gain from applying for the Malcolm Baldrige National Quality Award. The seven quality categories identified in Exhibit 3.9 list areas for objective setting that are ignored by many organizations. To demonstrate proficiency in these areas, a firm must first establish benchmarks, which typically are the quantitative performance levels of the leaders in the industry. The firm then develops objectives that center on improving performance in each area. Companies that have applied for the award feel that one of its most positive aspects has been the impetus it has had on organizations to set discontinuous objectives. This is true both for organizations that formally enter the competition as well as for those that use the Baldrige guidelines as a planning aid.

EXHIBIT 3.9	2000 MALCOLM BALDRIGE AWARD CRITERIA FOR PERFORMANCE EXCELLENCE

Categories/Items		Point Values
1 **Leadership**		125
1.1	Organizational leadership	85
1.2	Public responsibility and citizenship	40
2 **Strategic Planning**		85
2.1	Strategy development	40
2.2	Strategy deployment	45
3 **Customer and Market Focus**		85
3.1	Customer and market knowledge	40
3.2	Customer satisfaction and relationships	45
4 **Information and Analysis**		85
4.1	Measurement of organizational performance	40
4.2	Analysis of organizational performance	45
5 **Human Resource Focus**		85
5.1	Work systems	35
5.2	Employee education, training, and development	25
5.3	Employee well-being and satisfaction	25
6 **Process Management**		85
6.1	Product and service processes	55
6.2	Support processes	15
6.3	Supplier and partnering processes	15
7 **Business Results**		450
7.1	Customer-focused results	115
7.2	Financial and market results	115
7.3	Human resource results	80
7.4	Supplier and partner results	25
7.5	Organizational effectiveness results	115
TOTAL POINTS		1000

Timeframe Another key consideration in setting objectives is the timeframe for their achievement. Though marketing plans are often established on an annual basis, marketing objectives may differ from this period in their timeframe. Sales volume, market share, customer service, and gross margin objectives may be set for terms less than, equal to, or greater than one year. The timeframe should be appropriate and allow for accomplishment within the period with reasonable levels of effort. To set a target of doubling sales for a well-established company within six months would likely be unreasonable. On the other hand, objectives having an excessively long timeframe may be attained without any increased effort or creativity. The combination of managerial expertise and experience, along with the information acquired during the situation and SWOT analyses, should lead to the establishment of an appropriate timeframe.

For objectives with longer timeframes, it is important to remind employees of the objective on a regular basis and to provide feedback on progress toward its achievement. For example, employees at FedEx's main terminal in Memphis, Tennessee, can see a real-time "accuracy gauge" that displays the company's current performance in terms of getting packages to the right place. Whether a weekly announcement, a monthly newsletter, or an up-to-date "thermometer" on the wall that charts progress toward the objective, feedback should be a large part of the objective-setting process, particularly for longer term objectives.

Assignment of Responsibility   One final aspect of objectives that sets them apart from goals is that the person, people, or business function/unit responsible for their achievement is identified. By explicitly assigning responsibility, the firm can limit the problems of stealing credit and avoiding responsibility. A bank might give the marketing department the responsibility of achieving an objective of "Having 40 percent of its customers list the bank as their primary financial institution within one year." If by the end of the year, 42 percent of all customers list the bank as their primary financial institution, the marketing department gets credit for this outcome. If the figure is only 38 percent, the marketing department must provide an explanation.

Moving from Goals to Objectives and Beyond

Marketing goals and objectives identify the desired ends, both general and specific, that an organization hopes to achieve during the planning period. However, properly set goals and objectives are not attained automatically or through wishing and hoping. They set in motion a chain of decisions and serve as a catalyst for the subsequent stages in the strategic planning process. Organizational goals and objectives must lead to the establishment of consistent goals and objectives for each functional area of the firm. Having recognized the desired ends, each area, including marketing, must next determine the means that will lead to these targeted results.

As we move forward in the book, we will focus our attention on this means issue as we address marketing strategy development. Although the steps of the market planning process are considered sequentially, in reality the firm must move back and forth between steps. If marketing strategies that have the potential to achieve the marketing goals and objectives cannot be developed, the goals and objectives may not be reasonable and may require adjustments before the marketing strategy is developed. Given that the marketing plan must be a working document, it is never truly finalized.

Lessons from Chapter 3

SWOT analysis:

- links a company's ongoing situation analysis and the development of the marketing plan.

- structures the information from the situation analysis into four categories: strengths, weaknesses, opportunities, and threats.

- uses the structured information to drive the selection of the firm's strategy.

Major benefits of SWOT analysis are:

- simplicity—SWOT analysis can be conducted without extensive training or technical skills.

- lower costs—SWOT's simplicity eliminates the need for and the expense of formal training.

- flexibility—SWOT analysis can be performed with or without extensive marketing information systems or intranets.

- integration—SWOT analysis has the ability to integrate and synthesize diverse types of information, both quantitative and qualitative, from various areas of the firm.

- collaboration—SWOT analysis has the ability to foster collaboration between functional areas of the firm that are interdependent but that may have little additional contact with each other.

Five key directives for a productive SWOT analysis are:

- stay focused by using a series of SWOT analyses, each focusing on a specific product/market combination.

- search extensively for competitors, whether they are a present competitor or one in the future.

- collaborate with other functional areas by sharing information and perspectives.

- examine issues from the customers' perspective by constantly asking the question "What do our customers think/believe, and what does this issue mean for them?" This includes examining the issues from the perspective of the firm's internal customers, its employees.

- separate internal issues from external issues. The key test to differentiate an internal issue from an external issue is to ask this question: "Would this issue exist if the firm did not exist?" If the answer is yes, the issue should be classified as external.

Strengths and weaknesses:

- exist inside the firm or in key relationships between the firm and its other channel members, suppliers, or customers.

- are meaningful only when they assist or hinder the organization in satisfying a customer need.

- should focus on the business processes or "solutions" that are key to meeting consumer needs.

Opportunities and threats:

- are not potential marketing actions. Rather, they involve issues or situations that occur in the firm's external environments.

- should not be ignored as the firm gets caught up in developing strengths and capabilities, for fear of creating an efficient, but ineffective, organization.

- may stem from changes in the competitive, sociocultural, political/legal, and internal organizational environments.

SWOT-driven strategic planning:

- should serve as a catalyst to structure the generation of marketing strategies that will produce desired results.

- is facilitated by using the four-cell SWOT matrix to categorize information at the conclusion of the analysis. As a part of this process, the magnitude and importance of each strength, weakness, opportunity, and threat is evaluated, quantitatively if desired.

- should always be based on customer perceptions, not on the perceptions of the manager.

- strives to create capabilities by matching the firm's strengths with its opportunities.

- focuses on creating competitive advantages by matching company strengths to market opportunities. Many successful firms use one of three strategies to create competitive advantages.

- provides guidance on how the firm might structure its marketing strategy to convert weaknesses and threats and minimize/avoid those weaknesses and threats that cannot be converted.

Marketing goals:

- are desired general accomplishments that are stated in general terms.

- indicate the direction the firm is attempting to move and the set of priorities it will use in evaluating alternatives and making decisions.

- should be attainable and realistic.

- should be internally consistent.

- should be comprehensive and help to clarify the roles of all parties in the organization.

- should involve some degree of intangibility.

Marketing objectives:

- provide specific and quantitative benchmarks that can be used to gauge progress toward the achievement of the marketing goals for which they are developed.

- should be attainable with a reasonable degree of effort.

- may be either continuous or discontinuous, depending on the degree to which they depart from present objectives.

- should specify the timeframe for their completion.

- should assign responsibility for accomplishment to specific areas, departments, or individuals.

Questions for Discussion

1. Of the four elements in SWOT analysis, which do you feel is the most important? Why? Does your answer change if you take a different point of view (i.e., if you were the CEO, a company employee, a customer of the firm, a supplier to the firm)?

2. The most common mistake that analysts make in performing a SWOT analysis is to confuse internal issues with external issues. This is particularly true with respect to opportunities, which refer to issues or situations in the environment— not to the firm's strategic options. Why do you think this happens? Does the simplicity of SWOT analysis get in the way?

3. State whether you agree or disagree with the following, and defend your position: "Given the realities of today's business environment, and the rapid changes in business technology, there is no such thing as a *sustainable* competitive advantage. All competitive advantages are short-term advantages."

Exercises

1. Choose two products: one that you absolutely love and one that you despise (will not buy). Then, for each product, list every strength and weakness you believe it possesses. Compare your answers with those of your colleagues. What can the maker of each product learn from your analysis?

2. Make a list of the schools you considered before deciding on the one you now attend. If you had to identify a single competitive advantage for each school, what would they be? How sustainable are these advantages in the long run? Did the advantage possessed by your school influence your decision?

3. Perform a SWOT analysis using yourself as the product. Be candid about your strengths and weaknesses. Based on the opportunities and threats you see in the environment, where do you stand in terms of your ability to get a job, begin a career, or attend graduate school?

4

Market Segmentation, Target Marketing, and Positioning

Introduction

Marketing strategy involves selecting a specific target market and making decisions regarding the crucial elements of product, price, promotion, and distribution in order to satisfy the needs of customers in that market. Choosing the "right" strategy from among many possible alternatives is the ultimate test in developing good marketing strategy. There are literally hundreds of possible marketing mix combinations that, when matched with a good situation analysis, can give a firm a chance to satisfy the needs of target customers, differentiate its products from competitors, and achieve its marketing goals and objectives.

This chapter explores several issues that need to be considered in selecting the "right" marketing strategy. We begin our examination with the customer and decisions related to target market selection, such as mass marketing, market segmentation, niche marketing, and customized (one-to-one) marketing. Until a firm has chosen and analyzed a target market, it cannot make effective decisions regarding other elements of marketing strategy. Next, we look at the characteristics of both consumer and business markets, including the most common bases for segmenting these markets. We will conclude by considering strategies associated with differentiating and positioning products.

Market Segmentation

Because marketing strategy has the primary role of placing the firm in an optimal position with respect to customer needs, we first consider decisions related to target markets and market segmentation. The information used to make these decisions should come from the situation analysis, particularly the analysis of the customer environment as described in Chapter 2. Based on this information, the marketing manager must decide whether to target the entire market for a product or one or more segments of the total market. All firms have two basic alternatives in determining the scope of the markets they will serve or attempt to attract—mass marketing and market segmentation. Some firms opt to target small niches of a market or even the smallest of market segments, individuals.

Traditional Approaches to Market Segmentation

The segmentation approaches discussed in this section—mass marketing, differentiated marketing, and niche marketing—are traditional approaches only to the extent that they have been used successfully by firms for decades. It is not our intention to depict these approaches as old or out of date, especially when compared to emerging individualized segmentation strategies that we discuss later in the chapter. In fact, many of today's most successful firms used these tried-and-true approaches. Some organizations actually use more than one type of segmentation, depending on the brand/product or market in question. An overview of traditional segmentation approaches is illustrated in Exhibit 4.1.

Mass Marketing   It seems odd to call mass marketing a segmentation approach, for it involves no segmentation whatsoever. Mass marketing is aimed at the total (whole) market for a particular product. Companies that adopt mass marketing take an undifferentiated approach that assumes that all customers in the market have similar needs and wants that can be reasonably satisfied with a single marketing mix. This marketing mix typically consists of a single product or brand (or, in the case of retailers, a homogeneous set of products), one price, one promotional program, and one distribution system. Wal-Mart, for example, offers a set of quality name brands to consumers who tend to be both price and quality conscious. Likewise, Duracell offers a collection of different battery sizes (D, C, A, AA, AAA, 9-volt), but they are all disposable batteries marketed to consumers for use in toys and appliances.

Mass marketing works best when the needs of an entire market are relatively homogeneous. Good examples include commodities like oil and agricultural products. In reality, very few products or markets are suited for mass marketing, if for no other reason than companies wanting to reach new customers often modify their product lines. For most of its existence, Vaseline manufactured and offered a single product to consumers. To reach new consumers, Vaseline modified this strategy by launching its Intensive Care line of products and extending customers' perception of Vaseline's uses to various needs in the home, including the garage/workshop. Further, think of the many products that contain Arm & Hammer baking soda, a product that at one time was sold only as a baking ingredient.

While mass marketing is advantageous in terms of production efficiency and lower marketing costs, it is inherently risky. By offering a standard product to all consumers, the organization becomes vulnerable to competitors that offer specialized products that better match customers' needs. In industries where barriers to entry are low, mass marketing runs the risk of being seen as too generic. This situation is very inviting for competitors who use more targeted approaches. Mass marketing is also very risky in global markets, where even global brands like Coke must be adapted to match local tastes and customs.

Differentiated Marketing   Most firms use some form of market segmentation by dividing the total market into groups of customers having relatively common or homogeneous needs and attempting to develop a marketing mix that appeals to one or more

TRADITIONAL SEGMENTATION APPROACHES

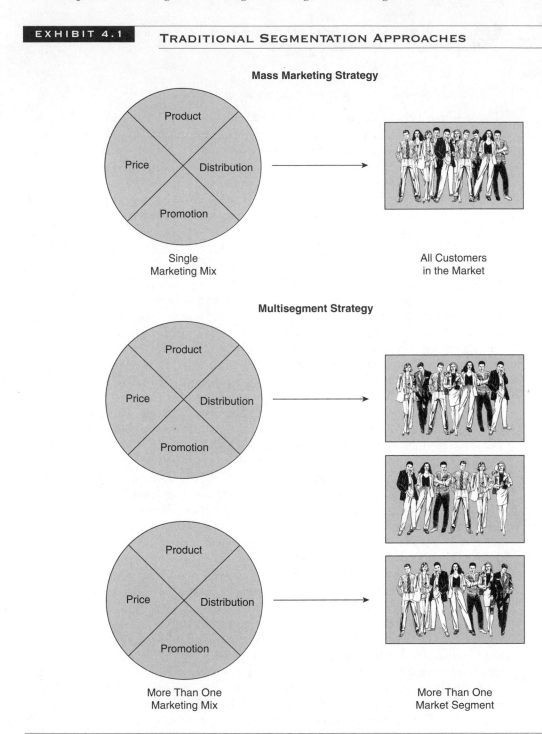

Mass Marketing Strategy

Single
Marketing Mix

All Customers
in the Market

Multisegment Strategy

More Than One
Marketing Mix

More Than One
Market Segment

EXHIBIT 4.1   **TRADITIONAL SEGMENTATION APPROACHES** (*continued*)

Market Concentration Strategy

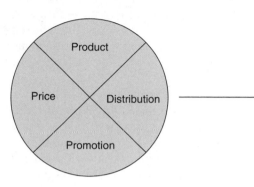

Single
Marketing Mix

Focused on a Single
Market Segment

Niche Marketing Strategy

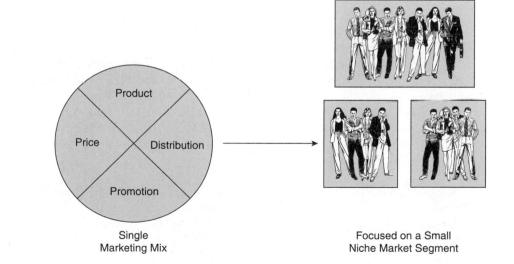

Single
Marketing Mix

Focused on a Small
Niche Market Segment

of these groups. This approach may be necessary when customer needs are similar within a single group but their needs differ across groups. Through well-designed and carefully conducted research, firms can identify the particular needs of each market segment to create marketing mixes that best match those needs and expectations. Within this differentiated approach, there are two options: the multisegment approach and the market concentration approach.

Firms using the multisegment approach seek to attract buyers in more than one market segment by offering multiple marketing mixes that will appeal to more parts of the total market. In using this option, the firm can increase its share of the market by responding to the heterogeneous wants and desires of different segments or submarkets. If the segments have enough buying potential, and the product is successful, the resulting sales increases can more than offset the increased costs of offering multiple marketing mixes.

The multisegment approach is the most widely used alternative in medium- to large-size firms. Packaged goods firms often make liberal use of multisegmentation. Maxwell House, for example, began by marketing one type of coffee and one brand. Today, this division of Kraft Foods offers twenty-three different brand varieties under the Maxwell House label in addition to providing private label brands for retailers. A walk down the cereal aisle of your local supermarket offers additional examples; firms such as Kellogg and Nabisco offer seemingly hundreds of brands of breakfast cereals targeted at specific segments, including children (Fruit Loops, Apple Jacks), health-conscious adults (Shredded Wheat, Total), parents looking for healthier foods for their children (Life, Kix), and so on.

Firms using the market concentration approach focus on a single market segment. These firms often find it most efficient to seek a maximum share in one segment of the market. Both Porsche and Ferrari use this strategy. Armor All markets appearance chemicals primarily to young, driving-age males. Small book publishers tend to focus their offerings toward readers with certain tastes. The market concentration approach is almost universal in the fine arts. For instance, musical groups hone their talents and plan their performances to satisfy the tastes of one market segment, such as country, rock, or classical music.

The main advantage of market concentration is specialization, because it allows the firm to focus all its resources on understanding and serving a single segment. Specialization is also the major disadvantage of this approach. By "putting all its eggs in one basket," the firm can be vulnerable to changes in its market segment, such as economic downturns and demographic shifts. Gerber experienced this effect in the 1970s and 1980s when birth rates declined just as it was proclaiming, "Babies are our business. Our only business."

Niche Marketing Some companies narrow the market concentration approach even more and focus their marketing efforts on one small, well-defined market segment or niche that has a unique, specific set of needs. One example of successful niche marketing is sports camps for youth. Such camps offer a specific level of sports training for children of a well-defined category of ages and specific ability levels. Nike, for example, sponsors minicamps for sports ranging from white-water rafting to golf and in-line skating for $500–$625. Many of Nike's full-service golf camps run $1,500 to $2,000 for ten days of instruction.[1] Obviously, these offerings are for a small and very well-defined set of parents who have the money and children with the athletic interest and potential to send to such camps. The key with niche marketing is to understand

and meet the needs of target customers so completely that, despite the small size of the niche, the firm's substantial share makes the segment highly profitable.

Individualized Approaches to Market Segmentation

Individualized segmentation approaches are beginning to emerge due to advances in technology, particularly communication technology and the Internet. These segmentation approaches are possible because organizations now have the ability to track customers with a high degree of specificity. By combining demographic data with information on past and current purchasing behavior, many organizations are able to tweak their marketing mixes in ways that allow them to precisely match customer's needs, wants, and preferences.

One-to-One Marketing   When a company creates an entirely unique marketing mix for each customer in the target segment, it is employing one-to-one marketing. This approach is common in business-to-business marketing, where unique programs and/or systems are designed for each customer. Airborne Express, for example, customized an 8:30 A.M. early delivery of parts to repair technicians for Xerox. Insurance companies, such as The Royal, and insurance brokers, such as Sedgwick, often design programs to meet a corporation's specific needs. The unique needs of moderate- to large-size companies dictate that promotion, price, product, and distribution are all modified to meet the specifics of the client's situation.

Historically, this type of one-to-one marketing has been used less often in consumer marketing, although Burger King heavily promoted this approach in its "Have It Your Way" campaign. Here the price, distribution, and promotion were the same for all consumers, but the product varied slightly (depending on what the customer wanted on the Whopper). One-to-one marketing is quite common in luxury and custom-made products, such as when a consumer buys a large sailboat or motorboat, a jet plane, or a custom-built home. In such instances, the product is significantly modified to meet unique customer needs and preferences. Many service firms—such as hairstylists, lawyers, doctors, and educational institutions—also customize their marketing mixes to match individual customer needs. One-to-one marketing is growing rapidly in electronic commerce, where customers can be targeted very precisely.[2]

Mass Customization   Mass customization, an extension of one-to-one marketing, refers to providing unique products and solutions to individual customers on a mass scale. Advances in supply chain management, including just-in-time inventory control and enterprise resource planning, allow companies to customize products in ways that are both cost effective and practical. For example, consumers can log onto Barbie.com to custom build Barbie dolls. Customers choose Barbie's ethnicity, eye color, lip color, hairstyle, clothing, and accessories and have the doll custom built for $39.95 plus shipping. A similar service is offered by the Build-a-Bear Workshop, where customers can select, stuff, wash, and dress a teddy bear of their choice. Dell Computer also uses a mass customization approach.

Mass customization also occurs in business-to-business markets. Via a buying firm's local area network (LAN), employees can order products ranging from office supplies to travel services through an electronic procurement system. The system allows employees to requisition goods and services via a customized catalog—unique to the firm—where the products and prices have been negotiated by the buying firm.

EXHIBIT 4.2   CUSTOMIZATION TOOLS OF PERMISSION MARKETING

Company-Side Tools	Client-Side Tools
Cookies Small files written to a user's hard drive while visiting a Web site. When the user returns to the site, the cookie files are used to personalize the site.	*Individualized Web Portals* Allowing users to create personalized start pages. Each user can customize the page with his or her own content, such as stocks, local news and weather, and sports information.
Web Site Log A file maintained on a Web server that tracks page visits, duration of visits, and purchasing behavior. The firm can analyze the log to customize a session for individual users.	*Wireless Data Services* Essentially wireless Web portals, with data and information customized for wireless phones, pagers, and personal digital assistants.
Real-Time Profiling Software that tracks users' movements through a Web site. Allows the firm to track "clickstream" behavior in real time to make instantaneous adjustments to Web pages.	*Web Forms* HTML forms that allow users to type information directly into a Web page. Firms use Web forms to register users, take orders, and conduct surveys.
Automated E-Mail Sending e-mail to registered users on a regular basis (usually weekly). Allows the firm to promote special offers and remind users of certain events, such as birthdays and anniversaries.	*FAX-on-Demand* Used a great deal in the business-to-business market, this system allows users to request detailed information on goods or services. This automated system can be accessed with or without an Internet connection.
	E-Mail Users can ask questions, request information, or make complaints using a firm's e-mail system.

Source: Adapted from Judy Strauss and Raymond Frost, *E-Marketing*, 2nd edition. (Upper Saddle River, NJ: Prentice Hall, 2001), 304–310.

E-procurement systems like these are becoming quite popular, for good reason: They allow firms to save a great deal of money, not only on prices but also on the costs of placing orders. Selling firms benefit as well, by customizing their catalogs to specific buying firms, and they are able to sell more goods and services at a reduced cost.

Permission Marketing   Permission marketing is a one-to-one technique whereby customers give companies permission to specifically target them in their marketing efforts. Examples of customization tools used in permission marketing are described in Exhibit 4.2. The most common form of permission marketing is the opt-in e-mail list, where customers permit a firm to send periodic e-mail about goods and services that they are interested in purchasing. This type of scenario is ubiquitous in business-to-consumer e-commerce, so much so that many consumers fail to notice it. When customers order products online, they are given the option of receiving or not receiving future e-mail notifications about new products. Unless the customer deselects the box at the end of the order form, they will be added to the e-mail list.

Permission marketing has one huge benefit: Customers who opt in are already interested in the goods and services offered by the firm. This allows the firm to target only those individuals with an interest in their products, thereby eliminating the problem of wasted promotion.[3] For example, many airlines have the permission of their customers to send weekly e-mail notices of airfare and other travel-related specials. This type of system is in stark contrast to traditional mass media advertising, where only a portion of the viewing or reading audience is truly interested in the company's product.

Identifying the Characteristics and Needs of the Target Market

Once the marketing manager has selected the target market—whether it be the total mass market or one or more segments of it—he or she must next identify the characteristics and needs of customers within that target market. This step involves selecting the most relevant variables to identify and define the target market. Many of these variables, including customer demographics, lifestyles, and product usage characteristics, are derived from the situation analysis section of the marketing plan.

It is at this stage of market planning where the target market variables are revised or carried over from previous planning periods. A new or revised marketing strategy often requires changes in target market definition or identification to correct any problems in the previous marketing strategy that led to reduced performance, or that are likely to do so in the future. Changes here might include reducing price (to enhance value), increasing price (to connote higher quality), updating the advertising message to keep the communication current, adding a new product feature to make the benefits delivered more meaningful, and selling through retail stores instead of direct distribution to add the convenience of immediate availability. Sometimes it takes major changes to deliver fairly minor improvements in mix performance, while at other points a relatively minor modification can deliver significant improvements.

Consumer Markets

The goal in segmenting consumer markets is to isolate personal characteristics that distinguish one or more segments from the total market. The difficulty often lies in isolating multiple characteristics to get a better feel for customer's needs and wants. Marketers of soft drinks are not only concerned about age and gender in marketing their products; they are also interested in consumer attitudes and lifestyles. To get a better idea of how to approach these market segments, marketers must first understand the differences between customers' needs and wants. Then they can focus on identifying characteristics that uniquely identify segments of customers in ways that make them more appealing than other segments.

Needs vs. Wants   Typically, we think of needs as being necessities, particularly with respect to the necessities of life (food, water, clothing, safety, shelter, health, love). However, this definition is limited, because everyone has a different perspective on what constitutes a need. For example, many people would argue that they "need" a car, when their real need is for transportation. Their need for a car is really a "want" for a car. This is where we draw the distinction between needs and wants. A *need* occurs when an individual's current level of satisfaction does not equal the desired level of satisfaction. A *want* is a consumer's desire for a specific product that will satisfy the need. Hence, people need transportation, but they choose to fulfill that need with a car rather than with alternative products that can also meet the need (motorcycles, bicycles, pubic transportation, a taxi, horses, etc.).

The distinction between needs and wants is not simply semantic. In any marketing effort, the firm must always understand the basic needs fulfilled by their products. For example, people do not need drills; they need holes. Similarly, they do not need lawnmowers; they need shorter grass. Understanding these basic needs allows the firm to segment markets and create marketing programs that can translate consumer needs into wants for their specific products. The idea is to build on the basic need and convince customers to want your product because it will fulfill their need better than any competing product. Of course, some consumers may have to be convinced that they actually have a need before they can want a specific product. So-called unsought products such as life insurance, cemetery plots, long-term health insurance, and education are good examples. In these cases, the marketer must first build the need and then convince customers to want their products over competing products.

It is at this point where segmentation becomes critical. Some products and markets can be segmented on the basis of needs alone. For example, college students have needs that are obviously different from senior citizens, and single consumers have very different needs than families with small children. However, most product categories are not marketed on the basis of need-fulfillment alone. Take the car market, for example. Not one single manufacturer promotes their product as being the best car to get you from point A to point B (the basic need of transportation). Rather, they market their product on the basis of consumer wants, such as luxury (Lexus), image (Mercedes), sportiness (Pontiac), durability (Ford Trucks), fuel economy (Honda Insight), and safety (Cadillac). As we examine the different bases for segmentation in the next section, keep in mind that in many cases the need does not change; what really changes from one segment of consumers to the next are the wants.

Bases for Segmentation   The purpose of segmenting markets is to divide the entire population into groups with relatively homogeneous needs. There are a variety of factors that can be used to divide markets into these homogeneous groupings. Most fall into one of three general categories—state of being, state of mind, and benefit(s) sought.

State-of-being segmentation divides markets into segments using demographic factors, such as gender (e.g., Virginia Slims cigarettes for women), age (e.g., Limited Express retail clothing stores for young women/teenagers), income (e.g., Lexus automobiles for wealthy consumers), and education (e.g., Executive MBA programs for business professionals with an undergraduate degree). *State-of-mind segmentation* deals not with the way consumers actually are, but how they think and feel. Attitudes, interests, and opinions are generally used to categorize consumers into state-of-mind segments. For example, "True Greens" tend to be the most environmentally conscious consumers and therefore those to whom recycled products are most likely to appeal.

Both state-of-being segmentation and state-of-mind segmentation are really surrogates for the true issue in market segmentation: *benefits sought* (wants). While some consumers certainly buy a new car solely for transportation, most buy specific car makes and models for other reasons. Younger consumers want cars that are sporty and fun to drive and that enhance their image. Families purchase minivans because they want more room for their children and cargo. Older consumers opt for comfortable and luxurious models. All have the same basic need for transportation. The explosion in demand for sport utility vehicles is partly due to consumers' desire for cargo capacity, image, and styling (many people would never consider the more practical minivan because it does not fit their image). Carmakers can be the most effective in marketing products to each of these segments when they know what specific benefits those consumers are seeking.

State-of-being segmentation tends to be the most widely utilized because demographic variables are relatively easy to measure. In fact, much of this information is easily obtained during the situation analysis through secondary sources. For example, the U.S. Census Bureau offers data about the size of state-of-being segments by state, county, and zip code. State-of-mind issues are more difficult to measure, and often require primary marketing research (e.g., survey questions) to classify people properly and assess the size of various segments. One of the most widely used state-of-mind approaches is VALS2 (http://future.sri.com/VALS/VALSindex.shtml).

Business-to-Business Markets

As with consumer marketing, business-to-business marketing does not totally depart from the issues regarding marketing strategy discussed to this point, but it does raise some additional considerations that must be addressed for successful strategies to be developed and implemented. The foundation, however, remains the same. The marketing manager must determine target customers' needs, assess the extent to which those needs are being met with existing products from the firm and its competitors, and then determine the ways in which these needs and competitive offerings may be changing in the future.

Unique Characteristics of Business-to-Business Markets   Business-to-business marketing differs from consumer product marketing in at least four ways. These key differences relate to the nature of the decision-making unit, the role of hard and soft costs in making and evaluating purchase decisions, reciprocal buying relationships, and the dependence of the two parties on each other. As a general rule, these differences are more acute for firms attempting to build client relationships than for those businesses that practice transactional marketing. Traditional transactional marketing focuses on delivering largely standardized products to a sizable group of customers at the lowest price possible. Relationship-based marketing is longer term in nature and tends to focus more on overall goal attainment than simply getting the lowest possible price. At the present time, relationship-based marketing is a fast-growing trend in business-to-business marketing.

The Buying Center   The first key difference relates to the role of the buying center—the group of people responsible for making purchasing decisions. For consumer products, the buying center is fairly straightforward: The adult head-of-household tends to make most major purchase decisions for the family, with input and assistance from children and other family members if applicable. In an organization, however, the buying center tends to be much more complex and difficult to identify, in part because it may include three distinct groups of people—economic buyers, technical buyers, and users—each of which may have its own agenda and unique needs and desires in the buying decision.

Any effort to build a relationship between the selling and buying organizations must include *economic buyers*—those senior managers with the overall responsibility of achieving the buying firm's objectives. In recent years, economic buyers have become increasingly important as major product purchase decisions, based on value factors beyond price, have moved up the organization chart. This has made economic buyers a greater target for promotional activities.

Technical buyers—employees with the responsibility of procuring products to meet the needs of the firm on an ongoing basis—include purchasing agents and materials managers. They have the responsibility of delivering product solutions within budget and to narrow the number of product options that are presented to the economic buyer(s). They are critical for transactional marketing and are important to the day-to-day maintenance of long-term marketing relationships.

Users—managers and employees who have the responsibility of using a product purchased by the firm—comprise the last segment in the buying center. The user is often not the ultimate decision maker, but frequently is included in the decision process, particularly in the case of technologically advanced products. For example, a vice president of information technology often has a major role in hardware and software purchase decisions.

Hard and Soft Costs   The second difference between business-to-business marketing and consumer marketing relates to the significance of hard and soft costs. Consumers and organizations both consider *hard costs*, which include monetary price and costs associated with the purchase, such as shipping and installation. Organizations, particularly those attempting to build client relationships, also consider *soft costs*, such as downtime, opportunity costs, and human resource costs associated with the compatibility of systems in the buying decision. Activity-based costing is a critical part of the process of building client relationships as hard and soft costs are identified and total cost targets are set for all major purchase decisions.

Reciprocity   The third key difference involves the existence of reciprocal buying relationships. With consumer purchases, the opportunity for buying and selling is usually a one-way street: The marketer sells and the consumer buys. Business-to-business marketing, however, is more often a two-way street, with each firm marketing products that the other firm buys. For example, a company may buy office supplies from another company that in turn buys copy machines from the first firm. In fact, such arrangements can be an upfront condition of purchase in transactional marketing. Reciprocal buying is less likely to occur under relationship-based marketing unless it helps both parties achieve their respective goals.

Mutual Dependence   Finally, in business-to-business marketing, the buyer and seller are more likely to be dependent on one another, particularly in client relationships. For consumer–marketer relationships and transactional marketing, the level of dependence tends to be low. If a store is out of a product or a marketing organization goes out of business, customers simply switch to another source to meet their needs. Likewise, the loss of a particular customer through competitive inroads, geographic relocation, or death is unfortunate for a company but not itself particularly damaging.

This is not the case with relationship-based marketing where sole-source or limited-source buying may leave an organizational customer's operations severely distressed when a supplier shuts down or cannot deliver. The same is true for the loss of a customer. The selling firm has invested significantly in the client relationship, often modifying products and altering information systems and other systems central to the organization. Each client relationship represents a significant portion of the firm's profit, and a single lost customer can take months and even years to replace, if that can be done at all. After Rubbermaid and Wal-Mart experienced a rift in their relationship, the impact for both firms was significant. Wal-Mart used the situation, along with its significant resources and buying power, to build Sterilite, a small Massachusetts-based manufacturer, into a major competitor for Rubbermaid. Similar dependent relationships exist between Dell and Federal Express as well as Toys "Я" Us and Amazon.com.

Business-to-Business Relationship Management Though our discussion certainly involves generalizations (e.g., some consumer product marketers are much better at building close relationships than many business-to-business marketers), business-to-business marketing mixes do tend to have some key differences from consumer marketing mixes, particularly as a firm moves toward client-relationship building. Central to this switch for relationship-focused buyers and sellers is a shift from a win–lose strategy—the only way for one side to get more is for the other side to get less—to a win–win strategy—a focus more on growing the "size of the pie," where both sides win. Some of the more prominent changes include:[4]

- *A change in buyers' and sellers' roles.* To build stronger marketing relationships, buyers and sellers must shift from being competitive negotiators trying to drive prices up or down to being true communications specialists. This represents a major change in all aspects of the promotion mix for the selling firm.

- *An increase in sole sourcing.* Supplier firms will continue to sell directly to large customers or move to selling through "systems suppliers" that put together a set of products from various suppliers to deliver a comprehensive solution to buyers. This is happening today with the growth of online e-procurement systems.

- *An increase in global sourcing.* Increasingly, both buyers and sellers are scanning the globe in search of suppliers or buyers that represent the best match with their specific needs and requirements. The relationship-building process is costly and complex enough that only the best potential partners will be pursued.

- *An increase in team-based buying decisions.* Increasingly, purchase decisions are being made among teams from both supply-side and buy-side firms. These teams consist of employees from different areas of expertise that are central to the success of both firms. More and more, senior management of both the buying and the selling firm will be represented on these teams as economic buyers for both sides play a major role in setting goals and objectives.

- *Advanced earning power though productivity enhancements.* Firms that closely align their buying and selling operations are able to identify and remove any inefficiency in the process. Increased productivity leads to a reduction in both hard and soft costs, thereby enhancing the bottom line of both firms. Only the most efficient channels will survive, particularly as more procurement moves into the electronic arena.

The fundamental shift in the structure of most buyer–seller relationships will lead to dramatic changes in the way marketing and buying organizations work together. Only those firms willing to make strategic, as opposed to cosmetic, changes in the way they deal with their customers/suppliers are likely to prosper as we move forward in this century.

Differentiation and Positioning

After selecting a target market(s) and developing a mix of marketing elements to satisfy the needs of members of that target market, the marketing manager should attempt to differentiate the product from competitive offerings and position it so that it seems to possess the characteristics the target market most desires. While differentiation and positioning can be based on actual product features or characteristics, the principle task for the marketer is to develop and maintain a *relative perception* of the product in customers' minds. That is, customers must hold a favorable mental image or perception of a product relative to all other competing products.

Differentiation Strategies

Product differentiation is one of the most important goals of any marketing strategy. Customers' perception is of utmost importance in this process because differences among products can be based on real qualities (product characteristics, features, and style) or psychological qualities (perception and image). Generally, the most important tool of product differentiation is the brand, as discussed in Chapter 6. However, there are other important bases for differentiation, including product descriptors, customer support services, and image.

Product Descriptors   Information about products is generally provided in one of three contexts, as shown in Exhibit 4.3. The first context is *product features*, which are factual descriptors of the product. A feature of Pepsi One, for example, is that it contains only one calorie per serving. A feature of the Xerox Phaser color laser printer is that it produces five color pages per minute. However, features—while telling customers something about the nature of the product—are not generally the pieces of information that lead people to buy. Features must be translated into the second context, advantages. *Advantages* are performance characteristics that communicate how the features make the product behave, hopefully in a fashion that is distinctive and appealing to the customers. The advantage of a one-calorie drink is lower daily calorie intake, while an advantage of the color printer is less waiting time. But, as we have said before, the real reason people buy products is to gain *benefits*, the positive outcomes or need satisfaction they acquire from purchased products. Thus, the benefits of Pepsi One may include weight loss, a more attractive figure, and longer life. Likewise, at five color pages per minute, the Xerox Phaser will reduce employee waiting time, which increases their satisfaction and productivity and ultimately helps the organization attain its goals.

For Pepsi One, the brand manager can differentiate and position the product simply by communicating the product's features. The price is low, the product is simple, and consumers can make their own translation to health and appearance benefits. However, Xerox's task is more difficult, in that promotional messages must incorporate all product descriptors to help customers recognize the attractiveness of the product: "At five color pages per minute, your employee waiting time will be reduced, freeing employees for more productive activities than watching pages slowly appear from your existing printer." In the case of Xerox, the product is expensive, somewhat complex, and the benefits are not clearly apparent. Despite differences in product complexity and cost, many firms simply communicate their product's features, leaving customers to ascribe their own benefits.

EXHIBIT 4.3   **USING PRODUCT DESCRIPTORS TO DIFFERENTIATE AND POSITION A PRODUCT**

Product	Features	Advantages	Benefits
Dell Inspiron 5000e laptop computer	850-MHz Pentium III Weighs 6.75 lb	Blazingly fast Lightweight	Applications run faster Greater mobility
Pontiac Gran Prix GTP automobile	240-HP engine WideTrack design	Speed and power Excellent handling	Better self-image Safety Fun to drive
Crest MultiCare Advanced Cleaning Toothpaste	Dissolving micro-cleansing crystals	Teeth stay cleaner longer	Fresher breath
Bounty Extra Paper Towels	20% larger sheets More sheets per roll	Superior absorbency Won't run out as often	Handles bigger messes Fewer buying trips

Increasingly, one aspect of a product's description that is highly valued by customers is *quality*, which refers to the overall degree of excellence or superiority of a firm's product. Product characteristics that consumers associate with quality include reliability, durability, ease of maintenance, ease of use, and a trusted brand name. For business-to-business customers, characteristics such as technical suitability, ease of repair, and company reputation are significant indicators of quality. In general, higher product quality—real or imagined—means that a company can charge a higher price for their product and simultaneously build customer loyalty. This relationship between quality and price (inherent in the concept of value) forces the marketing manager to consider product quality carefully in his or her marketing mix decisions. We will look at the role of quality more closely in Chapter 5.

Customer Support Services   A firm may have difficulty differentiating its products when all products in a market have essentially the same quality, features, and benefits. In such cases, providing good customer support services—both before and after the sale—may be the only way to differentiate the firm's products and move them away from a price-driven commodity status. In the face of low-price competitors such as Barnes and Noble, Books-a-Million, and Amazon.com, small, local bookstores have been disappearing at an alarming rate. Those that remain do so because of the exceptional, personalized service they provide to their customers. Many local bookstores create customer loyalty by being actively involved in the community, including local charities. Many customers value this level of personalization so highly that they are willing to pay slightly higher prices and remain loyal to *their* bookstore.

Support services include anything the firm can provide in addition to the main product that adds value to that product for the customer. Examples include assistance in identifying and defining customer needs, delivery and installation, technical support for high-tech systems and software, financing arrangements, training, extended warranties and guarantees, repair, layaway plans, convenient hours of operation, affinity programs (e.g., frequent flier/buyer programs), and adequate parking. If you buy a Kenmore refrigerator, for example, you can expect Sears to provide financing, delivery and installation, and warranty repair service. Through research, the marketing manager can discover the types of support services that customers value most. The importance of having good support services has increased in recent years, directing many firms to design their customer services as carefully as they design their products.

Image The image of a product or an organization is the overall impression, positive or negative, that customers have of it. This impression includes what the organization has done in the past, what it presently offers, and projections about what it will do in the future. All aspects of the firm's marketing mix as perceived by customers will affect this overall impression. Consider the Macintosh computer. Despite Apple's financial woes, the Mac maintains a fiercely devoted following of customers who perceive the computer as being easier to use and more versatile than Windows-based PCs. In another example, the recent troubles of Firestone and their tire recall debacle will be felt by the company for years. Faced with mounting consumer criticism of the tire maker, many dealers began pulling away from Firestone in 2000. Firestone countered by enhancing its already lucrative dealer affiliate program. Still, Firestone's image may have been irreparably damaged.[5]

Positioning Strategies

Marketers can manipulate their marketing mix to position and enhance a product's image in customers' minds. To create a positive image for a product, a firm can choose from among several positioning strategies, including strengthening the current position, moving to a new position, and attempting to reposition the competition.

Strengthen the Current Position The key to strengthening a product's current position is to monitor constantly what target customers want and the extent to which the product or firm is perceived as satisfying those wants. Any complacency in today's dynamic marketplace is likely to result in lost customers and sales. It can be easy for a company known for excellent customer service after a sale to stagnate in this area as it focuses on improving other areas. But if after-sale service is a key ingredient in the company's strategy, this just simply cannot be allowed to happen. The firm must continue to invest time, money, talent, and attention in after-sale service to protect its market share and sales from competitors.

Strengthening a current position is all about continually "raising the bar" of customer expectations and being perceived by customers as the only firm capable of reaching the new height. For example, in the crowded minivan market, Ford strives to differentiate its Windstar by positioning it on the cutting edge of safety features. Consider the following statement from Ford's Web site:[6]

> Safety has always been a priority with Windstar. It was the first minivan to earn the U.S. government's five-star front crash test rating. And since no single safety feature is more important than the next, we've equipped Windstar with over 40 others, all standard, including a new low-tire-pressure warning system for 2001.

Ford understands that it must constantly raise expectations about safety if the Windstar is to remain competitive. Companies that fail to strengthen their position often find themselves sliding backward on key dimensions of their market offering.

Move to a New Position   At times, declining sales or market share may signal that customers have lost faith in a product's ability to satisfy their needs. In such cases, strengthening the present position may well accelerate the downturn in performance; a new position may be the best response. Repositioning may involve a fundamental change in any of the marketing mix elements and perhaps even all of them. J. Crew, for example, dropped its "preppy" style of clothing in favor of more "urban and hip" merchandise. The traditional catalog-based retailer also expanded the number of stores where its clothes are sold. As its traditional baby boom customers age, J. Crew needs to attract younger shoppers, who have traditionally favored stores like Banana Republic.

Some of the most memorable ad campaigns involve attempts to move to new positions. The "not just for breakfast anymore" campaign for orange juice is a good example. An ongoing example is Cadillac's "The Fusion of Design and Technology" campaign. As its traditional target market ages, Cadillac's share of the luxury market is eroding—forcing the company to focus on technology in an attempt to lure younger buyers. Another good example is Sears. Several years ago, the company launched its "Come see the softer side of Sears" campaign in an attempt to shift its image away from appliances and hand tools. Recently, Sears has shifted the focus to convenience and selection in its "Designed Around You" campaign:[7]

> Sears like you've never seen us before. Look around. You'll find shopping carts, wider and brighter aisles, and a quicker, easier checkout, all for your added convenience. Best of all, our fantastic selection of the items you need has gotten even bigger, which means easy, one-stop shopping for you.

Reposition the Competition   Sometimes it is advantageous to attempt to reposition the competition rather than change your own position. A direct attack on a competitor's strength may put its products in a less favorable light or even force the competitor to change its positioning strategy. We are all familiar with the dueling campaigns of AT&T and MCI, Coke and Pepsi, and McDonalds and Burger King. The latest duel is set to occur in online book retailing. In the late 1990s, Barnes & Noble launched its online store, bn.com, to compete with online bookstore pioneer Amazon.com. Back then, B&N's electronic storefront forced Amazon.com to reposition on two fronts: price and product availability. B&N inaugurated its site with 30 percent discounts and 400,000 in-stock titles, forcing Amazon to respond to remain competitive. Now, with the backing of the world's largest media company, Bertelsmann AG, B&N is set to make a serious run at Amazon to become the world's largest online book retailer. Barnes & Noble won the first salvo in late 2000 when Yahoo dropped Amazon as its portal partner in favor of a new deal with B&N. Many analysts believe that B&N's status as a clicks-and-mortar retailer gives it significant long-term, competitive advantages over the purely online Amazon.com.[8]

Whether to strengthen or reposition is just one of the many complex decisions required in the development of a marketing strategy. The key is to develop a strong marketing mix that effectively differentiates and positions a firm's products in such a way that customers perceive those products as being the most likely to satisfy their needs and wants. What is a strong marketing mix? In today's economy, it is one that provides the level of quality, satisfaction, and value that customers desire. In the next chapter, we turn our attention to these critical issues in developing the "right" marketing strategy.

Lessons from Chapter 4

Marketing strategy involves:

- selecting a specific target market.
- making decisions regarding the crucial elements of product, price, promotion, and distribution in order to satisfy the needs of customers in that market.
- choosing the "right" strategy from among many possible alternatives.

Market segmentation involves:

- a careful analysis of the customer environment.
- two basic alternatives in determining the scope of the markets to be served: mass marketing and market segmentation.

Traditional approaches to market segmentation:

- have been used successfully for decades.
- are not out of date. In fact, they are used by many of today's most successful firms.
- are sometimes used in combination by the same firm, depending on the brand/ product or market in question.

Mass marketing:

- involves no segmentation whatsoever.
- is aimed at the total (whole) market for a particular product.
- is an undifferentiated approach that assumes that all customers in the market have similar needs and wants that can be reasonably satisfied with a single marketing mix.
- works best when the needs of an entire market are relatively homogeneous.
- is advantageous in terms of production efficiency and lower marketing costs.
- is inherently risky because a standardized product is vulnerable to competitors that offer specialized products that better match customers' needs.

Differentiated marketing:

- involves dividing the total market into groups of customers having relatively common or homogeneous needs and attempting to develop a marketing mix that appeals to one or more of these groups.
- may be necessary when customer needs are similar within a single group but their needs differ across groups.
- involves two options: the multisegment approach and the market concentration approach.

Niche marketing:

- involves focusing marketing efforts on one small, well-defined market segment or niche that has a unique, specific set of needs.
- requires that firms understand and meet the needs of target customers so completely that, despite the small size of the niche, the firm's substantial share makes the segment highly profitable.

Individualized approaches to market segmentation:

- are beginning to emerge due to advances in technology, particularly communication technology and the Internet.
- are possible because organizations now have the ability to track customers with a high degree of specificity.
- allow firms to combine demographic data with information on past and current purchasing behavior so that they are able to tweak their marketing mixes in ways that allow them to precisely match customers needs, wants, and preferences.

One-to-one marketing:

- involves the creation of an entirely unique marketing mix for each customer in the target segment.
- is common in business-to-business marketing, where unique programs and/or systems are designed for each customer.
- is growing rapidly in consumer marketing, particularly in luxury and custom-made products, as well as in services.

Mass customization:

- refers to providing unique products and solutions to individual customers on a mass scale.
- is now cost effective and practical due to advances in supply chain management, including just-in-time inventory control and electronic data interchange.
- is used quite often in business-to-business markets, especially in electronic procurement systems.

Permission marketing:

- is a one-to-one technique whereby customers give companies permission to specifically target them in their marketing efforts.
- is commonly executed via the opt-in e-mail list, where customers permit a firm to send periodic e-mail about goods and services they are interested in purchasing.
- has one huge benefit: Customers who opt in are already interested in the goods and services offered by the firm.

- allows a firm to precisely target individuals, thereby eliminating the problem of wasted promotion.

- is in stark contrast to traditional mass media advertising, where only a portion of the viewing or reading audience is truly interested in the company's product.

Identifying the characteristics and needs of consumer markets:

- involves selecting the most relevant variables to identify and define the target market, many of which are derived from the situation analysis section of the marketing plan.

- involves the isolation of personal characteristics that distinguish one or more segments of the total market.

Keys to understanding needs and wants:

- Needs as "necessities" is a limited definition because everyone has a different perspective on what constitutes a need.

- Needs occur when an individual's current level of satisfaction does not equal the desired level of satisfaction.

- Wants are a consumer's desire for a specific product that will satisfy a need.

- The firm must always understand the basic needs fulfilled by its products.

- The key is to segment markets and create marketing programs that translate consumer needs into wants for specific products.

- While some products and markets can be segmented on the basis of needs alone, most product categories are marketed on the basis of wants, not need-fulfillment.

State-of-being segmentation in consumer markets:

- divides markets into segments using demographic factors such as gender, age, income, and education.

- tends to be the most widely used form of segmentation because demographic variables are relatively easy to measure.

State-of-mind segmentation in consumer markets:

- deals with how consumers think and feel.

- uses consumers' attitudes, interests, and opinions to create market segments.

- is more difficult to measure, and often requires primary marketing research to classify people properly and assess the size of various segments.

Consumer segments based on benefits sought (wants):

- are the key to market segmentation but are difficult to identify without state-of-being and state-of-mind characteristics.

- are the most effective because marketers know the specific benefits that consumers are seeking.

Identifying the characteristics and needs of business-to-business markets:

- deals with the same basic issues as consumer marketing.

- requires an understanding of the unique characteristics of business markets, including the role of the buying center, the nature of hard and soft costs, reciprocity, and mutual dependence.

- is critical for firms attempting to build client relationships.

Business-to-business relationship management:

- includes a fundamental shift from a win–lose strategy (one side gets more, the other side gets less) to a win–win strategy (both sides win and get more).

- leads to a host of changes in the way that business is conducted, including a change in buyers' and sellers' roles, an increase in sole sourcing, an increase in global sourcing, an increase in team-based buying decisions, and advanced earning power though productivity enhancements.

- requires that firms closely align their buying and selling operations to identify and remove any inefficiencies in the process.

Differentiation and positioning:

- involves the development and maintenance of a *relative perception* for a product in customers' minds. That is, customers must hold a favorable mental image or perception of a product relative to all other competing products.

- is fundamentally based on the brand.

- is often based on product descriptors, customer support services, and image.

- includes the basic positioning strategies of strengthening the current position, moving to a new position, or repositioning the competition.

Questions for Discussion

1. Can you think of a product that could be marketed effectively using a mass marketing approach? If so, explain and justify your answer. If not, what types of changes would have to be made to the product to make it appropriate for a mass marketing approach?

2. People sometimes criticize marketing as being manipulative, based on the argument that marketing activities can create needs where none previously existed. Marketers that are often implicated include makers of sport utility vehicles, larger homes, cellular phones, microwave ovens, luxury products, and gourmet foods. Are consumers being manipulated into believing that they need these products? Or are marketers creating products that fulfill previously unmet needs?

3. Many consumers and consumer advocates are critical of the one-to-one marketing approach due to issues surrounding personal privacy. Marketers counter that one-to-one marketing can lead to privacy abuses but that the benefits to both consumers and marketers far outweigh the risks. Where do you stand on this issue? Why?

Exercises

1. Think about the last purchase you made in each of the following product categories. What were the features, advantages, and benefits of the specific product/brand that you selected? After completing the table, explain how the product/brand is positioned in the market.

Category	My Purchase	Features	Advantages	Benefits
Athletic shoes				
Restaurant				
Personal computer				

2. One of the most exciting advances in market segmentation is the increasing use of geographic information systems (GIS) to map target markets. Go to http://gis.about.com to get a feel for how GIS is used in business and many other fields. What are the advantages of using GIS in market segmentation?

3. One of the more popular proprietary segmentation tools is the PRIZM system developed by Claritas (http://www.claritas.com/index.htm). PRIZM describes every neighborhood in the United States in terms of demographic and behavioral "clusters." Go to the Claritas Web site and click on PRIZM ZIP Code Lookup under the "Express Solutions" tab. Try your zip code and see if you agree with their clustering scheme.

5

Developing Customer Relationships Through Quality, Value, and Satisfaction

---

Introduction

Developing a solid marketing mix that effectively satisfies customers' needs and wants has become difficult in today's rapidly changing business environment. The simple fact is that good situation and SWOT analyses, along with effective segmentation and differentiation, may not be enough to guarantee success, given the rapid pace of change. In times past, developing the "right" marketing strategy was really more about creating a large number of transactions with customers—or market share—than about finding better ways to solve customers' problems and satisfy their needs. In today's economy, the best marketing strategy is one that provides the level of quality, value, and satisfaction necessary to retain customers over the long term. Developing long-term relationships with customers is perhaps the best way to insulate a firm from the rapid pace of change in today's environment.

In this chapter, we first examine the concept of customer relationship management, including its basic principles. Then we explore three related issues in developing long-term customer relationships: quality, value, and satisfaction. While each issue involves a distinct concept, we address the interplay between quality, value, and satisfaction in a firm's efforts to effectively manage its relationships with customers. It is important to remember that quality, value, and satisfaction are tools or strategies, while maintaining long-term relationships with customers is the ultimate goal.

Customer Relationship Management

In order to fully appreciate the concepts behind customer relationship management (CRM), we have to develop a new perspective on the customer. In fact, we must shift our emphasis from "acquiring customers" to "maintaining clients," as shown in Exhibit 5.1. While this strategic shift has been under way for some time in business-to-business markets, it is now being embraced in consumer markets. A good definition of CRM is:

EXHIBIT 5.1	STRATEGIC SHIFT FROM ACQUIRING CUSTOMERS TO MAINTAINING CLIENTS

Acquiring Customers	**Maintaining Clients**
Customers are "customers"	Customers are "clients"
Mass marketing	One-to-one marketing
Acquire new customers	Build relationships with current customers
Discrete transactions	Continuous transactions
Increase market share	Increase share of customer
Differentiation based on groups	Differentiation based on individual customers
Segmentation based on homogeneous needs	Segmentation based on heterogeneous needs
Short-term strategic focus	Long-term strategic focus
Standardized products	Mass customization
Lowest cost provider	Value-based pricing strategy
One-way mass communication	Two-way individualized communication
Competition	Collaboration

CRM is the holistic process of identifying, attracting, differentiating, and retaining customers. It involves more than simply listening to customers or providing better products and services. It means integrating a firm's entire supply chain to create customer value at every step, either through increased benefits or lowered costs. It results in higher profits through increased business from a firm's customer base.[1]

It is important to note that CRM does not focus solely on end customers. Rather, CRM involves a number of stakeholders:[2]

Employees: Firms must manage relationships with their employees if they are to have any hope of fully serving customers needs. This is especially true in service firms, where employees *are* the service in the eyes of customers.

Supply chain partners: Virtually all firms buy and sell products upstream and/or downstream in the supply chain. This involves the procurement of materials or the sale of finished products to other firms. Either way, relationships with supply chain partners are critical to satisfying customers.

Lateral partners: Relationships with other stakeholders must also be managed effectively. These include government agencies, nonprofit organizations, and facilitating firms that help a firm achieve its goals but are not included in the supply chain.

Customers: The end users of a product, whether businesses or individual consumers.

Increasing Share of Customer

One of the most basic principles of CRM is the shift away from market share toward share of customer. This involves abandoning the old notions of acquiring new customers and increasing transactions to focus on more fully serving the needs of current customers. Financial services are a great example of this strategy in action. Most consumers acquire financial services from many different firms. They bank at one institution, purchase insurance from a different institution, and handle their investments through another. To counter this fact of life, most large banks now offer all of these services under one roof. For example, AmSouth Bank, a large regional financial institution with 600 offices throughout the southeastern United States, promotes itself as "The Relationship Bank." It offers every conceivable financial service that businesses or consumers could need. Rather than focus on the acquisition of new customers, AmSouth tries to more fully serve the financial needs of each individual customer, thereby acquiring a larger share of each customer's financial business.

Focusing on share of customer requires understanding that all customers have different needs and therefore that not all customers have equal value to a firm. The most basic application of this idea is the 80/20 rule: 80 percent of business profits come from 20 percent of customers. Though this idea is not new, advances in technology and data collection techniques now allow firms to profile customers in real time. The goal is to estimate the worth of individual customers to express their lifetime value (LTV) to the firm. Some customers—those that require considerable handholding or that frequently returns products—are simply too expensive to keep, given the low level of profits they generate. These unprofitable customers can be "fired" or required to pay very high fees for additional service. For example, many banks and brokerages slap hefty maintenance fees on small accounts. This allows the firm to spend its resources to more fully develop relationships with its profitable customers.

One-to-One Marketing and Mass Customization

In Chapter 4, we discussed one-to-one marketing and mass customization as segmentation strategies. Since these strategies focus on individual customers, they are critical to the development and maintenance of long-term relationships. The simple truth is that customers will maintain relationships with firms that best fulfill their needs and solve their specific problems. However, this type of one-to-one marketing can be prohibitively expensive to deliver. To make customized marketing mixes viable, two issues are critical. First, the delivery of the marketing mix (product, pricing, distribution, and promotion) must be automated to a degree that makes it cost efficient. The Internet makes this possible by allowing for individual customization in real time. As mentioned in Chapter 4, Dell's ability to offer customized product configuration via the Internet is both cost effective and driven by the needs of individual customers.

The second critical issue in mass customization is the notion of *personalization*. Today, personalization means much more than calling customers by name. We use the term to describe the idea of giving customers choices, not only in terms of product configuration, but also in terms of the entire marketing mix. Amazon.com, for example, offers a great deal of personalization by effectively mining its customer database. Customers can choose payment terms, shipping terms, delivery locations, gift wrapping, and whether to opt in to future e-mail promotions. Also, by monitoring its clickstream data in real time, Amazon.com can offer product suggestions on the fly—while customers are visiting the site. This sort of customized point-of-sale information not only increases sales, but also better fulfills customer's needs.

To grow in today's business environment, a firm must build its *relationship capital*—the ability to build and maintain relationships with customers, suppliers, and partners. In fact, many experts argue that relationship capital is more important than any tangible asset, such as land or property.[3] To build relationship capital, a firm must be able to fulfill the needs of its customers better than its competitors. And it must be able to fulfill those needs with high-quality goods and services, offer products that are a good value for the price, and achieve a high level of customer satisfaction. Let's now take a closer look at the role of quality, value, and satisfaction in developing customer relationships.

The Role of Quality in Developing Customer Relationships

When it comes to developing and maintaining customer relationships, quality is a double-edged sword. If the quality of a good or service is bad, the organization obviously has little chance of satisfying customers or maintaining relationships with them. The adage of "trying something at least once" applies here. A firm may be successful in generating first-time transactions with customers, but poor quality guarantees that repeat purchases will not occur. On the other hand, good quality is not an automatic guarantee of success. Think of it as a necessary but insufficient condition of customer relationship management.

What Is Quality?

Quality is a relative term that refers to the degree of superiority of a firm's goods or services. At issue here is the fact that quality applies to many different aspects of a firm's total product offering. The total product consists of at least three components, as illustrated in Exhibit 5.2: the core product, customer services, and symbolic attributes. The heart of the offering, the core product, is the firm's *raison d'être*, or justification for existence. The core can be a tangible good or an intangible service. The *core product* is the part of the offering that delivers the core benefit desired by customers. If the core product is of inferior quality, the firm has little chance of success, because the product will not be sufficient to meet customer needs. However, providing a high-quality core product is not enough to ensure customer satisfaction and develop long-term relationships. This occurs because customers expect the core product to be of high quality, at least at a level necessary to meet their needs. When the core product meets this level of expected quality, customers begin to take it for granted. For example, customers take their telephone service for granted because they expect it to work. The same thing can be said for a restaurant that consistently delivers high-quality food. Over time, the core product no longer stands out at a level that can maintain the customer relationship over the long term.

It is at this point that customer services become critical. Customer services involve activities that add value to the core product, thereby differentiating the core product from competing offerings. In many product categories, the true difference between competing products lies in the customer services provided by the firm. For example, every hotel is capable of delivering on the core product—a bed or room in which to spend the night. The important differences, however, lie in the customer services. Upscale hotels such as Hyatt and Hilton offer many amenities—spas, restaurants, health clubs, valet parking, room service, etc.—that budget hotels like Motel 6 do not. Wireless phone service is another example. Though all can fulfill their customers' communication needs, customer services such as rate plans, free minutes, rollover minutes, and free roaming and long distance are used by customers to distinguish one company

EXHIBIT 5.2   COMPONENTS OF THE TOTAL PRODUCT OFFERING

Example	Core Product	Customer Services	Symbolic Attributes
Sprint PCS Wireless Phone	Communication	Rate plans Free long distance Rollover minutes	Leather slipcase Changeable faceplates
Chevrolet Silverado Pickup	Transportation Hauling/towing	Financing Service department "Build your own"	"Like a rock" "Work and fun"
John Deere Lawn Tractor	Grass cutting	Financing Delivery	John Deere "green" "Nothing rides like a Deere"
Michelin Tires	Tires Safety	Availability Installation Financing	Security—"Because a lot is riding on your tires"
Waldorf Astoria, New York City	Bed/room	Mid-Manhattan location Restaurants/room service Executive lounge	"Extraordinary hospitality" The first "Grand Hotel" Art-Deco style

from another. In business markets, customer services are often the most important factor in developing long-term relationships. Services such as financing, training, installation, and maintenance must be of top quality to ensure that customers are willing to maintain a relationship with the supplier firm.

It is interesting to note that many products are not marketed with the core product in mind. When was the last time an automaker touted a car or truck on its ability to fulfill your transportation needs (i.e., getting you from point A to point B)? Rather, they focus on customer service attributes such as financing, roadside assistance, and warranties. They also focus on symbolic differences, such as image, style, prestige, and brand. In fact, many products—e.g., Mercedes, DeWALT power tools, Rolex, and Ruth's Chris Steak House—only have to say their names to get the message across. The power of brands like these is that they can project the entire product offering (core, service, and symbolic) with one word. Because branding and quality are so closely related, we discuss branding in more detail in Chapter 6.

Delivering Superior Quality

Delivering superior quality day in and day out is one of the most difficult things any organization can do with regularity. In essence, it is difficult to get everything right all or even most of the time. During the 1980s and into the 1990s, strategic initiatives such as total quality management and ISO 9000 were quite successful in changing the way businesses thought about quality. As a result, virtually every industry saw dramatic improvements in core product quality during that time.

However, most businesses today struggle with improving the quality of service—either as a core product or as customer services that add value to a core product. This happens because, unlike the quality of manufactured goods, service quality is inherently people driven. Since services are delivered by people for people, any number of things can and do go wrong in the delivery of service quality. A great deal of research has been conducted to determine how businesses can improve the quality of their services. The following four issues stand out.[4]

Understand Customers' Expectations, Needs, and Wants   It is not surprising that the basis of improving service quality is also the starting point for effective customer relationship management. The delivery of superior quality begins with a solid understanding of customers' expectations. This means that managers must stay in touch with customers by conducting research to better identify their needs and wants. This research can include large-scale and expensive efforts, such as surveys and focus groups; but it can also include simple and inexpensive efforts such as customer comment cards or having managers that are willing to interact with customers. Advances in technology, such as Web site cookies, bar code scanners, and Web site logs, have greatly improved our ability to collect and analyze information from individual customers.[5] New tools such as data warehousing and data mining hold great promise in enabling firms to better understand customers' needs.

Translate Customer Research into Specifications for Quality   Firms that can successfully convert customer information into quality specifications ensure that the voice of the customer is heard. If customers want better ingredients, friendlier employees, or faster delivery, then specifications should be set to match these desires. It is often the case, however, that managers set specifications that meet organizational objectives, with no consideration for customer expectations. A common example in retailing occurs when managers insist that employees stock shelves or clean floors when customers really want better selection, friendlier service, and speedier checkout. To truly achieve this goal, managers must be committed to giving customers what they want and expect.

Deliver on Specifications   The best service quality specifications are of little use if they are not delivered. At issue is the ability of managers and employees to deliver quality that is consistent with established specifications. Greeting customers by name, answering the phone on the second ring, and delivering a hot pizza within an hour are all examples of quality specifications that may, or may not, be delivered. Successfully achieving specifications depends mostly on the training and motivation of the firm's employees. However, it also depends on the ability of the firm to fully fund the quality effort. For example, many retailers—including Wal-Mart—at one time had specifications for opening additional checkout lanes when there were more than three people in line. However, these retailers failed to deliver on this specification due to the expense of staffing additional employees to operate the registers.

Promise Only What Can Be Delivered   It goes without saying that customers will be disappointed if an organization fails to deliver on its promises. The key is to create realistic customer expectations for what can and cannot be delivered. All communication to customers must be honest and realistic with respect to the degree of quality that can be delivered. This goal became a problem for electronic retailers during the 1999 Christmas season when they promised delivery by December 24. When many e-tailers failed to fulfill their promises that year, the Federal Trade Commission (FTC) stepped in during Christmas 2000 to warn these firms about setting unrealistic customer expectations.[6]

For many firms, improving quality has been the hallmark of a successful marketing strategy for many years. The growth and prestige of the Malcolm Baldrige National Quality Award since its inception in 1987 is proof of this. Despite its importance, however, quality is only one part of the equation in developing long-term relationships with customers. We now turn our attention to another important part of the equation: creating good value.

Creating Value to Develop Customer Relationships

A second important aspect of developing and maintaining solid relationships is to create good value for customers. As a guiding principle of marketing strategy, value is quite useful because it (1) includes the concept of quality, but is broader in scope, (2) takes into account every marketing mix element, and (3) can be used to consider explicitly customer perceptions of the marketing mix in the strategy development process. Value can also be used as a means of organizing the internal aspects of marketing strategy development.

The Value Formula

Value is a difficult term to define, because it means different things to different people.[7] Some people equate good value with high product quality, while others see value as nothing more than a low price. The most common definition of value relates customer benefits to costs, or to use a more colloquial expression, gives "more bang for the buck." Value is also a relative term, in that it can be judged only in comparison to the offerings of other firms. For our purposes, we define value as a customer's subjective evaluation of benefits relative to costs to determine the worth of a firm's product relative to the offerings of other firms. A simple formula for value might look like this:

$$\text{Perceived Value} = \frac{\text{Customer Benefits}}{\text{Customer Costs}}$$

Although this formula is simple in design, it is not very useful in developing marketing strategy. To see how each marketing mix element relates to this formula, we need to break down customer benefits and customer costs into their component parts, as shown here (and in Exhibit 5.3).

$$\text{Perceived Value} = \frac{\text{Core Product Quality} + \text{Customer Service Quality} + \text{Experience-Based Quality}}{\text{Monetary Costs} + \text{Nonmonetary Costs}}$$

Customer Benefits: Core Product, Service, and Experience-Based Quality Customer benefits can include anything that a customer receives in his or her dealings with the firm. These benefits are most closely associated with the product element of the marketing mix. Examples include the benefits that customers receive from the quality of the firm's core products, including all of the features possessed by its products. For service firms, product quality refers to the inherent quality of the core service, such as a bed or room in a hotel or education at a college or university. Customers also receive benefits from customer (product support) services, such as installation, delivery, training, and layaway programs. The quality of customer service depends on how reliable

| EXHIBIT 5.3 | COMPONENTS OF CUSTOMER BENEFITS AND CUSTOMER COSTS |

Customer Benefits	Customer Costs
Core Product Quality	*Monetary Costs*
Product features	<u>Transactional Costs</u>
Brand name	Retail or wholesale price
Styling and design	Delivery charges
Durability	Installation charges
Ease of use	Sales tax
Image	Usage tax
Reputation	Registration fees
Warranties and guarantees	Licensing fees
	Additional fees or charges
Customer Service Quality	
	<u>Life Cycle Costs</u>
Reliability	Maintenance costs
Responsiveness	Repair costs
Timeliness	Replacement costs
Friendliness of employees	
	Nonmonetary Costs
Experience-Based Quality	
	Time
Retail atmosphere and decor	Effort
Advertising and publicity	Risk
Entertainment benefits	Safety and security
	Opportunity costs

and responsive the firm is to customer requests and on employee characteristics, such as friendliness and empathy.

Customers also receive benefits based on their experiences. For example, many customers derive benefits from the act of shopping itself. These benefits are affected by the atmosphere and decor of the retail store. In sports marketing, the quality of the fan experience is often more important than the core product of the game or event. This happens because the marketer cannot guarantee the outcome due to the lack of control over the game or event.[8] Experience-based quality is also important in business-to-business marketing. Business customers receive benefits from their experiences, such as interacting with salespeople and working with an e-procurement system. Many promotional activities are included in experience benefits. These activities range from in-store promotion(s) (e.g., point-of-purchase displays, demonstrations, and fashion shows) to out-of-store promotion (e.g., advertising and publicity, trade shows, Web-based communication). Promotional activities are also partly responsible for creating the image and prestige characteristics that are a portion of core product quality.

Monetary and Nonmonetary Customer Costs   Customer costs include anything that the customer must give up to obtain the benefits provided by the firm. The most obvious cost is the monetary cost of the product, which comes in two forms: transactional costs and life cycle costs.[9] *Transactional costs* include the immediate financial outlay or commitment that must be made to purchase the product. Other than the purchase price of the product, examples of these costs include sales taxes, use taxes, licensing fees, registration fees, delivery, and installation. *Life cycle costs* include any additional costs that customers will incur over the life of the product. The costs for maintenance and repair are good examples. Firms that are able to reduce one or more of these costs are often seen as providing a better value than their competitors. For example, appliance retailers can increase value by offering free delivery and installation when their competitors charge for these services. Likewise, manufacturers of durable goods are able to charge higher prices if customers perceive their life cycle costs as being lower. Product quality, warranties, and the availability of repair services all play into the equation when customers judge monetary costs.

Nonmonetary costs are not as obvious as monetary costs. Two such costs are the time and effort customers expend to find and purchase goods and services. These costs are closely related to a firm's distribution activities. To reduce time and effort, the firm must increase product availability, thereby making it more convenient for customers to purchase the firm's products. The growth in nonstore and electronic retailing is a direct result of firms taking steps to reduce the time and effort required to purchase their products and thereby reduce these costs to customers. The sheer number of products that customers can have delivered directly to their homes is a testament to the growing importance of customers' time.

Another nonmonetary cost, risk, can be reduced by offering good basic warranties or extended warranties for an additional charge. Retailers reduce risk by maintaining liberal return and exchange policies. The final nonmonetary cost, opportunity costs, is harder for the firm to control. Some firms attempt to reduce opportunity costs by promoting their products as being the best or by promising good service after the sale. To anticipate opportunity costs, the firm must consider all competitors, including total budget competitors, that offer customers alternatives for spending their money.

Competing on Value

After breaking down value into its component parts, we can better understand how a firm's marketing strategy can be designed to optimize customer value. By altering each element of the marketing mix, the firm can enhance value by increasing core product, customer service, or experience-based quality and/or reducing monetary or nonmonetary costs. Retailers offer good examples of how value can be delivered by altering one or more parts of the value equation. Convenience stores offer value to customers by reducing nonmonetary costs (time and effort) and increasing monetary prices. These high-priced (in dollars) stores stay in business because in some situations customers value their time and effort more than money.

Customers who want the best quality may be willing to spend large sums of money and/or spend more time searching for top-quality merchandise because they consider their nonmonetary costs to be less important. These consumers are likely to shop at retailers such as Macy's, Nordstrom, and Saks rather than in discount chains. Electronic retailing also holds great promise in being able to deliver exceptional value in many product categories. Consumers who shop for toys at Amazon.com or KBkids.com can find low prices and quick delivery (often with free shipping) without fighting crowded toy stores. In an added bonus, many of these online purchases can be made free of sales tax, at least until the government solves the problems associated with Internet taxation.

Obviously, different target markets will have different perceptions of good value. The marketing manager must understand the different value requirements of each target market and adapt the marketing mix accordingly. From a strategic perspective, it is important to remember that all four marketing mix elements are important to delivering value. Strategic decisions about one element alone can change perceived value for better or worse. If these decisions lower overall value, the marketing manager should consider modifying other marketing mix elements to offset this decrease.

Maintaining Customer Satisfaction Over the Long Term

In the final part of this chapter, we look at customer satisfaction and the role it plays in maintaining long-term customer relationships. To maintain and manage customer satisfaction from a strategic point of view, managers must understand the differences between satisfaction, value, and quality. They must also make customer satisfaction measurement a long-term, continuous commitment.

Satisfaction vs. Value vs. Quality

How is customer satisfaction different from value and quality? The answer is not so obvious, because the definition of each term closely overlaps those of the others. *Customer satisfaction* is typically defined as the degree to which a product meets or exceeds the customer's expectations about that product. The difficulty in separating satisfaction from value and quality involves the word *expectations*. It should be obvious that customers can hold expectations about any part of the product offering, including value and quality. So how are value and quality different from satisfaction?

To solve this issue, think of each concept not in terms of what it is, but in terms of its size. The most narrowly defined concept is quality, which customers judge on an attribute-by-attribute basis. Consider a meal at a restaurant. The quality of that meal stems from specific attributes: The quality of the food, the drink, the atmosphere, and the service are all important. We could even go so far as to judge the quality of the ingredients in the food. In fact, many restaurants—such as Papa John's Pizza and Ruth's Chris Steak House—promote themselves based on the quality of their ingredients. When the customer steps up to consider the broader issue of value, they now include things other than quality: the price of the meal, the time and effort required to get to the restaurant, parking availability, and opportunity costs. In this case, even the best meal in a great restaurant can be viewed as a poor value if the price is too high in terms of monetary and/or nonmonetary costs.

When a customer considers satisfaction, he or she will typically respond based on his or her expectations of the item in question. If the quality of the food is not what the customer expected, then the customer will be dissatisfied with the food. Similarly, if the value of the meal is not what the customer expected, the customer will be dissatisfied with the value. Note that these are independent judgments. It is entirely possible for a customer to be satisfied with the quality of the meal but dissatisfied with its value. The opposite is also true.

However, most customers do not make independent judgments about satisfaction. Instead, customers think of satisfaction based on the totality of their experience, without overtly considering issues like quality and value. We are not saying that customers do not judge quality or value. Rather, we are saying that customers think of satisfaction in more abstract terms than they do quality or value. This happens because customers' expectations—hence their satisfaction—can be based on any number of factors, *even factors that have nothing to do with quality or value.* Continuing with our restaurant example, it is entirely possible for a customer to receive the absolute best quality and value yet still be dissatisfied with the experience. The weather, other customers, a bad date, and being in a bad mood are just a few examples of nonquality and nonvalue factors that can affect customers' expectations and cloud their judgments of satisfaction.

Maintaining Customer Satisfaction

There are three keys to leveraging customer satisfaction from a strategic point of view:

1. *Understand what can go wrong:* Managers, particularly those on the frontline, must understand that an endless number of things can and will go wrong in fulfilling customers' needs and wants. Even the best strategies will not work in the face of customers who are in a bad mood. Other things are simply uncontrollable. Sport and event marketers, for example, are often at the mercy of the weather.

2. *Focus on issues that are controllable:* With an eye toward #1, managers must focus on issues they can control—the marketing mix. Core product quality, customer service, atmosphere, experiences, pricing, convenience, distribution, and promotion must all be managed in an effort to increase share of customer and maintain loyal relationships. It is especially important that the core product be of high quality. Without that, the firm stands little chance of developing or maintaining long-term customer relationships.

3. *Make customer satisfaction measurement an ongoing priority:* If you don't know what customers want, need, or expect, everything else is a waste of time and resources. A permanent, ongoing program to measure customer satisfaction is the cornerstone of customer relationship management.

The ongoing measurement of customer satisfaction has changed dramatically over the last decade. While simple questionnaires using 5-point satisfaction scales still have their place, most firms that are serious about customer relationship management have adopted more robust means of tracking satisfaction that are based on actual customer behaviors. Some of these new metrics include:[10]

Lifetime value (LTV) of a customer: the net present value of the revenue stream generated by a specific customer over a period of time. LTV recognizes that some customers are worth more than others. Companies can better leverage their customer satisfaction programs by focusing on valuable customers.

Average order value (AOV): a customer's purchase dollars divided by the number of orders over a period of time. The AOV will increase over time as customer satisfaction increases and customers become more loyal.

Customer acquisition/retention costs: It is typically less expensive to retain current customers than to acquire new customers. As long as this holds true, a company is better off keeping its current customers satisfied.

Customer retention rate: the percentage of customers who are repeat purchasers. This number should remain consistent or grow slowly. A declining retention rate is a cause for concern.

Referrals: dollars that are generated from customers referred to the firm by current customers. A declining referral rate is a cause for concern.

Viral marketing: an electronic form of word-of-mouth communication. The number of Internet newsgroups and chat rooms where customers praise and complain about companies is staggering. Companies can track customer satisfaction by closely monitoring this online commentary.

Firms also have another research method at their disposal: the focus group. Long used as a means of understanding customers' wants and needs during product development, focus groups are being used more often in the measurement of customer satisfaction. Recent research in customer satisfaction measurement indicates that satisfaction is a more holistic concept than previously thought.[11] Focus groups allow firms to more fully explore the subtleties of satisfaction, including its emotional and psychological underpinnings. By better understanding the roots of customer satisfaction, marketers should be better able to develop marketing strategies that can meet customers' needs.

Lessons from Chapter 5

The best marketing strategy:

- is difficult to develop in today's fast-paced business environment.

- is not about creating a large number of customer transactions.

- is one that provides the level of quality, value, and satisfaction necessary to retain customers.

- develops long-term relationships with customers in order to insulate the firm from the rapid pace of change in today's environment.

Customer relationship management:

- is the holistic process of identifying, attracting, differentiating, and retaining customers.

- shifts the firm's marketing emphasis from "acquiring customers" to "maintaining clients."

- involves a number of stakeholders, including employees, supply chain partners, lateral partners, and customers.

- involves the creation of relationship capital—the ability to build and maintain relationships with customers, suppliers, and partners.

To increase share of customer, rather than market share, firms must:

- abandon the old notions of acquiring new customers and increasing transactions to focus on more fully serving the needs of current customers.

- understand that all customers have different needs and therefore that not all customers have equal value to a firm.

- recognize that some customers are simply too expensive to keep, given the low level of profits they generate.
- use one-to-one and mass customization strategies that automate and personalize the delivery of the marketing mix.

Quality:

- is a relative term that refers to the degree of superiority of a firm's goods or services.
- is a double-edged sword: Good quality can successfully generate first-time transactions, but poor quality guarantees that repeat purchases will not occur.
- is not an automatic guarantee of success—it is a necessary but insufficient condition of customer relationship management.
- is often taken for granted in the core product because customers expect the core product to be of high quality, at least at a level necessary to meet their needs.
- is critical in customer services that add value to the core product. In most cases, the customer services, not the core product, are responsible for product differentiation.
- is hard to maintain on a daily basis. Delivering superior quality involves understanding customers' expectations, needs, and wants, translating customer research into specifications for quality, delivering on specifications, and promising only what can be delivered.

Value:

- is a difficult term to define, because it means different things to different people.
- is a customer's subjective evaluation of benefits relative to costs to determine the worth of a firm's product relative to the offerings of other firms.
- breaks down into benefits (core product quality, service quality, experience-based quality) and costs (monetary and nonmonetary costs) that are useful for strategic planning.

Customer satisfaction:

- is typically defined as the degree to which a product meets or exceeds the customer's expectations about that product.
- is typically judged by customers within the context of the total experience, not just with respect to quality and value. Customer satisfaction can also include any number of factors that have nothing to do with quality or value.
- should be an ongoing priority for the firm, particularly the continuous measurement and management of the process.
- is now assessed using a number of new metrics, including lifetime value of a customer, average order value, customer acquisition/retention costs, retention rates, referrals, and viral marketing.

Questions for Discussion

1. How can one-to-one marketing and mass customization be used to develop customer relationships and increase a firm's share of customer? Is the strategic shift from "acquiring customers" to "maintaining clients" universally applicable, or are there firms or industries where "acquiring customers" is still a viable strategy?

2. What ethical issues are involved in "firing" customers because they are unprofitable for the firm?

3. Why do you think many firms do such a poor job of understanding the needs, wants, and expectations of their customers? Do they buy into the "better mousetrap" philosophy and believe that quality is the only necessary requirement of maintaining customer relationships? Explain.

4. As a marketing manager, what might you do to better understand the things that can go wrong with respect to customer satisfaction? How can you be more responsive to customers even if their expectations have nothing to do with the quality or value that your product delivers?

Exercises

1. Visit Peppers and Rogers Group's 1-to-1 Web site (http://www.1to1.com) to learn more about customer relationship management.

2. J. D. Power and Associates is a well-known research company specializing in the measurement of product quality and customer satisfaction. Explore their Web site at http://www.jdpa.com. What role will third-party firms like J. D. Power play in the future, given the increasing use of internal customer satisfaction metrics?

3. Think about all of the organizations with which you maintain an ongoing relationship (banks, doctors, schools, accountants, mechanic, etc.). Would you consider yourself to be unprofitable for any of these organizations? What would you do if one of these organizations fired you as a customer?

6

Product Strategy

Introduction

The product is at the core of the marketing strategy. It is important to keep in mind that *products* means more than tangible goods. Products are usually a combination of goods, services, ideas, and even people. The best way to view a product is as a set of features and advantages that have the capacity to satisfy customer needs and wants, thus delivering valued benefits. Products can also be exchanged for something else of value. When a consumer buys a Lexus automobile, for example, transportation is only one benefit of the product that he or she obtains. The buyer may also receive luxury, prestige, social appeal, comfort, a brand name, and countless other attributes in exchange for the price he or she pays.

As we consider product decisions through the reminder of this chapter, and throughout the rest of this book, it is important to remember that products in and of themselves are of little value. The real value a product provides is derived from its ability to deliver benefits that enhance the buyer's situation. Consumers don't buy pest control; they buy a bug-free living environment. Students frequenting a nightspot are not really thirsty; they want to fulfill their need for social interaction. Likewise, companies do not really want computers; they want tools to store, retrieve, distribute, network, and analyze data and information. Thus, organizations that keep their sights set on developing products, systems, and processes that identify and meet needs of the target market are more likely to be successful, while those that take an internal focus of designing the best product possible are following a map to failure once that product is no longer the best method of meeting a need.

On the other hand, consider the following example of how a product utilizing available technology can solve an important problem for consumers. Motorola's CreatalLink® 2XT two-way wireless data transceiver has been integrated into an innovative security device designed exclusively for Harley-Davidson motorcycles. The new security device helps deliver to Harley-Davidson owners wireless remote control and tracking capability to enable them to track their bike's location and even control its ignition. When someone tampers with the motorcycle, a compatible messaging device can be used by the owner to send wireless remote control commands back to the bike, triggering a siren and flashing lights and immobilizing two electrical circuits. To aid in the recovery of a stolen bike, users can track the location of their motorcycle through a compatible PC or by phone through a 24-hour control center.[1]

This example illustrates the importance of creating new products to satisfy customer needs. Most new products result from the creative application of existing knowledge to help provide something customers desire.

Developing New Products

One of the key decision areas related to products deals with the introduction of new products. Strategic considerations that relate to new product success include overall fit with the organization's strengths and a defined opportunity in the environment. The competitive situation as well as market need, growth, and size might be analyzed and defined relative to the potential new product project. The organization's ability to develop product superiority and technological compatibility with markets that are familiar to organizations will be helpful in improving the odds of success. Leveraging core competencies to take advantage of market characteristics and conditions should yield a competitive advantage.

What is considered to be a new product depends on the point of view of both the firm and its customers. There are at least six marketing strategy options related to the newness of products. These options follow, in decreasing degree of product change:

1. *Innovation,* the most radical option, involves the firm in a pioneering effort, as did FedEx in providing an overnight, small-package delivery service. Innovations of this type can even result in new product categories (e.g., Henry Ford with cars and Xerox with copy machines).

2. *New product lines* allow a firm to enter new markets with a new group of closely related product items that are considered as a unit, based on technical or end use considerations. For instance, Caterpillar, long known for powerful construction equipment, has in recent years developed engines for boats, trucks, and generators.[2]

3. *Product line extensions* supplement an existing product line with new styles or models. BMW, for example, introduced the Z3 to compete in the market for small, two-seat sports cars, while both Lincoln (Navigator) and Mercedes Benz (ML320 and ML420) added sport utility vehicles to their product lines.[3] WaterPik Technologies added a shower filter that reduces chlorine in shower water, resulting in softer, healthier skin, scalp, and hair.

4. *Improvements or changes in existing products* offer customers improved performance or greater perceived value, such as the yearly design changes in the automobile industry. This option also includes changes to make an existing product "new and improved," a common option in packaged goods. Clorox Co., for example, spiced up sales after adding lemon and floral scents to its perennial bleach product and a lemon fragrance to Pine-Sol. Cascade Complete dishwasher detergent has been successful in eliminating the need to presoak dishes.[4]

5. *Repositioning* involves the modification of existing products (either real or through promotion) so that they can be targeted at new markets or segments.

An example is Carnival Cruise Line's effort to attract senior citizens to supplement its younger crowd. Cell phone manufacturers can now promote the safety and security aspects of their product as a result of mobile positioning technology. As long as the phone is switched on, it can be located.[5]

6. *Cost reductions* involve modified products that offer similar performance at a lower price, such as Plymouth's Neon, a lower-cost version of Plymouth's entry-level cars, to compete with Kia and Chevrolet's Metro and Prizm. Phone companies have been able to offer reduced prices for services through bundling. AT&T@Home is trying to sell high-speed Internet access, long-distance service, and cable through bundling.

The first two options are the most effective and profitable when the firm wants to differentiate itself significantly from competitors. The consulting firm of Booz-Allen found that 30 percent of the product introductions they studied were innovations or new product lines, and 60 percent of the profitable product changes were of this type.[6] A firm may have ample reason, nevertheless, to pursue one of the last four product modification options, particularly if resource constraints are a significant issue.

Of these criteria, building a differential advantage is perhaps the most critical for long-term success and survival. What unique benefit does, or can, the firm offer to customers? A differential advantage can be either real or based exclusively on image. In either case, creating the *perception* of differentiation is the key. For example, lacking anything exclusive, a firm might find some feature that no competitor has claimed and promote it before the competition can retaliate. This is often a highly creative process. Consider the car rental industry. In the industry's early years, Hertz not only stood first but maintained a vast lead over second-place Avis. The management of Avis, intent on capturing a larger portion of Hertz's customers, asked its advertising agency to find an effective marketing strategy. After searching for any advantage that Avis held over Hertz, the agency concluded the only difference was that Avis was number two! Avis management decided to claim this fact as an advantage, using the theme, "We're number two. We try harder!" Avis rentals soared, putting the company in a much stronger number-two position.

The criteria for a good marketing strategy will vary across companies, markets, and products and over time. In some cases, what makes a good marketing strategy depends on the person reviewing it. In some firms, the best marketing strategy may be the one that is capable of being approved by top management. Thus, in the process of selecting a marketing strategy, it is important for the SBU or marketing manager to do an occasional "reality check" to understand better what can and cannot be achieved. The manager should also do a reality check of the firm's own strengths and weaknesses. Key weaknesses that cannot be overcome in the short term can make an otherwise attractive marketing strategy impossible to implement.

Life Cycle Considerations

Because many marketing strategy decisions are made at the strategic business unit (SBU) level, it is beneficial to consider the issue of life cycle stages of the product, brand, or market. Other approaches to planning and managing products are equally valid, but you are probably most familiar with the product life cycle in terms of how sales, resources, investments, and profits vary over time. To the usual four stages, we

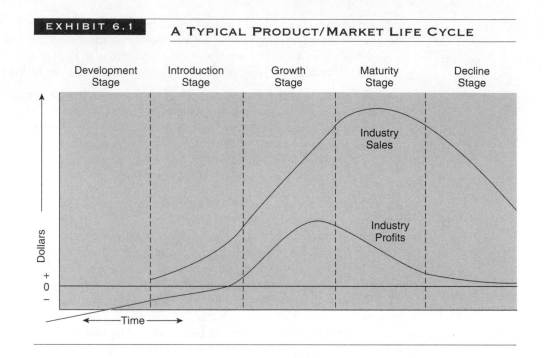

| EXHIBIT 6.1 | A TYPICAL PRODUCT/MARKET LIFE CYCLE |

EXHIBIT 6.2 — DESCRIPTION OF LIFE CYCLE STAGES

Development	Determine target customers' desired benefits. Conceive or select product ideas. Develop direction and specifications for marketing strategy. Move rapidly but prudently toward commercialization that begins in the next stage.
Introduction	Determine the best strategy for introducing the new product and gaining customer acceptance. Launch marketing strategy.
Growth	Establish the product in a defensible competititve position and broaden its market. Sales should rise rapidly and profits should peak.
Maturity	Extend the life of the product. Innovate to maintain profits while sales curve peaks and starts to decline. Severe competition with many brands. Curtail, but do not eliminate, resource investments of financial and human capital.
Decline	Find solutions that will slow or postpone the decline of demand, or find ways to terminate the product. Cut marketing expenses to maximize profits.

add a fifth: the product's development period, from conception to commercialization. With that addition, Exhibit 6.1 charts the typical life cycle.

Exhibit 6.1 shows the growth and decline in sales volume over the life of a product in a curve that, though a generalization, is appropriate for our discussion. The relative time length of the stages can vary greatly. For a fad, such as Tamagotchi virtual pets or specific Beanie Babies, the life cycle might be measured in weeks or months, while the cycle for a staple item may last for years or even decades. Exhibit 6.2 describes each of the life cycle stages. Let's briefly consider these stages and how they relate to marketing strategy development.

Development Stage

As Exhibit 6.1 shows, a firm has no sales revenue during the product development stage. In fact, the firm experiences a net cash outflow due to the expenses of product invention and development. For most innovations, a substantial investment of financial resources and time, as well as risk assumption, are necessary for invention and development. For example, the development of the Gulfstream V, an ultra-long-distance corporate jet aircraft, required four years and an $800 million investment.[7] Such investments are no guarantee of success, and in fact many products fail. A study of 11,000 new products manufactured by 77 firms found that only 56 percent were still on the market five years after introduction. In the food and beverage industry alone, 80 percent of all new products fail.[8] The high product failure rate underscores the need to identify target customer needs correctly *before* developing a marketing strategy.

The development stage usually begins with a product concept, which has several components:

- An understanding of the specific uses and benefits that target customers seek in a new product.

- A description of the product, including its potential uses and benefits.

- The potential for creating a complete product line that can produce synergy in sales and income and place the firm in a strong market position.

- An analysis of the feasibility of the product concept, including such issues as anticipated sales, required return on investment, time of market introduction, and length of time to repay investment.

Although marketing activities do not typically occur in the development stage, planning efforts at this point can greatly influence marketing activities in later stages of the life cycle. In creating a new product or product line, a group of closely related product items is desired because of the scale economies that are created, along with increased efficiency in operations and marketing. New products that match customers' needs and have strong advantages over competing products are simply easier to market as the new product enters the introduction stage of its life cycle.

Introduction Stage

The introduction stage begins when development is complete and ends when sales indicate that target customers are widely accepting the product. The marketing strategy devised during the development stage should be fully implemented during the introduction stage, and should relate to issues that arose during the SWOT analysis. Marketing strategy goals that are common to the introduction stage include:

- Attract customers by raising awareness of and interest in the product through advertising, public relations, and publicity efforts that stress key product features and benefits.

- Induce customers to try and buy the product through the use of various sales tools and pricing activities.

- Strengthen or expand channel relationships to gain sufficient product distribution to make the product accessible to target customers.

- Build on the availability and visibility of the product through trade promotion activities.

- Engage in customer education activities that teach target market members how to use the new product and convince them to repurchase the product.

Although all marketing mix activities are important during the introduction stage, good promotion and distribution are essential to make customers aware that the new product is available and to inform them on how to use it and where to purchase it. Nike has developed new technology, called "Shox," that provides a springlike sole. Nike has effectively used the word *boing* in their introductory advertising. *Boing* means basically the same thing in any language and accurately describes the spring-loaded mechanism in the shoe.[9]

After a product is introduced, the marketing manager must employ the firm's marketing information system to determine market share, revenues, store placement/channel support, costs, and rate of product usage to assess whether the new product is paying back the firm's investment. Even when the firm has patent protection or hard-to-copy technology, the manager must carefully track competitors' reactions. Tracking this information is critical if the firm is to continue along the gradually rising sales curve shown in Exhibit 6.1.

Industrial products often have long periods of introduction while buyers are being convinced to adopt them. Pharmaceuticals in particular may experience long delays while being tested and before doctors become convinced of drug safety and efficacy. A packaged consumer good, on the other hand, may see an immediate upsurge in sales as consumers and retailers take advantage of special introductory offers. Unfortunately, many product introductions never enjoy rising demand, leading to significant losses for an organization.

The future of digital subscriber lines (DSL) remains uncertain. Customers want high-speed Internet access, and a clear victor in this industry remains undetermined. Phone access, cable access, satellite, and DSL are all vying to provide the most efficient and accessible service. The success of product introduction determines whether the product will make the grade and enter the profitable growth stage, where bottom-line enhancement occurs and resources for subsequent revisions and additional new product introductions are found. Crest introduced teeth-whitening strips but made them available through direct Internet sale only. Such a limited distribution introduction of a new product may be a "test" of the product's potential success.

Growth Stage

Marketing managers should be ready for growth, because sustained sales increases may begin quickly. The product's upward sales curve may be steep, as shown in Exhibit 6.1. The length of the growth stage varies according to the nature of the product and competitive reactions. Disposable diapers had a long growth stage as they experienced over 30 percent yearly growth for a decade. A short growth stage is typical for games and toys—Barbie dolls notwithstanding.

Regardless of the length of the growth stage, the firm has two main priorities: (1) establish a strong market position and defend it from competitors, and (2) achieve financial objectives that repay investment and earn enough to justify a long-term commitment to the product. Within these two priorities, there are a number of pertinent marketing strategy issues:

- Utilize the product's *perceivable* differential advantages in terms of quality, price, value, etc., to secure market leadership.

- Establish a clear product/brand identity through image-oriented advertising and personal selling campaigns.

- Create a unique product position, or niche, through the use of advertising that stresses product features and benefits for target customers relative to other solutions/products available to target market members.

- Maximize availability of the product through extensive trade promotion activities that capitalize on the product's popularity at this stage and thereby enhance the firm's ability to deliver profits to key channel members, especially retailers.

- Find the ideal balance between price and demand and determine a general estimate of price elasticity.

- Maintain control over product quality to ensure customer satisfaction.

The overall strategy in the growth stage shifts toward generating repeat purchases and building brand loyalty. Typically, the overall product/market is growing as well, thus the firm should focus not only on sales increase percentages, but also on achieving as high a market share as possible. For example, perfume targeted at kids, from newborns to young teenagers, is one of the fastest-growing segments in this market. Designer children's perfumes from Bulgari, Givenchy, and Versace can cost as much as $50. While children's perfumes represent only 2 percent of the world's $15 billion prestige perfume market, it has been growing at a 6 percent rate for a number of years. The number of girls 11 to 16 years old using perfume has jumped 50 percent in the last several years.[10]

The growth stage is the most expensive stage for marketing. A deep negative cash flow is likely because strong marketing efforts are needed to sustain growth. One of the most difficult questions that a marketing manager must ask is: how long should the firm expend cash and other resources to establish the product? This decision should be influenced by the growth rate of the *total* market. The answer to this question is complicated by the price/quality/earnings tradeoff: Low prices build market share but sacrifice profit and can lower customer perceptions of the product's quality. A good estimate of *price elasticity* (percentage change in quantity demanded for a particular percentage change in product price) is important. One option at this point is to create a prestige image by fortifying quality perceptions and holding to premium prices.

Increasing competition should be expected as the product moves through the growth stage and into the maturity stage, and the product's sales growth and emerging profitability encourages other firms to develop competitive product entries. These firms may be traditional rivals or nontraditional competitors. Photography giant Kodak, for example, now faces competition from Hewlett-Packard, best known for its laser and inkjet printers, in the emerging market for digital photography products.[11] If a firm is the first to market a new product, it has a better chance of capturing and maintaining market leadership, assuming that the product's competitive advantages can be sustained against competitive inroads. Whatever competitive role the marketing manager selects during the growth stage, it is important to commit to it. Competitors who enter with comparable products later have narrower options.

Maturity Stage

In the typical product life cycle, we expect maturity to be the longest stage. When the relatively fast growth has tapered, there will be some "shakeout" of the competition that built during the growth stage. Because the strategic window of opportunity has all but closed for the product/market, no more firms will enter the market, unless they have found some product innovation significant enough to attract large numbers of target customers. The window of opportunity often remains open, however, for new product features and variations. A good example in the beer industry is the introduction of light, dry, ice, microbrew, and low-alcohol products. These variations can be quite important as firms attempt to gain market share. In the face of limited or no growth within the product market, the only way for a firm to gain market share is to steal it from a competitor. Such theft often comes only with significant promotional investments or cuts in gross margin as prices are lowered.

For the manager who has survived the growth stage, maturity can be a relatively status quo stage. As long as sales volume is maintained, keeping market share constant, a more long-term perspective can be taken due to decreasing market uncertainty. Typically, the marketing manager has three general objectives that can be pursued during the maturity stage:

1. *Generate cash flow.* By the time a product reaches maturity, it should be yielding a very positive cash flow. This is essential to recoup the initial investment and to generate the excess cash necessary for the firm to grow and develop new products.

2. *Hold market share.* Marketing strategy should still stress holding market share among the dominant brands in the market. Firms having marginal market share must decide whether they have a reasonable chance of improving their position or whether they should drop out.

3. *Increase share of customer.* Where market share refers to the percentage of total customers held by the firm, *share of customer* refers to the percentage of each customer's needs being met by the firm. Many banks, for example, have added a variety of services to gain more of each customer's business in financial services (brokerage, auto leasing, retirement planning, etc.). Likewise, many larger grocery stores gain share of customer by adding features ranging from restaurants to video rentals to dry cleaning services in an effort to create one-stop shopping for household needs.

To achieve these objectives, the marketing manager has at least four general options for strategy selection throughout the maturity stage: (1) develop a new product image; (2) find and attract new users to the product; (3) discover new applications and uses for the product; or (4) apply new technology. Kraft Foods, for example, launched a massive advertising campaign to create a new product image for Jell-O after a nine-year decline in sales. Today, Jell-O has once again achieved gourmet status with American children. After sales of baking soda went flat, Arm & Hammer began touting the product's uses as a deodorizer. Today, baking soda is found in products ranging from toothpaste to kitty litter.

Holding market share or increasing share of customer often requires heavy expenditures in marketing, particularly in promotion. Increasing share of customer may also require additional expenditures in creating new product features or modifications, as was the case in the beer industry. Likewise, when Clorox added lemon and floral scents to its bleach product and a lemon fragrance to Pine-Sol, sales for both products accelerated despite a slow-growing market.[12] A holding strategy also requires a careful coordination of marketing activities as the firm attempts to maintain its image against possible attacks by competitors. Due to the expense, only firms in an already strong market position should attempt a holding strategy.

Decline Stage

A product's sales plateau will not last forever, and eventually it begins a persistent decline in revenue that marks the beginning of the decline stage. Very popular brands can postpone this stage longer than weaker brands. The decline stage, and the product's life, ends when the product is terminated. Consider Ty Inc., the marketer of Beanie Babies. Ty experienced nearly four-digit sales increase rates in the 1990s by continuously introducing new stuffed animals and retiring mature editions of these cuddly collectibles. The firm has seen its collectibles reach a decline stage as collectors now sell retired Babies at lower prices than a few years ago via classified newspaper ads and Web sites.

The marketing manager must choose one of two options during the decline stage: attempt to postpone the decline or accept its inevitability. Should the firm decide to attempt to postpone the decline, the manager must find ways to renew the product's demand, perhaps through repositioning, developing new uses or features for the product, or applying new technology. Oldsmobile is phasing out its brand over several years by offering discounts and other special incentives. Whatever the method, postponing the decline stage often takes a great deal of time and a substantial investment of resources. Many firms, however, do not have the resources or opportunity to renew a product's demand and are forced to accept the inevitability of decline. In such instances, the marketing manager can either harvest profits from the product while demand declines or divest the product, taking steps to abandon it or sell it to another firm.

The *harvesting* approach calls for a gradual reduction in marketing expenditures and uses a less resource-intensive marketing mix. A harvesting strategy allows the firm to funnel its increased cash flow into new products. Chrysler, for example, gradually pulled all resources and development efforts from the Eagle brand of its Jeep/Eagle SBU. Harvesting the Eagle brand enabled the automaker to consolidate its organizational structure and funnel extra resources into its more prosperous Jeep, Chrysler, and Plymouth brands.[13] The Plymouth brand is now moved into a position for harvesting and is destined to join Eagle because it will probably be eliminated from the product mix. General Motors' plans to eliminate the Oldsmobile brand include increased length of warranties and promises to service Oldsmobiles at all General Motors dealers.

A company using the *divesting* option withdraws all marketing support from the product or SBU. It may continue to sell the product until losses are sustained, or arrange for the product to be acquired by another firm. Home Depot, for example, made the tough decision to divest its Crossroads stores for farm dwellers and to move human and financial resources to Home Depot Expo (a chain for upscale consumers doing significant renovations or remodeling projects) and a program to attract more professional contractors into its home improvement centers.[14]

There are several factors that the marketing manager should examine before making a decision to harvest or divest:

- The rate of market deterioration—the faster the rate, the sooner the manager should divest.

- Market segment potential—loyal customer segments might continue to buy.

- The market position of the product—a leading product with a good image in a declining industry may be profitable and generate excess cash by attracting customers from competitors' abandoned products.

- The firm's price and cost structure—this may remain strong in the face of declining sales if the firm no longer has to invest significantly in maintaining the product.

Although the marketing manager should study all of these factors, he or she should not be sentimental about dropping a failing product. On the other hand, the marketing manager should not quickly dismiss a renewal attempt, particularly if the firm does not have a better alternative use for its resources.

Bear in mind that throughout all of these life cycle stages, the marketing manager should stay focused primarily on changes in the market, not the firm's products. Products have life cycles only because markets and customer needs—and options for meeting those needs—change. By focusing on changing markets, the manager can attempt to create new and better quality products to match customer needs. Only in this way can a firm grow, prosper, remain competitive, and continue to be seen as a viable source of solutions for the target market members' needs.

Marketing Strategy for Services

Although we have focused largely on strategies for tangible goods thus far, it is important to remember that products can be more intangible services and ideas as well. Recall also that marketing strategies can be applied to nonprofit organizations, government agencies, and individuals as well as for-profit businesses. In many cases, the products offered by a nonprofit organization such as the American Cancer Society (information, research funding) or the National Wildlife Federation (financial assistance for endangered species and habitats) lie closer to the intangible end of the service continuum. Although most aspects of marketing planning can be applied regardless of type of organization or product, we believe it will be beneficial to explore a few issues regarding marketing strategies for services.

Nonprofit and for-profit organizations that market services and ideas face additional considerations in creating an appropriate marketing mix. These factors are the direct result of the unique characteristics of services that distinguish them from goods; these distinctions and their resulting challenges are summarized in Exhibit 6.3. Obviously, the primary difference between a good and a service is that a service is less tangible. Some services, such as business consulting and education, are almost completely intangible, while others have more concrete elements. The services provided by UPS

EXHIBIT 6.3　　**UNIQUE SERVICE CHARACTERISTICS AND RESULTING MARKETING CHALLENGES**

Unique Service Characteristics	Resulting Marketing Challenges
Intangibility	• Difficult for customers to evaluate • Firm is forced to sell a promise • Difficult to advertise and display • Prices are difficult to set and justify
Inseparability of production and consumption	• Service employees are critical to delivery • Customers must participate in production • Other customers affect service outcomes • Customers cannot derive possession utility • Services are difficult to distribute
Customer contact	• Service employees are critical to delivery • Training and motivating service employees • How to change a high-contact service into a low-contact service to lower costs
Perishability	• Services cannot be inventoried • Difficult to balance supply and demand • Unused capacity is lost forever • Demand is very time sensitive
Heterogeneity	• Service quality is difficult to control • Service delivery is difficult to standardize
Client-based relationships	• Success depends on satisfying and keeping customers over the long term • How to generate repeat business • Relationship marketing becomes critical

Sources: J. Paul Peter and James H. Donnelly, Jr., *A Preface to Marketing Management*, 6th edition (Burr Ridge, IL: Richard D. Irwin, 1994), 220–228; and Valarie A. Zeithaml, A. Parasuraman, and Leonard L. Berry, *Delivering Quality Service: Balancing Customer Perceptions and Expectations* (New York: The Free Press, 1990).

and FedEx, for example, include tangible airplanes, trucks, boxes, and air bills. Still other firms, such as restaurants, market products that are a mixture of both goods and services. As the intangible elements begin to dominate the total product offering, the firm will experience a new set of considerations in designing a marketing mix.

Product Considerations

Because of the intangibility of services, it is quite difficult for customers to evaluate the product before they actually use it. This forces customers to place some degree of trust in the service provider to perform the service correctly and in the timeframe promised or anticipated. One way companies can address this issue is by providing satisfaction guarantees to customers. For example, Hampton Inn, a national chain of mid-priced hotels, offers guests a free night if they are not 100 percent satisfied with their stay.[15]

Moreover, because most services are people-based, they are susceptible to variations in quality and inconsistency. Such variations can occur from one organization to another, from one outlet to another within the same organization, from one service to another within the same outlet, and even from one employee to another within the same outlet. Service quality can further vary from week to week, day to day, and even hour to hour. And because quality is a subjective phenomenon, it can also vary from customer to customer and for the same customer from one visit to the next. As a result, standardization and service quality are very difficult to control. The lack of standardization, however, actually gives service firms one advantage: Services can be customized to match the specific needs of any customer. Such customized services are frequently very expensive for both the firm and its customers. This creates a dilemma: How does a service firm provide efficient, standardized service at an acceptable level of quality while simultaneously treating every customer as unique? This dilemma is especially prevalent in the health care industry today.

Pricing Considerations

Pricing is a key issue in the marketing mix for services because it can be used to connote quality in advance of the purchase experience. However, determining the costs of producing and delivering a service is complicated for service providers. Part of this complexity stems from the fact that some services do not have well-defined units of measure. While some services have clearly defined pricing units—airlines (by the seat), college courses (by the credit hour), and consulting (by the hour)—other services are not as clearly defined. For example, what is the unit of measure for hairstyling services? Is it time, hair length, type of style, or gender of the customer? Many female customers complain that they are charged more for a cut and style than men, even when a man's hair is longer. Likewise, the pricing of health care services is confusing and not well defined. This illustrates the challenge that service firms often face in justifying their prices to customers.

Customers often balk at the high prices of legal, accounting, or medical services because they have no way to evaluate the product's worth prior to purchase. This issue can be especially critical when customers emphasize price in selecting a service provider. Consider the pricing challenges of the airline industry, given that many customers perceive all airlines as being about the same. Airlines often resort to fare wars to ensure that they get their desired share of customers' business. Pricing tactics can also help a firm balance peak and off-peak demand times. Most service firms offer lower prices during off-peak demand times to encourage more customers to use the service. Good examples include half-price movie matinees, lunch specials at a restaurant, and off-season vacations.

Promotion Considerations

Because a service cannot be directly shown or displayed, the marketer faces the difficult task of explaining the service to customers. As a result, service advertising typically focuses on tangible cues that symbolize the service.[16] Insurance firms are good examples: Prudential's rock, Allstate's good hands, and Travelers' umbrella. Although these symbols have nothing to do with the service, they make it easier for customers to understand the intangible features and benefits associated with insurance.

Endorsements from other customers in the target market who have had a positive experience are often a key to successful promotion. In fact, in order to create a group of satisfied clients, the service provider must be able to generate positive word-of-mouth advertising. For example, some doctors provide such good service and generate so much good word-of-mouth that they actually have to turn clients away. Consistently bad service can have the opposite effect.

Distribution Considerations

It is practically impossible to distribute services in the traditional sense because customers cannot take physical possession of a service. Distribution systems must be developed to provide service in a convenient manner (e.g., Enterprise Car Rental's pickup and drop-off service) and in locations where they are expected to be found (e.g., shoeshine stands in airports and hotels). Service distribution often requires multiple outlets to increase customer convenience.

Another way to distribute a service is to separate production and consumption by creating a tangible representation of the service. A credit card, for example, is not a service, but rather a tangible representation of a line of credit service offered by a bank or other financial institution. Although the production and consumption of this service remain inseparable, the credit card increases convenience by giving the customer something tangible to possess. This also allows the firm to distribute its credit services through the mail.

If any one of these marketing mix elements is inappropriately designed or implemented, it can lead to the failure of the entire mix to reach developed goals and objectives. Many service providers have found that successful marketing mixes create and maintain client-based relationships, with satisfied customers who repeatedly use a service over time.[17] Some service providers, such as doctors, lawyers, accountants, and financial consultants/advisers, actually refer to their customers as clients. These service providers are successful only to the degree that they can develop a marketing mix that builds relationships with a group of clients who use their services on an ongoing basis.

Branding Strategy

One of the key decisions that marketers must make relates to product branding. *Branding* is the identification a product maintains through name, symbol, or design. Such identification seeks to differentiate one manufacturer or marketer's products from another. Nike has a unique and distinct brand mark (Swoosh symbol uniquely associated with the brand). Some of the world's most recognized brands are McDonald's, Coca-Cola, Disney, Kodak, Sony, Gillette, Mercedes-Benz, Levi's, Microsoft, and Marlboro.[18] Exhibit 6.4 summarizes some of the key advantages of branding.

Strategic planning often focuses on branding decisions as one of the most important decisions in developing a marketing strategy. Understanding concepts such as brand loyalty and brand equity, co-branding, and brand licensing are critical to properly developing and managing a product strategy. A *brand name* is the part of a brand that can be spoken. It could be letters, words, and numbers—such as the Intel Pentium IV processor. One danger in gaining wide acceptance of a brand is that it could become synonymous with the product, such as Scotch tape or Xerox copiers. Owners of brand names such as these, as well as Coca-Cola, Tide detergent, Crest toothpaste, and Levi jeans try to protect them from being used as generic names for their products. The element of a brand that is not words but often a symbol or design is called

EXHIBIT 6.4	ADVANTAGES OF BRANDING

- Helps buyers identify brands they support
- Speeds up the buying process
- Provides status and psychosocial identification
- Assists in evaluating product quality and price
- Reduces the risk of purchasing
- Makes repeat purchases easier
- Allows for greater acceptance of new products under the brand name
- Generates consumer loyalty

a *brand mark*. A good example is the swoosh for Nike or the golden arches for McDonald's restaurants. A *trademark* is a legal designation indicating that the owner has exclusive use of the brand or a part of the brand and that others are prohibited by law from using the brand in any form or way. A *trade name* is the full and legal name of an organization, such as General Motors or Campbell's Soup.

Brand loyalty is the positive attitude toward a specific brand that draws a customer to consistently purchase the brand when the customer needs a product in that product category. Although brand loyalty may not lead the customer to purchase a specific brand every time, potentially the customer considers that brand the most favorable or viable brand in the set of brands being considered for purchase. The three degrees of brand loyalty include brand recognition, brand preference, and brand insistence. *Brand recognition* exists when a customer knows about the brand and is thinking about it as a possible purchase. This is the lowest form of brand loyalty, and it exists mainly due to the awareness of the brand rather than a strong desire to buy that specific brand. *Brand preference* is a stronger degree of brand loyalty. The customer prefers one brand over competing brands and will usually purchase that brand if available. For example, there may be a brand preference for Diet Coke. If this brand is not available, the customer will usually accept a substitute brand, such as Diet Pepsi, rather than expending extra effort to find the Diet Coke. *Brand insistence* is the strongest degree of brand loyalty. Here the customer will accept no substitute and will go out of his or her way to obtain that brand, perhaps spending a great deal of time and effort in the process. Even though there is no Mercedes dealer in the state of Wyoming, a customer may drive to Colorado to purchase a new Mercedes because the customer is brand insistent for that product. Customers could also be brand insistent for a particular computer, cell phone, soft drink, or even restaurant.

The value of a brand is often referred to as *brand equity*. Another way of looking at brand equity is to consider the marketing and financial value associated with a brand's position in the market place. Brand equity is usually associated with brand name awareness, brand loyalty, brand quality, and the association with the brand's organization. Although brand equity is hard to measure, it represents the value of the brand to an organization. Exhibit 6.5 provides estimates of the world's most valuable brands. Often an organization may buy a brand from another company at a premium price because it is perceived as less expensive than creating and developing a new brand. Among the most valuable brands are Coca-Cola, Marlboro, IBM, McDonald's, and Disney.

Co-branding—the use of two or more brands on one product or set of products— is a way for an organization to differentiate its product from those of competitors by

EXHIBIT 6.5	THE WORLD'S MOST VALUABLE BRANDS

Brand	Brand Value ($million)	% Change from 1999 to 2000
Coca-Cola	72,537	(13)
Microsoft Windows	70,197	24
IBM	53,184	21
Intel	39,049	30
Nokia	38,528	86
General Electric	38,128	14
Ford	36,368	10
Disney	33,553	4
McDonald's	27,859	6
AT&T	25,548	6
Marlboro	22,111	5
Mercedes-Benz	21,105	19
Hewlett-Packard	20,572	20
Cisco Systems	20,068	—
Toyota	18,824	53

Source: Beth Snyder Bulik, "The Brand Police," *Business 2.0*, November 28, 2000, 154.

using the co-branded partner to create a distinctive offering. A Compaq computer with an Intel Pentium IV processor is an example of co-branding by two different companies. Sometimes co-branding involves two brands owned by the same company. For example, Taco Bell and KFC restaurants are sometimes a part of the same store because these two companies have the same parent company. Co-branding can also be potentially harmful if the right partner is not a part of the alliance. Kellogg co-branded some cereal products with Toysmart.com. Three weeks after the Froot Loops and Frosted Flakes products were on store shelves, Toysmart.com went bankrupt.[19] *Brand licensing* is a licensing agreement by which a company, for a fee, permits an organization to use its brand on other products. Royalties may be paid for use of the brand. Fashion brands such as Calvin Klein, Ralph Lauren, Bill Blass, and Tommy Hilfiger appear on numerous products in a variety of product categories through licensing agreements. Even Jack Daniels and Jim Beam whiskeys have licensed barbecue sauce brands.

Building successful brands is a very challenging process. But perhaps the biggest challenge for successful brands is protecting a reputation, which has tremendous long-term equity and millions of dollars in value. Brand names are often copied illegally in an attempt to boost sales. For this reason, many companies expend significant amounts of money and effort to monitor potential brand abuses. Exhibit 6.6 shows the ten most common forms of online brand abuse. While the legal system provides many laws to protect brands, most of the responsibility for enforcing this protection relies on the company to find and police abuses.

In many ways, product strategy is the most important element of the marketing mix. It matters little if pricing, promotion, and distribution exceed customer requirements and expectations if the product does not match the needs and wants of the target market. The role of branding will become even more important as products jockey for position in crowded markets. As electronic commerce becomes more mainstream,

EXHIBIT 6.6 MOST COMMON TYPES OF ONLINE BRAND ABUSE

> Unauthorized use of logos and images.
> Diverting users away from a Web site by hiding keywords in background text.
> Unauthorized use of a company's name or product in metatags.
> Software, music, or video piracy.
> Unauthorized distribution or sale of consumer goods.
> Unauthorized framing, where one Web site appears within another Web site.
> Use of a company's name on a competitor's site.
> Use of logos or images in a pornographic context.
> Domain name abuse and parody sites.
> Gripe sites and negative newsgroup postings.

Source: Beth Snyder Bulik, "The Brand Police," *Business 2.0*, November 28, 2000, 146.

companies will also find that they need a solid brand reputation in the offline world in order to be competitive in the online world.

Despite the overall importance of product strategy, other elements of the marketing mix are gaining in importance. Business customers and individual consumers increasingly demand better value and more convenience when examining product offerings. In the next chapter, we explore the growing importance of pricing in the marketing mix. To be successful, product strategy and pricing strategy must work in harmony to maximize product differentiation and brand image.

Lessons from Chapter 6

Product decisions may involve:

- innovation—the most radical and pioneering approach, which can lead to new product categories.

- new product lines—closely related products developed from existing products that allow the firm to enter into new markets.

- product line extensions—supplement of an existing product line with new styles or models.

- improvements or changes in existing products—improved performance or efficiency of an existing product.

- repositioning—modifying existing products so that they can target new markets or segments.

- cost reductions—providing similar products at lower prices.

Stages in the product life cycle that relate to marketing strategy development:

- development—involves the successful development, testing and refinement of the product concept. Key issues to address include: target market needs, potential benefits and uses, potential for product line development, and product feasibility.

- introduction—involves attracting customers by raising awareness of the product's existence and attributes through advertising, public relations, and publicity efforts. Consumer trial is encouraged and customer education is ongoing.

- growth—involves positioning the product so that consumers perceive a differential advantage in quality, price, or value. Brand image is strengthened through image-oriented advertising and personal selling. Distribution of the product is expanded, and quality control efforts are maximized.

- maturity—involves an attempt to maintain market share. Generally this phase entails one of the following: developing a new product image; finding and attracting new users to the product; discovering new applications and uses for the product; applying new technology.

- decline—involves considering whether to divest or to maintain the product to satisfy current customers.

Marketing strategies for services:

- product considerations—intangibility forces the buyer to trust the seller, and sellers frequently utilize satisfaction guarantees.

- pricing considerations—unclear units of measure for services create challenges in pricing, particularly with respect to justifying prices in customers' minds. Price changes are a viable means of balancing supply and demand between peak and off-peak demand times.

- promotion considerations—tangible items are often used to represent intangible services.

- distribution considerations—services must be provided in a convenient location where consumers are found or are willing to go.

Branding strategies:

- Branding is the identification of a product that maintains an image through the use of a symbol, design, or brand name.

- Branding's strategic value is differentiation from competition.

- Brand loyalty is the positive attitude toward a brand that results in purchases by customers.

- Brand equity is the financial and marketing value associated with the brand's position in the marketplace.

- Co-branding is the use of two or more brands on one product or set of products.

- Brand licensing is an agreement to permit an organization, for a fee, to use another company's brand.

Questions for Discussion

1. Of the six marketing strategy options related to new products, which are the most effective in differentiating a firm's products from the competition? Which would

be the easiest (costing the company the least amount of time and effort) to implement? If you were defending a strategy for the long-term success and survival of a product, what would be the key criteria for success?

2. Describe the different product decisions that impact each phase of the product life cycle. If you were still losing money with a product in the decline stage, why might you consider retaining that product?

3. Given the unique characteristics of services, what potential ethical issues could arise in service marketing and delivery? How can a service marketer prevent ethical challenges and convey a sense of trust to customers?

Exercises

1. Go to the Amazon.com Web site. What customer support services do they provide? If you were ordering a book, would they offer any competitive advantages over Barnes & Noble (http://www.bn.com)? Are there any additional services that Amazon.com could provide to further differentiate themselves from the competition?

2. What are some of the key attributes of successful brands? Are there any companies on the list of "The World's Most Valuable Brands" (Exhibit 6.5) that surprise you? If you were to project 5 to 10 years into the future, what brands on the market today might be atop this list?

3. Evaluate the auto industry, and discuss how different brands fit into the product life cycle. Why did the Oldsmobile brand fail? Why might companies like Toyota consider introducing a new brand of cars to appeal to a younger target audience?

7

Developing a Pricing Strategy

Introduction

Keeping track of competitors' prices has long been considered an important part of competitive intelligence. Salespeople learned to read a competitor's price sheets upside down at a buyer's desk. Retail firms sent "secret shoppers" to learn what other stores were charging for the same or similar merchandise. Even the great Sam Walton was known to take a pencil and pad of paper into other discount stores and jot down the prices charged by Wal-Mart competitors. In this age of e-commerce, tracking what competitors charge for books, tapes, airline flights, hotel rooms, and many other items has become even more difficult. Prices now change more rapidly (even by the minute), and the number of sellers seems to be exploding at an exponential rate. The task became so large that Fatbrain.com had two full-time temporary employees doing nothing but tracking competitors' prices on the Web. Even with this level of effort and investment, the consensus was that a lot of information was sliding through the cracks.

E-tailers (e-based retailers) must be particularly attuned to price. They often find themselves offering identical merchandise to what competitors have (a book from Fatbrain.com is identical to the same book from Amazon.com or Barnes & Noble). There is little chance to differentiate on service or promotion. That makes pricing king. Get the reputation for pricing a little high, and people will run away in droves. Get too aggressive in price-cutting, and your margins go down the tubes. That makes operating from timely and accurate information about competitive pricing not a luxury, but a necessity.

Recognizing this growing need, the founders of RivalWatch decided that an opportunity for a new venture was present. Using superior computer expertise, they developed a software program that would track e-based prices with varying degrees of frequency and provide regular reports on all aspects of competitive marketing mixes to subscribing firms. The price for this intelligence service is $150,000 to $250,000 annually, depending on the number of competitors to be watched, the number of issues to be tracked, and the frequency of checks and reports. The mission of RivalWatch is "to provide actionable, real-time competitive information to the leading click-and-mortar companies throughout the world." This firm provides more than reams of data to its clients. Its service mix includes: (1) product assortment analysis, (2) pricing analysis, and (3) promotions analysis. This is all done with flexibility and customization. While some have expressed concerns about the sources of information used by RivalWatch, its management contends that only readily available Internet sources of information are used, analyzed, and communicated to clients. Early results show clients spending more than they have in the past, but feeling much more confident about the quality of the information they use to make their pricing decisions. So the next time you see a price change on one of your favorite Web sites, know this: Someone is definitely watching—RivalWatch.[1]

The Importance of Pricing

There may well be no other component of the marketing mix that managers become more infatuated with than price. "Is our price too high, and is that why our sales are not higher?" Conversely, "Is our price too low? And while our sales are up, are we leaving money on the table? Should we be charging more?" These are common concerns that run through the minds of decision makers. There are at least two reasons for the attention given to pricing. First, the revenue equation is pretty simple: price times quantity. There are only two ways to grow revenue. You can raise your price, increase the quantity you sell, or, in the best-case situation, do both. While there are literally hundreds of ways to raise profits by managing costs, the revenue side only has two variables, with one being price and the other heavily influenced by price.

The second reason pricing gets such extensive attention from management is that it is the easiest of all marketing variables to influence, and the changes can take place immediately. Changing the product can take months and even years, and can be very expensive in terms of research and development as well as production changes. As you will see in the next chapter, changes in distribution strategies can be very costly, take long periods of time, and end up producing hard-to-predict results. Changes in the promotion mix are also quite costly and time consuming. In the end, your new advertising campaign may end up confusing consumers and sell more of your competitor's products than your own. Pricing, conversely, is relatively easy and simple to change, and those changes can be implemented instantaneously. A Kroger manager in Cincinnati can decide that Green Giant Brussels sprouts should be $1.29 instead of $1.42 and put the change in the system computer, and the next item that is scanned can be at the thirteen-cents-lower price. Try that with a new concept for an advertising agency.

The fact that prices are easy to change, and in fact do change quite frequently (particularly in this age of e-commerce), should not be taken to mean that most firms do a good job of setting prices. Many manufacturers, wholesalers, and retailers readily admit that they *worry* more about price than they actually *manage* price. Consumers are so frustrated by pricing in the auto industry that the Saturn strategy of fixed pricing for a particular model has caught on across the country in dealerships for many other car makers.

In this chapter, you will be exposed to some of the key elements managers must consider in developing a pricing strategy that drives the development of prices for individual items. Far too often managers guess more than they should, and use strategy less than they should, in managing this critical marketing mix component.

The Role of Pricing in Marketing Strategy

In this section, the role of pricing for both the selling organization and the buying organization will be considered. Pricing can be a major source of confrontation between sellers and buyers. Sellers obviously want to sell the item for as much as possible, while buyers would love to get the items they want for free. Somewhere between these extremes the two parties must find a way to meet.

The Seller's Perspective on Pricing

You may love your home or your parent's home. Because of the memories and your strong feelings, you may feel that your home is worth $1 million. To determine if it is really worth that amount, you need to find a buyer willing to pay that much to own the home. If you can, then your assessment is correct. If you can't, then you are just a sentimental person. Sellers must go beyond mere feelings to set prices for the items they make available to their target market(s). Managers developing a pricing strategy should base their decisions on a careful consideration of several factors: (1) costs, (2) demand, (3) customer impacts, and (4) competitors' prices.

Costs are an important consideration in any pricing model. A firm that fails to cover both its *direct* costs (finished goods/components, materials, supplies, sales commission, and transportation) and its *indirect* costs (primarily overhead issues such as administrative expenses, utilities, rent, and equipment) will not make a profit. Higher volumes of sales will only mean larger losses. Most smart pricing models build in a target profit margin as if it were a cost. A dollar reduction is a dollar off the bottom line, whether it comes out of a product that has covered its costs or one that has failed to cover its costs.

When the availability of a product is limited, innovative firms today are also addressing a new cost: opportunity cost. This is particularly appropriate for service firms. Sell one hour of home cleaning next Wednesday for $50 and that hour is gone from inventory. If someone else would be willing to pay $70 for the same time slot and is not willing to go with another time, the cleaning firm just lost $20 worth of profit. Goods producers who do not sell a car today can sell that same car tomorrow. Not so for a service firm. This is why airline firms use complex yield management systems in an attempt to squeeze every dollar out of every seat on every plane. Northwest Airlines makes remaining seats for weekend flights available the Wednesday morning before departure. Many restrictions apply, but great deals can be had for last-minute travelers because Northwest realizes that an empty seat generates no revenue and with almost an identical cost of operation as a full seat. Northwest calls these last-minute fares "Cybersavers." The company sends information on prices and routes in e-mails to regular fliers and posts them on the firm's Web site at NWA.com.

The fact that costs are covered with a set amount from a pricing model does not mean that people are willing to pay that price. Inefficient firms are quickly run from the marketplace as consumers go with more efficient competitors. The manager must know what consumers are willing to pay for an item or service. Business travelers who get their expenses reimbursed by their own firm or by a client are willing to pay more for an airline seat than are pleasure travelers, who might just drive, take a bus, or stay home to avoid putting a big dollar amount on their charge card. This consideration will be addressed in greater depth in the next major section on price elasticity.

Particularly in business-to-business sales, the bottom-line impacts delivered for the customer should be a consideration for the selling firm. If an insurance broker shows a client how to reduce risk costs by $10 million dollars, what is that worth? It is obviously not worth more than $10 million, but it is worth more than $10. Firms in sectors such as marketing research and consulting, information technology, and other professional services are increasingly investing in charting the impacts their services provide. The same is true for a new piece of production machinery that increases capacity by 25 percent while utilizing 50 percent less labor. These impacts may have little to do with costs, but instead are based upon the innovation and intellectual capital of the selling firm. There can be instances where consumer service firms can consider the impacts they provide to their customers in their pricing (for example, a mortgage search firm), but in most instances this is a business-to-business concern.

A selling organization should be very much aware of what its competitors are charging for the same or comparable items. In the case of a commodity, there can be no variability between product providers in terms of the amount they receive for a unit of product (a bushel of wheat, for example). Very few firms are selling pure commodities, and most of the marketing efforts discussed in this textbook are designed to help firms create real or perceived differentiation that separates their product from the pack. While all firms should be aware of competitive prices, they should resist the temptation to blindly meet or beat all prices. Unless the company promotes itself as always having the lowest price (e.g., Priceline.com), it should think in terms of being in a price range when it comes to its competitive set. Mercedes does not have to match BMW's pricing, but if the price comparison for comparable models from these two manufacturers shows one firm as 30 percent higher than the other, a large number of consumers will be pulled to the cheaper model. An innovative promotional campaign or a superior distribution strategy can allow the stronger firm to widen the gap. Terms should also be factored into the equation. A furniture store offering two years, no interest can get more money for a comparable sofa than a competitor down the street that only offers 90 days same as cash. The best advice when it comes to tracking competitors' pricing is to know, but not to blindly follow, what the competition is doing.

Customer Issues in Pricing

As marketing managers work to set prices that give the firm and the product the greatest chance for financial success, one eye must be kept on how the price will meld with other mix elements to create an overall positive evaluation of the purchase decision. Over the years, marketers have used many approaches to organize marketing strategy decisions to achieve this end, including the recent interest in product/service quality and total quality management. One of the more prevalent approaches to looking at the product offering though the target customer's eyes is the concept of *value*. As discussed in Chapter 5, value assessment is an effective way to integrate marketing activities because: (1) it includes the concept of quality, although it is a much broader term, (2) it takes into account all four marketing mix elements, and (3) it can be used to consider explicitly customer perceptions of the marketing mix in the strategy development process.

Though pricing is an integral part of the value equation (refer to Chapter 5), it is not the only consideration. By understanding the relationships among the components of value (product quality, service quality, experience-based quality, monetary costs, and nonmonetary costs), the marketing manager is in a much better position to set prices accordingly. It is important to remember that different target markets will have different perceptions of good value. For some, good value means good service. For the 2000 holiday season, Gateway Computer began offering in-home setup of systems—a big plus for many technophobes. In many cases, services such as setup, delivery, financing, gift wrapping, and 1-800 information lines are more important than the actual price of a product. For other target markets, good value means the lowest price. In the end, the key for the marketing manager is to recognize that any change in price will have repercussions throughout the marketing mix. Thus, all marketing mix elements are important considerations in delivering good value to customers.

A Shift in the Balance of Power

You may have heard the phrases "It's a buyer's market" and "It's a seller's market." These refer to who holds the power in the exchange relationship. In the former it is the buyer. There may be a large number of sellers and/or a large number of options in the marketplace. The economy may be tight and few people may have the money, or be willing to part with their money, to buy an item. During a seller's market, prices go up and terms and services become less favorable. At the present time, for most items, the perception is that it is a buyer's market. Particularly with all of the e-commerce startups, buyers have more choices than ever before. While the economy has generally been on an upward trend, consumer spending and confidence remain in a somewhat guarded state. Both business and consumers are certainly still buying, but they are buying smart. They have more and better information about product options and prices than ever before. For these reasons a firm that gets overly aggressive in its pricing may find no one in line. The impact of such price changes will be the focus of the next section, on price elasticity.

Understanding Price Elasticity

Simply defined, price elasticity is the relative impact on the quantity demanded for a product for a given increase or decrease in the price charged for that item. The following formula is used to calculate elasticity:

$$\text{Price Elasticity of Demand} = \frac{\text{Percent Change in Quantity Demanded}}{\text{Percent Change in Price}}$$

For products where this calculation produces a negative fraction (negative due to the general inverse relationship between price and quantity demanded, a downward-sloping demand curve), the item is said to have an *inelastic* demand. Given that the quantity demanded is not very responsive to price changes, an increase in price will increase revenue from the product, and a decrease in price will decrease revenue from the product. When elasticity is a number less than or equal to a negative 1.0 the item is said to have an *elastic* demand. Here quantity demanded is very sensitive to price fluctuations, and thus an increase in price will decrease revenue and a decrease in price will increase revenue. Marketing managers will rarely know the price elasticity for an item with great precision over time, and considering the factors that follow in this section, the type of elasticity should become fairly clear. Understand that a major change in another factor can cause a significant shift in the item's elasticity, perhaps even moving it from elastic to inelastic.

Substitute and Complementary Products

The price and other marketing factors associated with products that can be used instead of or with an item must be considered in assessing elasticity. When a new competitor enters the market place with a product that customers see as comparable to the item in question, the elasticity of that item will increase. This is the case when a new air carrier enters a market. When Value Jet (now Airtran) started flying out of Atlanta in the 1990s, many travelers saw it as an acceptable alternative to Delta and other existing carriers. As a result, the fare for a flight between Atlanta and Miami became more elastic. If Delta did not match the new competitor's lower fares on that route, their planes would have started to fly with much smaller passenger lists.

Complementary products demonstrate the exact opposite relationship when it comes to impacts on elasticity. When the price of a cruise goes down, the price of shore trips at each port becomes more inelastic. With more travelers on board, and each having more spending money left after paying for the trip, the operators of the shore trips should realize that the number of people on each trip is now less sensitive to the price they charge. The same is true for strawberries and shortcake as well as any other set of complementary goods or services.

Product Differentiation

The basic goal of differentiation is to make the demand curve for a product more inelastic. Differentiation reduces the number of perceived substitutes for a product, ideally to zero. Coke's marketing strategy is to make the product seem different from and better than Pepsi, and vice versa. Loyal Coke drinkers will buy the firm's soft drinks at $1.25 per six-pack or $2.25 a six-pack, it does not matter. In some instances extensive research and development result in a product that is factually differentiated. Intel Pentium processors were faster than any other available computer processor when they hit the market. Other times it may be a perceptual difference that matters. Blindfolded, a person may not know the difference between Coke and Pepsi, but consumers do not drink soft drinks blindfolded. The look of the can, the advertising, and prior experiences with the product all come together to differentiate the alternative and make price increases have a smaller impact on the quantity demanded. In many instances it is both real and perceived differentiation that matters. A lot of people who demand a computer with "Intel Inside" do not know the difference between a Pentium chip and chips from other makers. They want a Pentium because Intel has done a great job of differentiating its products.

Total Expenditure

As a general rule, the smaller the total expenditure to purchase and use an item, the more inelastic the demand for the item will be. A 20 percent increase in the price of Q-tips would not have much of an impact on your purchase of the item. Before the increase, a 100-count box that might last you three months was $1.00, and after the increase it is $1.20. Most people would not even notice the change. If the price of a $20,000 boat increases 20 percent, then the impact is another $4,000. That is something people will notice. Some people may look for another brand of boat, while others will decide that at $24,000, they don't really need a boat.

There are some exceptions to this guideline. Products that have their prices heavily promoted tend to be more elastic. Gasoline is a classic example. An additional three cents a gallon is only 45 cents on a 15-gallon fill-up, but a large number of consumers will drive all over town to find what they believe is an available lower price (often spending more in gas consumption than they save on price). There are also thresholds that come into play that will change the elasticity of an item. Using the gasoline example, a large segment of the market may not even notice that the price is going up until it hits $2.00 per gallon. At this price they move from an inelastic mindset to an elastic mindset. "Two dollars! Are you kidding me? I will walk before I spend that much for gas," may suddenly be their reaction. The move from $1.90 to $1.95 may not have had any impact, but the jump from $1.95 to $2.00 totally changed their view of the world.

Situational Influences

The circumstances that surround a purchase situation can vastly alter the elasticity of demand for an item. Such situations can alter the number of substitutes available and make an immediate purchase mandatory. To help explain this point the example of car tires works well. Let's say you are walking to a car to go to class and notice your front tires are a little worn. You may make a mental note to start shopping for tires. You may even jot down the size of your tires. That weekend you look in the newspaper and compare prices from several local tire dealers. You might select the lowest-price tire source, or you may decide that you do not have the money for two new ones and opt to replace just the one that is in worse shape. You might even go against safety concerns and keep driving on both of the old ones. You are in a very elastic state in this circumstance of an optional purchase.

Now let's change the situation significantly. You are driving to visit relatives, and out in the middle of nowhere your tire goes flat. Using your cell phone you summon help. The repairperson that arrives from AAA also happens to be a tire dealer. He tells you your tire is not fixable. You want to get where you are going as soon as possible, so you ask if he has a tire the size you need. You don't even ask what the price is. You are now in an inelastic mode, and all that has changed is the circumstances that reduced your options to one and eliminated the status quo from that set. Tire dealers are not the only marketers who have noticed this. Consider what a plumber charges in the middle of the night, on a weekend. That is inelastic demand at its best.

The Revenue/Profit Relationship

The discussion regarding elasticity in this section considers only top-line revenue that is generated from the sale of a product at various price levels. Up to this point the issue of gross margin has not been addressed. As you know, firms do not stay in business by selling products; they stay in business and prosper by making a profit on the products they sell. Cutting prices is seen by many managers as a quick way to move excess inventory and generate short-term revenue, but it may end up having severe, negative consequences on the firm's bottom line.

Another example should help clarify this issue. A firm making and marketing stereo systems has traditionally charged $1,000 per system. The cost to manufacture this system is $600. That leaves a margin of $400. The firm experiences a drop in sales and decides to cut the price to increase revenues. After some debate the decision is made to offer a $100 rebate to anyone who buys a system over the next three months. That decision is consistent with a 10 percent price cut, but it is in reality a 25 percent reduction in margin (from $400 down to $300). That means that the firm must sell 25 percent more units than would have been purchased under the old price just to get to the same margin level. In all cases the impact of the price decrease must be greater than the percentage margin decrease for the price cut to work. The message is fairly clear. It is better for a manager to find ways to build value and justify the current price, or even a greater price, than it is to cut the price in search of volume. Giving $150 worth of CDs to anyone who buys the stereo system in the next three months (which, due to volume purchases, are being secured by the stereo manufacturer for a total of $22) is a far better option than a price cut. Decision makers often misunderstand the dynamics of the relationship between price cuts and margins.

Major Pricing Strategies

While prices for individual products must be made on a case-by-case basis, most organizations have developed a general and consistent approach to be used in determining those prices. That approach is known as a *pricing strategy*. The selection of a pricing strategy should not take place in isolation from other strategic decisions, and the final selection may result in a modification of the product, distribution, or promotion strategy. As has already been discussed, it is not so much the actual price being charged that influences buying decisions as the way that price is perceived by members of the target market. Strategies that put the actual price in as positive a light as possible under the circumstances are known as *psychological pricing*. In this section some of the more common approaches to psychological pricing are addressed.

Prestige Pricing

Firms using prestige pricing set their prices at the top end of all the available products in a category. This is done to promote an image of exclusivity and superior quality. Ritz Carlton Hotels never want to find themselves competing with other hotels on price. Ritz Carlton competes only on service and the value of the "It would be a pleasure" experience. It lets Red Roof Inn and Motel 6 fight it out at the low end of the industry. Particularly where it is hard to objectively judge the true value of a good, and especially a service, a higher price may indicate a better product, even to the extent that the demand curve slopes up instead of down. Most people assume a $40 bottle of wine is better than a $25 bottle. Only a real wine connoisseur would know, but the average wine-buying public would see the $40 bottle as more appropriate for a celebration. Consulting and research services are often sold in this fashion as well. Former President George Bush gets $50,000 for a one-hour speech to a company's employees. The meeting planner would likely assume that his message will have a better impact than a local professional speaker getting $5,000 for the same amount of time.

Odd/Even Pricing

You must have noticed that most prices are not nice, round numbers. The concert tickets are $49.95, and the breakfast special is $3.95. A couple of factors drive the prevalence of such odd prices over nice, even pricing. The first is that demand curves are not a straight line. As was discussed earlier in this chapter, the elasticity of a product's demand will change significantly at various points. The move from $45.95 to $49.95 may result in very little drop in demand. When the price hits $50.00, just 5 cents more, the drop in demand may be sizable. Concertgoers see $49.95 as $40, even though with taxes the price might raise well over $50. They will tell a friend, and particularly a parent, that they spent about $40 to go, or that it certainly was not $50 to get a ticket. Another reason the odd/even price works is the impression it makes that the seller did everything possible to get the price as fine (and thus as low) as he or she possibly could. To say you will clean my gutters for $47 sounds like you put a lot more thought into it than if you just said, "Oh I will do it for about $40," even though the first figure is $7 higher.

Reference Pricing

Contrary to prestige pricing, reference pricing has a strategy of going to market with products priced just slightly below most of the competitors. There is always a segment of shoppers who will pick the lowest-price option. Cut a few extra features off the VCR, and the unit can be on the shelf at $195 when all other choices are above $200. While consumers may not know what they intend to spend for a new VCR or DVD player when they go to the store, they use the mix of products and prices as an information source to create the range of available options. This is also done on the Web at MySimon.com, which asks shoppers to chose options below $100, below $150, below $200, etc. Go over the threshold, and a particular firm's offering will not be in the set provided.

Reference pricing is also used when sale prices are compared to regular prices. A retailer might offer a television as "Regularly $399.99, On Sale for $349.99." To be effective, the reference price—$399.99 in this case—must be seen as a legitimate, regular price. In other words, the retailer could not inflate the reference price in order to make the sale price more attractive. Further, the sale price of $349.99 must be available for just a limited time, or else customers will come to see the sale price as the regular price. This is an important legal issue involved with reference pricing: The reference price must truly be the regular price. Retailers that offer nothing but sale prices essentially mislead customers by comparing the sale price to a higher, but never used, reference price.

Price Bundling

Price bundling has also been called *solution-based pricing* or *all-inclusive pricing*. This approach brings together two or more complementary products for a single price. At its best the bundled price is less than if the items were sold separately. Slow moving items can be bundled with hot sellers to expand the scope of the solution, build value, and manage inventory. The SuperClubs resorts have gone to price bundling due to the desire of a large segment of the vacationing public to simplify their vacations and stick to a budget. The room, food, beverages, and entertainment are all included in a per-person price for a class of room. This lets guests leave their credit cards and their money in their safe and just enjoy themselves. Some packages even include the airfare, purchased in large quantities of seats from major departure points for reduced prices. Bundling is an attraction to the people in the convenience segment, but those who believe they can do a better job of creating their own solution and building a better value can see it as a negative. It is key to know the target segment's perceptions well for any and all of these psychological pricing strategies.

Fixed versus Negotiated Prices

Up to this point the discussion has assumed that once a price is set, everyone who buys an item from a marketer will pay the same price. Historically this has been the case for almost all products in the United States except cars. It was expected that one would haggle and bargain to get the best price when buying a new or used car. The sticker price for the vehicle was only the starting point and the highest price anyone would have to pay. As cars have moved toward fixed pricing, it seems that almost everything else has become negotiable. The Internet has played a large role in fostering the "let's make a deal" approach to buying everything, from airline tickets to food and hotel rooms and rental cars. Priceline.com was a major pricing trendsetter when it was launched in 1998. The approach has been simple: Create a competitive bidding process for an identified unit of demand. Critics of the competitive bidding process via the Internet contend that it is inconvenient (haggling takes time, and you may end up with an unattractive option) and unfair (the person in the next room may have paid 20 percent less than you did), and it promotes disloyalty (price is the only marketing mix element that matters). Others would say that it does not promote these negatives, but only capitalizes on what has been present for some time. Whatever your opinion, Priceline.com has been a success in several segments of the market. Its sales approached $1.3 billion in 2000, and the system sells about 4 percent of all airline tickets. Sales of hotel rooms and rental cars continue to climb rapidly. About half of all sales are made to repeat users, an indication that satisfaction and loyalty are continuing to mount.[2]

While generally new to the consumer marketplace, negotiated pricing has long been widespread in business-to-business marketing. Salespeople with many firms had a great deal of flexibility in terms of what was charged to organizational buyers, with big discounts for volume purchases. Buyers went through comprehensive training programs to learn how to squeeze every dime out of every deal. In a negotiated situation of this type, there are three levels of price (and any other issue being negotiated for that matter) that both the buyer and the seller need to understand and plan. The first is the *opening position*. This is the figure that each side will put on the table as a starting point. For 500 cases of 20-pound paper the salesperson might put out an opening position of $23.50 per case. The buyer might counter with his or her opening position of $17.50. It is important to note that neither side expects to get the number it is initially proposing, if the negotiators are skilled. All that the two opening positions do is establish the *negotiation range*. If there is to be a deal, it will take place somewhere between $23.50 and $17.50.

Behind these opening positions, each side should know its *aspiration*. The aspiration is the number that each side will use to distinguish between a successful negotiation and an unsuccessful negotiation. For the seller this number might be $20.25, and for the buyer it might be $20.00. If the agreement is reached at a price higher than $20.25, the salesperson will be happy; if it is below $20.00, the buyer will feel that he or she successfully negotiated a favorable outcome. Each side moves via concessions from its opening position toward its aspiration in an effort to find common ground. A *concession* is a reduction in the asking or buying price as one moves away from an opening position to subsequent positions. Several guidelines come into play when making concessions: (1) Try not to be the first one to make a concession; (2) start with modest concessions and make them smaller as you go along (for the salesperson a sample series would be $23.50 to $22.50 to $22.10 to $21.85, and so on as needed); (3) do not make any concessions early, try to support your opening position with facts consistent with what you have proposed (for the salesperson high quality and good service, and for the buyer high volume and the potential for additional business); and (4) don't give anything up unless you get something in return (the salesperson might offer to drop the price by seventy-five cents if the buyer can commit to a longer-term commitment or a larger-volume order).

The third number in the set is the least favorable amount either side is willing to agree to in this meeting. This level is referred to as one's *limit*. In our continuing example, the limit for the salesperson might be $18.50 and the limit for the buyer might be $20.50. In this example, since the two limits overlap, we know that if the two parties keep negotiating, they will come to an agreement. Unless something changes, that agreement will lie somewhere between $18.50 and $20.50. Whether it is the buyer or the seller that feels good about the deal depends on the relationship of the final amount to the aspiration levels.

Negotiating prices can be a long and frustrating process, but it is the most logical and systematic way two parties who don't initially agree with each other can work to reach an agreement. Some firms give their salespeople and buyers total authority to negotiate prices within a broad range. Others require management involvement, and some decide they will not negotiate off their published prices. Increasingly in today's challenging business-to-business marketplace, the development of negotiation skills is a prerequisite for survival, much less success.

Legal and Ethical Issues in Pricing

Pricing is one of the most heavily watched and regulated of all marketing activities. Given that a difference in price can create such a significant competitive advantage, any effort to artificially give one company an edge over another is subject to judicial action. While managers in a company need to talk about pricing strategies and pricing decisions on a regular basis, they should *never* discuss pricing with a competitor or in the presence of a competitor. Such "collaboration" is known as *price fixing*, which is illegal under the Sherman Antitrust Act. Sizable fines and prison terms for those who are convicted are the norm. Usually one firm in an industry will be a price leader and others will be the price followers when it comes to increases and decreases. The Justice Department has determined that while following a competitor's lead in an upward or downward trend is acceptable, there can be no signaling of prices for particular products or services in this process. Several airlines were involved in cases where a sharp price drop or increase in one route told competitors what to do and what not to do. Such indirect price fixing is also illegal.

Intentionally misleading consumers with promoted prices is another area that has seen significant court action in recent years. This pricing tactic, known as *deceptive pricing*, is illegal under the Federal Trade Commission Act and the Wheeler-Lea Act. One form of deceptive pricing that is the most carefully watched for is *superficial discounting*, which is associated with reference pricing. This form of deception provides the indication that an advertised sale price is a reduction below the regular, reference price when that in fact is not the case. The product may not have been sold at the regular price in any meaningful quantities, or the sale price period may be excessively long. To avoid this legal violation, the product should be offered at the regular price, discounted in a specified dollar amount and for a specified period, and then at the end of that period revert to the regular price. If the product is a discontinued item, that should be stated in the advertisement. Most of the activity on superficial discounting has taken place at the state attorney general level.

One final form of price regulation is *price discrimination*. Charging different prices to two different-channel intermediaries and retailers who will in turn sell the product to consumers may be illegal. The most important question is: "Does this price differential injure competition"? There are essentially two ways of defending a price difference. One is to base the reduced price on lower costs of doing business with one customer compared to another. For example, large-volume orders are generally cheaper per item to deliver than small-volume orders. These cost savings must be documented, and the reduction cannot exceed the amount of the savings. The second defense is that the lower price was necessary to meet competitive pricing for the customer getting the reduction. This lower pricing must be documented, and the selling organization can only match, and not beat, the lower price at the more competitive customer. Discriminatory pricing is regulated under the Robinson-Patman Act and the Clayton Act. The intent of these regulations is to provide a playing field that is as level as possible for all competitors, where large retailers can't demand unfair price reductions from their suppliers, which would make it hard for smaller retailers with lower gross margins to compete.

Lessons from Chapter 7

Pricing in the marketing mix:

- is the focus of great concern by management today.

- is one of only two ways to grow revenue.

- sells your items at a higher price.

- sells more items.

- is the easiest of all marketing mix variables to change.

- is the marketing variable that can be changed in the shortest period of time.

- often is not set properly to maximize the profitability the product provides to the firm.

Pricing in marketing strategy:

- is often a major source of confrontation between buyers and sellers.

- must consider a variety of factors, including:

- costs

- demand

- customer impacts

- competitors' prices

- should be based on all costs, including opportunity costs.

- can't cover cost levels that are driven by inefficiencies.

- should involve the selling firm's attempting to communicate not just prices but bottom-line impacts whenever this can create favorable differentiation.

- must reflect an understanding of competitive pricing, but should not be driven by a blind urge simply to meet or beat what competitors are charging.

Customer issues in pricing:

- ultimately must be considered in an effort to create an overall positive evaluation of the purchase decision.

- are driven by the concept of value.

- must be driven by the understanding that members of different target market segments have different perceptions of value.

- have been significantly influenced by the move from a market where sellers have the power to one where buyers have the power.

Price elasticity:

- is calculated by contrasting the percentage change in quantity demanded for a product with a given percentage change in price.

- is influenced to be more elastic when the prices for substitute products fall.

- is influenced to be more inelastic when the prices for complementary products fall.

- becomes more inelastic when marketing managers successfully achieve product differentiation.

- is more inelastic when the total expenditure to buy an item is small than when it is large.

- is made more inelastic when situational influences reduce the choices a customer has or make an immediate purchase mandatory.

- should not be considered from just a total revenue perspective, but must also address the consequences on total margin of cutting or raising prices.

Pricing strategies:

- provide general and consistent approaches for firms as they come up with prices for their products.

- can use higher prices to promote a perception of higher quality via the use of a prestige pricing approach.

- may use prices ending in odd numbers ($3.95) to create the perception of a lower price (odd–even pricing).

- can be driven by the price levels of other brands on the shelf to create a favorable relative position (e.g., being the only item in a category below $200). This is known as reference pricing.

- have been based on an approach called price bundling, where the entire set of products that make up the solution is based on one total price.

Fixed vs. negotiated prices:

- contrasts a situation where all buyers pay the same amount with one where each transaction is based on a negotiated agreement between buyer and seller.

- begin with an opening position when the price is to be negotiated.

- operate in a range between the two sides' opening positions when negotiations take place.

- involve an understanding of the aspiration, or desired outcome, each side wants in a negotiation.

- incorporate concessions as each side negotiates from its opening position toward its aspiration and ultimately its limit, or stopping point, in a negotiation.

Legal and ethical issues in pricing:

- are critical considerations as firms go about the business of establishing prices.

- exclude discussions with competitors as prices are being established.

- make illegal any attempt to deceive consumers as prices are set.

- preclude companies from discriminating against one customer by the prices that are charged in comparison to another customer.

Questions for Discussion

1. One of the key decisions a manager has to make is to change prices that have been set inappropriately. What considerations should be taken into account in deciding whether it is the price that is wrong or whether the problem lies in some other element of the marketing mix?

2. Discuss the variety of situational factors that could come into play and impact elasticity in the purchase of each of the following products: (a) sporting event and concert tickets, (b) staples such as milk, eggs, and bread, (c) an electric generator, (d) an airline ticket to a beach resort.

3. As you negotiate with someone to give you a ride home from school, what factors might determine how you set your opening position, your aspiration, and your limit in terms of what you would pay to get a ride?

Exercises

1. Pick a departure date, departure location, and destination. Go to the Web sites for three airlines, and compare the prices for this trip (e.g., NWA.com for Northwest). Try dates that include a Saturday night layover and those that do not. Try dates less than seven days away, and compare these prices with those for dates that are more than twenty-one days out. How do you explain the similarities and differences you see in these prices?

2. Pick three different restaurants in your city. Choose a comparable meal for each location (e.g., a grilled chicken breast dinner or a vegetable plate). For each option, do a value assessment that addresses all positive and negative consequences of eating there.

3. Pair up with another student. Find an item you have that the other student wants or one they have that you want. Negotiate the sale of this item between you. Be sure to plan your opening position, your aspiration, and your limit before you begin. Keep track of each side's concessions, and evaluate the concession sequence once you are done.

8

Distribution and Supply Chain Management

Introduction

One of the major concerns consumers have with shopping on the Web is that they might want to return what they purchased. There is a vast number of reasons why a buyer would want to return an item. It might not fit, or it may look better on a computer screen than it does in reality. The item also may not function properly, or it may just be a well-intentioned gift gone wrong. If the purchase is from a store, the mindset is no problem: I will just take it back to the place where it was purchased. If the item was bought online, new concerns arise. How will I send it back? Will I get my money refunded or my charge card credited? Who will pay for the postage, and what if it gets lost in transit? These concerns are very real. One study showed that almost 40 percent of e-shoppers would buy more online if they were assured of easy returns or exchanges. The Boston Consulting Group found that concerns about returns were one of the top two reasons people do not buy apparel on the Web. Even those who buy clothes online send the item back to the e-tailer one time in five. Footwear returns can run even higher.

Seeing an unmet need for both retailers and consumers, The Return Store (TRS) was founded to come to the rescue. This firm, based in Fair Lawn, New Jersey, has plans to open 2,000 locations across the United States where consumers can return electronically purchased merchandise or gifts. The premise of TRS is simple: "Offer prompt, courteous, friendly, and intelligent service" to people with an item not purchased from a store. There is no need to repack and wrap the merchandise; just take it to TRS and they do the rest. Within minutes the consumer has his or her credit and is out the door. A Web site (http://www.thereturnstore.com) provides a listing of policies for any represented merchant and a map to the person's closest two or three TRS locations, with days and hours the locations are open. For those who won't leave their home to shop or return, a "Platinum Pick-Up Service" is available for a small fee.

One key to the success of TRS is the software program it developed: Merchandise Return System (MRS). This system links all the store locations, pulls up data about the item being returned, maintains a customer record, keeps track of all returned items, and efficiently schedules shipments back to the seller.

When most people think of marketing channels, they only think of the product moving one way (seller to buyer) and the payment moving the other (buyer to seller). In the case of TRS there is a firm that knows it goes both ways.[1]

The Importance of Distribution and Supply Chain Management

Throughout most of the twentieth century, *distribution* was the forgotten component of marketing strategy. After all, marketing was known as being made up of the four Ps: product, price, promotion, and something most people had a hard time remembering. That fourth P really didn't fit. Marketing textbook authors passed it off as *place*, but it was really a D, for *distribution*. Beginning in the 1980s and certainly in the 1990s, organizations that neglected the distribution component of their marketing strategy were faced with a different D: death.

Distribution and supply chain management have moved to the top of the list when it comes to achieving a sustainable advantage and true differentiation in the marketplace. Prices can easily be copied, even if only for the short run. Products may become obsolete almost overnight. Good promotion and advertising in September can easily be passé by the prime selling season of November and December. A solid distribution system, while costly to construct (in both money and time), will generate profits for years to come. With great distribution you can overcome some weaknesses in pricing, products, or promotion. A poor distribution strategy will kill a firm's efforts to market a superior product, at a good-value price, using effective communication media. Such importance is realized by top managers of North American manufacturing firms, who nearly unanimously rank supply chain management as critical or very important to their firm's success. High importance comes along with a high level of difficulty, for only 2 in 100 responding managers rank their supply chains as world class, and less than half of the firms claim to have formally developed a supply chain strategy.[2]

The development of a distribution strategy involves multiple components that will be discussed in this chapter. These generally fall into two basic categories: marketing channels and physical distribution. Distribution decisions address either or both of these components.

1. *Marketing channels:* a system of organizations through which products, resources, information, funds, and/or product ownership flows between producers and consumers.

2. *Physical distribution:* moving products to the right place in the right quantities at the right time, and in a cost-efficient manner. Logistics strategies address physical distribution issues. Included here are tangible product movements down channel as they are sold, and increasingly up channel as they are returned. This set includes functions such as transportation, storage, materials handling, and the systems and equipment necessary for these activities.

The evaluation of distribution decisions is increasingly made using two criteria. First, is the channel *effective?* Second, is the channel *efficient?* More and more today the answer from a significant portion of the members in the organization's target market must be yes to both questions. On the issue of effectiveness, the key concerns are the extent to which the channel provides time, place, and possession utility. In terms of time, the new standard is 24, 7, 365. Businesses as well as consumers want to be able to purchase products and have access to information every hour of every day, every day of the week, and every day of the year (holidays included). In addition to the issue of *when* consumers can interact with product suppliers, *where* they do this has become more important. In the past consumers and businesses would often travel great distances to get to a source of products. Today, they do not even want to leave their home or office. Products are ordered over the phone or via the Internet and shipped directly to the purchaser or the receiver of the gift. "I want to be able to shop for underwear in my underwear" is the motto of many of today's consumers.

Significant efficiencies can be realized at all levels of the channel with a supply chain management strategy for distribution. As a general rule, a traditional distribution channel is filled with a good deal of uncertainty and competition (as will be discussed later). Both lead to inefficiencies via redundancies and waste. Office Max was able to cut its inventory investment by $200–300 million for a comparable volume of sales when it implemented a comprehensive supply chain approach.[3] Best-in-class supporters of a coordinated supply chain strategy have seen their total supply chain costs reduced to just 4–5 percent of total sales, a good 5–6 percent less than average performers. This may not sound like a lot, but given the large volume of the firms involved, it could easily result in a $25–30 million cost advantage over a mid-level efficiency channel participant.[4] For a firm with a 10 percent net margin, that would require an additional $250–300 million in sales activity just to catch up with the top supply chain strategist.

Possession utility relates to the ease of the actual purchase process. Customers want to buy both goods and services only in the amounts they need and using the means of payment they most prefer. When they buy in large volume, they want to receive significant discounts. Sam's, Costco, and other wholesale clubs have made it possible for people who have the storage space to save 20 percent or more per roll of paper towels if they will buy a package of 20 rolls. On the other hand, the consumer living alone in a small, efficiency apartment can buy the single roll and also single servings of a wide variety of food items and complete meals.

The important steps for a manager developing his or her distribution strategy are first to know who the best-chance customers are and then to design a distribution strategy and network that will provide target customers with the products they want, in the right quantities, for an acceptable price, when and where they want to buy them. This may sound simple, but as many firms find out on an annual basis, it is not easy. It is also a moving target. What works today will almost certainly need to be modified and updated to achieve continued success tomorrow.

Strategic Issues in Distribution and Supply Chain Management

While the terms are often used interchangeably, there is a key distinction that separates a traditional channel from a true supply chain. With the *traditional channel*, each member or level is concerned primarily with how much profit it makes, the size of one's own slice of the pie, if you will. In a *supply chain* (also called by names such as *value-added partnership* and *seamless pipeline*), the major concern is the share of the market the entire channel captures. There is a clear understanding that our channel is competing against other channels. For an organization to have any chance of reaching its objectives, the channel must win the customer's business. Here the focus shifts from the size of one's slice to the size of the overall pie.

As Exhibit 8.1 shows, a firm can demand a larger portion of the profit made from channel activities. But if the share of the market or pie shrinks, that firm may actually

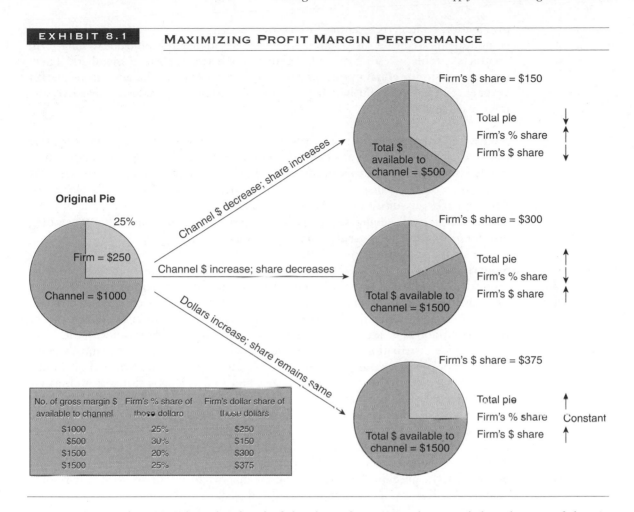

EXHIBIT 8.1   **MAXIMIZING PROFIT MARGIN PERFORMANCE**

No. of gross margin $ available to channel	Firm's % share of those dollars	Firm's dollar share of those dollars
$1000	25%	$250
$500	30%	$150
$1500	20%	$300
$1500	25%	$375

lose. On the other hand, if the channel grows its share, and thus the size of the pie grows, an organization may get a smaller share of the margin/profit dollars available and still come out ahead. Results clearly indicate that firms involved in supply chains tend to outperform, by a wide margin, those in traditional marketing channels. This shows that a focus on the size of the channel's market share is good not just for the viability of the channel, but for all of the players involved

Procter & Gamble realized such benefits as it moved forward with a major supply chain initiative. In the five years after the start of this strategic shift the firm saw its market share go up by 3.5 percent to 28 percent, and its net profit margin climbed from 6.4 percent to a vastly improved 9.5 percent.[5]

This section will consider three key strategic aspects of any supply chain: the structure of the channel, the means to build value in the channel, and the power and conflict that naturally exist (and may or may not be managed) in the channel. All of these combine to determine the extent to which the firms involved can advance their relationship from a loosely configured marketing channel to a true supply chain.

Marketing Channel Structures

There are many strategic options for the structure of a channel of distribution, and these strategies are often complex and very costly to implement. However, a good distribution strategy is essential for success because once a channel is selected and commitments are made, distribution often becomes highly inflexible due to long-term contracts, sizable investments, and commitments between channel members. There are three basic structural options for distribution in terms of the amount of market coverage and level of exclusivity between vendor and retailer: exclusive, selective, and intensive distribution.

Exclusive Distribution   Exclusive distribution gives one merchant or outlet the sole right to sell a product within a defined geographic region. This option is most commonly associated with prestige products or with firms that are attempting to give their products an exclusive image. Many carmakers, such as BMW, Jaguar, and Mercedes-Benz, use exclusive distribution. Manufacturers that pursue this option are usually targeting a single, well-defined segment and need a significant amount of input regarding how their products are presented to the ultimate consumer.

Selective Distribution   Selective distribution gives several outlets the right to sell a product in a defined geographic region. McDonald's and most other franchisers utilize selective distribution in the allocation of franchises. Such selectivity may be based on population (e.g., one franchise per 250,000 people), dollar volume (e.g., when sales reach $5 million in an area, another franchise is awarded), or some other factor.

Selective distribution is desirable when customers need the opportunity to comparison shop, and after-sale services are important. For example, Kodak digital cameras are available at Circuit City, Best Buy, and Office Depot stores as well as via MySimon.com. This broader degree of distribution allows shoppers to collect information on Kodak and competing manufacturers, compare prices, shop at their favorite store, use a variety of means of payment, and get the model they want even when one location is sold out, even from their own computer. Kodak does not make the cameras available in convenience stores and most grocery stores due to the relatively high price of the item, the need for information, and the manufacturer's desire to maintain some control over how its cameras are displayed and sold.

Intensive Distribution   Intensive distribution makes a product available in the maximum number of outlets in each region to gain as much exposure and as many sales opportunities as possible. This option is closely associated with consumer convenience goods, such as bread, candy, soft drinks, and cigarettes. Firms that take the mass marketing approach to segmentation often employ an intensive distribution strategy. If consumers can't find one firm's products in a given location, they will simply substitute another brand to fill the need. The manufacturer is giving up a good degree of control in order to get as much visibility, and as large a share of sales, as possible. As brands and product classes age they often move toward more extensive distribution. In the 1970s, calculators were available only on a selective basis. Today they can be purchased at almost every convenience store around the globe.

Enhancing Value

A key consideration in making strategic decisions about the structure of one's marketing channel is to know the value components target customers will see as attractive as they make selections. Included here are information, communication, and sales, after-sale service, delivery, enhancements (such as gift wrap), and solution development.

Solution development involves the combination of complementary products that yield a greater overall value. Combining wine, cheese, other snacks, plates, flatware, napkins, a table cloth, and a picnic basket results in a combined value much greater that the sum of the individual parts in the mix. We call this *synergistic value building* in the channel.

Such value building also takes the focus off the price of the individual items, because consumers and business customers tend to put less margin pressure on a solution to a need or problem than they do on isolated products. The value of an Epson printer would be perceived differently depending upon whether it is a stand-alone item, is part of a system for a student, is one piece of equipment in a home office, or will be used in an office building. The desire for rapid service and training/information close to the consumer will tend to push a manufacturer to use a sizable number of local distributors to perform the value-adding functions. In contrast to traditional marketing channels, supply chains tend to have value building as one of their greatest competitive differentiators.

Power and Conflict in the Supply Chain

Although relatively simple to describe, the implementation of a relationship driven by supply chain management is quite difficult to achieve. It requires a fundamental change in how distribution channel members work together. Among these changes is a move from a "win–lose" competitive attitude to a "win–win" collaborative approach, in which there is a common realization that all parties in the chain must prosper. This change shifts the participants from short-term to long-term assessments in evaluating decisions affecting the relationship. The focus is modified from one of selling to the next level in the channel to one of selling products through the channel to a satisfied ultimate customer. Information flows move from a guarded "as needed" basis, to open, honest, and frequent communications. Perhaps most importantly, the points of contact in the relationship expand from one-on-one at the salesperson–buyer level to multiple interfaces at all levels and in all functional areas of the various organizations. The desired result of this shift is to create channels with all members working together to reduce costs, waste, and unnecessary movement in the entire marketing channel in order to satisfy ultimate customers.[6]

The sources of power or influence that are utilized also change with the move from a traditional channel to a collaborative supply chain approach. *Power*, or *influence*, can be defined as the ability to get other parties to do or say something they would otherwise not do or say. This does not mean that you use power to get them to take action or communicate information that will hurt them. It only means that they would not be doing or saying this without the influence of the powerful party.

The sources of channel power can be broken down into a fairly limited set: legitimate, reward, coercive, information, and referent power. These sources are identified and briefly discussed next.[7]

> *Legitimate power*—This power source has to do with the firm's position in the marketing channel. Historically, manufacturers have been seen as holding most of the power, but in the 1990s this power balance shifted to retailers (as we will discuss later). Here in the twenty-first century the only channel member that can lay claim to power with any consistency is the final level of customer or consumer.

Reward power—The ability to help other parties reach their goals and objectives is the crux of reward power. Rewards may come in terms of higher-volume sales, sales with more favorable margins, or both. Individual salespeople at lower levels in the channel may be rewarded with cash payments, merchandise, or trips to motivate more favorable presentations of a manufacturer's or wholesaler's products. Consumers can be rewarded with free airline tickets, car rentals, or hotel rooms based upon their purchases of a company's goods or services.

Coercive power—In contrast to reward power, coercive power is the ability to take positive outcomes away from, or even to inflict punishment on, another channel member. Coercive power has been limited by legislation and judicial actions, but a manufacturer may still slow down deliveries and postpone the availability of some portions of the product line to a wholesaler or retailer. A retailer can decide not to promote, give favorable shelf space to, or even carry the new products from a particular manufacturer.

Information power—Having and sharing knowledge is at the very root of information power. Such knowledge makes channel members more effective and efficient. Knowledge may relate to topics such as sales forecasts, market trends, competitive intelligence, product uses, and use rates, or some other critical pieces of information.

Referent power—This power source comes from the liking of the other party or organization. It has long been said that buyers like to do business with salespeople they enjoy being with. This is still true, but increasingly referent power has its roots in businesses wanting to associate with other businesses, as opposed to just people liking people. Similar cultures, values, and even computer information systems can lead to the development of referent power.

Collaborative Supply Chains

Traditional marketing channel members have made heavy use of legitimate, reward, and coercive power sources. The use of such sources is consistent with the high level of conflict that exists in such channels. The seller wants to sell the item for as much as possible, provide as few additional services as it can get away with, get the money in advance, and deliver the product (good or service) at its convenience. By contrast, the buyer wants to purchase the product for as little as possible, get a large number of additional services both now and in the future, pay months or even years later with no interest, and get the product immediately. The collaborative supply chain that focuses on win–win outcomes works to get past these natural sources of confrontation. Reward and referent power are used, with the most important source of influence being information. Whether the problems that naturally materialize in a marketing channel are confronted successfully is dependent on the successful development, communication, and utilization of information.

Toshiba has been among the most aggressive and innovative firms in its efforts to convert traditional competitive relationships into collaborative partnerships. Toshiba and its supply partners focus first on creating more wealth in the channel and then on sharing that wealth based on the contributions of all players. Exhibit 8.2 lists the seven steps this channel has found to be essential to move competitive opponents in a traditional channel to collaborative partners in a supply chain.

EXHIBIT 8.2	SEVEN STEPS TO A SUCCESSFUL COLLABORATIVE SUPPLY CHAIN INITIATIVE

Step 1 Get ready to share in all realized cost savings from collaboration. Agree that efforts in this area will not erode margins, or overall profits, for any party involved.

Step 2 Make sure all parties are clear on the objectives of the initiative.

Step 3 Top management at each company must be fully committed to the initiative's success, and invest accordingly.

Step 4 The mindset of the way things have always been done must change to one where anything is possible. "Up to now," must be replaced with "From now on" as a mental timeline. Everything must be analyzed as the status quo is placed under attack.

Step 5 Each member must be willing to fully share information and logistics capabilities and processes with all other partners.

Step 6 Technology must receive increased emphasis from all parties as a source of data to drive information for intelligent solutions and modifications.

Step 7 Follow-up and general communications must be increased in quantity and quality.

Source: Adapted from "Collaborative SCM: Adversaries to Allies," *Inbound Logistics*, July 2000, 124.

A further example of the move to form collaborative supply chains is the ongoing and highly successful initiative called *category management*. A group of consumer food product manufacturers and leading supermarket chains that were dissatisfied with the highly competitive/traditional channel relationship that existed among them created a task force to reduce channel conflict and its accompanying inefficiencies. To improve their relationship, the group developed the concept of category management through their Joint Industry Project on Efficient Consumer Response (ECR). This group defines category management as "a supplier process of managing categories (of products) as strategic business units, producing enhanced business results by focusing on delivering continuously enhanced consumer value."[8] This group has determined that category management should also be:

Customer driven: Manufacturers and wholesalers should make all decisions with a concern for the challenges facing retailers in the channel.

Strategically driven: The relationship between the parties should be driven by a strategic plan to advance the relationship and, through this, to advance the outcomes for the parties involved.

Multifunctional: Contact points should go beyond marketing and buying to include areas such as finance, logistics, quality control, and facilities management, in addition to the senior management teams of all firms.

Financially based: Solid financial targets should be set and met in terms of profitability and hard and soft cost management.

Systems dependent: Systems (operational and technical) should be designed and put in place to support the activities of the relationship.

EXHIBIT 8.3	MAJOR COMPONENTS OF CATEGORY MANAGEMENT

Component	Description
1. Strategy	This step involves an informed choice by the retailer to move from managing brands or SKUs (stock-keeping units) to managing groups of products that satisfy similar consumer needs. Such groups are known as categories (e.g., deli meats, fresh cut floral, appearance chemicals, home bath cleaning products).
2. The Business Process	This is an eight-step process that includes: (1) defining categories and subcategories; (2) determining the categories' role in meeting retailer goals and objectives; (3) assessing the present performance of the defined category; (4) setting scorecard targets for measuring performance; (5) jointly developing strategies for achieving scorecard targets; (6) selecting specific tactics to implement selected strategies; (7) implementing plans with calendars and assigned responsibilities; and (8) appraising categories and refining plans for return to step 1.
3. Scorecard	An ongoing process of setting targets and setting up the means to monitor and improve performance in targeted areas (e.g., profit per square foot of category space, or average dollars purchased in the category per consumer).
4. Organization Capabilities	Changes in the design and structure of organizations, the required skill bases of the parties to the relationship, and the performance measurement and reward and recognition systems of the people involved.
5. Information Technology	Address the acquisition, analysis, and movement of information within and between the organizations involved. It must involve the supplier's marketing information system (MIS), the retailer's MIS, and external syndicated data suppliers (e.g., Nielsen).
6. Collaborative Trading Partners	The methods used to structure and conduct interactions between members of both the supplier and retailer organizations in a win–win fashion, with the open and honest exchange of information for the purpose of identifying and solving problems.

Source: *Category Management Report* © 1995 by the Joint Industry Project on Efficient Consumer Response.

Focused on immediate consumer response: Successful channel members implementing category management should be able to give consumers what they want more rapidly than firms operating as traditional marketing channels.[9]

Exhibit 8.3 outlines six components of an ongoing category management process that must be jointly managed by both the category manager (retail buyer and merchandising position) and channel consultant (manufacturers' or wholesalers' account manager or salesperson). Each of the components in the process depends on the quality planning and performance of the other five components. In recent years, firms outside the consumer products industries have begun to adopt components of the ECR category management process to drive their own relationships.

Trends in Marketing Channels

In addition to the issues discussed to this point in the chapter, a number of other key trends are occurring in the ways in which marketing channels and supply chains function.

Growth of Direct Distribution

The traditional marketing channel of producer to wholesaler to retailer is alive and well today and is used to distribute a wide range of products. However, some changes have occurred in this traditional arrangement for very large retailers, such as Sears, Kmart, Circuit City, Toys "Я" Us, Home Depot, and Wal-Mart, are now performing their own wholesaling activities and buying directly from producers.

Distribution activities have also changed as a result of increased distribution from producers directly to consumers. In some cases, producers are selling to consumers through their own retail outlets. Nike, for example, continues to expand its Nike Town locations. The continued popularity of factory outlet malls also testifies to this trend. However, most of the increased activity in direct distribution stems from nonstore retailing.[10] Millions of satisfied customers are now purchasing products from catalog marketers, such as Lands' End and J. Crew; door-to-door marketers, such as Avon and Fuller Brush; home shopping TV programs, like QVC and the Home Shopping Network; and interactive marketers, such as those found on the World Wide Web (as will be discussed in greater depth later in this section).

Intermediary Pressures

Given the demand by consumers for products at lower prices and the number of nontraditional channels that are willing to accommodate this desire, the pressure on all channel member intermediaries to justify their existence continues to mount. The move toward direct marketing has led to the elimination of some retailers from marketing channels. It has also put great pressure on wholesalers, brokers, agents, and all other forms of intermediary organizations to continually justify their presence in the channel. When margins get squeezed, there just may not be enough to go around for everyone in an existing channel. Under such circumstances the channel must either evolve into a more direct form or fail to survive.

An important point to keep in mind is that while channel members may go away, the functions those members perform must continue to be fulfilled. Some other channel member, possibly including the consumer or business customer, will have to step up and take on the function. This must take place at a time when every entity's resources are strained. Firms today are increasingly focusing on their core competencies and outsourcing all noncore functions. This has led some customers in industrial service supply chains to make even greater use of brokers or agents, to evaluate alternatives and make recommendations, and innovative service providers, to perform required (but noncore) functions. When a firm has significant needs and insufficient in-house expertise, the role of such intermediaries may tend to expand, not be eliminated. An entire industry known as 3PLs (third-party logistics providers) has sprung up in the United States and Europe as retailers look for outside expertise to make their products more readily available and to reduce key costs.[11] These firms manage inventories and handle the physical movement of product in the channel to make sure that items are in the right amounts and in the right places when they are needed at a particular channel location.

Power Shifts in the Channel

Distribution strategy is also changing as a result of the growing power of discount mass merchandise retailers like Wal-Mart, Kmart, and Target, which have gained increasing power relative to their suppliers. Attracting consumers broadly and in a large number of product categories gives them a significant power advantage when working with consumer product manufacturers such as Procter & Gamble and Levi Strauss. In addition, category-focused retailers (sometimes referred to as *category killers*), such as Toys "Я" Us, Home Depot, Office Depot, Auto Zone, and Best Buy, move large volumes of merchandise and attract large numbers of consumers in their specific category. This can give them great power when negotiating with suppliers such as Mattel, Black & Decker, International Paper, A. C. Delco, and RCA. This higher level of retailer power compels manufacturers to accommodate the objectives and methods of these large retailers. Indeed, these retailers have become the distribution strategists for many lines of consumer goods.

Dual Distribution

Distribution strategies often need multiple channels to reach various markets. The use of multiple channels may arise either to meet customer needs or by design. Multiple channels enable a producer to offer two or more lines of the same merchandise through two or more means, thus increasing sales coverage. The Hallmark Cards organization has made extensive use of dual distribution. It sells its highly respected Hallmark line primarily through the selective distribution of Hallmark stores. Its Ambassador line is made available on an extensive basis through supermarkets, drugstores, and discount stores. In addition, the firm offers both e-cards and paper cards online at Hallmark.com.

Whether to use dual distribution is a strategic decision that manufacturers must consider very carefully. It spreads marketing mix resources across two or more channels, instead of focusing them on just one. Dual distribution can also create channel conflict, particularly when the target segments are not clearly defined and distinct for each channel. The wall covering industry has seen great conflict between traditional decorating centers, 1-800-number locations, and Web sites. Traditional retailers resent doing all of the presale service to help a shopper find a wallpaper that meets the shopper's needs, only to have that person take the pattern number and buy the rolls from a distributor who has neither the costs of a store nor the knowledgeable salespeople. This has led some retailers to boycott the products of manufacturers engaged in aggressive dual distribution.

Order Fulfillment and e-Commerce

Significant advances in information processing and computer-to-computer communications have made possible the introduction of new ways to place and fill orders. The two biggest hurdles that have restricted the use of e-channels, by consumers as well as business organizations, are the costs of shipping and the dependability of deliveries.[12] Advances that have taken place in shipping technology and capabilities have recently significantly reduced both of these concerns.

E-fulfillment is based on a true partnership between areas that have historically often been at odds with one another: marketing and logistics. Both sides must communicate capabilities on a continuous basis so that marketing does not make promises that logistics cannot keep.[13]

The growth in e-commerce has been sparked primarily by consumer demands for convenience and safety and by increased pressure for producers to cut distribution expenses to survive against other, highly competitive marketing channels. "Faster, better, and cheaper" is what business customers and consumers alike have been demanding with a thunderous voice. As the ownership of personal computers and Internet access have exploded, the World Wide Web has become a critical channel component for both manufacturers and retailers to consider. One projection places the volume of consumer purchases via Internet channels at $108 billion by the year 2003. Europe will not be left behind, with sales of goods and services growing 140 percent annually and 100 million Europeans using e-tailers by 2004. Such a sizable opportunity has led many brick-and-mortar retailers to become "click-and-mortar" e-tailers.[14] Even when the purchase is not made via the Web, the Web is increasingly viewed as an important source of information in the decision-making process of both consumers and organizational buyers.

Legal and Ethical Issues in Distribution Strategy

Like every other aspect of marketing strategy, distribution decisions must be made with an eye toward ethical and legal considerations. This chapter concludes with a discussion of several of the most important distribution concerns of this type.

Counterfeit and Gray-Market Products

Both providers of a product and buyers of a product must make reasonable efforts to be aware of the item's origin. Counterfeit products abound today, particularly in the areas of clothing, audio and video products, and computer software. Anything that can easily be copied is prone to counterfeit activities. Some might feel that only manufacturers get hurt when counterfeit products are purchased. This is clearly mistaken reasoning. Governments are affected by the loss of tax revenues. In 1998 in the United Kingdom, for example, over 1 billion pound sterling in direct and indirect taxes was not collected due to the sale of counterfeit products. Profits necessary for ongoing product development are removed from the channel, as well as thousands of jobs at legitimate companies. Counterfeit firms give nothing to the marketplace, they merely take. The consumer is also affected because the quality of counterfeit products almost never matches that of the original. This can be more than just an inconvenience, as in the case of counterfeit auto parts. Counterfeiting has also become a convenient way for organized crime to support its activities, with all of the attendant social costs.[15]

The Internet has made the purchase of counterfeit products that much more prevalent. The Counterfeit Library Web site (http://www.counterfeitlibrary.com) provides the following guidelines to reduce your probability of purchasing counterfeit items online. First, look for sites that accept credit cards. Banks and credit card companies conduct checks on such firms. Second, avoid sending cash whenever possible. Third, check out any unfamiliar source with friends and trusted individuals. Fourth, avoid buying from contacts made via discussion groups or chat rooms, unless you have good information about their legitimacy. Finally, if the match between the price and the description of the item sounds too good to be true, it probably is too good to be true.

Exclusive Channel Arrangements

An exclusive arrangement benefits a manufacturer by requiring that an intermediary, such as a wholesaler, broker, agent, or retailer, not carry or represent products from any of the manufacturer's competitors. Violations of exclusive dealings can cause the manufacturer to cut off supply to the intermediary in question. Not all exclusive dealing agreements are legal. There are three tests that determine their validity. First, the arrangement cannot block competitors from 10 percent or more of the overall market. Second, the sales revenue involved can't be sizable, and finally the manufacturer can't be much larger (and therefore more intimidating) than the intermediary. Such arrangements are viewed most favorably when consumers and business customers have access to other, similar products from other channels and when the exclusivity strengthens the otherwise weak position of a manufacturer.[16]

Dual Distribution

Earlier in this chapter the topic of dual distribution was discussed. With dual distribution, a manufacturer uses two channels to distribute the same product, often both direct sales and traditional retailers, as exemplified by Nike and Hallmark Cards. The only situation in which legal concerns arise is when the manufacturer uses its own retail or e-tail (Internet) distribution to drive independent retailers out of business or to totally dominate them. To avoid this problem, the manufacturer should not undercut the prices that independent retailers can charge with a reasonable margin. Besides being ethical, Nike is very careful to protect the retailers who sell its products. Manufacturers who do not stay legal or use a solid ethical approach and sound judgment may find themselves the only firm that wants to retail their products. Most manufacturers do not want to run, and cannot profitably run, a comprehensive retail venture.

Lessons from Chapter 8

Distribution in the marketing mix:

- was the forgotten element during most of the twentieth century.
- has been advanced by a supply chain management approach.
- has recently moved to the top of the list when it comes to achieving a sustainable competitive advantage.
- is a costly component to do well, but can have long-term positive impacts when successful.
- can be used to effectively overcome some weaknesses in pricing, product, and promotion.
- can rapidly kill a firm if it is not done well.
- is seen as critical by managers in the United States, most of whom feel they should do it much better.

The role of distribution in marketing strategy:

- is divided into two major components: marketing channels and physical distribution.

- should be evaluated from the target market's perspective using both effectiveness and efficiency criteria.

- faces ever-greater challenges on the effectiveness dimension from increasingly demanding customers.

- does not score well on the efficiency dimension when it comes to traditional marketing channels that are filled with conflicts.

- can lead to significant cost reduction through additional efficiencies when a supply chain strategy is developed and implemented.

- must consider possession utility, because customers want to buy both goods and services in the amounts they need using payment means they most prefer.

- must be based on the firm foundation of knowing who your customers are and how they want to acquire the products they need.

- requires constant evaluation and updating, because what works well today may need to be modified for success in the future.

Strategic issues in distribution:

- differ between traditional distribution channels ("I must win") and true supply chains ("We must win").

- shift from the size of the firm's percentage of channel profits to the size of the channel's share under a supply chain approach.

- show significant success, for both the firms involved and the overall channel, with a shift toward a coordinated and effectively managed supply chain.

- include the selection of the proper degree of market coverage delivered by any of the following marketing channel structures:

    - exclusive distribution, where only one firm offers a product to customers in a large geographic marketplace, provides the least amount of market coverage.

    - selective distribution expands coverage to multiple, but a very limited number of, product providers.

    - intensive distribution, where a product is distributed in as many locations as realistically feasible.

Enhancing value:

- must first be driven by a clear and comprehensive understanding of what target customers value.

- is often based on moving beyond simply providing a product to providing a true solution to the target customers' needs.

- through a solution that results in synergistic value building can reduce the customers' emphasis on price in their selection process.

- must be a concern at all levels of the supply chain, not just at the manufacturer or retailer level.

Power and conflict in the supply chain:

- can be effectively dealt with only when supply chain partners shift their mindset from one of win–lose to a true win–win approach.

- can be overcome via win–win only when a longer-term perspective is taken by all parties.

- is a natural phenomenon unless firms move from simply selling to the next level in the channel, to moving a product completely through the channel, to successful consumption by the ultimate user.

- can involve the use of several power or influence sources, including:

  - legitimate power, which is based on a person's or firm's title or position in the marketing channel.

  - reward power, which delivers positive results to the other members of the channel that assist in their goal attainment.

  - coercive power, which imparts negative consequences on other channel members that diminishes their goal attainment.

  - information power, which has risen in importance as people with information are seen as the key to everyone's success when that information is effectively shared.

  - referent power, which is based on the degree to which other parties like and trust the individual or firm in question.

- can be more effectively managed when the people and firms involved shift to a collaborative (win–win) supply chain approach, with seven steps capable of overcoming the natural issues of confrontation.

- has led the most progressive firms in the consumer products industry to develop a powerful tool for success known as category management, based on six criteria:

  1. a customer-driven approach to all decisions.

  2. an overall strategy that directs the actions of each party in the channel.

  3. considers multifunctional issues that go well beyond simply marketing and buying issues, including finance, logistics, quality control, and facilities.

  4. financially based targets to track results beyond sales, to profitability and hard- and soft-cost management.

  5. supported by operational and technical systems to direct and monitor channel activities.

  6. immediate response to customers, to ensure that the channel moves almost instantaneously to changes in customer tastes or preferences.

Trends in marketing channels:

- include the growth of direct distribution, which moves products directly from manufacturers to consumers or business customers who use the products.

- can utilize manufacturer-owned stores for direct distribution, but increasingly is based on electronic/Web-based channels.

- have placed increasing pressure on intermediaries to justify their existence as direct distribution expands.

- include the reallocation of channel functions, for, while levels of channels may disappear, the functions performed by those levels do not go away.

- have resulted in the creation of entirely new types of firms (e.g., third-party logistics firm's, that is, 3PLs) to take on limited outsourced functions in streamlined channels.

- include a major power shift in the channel, from producers and wholesalers to retailers, due to the larger percentage of total sales each store represents today.

- have led some firms to go with a dual distribution strategy to reach different segments of consumers via distinct marketing channels.

- have placed a premium on the development and ongoing advancement of a firm's information system due to the growing importance of effective order fulfillment and the expanded importance of e-commerce.

- are influenced by the growing desire by customers for purchases that can be conducted faster, better, and cheaper, thus really moving the ultimate power in any channel to their level.

Legal and ethical issues in any distribution strategy:

- have grown in importance as distribution channels and supply chains have become more complex, more closely watched, and more heavily regulated than ever before.

- include the concern that the products a firm is selling are legitimate and not some of the growing number of counterfeit items around the globe.

- require very careful consideration and justification of any exclusive arrangements between channel members.

- do not allow manufacturers to drive other channel members out of business through predatory use of a dual distribution strategy.

Questions for Discussion

1. What are the major differences you have experienced in buying a product through a retail store, a manufacturer store, a catalog, and an e-commerce source? What have some retailers in your area done to justify their ongoing presence in the channel?

2. Talk about what makes a product something you would go to great lengths to get, thus supporting a manufacturer's use of an exclusive distribution strategy. What items do you expect to find at any quick shop or grocery store? How much more knowledgeable are the salespeople at an exclusive distribution location versus those at an extensive distribution location at explaining the product? Why is this so?

3. Some manufacturers and retailers advertise that you should shop with them because "We eliminate the middleman." Evaluate this comment in light of the functions that must be performed in a marketing channel. Does a channel with fewer members always deliver cheaper products to customers? Defend your position.

Exercises

1. Find a product offered by a manufacturer under a dual distribution approach. Speculate about the target customer the manufacturer is attempting to reach using each of the two channels. In what ways is the purchase experience different under each channel?

2. During a trip to a local supermarket, visit at least three product areas besides produce and other fresh items. What evidence of a category management approach do you see in each area? Which manufacturer do you feel is the category captain in each area where you see such evidence? Defend you position. Why do you feel the retailer chose that manufacturer to be the category captain?

3. Visit five Web sites offering products you might purchase. Evaluate each site in terms of pricing, terms, and the information it provides in assisting you to make a selection and a purchase.

9

Integrated Marketing Communications

Introduction

Marketing communications includes conveying and sharing meaning between individuals or between organizations and individuals within a marketing context. Integrated marketing communications is a long-term view of influencing customers through a coordinated strategic use of the promotion elements available to marketing. Integrated communications starts with the customer and develops a strategic program of persuasive communications that considers all contacts a customer will have in a marketing relationship. The traditional elements of the promotion mix include advertising, public relations, personal selling, and sales promotion, as illustrated in Exhibit 9.1. There are many ways to describe the promotion mix available to use in an integrated marketing communications program. The most important concern is using the variety of methods available and integrating the promotional effort into a coordinated, customer-focused marketing strategy.

Promotional activities are necessary to communicate the features and benefits of a product to its intended target market(s). For example, to raise awareness of its newly acquired Altoids peppermints beyond their limited counterculture devotees, Kraft employed the Leo Burnett ad agency to develop a campaign to tout the mints without diluting their already "curiously strong" word-of-mouth advertising. The resulting low-key campaign, which featured quirky posters in bus shelters, subways, and alternative weekly newspapers, helped swell the product's share to nearly 10 percent of the market in just two years.[1] The role of advertising, sales promotion, personal selling, and public relations (the promotion mix) in a particular marketing strategy will vary depending on the nature of the product. Industrial products, such as heavy equipment, tend to rely more heavily on personal selling, while consumer products often require greater use of advertising, sales promotion, and publicity. Simple products, like the Altoids peppermints, are more suited for advertising, while technologically complex products rely more heavily on personal selling.

The role of promotion mix elements also varies by stage in the product purchase process (awareness, interest, desire, and action). Mass elements such as advertising and publicity tend to be used more heavily to stimulate awareness and interest due to their efficiency per target member contact. The enhanced communication effectiveness of

| EXHIBIT 9.1 | ELEMENTS OF THE PROMOTION MIX USED IN INTEGRATED MARKETING COMMUNICATIONS |

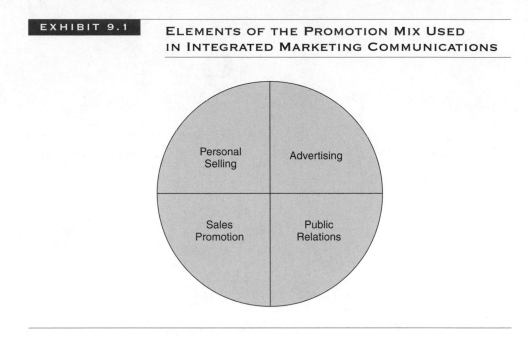

personal selling makes it better suited for moving target members through desire and into action. Promotion mix decisions are also affected by product price, because lower-priced products tend to have a lower profitability per unit that would dictate advertising (e.g., chewing gum and soft drinks), while higher-priced products include a level of margin that makes covering the costs of personal selling feasible (e.g., cars, jet skis, dress clothing, and accessories).

The wide variety of promotion methods makes it necessary to assess the promotional mix in terms of its role in a long-term, effective integrated marketing communications strategy. The advantages and disadvantages of each promotion method must be carefully weighed against their costs and the firm's marketing and the integrated marketing communication objectives. The marketing manager must also decide on the relative weight to give to each method in the total promotion mix. This decision typically comes down to how best to divide the promotion budget across different methods. As the SBU or marketing manager selects promotional methods for the marketing plan, the product's current position should be assessed with respect to customers. Then promotion objectives can be set for the upcoming planning period. Making these decisions requires the marketing manager to specify what each method is capable of delivering in terms of customers' decision-making processes. Supply chain management coordination is also requiring more integration and coordination of communication strategies to develop an effective marketing strategy. Personal selling expenses, roughly two-thirds of business-to-business promotional expenses, are directed toward efforts to move products through the channel of distribution.

When selecting promotion methods to include in the promotion mix, it is important to take an integrated marketing communication perspective, that is, to coordinate promotion elements and other marketing efforts that communicate with target customers to maximize the total impact on those customers. This requires a marketer to look at the "big picture" when planning marketing and promotional programs and co-ordinating the total set of communication functions to deliver the intended message

| EXHIBIT 9.2 | NATIONAL ADVERTISING SPENDING: 2001 PROJECTIONS | |

Advertising Media	Projected 2001 Spending (in billions)	Percent Change Over 2000 Spending
Four TV networks	$15.87	+1.0%
Spot TV	11.85	−1.0
Cable TV	10.13	+12.5
Syndication TV	3.32	+6.0
Radio	4.93	+5.5
Magazine	12.97	+5.0
Newspapers	7.69	+7.0
Direct mail	46.95	+5.0
Yellow Pages	2.23	+5.0
Internet	5.12	+60.0

Source: *Bob Coen's Insider's Report*, McCann-Erickson WorldGroup (http://www.mccann.com).

on a consistent basis.[2] For example, if the promotional campaign stresses quality while the sales force is talking about low price and the Web site features product innovations, what is the customer to believe? Not readily seeing that a product can deliver all of these, the customer is likely to become confused and go to a competitor with a more consistent set of messages.

All too frequently, managers find themselves in the midst of promotion campaigns or activities that have no *clear* promotion objectives. Marketing managers must understand that most promotion activities do not create results simply in the short term. Thus, the firm must have long-term promotion objectives and the patience to continue the promotion strategy long enough to gauge true success and, hopefully, to build a solid market position. Promotion activities based on creativity alone and not linked to the rest of the marketing strategy can waste precious marketing resources.

Coordinating promotional methods in the context of a marketing strategy requires a complete understanding of the role, function, and benefits of each element of the promotion mix. Marketing communications should send a constant and synergistic message to target markets. Let's now turn our attention to the four major elements of the promotion mix: advertising, public relations, personal selling, and sales promotion.

Advertising

Advertising is a key component of promotion and is usually one of the most visible components of integrated marketing communications. Advertising is identified as paid, nonpersonal communication that is transmitted through the mass media. Exhibit 9.2 shows the projected number of dollars spent in 2001 on various advertising media. Most advertising is transmitted through television, newspapers, magazines, direct mail, outdoor displays, the Internet, and even signs on moving vehicles. For example, the city of Orlando has begun a pilot advertising program on city buses. Closed-circuit TV systems were installed by Orbital-Itec on the bus interiors to broadcast news, weather, and ads to riders. To attract manufacturers, Orbital-Itec guaranteed 1 million viewers

| EXHIBIT 9.3 | TOP TEN WEB ADVERTISERS BY IMPRESSIONS AND REACH | |

Advertiser	Impressions	Reach %
1. TRUSTe	2,006,977,220	30.44
2. Microsoft	1,887,905,431	46.46
3. Amazon	1,001,779,067	54.18
4. ClassMates	744,813,672	39.55
5. Yahoo!	714,093,746	33.91
6. ConsumerInfo	612,850,972	9.60
7. Columbia House	592,924,884	29.22
8. Barnes & Noble	520,761,185	43.97
9. America Online	500,617,355	36.81
10. eBay	355,452,683	30.43

Source: Nielsen Net Ratings, http://www.netratings.com, March 23, 2001.

per six-month period, with thirty-second advertisements for $1,500 a month, considerably less than the $3,500 a month to reach homes.[3]

Because advertising is so flexible, it can be used to reach an extremely large target audience or focus on a very small, precisely defined market segment. For example, Internet Web sites and magazines often focus on a narrow market segment, such as organic gardening, skiing, or women's health. Herplanet.com is one such Web site that targets women to provide information and sell products from a wide array of businesses.

Research has shown, however, that spending a large amount of money on advertising for Internet companies does not always result in strong brand awareness. For example, a study conducted by Greenfield Online showed Ameritrade spent $103.7 million on advertising in 1999 but earned only approximately $0.10 for every dollar spent. Meanwhile, eBay spent merely $5.5 million on ads in 1999 but earned about $4.00 for every dollar spent. Overall, this study concluded that it is not how much money you spend on advertising, but how you spend it. Success in advertising on the Internet is finding the most effective way and place to allocate available resources.[4] Exhibit 9.3 shows the top 10 Internet advertisers in terms of impressions and reach.

Targeting advertising to market segments such as African Americans, gays, Hispanics, and women has been an accelerating trend among advertisers over the last decade. Regardless of the medium used, targeting a group of buyers with messages in tune with various lifestyles is important in many marketing strategies. John Hancock ads have incorporated customers from all walks of life as they interact with other customers and with service agents. Many of these ads portray divorce, gay partners, and other nontraditional themes. John Hancock's marketing and advertising vice president indicates the firm is not targeting a specific audience as much as trying to communicate an understanding of what is going on in people's lives and how the company can help. The effort seems to be working: One *USA Today* poll found that 26 percent of respondents liked the ads a lot, while only 18 percent disliked them.[5] Often, effective advertising can be very controversial. In the case of John Hancock, a TV advertisement featuring two women adopting a baby from Asia set off concerns in the international adoption community. Adoption agencies began to protest, fearing that Asian

EXHIBIT 9.4	GLOBAL ONLINE AD SPENDING PROJECTIONS (IN MILLIONS OF U.S. DOLLARS)

	1999	2000	2001	2002	2003	2004	2005
North America	3,509	5,390	7,444	9,768	12,237	14,623	16,913
Western Europe	434	906	1,535	2,258	3,118	4,111	5,263
Asia	225	502	880	1,375	1,922	2,556	3,324
Latin America	52	127	240	402	628	888	1,168
Australia/New Zealand	24	74	135	208	288	373	462
Other	9	28	61	118	211	351	578
Total	4,253	7,027	10,296	14,129	18,402	22,903	27,708

Source: Jupiter Internet Advertising Model, http://www.jup.com, March 26, 2001.

governments would assume that the child is being placed with a homosexual couple and has been approved by American adoption officials. Since 1998 the Chinese government has made it clear that it will not accept applications from gay couples, according to U.S. adoption agencies.[6]

Advertising offers many benefits because it is often extremely cost efficient when it reaches a large number of people. For example, because a magazine such as *Time* reaches over 4 million subscribers, the cost of reaching a thousand subscribers may be less than $50. The cost of a thirty-second spot on a recent Super Bowl broadcast was $2.4 million. But it is possible to purchase a part of a thirty-second spot (3.75 seconds) for an estimated cost per viewer of $.0014.[7] Advertising on television, in magazines, in outdoor displays, and over the Internet, as well as other promotional activities, can add up to a cost-efficient key component of an integrated marketing communication strategy.

There are certainly some disadvantages of advertising even when the cost per person reached may be low. The aggregate dollar layout can be extremely high, especially for television advertising and magazines that reach millions of consumers. On the other hand, Internet advertising provides the opportunity to reach highly specialized markets, sometimes at a low cost per individual that clicks on an ad. The Internet Advertising Bureau estimates that total online advertising for 2000 cost $4.2 billion, and half the ads were banner ads.[8] One of the disadvantages of advertising, especially online, is that its effect on sales is difficult to measure, and advertising is less persuasive than personal selling. In addition, research indicates that getting a target market to listen to a message, click on a banner ad, or look at a print advertisement for only a few seconds is difficult. However, online ad spending continues to grow at an accelerated rate, with projections heading further into the billions of dollars, as shown in Exhibit 9.4.

Types of Advertising

Advertising is used to promote all types of products, including goods, services, ideas, issues, people, and anything that advertisers want to communicate. Since the total expenditures for advertising may be great, larger firms with greater market shares tend to advertise the most. The following are some examples of different types of advertising.

Institutional Advertising   Institutional advertising promotes organizational images, ideas, and culture. It is used to create or maintain an organizational image. For example, IBM advertises that it provides e-solutions with its e-business products, without naming specific products or explaining how e-solutions are provided. The goal is to cultivate the image of IBM as a company that understands electronic commerce and helps companies incorporate the Internet into their business strategies. Aimed at various stakeholders, including shareholders, consumer advocacy groups, government regulators, and the general public, institutional advertising can create a positive view of the organization.

When a company or an organization promotes a position on a public issue, for example, tax cuts, international trade regulations, or social issues, it is referred to as *advocacy advertising*. Advocacy advertising is often used to promote socially approved behavior, such as recycling, responsible use of alcohol beverages, and support for diversity. This type of advertising not only benefits a company's image but can also be a significant contribution to improving the quality of life in our society. Home Depot advertises that it sells only environmentally certified lumber, to protect endangered forests.

Product Advertising   Product advertising promotes the image, features, uses, benefits, and attributes of products. One type of product advertising, *pioneer advertising*, focuses on stimulating demand for a product category rather than a specific brand. For example, Handspring might promote the uses and benefits of its personal digital assistants without promoting individual products. Handspring's advertising would be used in the introduction stage of the product lifecycle.

Another type of product advertising is *competitive advertising*, which attempts to stimulate demand for a specific brand by promoting the brand's image, features, uses, or benefits through indirect or direct comparisons with competing brands. For example, Handspring might compare its Visor Deluxe product to Palm's IIIxe product. The use of such *comparative advertising*, a form of competitive advertising, is appropriate when two or more brands are compared on one or more product characteristics. For example, the BMW 3 series may be compared directly to the Mercedes C series in terms of features, horsepower, or performance. Product categories in which comparative advertising is common include soft drinks, automobiles, computers, and pain relievers. Under the provisions of the Trademark Law Revision Act, marketers using comparative advertisements must make sure they do not misrepresent the characteristics of competing products. A visit to the Federal Trade Commission Web site, http://www.ftc.gov, usually provides examples of companies who have crossed the line and misrepresented competitors in comparative advertisements. Other forms of competitive advertising include *reminder advertising*, which lets customers know that a brand is still available and that it has certain attributes, uses, or benefits, and *reinforcement advertising*, which ensures current purchasers of a brand that they have made the right choice and should continue to use the brand in the future.

Determining the Advertising Budget

The advertising budget, the total amount of money a marketer allocates for advertising for a specific time period, is difficult to set, because the effects of advertising are so difficult to measure. There are many factors that will determine the organization's decision about the appropriate advertising budget, including geographic size of the market, distribution of customers, types of products advertised, sales volume relative to competitor sales, as well as historic trends in the firm's advertising budget. Usually the advertising budget for business-to-business products is small relative to product sales, whereas consumer convenience products, such as cigarettes, soft drinks, detergents, and cosmetics, have a very large budget as a percentage of sales. The following approaches to determining the advertising appropriation are most widely used.

The *objectives-and-task approach* requires the marketing strategist to determine what is to be accomplished in a campaign and attempt to list the tasks required to accomplish those objectives. The cost of the tasks are calculated and used to determine the total budget. Of course, this approach has major problems, including the fact that even with a good marketing plan it is difficult to determine accurately the level of effort needed to obtain certain objectives. For example, Starbucks might find it very difficult to determine exactly how much of an increase in national television advertising it would require to increase by 3 percent the brand's market share of coffee sold in supermarkets.

The *percentage-of-sales approach* is the most widely used method firms implement when planning advertising expenditures. It is simple and straightforward and is based on both what the firm traditionally spends on advertising and the industry average. It is obvious that this method has a major flaw, in that it appears that sales creates advertising rather than a good advertising campaign increasing sales. It should be recognized that a reduction in advertising during a period of declining sales may continue to significantly diminish sales. While this approach is not scientific or logical, it seems to work for many companies and it is very easy to implement.

The *competition-matching approach* is used when setting the advertising allocation by trying to match major competitors' appropriations in absolute dollars. It is hard to allocate the same percentage of sales for advertising as competitors. Again this method may be illogical, because a firm's competitors may have different advertising objectives, and many firms have different resources. Many organizations review competitive advertising and compare competitor's expenditures for various media, such as print, radio, and television, with their own spending levels. This competitive tracking can occur at the national and regional levels and at the least provides a benchmark for comparing advertising resources to market share movements.

The *arbitrary approach* means that someone in the organization determines how much to spend on advertising for a certain period of time based on intuition and personal experience. This approach can lead to mistakes in budgeting because it is not scientific, objective, or logical. On the other hand, deciding how much to spend on advertising is not an exact science. When the appropriation is set too low, advertising cannot achieve its full potential. When too much money is appropriated, overspending and lowered profits results. Many of the dot-com companies, such as Pets.com, went out of business after spending millions of dollars on institutional advertising to create a brand image. The Pets.com URL was purchased by PETSMART.com to obtain the brand name.[9] These decisions were based on an arbitrary approach and did not take into account the realistic amount of benefits that could come quickly from increasing the public's awareness of the organization's Web site.

Evaluating Advertising Effectiveness

A study of the top 100 advertisers determined that 20 percent of ad spending was not efficient in generating sales volume.[10] There are as many ways to test the effectiveness of advertising as there are ways to advertise. Some measures include assessment of the achievement of advertising objectives, assessing the effectiveness of copy, illustrations, and layouts, and evaluating the effectiveness of various media. All of these can involve looking at the response of different market segments to advertising, including images, attitudes, and purchase behavior. Advertising can be evaluated before, during, and after the campaign. A *pretest* usually attempts to evaluate the potential effectiveness of one or more elements of the advertising, usually the message. To pretest advertisements, marketers sometimes ask members of a panel of actual or potential buyers to judge one or more dimensions of the advertisement. A pretest is based on the belief that consumers are more likely than marketers to know what type of advertising would influence them to achieve the desired action. To measure advertising effectiveness during an advertising campaign usually relies on communication or inquiries from the targeted audience, including calls to toll-free numbers, return of coupons, Web site hits, and even personal communication. The advertiser may record the number of inquiries or communication contacts for advertisements and judge the effectiveness based on industry norms or the organization's previous benchmarks.

The evaluation of advertising effectiveness after the campaign is called a *posttest*. Advertising objectives, if measurable, often determine what kind of posttest is most appropriate to measure effectiveness. For example, if the purpose of the advertising were to increase brand awareness or to create a more favorable attitude toward the firm, then the posttest might measure changes in these variables. Consumer surveys, panels, and experimental designs may be used to evaluate a campaign based on communication objectives. If the advertising campaign's objectives were stated in terms of sales, then the marketer would examine the change in sales or market share attributable to the campaign. For example, a study of sixty sports stadiums sponsored by corporations showed that the stock prices of the sponsoring companies fell by 22 percent on average during 2000, thus indicating that putting a corporation's name on a stadium might not be a wise move.[11]

Such posttests can be difficult to interpret because sales or market share changes can be caused not only by advertising but by many other independent factors as well. For instance, competitors' actions, regulatory decisions, changes in economic conditions, and even weather might influence or diminish a firm's sales or market share during the specific time period the advertising effectiveness is being measured.

Public Relations

Public relations is an intricate part of integrated marketing communications. It is used to create and maintain positive relationships between an organization and its stakeholders. An organization communicates with various stakeholders for the same reasons that it develops advertisements. Public relations can be used to promote the organization, people, ideas, and images and even to create an internal shared understanding of the values involved in daily decision making. It usually focuses on creating, enhancing, and maintaining the image of the total firm or organization. A part of public relations is assessing the public's image and opinion of the organization and creating a favorable image of the organization and its products. Because various stakeholders' attitudes toward the firm affect their decisions relative to the firm, it is very important to maintain positive public opinion.

Public relations can improve the public's general awareness of a company and create specific company images, such as high quality, innovativeness, and value. Ben & Jerry's has a reputation for being socially responsible because of mass media reports of their initiatives and other contributions. For example, Ben & Jerry's issued a news release on their plan to use unbleached paperboard, an environmentally friendly packaging material.[12] Starbucks has garnered international awareness through its fair treatment of employees, and small farmers who supply the coffee beans for its products. The company was the first coffee retailer to establish a global code of conduct for fair treatment of agricultural suppliers.

By encouraging the mass media to report on a firm's accomplishments, public relations helps maintain positive public awareness and visibility and creates a desired image. Public relations can be used for a single purpose, such as to diminish the public's opinion concerning a negative event, or it can be used to enhance several dimensions of the company's activities and products.

Public Relations Methods

Organizations use a number of public relations methods to convey messages and to create the right attitudes, images, and opinions. Often a firm may use a public relations agent, professional, or firm to prepare materials such as brochures, newsletters, annual reports, and news releases that reach and influence desired stakeholders. Publicity is a highly visible part of public relations and relates to communication transmitted through a mass medium at no charge. Public relations has a larger and more comprehensive communication function than publicity, but publicity is important because it can have the same effect as advertising, often with more credibility, if reported through an independent source. Some of the more commonly used publicity-based public relations methods include news releases, feature articles, and press conferences.

News releases, sometimes called *press releases*, are usually a few pages of typewritten copy (fewer than 300 words) describing a company event or product. A news release provides the organization's name, address, phone number, e-mail address, Web site, and other contact information. When Dell Computers or Compaq Computers decides to make a significant overall price reduction, it may submit news releases to newspapers, magazines, television contacts, and suppliers, resulting in public relations in the form of magazine articles, newspaper acknowledgments, and television coverage.

A feature article is a manuscript of up to 3,000 words prepared for a specific publication. For example, if Hewlett-Packard decided to build a new production facility in Fort Collins, Colorado, it could supply an approximately 3,000-word manuscript for regional newspapers to report the economic impact and job market implications. Feature articles also might be appropriate if a company was dealing with negative publicity. Microsoft released a number of feature articles on its Web site and through other communication channels when the U.S. Justice Department was investigating alleged antitrust violations.

A *press conference* is a meeting called to announce major news events. Media personnel are usually invited to a specific location and supplied with written materials, photographs, exhibits, and even products. Videos and audiotapes may be distributed to broadcast stations in hopes that they air some of the events covered at the press conference. Many companies try to hold a press conference when announcing a new patent, acquisition, or philanthropic effort.

A publicity-based public relations method has the advantage of credibility because it is perceived as being endorsed by the media that carries the story. Usually the public and stakeholders will consider news coverage more truthful and believable than an advertisement because the organization has not paid for the media message. One negative aspect of publicity is that it is difficult to control exactly how the message will be delivered. Many media personnel are known for inserting their own opinions and sometimes making mistakes in communicating the desired message. Also, there is the danger of spending a great deal of time developing publicity releases that fail to attract mass media attention.

Negative Public Relations

One important aspect of public relations is dealing with the unexpected and often-unfavorable public reactions resulting from an ethical or legal inquiry, an unsafe product, an accident, or some other controversial action of employees or top management. For example, every time an airline has a plane crash it is faced with a very difficult and distressing situation. Most airlines have very careful planning and personnel available to handle these tragic situations. Charges of deceptive pricing by Columbia HCA, the largest hospital organization in the country, resulted in negative publicity for the company. Microsoft has worked hard to create an image of quality and innovativeness, but its image was diminished considerably when it was reported, and eventually a judge ruled, that it was guilty of anticompetitive conduct. Ford Motor Company and Bridgestone–Firestone tire manufacturers defended their image and product quality in their recall of 6.5 million tires.

Negative coverage of a company's problems can have quick dramatic effects. A single negative event, such as the recall of a food product that is potentially dangerous to consumers, can wipe out a company's wholesome image or destroy positive consumer attitudes developed through many years of expensive advertising campaigns. Mass media can report incidents through television and the Internet faster than ever before, and negative stories generally receive more of such attention.

In order to avoid negative public relations it is important to avoid negative incidents and events that could create a problem. Ethical and legal compliance programs, safety programs, and effective quality control procedures are important to maintain a good image of employee conduct and product integrity. But no matter how hard a company tries, negative events are bound to happen. Therefore, organizations should have plans in place to handle them when they occur. Specific policies and procedures for news coverage of a crisis or controversy are absolutely necessary. Major theme parks such as Disney World, Sea World, and Six Flags are prepared for any accident or tragic event that might occur in their parks. These organizations have learned that they need to expedite news coverage of negative events rather than trying to block the release of facts or cover them up. Exxon learned how important it is to convince the public of honest attempts to deal with a situation when it failed to communicate effectively with the press and various stakeholders concerning the Exxon Valdez accident. It took days before top executives communicated clearly how Exxon was going to deal with the massive oil spill in Alaska. In contrast, when Johnson & Johnson was faced with possible tampering with some packages of its Tylenol brand pain killer, it generated even more consumer support by recalling the entire product batch from retail stores. They assured the public that the firm would take no chances in risking use of a product that had been tampered with.

The Nature of Personal Selling

Personal selling is paid personal communication that attempts to inform customers about products and persuade them to purchase those products. Salespersons trying to convince a large industrial organization to purchase photocopy machines is a good example. Compared to other forms of promotion, personal selling is the most precise form of communication because it assures companies that they are in direct contact with an excellent prospect.

Though one-on-one contact with a prospect is highly advantageous, it does not come without disadvantages. Probably the most important disadvantage of personal selling is the cost per contact. In business-to-business selling one sales presentation can take months to prepare and cost thousands of dollars. The recruiting, selecting, training, and motivating of salespeople is a large expense that must be considered in relations to the market opportunity and expected sales revenue from engaging in personal selling. Personal selling plays an increasingly important role in integrated marketing communications and overall marketing strategies. In general, personal selling is becoming more professional and more accepted as an important service that organizations provide their customers.

The goals of personal selling vary tremendously, depending on its role in a long-term approach to integrated communications. Whatever the goals, the activities of personal selling usually involve finding prospects, informing prospects, persuading prospects to buy, and keeping customers satisfied by following up and providing service. Two of the most important roles that salespersons play are in providing information and assistance for making the purchase decision and then ensuring that the customer has all the information, service, and assistance needed for using the product. This means that sales personnel must be well trained and must understand the customers' needs, the product's technical characteristics, as well as the various issues involved in using the product for its intended purpose. For example, salespersons involved in marketing products to physicians and hospitals often have to have detailed training in the technical medical applications of the pharmaceuticals and devices they sell. It is not unusual for people who sell implants such as knee or hip replacement parts to have almost as much technical knowledge of the products as the physicians who use them in performing surgery. Much training and observation is required to be prepared to serve highly sophisticated buyers of medical products.

Relationship marketing is viewed today as the alternative to trying to survive on one-time customer purchases. Professional marketers depend on repeat sales and consider that providing a high level of service is the best way to keep customers satisfied. Since the whole organization is responsible for providing customer satisfaction, much of the responsibility is delegated to the salesperson, since this person is usually closer and in better communication with customers than anyone else in the company. Every customer contact gives a salesperson an opportunity to learn about customer needs and find out about the strengths and weaknesses of the company's products. The salesperson's knowledge gained from maintaining a good relationship with customers is often one of the most important assets to be considered during strategic planning.

Strategic Management of the Sales Force

Since the sales force is one of the most important units in an organization's contact with customers and often directly determines the sales revenue, without successful management of this unit no strategic plan can be effectively implemented. In addition to generating sales revenue, the sales force often builds the firm's reputation. How ethical the company is perceived as being is frequently a function of the salespersons' conduct. The motivation and ultimate success of the firm's sales force usually depends on their product knowledge, training, and management support. Strategic implementation of effective sales management as an important communication component of promotion requires a number of activities.

Sales Force Objectives

The objectives of the sales force must be derived as one component of the overall strategy for integrated marketing communications. When evaluating the role of communications and the appropriateness of advertising, public relations, personal selling, and sales management, the objectives of personal selling must be seen in conjunction with other promotion mix elements. The objectives of the sales force will determine the type of salesperson the company needs to hire. For example, some salespeople may be needed to find new customers as well as increase sales to current ones. This task, sometimes called *creative selling*, requires that salespeople recognize potential buyers' needs and give those buyers necessary information and service. Other salespeople seek repeat sales and to some extent take orders for standardized products purchased routinely. Finally, many salespeople act to support customers by educating them and providing both postsale service and expert advice. Hewlett-Packard redirected its sales force to use a team approach to sell to corporate customers. These twenty-person teams create an "opportunity map" for each customer that details any and all products HP has to offer that company. At the same time, the team is able to analyze the deal to ensure it maximizes earnings for HP.[13]

The technical aspects of establishing sales force objectives involve determining desired sales volume and market share. Sales objectives can be translated into sales quotas for individual salespersons and are commonly stated in terms of dollar or unit sales volume. Depending on the type of salesperson, individual sales objectives could include order size, calls per time period, and the ratio of orders to calls.

Sales Force Size

The size of the sales force is a function of many other variables, including the type of salespeople used, the sales objectives, and the role of personal selling in the entire promotion mix. The size of the sales force is important, because it is often the final opportunity a company has to close the sale and finalize the customer relationship. In general sales force size has been declining over the past ten years due to many factors, including e-commerce. The development of long-term supply chain relations and the ease of buying standardized products over the Internet has reduced the need for salespeople in many industries. An important challenge in managing the sales force today is to determine how salespeople can be most effective in building one-to-one relationships that can also be extended through less expensive communication methods. The growth of e-commerce in business-to-business relationships illustrates how cost can be reduced by leveraging relationships and long-term commitment.

Since salespersons' compensation can be a major marketing strategy expense, synchronizing the right number of salespersons to the marketing plan is a continuous process. One of the quickest ways to reduce sales and profits is to cut back the size of the sales force and allow competitors an opportunity to improve their position with valued customers.

While there is no exact analytical method for determining the optimum sales force size, there are several general approaches. Determining specific objectives and tasks that are important in the overall promotional effort is one effective approach for determining sales force size. This method could include determining how many sales calls per year are necessary for the organization to effectively serve its market and then dividing this total by the average number of sales calls a salesperson can make in one year. This is a very simple and straightforward way to estimate the number of salespeople needed for a specific organization. Another method could be based on marginal analysis, where salespeople are either added to or taken away from the sales force until the sales generated by the number of salespeople are maximized. It is very unusual for an organization to be sophisticated enough to be able to quantify the exact number of salespeople needed to achieve specific objectives. While a particular organization may develop a fairly effective quantifiable model to determine the optimal number of salespeople, most companies make such decisions subjectively based on the experience of sales managers.

Recruiting Salespeople

To have an effective sales force, sales managers must find the right type of salesperson to fulfill assigned responsibilities. The cost of hiring and training a salesperson can be over a hundred thousand dollars in some industries. In recent years, successful salespeople have had many opportunities to leave organizations and get even higher salaries once they are trained. The turnover of salespeople in highly technical fields represents a considerable cost of doing business. The sales manager usually recruits applicants from a number of sources, including within the firm, competing firms, employment agencies, educational institutions, and direct response advertisements that may be placed on the Internet, in magazines, or in newspapers.

Recruiting the right type of salesperson should be closely tied to personal selling within the integrated marketing communication strategy. The job description and analysis of traits needed should be important to developing both a set of specific requirements and an awareness of potential weaknesses that could limit the success of the marketing strategy.

Companies that wish to reduce sales force turnover are likely to have very restrictive recruiting and selective procedures and highly specialized training. For example, State Farm Insurance Company strives to retain customers by having low sales force turnover. Applicants for State Farm Insurance agent must go through a yearlong series of interviews, tests, and visits with agents before finding out if they will be hired. Most State Farm agents are employed for years after being hired.

For most companies, the effective recruiting and selection of salespeople comes from a system that satisfies the company's needs, usually from a series of steps that yield information required for making accurate selection decisions. For most companies, continuous activities to find the best applicants by systematically and effectively matching applicants' characteristics and needs with the requirements of the sales program should ensure the availability of new sales people to sustain the sales program. Contrary to popular belief, the best applicant these days may be male or female. A study that examined gender differences in sales organizations revealed but a few significant differences in areas such as job satisfaction, expectations, compensation, and performance.[14]

Training the Sales Force

Corporate training is an important component of implementing a marketing strategy. Most organizations have moved toward formal training programs, although some companies depend on on-the-job training and less formal methods. Whether the training program is long and detailed or simple and on the job, sales managers must determine what to teach, when to train, and how to effectively train salespeople to reach sales objectives. Today, formal training is moving more toward self-directed, on-line training modules and away from classroom experience. While the majority of formal training continues to be offered in the classroom, within a few years most such training will probably be online. Of course, in situations where online learning does not help to properly motivate and socialize salespeople, classroom training will still be an important element.

Training programs usually concentrate on the company, its culture, and its products and on effective selling methods. Training programs are, of course, most desired for newly hired salespeople, but experienced salespersons benefit from continuous training. Training for experienced salespeople usually emphasizes new-product information and how to deal with changing competitive situations. Experienced salespeople also need to become informed about changes in the company's marketing strategies, policies, and plans for implementation. New sales personnel require complete training and socialization. Training can be modified to deal with special situations, components of the sales force that seem to need additional information, or many variations of special situations.

Sales training today is often accomplished in corporate university environments, where the company develops facilities at specific locations to train employees. Sometimes companies work with educational institutions or consulting firms that handle specific training experiences. One important sales management decision is determining the frequency, sequencing, and duration of sales training. The choice of methods and materials for sales training will depend on the objectives of the sales program and a number of situational variables, such as the number of trainees and the complexity of program content.

Controlling and Evaluating the Sales Force

To control and evaluate the performance of the sales force requires a comparison of sales objectives with actual performance. Without a formal evaluation and control system, many other decisions related to the promotional program cannot be made effectively. The variables used to measure salesperson performance are determined by the sales objectives set by the sales management team. For individuals, this includes their specific sales objectives, stated in terms such as sales volume, number of sales calls, or other sales performance criteria.

To effectively evaluate a salesperson, predetermined salesperson performance standards must be in place. Sales managers commonly compare a salesperson's performance with that of other employees operating under similar sales situations or with the salesperson's previous performance.

After evaluating salespeople, sales managers have to make sure that corrective action to improve sales performance is taken. They can change performance standards, provide additional training, or try other methods, such as motivation. Corrective action may demand comprehensive changes in the sales force or a change in the entire promotional strategy.

Sales Promotion

Sales promotion is any activity or object that acts as an incentive or inducement providing added value for a buyer. Sales promotion can be targeted toward resellers, salespersons, or consumers. Sales promotion includes all promotional and communication activities other than personal selling, advertising, and public relations. Sales promotion in general attempts to persuade or encourage product trial and purchase decisions. Sometimes the added incentive attempts to add image to the brand. For example, champagne marketer Pommery has promoted its Pop brand with three CD samplers. The Pop brand has used customized dance mixes by different artists, such as Prince Dred, that also feature guest disc jockeys. The CDs are handed out in bars and restaurants where the company is trying to promote champagne in seven-ounce bottles to younger consumers.[15] Brunswick pool tables has been providing a free air hockey game with every pool table purchase. McDonald's and Burger King are well known for offering free toys with every child's meal.

Most businesses use sales promotion to facilitate personal selling, advertising, and public relations. Advertising may be used to promote free samples, premiums, or added-value incentives. For example, a computer company such as Compaq might advertise their offer of one-year's free Internet service with the purchase of a new computer. A business-to-business customer might be offered free merchandise to retailers who purchase a stated quantity of merchandise. For example, a 7-Up wholesaler might offer a free case of 7-Up for every ten cases purchased by the retailer.

Consumer Sales Promotion Methods

Consumer sales promotion methods can be initiated by retailers or manufacturers. Retailers are usually trying to use sales promotions to attract customers to specific locations, while manufacturers are generally introducing new products or promoting established brands.

Coupons are used to reduce the price of a product and encourage customers to try new or established brands. Coupons can be used to increase sales volume quickly, to attract repeat purchasers, or even to introduce new sizes, models, or features. For example, when Starbucks introduced Frappuccino in supermarkets, price-reduction coupons were distributed through advertising and in retail stores. For coupons to be effective, they need to be accessible and easy to recognize and involve products where a price reduction will provide an adequate incentive for a purchase.

Coupons can be distributed on packages, through inserts in print advertising, via direct mail, in stores, at checkout counters, and over the Internet. Here are some sites: http://www.hotcoupons.com, http://www.coupons.com, http://www.onlinecoupons.com, http://www.centsoff.com. In general, consumers prefer receiving coupons through newspapers and the mail, but accessing coupons via the Internet is increasing.

Before using coupons as a part of a promotional strategy, marketers should consider the objectives and purpose of the coupon in an integrated marketing communications strategy. For example, print advertisements with coupons are often more effective at generating brand awareness than print ads without coupons. Coupons can be used to reward the users, win back former users, or even encourage purchasers to buy larger quantities. At any rate, there should be objectives tied to an overall strategy when coupons are used as a part of promotions.

Demonstrations are another example of a consumer sales promotion method. For instance, cosmetics manufacturers such as Clinique sometimes offer potential customers demonstrations of product benefits with proper application.

Frequent-user incentive programs reward customers who engage in repeat purchases. For example, most major airlines offer frequent-flier programs through which customers can be awarded free tickets for accumulating a specific amount of mileage. Other companies, such as hotels, auto rental agencies, and even credit card companies, offer free products and services for repeat purchases. For example, Discover card provides a 1 percent cash-back bonus at the end of each year.

Point-of-purchase (POP) displays include outdoor signs, window displays, counter display racks, and self-service cartons. They also include computerized interactive displays supplied by producers to attract and inform customers and to encourage retailers to carry a particular product. High-tech interactive displays are more likely to be used for selling products such as boats, motorcycles, and automobiles.

Free samples are one of the most widely used consumer sales promotion methods. They serve to stimulate trial of a product to increase volume in the early stages of the product's life cycle and to encourage consumers to demand the product. Most consumers prefer to get samples by mail, but samples can be distributed in stores, at special public events, or in any environment where they can be made available. For example, free samples of sunscreen might be placed in beach hotel rooms as a service to guests and to help a manufacturer promote a specific brand.

Other consumer sales promotion methods include *premiums,* which are items offered free or at minimum cost as a bonus for purchasing a product. Examples of premiums include a free car wash with a gasoline fill-up and a free toothbrush with purchase of a tube of toothpaste.

Consumer contests, games, and sweepstakes encourage potential consumers to compete for prizes or a reward for entering a contest or game. Consumer sweepstakes entrants submit their names for inclusion in a drawing for prizes. Successful sweepstakes can attract a large number of participants and generate widespread interest in a product. In general, sweepstakes are more effective for short-term increases in sales or market share.

Business-to-Business Trade Sales Promotion

In business-to-business markets, resellers are the most popular sales promotion target. Some of the most common sales promotion methods used in this market follow.

A *buy-back allowance* is a sum of money a producer gives to a reseller for each unit the reseller buys. With this method, the incentive, the total amount of money resellers receive, is proportional to their purchases during a promotional offer. Buy-back allowances tend to stimulate repurchase after the incentive period is over.

A *buying allowance* is a temporary price reduction to resellers for purchasing specified quantities of a product. For example, a 7-Up distributor might provide a $1 rebate for each case of soda purchased. A buying allowance may act as an incentive to handle new products or to achieve temporary price reductions to stimulate consumer purchase of the products.

Manufacturers sometimes offer *free merchandise* to resellers who purchase a specific quantity of products. Occasionally, free merchandise is provided to avoid bookkeeping problems. Sometimes merchandise is given away free to lower the invoice amount or as part of some other promotional activities that the reseller may be engaging in to assist the manufacturer in product distribution.

A *merchandise allowance* is a manufacturer's agreement to pay resellers a specific amount of money in exchange for the resellers' promotional efforts, such as special displays and advertising.

A sales promotion method that is very popular with resellers is *cooperative advertising*. This is an arrangement whereby a manufacturer agrees to pay a certain amount of a retailer's media cost for advertising the manufacturer's products.

There are a number of sales promotion techniques in which manufacturers offer additional compensation to salespeople to encourage a more aggressive selling effort for a particular product category. A *premium*, or *push money*, is appropriate when personal selling is an important part of the marketing effort. Though it can be effective in gaining a commitment from the sales force, this method is expensive and should be used with caution to avoid any ethical or legal problems. *Sales contests* are another sales promotion technique involving salespeople. Sales personnel can be recognized for outstanding achievements, including meeting or exceeding certain sales targets.

Lessons from Chapter 9

Integrated marketing communications:

- Marketing communications involves conveying and sharing meaning between individuals or between individuals and organizations.

- Integrated marketing communications takes a long-term view of influencing customers through a coordinated strategic use of the promotion elements available to marketing.

- Traditional elements of the promotion mix include advertising, public relations, personal selling, and sales promotion.

- Promotion activities are necessary to communicate the features and benefits of a product to its intended target market.

- The wide variety of promotion methods makes it necessary to assess the promotional mix in terms of its role in the overall promotional strategy and its contribution to the long-term integrated marketing communication strategy to represent the product.

Advertising:

- Advertising is one of the most visible and key components of promotion and is identified as paid, nonpersonal communication that is transmitted through the mass media. Because of the various methods for transmitting mass messages—through the Internet, television, newspapers, magazines, direct mail, outdoor displays, and even signs on moving vehicles—advertising can be used to focus on very small, precisely defined market segments or general audiences.

- Advertising offers many benefits because it is extremely cost efficient when it reaches a large number of people. On the other hand, its effectiveness on sales is hard to measure.

- Institutional advertising promotes organizational images, ideas, and culture.

- Product advertising promotes the image, features, uses, benefits, and attributes of products.

- Methods that can be used to determine the advertising budget include the objectives-and-task approach, the percentage-of-sales approach, the competition-matching approach, and the arbitrary approach. There are a variety of ways to measure advertising effectiveness, both before and after the advertising campaign is conducted. Consumer panels, surveys, and experimental designs may be used to evaluate a campaign based on communication objectives.

Public relations:

- Public relations is an intricate part of integrated marketing communications that is used to create and maintain positive relationships between an organization and its stakeholders.

- An organization communicates with various stakeholders to promote the organization, people, ideas, and images and even to create an internal shared understanding of values used in daily decision making.

- Public relations methods include news releases, feature articles, and press conferences.

- One of the most important aspects of public relations is dealing with unexpected and often-unfavorable public relations resulting from a legal inquiry, unsafe product, or other action that sullies the reputation of the organization.

- The best way to avoid negative public relations is to avoid negative incidences and events that could create a problem. But even when trying hard, there will always be some negative events, so an organization should have a plan in place to handle negative events when they occur.

The nature of personal selling:

- Personal selling is paid personal communication that attempts to inform and persuade customers to purchase products.

- Personal selling goals must be synchronized to play an appropriate role in integrated marketing communications.

- The most important roles that salespersons play are providing information and assistance in making the purchase decision and then making sure that the customer has all the information, service, and assistance needed to use the product.

- The strategic management of the sales force is an important communication component of promotion and the overall marketing plan.

- Some of the activities required to carry out effective sales management include the development of sales force objectives, determining the sales force size, recruiting salespeople, training the sales force, and controlling and evaluating the sales force.

Sales promotion:

- Sales promotion is any activity or object that acts as an incentive or inducement providing added value for a buyer.

- Sales promotion can be targeted at resellers, salespersons, or consumers.

- Sales promotion, as a part of integrated marketing communication, can facilitate personal selling, advertising, or public relations.

- Consumer sales promotions methods can be initiated by retailers or manufacturers and are used to attract customers to specific locations or to purchase new or established brands.

- Consumer sales promotion methods include coupons, demonstrations, frequent-user incentives, and point-of-purchase (POP) displays, such as outdoor signs. Free samples are one of the most widely used consumer sales promotion methods. In addition, consumer contests, games, and sweepstakes encourage potential customers to compete for prizes or rewards for entering a contest or game.

- Business-to-business trade sales promotions include buy-back allowances and co-operative advertising, among others.

Questions for Discussion

1. What role does integrated marketing communications play in the overall marketing strategy? What is the difference between the promotion mix and the marketing mix?

2. Comment on how the highly visible nature of advertising relates to the development of a long-term brand image. What are the advantages and disadvantages of advertising versus other elements of the promotion mix?

3. How can public relations be used as an integral part of integrated communications? Which public relations method might be more appropriate for a dot-com company?

4. Explain the role of effective management of the sales force in implementing a marketing strategy. How can the sales force be involved in developing a successful marketing plan?

Exercises

1. Access Gap.com, and evaluate the effectiveness of the Gap Web site in building the Gap brand image. How does the Gap Web site complement the integrated marketing communications of the Gap?

2. Talk with a salesperson about the need for sales objectives and the role of sales in the overall marketing strategy for a company. What opportunities exist for the salespeople to participate in marketing planning activities?

3. Find an example of an advertisement that integrates a sales promotion device in a print or Internet advertisement.

10

Marketing Implementation and Control

Introduction

Throughout the history of business, many organizations and their top managers have emphasized strategic planning at the expense of strategic implementation. This emphasis occurred because managers believed that strategic planning, by itself, was the key to marketing success. This belief was—and is today—based on the logical premise that before a company can determine where it is going, it must have a plan for getting there. Unfortunately, many firms are quite effective at devising strategic plans but totally unprepared to cope with the realities of implementation. Strategic planning without effective implementation can produce unintended consequences that result in customer dissatisfaction and feelings of frustration within the firm. In addition, ineffective implementation will most likely result in the firm's failure to reach its organizational or marketing objectives.

In this chapter, we examine the critical role of marketing implementation and its relationship to the overall strategic market planning process. First, we define implementation and discuss a number of issues associated with implementing marketing strategies. Second, we discuss the major components of marketing implementation—all of which must work together effectively in order for implementation to be successful. Then we examine the relative advantages and disadvantages of four major approaches to marketing implementation. This discussion also describes how an internal marketing approach can be used to motivate employees to implement the marketing strategy. Finally, we look at the process of marketing control.

Before we continue, it is important to reiterate a point from Chapter 1: Though a well-developed plan for implementation involves several considerations, the most important consideration is gaining the support of employees. Because a strategy cannot implement itself, organizations depend on employees to carry out all marketing activities. As a result, the organization must devise a plan for implementation just like it devises a plan for marketing strategy.

Marketing Implementation Defined

Marketing implementation is the process of executing the marketing strategy by creating specific actions that will ensure that the marketing objectives are achieved. Simply put, implementation refers to the "how" part of the marketing plan. Because marketing implementation is a very broad term, it is often used but frequently misunderstood.

Some of this misunderstanding may stem from the fact that marketing strategies almost always turn out differently than anticipated because of the difference between intended marketing strategy and realized marketing strategy.[1] *Intended* marketing strategy is what the organization wants to happen—it is the organization's planned strategic choice. The *realized* marketing strategy, on the other hand, is the strategy that actually takes place. More often than not, the difference between the intended and the realized strategy is the result of the way the intended marketing strategy is implemented. This is not to say that an organization's realized marketing strategy is necessarily better or worse than the intended marketing strategy, just that it is different in some way. Such differences are often the result of internal and external environmental factors that change during implementation. As a result, when it comes to marketing implementation, Murphy's Law usually applies: If anything can possibly go wrong, it will. This serves as a warning to managers that the implementation of marketing strategy should not be taken lightly.

Issues in Marketing Implementation

Marketing implementation is critical to the overall success of any organization because it is responsible for putting the marketing strategy into action. Unfortunately, many organizations repeatedly experience failures in marketing implementation—out-of-stock items, overly aggressive salespeople, long checkout lines, and unfriendly or inattentive employees. Such examples illustrate that even the best-planned marketing strategies are a waste of time without effective implementation to ensure their success. In short, a good marketing plan combined with bad marketing implementation is a guaranteed recipe for disaster.

One of the most interesting aspects of marketing implementation is its relationship to the strategic planning process. Many managers assume that planning and implementation are interdependent but separate issues. In reality, planning and implementation are intertwined within the marketing planning process. Many of the problems of marketing implementation occur because of this relationship to strategic planning. Let's look at three of the most common issues.

Planning and Implementation Are Interdependent Processes

Many marketing managers assume that the planning and implementation process is a one-way street. That is, strategic planning comes first, followed by marketing implementation. Although it is true that the content of the marketing plan determines how it will be implemented, it is also true that how a marketing strategy is to be implemented determines the content of the marketing plan. This two-way relationship between marketing strategy and marketing implementation is depicted in Exhibit 10.1.

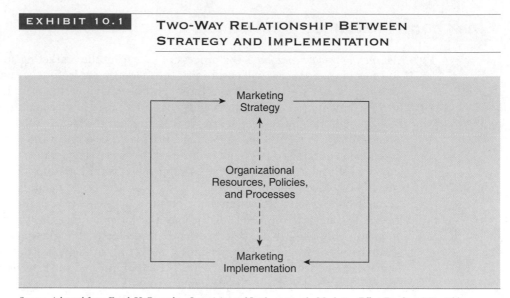

EXHIBIT 10.1 TWO-WAY RELATIONSHIP BETWEEN STRATEGY AND IMPLEMENTATION

Source: Adapted from Frank V. Cespedes, *Organizing and Implementing the Marketing Effort* (Reading, MA: Addison-Wesley, 1991), 18.

Certain marketing strategies will dictate some parts of their implementation. For example, a company such as Southwest Airlines with a strategy of improving customer service levels may turn to employee training programs as an important part of that strategy's implementation. Through profit sharing, many Southwest Airlines employees are also stockholders with a vested interest in the firm's success. Employee training and profit-sharing programs are commonly used in many companies to improve customer service. However, employee training, as a tool of implementation, can also dictate the content of the company's strategy. A Southwest Airlines competitor, in the process of implementing its customer service program, may realize that it does not possess adequate resources to carry out extensive employee training. Perhaps the company lacks the financial resources for a profit-sharing program and does not employ, or cannot acquire, a staff that is qualified to perform the training. As a result, the company must go back to the planning stage to adjust its customer service strategy. These continual changes in marketing strategy make implementation more difficult. Clearly a SWOT analysis conducted with an eye toward what the company can reasonably implement can reduce, but not completely eliminate, this problem.

Planning and Implementation Are Constantly Evolving

Marketing managers face a simple truth: Important environmental factors constantly change. As customers change their wants and needs, as competitors devise new marketing strategies, and as the organization's own internal environment changes, the firm must constantly adapt. In some cases, these changes occur so fast that once the organization decides on a marketing strategy, it is already out of date. Because of the interrelationship between marketing strategy and marketing implementation, both must constantly adapt to fit the other. The process is never static because environmental changes require changes in strategy, which require changes in implementation, which require changes in strategy, and so on.

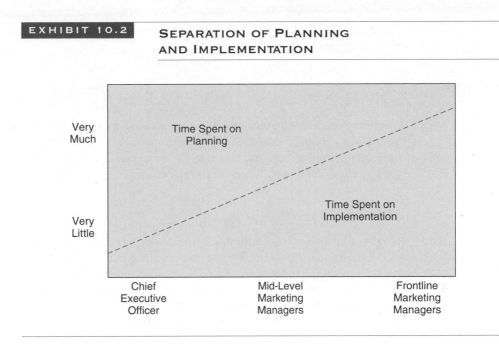

EXHIBIT 10.2 SEPARATION OF PLANNING AND IMPLEMENTATION

A related issue is that managers often assume there is only one correct way to implement a given strategy. This is simply not true. Just as strategy often results from trial and error, so does marketing implementation. The fact that marketing is customer driven requires that the organization be flexible enough to alter its implementation to counter changes in its customers' preferences or the competitive environment. The airline industry provides a good example. Regardless of any one company's marketing strategy, all airlines quickly alter their pricing strategy when a competitor announces a fare reduction. Such rapid changes require that the organization be flexible in its marketing strategy and its implementation.

Planning and Implementation Are Separated

The ineffective implementation of marketing strategy is often a self-generated problem stemming from the planning process itself. Although top managers carry out strategic planning, the responsibility for implementing marketing strategy falls on lower-level managers and frontline employees. This separation of planning and implementation is depicted in Exhibit 10.2. Top managers often fall into a trap of believing that a good marketing strategy will implement itself. Because these managers are separated from the "frontline" of the organization, they often do not understand the unique problems associated with implementing marketing strategies. Conversely, those employees who do understand the problems of marketing implementation usually have no voice in developing the marketing strategy.

Another trap that top managers often fall into is believing that lower-level managers and frontline employees will be excited about the marketing strategy and motivated to implement it. However, because they are separated from the planning process, these managers and employees often fail to identify with the organization's goals and objectives or to understand the marketing strategy.[2] It is unrealistic for top managers to expect lower-level managers and employees to be enthused about or committed to a strategy they had no voice in developing or to a strategy they do not understand or feel is inappropriate.[3]

The Components of Marketing Implementation

Marketing implementation involves a number of interrelated components and activities, as shown in Exhibit 10.3. These components must work together for strategy to be implemented effectively. Because we examined marketing strategy in Chapters 6 through 9, we now look briefly at the remaining components.

Shared Goals and Values

Goals and values shared among all employees within the organization are the "glue" of successful marketing implementation because they bind the entire organization together as a single, functioning unit. When all employees share the firm's goals and values, all actions will be aligned and directed toward the betterment of the organization. Without a common direction to hold the organization together, different areas of the company may work toward different outcomes, thus limiting the success of the entire organization.

Institutionalizing shared goals and values within a firm's culture is a long-term process. The primary means of creating shared goals and values is through employee training and socialization programs.[4] Although creating shared goals and values is a difficult process, the rewards are worth the effort. Some have argued that creating shared goals and values is the most important part of marketing implementation because it stimulates organizational commitment so that employees become more motivated to implement the marketing strategy and meet customer needs.[5]

Marketing Structure

Marketing structure refers to how an organization's marketing activities are organized. The organization's marketing structure establishes formal lines of authority (i.e., who reports to whom) as well as the division of labor within the marketing function.

One of the most important decisions that managers must make is how to divide and integrate marketing responsibilities. This question typically comes down to the centralization versus decentralization issue. In a centralized marketing structure, all marketing activities and decisions are coordinated and managed from the top of the marketing hierarchy. Conversely, in a decentralized marketing structure, marketing activities and decisions are coordinated and managed from the frontline of the organization. Typically, decentralization means that frontline marketing managers are given the responsibility of making day-to-day marketing decisions.

Both marketing structures have advantages. Centralized structures are very cost efficient and effective in ensuring standardization within the marketing program. These advantages can be particularly critical to organizations whose competitiveness depends upon maintaining a tight control over costs and programs.[6] For example, companies employing a strategy of operational excellence, such as Wal-Mart and Southwest Airlines, may find a centralized structure beneficial for ensuring operational efficiency and consistency. Decentralized marketing structures have the important advantage of placing marketing decisions close to the frontline, where customer needs

| EXHIBIT 10.3 | COMPONENTS OF MARKETING IMPLEMENTATION |

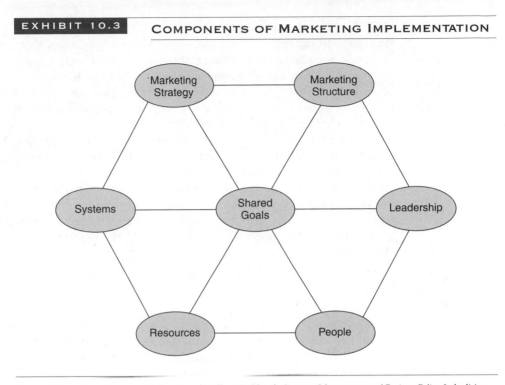

Source: Adapted from Lawrence R. Jaunch and William F. Glueck, *Strategic Management and Business Policy*, 3rd edition (New York: McGraw-Hill, 1988), 305.

are the priority. By decentralizing marketing decisions, frontline managers can be creative and flexible, allowing them to adapt to changing market conditions.[7] For this reason, companies employing a strategy of customer intimacy, such as Airborne Express and Nordstrom's, may decentralize to ensure that they can respond to customers' needs. In many cases, the decision to centralize or decentralize marketing activities is a tradeoff between reduced costs and enhanced flexibility. However, there is no one correct way to organize the marketing function. The right structure will depend on the specific organization, the nature of its internal and external environments, and its chosen marketing strategy.[8]

Systems and Processes

Organizational systems and processes are collections of work activities that take in a variety of inputs to create information and communication outputs that ensure the consistent day-to-day operation of the organization.[9] Examples include information systems, strategic planning, capital budgeting, procurement, order fulfillment, manufacturing, quality control, and performance measurement. Although all systems are important, the marketing information system (MIS) is a critical part of the planning and implementation process. By providing a continuous flow of information, the MIS can assist in the analysis of the internal and external environments before marketing strategies are developed. The MIS is also used during implementation to assist in the evaluation and control of all marketing activities.

Resources

An organization's resources can include a wide variety of assets that can be brought to-gether during marketing implementation. These assets may be tangible or intangible. *Tangible* resources include financial resources, manufacturing capacity, facilities, and equipment. Though not quite as obvious, *intangible* resources, such as marketing ex-pertise, customer loyalty, brand equity, corporate goodwill, and external relationships/strategic alliances, are equally important.

Regardless of the type of resource, the amount of resources available can make or break a marketing strategy. However, a critical and honest evaluation of available re-sources during the situation and SWOT analyses can help ensure that the marketing strategy and marketing implementation are within the realm of possibility. Once the marketing plan is completed, the planner must seek the approval of needed resources from top management. It is important to remember that resources will be allocated for the marketing plan based on its ability to help the organization reach its goals and objectives.

People

The quality, diversity, and skill of an organization's workforce are all important con-siderations in implementing marketing strategy. Consequently, human resource issues are becoming more important to the marketing function, especially in the areas of em-ployee selection and training, evaluation and compensation policies, and employee motivation, satisfaction, and commitment. In fact, the marketing departments of many organizations have taken over the human resources function to ensure that employees are correctly matched to required marketing activities.[10] Due to the importance of people in the process, let's look at several issues in the human side of implementation.

Employee Selection and Training   One of the most critical aspects of marketing implementation is matching employees' skills and abilities to the marketing tasks to be performed.[11] The first step in this process is employee recruitment and selection. It is no secret that some people are better at some jobs than others. All of us know individ-uals who are born salespeople. Some individuals are better at working with people, while others are better at working with tools or computers. The key is to match these employee skills to marketing tasks. Corporate downsizing and tight job markets in re-cent years have forced companies to become more demanding in finding the right em-ployee skills to match their required marketing activities.

An increasingly important aspect of selection and training practices is the man-agement of employee diversity, whether it be ethnic or generational. As the U.S. pop-ulation becomes more ethnically diverse, many companies are taking steps to ensure that the diversity of their employees matches the diversity of their customer groups. Many firms also face challenges with generational diversity, in that most middle and upper managers are baby-boomers (born 1946–1964), whereas most entry-level posi-tions are filled by members of Generation X (born 1965–1976) or Generation Y (born after 1976).[12] In many cases, these younger employees are better trained, more tech-nologically sophisticated, and less politically minded than their baby-boomer bosses. Managers must recognize these issues and adapt selection and training practices accordingly.

Employee Evaluation and Compensation Policies   Employee evaluation and compensation are also important to successful marketing implementation. Although employee compensation is a highly visible part of managing the human side of marketing, it is not always the most important. Simply doing a job well rewards many individuals. Others are interested only in financial gains. The key is to balance these differing perceptions and develop an evaluation and compensation program that ties employee rewards to performance levels on required marketing activities.

An important decision to be made with respect to employee evaluation and compensation is the choice between outcome- and behavior-based systems.[13] An *outcome-based* system evaluates and compensates employees based on measurable, quantitative standards, such as sales volume and gross margin levels. This type of system is fairly easy to use, requires less supervision, and works well when market demand is fairly constant, the selling cycle is relatively short, and all efforts directly affect sales or profits. However, outcome-based systems are not tied directly to customer satisfaction levels and may penalize employees for factors beyond their control (e.g., a recession). Conversely, *behavior-based* systems evaluate and compensate employees based on subjective, qualitative standards, such as effort, motivation, teamwork, and friendliness toward or problem solving with customers. This type of system is tied directly to customer satisfaction and rewards employees for factors they can control. However, behavior-based systems are expensive and difficult to administer because of their subjective nature and the amount of supervision required. The choice between outcome- and behavior-based systems depends on the type of company, type of product, type of market, and customer needs. The important point is to match the employee evaluation and compensation system to the activities that employees must perform in order to implement the marketing strategy.

Employee Motivation, Satisfaction, and Commitment   Other important factors in the implementation of marketing strategy are the extent to which employees are motivated to implement a strategy, their overall feelings of job satisfaction, and the commitment they feel toward the organization and its goals.[14] For example, one of the contributors to the highly successful implementation at FedEx is the motivation and commitment of the company's employees. These employees are so dedicated to FedEx that they are often said to have purple blood—one of the company's official colors.[15] Likewise, Home Depot employees wear orange aprons to indicate stock ownership in the company.

Although factors such as employee motivation, satisfaction, and commitment are critical to successful implementation, they are highly dependent on other components, especially training, the evaluation/compensation system, and leadership. Marketing structure and processes can also have an impact on employee behaviors and attitudes. The key is to recognize the importance of these factors to successful marketing implementation and to manage them accordingly.

Leadership

The leadership provided by an organization's management and the behaviors of employees go hand in hand in the implementation process. As the art of managing people, leadership includes how managers communicate with employees as well as how they motivate their people to implement a marketing strategy. Leaders are responsible for establishing the corporate culture necessary for implementation success.[16] A good deal of research has shown that marketing implementation is more successful when leaders create an organizational culture characterized by open communication between employees and managers. In this way, employees are free to discuss their opinions and ideas about the marketing strategy and implementation activities. This type of leadership also creates a climate where managers and employees have full confidence and trust in each other.

Whether good or bad, all leaders possess a leadership style, or way of approaching a given task. Because a manager's leadership style is important to implementation success, we devote the next section to a discussion of several approaches that managers can take in implementing marketing strategies.

Approaches to Marketing Implementation

Managers can use a variety of approaches in implementing marketing strategies and motivating employees to perform implementation tasks. In this section, we'll examine four of these approaches—the command approach, the change approach, the consensus approach, and the cultural approach.[17]

The Command Approach

With the command approach, marketing strategies are evaluated and selected at the top of the organization and forced downward to lower levels, where frontline managers and employees are expected to implement them. The approach has two advantages: (1) It makes decision making easier, and (2) it reduces uncertainty as to what is to be done.

Unfortunately, the command approach suffers from several disadvantages. First, it does not consider the feasibility of implementing the marketing strategy. The only consideration in the command approach is that top managers have the power to force the implementation of the strategy. Second, the approach divides the organization into strategists and implementers, with no consideration for how strategy and implementation affect each other. Those developing the strategy are often far removed from the targeted customers it is intended to attract. Third, the command approach often creates employee motivation problems. Many employees are not motivated to implement strategies in which they have little confidence. This can create problems in the implementation of the chosen strategy.

McDonald's came to appreciate the limitations of the command approach when it tried to force franchisees to implement its "Campaign 55" promotion. The promotion offered discounted prices on select sandwiches when customers purchased fries and a drink. However, the company's franchisees balked at the plan when they lost money because customers bought only small fries and drinks to get the discounts. The original "Campaign 55" strategy also included a 55-second service guarantee, or customers would get their food for free. Franchisees flatly refused to implement the guarantee. In total, "Campaign 55" lasted less than 55 days.[18]

The experience of McDonald's illustrates how a marketing strategy can fail when those responsible for its implementation do not believe in it. However, the command approach can be a viable method of marketing implementation under the proper conditions. The command approach tends to work best when a powerful leader heads the organization, the strategy is simple to implement, and the strategy poses few threats to employees. Faced with the difficulty of meeting these criteria in today's business environment, few companies practice the command approach.

The Change Approach

The change approach is similar to the command approach except that it focuses explicitly on implementation. The basic premise of the change approach is to modify the organization in ways that will ensure the successful implementation of the chosen marketing strategy. For example, the organization's structure can be altered; employees can be transferred, hired, or fired; new technology can be adopted; the employee compensation plan can be changed; or the organization can merge with another firm.

As opposed to the command approach, the manager taking the change approach toward implementation is more of an architect and politician, skillfully crafting the organization to fit the requirements of the chosen marketing strategy. A good example of the change approach in action occurred during Lee Iacocca's tenure at the Chrysler Corporation. His purchase of AMC and Jeep/Eagle were crucial steps in the slow process of rebuilding Chrysler. Similarly, FedEx has undergone numerous changes in its history. Its purchase of Caliber System, Inc., in 1998 created the FDX Corporation (later renamed the FedEx Corporation), a global logistics and distribution powerhouse.

Because many top managers are reluctant to give up control over the organization, the change approach is used quite often in business today, sometimes with great success. However, despite its advantages, the change approach still suffers from the separation of planning and implementation. By clinging to this "power-at-the-top" mentality, employee motivation often remains an issue. Likewise, the changes called for in this approach often take a great deal of time to design and implement. This can create a situation where the organization becomes frozen while waiting for the chosen strategy to take hold. As a result, the organization can become vulnerable to changes in the marketing environment.

The Consensus Approach

In the consensus approach, top managers and lower-level managers work together to evaluate and develop marketing strategies. The underlying premise of this approach is that managers from different areas and levels of the organization come together as a team to "brainstorm" and develop the marketing strategy. Each participant has different opinions as well as different perceptions of the marketing environment. The role of the top manager is that of a coordinator, pulling different opinions together to ensure that the best overall marketing strategy is created. Through this collective decision-making process, a marketing strategy is agreed upon and a consensus is reached as to the overall direction of the organization.

The consensus approach is more advantageous than the first two approaches in that it moves some of the decision-making authority closer to the frontlines. Lower-level managers who participate in the strategy-formulation process have a unique perspective on the marketing activities necessary to implement the strategy. These managers are also more sensitive to the needs and wants of the organization's target market customers. In addition, because they are involved with developing the marketing strategy, these lower-level managers are often much more committed to the strategy and more motivated to see that it is implemented properly.

However, like the first two approaches, the consensus approach often retains the barrier between strategists and implementers. This occurs because top managers are unwilling to give up their centralized decision-making authority. The end result of this barrier is that the full potential of the organization's human resources is not realized. Thus, for the consensus approach to be truly effective, managers at all levels within the organization must communicate openly about strategy on a daily basis, not just during formal strategy-development sessions. The consensus approach tends to work best in complex, uncertain, and highly unstable environments. The collective strategy-making approach works well in this environment because it brings multiple viewpoints to the table.

The Cultural Approach

The cultural approach carries the participative style of the consensus approach to the lower levels of the organization. Its basic premise is that marketing strategy is a part of the overall organizational vision. Thus, the goal of top managers using this approach is to shape the organization's culture in such a way that all employees—top managers to janitors—participate in making decisions that help the organization reach its objectives. As a result, the cultural approach breaks down the barrier between strategists and implementers so that all employees work toward a single purpose.

With a strong organizational culture and an overriding corporate vision, the task of implementing marketing strategy is about 90 percent complete.[19] Employees are allowed to design their own work procedures, as long as they are consistent with the organizational mission, goals, and objectives. This extreme form of decentralization is often called *empowerment*. Empowering employees means allowing them to make decisions on how to perform their jobs. The strong organizational culture and a shared corporate vision ensure that empowered employees make the right decisions.

While creating a strong culture does not happen overnight, it is absolutely necessary before employees can be empowered to make decisions. Employees must be trained and socialized to accept the organization's mission and to become a part of the organization's culture.[20] Despite the enormous amount of time involved in developing and using the cultural approach, its rewards of enhanced implementation and increased employee commitment are often well worth the investment.

To summarize, managers can use any one of these four approaches for implementing marketing strategy. They all have advantages and disadvantages, as shown in Exhibit 10.4. The choice of any approach will depend heavily on the organization's resources, its current culture, and the manager's personal preference. Many managers today are unwilling to give up total control over marketing decision making. For these managers, the cultural approach may be out of the question.

Regardless of the approach taken, one of the most important issues that a manager must face is how to deal with the people who are responsible for implementing marketing strategy. To examine this issue, we now turn our attention to internal marketing—an increasingly popular approach to marketing implementation.

Internal Marketing

As more companies come to appreciate the importance of people to the implementation process, they are becoming disenchanted with traditional approaches to

EXHIBIT 10.4   ADVANTAGES AND DISADVANTAGES OF IMPLEMENTATION APPROACHES

Command Approach

Basic Premise: Marketing strategies are evaluated and selected at the top of the organizational hierarchy and forced downward to lower levels, where frontline managers and employees are expected to implement them.

Advantages: Makes decision making easier.
Reduces uncertainty.
Good when the organization is headed by a powerful leader.
Good when the strategy is simple to implement.

Disadvantages: Does not consider the feasibility of implementing the strategy.
Divides the organization into strategists and implementers.
Does not consider how strategy and implementation affect each other.
Can create employee motivation problems.

Change Approach

Basic Premise: The organization is modified in ways that will ensure the successful implementation of the chosen marketing strategy.

Advantages: Specifically considers how the strategy will be implemented.
Considers how strategy and implementation affect each other.
Used successfully by a large number of U.S. businesses.

Disadvantages: Clings to a "power-at-the-top" mentality.
Requires a skilled leader who can be both an architect and a politician.
Changes often take a great deal of time to design and implement.
Organization can become frozen while waiting for the chosen strategy to take hold.
The time required for changes to occur can make the organization vulnerable to changes in the marketing environment.

Consensus Approach

Basic Premise: Managers from different areas of the organization come together to "brainstorm" and develop the marketing strategy. Through this collective decision-making process, a marketing strategy is agreed upon and a consensus is reached as to the overall direction of the organization.

Advantages: Incorporates multiple opinions and viewpoints into the marketing strategy.
Leader coordinates by pulling different opinions together.
Organizationwide commitment to the strategy makes implementation easier.
Top-level and lower-level managers work together, thus moving some of the decision making closer to the frontlines of the organization.
Good in complex, uncertain, and highly unstable environments.

Disadvantages: Top managers are often unwilling to give up their decision-making authority.
Can lead to groupthink.
Process of strategy development and implementation is very slow.
Requires ongoing, open communication between all levels of the organization.

Cultural Approach

Basic Premise: Marketing strategy is a part of the overall organizational vision. The goal of top managers using this approach is to shape the organization's culture so that all employees participate in making decisions that help the organization reach its objectives.

continued

EXHIBIT 10.4	ADVANTAGES AND DISADVANTAGES OF IMPLEMENTATION APPROACHES (*continued*)

Advantages:	Completely breaks down the barrier between strategists and implementers. Increases employee commitment to a single organizational goal. Participative style leads to an overriding corporate vision. If done correctly, the approach makes implementation easier to accomplish. Allows for the empowerment of employees.
Disadvantages:	Must spend more money on employee selection and training. Creating the needed culture is a painful, time-consuming process. Quickly changing to this approach from another approach causes many problems.

marketing implementation. These forces for change have been caused by several factors: the losing out of American businesses to foreign competitors, high rates of employee turnover and its associated costs, and continuing problems in the implementation of marketing strategy. These problems have led many organizations to adopt alternative approaches to marketing implementation. One of these alternatives is internal marketing.

The Internal Marketing Approach

The concept of internal marketing comes primarily from service organizations, where it was first practiced as a tactic for making all employees aware of the need for customer satisfaction. Generally speaking, internal marketing refers to the managerial actions necessary to make all members of the organization understand and accept their respective roles in implementing marketing strategy.[21] This means that *all* employees, from the chief executive officer to frontline marketing personnel, must realize how their individual jobs contribute to the implementation of the marketing strategy.

Under the internal marketing approach, every employee has two sets of customers: external and internal. For retail store managers, for example, the people who shop at the store are external customers, while the employees who work in the store are the manager's internal customers. In order for implementation to be successful, the store manager must serve the needs of both customer groups. If the internal customers are not dealt with properly, then it is unlikely that the external customers will be completely satisfied.

This same pattern of internal and external customers is repeated throughout all levels of the organization. Even the CEO is responsible for serving the needs of his or her internal and external customers. Thus, unlike traditional approaches, where the responsibility for implementation rests with lower levels of the organization, the internal marketing approach places this responsibility on all employees, regardless of organizational level. In the end, successful marketing implementation comes from an accumulation of individual actions where all employees are held responsible for implementing the marketing strategy.

Wal-Mart founder Sam Walton was keenly aware of the importance of internal marketing. He visited Wal-Mart stores on a regular basis, talking with customers and employees about how he could better serve their needs. He felt so strongly about the importance of his associates (his term for store personnel) that he always allowed them

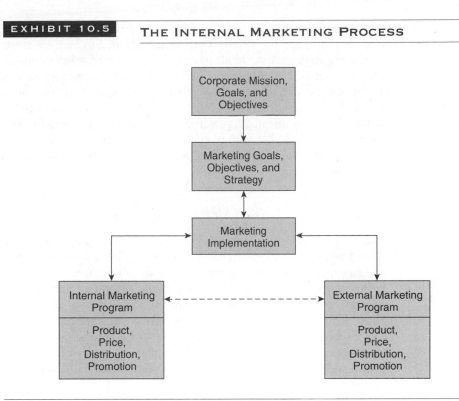

EXHIBIT 10.5 THE INTERNAL MARKETING PROCESS

Source: Adapted from Nigel F. Piercy, *Market-Led Strategic Change* (Stoneham, MA: Butterworth-Heinemann, 1992), 371.

the opportunity to voice their concerns about changes in marketing activities. He felt that if he took care of his associates, they would take care of Wal-Mart's customers.

The Internal Marketing Process

The process of internal marketing is straightforward and rests on many of the same principles used in external marketing. As shown in Exhibit 10.5, internal marketing is seen as an output of and input to both marketing implementation and the external marketing program. That is, neither the marketing strategy nor its implementation can be designed without some consideration for the internal marketing program.

The product, price, distribution, and promotion elements of the internal marketing program are similar to the elements of the external marketing program. *Internal products* refer generally to marketing strategies that must be sold internally. More specifically, however, internal products refer to any employee tasks, behaviors, attitudes, and values necessary to ensure implementation of the marketing strategy.[22] The implementation of a marketing strategy typically requires changes on the part of employees. They may have to work harder, change job assignments, or even change their attitudes and expand their abilities. The increased effort and changes that employees must exhibit in implementing the strategy are called *internal prices*. Employees pay these prices through what they must do, change, or give up when implementing a new marketing strategy.

Internal distribution refers to how the marketing strategy is communicated internally. Planning sessions, workshops, formal reports, and personal conversations are all examples of internal distribution. Internal distribution also includes employee education, training, and socialization programs designed to assist in the transition to a new marketing strategy. Finally, all communication aimed at informing and persuading employees about the merits of the marketing strategy comprise *internal promotion*. Internal promotion can take the form of speeches, video presentations, audiotapes, and/or internal company newsletters. Given the growing diversity of today's employees, it is unlikely that any one medium will communicate with all employees successfully. Managers must realize that telling employees important information once in a single format is not good communication. Until the employees "get it," communication has not taken place.

Implementing an Internal Marketing Approach

Successfully using an internal marketing approach requires an integration of many factors already discussed in this chapter. First, the recruitment, selection, and training of employees must be considered an important component of marketing implementation, with marketing having input to the personnel function as necessary.[23] This ensures that employees will be matched to the marketing tasks to be performed. Second, top managers must be completely committed to the marketing strategy and overall marketing plan. It is naive to expect employees to be committed when top managers are not. Simply put, the best-planned strategy in the world cannot succeed if the employees responsible for its implementation do not believe in it or are not committed to it.[24]

Third, employee compensation programs must be linked to the implementation of the marketing strategy. This means that employees should be rewarded on the basis of behaviors that are consistent with the marketing strategy. Fourth, the organization should be characterized by open communication among all employees, regardless of organizational level. Through open, interactive communication, employees come to understand the support and commitment of top managers and how their jobs fit into the overall marketing implementation process.

Finally, organizational structures, policies, and processes should match the marketing strategy to ensure that the strategy is capable of being implemented. On some occasions, the organization's structure and policies constrain employees' ability to implement the strategy effectively. Although eliminating these constraints may mean that employees should be empowered to creatively fine-tune the marketing strategy or its implementation, empowerment should be used only if the organization's culture can support it. However, if used correctly as a part of the internal marketing approach, the organization can experience more motivated, satisfied, and committed employees as well as enhanced customer satisfaction and improved business performance.[25]

Evaluating and Controlling Marketing Activities

A marketing strategy can achieve its desired results only if it is implemented properly. *Properly* is the key word. It is important to remember that a firm's intended marketing strategy often differs from the realized strategy (the one that actually takes place). This also means that actual performance is often different from what was expected. Typically, there are three possible causes for this difference:

1. The marketing strategy was inappropriate or unrealistic.

2. The implementation was inappropriate for the strategy or was simply mismanaged.

3. The internal and/or external environments changed substantially between the development of the marketing strategy and its implementation.

To reduce the difference between what actually happened and what was expected and to correct any of these three problems, marketing activities must be evaluated and controlled on an ongoing basis. While the best way to handle implementation problems is to recognize them in advance, no manager can successfully recognize all of the subtle and unpredictable warning signs of implementation failure.

The best way to prevent implementation problems is to have a system of marketing controls in place that allows the manager to spot potential problems before they cause real trouble. Exhibit 10.6 outlines a framework for marketing control that includes two major control types: formal controls and informal controls.[26] While we discuss each type of marketing control separately, most organizations use a combination of these control types at the same time.

Formal Marketing Controls

Formal marketing controls are mechanisms designed by the marketing manager to help ensure the implementation of the marketing strategy. The elements of formal control are designed to influence the behaviors of employees before, during, and after implementation. These elements are referred to as input, process, and output control mechanisms.

Input Control Mechanisms Any actions taken prior to the implementation of the marketing strategy are referred to as input control mechanisms. The premise of input control is that the marketing strategy cannot be implemented unless the proper tools are in place for it to succeed. Among the most important input control mechanisms are recruiting, selecting, and training employees. Most marketing strategies require that the right employees be matched to the job. These employees must then be trained on the best way to perform their jobs. For example, a marketing strategy that focuses on increased customer service must also emphasize the selection and training of people-oriented employees. Other examples of input controls include resource allocation decisions (manpower and financial), capital outlays for needed facilities and equipment, or increased expenditures on research and development.

Process Control Mechanisms Process control mechanisms include activities that occur during implementation that are designed to influence the behavior of employees so that they will support the strategy and its objectives. While the potential number of process controls is limitless and will vary from one organization to the next, there are examples of universal process controls that all organizations must use and manage well (see Exhibit 10.6).

One of the most important process control mechanisms is the system used to evaluate and compensate employees. In general, employees must be evaluated and compensated based on criteria that are relevant to the marketing strategy.[27] For

| EXHIBIT 10.6 | FRAMEWORK FOR MARKETING CONTROL |

Formal Control Mechanisms—initiated by the marketing manager

Input control mechanisms—actions taken prior to implementation
- Employee recruitment and selection procedures
- Employee training programs
- Employee manpower allocations
- Financial resources
  Capital outlays
- Research and development expenditures

Process control mechanisms—actions taken during implementation
  Employee evaluation and compensation systems
  Employee authority and empowerment
- Internal communication programs
  Lines of authority/structure (organizational chart)
- Management commitment to the marketing plan
- Management commitment to employees

Output control mechanisms—evaluated after implementation
  Performance standards (e.g., sales, market share, promotion)
  Marketing audits

Informal Control Mechanisms—unwritten controls initiated by employees

Employee self-control—individualized control
  Job satisfaction
  Organizational commitment
  Commitment to the marketing plan

Employee social control—small-group control
  Shared organizational values
  Social and behavioral norms

Employee cultural control—culture of the entire organization
  Organizational culture
  Organizational stories, rituals, and legends
  Cultural change

Source: Adapted from Bernard J. Jaworski, "Toward a Theory of Marketing Control: Environmental Context, Control Types, and Consequences," *Journal of Marketing* 52 (July 1988), 23–39.

example, if the strategy requires that salespeople increase their efforts at customer service, they should be rewarded on the basis of this effort, not on other criteria, such as sales volume and new accounts. Another important control issue is the amount of authority and empowerment granted to employees. While some degree of authority or empowerment can lead to increased performance, employees who are given too much authority often become confused and dissatisfied with their jobs.[28] Having good internal communication programs—another type of process control—can help to alleviate these problems.

The process control mechanism that stands out above all others is management commitment. Several research studies have confirmed that management commitment to the marketing strategy is the single most important determinant of whether the strategy will succeed or fail.[29] Management commitment is critical because employees learn to model the behavior of their managers. If management is committed to the marketing strategy, it is more likely that employees will be committed as well. Commitment to the marketing strategy also means that managers must be committed to employees.

Output Control Mechanisms   Output control mechanisms are designed to ensure that marketing outcomes are in line with anticipated results. The primary means of output control is setting performance standards against which actual performance can be compared. To ensure an accurate assessment of marketing activities, all performance standards should be based on the marketing objectives. Some performance standards are broad, such as those based on sales, profits, or costs. We say these are broad standards because many different marketing activities can affect them. Other performance standards are quite specific, such as many customer service standards (e.g., number of customer complaints, repair service within 24 hours, overnight delivery by 10:00 A.M.). In many (if not most) cases, how the firm performs relative to these specific standards will determine how well it performs relative to broader standards.

But how specific should performance standards be? Standards should reflect the uniqueness of the firm and its resources as well as the critical activities needed to implement the marketing strategy. In setting performance standards, it is important to remember that employees are always responsible for implementing marketing activities and, ultimately, the marketing strategy. For example, if an important part of increasing customer service requires that employees answer the telephone by the second ring, then a performance standard should be established in this area. Performance standards for marketing personnel are typically the most difficult to establish and enforce.

One of the best methods of evaluating whether performance standards have been achieved is to use a marketing audit to examine systematically the firm's marketing objectives, strategy, and performance.[30] The primary purpose of a marketing audit is to identify problems in ongoing marketing activities and to plan the necessary steps to correct those problems. A marketing audit can be long and elaborate or short and simple. A sample marketing audit is shown in Exhibit 10.7. This example is just that, a sample. In practice, the elements of the audit should match the elements of the marketing strategy. The marketing audit should also be used in concert with the actual implementation of marketing activities—not just when problems arise.

Regardless of how the audit is organized, it should aid the marketing manager in evaluating marketing activities by:

1. Describing current marketing activities and their results.

2. Gathering information about changes in the external or internal environments that may affect ongoing marketing activities.

3. Exploring different alternatives for improving the ongoing implementation of marketing activities.

4. Providing a framework to evaluate the attainment of performance standards as well as marketing goals and objectives.

The information in a marketing audit is often based on a series of questionnaires that are given to employees, managers, customers, and/or suppliers. In some cases, people outside the firm do this ongoing evaluation. Using outside auditors has the advantages of being more objective and less time consuming for the firm. However,

| EXHIBIT 10.7 | A SAMPLE MARKETING AUDIT |

Identification of Marketing Activities

1. In what specific marketing activities is the company currently engaged?

   Product activities: research, concept testing, test marketing, quality control, etc.
   Customer service activities: installation, training, maintenance, technical support, complaint handling, etc.
   Pricing activities: financing, billing, cost control, discounting, etc.
   Distribution activities: availability, channels used, customer convenience, etc.
   Promotion activities: media, sales promotion, personal selling, public relations, etc.

2. Are these activities conducted or provided solely by the company, or are some conducted or provided by outside contractors? If outside contractors are used, how are they performing? Should any of these outside activities be brought in-house?

3. What additional marketing activities do customers want, need, or expect?

Review of Standard Procedures for Each Marketing Activity

1. Do written procedures (manuals) exist for each marketing activity? If so, are these procedures (manuals) up to date? Are these procedures (manuals) being followed by employees?

2. What oral or unwritten procedures exist for each marketing activity? Should these procedures be formally included in the written procedures, or should they be eliminated?

3. Do marketing personnel regularly interact with other functional areas to establish standard procedures for each activity?

Identification of Performance Standards for Each Marketing Activity

1. What specific, quantitative standards exist for each activity?

2. What qualitative standards exist for each activity?

3. How does each activity contribute to customer satisfaction within each marketing mix element (i.e., product, pricing, distribution, promotion)?

4. How does each activity contribute to marketing goals and objectives?

5. How does each activity contribute to the goals and objectives of the company?

Identification of Performance Measures for Each Marketing Activity

1. What are the internal, profit-based measures for each marketing activity?

2. What are the internal, time-based measures for each marketing activity?

3. How is performance monitored and evaluated internally by management?

4. How is performance monitored and evaluated externally by customers?

Review and Evaluation of Marketing Personnel

1. Are the company's current recruiting, selection, and retention efforts consistent (matched) with the requirements of the marketing activities?

2. What is the nature and content of employee training activities? Are these activities consistent with the requirements of the marketing activities?

3. How are customer-contact personnel supervised, evaluated, and rewarded? Are these procedures consistent with customer requirements?

4. What effect do employee evaluation and reward policies have on employee attitudes, satisfaction, and motivation?

5. Are current levels of employee attitudes, satisfaction, and motivation adequate?

EXHIBIT 10.7	A SAMPLE MARKETING AUDIT *(continued)*

Identification and Evaluation of Customer Support Systems

1. Are the quality and accuracy of customer service materials (e.g., instruction manuals, brochures, form letters) consistent with the image of the company and its products?

2. Are the quality and appearance of physical facilities (e.g., offices, furnishings, layout, store decor) consistent with the image of the company and its products?

3. Are the quality and appearance of customer service equipment (e.g., repair tools, telephones, computers, delivery vehicles) consistent with the image of the company and its products?

4. Is the record-keeping system accurate? Is the information always readily available when it is needed? What technology could be acquired to enhance record-keeping abilities (e.g., bar code scanners, portable computers, cellular telephones)?

Source: Adapted from Christopher H. Lovelock, *Services Marketing*, 3rd edition (Upper Saddle River, NJ: Prentice Hall, 1996), 504.

outside auditors are typically quite expensive. A marketing audit can also be very disruptive, especially if employees are fearful of the scrutiny.

Despite their drawbacks, marketing audits are usually quite beneficial for the firms that use them. They are flexible, in that the scope of the audit can be broad (evaluate the entire marketing strategy) or narrow (evaluate only a specific marketing mix element). The results of the audit can be used to reallocate marketing efforts, to correct implementation problems, or even to identify new opportunities. The end results of a well-executed marketing audit are usually better performance and increased customer satisfaction.

Informal Marketing Controls

Although formal marketing controls are overt in their attempt to influence employee behavior, informal controls are more subtle. Informal marketing controls are unwritten, employee-based mechanisms that subtly affect the behaviors of employees, both as individuals and in groups.[31] Here we are dealing with personal objectives and behaviors as well as group-based norms and expectations. There are three types of informal control: employee self-control, social control, and cultural control. As you read the descriptions of each type, note that the elements of informal control are affected to a great extent by the formal control mechanisms employed by the marketing manager. However, the premise of informal control is that some aspects of employee behavior cannot be influenced by formal mechanisms and therefore must be controlled informally through individual and group mechanisms.

Employee Self-Control   Through employee self-control, employees manage their own behavior (and thus the implementation of the marketing strategy) by establishing personal objectives and monitoring their results. The type of personal objectives that employees set depends on how employees feel about their jobs. If they are satisfied with their jobs and committed to the organization, they are more likely to establish personal objectives that are consistent with the aims of the organization. Further, when employees are committed to the marketing strategy, they are more likely to establish personal objectives that are consistent with the marketing goals and objectives.

Employee self-control also depends on how employees are rewarded. Some employees prefer the intrinsic rewards of doing a good job rather than the extrinsic rewards of pay and recognition. Employees who are intrinsically rewarded are likely to exhibit more self-control by managing their behaviors in ways that are consistent with the marketing strategy.

Employee Social Control   Social, or small-group, control deals with the standards, norms, and ethics that are found within work groups within the organization.[32] The social interaction that occurs within these work groups can be a powerful motivator of employee behavior. The social and behavioral norms of work groups provide the "peer pressure" that causes employees to conform to expected standards of performance. If employees fall short of these standards, the group will pressure them to increase effort and performance.

Employee Cultural Control   Cultural control is very similar to social control, only at a much broader level. Here we are concerned with the behavioral and social norms of the entire organization. One of the most important outcomes of cultural control is the establishment of shared values among all organizational members. Marketing implementation is most effective and efficient when every employee is committed to the same organizational goals and guided by the same organizational values.[33] Companies such as FedEx and Hewlett-Packard are noted for their strong organizational cultures that guide employee behavior. Unfortunately, cultural control is very difficult to master, in that it takes a great deal of time to create the appropriate organizational culture to ensure implementation success.

Implementing Marketing Activities

Through good planning and organizing, marketing managers provide purpose, direction, and structure for marketing activities. However, the manager must understand the problems associated with implementation, understand how the various components of implementation are coordinated, and select an overall approach to implementation before actually executing marketing activities. As we have stated before, people (employees) are ultimately responsible for implementing marketing activities. Therefore, the manager must be good at motivating, coordinating, and communicating with all marketing personnel. In addition, the manager must establish a timetable for the completion of each marketing activity. Good communication is the key to motivating and coordinating marketing personnel. One of the most important types of communication flows upward from the frontline of the firm to management. Frontline employees interact daily with customers, putting them in a unique position to understand their perceptions, wants, and needs. By taking steps to encourage upward communication, managers gain access to a fertile source of information about customer requirements, how well products are selling, whether marketing activities are working, and the problems that occur during implementation.[34] Upward communication also allows management to understand the problems and needs of employees, an integral part of the internal marketing approach.

Successful implementation also requires that employees know the specific activities for which they are responsible and the timetable for completing each activity. Establishing an implementation timetable involves several steps:

1. Identifying the specific activities to be performed.

2. Determining the time required to complete each activity.

3. Separating the activities that must be performed in sequence from those that can be performed simultaneously.

4. Organizing the activities in the proper sequence.

5. Assigning the responsibility for completing each activity to one or more employees, teams, or managers.

Although some activities must be performed before others, other activities can be performed simultaneously or later in the implementation process. This requires tight coordination between departments—marketing, production, advertising, sales, etc.—to ensure that all marketing activities are completed on schedule. Pinpointing those activities that can be performed simultaneously can greatly reduce the total amount of time needed to execute a given marketing strategy. Because scheduling is a complicated task, most organizations use sophisticated computer programs to plan the timing of marketing activities.

Lessons from Chapter 10

Marketing implementation:

- is every bit as important as planning the marketing strategy.

- is the process of executing marketing strategies by creating specific actions that will ensure that marketing objectives are achieved.

- usually causes the difference between intended marketing strategy—what the organization wants to happen—and realized marketing strategy—the strategy that actually takes place.

Three issues in marketing implementation are:

- Planning and implementation are interdependent.

- Planning and implementation are constantly evolving.

- Planning and implementation are separated.

The components of marketing implementation include:

- marketing strategy

- shared goals and values

- marketing structure

- systems and processes

- resources

- people
- leadership

Four approaches to implementing marketing strategy:

- *Command approach:* evaluating and selecting marketing strategies at the top of the organization and forcing them downward to lower levels, where frontline managers and employees are expected to implement them.
- *Change approach:* modifying the organization in ways that will ensure the successful implementation of the chosen marketing strategy.
- *Consensus approach:* top managers and lower-level managers working together to develop and evaluate a marketing strategy.
- *Cultural approach:* carrying the participative style of the consensus method to the lower level of the organization. The organization's culture guides the implementation of the marketing strategy.

Internal marketing:

- refers to the managerial actions necessary to make all members of the organization understand and accept their respective roles in implementing marketing strategy.
- involves two sets of customers: external and internal. Every employee in the organization has these two sets of customers.

Evaluating and controlling marketing activities:

- is an important step in the planning process because the marketing plan must be implemented before the expected financial results can be realized.
- is necessary if the manager is to reduce the difference between expected performance (the intended marketing strategy) and actual performance (the realized marketing strategy).

Differences between the intended marketing strategy and the realized marketing strategy may be due to:

- an inappropriate or unrealistic marketing strategy.
- mismanaged or inappropriate implementation for the strategy.
- substantial changes in the internal and/or external environments between the development of the marketing strategy and its implementation.

Formal marketing controls:

- involve mechanisms that are initiated by managers in an attempt to influence employee behavior toward implementing the marketing plan.
- include input controls (actions taken prior to implementation), process controls (actions taken during implementation), and output controls (setting performance standards and monitoring the results).

Informal marketing controls:

- are unwritten, employee-based mechanisms that center on individual objectives and behavior as well as group-based norms and expectations.

- include employee self-control (individual objectives and behavior), social control (norms and expectations of small groups), and cultural control (norms and expectations of the entire organization).

Implementing marketing activities:

- requires good communication to motivate and coordinate marketing personnel properly. Upward communication is especially important to implementation.

- requires that employees know the specific activities for which they are responsible and the timetable for completing each activity. The steps in this process are:

  1. Identify the specific activities to be performed.

  2. Determine the time required to complete each activity.

  3. Separate the activities that must be performed in sequence from those that can be performed simultaneously.

  4. Organize the activities in the proper sequence.

  5. Assign the responsibility for completing each activity to one or more employees, teams, or managers.

Questions for Discussion

1. Debate question: Which is more important—planning the marketing strategy or implementing the marketing strategy? Forget for a moment that they are equally important. What arguments can you make that one is more important than the other?

2. If you were a marketing manager, which approach to implementation would you be most comfortable using, given your personality and personal preferences? Would your approach be universally applicable to any given situation? If not, how would you adapt your approach? Remember, adapting your basic approach means stepping out of your personal comfort zone to match the situation at hand.

3. What do you see as the major stumbling blocks to the successful use of the internal marketing approach? Given the stratification of employees in most organizations (e.g., CEO, middle management, staff employees), is internal marketing a viable approach for most organizations? Why or why not?

Exercises

1. Find a recent article about an organization that changed its marketing strategy. What were the reasons for the change? How did the organization approach the development and implementation of the new strategy?

2. Think about several well-known leaders from business, politics, religion, or social causes. How would you characterize each person's implementation style? Would you say each leader was effective in their use of that style? Why or why not?

3. Think about the unwritten, informal controls that exist in your life. Then develop a list of the controls that exist at work, at home, or at school. Are these controls similar or different?

	Controls at Work	Controls at Home	Controls at School
Self-Control (personal objectives and behavior)			
Social Control (norms and expectations in small groups)			
Cultural Control (norms and expectations in the organization)			

Financial Analysis for Marketing Decision Making

Introduction

Will the marketing plan and marketing strategy assist a firm in reaching its goals and objectives? This is a complex question for the marketing manager that, despite its difficulty, simply cannot be ignored. As we consider the tools related to assessing the financial impact of the marketing plan, you will see that we have come full circle. We have moved from analyzing the environment, to establishing goals and objectives, to developing and selecting specific marketing strategies, to marketing implementation. We are now ready to consider the extent to which the marketing strategies are likely to deliver the desired outcomes.

In reality, budgetary considerations must play a role in the identification of alternative strategies as well as the evaluation and control of those strategies. Developing a marketing plan that ignores the financial realities of the organization is a waste of time and shows great naiveté on the part of the marketing manager. Even when funds are available for marketing activities, they are not assured. Top managers must be convinced that the marketing plan and strategy are a good value for the firm. Like external customers, these executives will determine value by assessing the relationship between benefits and costs. The ratio of the plan's cost compared to expected returns will be a critical deciding factor in determining which plans receive management approval and funding. This is true regardless of the size of the firm and the cost of the plan. In larger firms, the sophistication and depth of the assessment will be greater, but the same principles apply. Marketing managers must prepare and submit convincing proposals to compete successfully against the plans of other product or business-unit managers as well as against managers from other functional areas, who are also seeking their share of a limited set of resources.

Performing a financial assessment of the marketing plan requires a working understanding of both finance and statistical analysis. It also involves basic concepts from microeconomics. Our discussion in this appendix will combine all of these areas using a hypothetical case for illustration. We will be looking at the financial assessment process, including several tools that marketing managers can use to estimate the financial results of implementing specific marketing strategies.

The Financial Assessment Process

Determining the potential financial impact of a marketing plan is a similar process at all levels of the organization. Our discussion and example here are oriented around the activities of a marketing manager for a single product/market combination. This approach allows for simplicity, because only one product and market are involved, and it is this first level of the organization where comprehensive financial analysis is likely to occur. Like other area managers, the marketing manager strives to develop a plan that will achieve goals and objectives set at higher levels of the organization. The question then becomes the same for managers at all levels of the firm: Does the proposed plan (or combination of plans) lead to the outcomes that must be generated within my unit?

To introduce our ongoing example, let us assume that it is late 2001. Mallory James is the marketing manager for a line of convection ovens sold by Zonic Electronic Products, Inc. (ZEP)—a firm that manufactures and markets electronics and appliances for household markets. Although ZEP's convection ovens have been quite successful, Mallory faces the challenge of increasing sales to a level that will generate a $1 million increase in gross margin—a goal set by ZEP's top management. Achieving this goal will be critical if Mallory is to secure more marketing funds to expand promotional efforts to the extent called for in her marketing plan. We will now consider the tools Mallory can use in her effort to justify the desired budget increase. These tools or techniques are contribution analysis, response analysis, and the systematic planning model.

Contribution Analysis

Contribution analysis attempts to determine the amount of output (revenues) that can be expected from a given set of inputs (costs). You are probably familiar with break-even analysis, a type of contribution analysis used to determine the amount of revenue necessary to cover both variable and fixed costs. In our example, Mallory is trying to demonstrate the ability of her marketing plan to increase gross margin. Gross margin is calculated by subtracting the cost of goods sold and all marketing costs from sales volume in dollars. Four different factors figure into this form of contribution analysis: expected sales in dollars, fixed costs, variable costs, and the gross margin objective. Fixed costs (such as rent, salaries, utilities) do not fluctuate with changes in volume, while variable costs (such as costs of product inputs, commissions, transportation charges) do fluctuate. Mallory's motive in using contribution analysis is to find the level of sales that will be required, given the costs that are within her control, to generate the desired increase in gross margin. The formula for this type of contribution analysis is:

$$\text{Required sales volume in units} = \frac{\text{Total fixed costs (\$)} + \text{Desired gross margin (\$)}}{\text{Unit selling price} - \text{Variable costs per unit}}$$

Mallory has been able to collect the following information about the costs associated with producing convection ovens:

Selling price per unit: $200

Variable costs per unit: $110

Total fixed costs: $5,000,000

Gross margin: $4,000,000

Using these numbers, the gross margin contribution per unit is $200 − $110 = $90. Substituting these numbers into the formula yields the following result:

$$\text{Required sales volume in units} = \frac{\$5,000,000 + \$4,000,000}{\$90} = 100,000 \text{ units}$$

At the current 100,000-unit sales level, total revenues are $20 million and total variable costs are $11 million. Mallory now wants to determine how changes in any one of these numbers will affect the results. For example, ZEP's management has asked for a $1 million increase in gross margin. This changes Mallory's gross margin target from the current $4 million to $5 million. The required sales volume increase can be estimated by substituting this larger gross margin figure into the equation, as follows:

$$\frac{\$5,000,000 + \$5,000,000}{\$90} = 111,111 \text{ units}$$

The size of the convection oven market is approximately 500,000 units per year. ZEP holds a 20 percent share of this market (Mallory sells 100,000 units per year)—exactly what is needed to meet the $4 million gross margin goal. To increase gross margin by $1 million, Mallory must find a way to sell 11,111 more ovens per year, an 11.1 percent increase. This increase may be quite difficult to achieve because the total convection oven market is growing at only 4 percent per year. Thus, to achieve the required increase in sales, Mallory must capitalize on overall industry growth *and* find ways to take market share away from her competitors.

Let's assume that in her search for options, Mallory considers a price cut to generate increased sales. If the price is reduced by $10 to $190 (a 5 percent decrease), what would be the impact on sales? Keeping other factors constant, gross margin per unit would fall to $190 − $110 = $80. Substituting the $80 figure into the contribution analysis equation yields the following result:

$$\text{Required sales volume in units} = \frac{\$5,000,000 + \$5,000,000}{\$80} = 125,000 \text{ units}$$

Mallory must now address the likelihood that a 5 percent price decrease will generate a 25 percent increase in unit sales volume. This issue is assessed by considering demand response by means of our second tool, response analysis.

Response Analysis

Accurate financial assessment depends on the marketing manager's ability to predict costs and revenues over the course of the planning period. A key aspect of this prediction centers on the question of how large a percentage change in sales can be anticipated when a variable in the marketing mix is altered. Response analysis is the category of tools used to address this question of incremental change. The goal of response analysis is to estimate accurate response coefficients that can be used to predict the change in sales volume based on a change in one or more elements of the marketing mix.

Let us first address the issue of price changes. Price and sales volume should vary inversely, with the exception of certain prestige products (which have upward-sloping demand curves) or products with totally inelastic demand (the quantity sold is constant at all price levels). Thus, higher prices should result in a smaller number of units sold, and vice versa. A response coefficient of −2.0 means that if price falls 5 percent, as was the case in our example, sales would be expected to grow by twice that level, or 10 percent.

Other marketing mix elements would be expected to have positive response coefficients, whereby increased spending would be expected to result in increased sales volume. Let's assume that Mallory is considering an increase in advertising

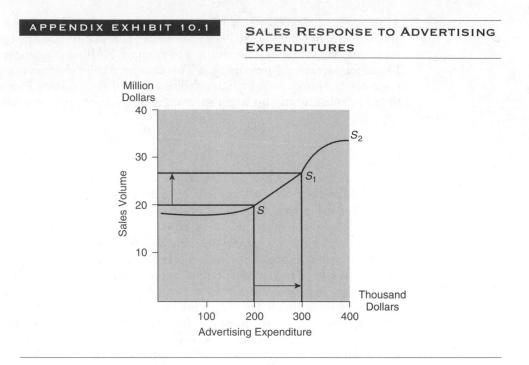

APPENDIX EXHIBIT 10.1   SALES RESPONSE TO ADVERTISING EXPENDITURES

expenditures for the 2002–2003 planning period. In 2001, $200,000 was budgeted for advertising. Now Mallory wants to analyze the impact of a 50 percent increase in this budget to a total of $300,000. The change in sales volume from such an increase in expenditures would be expected to be positive, but would it contribute to the objective of a $1 million increase in gross margin?

Estimating response coefficients can be a very difficult process. However, several sources of information are usually available. Historical relationships between advertising and sales volume for the convection oven market, or a similar market, could be calculated. Trade association figures may also be used to estimate response coefficients. These figures are usually provided as averages for the items addressed. ZEP might also conduct primary research to better understand these relationships when no historical data is available. Such research usually involves manipulating advertising, pricing, or another element, with the goal of determining the effect of these changes on sales volume. The use of multiple methods should increase the manager's confidence in the coefficients that are estimated.

For the sake of example, we will assume that Mallory has evidence allowing her to estimate a response coefficient of $+0.3$ for advertising expenditures. Based on this estimate, her proposed 50 percent increase in advertising will increase sales volume by 15 percent (0.5×0.3) from $20 million to $23 million. This, of course, assumes that all other marketing mix elements remain unchanged from the previous period.

Marketing managers should not use response coefficients without understanding the implicit assumptions associated with them. These assumptions are displayed graphically in Appendix Exhibit 10.1. The line from S to S_1 shows what Mallory expects to happen as advertising expenditures rise from $200,000 to $300,000. The 15 percent increase in sales is associated with the single-year planning period. Although the primary interest in our example is the particular change in question, it is useful for the analyst to have an understanding of how the response varies over a range of values. This issue is addressed by the line from S_1 to S_2. Above a certain point, increases in advertising expenditures have a decreasing marginal impact on sales volume. In Appendix Exhibit 10.1, increases above the $300,000 level, while generating marginal increases in sales volume, may not be worth the effort, especially if competitors are well entrenched and spending large sums on their own advertising.

In practice, it would be rare if a marketing plan called for the modification of a single marketing mix element. As multiple changes in planning elements are considered, response analysis becomes more sophisticated, using tools such as regression analysis to analyze the impact of multiple independent variables (marketing mix elements) on a single dependent variable (sales volume). The estimated response functions can be used to make predictions and to develop a hypothetical (pro forma) income statement for the marketing plan. For a comprehensive discussion of regression analysis, you should consult a multivariate statistics text.

Systematic Planning Models

Marketing managers often use a model that indicates the financial effects of marketing activities proposed in the marketing plan. The systematic planning model that we will use to map out the impact of these decisions is outlined in Appendix Exhibit 10.2. This model has nine steps that collectively show the projected bottom-line impact of all aspects of the plan. We will examine each of these steps in this section.

Several essential predictions, representing the first three steps, are critical pieces of input for the model. First, industry sales for the product are required. This figure should be expressed in units, not dollars, because dollar sales is dependent on the prices charged by competing firms. Industry sales in units can then be used to develop a forecast for the planning period. Second, the firm's market share is needed. This can be expressed as the number of units sold by the firm divided by the total units sold in the industry. This figure is then used to forecast market share for the planning period. Because this forecast is the base level for the planning period, it should be calculated with the assumption that the present marketing strategy will be continued.

In step 3, response coefficients are estimated for each element of the new marketing strategy. The estimation of these coefficients was discussed in the previous section. Calculating a group of coefficients for a strategy is more complex, because interactions between marketing mix elements may produce a combined effect that is different from each separate coefficient if estimated independently. Both the positive and negative effects for the various elements are combined into an aggregate rate of sales change for the new marketing mix. At the bottom of step 3 this is referred to as "Combined market-response impact."

In steps 4 through 9, the bottom-line effects of the three input categories are calculated. In step 4, modified market share is calculated by multiplying the projected share (step 2) by the combined market-response impact (step 3). The result indicates the relative merits of continuing the old strategy versus adopting the new strategy. In step 5, modified market share is multiplied by the projected total market in units (step 1). The result is a unit sales prediction for the product. Step 6 adds the unit's sales price to the process, because it is multiplied by the unit sales prediction to estimate projected sales in dollars (international operations would require the use of multiple currencies here).

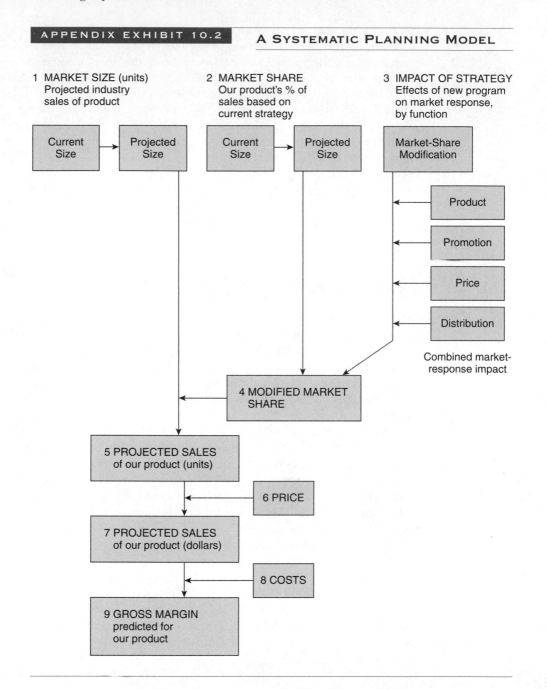

APPENDIX EXHIBIT 10.2 **A SYSTEMATIC PLANNING MODEL**

1 MARKET SIZE (units)
Projected industry
sales of product

2 MARKET SHARE
Our product's % of
sales based on
current strategy

3 IMPACT OF STRATEGY
Effects of new program
on market response,
by function

Current Size → Projected Size

Current Size → Projected Size

Market-Share Modification

Product

Promotion

Price

Distribution

Combined market-
response impact

4 MODIFIED MARKET SHARE

5 PROJECTED SALES
of our product (units)

6 PRICE

7 PROJECTED SALES
of our product (dollars)

8 COSTS

9 GROSS MARGIN
predicted for
our product

In steps 8 and 9, we move from sales to gross margin. In step 8, the cost of the new marketing mix is subtracted from projected sales volume. All costs, excluding those associated with administration and finance, are subtracted at this time. The result in step 9 is the gross margin predicted for the product under the new marketing strategy. Gross margin was chosen as the outcome in this case because it was the targeted goal for Mallory's new marketing strategy. With slight modifications, the model could produce whatever outcome is being considered by top management.

APPENDIX EXHIBIT 10.3

PROJECTED FINANCIAL IMPACT FOR CONVECTION OVEN MARKETING PLAN

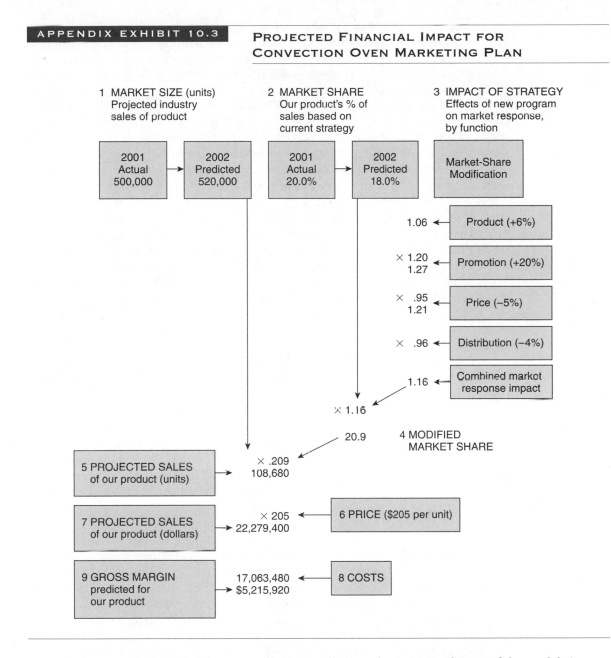

1 MARKET SIZE (units)
Projected industry
sales of product

2 MARKET SHARE
Our product's % of
sales based on
current strategy

3 IMPACT OF STRATEGY
Effects of new program
on market response,
by function

| 2001 Actual 500,000 | → | 2002 Predicted 520,000 |
| 2001 Actual 20.0% | → | 2002 Predicted 18.0% |

Market-Share Modification

1.06 ← Product (+6%)

× 1.20
1.27 ← Promotion (+20%)

× .95
1.21 ← Price (−5%)

× .96 ← Distribution (−4%)

1.16 ← Combined market response impact

× 1.16

20.9   4 MODIFIED MARKET SHARE

5 PROJECTED SALES
of our product (units)   × .209   108,680

7 PROJECTED SALES
of our product (dollars)   × 205   22,279,400   ← 6 PRICE ($205 per unit)

9 GROSS MARGIN
predicted for
our product   17,063,480 $5,215,920   ← 8 COSTS

Now let's return to Mallory's efforts to demonstrate the use of the model. Appendix Exhibit 10.3 provides an example of how valuable the model can be for managers in the financial analysis phase. Hypothetical numbers have been inserted for each of the steps to show how the model progresses toward the desired outcomes.

In step 1, Mallory takes the 500,000-unit sales level for convection ovens in 2001 and combines it with the current industry growth rate of 4 percent to get the projected industry sales figure of 520,000 units for 2002. Although ZEP's marketing plan for 2001 yielded a 20 percent market share in convection ovens, Mallory projects that a repeat of the same strategy would lead to a 10 percent decline in market share—down to 18 percent (step 2).

In step 3, the effects of the proposed marketing plan on ZEP's market share are addressed. Mallory is proposing a fresh look for the product as well as the addition of a warming feature that keeps food left in the oven at a constant temperature once the timer goes off. Mallory has reason to believe that this change will represent the greatest product improvement in the industry. Thus, she expects a 6 percent share increase from changes in the product element (calculated using a 1.06 multiplier). The proposed advertising program has tested well, and with an increase in media expenditures of $50,000 (from $200,000 to $250,000), Mallory projects a 20 percent increase in share from changes in the promotion element (multiplier of 1.20).

Not all elements of the new plan will have positive effects on the product's market share. The termination of excessive discounting to dealers, as well as a slight price increase that will likely not be matched by major competitors, will hurt ZEP's share by an estimated 5 percent (multiplier of 0.95). In the distribution area, the elimination of small dealers, who are unprofitable for ZEP to maintain, will cut market share. Although these dealers represent 6 percent of unit volume, it is anticipated that ZEP will lose only 4 percent in market share as a result of dropping them (multiplier of 0.96). Sequentially multiplying for each element ($1.06 \times 1.20 \times 0.95 \times 0.96$) yields a combined market response impact of 1.16 for the new marketing strategy.

Mallory uses the combined market response figure to calculate modified market share in step 4. Taking the projected share for 2002 that would occur using the existing plan, and correcting it for the anticipated impact of the new marketing plan, yields a modified market share of 20.9 percent—a gain in share of just under 1 percent. In step 5, modified market share is multiplied by the projected 520,000-unit industry sales for 2002 to arrive at ZEP's projected sales level of 108,680 units. Because Mallory proposes a selling price of $205 per unit, the resulting projected revenues for the new plan are $22,279,400 (step 7). Now that revenues have been estimated, Mallory must consider costs in step 8. Working with the cost accounting department, Mallory expects a $1 increase in unit variable costs (from $110 to $111), while fixed costs are expected to remain the same. Based on these numbers, Mallory arrives at a figure of just over $17 million to produce and market the 108,680 units:

$$(108,680 \times \$111) + \$5,000,000 = \$17,063,480$$

Costs are usually much easier to predict than revenues because the firm has more control over its costs. In the final step, Mallory gets to the bottom-line result of her proposed marketing plan: a gross margin of over $5.2 million for ZEP's line of convection ovens. Thus, based on the new marketing strategy, Mallory expects to generate roughly $1.2 million more in gross margin—a result that should please ZEP's top management.

The systematic model has allowed Mallory to conduct a thorough assessment of the cost and revenue generation associated with her proposed marketing plan. The inclusion of a detailed model (like the one shown in Appendix Exhibit 10.3) can assist the marketing manager in convincing top management that all the implications of the proposed plan have been carefully considered. Management can clearly see the route that the planner has taken to arrive at the bottom-line impact of the proposed plan. This does not mean that management will not question the estimates utilized, but only that the process will be clear and sound.

CASES

1

Saturn

In 1990, after seven years of incubation, Saturn, a division of General Motors Corp., debuted in the crowded market of compact cars. Since 1985, GM's share of the U.S. passenger car market had fallen 11 points to 33 percent. Moreover, a J. D. Powers & Associates study revealed that 42 percent of all new car shoppers didn't even consider a GM car. Saturn's mission, then, was to sell 80 percent of its cars to drivers who would not otherwise have bought a GM car.

GM established Saturn as a separate and independent subsidiary in 1985 with an investment of $5 billion. Former GM Chairman Robert B. Smith envisioned Saturn as a "laboratory" to find better ways to manufacture and market cars. GM believed that Saturn was the key to its long-term competitiveness and survival. Saturn managers spent years developing the new company from scratch. They viewed partnerships as a key element of Saturn's future relationships between management and labor, between company and supplier—with everyone sharing the risks and rewards. To truly separate Saturn from the traditional Detroit auto-building mentality, GM decided to build Saturn in Spring Hill, Tennessee. GM lent its financial support to Saturn by providing the latest technology, manufacturing methods, pacesetting labor relations, and participatory management ideas. Saturn represents the largest single construction project in the history of GM. While other GM plants merely assemble parts, Saturn manufactures almost everything at its facility, including power trains, moldings, and instrument panels.

Production Quality and Employee Participation

At first, management expected to totally automate the Saturn assembly line. However, GM has learned many costly lessons about robotics, including the fact that robots do not always perform as expected. A joint venture with Toyota in California taught GM and Saturn that good labor–management relations could do more for productivity and quality. Consequently, Saturn adopted the outlook that technology takes a backseat to people.

The United Auto Workers Union (UAW) and General Motors management both wanted Saturn to succeed from the start and, in a partnership unprecedented in the

This case was prepared by Don Roy, Middle Tennessee State University, for classroom discussion rather than to illustrate either effective or ineffective handling of an administrative situation. An earlier edition of this case was prepared by O. C. Ferrell, Colorado State University.

auto industry, the two entities joined hands and decided to work side by side. All decisions at Saturn are reached by consensus. UAW members, for example, help select Saturn "partners," such as suppliers, Saturn's advertising agency, and dealers. All employees, blue- and white-collar, have to be approved by both union members and management. New employees at Saturn's Tennessee plant also face extensive training to teach them how to work in teams and how to keep track of costs.

Even the plant's design reflects thought for cost efficiency and people. For example, there are many entrances to the plant instead of one main entrance, and each is designed to be no more than a five-minute walk to an employee's station. Parking was designed so that no one has to dodge delivery trucks. Street names around the plant— Handshake Road and Greater Glory Road—also reflect a people-oriented philosophy. Inside, cars on the assembly line can be raised or lowered to make the workers' jobs easier. Another first in North America is that the assembly line is made of wood, which is easier on employees' feet.

The Marketing Strategy

Promotion

The story of Saturn is inseparable from its advertising history, because Saturn involved all marketing entities, from the advertising agency to the dealers, in all decisions from the very beginning. In 1987, Saturn began looking for an advertising agency to handle what would become a more than $100 million account, searching for an agency that could understand the importance of partnership. After reviewing applications from more than 50 agencies, Saturn decided to widen its search. San Francisco's Hal Riney & Partners had already attracted attention in the car industry with its work for Austin Rover Cars of North America, with an ad for the Sterling that showed only brief glimpses of the car itself. In May 1988, after a review by a panel of company executives, two dealers, and a UAW representative, Saturn named Riney its advertising agency, 29 months before the first car went on sale. The agency, now known as Publicis Hal Riney & Partners, continues as Saturn's advertising agency partner today.

Riney immediately became involved with many aspects of the company's innovative start-up. Unlike other ad agencies handling automotive accounts, Riney did not open a satellite office in Detroit, because it wanted to remain free of Detroit's limited worldview, where 80 percent of the cars are domestic. Riney understood that Saturn had to cater to baby-boomers who preferred Japanese automobiles for their perceived higher quality and value.

Riney, along with a panel of 16 Saturn dealers, contributed to many Saturn decisions. Keeping in mind the target market of college-educated men and women aged 25 to 49, they decided to adopt a "straight talk" philosophy, which was applied to many aspects of the Saturn brand. For example, all Saturn retail stores would be called "Saturn of (Geographic Location)" to stress the Saturn name rather than the dealer's. Car color descriptions are also simple, using names like "red" rather than "raspberry red."

Riney's first real promotion task was internal communication. When members of his agency interviewed Saturn employees for this task, they found the Saturn employees enthusiastic and emotionally involved with their new company, a fact that Riney would use to advantage in both internal and external promotions. In April 1989, Riney produced a 26-minute documentary film called *Spring in Spring Hill*, which chronicled the start-up of a new company dedicated to building cars "in a brand new way." The film is used to help explain Saturn to new employees and suppliers and for training; dealers use it to make presentations; and the film has aired on some cable television networks. The film features employees explaining, often quite emotionally, just what Saturn is all about and what it means to them.

Riney applied the straight-talk, people-oriented philosophy in consumer advertising, stressing Saturn, the company, rather than the car. "A different kind of company. A different kind of car." was the theme line. The first commercials told stories about the Spring Hill heartland and about Saturn employees. All Saturn ads have a down-home feeling and feature ordinary people talking about the cars and the Saturn concept. They tell the story of how employees took a risk and left Detroit for something new and exciting—to start from the drawing board and "build cars again . . . but in a brand new way." The ads stress that, by recapturing the USA's can-do spirit, Saturn knows how to make cars.

Later ads featured the stories of Saturn customers, focusing on Saturn buyers' lifestyles and playing up product themes that baby-boomers hold dear, such as safety, utility, and value. One commercial, for example, highlighted a recall order Saturn issued to fix a seat problem and showed a Saturn representative traveling to Alaska to fix the Saturn owned by Robin Millage, an actual customer who had ordered her car, sight unseen, from a dealer in the continental United States. The result of Riney's folksy, straight-talk campaign is a sharply focused brand image for Saturn.

Most Saturn dealers have salespeople working in teams and avoid high-pressure sales techniques. Usually salespeople split commissions and cooperate in providing a relaxed, inviting showroom environment, allowing customers to browse and offering service and advice only as customers seek it.

Product

Initially, Saturn offered only four products: the Saturn SC1 and SC2 coupes and the Saturn SL1 and SL2 sedans. An SW1 and SW2 station wagon and entry-level coupe (SL) were introduced in 1993. The EV1 (a limited-production electric car) was introduced in late 1996. An innovative three-door version of the SC1 and SC2 appeared on the market in 1998. The long-awaited introduction of a midsize sedan and station wagon known as the L-Series took place in mid-1999. A sport utility vehicle is slated to be the next addition to the Saturn line. The CV1 is expected to be at dealerships by late 2001. The ad agency/dealer advisory panel felt the cars should not be given descriptive names (such as Chevrolet Camaro) because they did not want anything to dilute the Saturn name. Saturn's entire philosophy means that the cars have a higher level of quality than other General Motors–made vehicles.

Distribution

With marketing and distribution of new cars accounting for 30 to 35 percent of a car's cost, Saturn planned its distribution very carefully. Dealers are given large territories so that each competes with rival brands rather than with each other. Saturn generally has only one dealership in a metropolitan area. The first dealerships were set up in areas where import car sales are high, and most were located on the East and West coasts to avoid cannibalizing sales of other GM cars. In addition, Saturn chose dealers that know how to appeal to import car buyers.

Pricing

The revolutionary ideas employed at Saturn continue with its pricing strategy. Base prices for the 2000 models ranged from $10,685 (SL) to $21,630 (LW2), competitive with import car prices. Other base prices were SL1 ($12,345), SL2 ($13,775), SC1 ($13,395), SC2 ($16,005), SW2 ($15,150), LS ($15,010), LS1 ($17,610), LS2 ($20,135), and LW1 ($18,835). For most dealers, there are no rebates or promotions and no haggling or dealing. A price tag of $15,165 (base price plus an options package and transportation charge) means that the customer pays $15,165, period. Saturn cannot set prices or control the one-price policy because of legal considerations. However, dealers have found the one-price policy very desirable because of tight profit margins and the high-integrity sales approach that is part of this marketing strategy. Potential buyers can access the iShowroom, an interactive buying center, from Saturn's Web site (http://www.saturn.com) to obtain pricing information for all models as well as "build" their own Saturn, starting with a base car and adding options. Monthly payments can be estimated and financing options chosen.

Implementation of the Saturn Strategy

The marketing mix developed by Saturn was a resounding success in the first half of the 1990s. Initial sales of Saturn cars were tremendous. One Memphis dealership sold all nine of its Saturns on the first day, with a backlog of orders. Similar success stories occurred all over the country. However, the company experienced great difficulty meeting demand, with many customers waiting more than six weeks to receive their automobiles. For example, in late 1992, the Plymouth, Michigan, dealer had only four Saturns on hand instead of the usual 200, and she had sold the nine demonstration models her sales staff had been driving. Saturn officials say part of the problem with shortages was that they were unwilling to compromise on quality. Saturn expected to hit peak production of 300,000 cars per year at Spring Hill in 1993.

With serious troubles of its own, General Motors wanted Saturn to stand on its own and was reluctant to invest more money in the project. Specifically, GM wanted the Spring Hill plant to be more productive, saying there was room for improvement. However, Saturn employees said quality suffered when personnel and equipment were pushed too hard. Because their pay is tied to quality targets, they were especially concerned about the quality of Saturn cars. In October 1991, they held a slowdown during a visit by then–GM Chairman Robert C. Stempel to protest a production increase that resulted in high defect rates. Saturn president Richard G. "Skip" LaFauve tried to increase production without harming quality, partly by adding a third shift to the Spring Hill plant. Saturn's future was further threatened by the fact that GM had yet to commit money to fund new Saturn models beyond 1995. This could have been a real problem because it takes a minimum of three years to develop a new car. However, GM pinned hopes on today's baby-boom Saturn buyers graduating to larger, more expensive GM models, such as Buick and Cadillac, in future years.

Despite production restraints and other problems, Saturn sold 170,495 cars in the 1992 model year, a 236 percent increase over its first-year sales in 1991. That gave Saturn a 2.1 percent share of the U.S. auto market, helping it leapfrog over Hyundai, Subaru, Volkswagen, and Mitsubishi. More significantly, Saturn ranked third in J. D. Power & Associates' measurement of new-car buyer satisfaction, behind only Lexus and Infiniti.

May 1993 was the first profitable month for the Saturn Corporation since its first car was produced. Saturn expected to sell 300,000 cars in the 1993 calendar year but failed to reach this objective. A third production shift was added to cut overtime costs. With 20 hours of production, six days a week, quality was still the company's main concern. If a car is not up to standards, Saturn employees stop the assembly line.

Until 1996, Saturn was able to maintain its sales momentum by developing a cult-like following with its down-home advertisements and successful picnics, where all Saturn owners were invited to Spring Hill, Tennessee, to celebrate the joy of Saturn ownership. Since then, even creative advertising and high-profile customer events have not overcome decreasing sales in the subcompact market. Fewer people want to buy small, fuel-efficient cars. Another factor was the Asian currency crisis in 1997 that helped foreign small-car makers drop prices.

There is a question concerning Saturn's decision to focus on small cars. The company may have missed an opportunity to build on Saturn's success as a respected, high-quality small-car manufacturer. Should GM have developed Saturn into a company selling many different types and sizes of cars and trucks? Even Saturn workers suggested in 1996 that the company should be selling a small sport utility vehicle. Then they watched as Honda (CR-V) and Toyota (RAV4) sold all they could make.

The Need for New Products and Sales Growth

In the second half of the 1990s, Saturn's successes were replaced by challenges to remain competitive in the automotive industry. Unit sales peaked during calendar year 1994 at approximately 286,000 units. Since then, unit sales have declined while the industry has experienced record sales. In 1999, Saturn sold 232,570 cars, which was only a 0.3 percent increase from the previous year. Saturn's rather narrow product line is cited as one reason for the sales decline. The company's focus on small cars left it vulnerable to the shift in demand toward bigger vehicles, including minivans and sport utility vehicles.

In an effort to expand its limited product line, Saturn rolled out the L-Series sedans and station wagons in the summer of 1999. A midsize car, the L-Series represents Saturn's first models outside of its core subcompact line. Design of the L-Series sedan was based on the Opel Vectra, a GM Europe model. GM executives chose this route for developing an L-Series design rather than commissioning its domestic designers to create a unique design for Saturn. For the first time, production of Saturn models would take place outside of the Spring Hill plant. A former Chevrolet factory in Wilmington, Delaware, was selected as the site for L-Series production. Executives at GM expect the L-Series to compete with popular import sedans such as the Honda Accord and the Toyota Camry. One advantage the L-Series holds is price; the LS sedan is priced a couple of thousand dollars lower than both Accord and Camry. The L-Series was launched with an advertising campaign estimated to cost $116 million.

The first year for the L-Series was filled with problems. Difficulties arose for the L-Series before it ever debuted on the market. Clashes between GM designers in Europe and the United States led to delays in beginning production at the Delaware plant. Thus, Saturn dealers did not have enough of the new models to sell when the ad campaign began. As production was accelerated to increase inventory levels, demand for the new models decreased. The resulting inventory buildup forced GM to shut down the Delaware plant for several days in January 2000. Another factor contributing to the L-Series slow start was an unsuccessful advertising campaign. The "Next Big Thing" campaign failed to show consumers that the L-series models were larger than the Saturn compact. GM scaled back its annual production forecast to 150,000 units from the more than 200,000 units it originally planned to produce. Styling of the L-Series is cited as another reason for its unspectacular splash in the market. While some industry experts called the L-Series styling practical, many consumers saw the L-Series as plain and uninspired compared to such rivals as the Volkswagen Passat.

Keeping with GM's vision of Saturn as a laboratory for new product development, GM selected the Saturn unit to market the company's first electric vehicle, named EV1. This two-seat coupe, which goes from 0 to 60 miles per hour in 8.5 seconds, was introduced at select Saturn dealers in Arizona and California in late 1996 and was supported by a $25 million marketing campaign. The development of the EV1 is in response to mandates passed in California, Massachusetts, and New York that require a certain percentage of vehicles sold in any given year be "zero-emissions vehicles." GM was the first company to have an electric vehicle on the market, but other manufacturers, including Chrysler, Honda, and Nissan, have similar products available. True to Saturn's reputation for customer service, the company employs EV specialists, who work with customers throughout the leasing process. EV specialists assist customers by explaining how to install the battery charger, how to charge batteries, how to arrange a lease agreement, and how to obtain tax credits.

Electric vehicles may hold promise for the future, but their impact on Saturn today is minimal. Many consumers are not ready to change from gasoline-powered automobiles to ones powered by electricity. A survey by J. D. Power & Associates found that only 23 percent of consumers would consider buying or leasing an electric vehicle. Pricing is another reason electric vehicles have not enjoyed widespread acceptance. The manufacturer's suggested retail price (MSRP) for the EV1 is $33,995. Monthly lease payments for the EV1 range from $424 to $574, depending on the type of lease agreement signed. As of 2000, 34 Saturn dealers in Los Angeles, Orange County, San Diego, San Francisco, Sacramento, Phoenix, and Tucson lease and service the EV1. The number of dealers participating in the EV1 program represents a small percentage of Saturn's approximately 400 dealers.

Another challenge for Saturn lies in its attempt to establish itself in the Japanese market. Saturn began selling right-side-drive cars in Japan in 1997 and is working to build a network of exclusive Saturn dealers in that country. The entry into Japan was complicated by a strong dollar versus all Asian currencies, thus hurting Japanese consumers' purchasing power. Also, Saturn's small-car products face intense competition in Japan from domestic producers Toyota, Honda, and Nissan.

Saturn's struggles in recent years cannot be blamed solely on leadership within the division. Having GM as its parent company is a potential plus for Saturn, considering GM's vast resources. However, in the late 1990s GM appeared to be hesitant to support Saturn. GM executives decided to make heavy investments in the Oldsmobile brand in an attempt to revive it rather than strengthen the young Saturn brand. Another decision led Cadillac to develop a near-luxury sedan, the Catera, when Saturn could have benefited from the addition of a midsize sedan to its product line. Saturn was not included in GM's plans for development of sport utility vehicles. First, GM produced an SUV for Cadillac, the Escalade. Then it created a new category, sports recreation vehicles (SRVs), with the Pontiac Aztek. When Saturn's CV1 is introduced in late 2001 it will be several years behind in the SUV market.

With Saturn appearing to be at a crossroad at the beginning of the twenty-first century, GM faced a difficult decision about what to do with its once-prized brand. In

April 2000, GM announced that it would invest $1.5 billion in its Saturn unit for development of new products. About $1 billion of the investment will go to development and production of the CV1 and a sedan that will be powered by a Honda engine. Another $500 million will be invested in the Spring Hill plant to build a 450,000-square-foot facility where GM's new global four-cylinder engine will be manufactured. As Saturn goes forward, it faces the challenge of utilizing the resources of its parent company while maintaining the distinct brand image it developed during its first decade of operation.

Questions for Discussion

1. Analyze strategic market planning at Saturn. Has Saturn been successful in its planning efforts?

2. What should Saturn do as competitors attempt to copy its pricing and dealer service policies?

3. Can General Motors change its corporate culture and implement some of Saturn's successes within its organizational structure?

Sources

These facts are from http://www.gm.com (Apr. 22, 1998); http://www.saturn.com (Apr. 16, 1998); Kristine Breese, "First Saturn Day: Diary of a Dealer," *Advertising Age*, Oct. 29, 1990, 68; Rich Ceppos, "Saturn—Finally, It's Here, But Is It Good Enough?" *Car and Driver*, Nov. 1990, 132–138; Stuart Elliott, "Campaign Takes Aim at Heartstrings," *USA Today*, Nov. 1, 1990, 1B, 2B; Bob Garfield, "Down-to-Earth Ads Give Saturn an Underrated Liftoff," *Advertising Age*, Oct. 29, 1990, 68; James R. Healey, "Saturn Demand Delivers Excitement to Dealers," *USA Today*, Nov. 5, 1990, B1; James R. Healey, "Saturn, Day One: Business is Brisk," *USA Today*, Oct. 26, 1990, 1B, 2B; Barbara Lippert, "It's a Saturn Morning in America," *Adweek*, Oct. 15, 1990, 67; Micheline Maynard, "Fulfilling Buyers' Wishes, Saturn's Well Runs Dry," *USA Today*, Aug. 18 1992, B1; Michelle Maynard, "Sales Slump Forces Saturn to Cut Production," *USA Today*, Jan. 21, 1998, B1; Robyn Meredith, "As Sales Fall, Saturn Workers to Vote on Ditching Contract," *The Commercial Appeal*, Mar. 8, 1998, C1, C3; Ian P. Murphy, "Charged Up: Electric Cars Get Jolt of Marketing," *Marketing News*, Aug. 18, 1997, 1, 7; Raymond Serafin, "Saturn's Goal: To be Worthy," *Advertising Age*, Nov. 5, 1990, 21; Raymond Serafin, "The Saturn Story," *Advertising Age*, Nov. 16, 1992, 1, 13, 16; Raymond Serafin and Patricia Strand, "Saturn People Star in First Campaign," *Advertising Age*, Aug. 27, 1990, 1, 38; Neal Templin and Joseph B. White, "GM's Saturn, In Early Orbit, Intrigues Buyers," *The Wall Street Journal*, Oct. 25, 1990, B1, B6; James B. Treece, "Here Comes GM's Saturn," *Business Week*, April 9, 1990, 56–62; "23 More Dealers Open Doors to Saturn Buyers," *USA Today*, Nov. 15, 1990, 6B; Phil West, "Saturn Corp. Rings up First Profitable Month," *The Commercial Appeal*, June 11, 1993, B2; Joseph B. White and Melinda Grenier Guiles, "Rough Launch," *The Wall Street Journal*, July 9, 1990, A1, A12; Cindy Wolff, "First Saturn Here Runs Jag Off Road," *The Commercial Appeal*, Oct. 26, 1990, A1, A12; David Woodruff, with James B. Treece, Sunita Wadekar Bhargava, and Karen Lowry Miller, "Saturn: GM Finally Has a Real Winner. But Success is Bringing a Fresh Batch of Problems," *Business Week*, Aug. 17, 1992, 86–91.

2

Nissan Motor Company

In 1911 in Tokyo, the Kaishinsha Automobile Company was begun. Three years later, the first car rolled off its production lines. That model was an open-touring automobile typical of its day and was called the "Dat."

Post–World War II Period

Forty years later, when the postwar Japanese industrial revival began, the Kaishinsha firm was among the survivors. Soon it was given a simpler name—Nissan Motor Company. Nissan began to produce compact cars that were popular in its home market. Like other successful Japanese manufacturers, Nissan also built an export business around the Orient. Nissan prospered, as did its major rival, Toyota.

The 1950s economy facilitated strong markets for automobiles in all major nations. The United States continued to be the world's largest market, and its major automakers basked in the success of their ever-larger cars. Henry Ford's strategy of tapping popular demand with his low-priced cars seemed all but forgotten. However, the lesson had not been wasted on the West Germans. With their "people's car" (developed before WWII), they staged a peacetime invasion of other European countries, and by the early 1950s, Volkswagen was enjoying success in the United States. American car manufacturers underestimated the threat from the German (and English and French) compacts and responded weakly by importing compacts of their European subsidiaries, like the Opel.

Crossing the Pacific, 1958

In Japan, Nissan and Toyota controlled most of the automobile market. They watched Volkswagen gain solid success in the United States, where other European compacts were established as well. In 1958, Toyota first entered the U.S. market with its inexpensive Crown model. Americans found the car inadequate, and Toyota withdrew it.

Nissan was just a few months behind when it took a compact Japanese model to the United States, where it met a reception almost as chilly as Toyota's. Nissan persevered, and in 1960 sent over a top salesman, Yatuka Katayama, to cover the West Coast.

This case was prepared by Don Roy, Middle Tennessee State University, for classroom discussion rather than to illustrate either effective or ineffective handling of an administrative situation. An earlier edition of this case was prepared by David J. Luck, Emeritus, Southern Illinois University.

With him came another car, which the company named the Datsun 210 (reminiscent of their first model's name). It was so underpowered and boxy that Katayama struggled to enlist used car dealers to sell it.

However, Katayama put together a network of dealers who were eager to succeed in new-car sales. He taught them Japanese-class service and rewarded them well. Much of the credit for Nissan's new U.S. subsidiary (named Datsun Motors) forging ahead into the United States belonged to Katayama. Datsun's first solid success came with a well-designed 1.6-liter Datsun 510 (designed for the United States) in 1968. Sales zoomed in 1969, when the Datsun 240Z, a two-seater sports car fitting U.S. tastes, hit the United States and created a performance image for Datsun.

The Joys of Success

As the 1970s dawned, Toyota and Nissan were successful competitors in the Orient, the United States, and European markets. This was expanded by a 1973 windfall: the world oil crisis. As Middle Eastern sources withheld supply and prices at the pump soared, sales of gas-saving compacts surged in the United States. Nissan became the front-runner, and in 1975 moved ahead of Volkswagen as the number-one import in the United States. Its market share, over 3 percent, was greater than Toyota's. A third Japanese firm, Honda, then seized the opportunity to be an important player in the U.S. market.

At this time, Katayama was head of the Datsun subsidiary, but he did not hold this position long. His personality did not suit Nissan's president, nor was Katayama's boasting of his U.S. role deemed proper in Tokyo. He was recalled to Japan and soon retired. In 1977, a former accountant, Takashi Ishihara, became president of Nissan. He was conservative and domineering and clashed with Nissan's labor unions, ultimately depressing factory morale. Also, his people discouraged original car designs by haggling over new designs emerging from the studio.

The 1980s

Datsun won acclaim in 1980 by announcing it would be the first Japanese auto company to build a plant in the United States. The plant, built in Tennessee, had a 245,000-unit capacity. Shortly after, Honda announced that its U.S. plant would be built in Ohio. At that time, Datsun's U.S. market share had reached over 5.5 percent, its highest ever. The achievement was dimmed, though, when Toyota's share exceeded 6 percent (continuing the lead it had held for five years). Honda was doing well too, having tripled its U.S. share during the previous five years.

In 1981, Datsun was a very popular automobile manufacturer among Americans. Its slogan, "Datsun—We Are Driven!" was engraved in Americans' minds and stood for high performance. That image changed abruptly when the corporate headquarters decided that its cars throughout the world must carry the head company's nameplate, Nissan. Whatever the logic was in Tokyo, the name change confused U.S. consumers. Many Americans continued to refer to the company's cars and trucks as Datsuns because the Nissan name meant very little to them. Further, some even believed Nissan was a division of Toyota. The confusion over the name may explain why Nissan experienced a decline in sales and market share and trouble with its dealer network.

Datsun dealers in the United States reacted very negatively. Dealer resistance included refusal to pay for new Nissan signs or make further investments, a standoff that some maintained for five years. In 1981, an artificial shortage of Japanese cars developed in the United States as the respective governments agreed to limit Japan's exports to 1.68 million cars. This inflated the Japanese firms' U.S. profits, which they used to improve their position in the United States. Toyota employed them to strengthen its U.S. sales force and to ration cars to dealers willing to invest in better facilities and locations. Nissan, however, nervous about declining market share back home, used these excess funds to improve its Japanese dealerships. Given its strained relationship with the U.S. automobile market, Nissan missed the opportunity to develop successful partnerships with large, professionally managed dealerships. Instead, the firm struggled with the image problem presented by dealing with former used-car lots.

As gasoline prices decreased in the United States, motorists returned to larger cars. None of the Japanese car manufacturers had such models in their lines. Toyota, however, acted by introducing its family-size Camry line, while Honda brought out its comparable Accord. Nissan continued with its smaller Sentra and thus missed an opportunity to penetrate the higher-profit segment.

In 1985, Nissan's U.S. plant began producing Sentras, but Honda had already completed its Ohio plant earlier and produced 117,000 cars. The Nissan plant cost around 50 percent more than Honda's yet had only two-thirds the capacity. Nissan achieved higher U.S. sales that year, a peak of 831,000 cars, but from there its market share drifted downward against gradual growth in Toyota's share and even better growth in Honda's. In Japan, these rivals' market shares followed a comparable pattern.

In 1986, Yutaka Kume, a career engineer, became Nissan's president. Then the yen's value rose steeply against the dollar, hurting Nissan's U.S. profits and causing total earnings to fall into the negative category. However, the company recovered, and its operating profit soared to over a billion dollars by 1989. This was fueled in part by success in Europe, following the opening of Nissan's plant in England, where the new "Bluebird" was produced. With it, Nissan expanded its lead in European market share over Japanese rivals. Meanwhile, Kume shook the Tokyo bureaucracy: He put one engineer in charge of each car and supported more original styling.

A new president, Hagiwara, was named for the U.S. subsidiary. Lacking new car models, he concentrated on reforming the dealership system. He hired an American marketing executive from Ford, Thomas Mignanelli, to head Nissan's U.S. marketing activities. The new marketer started on Nissan's confused U.S. image. In 1987, the widely criticized theme "Built for the Human Race" was chosen to replace its weaker theme, "The Name Is Nissan." This advertising campaign failed to bring prospective buyers into the showroom as sales fell by 40 percent. The company kept the slogan but dropped the corresponding advertisements. Soon after, Nissan initiated a sales promotion offering rebates of up to $1,000 on selected cars. Many industry experts predicted that such sales promotions would bring only short-run sales results, not build the long-term image Nissan wanted. Mazda now had a tight grip on performance positioning, and Honda and Toyota were holding popularity with quality themes. A new image or positioning for Nissan was badly needed.

Meanwhile, under Hagiwara, important steps were taken toward U.S.-oriented car design. A design studio was opened near San Diego, with a GM designer, Gerald Hirshberg, as chief. The company brought out a luxury car designed in Japan for world markets—the Infiniti—in 1989. The introduction was preceded by novel "tease" commercials, showing images of waves, fields, or clouds but no automobiles. A market research firm named these Zen-inspired spots third in the top ten most-remembered television advertisements, the best showing ever for a new-car campaign. However, Toyota won the race to market with its Lexus luxury line and led Nissan's Infiniti in American sales. Although Infiniti dealers were overwhelmed with prospective buyers, sales lagged about 30 percent behind Nissan's goals. Largely in response to dealer insistence, later Infiniti ads were more typical of automotive advertising (i.e., the ads emphasized steering and comfort instead of rocks and trees). Two-page ads in newspapers across the country not only displayed the car at last, but did it from 15 different angles. For Infiniti, however, the goal remained to establish an identity that would make it stand out from its toughest competitor, the Toyota Lexus.

As the 1980s ended, Nissan's market share in Japan had declined to 23 percent but was steady. In the United States, its share revived slightly (after 1988) to around 4.5 percent. However, over 60 percent of Nissan's sales were for smaller, less expensive models. Overall corporate profits slipped moderately from their 1989 peak.

The 1990s

The 1990s began adversely for the automotive industry worldwide. The Japanese companies avoided the deep losses sustained in most countries, but profits shrank drastically. Nissan's profits fell to around $200 million in 1991 and kept declining. This occurred despite the success of Nissan's Maxima line. The Maxima SE represented a successful venture in image-building efforts. Selected by *Road & Track Magazine* as the best coupe/sedan of 1991, the Maxima SE represented a mid-price "family" car offering responsiveness, durability, and attractive styling. The Maxima helped Nissan's efforts to reposition itself as a leader in Japanese design. Described as a quiet, elegant sedan, the Maxima SE maintained a mid-level image and represented a major force behind the revival of Nissan's presence in the U.S. market. The luxury-market Maxima GXE met with similar success.

Continued profit pressures in 1992 put Nissan in a tough spot, because it was a relatively high-cost producer in Japan and was still trying to recover in the United States. Nissan took steps to meet the needs of the immediate future. Capacity was doubled at the Tennessee plant (with a $425 million investment) and at the English plant. New cars, including three from its California design center, were introduced: the Altima, a larger sedan intended to surpass the Accord and the Camry (and the reason for the U.S. plant expansion), the Infiniti J30, to expand the line with touches appealing to the U.S. luxury car market, and the Quest, a minivan that was Nissan's third effort to crack the U.S. minivan market.

By the mid-1990s, efforts were well under way to reorganize Nissan's U.S. operations. These steps included (1) moving decision-making authority to a dealer-operations manager who would live in the dealers' communities and be sole advisor to a group of them, (2) consolidating each model's marketing decisions at headquarters under a brand manager rather than have decisions diffused among functions, and (3) reducing regional offices from eleven to seven and move much of headquarters staff to them. The same reorganization was taking place in Tokyo, where Yoshifumi Tsuji—the former head of production—had become the new Nissan CEO. His mission was to increase Nissan's productivity by 10 percent during his first three years, a task to which he was well suited. By rationalizing production methods and reducing line workers by 2 percent per year, total cost savings reached $770 million. With the savings, Nissan tried to hold its place in the auto race.

In the United States, a new ad campaign was developed that featured "Mr. K" and the "Enjoy the Ride" slogan. The ads were seen as creative masterpieces, with consumers shown as being rejuvenated as they drove around in Nissan products. However, the ads did very little to sell cars. Despite early optimism, sales in the late 1990s were disappointing. In 1997 alone, total sales dropped over 45 percent from 1996 sales figures. In addition, sales for the Altima, one of Nissan's most successful car introductions fell to disappointing levels.

To combat these problems, Nissan began to take some bold and creative steps. First, Nissan announced an aggressive pricing strategy for the 1998 Altima—about $1,500 less than the 1997 model. However, a lower price does not always mean lower quality. Instead, Nissan's goal was to provide a higher-quality car at a lower price. This goal was achieved in part by using more U.S.-based plants to produce parts for the Altima. Literally hundreds of small improvements (both in manufacturing processes and operations) were made in order to introduce car buyers to an affordably priced luxury car. Nissan's "Value Strategy" was later universally adopted for all Nissan products, with hopes that consumers will think "extraordinary value" when they think of Nissan. Nissan was so confident in its new strategy, it forecasted sales to increase 13 percent—a very bold forecast, given the fiercely competitive market for midsize sedans.

Second, Nissan shifted its strategic focus to creating cohesion between manufacturing, finance, and marketing. In addition, Nissan moved aggressively into enhanced customer service. Nissan implemented a "no-pressure" customer-oriented buying situation, where consumers are treated fairly. In the future, Nissan will likely expand customer services to include such amenities as roadside assistance and postpurchase service. The new strategy will uphold the notion that the initial sale is merely the beginning of an overall long-term buyer–seller relationship.

Third, Nissan introduced a new advertising campaign in early 1998. The new ads kept the "Enjoy the Ride" slogan but no longer featured "Mr. K." Instead, the new ads focused on product features and Nissan's new worldwide positioning statement: "Dependability, Quality, and Reliability." The overriding goal of the new campaign was to focus on each product by touting the fun-to-drive benefits of each Nissan model.

A part of this new promotional effort was Nissan's launch of its restored vintage "Z-car" promotion. Z-cars refer to Nissan classic cars (e.g., 1969 Datsun 240Z). Nissan began efforts to market fully restored versions of their famed classics at ten select "Z-stores" across the United States. In doing so, Nissan became the first major car manufacturer to undertake this type of restoration and marketing effort. The restoration process lasts two months and involves locating original parts (when available) and rebuilding parts that are no longer manufactured. The cars are all being restored by Pierre Perrot (a former race car driver) along with Nissan's quality department. The goal is to make restored Z-cars virtually equal to the originals. Nissan's revitalization strategy may prove beneficial, as rare commodities—waterfront property, stamp collections, and now "Z-cars"—continue to be lucrative investments.

Fourth, new products were introduced to the market. Nissan North America, Inc., (NNA) announced its intentions to pioneer the U.S. electric vehicle (EV) market with the new "Altra EV." The compact van is equipped with cutting-edge lithium-ion (Li-ion) battery technology. Li-ion batteries allow drivers to travel approximately 120 miles at one time and provide acceleration levels comparable to gasoline-powered vans. The "EV" represents a high-tech van for practical use. Nissan began testing the "EV" under several driving conditions (e.g., summer weather and urban driving). The carmaker also began testing the concept with California and Arizona consumers. The purpose of this testing is to help Nissan deliver a reliable electric vehicle that meets the needs of American drivers. The Altra EV will be manufactured on an all-new platform at Nissan's Tochigi (Japan) plant. Nissan provided approximately thirty Altra EVs to some fleet users in 1998. Further, ninety demonstration units were to be tested by fleet users in 1999 and 2000. Given positive results, retail sales were to begin soon after. The NNA also plans to participate in a National Low Emission Vehicle (NLEV) Program. In 1999, the company was in the final process of certifying a gasoline-fueled, "super-ultra-low-emission vehicle" in California. The model is a 1.8-liter version of the Sentra compact sedan and emits one-fourth the unburned hydrocarbons and one-tenth the oxides of nitrogen of the average gasoline-burning car. The opportunity to market the low-emission Sentra is limited because most states' restrictions are not as tough as California's emissions laws. Production of the vehicle began in early 2000 and was to be available for sale before the end of the 2000 model year.

In early 1998, Nissan introduced two "new" vehicles to the U.S. market: the seven-passenger 1999 Quest minivan and the Frontier four-door pickup. The new Quest, a joint venture with Ford Motor Company, offers Nissan's minivan customers increased passenger roominess, more cargo space, many performance enhancements, and a refreshing new style. The hallmark of the new Quest is its ability to provide a carlike ride without compromising comfort or cargo space. The new Frontier represents uncharted territory for Nissan, for it boasts a family-sized cab and a much larger body. Nissan basically created the U.S. compact pickup market in 1959 and has stayed at the forefront of small-truck innovation ever since. In 1999, Nissan introduced the Xterra, a small sport utility vehicle that was an immediate success with Generation-X buyers.

A New Alliance and a "Revival Plan"

Despite the changes Nissan implemented in the late 1990s, the company found itself at a crossroad as years of misreading consumer preferences and losing ground to competitors such as Toyota and Honda created great financial difficulties. Nissan lost $264 million in fiscal year 1998, and the prospects for a turnaround were bleak, given its bloated production costs and a product line that was considered unstylish by many experts in the auto industry. Attempts to form an alliance with another automaker in the late 1990s had been unsuccessful as both Ford and Daimler-Chrysler passed on opportunities to enter into joint ventures with Nissan. A savior finally appeared in 1999: Renault, the French auto manufacturer that was on the brink of financial ruin in the mid-1990s. Renault invested $5.4 billion for a 37 percent stake in Nissan. In addition to the much-needed cash infusion provided by Renault, Nissan hoped to take advantage of Renault's strength in car design, while Renault planned to use its ties to Nissan to sell its models through Nissan dealerships worldwide. In an effort to ensure success of the new alliance, Renault Chairman Louis Schweitzer named Carlos Ghosn as Nissan's chief operating officer in 1999 and charged him with leading Nissan back to stability. Ghosn had developed a reputation as a master cost-cutter during stints at Michelin in the 1980s and at Renault during its period of financial difficulty in the mid-1990s.

The early months of the Ghosn reign went as expected. In October 1999, Ghosn unveiled what he termed the "Nissan Revival Plan." One key component of the plan was a call for a 20 percent reduction in purchasing costs over three years. Nissan's suppliers were called on to submit ideas for reducing costs. Ghosn made it clear that affiliated firms that were not willing to help Nissan reduce costs were in danger of losing the company's business. Nissan has an unwieldy supplier network of over 1,110 members. It plans to reduce that number to 600 members by 2002. One of the most surprising parts of the revival plan was the elimination of 21,000 jobs worldwide, including the closing of three assembly plants and two engine plants in Japan. This was surprising, given the Japanese custom of lifelong employment. Ghosn insisted that no employees would be laid off. Instead, workforce reductions would come from attrition and increased use of part-time employees. The plant closings were necessary because Nissan plants were operating at approximately 25 percent of capacity, well below production levels needed in order to be profitable.

While cost-cutting measures were needed to bring Nissan's costs in line with other automakers, changes in marketing strategy were needed to jump-start the brand. Nissan has a reputation for quality engines but uninspiring body designs. Ghosn pushed for a redesign of the Frontier pickup, Altima sedan, and Maxima sedan. Also, plans call for the introduction of 22 new models worldwide over the next three years. Four new models will be introduced in the United States by 2002, including a version of the popular Z series sports car. Ghosn has committed to increasing annual product development investments to five percent of sales over the next few years. The emphasis on product development is designed to help Nissan reach a goal of 1 million units sold in the United States by 2003. That figure represents an increase from unit sales of 700,000 in 1999. One advantage Nissan now possesses in the design area is that it has reduced the product development cycle over the past five years from 29 months to 15 months. This drastic improvement will allow the company to move cars from the design stage to the showroom floor much faster than before.

The next few years will be critical for the long-term stability of Nissan. Some strides have been made already under Ghosn's revival plan. Net automotive debt was reduced from $17.6 billion to $12.7 billion in fiscal 1999, bloated vehicle inventories have been reduced, and the amount of incentives per vehicle has declined from $2,500 to $1,800. It remains to be seen to what extent Nissan's affiliate suppliers will work to cut costs to help reduce purchasing costs. Even Ghosn, who was known as "Le Cost Cutter" during his days at Renault, acknowledges that cost cutting alone will not rescue Nissan. A return to the successes of the 1970s will require a focus on customers and differentiating itself not only from Toyota and Honda but from other import brands, such as Mitsubishi and Subaru, that are attempting to make inroads in the U.S. market.

Questions for Discussion

1. How would you characterize the strategy-making performance of Nissan in general and in the United States since World War II?

2. What were the major forces behind this performance?

3. Appraise Nissan's actions and programs as it begins the new millenium. What would you have changed or added?

4. Evaluate Nissan's plans to be a pioneer in the electric car market. Do you agree with their decision? How would you market such vehicles?

5. Nissan spends a great deal of resources on environmentally friendly strategies. Given the expense of these strategies in both time and cost, do you feel that these strategies are a wise decision? Will such strategies help the long-term profitability of Nissan? If so, how?

Sources

These facts are from Larry Armstrong, "In reverse at Nissan," *Business Week*, March 9, 1998, 42; James R. Crate, "Nissan Unveils Altra in Effort to Zoom Ahead in EV Race," *Automotive News*, October 27, 1997, 50; Paul J. Deveney, "Nissan Motor Co. Expects Domestic Sales to Fall," *Wall Street Journal*, December 18, 1997, A16; Jean Halliday and Alice Z. Cuneo, "Nissan Reverses Course to Focus on the Product," *Advertising Age*, February 16, 1998, 1; Michiyo Nakamoto, "Nissan Warning as Domestic Sales Slip," *Financial Times*, March 3, 1998, 29; Nissan's homepage, http://www.nissan.co.jp; "Nissan Says All Is Well with TBWA Chiat/Day," *ADWEEK Eastern Edition*, March 2, 1998, 6; "Nissan Says Profits Will Be Disappointing," *New York Times*, March 13, 1998, C2; Mark Rechtin, "Nissan Cleans House in U.S.," *Automotive News*, February 23, 1998, 1; Daniel Taub, "Nissan continues to flail, despite management change," *Los Angeles Business Journal*, Mar. 9, 1998, 8; "3 Nissan Executives in U.S. Are Removed as Sales Slump," *New York Times*, February 24, 1998, C9; James B. Treece, "Hanawa Tries to Stir the Stew at Nissan," *Automotive News*, March 16, 1998, 39; "Upping the EV Ante: Nissan Hopes to Charge Up Image of Electric Vehicles," *Ward's Auto World*, December 1997, 124; Lindsay Chappell, "Nissan to Boost Product Spending," *Automotive News*, January 17, 2000, 30; Gail Edmondson, "Dangerous Liaison: Renault and Nissan," *Business Week*, March 29, 1999, 48; "Image Problems: Falling Sales Hurting Nissan's Bottom Line," *Greensboro News Record*, February 3, 1999, B6; "Nissan Ponders Full-Size Pickups, SUVs," *Ward's Auto World*, March 2000, 33; "Nissan Unveils Revival Plan," Nissan Motor Company, Ltd., Press Release, October 18, 1999; "Nissan Motors Plans for California Launch of Low-Emission Car," *Wall Street Journal*, August 11, 1999; Mark Rechtin, "Nissan Speeds to Redo 3 U.S. Vehicles," *Automotive News*, January 17, 2000, 3, 79; Norihiko Shirouzo, "Renault, Nissan Seal Their $5.44 Billion Deal," *Wall Street Journal*, March 29, 1999, A19; Robert L. Simonson and Norihiko Shirouzu, "Nissan to Shut Five Plants, Cut Jobs in Retrenchment," *Wall Street Journal*, October 19, 1999, A18; Emily Thornton, "Remaking Nissan," *Business Week*, November 15, 1999, 38; James B. Treece, "Ghosn 'Confident' of Nissan Revival," *Automotive News*, May 29, 2000, 20; David Woodruff, "Renault Bets Ghosn Can Drive Nissan," *Wall Street Journal*, March 31, 1999, A14; Dave Zoia, "Nissan Cuts Cycle from 29 to 15 Months," *Ward's Auto World*, September 1999, 75–77.

Sigma Press

In the fall of 1970, Donald Sapit was faced with a dilemma. His company, Weston Laboratories, of which he was president, had been sold to a larger corporation. At the age of forty-one, he was faced with the prospect of unemployment for the first time in his life. Employment prospects in his town, Ottawa, Illinois, were not good for someone with a degree in mechanical engineering and an MBA from the University of Chicago. He was not looking forward to having to move his family of four school-age children, given the anticipated disruptions in their lives and resulting stress and unhappiness. He had received offers in Chicago, eighty miles away, but it would have required a full-fledged move to the city or suburbs. The alternative was to stick it out in Ottawa and rectify his company's badly damaged financial situation.

As president of Weston Laboratories, a small research facility, Sapit had gained an excellent background in the administration and operation of a small business. During the two years prior to the sale of Weston Laboratories, he had returned to school on a part-time basis to earn his MBA at the University of Chicago. As in most small businesses, Sapit wore many hats, one of which was supervising most of the purchasing functions. Over the previous two or three years, he had dealt, on a continuing basis, with a small printer, Dayne Printing Company, of Streator, Illinois, a town fifteen miles away. In 1967, Dayne, on the verge of bankruptcy, was offered to Weston Laboratories at an attractive price. Sapit saw it as an opportunity for a good personal investment that would not conflict with the Weston Labs operation. He felt the present Dayne managers, who indicated their desire to stay on after the sale, could manage the day-to-day operations with little outside help. Sapit personally made the purchase and felt that, with the increased volume that Weston would provide, the operation could become profitable within a twelve-month period.

One problem Dayne had experienced over the years had been establishing a sound, effective sales program. To help mend some of Dayne's image problems with its customers, the name was changed to Sigma Press, Inc., and the business was incorporated in the state of Illinois. A new salesman/manager was hired and given the authority to establish new sales policies. Sapit had decided to be involved only on a limited basis and, in effect, took the position of an absentee owner. Over the next few years, several salespeople came and went, and the sales effort provided only minimal increases in volume. The business held its own, but made little progress. The results were typical of those experienced by most absentee-owned businesses.

This case was provided by Donald and Mike Sapit, Sigma Press, 1543 Kingsley Ave., Bldg. 16, Orange Park, Florida 32073, for classroom discussion rather than to illustrate either effective or ineffective handling of an administrative situation. O. C. Ferrell, Colorado State University, developed the final draft of this case.

In spite of the fact that Sigma was making little progress, Sapit continued to see the potential for making it into a quality-oriented printing business that could make substantial gains against its local competition. The area served by the shop covered a radius of approximately thirty miles around the city of Streator. The area had a number of major manufacturing plants that were potential users of substantial quantities of printing. Unfortunately most of these plants were headquartered in other cities and did not have authority for local purchasing of anything beyond the basic necessities required for daily plant operations.

The Desk Calendar: A Strategic Opportunity

In seeking other alternatives to improve sales, Sapit and Sigma staff had developed an advertising desk pad calendar for distribution as a gift to its customers. Its purpose was to keep the Sigma name, phone number, and list of services in front of the customer as a constant reminder of its existence. It was freely offered to any customer thought to have sufficient volume potential to justify the expense of the calendar and its distribution costs.

One of the customers that had received the calendar, Oak State Products, an Archway Cookie Bakery, asked the salesman if Sigma could produce similar calendars for them with the Archway advertisement printed at the top. Sigma filled this initial order and it proved popular with Archway's customers. The next year Archway asked if the calendars could be produced with a color photo of its plant in the ad space. This version was so well received that Oak State recommended the use of the calendar as a marketing tool to all the other Archway Bakeries around the country. Sigma recognized that the opportunity for a new marketing strategy was developing.

The sales volume realized from the calendar sales was not substantial, but Sapit saw in it a good possibility for a totally new market, divorced from the limitations imposed by Sigma's present sales territory. Furthermore, he perceived a market that could be developed by a direct marketing effort. This direct marketing effort would permit sales penetration into a much larger geographical area than was practical to serve with Sigma's limited sales staff.

It was at this time that the sale of Weston Laboratories took place, and because of philosophical differences with the new management, Sapit was forced to make the decision to leave the company. Although Sigma was starting to show potential for very modest profitability and good growth, it was still just barely able to support itself. After a family council meeting where the decision was made to "tough it out," Sapit made the decision to enter the Sigma operation on a full-time basis and to prove that it really could become a first-class operation. The change was made in 1971.

A New Marketing Strategy

The first major strategic organizational decision for Sapit was to dismiss the one salesman and assume all sales and management responsibilities himself. He then developed a general marketing strategy. A definite sales territory was established and prime prospects targeted for personal calls on a regular basis. (Previous salespeople had been making calls on a hit-or-miss basis, with no real continuity.) Customer and prospect lists were developed so that a mailing program could be instituted on a scheduled basis. Each four to six weeks, a specially created mailing piece or a sample of the "job of the month" was sent to each firm. Additionally, a direct marketing calendar program was developed with a crude effort to target specific market segments. At the time, direct mail promotion of printing, and especially direct marketing efforts, were relatively unheard of in the printing industry.

The advertising desk calendar was marketed on the theme of "constant exposure advertising." It was given the name "Salesbuilder." Each customer was offered a standard calendar format with an individual ad imprint customized to fit the needs of the company's business. The imprint could contain line drawings, photos, product lists, or any special information necessary to convey the company's message to customers. Sigma's willingness to encourage attractive and creative designs received immediate attention and acceptance by customers. It set the company apart from the competition, which would allow "four lines of block type, not to exceed thirty-two letters." In effect, a whole new advertising medium was being created, and Sigma was at the front of the wave.

A Financial and Production Strategy to Promote Expansion

Within a year after Sapit's entry into the business, total volume was up 50 percent; even more important, the response to the calendar marketing effort was starting to show real promise. As a result, Sigma was experiencing the need for additional capital to finance the growth. Sapit offered one-third of the stock to Don Vonachen, a long-time friend, who was a practicing attorney from Peoria, Illinois. The transaction was completed, and the cash was used for capital to help fund the day-to-day operations and expanding accounts receivable resulting from the increased volume. Vonachen was not active in the day-to-day operations but functioned as corporate secretary, legal counsel, board member, and advisor.

In the summer of 1972, the sales of commercial printing were gaining at a modest rate of increase, but calendar sales were increasing at a rate of 40 percent per year. It was becoming apparent that larger manufacturing facilities would be required in the immediate future or the sales efforts would have to be scaled back. A search was started for a larger building in a better location. When no suitable building could be found, the board decided to construct its own building on a five-acre site at the intersection of Route 23 and Interstate 80 in Ottawa. It was a site with high visibility and a good measure of prestige. This was a rather ambitious move for a company that, only 18 months prior, was just barely holding its own. The move to the new building, attractively designed and fronting on the Interstate, created a then-unwarranted image of success for Sigma. It seemed to Sapit that Sigma should try to capitalize on its new image and high visibility. He decided to change the emphasis of the business and hoped to improve its record of growth and profitability.

A Three-Year Corporate Plan

Over the next few years, Sigma's marketing strategy was oriented toward building a reputation for producing the most creative and highest-quality printing in its service area, which had a thirty-five- to forty-mile radius around Ottawa. The firm took a calculated risk. Sapit anticipated that this new direction would give his firm a solid reputation as a quality printer, one that fully justified the higher prices it charged. Several of the larger local companies obtained permission from their corporate offices to procure their printing locally. The downstate division of Carson Pirie Scott & Company, a substantial department store chain, chose Sigma for the production of its catalogs. The new marketing strategy paid off, and total sales volume had increased 220 percent by 1976.

Sales of the calendar increased slowly but steadily. Management wanted growth, but it wanted it in an orderly and controlled manner. Management also wanted its growth to be more profitable than the industry average of approximately 5 percent on sales. It was becoming obvious that to be successful in the printing business, it was necessary to specialize. After long and deliberate discussion and investigation during 1976, the company management wrote a three-year corporate plan.

The corporate plan emphasized marketing, which at this time was considered unique for a small commercial printer. The marketing plan focused a major share of the sales and marketing effort on building a market for the "Salesbuilder" desk calendar. The target market consisted primarily of smaller corporate accounts, while the marketing mix emphasized product and promotion. Space advertising in sales and marketing-oriented publications created substantial numbers of inquiries, but sales levels did not follow. Direct mail, primarily to manufacturers, produced a much higher response and return on investment. Sigma had created a unique product that was very flexible in terms of unusual designs, advertising messages, photographic techniques, and other special requirements—a highly effective marketing tool.

Within the next few calendar seasons, solid accounts such as Serta Mattress, Domino Sugar, and Borden, Inc., were added to the list of satisfied customers. Reorder rates were very high, usually in the 88–90 percent range. Quantities ordered by individual companies tended to increase annually for three or four years and then level off. Total calendar sales had increased at a rate of approximately 40 percent per year during the 1976–1980 period, during which time commercial printing sales increased at a rate of about 15 percent annually.

The Calendar Becomes Sigma's Corporate Strategy

Because of the success of the marketing plan, production capacity was being taxed. In 1979–1980, major capital commitments were made to add a new high-speed two-color press and to purchase, redesign, and rebuild a specialized collating machine to further automate calendar assembly. This opened the way to mass marketing of the "Salesbuilder" calendar line. Direct mail techniques were improved to allow selection of prospects by SIC number and sales volume. A toll-free 1-800 number encouraged direct response by interested parties. Whenever possible, Sigma responded to inquiries by sending a sample calendar that contained advertising ideas related to the respondent's line of business. The sample would be followed up with a personal phone call within two to three weeks. Calendar sales continued to improve until, by 1983, they represented 40 percent of total sales and approximately 75 percent of net profit.

In spite of the success of the calendar marketing programs and attractive profit levels, Sapit was disturbed by trends in the printing industry that pointed toward a diminishing market and increased competition for the commercial segment, particularly in Sigma's local Rust Belt area. Rapid development of new technology and high-speed equipment had caused industry-wide investments in new equipment well beyond immediate need, creating excess capacity. The result was cost cutting and reduced margins.

Sigma's management had for some time been considering selling the commercial portion of its business in favor of becoming an exclusive marketer of calendar products. Through its membership in the Printing Industry of Illinois, a buyer was found for the plant, the equipment, and the goodwill of the commercial portion of the business. The buyer agreed to enter into a long-term contract to handle all calendar production for Sigma, using the same plant and staff that had been handling the production for the previous ten years. The sale was completed in June 1983.

Sigma's management now found itself free of the daily problems of production and plant management and able to commit all its efforts to creating and marketing new calendar products. Sapit had a long-standing personal desire to move the business to the Sun Belt for the better weather and, more important, for the better business climate. In May 1985, corporate offices were moved to Jacksonville, Florida. Concurrently, Sapit was joined in the business by his son, Mike, a graduate of Illinois State University in graphic arts.

Actions were taken to expand Sigma's product line to include several additional products, all designed to be highly personalized. The new products included a year-at-a-glance wall planning calendar, a desk diary, a pocket diary, and a smaller version of the original desk calendar.

Sigma had built its calendar business on items that were basically "off-the-shelf" products that could be imprinted with the customer's advertising message. It was now seeing a growing market and benefiting from the demand for products that were totally customized not only in graphic design, but in product specifications as well. Sigma's management perceived the market for their new line of "supercustomized" calendars to be the medium to large corporation with a substantial customer base. The audience was companies with large advertising budgets that were service-oriented, thus providing the potential for orders of larger magnitudes. The market being studied was relatively small in terms of number of companies but very large with respect to total sales potential. It would require a totally different marketing approach from those used in the past.

Test advertisements for custom-designed calendars were run in *Advertising Age* and in several marketing journals. These advertisements appealed to larger corporate accounts. In addition, the sales staff became much more aggressive in searching out individual accounts that appeared to have a high potential as customized-calendar customers. Prospects were contacted by phone and mail to determine the individual with the responsibility to specify and authorize this type of purchase. Unsolicited samples of several different customized products were sent by Federal Express in order to attract attention. Each prospect was followed up by a phone call within a few days to confirm interest and provide additional information.

The goal was to establish Sigma as a publisher of high-quality, creatively designed custom calendars. Initial response to the new marketing strategy was good, with indications that the blue chip companies could, in fact, be reached through this approach. To reach its growth goals, Sigma felt it had to be successful in this marketing strategy. This type of highly customized product design is very demanding on the creative staff. Because only ten to fifteen new accounts of this type could be handled each year, it was important that creative time be spent on high-potential accounts. The new strategy was successful in landing substantial orders from Nabisco, Fidelity Investments, and FedEx. Realizing that these blue chip companies were consumers, Sigma focused the entire organization on meeting five customer needs:

1. Flexibility

2. The ability to produce a quality product consistent with the client's image and marketing goals

3. Personal service and attention from beginning to end

4. Fair pricing

5. Timely, efficient fulfillment

With the blue chip accounts, Sigma realized that it had to be able to offer its products on a turnkey, or concept through fulfillment, basis. Many of these corporations wanted to use a calendar program but were not able to devote staff, time, or expertise to such a project. Sigma offered the solution—handling the entire calendar promotion so that customers could devote their time to more productive efforts, confident that their calendar program was running smoothly and efficiently. It installed new computer equipment and programs that would allow order fulfillment in small or single shipments, even for large-quantity orders. Special UPS manifest programs were developed to simplify the handling of large quantities of drop shipments.

The Total Service Package

The business grew rapidly from 1985 to 1990, and by 1991 Don and Mike Sapit saw a new opportunity to expand the business again. After carefully analyzing the characteristics of its buyers and their buying decisions, Sigma found new market opportunities. During its first fifteen years in the promotional-calendar business, Sigma focused on large companies, which usually distributed their promotional calendars through their sales forces to customers. These companies usually supplied Sigma with the basic idea for their calendar promotion, including an imprint or art design for the firm's individualized calendar. For years, Sigma heard the same story from several top prospects: An effective calendar program required too much of their staff's valuable time. Sigma seized this opportunity by marketing its "Total Service Package," a program in which it handled the entire calendar promotion, including conception, design, production, and delivery.

With its own computer order-tracking and manifest system in place, Sigma was able to offer its customers and prospects an efficient and cost-saving order and distribution system. From established customer lists or those generated through Sigma's direct order programs, calendars could be shipped to as many as 20,000 locations for a single account. This was particularly helpful to accounts that had dealers scattered across the country.

This achievement led Sigma to take its experience one step further. Using a customer-supplied list, it began marketing the calendars directly to the customer's distributors.

Flyers and samples were produced and mailed by Sigma. Orders were then returned directly to Sigma. This process allowed individual distributors or a single branch to include its own imprint on the calendar. Currently, a customer list may have over 10,000 names, and a single order may consist of over 1,000 different imprints. Because each customer has its own requirements, a staff member dedicated to personalized service is assigned to each customer. Sigma learned how its customers make decisions about specialty advertising purchases such as promotional calendars and then developed a program to satisfy the needs of purchasing agents and buyers in large organizations.

The strategy appears to be very successful. The company has added to its list of satisfied customers such prime accounts as Milwaukee Electric Tool Corp., Hoffman-LaRoche, Inc., International Paper Company, and Nabisco Brands, Inc.

Recent Developments

Since focusing on the "Total Service Package" approach as its marketing strategy, Sigma has experienced a large increase in corporate clientele with very specialized product and service requirements. Because of the high demand for the "Total Service Package," the workload soon placed a serious strain on Sigma's existing staff and physical space. When one additional full-time employee was added in 1993, Sigma began looking for a new facility. The company moved into its new building in 1995 knowing that the new office would allow for personnel growth for at least five to seven years. Adjacent land was secured in the same purchase, which made possible the early-1996 addition of a complete wing for graphics production. State-of-the-art equipment was purchased to keep Sigma in line with new technology, and two additional full-time employees were added between 1995 and 1997, along with one permanent part-time employee—a total of eleven full-time personnel. As Sigma's growth has continued, the company has faced additional space requirements. In 2001, Sigma began construction of an additional wing on the adjacent land.

Marketing

In 1994, Sigma's sales had leveled off at $2.5 million, and its new test product, the School Year Planner, was into its second year, with sales growing at about 3 percent per year. The School Year Planner had been developed as an ideal "off season" product that would not interfere with seasonal-calendar production, but Sigma found that coordination of sales and production was cumbersome and was spilling over into the seasonal-calendar production. The effort was not worth the increase in sales in terms of demand on staff time and energy, so Sigma ultimately decided to discontinue the project in 1998.

Sigma's reputation for its main product continued to grow. Companies were drawn to the custom-calendar vendor known for high-quality products and a staff with tremendous flexibility and creativity. In an effort to distance itself from competitors, Sigma improved on the "Total Service Package," which had become an important part of its marketing strategy. Customers are now surveyed before and after they receive the product, and large corporate account contacts receive a visit from their account representative early in the year to review the previous year's program and begin groundwork on the upcoming promotion. In addition, international promotions and shipping have become important aspects of several large accounts. Account representatives are developing large corporate accounts by promoting multiple products, while some promotional items beyond calendars are produced in an effort to maintain exclusivity with a client.

Customer demand led to changes in both the sales and administrative areas as well as the graphics department. A stronger focus on the service aspect of the business was a strategic move for the sales and administrative areas. However, the company has also seen tremendous growth in its graphics capabilities—a response to the printing industry itself as well as to the needs of its customers.

However, Sigma's focus on securing corporate accounts that rely heavily on service, rather than the traditional "salesbuilder, once-a-year accounts," is clearly the right formula. The company has added to its list of satisfied customers such prime accounts as Unisource, Volvo, DitchWitch, BetzDearborn, and Sears. But despite the additional staff and resources, the demand for the "Total Service Package" is so great that the company is in danger of overselling its production capabilities to its vendors. Recognizing that possibility, Sigma has become more selective in its marketing efforts.

Annual marketing meetings, held in a different city each year, have become a tradition. Since 1991, staff members have met to review the past year and solve internal and external problems. The meetings encourage teamwork, foster company loyalty, and increase employees' knowledge about Sigma's status in the marketplace. The firm is forecasting 30 percent annual sales growth over the next five years.

Technology

In the late 1980s and early 1990s, Sigma offered limited in-house design/layout services and had film shot manually on a camera—but utilized service bureaus for scans, separations, digital files, and special film needs. Sigma's capabilities were limited, but very few of its customers had complex needs or technologically capable marketing departments.

The advent of the "digital age" in the 1990s served as the catalyst to transform Sigma's prepress capabilities. Graphics workstations were given the speed and storage capacity to handle larger and more complex files that became an integral part of the business. In 1996, an imagesetter was installed—a tremendous commitment to switch to digital film output and to bring a portion of the production work in-house that had been going to outside vendors. The additional equipment also created an environment of more sophisticated hardware, software use, and training needs. The graphics applications used to create the page layouts and images are very complex and call for continual upgrades.

As more companies utilize desktop publishing, Sigma has taken on some of the functions of a service bureau. Converting disks into usable formats and correcting customer artwork have become routine and time consuming for the graphics department. The growth of the desktop publishing market has created a large number of self-proclaimed graphic artists, who serve as a reminder that the need for such functions will only continue to increase.

The graphics department continues to face more sophisticated product design, printing processes, and compatibility challenges with data and equipment. A commitment was made toward continued evaluation of resources and education on the part of management and the graphics staff.

Though the majority of the prepress work is now handled in-house, there are still some items that must be sent out. Certain capabilities are cost prohibitive to accommodate when the demand isn't great enough to justify the purchase of the resources. Sigma has developed strong relationships with service providers who complement its ability to respond to customer needs.

The mid-1990s also ushered in the company's Internet presence and online capabilities. With a corporate identity on the Web, Sigma is better prepared to compete in the increasingly high-tech world of business.

Upgrading technology on the administrative side has allowed the company to better serve its customers. Sigma is now online with several transportation companies, making package tracking an easy task. Networking the administrative computers has resulted in increased flexibility among the staff. In addition, the company is able to do direct invoicing; credit card sales are now offered as a service.

Management Change/Ownership Issues

During the expansion period, Don began to turn over the daily operations of the business to his son Mike. In early 1996, the transition was complete, with Mike in full charge of the business. Don has retired but remains chairman of the board, acting in an advisory capacity.

One of the major concerns is developing personnel strategies over the next few years. Sigma must plan for the transfer of duties as one key employee prepares for retirement in the next five years. This also raises the question of who would succeed the Sapits. Purchasing, production, and scheduling are fully understood only by Mike and Don. In the absence of both Mike and Don's leadership, the business would most likely flounder as it is structured today. Even if a successor were waiting in the wings, the internal knowledge of both men would be lost without documentation. The need for procedure manuals clearly needs to be part of a strategy to educate a successor and keep the business going in the event of the loss of one or both of the leaders. As of 2001, there was an active concern for developing a clear succession plan.

Questions for Discussion

1. Compare and contrast the need for long-range versus short-range marketing planning at Sigma Press.

2. Compare the changes in Sigma's marketing strategy before and after 1983—the date of the sale of the plant and production activities. What were the primary considerations for marketing strategy changes?

3. If you were Sigma's marketing consultant, what recommendation(s) would you make for future strategic market planning?

4. How was Sigma managed growth, and what do you see as its major environmental threats and opportunities for future growth?

Apple Computer, Inc.

Apple Computer, Inc., designs, manufactures, and markets microprocessor-based personal computers and related personal computing and communicating solutions for sale primarily to education, home, business, and government customers. Substantially all of the company's net sales to date have been derived from the sale of personal computers from its Apple Macintosh line of computers and related software and peripherals. Apple is considered the true American entrepreneurial legend. Founded in a garage in 1976 by two college dropouts, Steven Jobs and Stephen Wozniak, the company grew to reach its high point in 1995 with worldwide revenues of $11.1 billion. However, the company earned just $424 million on those phenomenal sales, and it lost $69 million in the last quarter of the year. Although Apple customers tend to be vehement in their support of the company's products, Apple's share of the world computer market fell to 7.1 percent in 1995, down from 8.2 percent in 1994. In 1996, Apple announced it would take a $125 million restructuring charge and lay off 1,300 employees. By 1997, Apple continued to decline, with sales decreasing 28 percent from 1996 to $7.1 billion, and the company posted a $1 billion loss. Apple's market share dipped to 3 percent. To many outsiders, it appeared that Apple had lost its technological edge, and its future as an independent entity looked doubtful. However, the period of 1997–1999 brought about a remarkable turnaround of Apple's fortunes. Apple posted profits of $309 million in 1998 and $601 million in 1999 on sales of $5.9 billion and $6.1 billion, respectively. To understand how the company rebounded from its bleak predicament, we will consider the firm's history, culture, and marketing strategy changes. Case Exhibit 4.1 provides an overview of Apple's financial performance over the last five years.

Birth of an Icon

Stephen Wozniak developed Apple's first product, the Apple I computer, which he and Steven Jobs built in Jobs' garage and sold without a monitor, keyboard, or casing. The Apple I's success helped Jobs recognize a demand for small, "user-friendly" computers. Wozniak added a keyboard, a color monitor, and eight slots for peripheral devices, giving the firm's next product, the Apple II, greater versatility and encouraging other firms to develop add-on devices and software. It worked: Jobs and Wozniak sold more than 13,000 Apple IIs by 1980, and revenues climbed from $7.8 million in 1978 to

This case was prepared by Don Roy, Middle Tennessee State University, for classroom discussion rather than to illustrate either effective or ineffective handling of an administrative situation. An earlier edition of this case was prepared by O. C. Ferrell, Colorado State University.

CASE EXHIBIT 4.1	APPLE COMPUTER, INC., FINANCIAL PERFORMANCE— FIVE FISCAL YEARS ENDED SEPTEMBER 25, 1999 (ALL FIGURES IN MILLIONS OF DOLLARS EXCEPT EARNINGS)				
	1999	**1998**	**1997**	**1996**	**1995**
Net sales	$6,134	$5,941	$7,081	$9,833	$11,062
Net income (loss)	601	309	(1,045)	(816)	424
Earnings (loss) per common share	4.20	2.34	(8.29)	(6.59)	3.45
Total assets	5,161	4,289	4,233	5,364	6,231
Long-term debt	300	954	951	949	303

Source: Apple Computer Inc. 1999 Annual Report; "Apple to Postpone Software Upgrade," *New York Times*, May 16, 2000, C6.

$117 million in 1980. The next ventures, the Apple III and Lisa computers, flopped, but Apple scored a huge success with the Macintosh, introduced in 1984. The Mac, which incorporated an easy-to-use graphical interface, was billed as the computer "For the Rest of Us." The Mac's rapid popularity soon established Apple as a leader in the expanding computer industry. Apple moved into the office market in 1986 with the Mac Plus and the LaserWriter printer. Wozniak left in 1983, and Jobs brought in John Sculley, a former PepsiCo executive, to manage the growing firm.

From Apple's garage-bound birth, Jobs and Wozniak, iconoclasts themselves, so engraved their personalities on Apple Computer's culture that it survived long after their departures. Their do-your-own-thing, ignore-the-Establishment philosophy gave Apple a unique culture of rebels, right down to the pirate flag flying over headquarters. Scorning dress codes, formal meetings, and other traditional business trappings, Apple's creative, defiant culture nurtured the development of the groundbreaking Macintosh computer and operating system, as well as numerous other successful products, and propelled Apple to the top of the computer industry.

Cultural Conflict

The do-it-your-way culture also created strife within the company, pitting the inventive "gearheads" and "wizards"—the engineers and programmers who developed products—against the managers Jobs imported to bring order and good business practices to the firm. Jobs, in fact, left the firm in 1985 in a power struggle with Sculley, largely over the future of the Macintosh platform. When Sculley took over the reins, he realized that Apple's employees would resent the big-business systems he wanted to implement. He also recognized that he had to retain Apple's technical wizards if the firm was to succeed. He decided not to tinker with Apple's unique culture. However, glorifying Apple's technical personnel made them very tough to supervise. This, combined with Sculley's feel-good approach to management, resulted in a company run largely by consensus, and decisions were rarely final. One joke on the Apple grapevine was that "a vote can be 15,000 to 1 and still be a tie."

Apple's culture contributed to frequent power struggles and a seemingly revolving door on management offices. In 1995 alone, fourteen of forty-five vice presidents left or were dismissed. Major management upheavals occurred in 1981, 1985, 1990, 1993,

1996, and 1997, with numerous minor ones in between. Several of these disturbances led to the removal of chief executives. Sculley, for example, was dethroned in 1993 after an 84 percent drop in earnings. His replacement, Michael "Diesel" Spindler, brought a focus on business basics to the firm and quickly worked to address Apple's problems: overpriced products, inflated costs, and sluggish product development. He laid off 2,500 workers, cut R&D costs by more than $100 million a year, and launched a new product line based on the PowerPC microprocessor (which Apple developed with IBM and Motorola). Spindler's back-to-the-basics approach helped Apple rebound, but Spindler soon stumbled under Apple's consensus culture. An insider close to Spindler says, "It was fine for a while. But the system converts people." Spindler was ousted in 1996 and replaced by Gilbert Amelio as president and CEO. By July 1997, Amelio departed and was replaced on an interim basis by Steven Jobs, who stepped in to reverse the company's declining performance. Jobs, who had sold all but one share of his Apple stock in disgust over the company's decline, went back onto the payroll with a $1 annual salary. The appointment of Jobs as interim CEO meant he was now head of two firms: Apple and Pixar, a computer animation company responsible for Disney's hit movies *Toy Story* and *A Bug's Life*. Jobs insisted his leadership role at Apple would be temporary and that he would step aside once a permanent CEO was selected. In January 2000, after more than two years as interim CEO, Jobs announced he was removing "interim" from his title and intended to remain as CEO. In the first two and one-half years of Jobs' second stint at Apple, he led drastic changes in the firm's marketing strategy. In order to understand the changes implemented, it is necessary to examine the frequent changes in marketing strategy between his first and second stints with Apple.

Frequent Strategy Changes

Frequent strategy changes may be the biggest source of Apple's disappointing performance in recent years. Over the years, Jobs, Sculley, Spindler, and then Jobs again reversed, delayed, or evaded outright key decisions while trying to push their own agendas. For example, in April 1995, Spindler implemented a major reorganization of Apple but was forced to recant that decision six months later under fiscal pressures. A late-1995 decision to launch an all-out bid for market share failed after executives misread the market. The result was a storehouse of low-end computers, at a time when consumers wanted expensive powerhouse machines, and an $80 million inventory write-off. Meanwhile, savvy rivals IBM, Hewlett-Packard, and Compaq raked in the bucks and made further inroads into Apple's market share.

In fact, Apple has been consistent only in its inconsistency over the years. For example, Apple has traditionally relied on high-priced products to fund development and marketing of new technology. However, in a desperate bid to boost market share and improve efficiency, the firm has occasionally deviated from this strategy by introducing lower-priced Apple machines. But management has never given the latter strategy time to work, and it failed to implement other tactics that might have generated the same results.

One of the most significant examples of this inconsistency and wavering was the issue of whether to license the Mac operating system to other computer makers in order to create a clone industry that would increase market share for the Mac platform, much as IBM had done with its personal computer. The clone decision was debated as early as 1985, but until 1994 every time top management came close to making the licensing decision, it was stymied by lack of consensus. As one former Apple executive says, "I've never understood why somebody didn't just say: 'I'm the leader. This is the way it's going to be. Thanks for the discussion, but if you don't want to do it, leave.'"

When Spindler finally made the decision to license the technology in 1994, the rising popularity of Microsoft's Windows operating environment for the IBM-PC platform made the clone decision too late. Apple executives asserted that they could raise the Mac's share of the global market to 20 percent in five years, adding 1 percent each year, with the clones bringing in the rest. However, even though Apple executives said they would "aggressively" pursue licensees, thus far, Apple has licensed the Mac design only to Pioneer, Power Computing, Unmax, and Daystar. Together, these firms sold about 200,000 Mac clones in 1995, a drop in the bucket compared with the 4.5 million shipped by Apple. In a last-ditch attempt to revive Mac software's faltering market share, Apple gave Motorola the rights to use its current and future operating systems, as well as the right to sublicense the operating system to other computer makers likely to produce Apple clones. However, Motorola grew tired of Apple's tough antilicensing stance and announced in late 1997 that it would halt development of Mac clones. In another move that signaled an about-face on licensing, Apple acquired Power Computing Corp., the largest cloner of Macs, in 1997. Jobs moved quickly to terminate other license agreements after returning to Apple in 1997. The company believes it made the correct decision in not using licensees, because 99 percent of customers who bought clones were Mac users. Thus, sales of Mac clones came at the expense of Apple products.

Other strategy changes were implemented by Jobs after he returned as CEO. The thrust of his strategy changes was to reduce the number of new product ideas and concentrate on a small number of key new products. Among the most notable products scrapped by Jobs was the Newton handheld computer. The company spent over a decade attempting to develop the handheld technology. Performance problems with the Newton Message Pad and competition from the 3Com Palm Pilot led to Newton's dismal performance. In early 1998, Apple announced it would cease all further development of Newton technology.

Another delayed decision may be riskier for Apple—whether to merge with or sell the company to another firm. During his tenure, Michael Spindler held serious talks with IBM starting in 1994. IBM seemed like a perfect match. The two firms had collaborated with Motorola on the PowerPC chip, which both were committed to using in their products, and they shared two software joint ventures—Kaleida Labs and Taligent (both now defunct). Negotiations between Spindler and IBM's Louis Gerstner even generated a proposed marketing strategy for the merged firm, with IBM bringing out a new line of PCs based on the PowerPC chip already used in Power Macs, and the two firms using Apple's software, beefed up with IBM's OS/2 for the merged PowerPC line. However, with Spindler making many demands, negotiations deteriorated, and the merger talks broke down. A second attempt at negotiating a merger with IBM in 1995 also failed.

Another major issue for Apple has been the thorn of Microsoft's Windows. Windows, with its graphical interface, makes PCs work much like the Macintosh. When the first successful version of Windows appeared in 1990, Apple executives dismissed the threat, although they filed a lawsuit against Microsoft and Hewlett-Packard, claiming copyright protection for the "look and feel" of the Macintosh user interface. Apple lost the suit in 1992. Macintosh users continued to be passionate in their insistence that the Macintosh is a better machine than a Windows-based PC, but Apple has failed to capitalize on their fervor. At the same time, Microsoft had been very aggressive in upgrading Windows to the point where buyers just entering the market failed to see significant differences between a PC and a Mac, beyond the fact that the Apple machine costs more. A new Mac operating system tentatively called Copland, the one project that could have countered Windows 95 and Windows 98, was several years behind schedule.

In August 1997, Apple and Microsoft entered into patent cross-licensing and technology agreements. Under these agreements, the companies provided patent cross-licenses to each other. In addition, for a period of five years beginning in August 1997, Microsoft agreed to make future versions of its Microsoft Office and Internet Explorer products for the Mac OS. Apple would bundle the Internet Explorer product with Mac OS system software releases and make that product the default Internet browser for such releases. In addition, Microsoft purchased 150,000 shares of Apple Series "A" nonvoting convertible preferred stock for $150 million. While the company believed that its relationship with Microsoft would be beneficial to Apple and its efforts to increase the installed base for the Mac OS, the Microsoft relationship was for a limited term and did not cover many of the areas in which the company competes with Microsoft, including the Windows platform.

Current Marketing Strategies

Due to the highly volatile nature of the personal computer industry, which is characterized by dynamic customer demand patterns and rapid technological advances, Apple must continually introduce new products and technologies and enhance existing products in order to remain competitive. Under Jobs, Apple clarified who its customers were and focused on developing products for those markets. The company sees itself serving two market segments: consumers and professionals. Consumer business targets include individuals and education (institutions and students). The professional business segment consists of customers who have computing needs for publishing and graphic arts.

One of Jobs' first moves was to slash Apple's product line from nineteen products to four: one desktop computer and one notebook computer targeting consumers and education customers (iMac and iBook) and a desktop and notebook designed to meet the needs of professional business customers (PowerMac G4 and PowerBook). The key product in Apple's resurgence has been the iMac, a uniquely designed computer that features a one-piece CPU and monitor enclosed in candy-colored casings. Launched in August 1998, iMac became an instant success with consumers, who loved the appearance and ease of use of the new machines. Apple estimates that as many as one-third of iMac buyers are first-time PC buyers. Fueled by the iMac's success, Apple's market share in the home computer market grew to 12 percent in 1999, compared with 3 percent in 1997. The company leveraged the success of the iMac by introducing the iBook notebook model in 1999. Like the iMac, the iBook is available in a variety of colors. Also, it is competitively priced with other notebook brands. Another product focus for Apple is computer operating systems. In 2001, the company released Mac OS X (ten), a major upgrade of the Mac operating system that could allow Apple to gain a competitive advantage over Microsoft's Windows. A key feature of OS X is a visually appealing graphic interface called Aqua. Jobs is so enthusiastic about the graphic interface that he says, "We made the buttons on the screen look so good you'll want to lick them."

In addition to focusing its product line on a few key products, Apple has made changes in its production and distribution strategies. The company has drastically reduced the amount of inventory it carries. At the end of 1997, Apple had $437 million in inventory, about one month's supply. One year later, it had reduced year-end inventory to $78 million, or about six days' worth of inventory. Improvements have been made in inventory turnover, too. Apple turned its inventory over 10 times in 1997, but by 1999 it achieved an inventory turnover of 180 times. Production schedules are based on weekly sales projections and can be adjusted daily. Production of the key iMac product has been shifted to one company, LG Electronics, a Korean firm with plants in Korea and Mexico. This change will allow Apple to reduce its workforce, although Apple employees will continue to assemble custom-ordered iMacs and PowerMac G4s.

Major changes in Apple's distribution strategy were implemented by Jobs after his return to Apple. A partnership was formed with CompUSA, the nation's largest computer retailer, to be Apple's key retail customer. And Apple discontinued relationships with retailers that were unenthusiastic about selling Macs. Apple is one of several computer manufacturers looking to the Internet as an important distribution channel for its products. In 1999, about 13 percent of Apple's PC sales were made online. Another opportunity being explored by Apple is entrance into the retail business. The company is reluctant to discuss reports that it may open its own stores. The operation would open with five to ten stores and could become as large as 100 stores. This strategy has been employed by one of Apple's chief competitors, Gateway, which operates Gateway Country stores in 45 states.

And, apparently like everyone else inside and outside the computer industry, Apple is turning to the Internet. In 1996, Apple acquired NeXT, which developed, marketed, and supported software that enables customers to implement business applications on the Internet, intranets, and enterprise-wide client/server networks. NeXT technology was instrumental in the development of a major Internet package for Apple customers. This package of services, named iTools, is considered improved versions of services already being offered on the Web. One feature offered with iTools is iDisk, a program that allows Mac users 20 megabytes of storage space on Apple's servers. It is an improvement over similar services offered on the Web because it looks and behaves more like an internal disk drive. HomePage is another service that will allow Apple customers to set up Web sites and utilize digital photos, sound bites, documents, and movie clips. A third feature of iTools is KidSafe, a service designed to ensure that children who are using the Internet do not view sites that are not suitable. Apple is beginning this service with 50,000 approved Web sites and plans to add 10,000 sites per month. An advisory board of teachers and librarians will certify specific sites as "KidSafe." The most ambitious undertaking of iTools is iReview, a ratings service for Web sites. Reviews will cover 15 categories, such as computers, news, and personal finance. Members can suggest sites to be reviewed or submit a review of their own. Jobs likens the utilization of iReview to book reviews provided on Amazon.com's Web site.

To capitalize on these opportunities, Apple must develop new products and market them astutely and consistently. Steven Jobs has brought to Apple much-needed focus, consistency, competitive products, and marketing strategies. Apple does not compete with other PC manufacturers on price. For example, while other PC makers, such as Compaq, Gateway, and Hewlett-Packard, have introduced models with a price below $1,000, Apple has shied away from low-end price points. Therefore, it is imperative that Apple provide exceptional benefits to its customers. Offering iMacs in fashionable colors won over many new computer buyers, but as Apple moves forward it will have to continue to offer customers new innovations in order to stand out in a highly competitive industry.

Questions for Discussion

1. Describe how Apple's unique culture contributed to its present situation. If you were the chief executive, how would you deal with this culture?

2. How have Apple's frequent strategy changes brought it to where it is today? What do you see as the single most costly error made by executives?

3. Describe Apple's current strategy.

4. Propose a strategy for Apple Computer. Keep in mind such factors as Microsoft Windows and the Internet. Describe how you would implement your strategy.

Sources

These facts are from Jim Canton, "Apple Drops Newton, An Idea Ahead of Its Time," *Wall Street Journal*, March 2, 1998, B1, B8; "Claris to Reorganize as FileMaker, Inc.," Apple Press Release, January 27, 1998; United States Securities and Exchange Commission Form 10-K for Apple Computer, Inc.; Peter Burrows, "A Peek at Steve Jobs' Plan," *Business Week*, November 17, 1997, 144; "Apple Buys Assets of Clone Maker Power Computing," Reuters, September 3, 1997; "Apple Drives Away Motorola from Cloning, IBM Next," Reuters, September 12, 1997; Peter Burrows, "An Insanely Great Paycheck," *Business Week*, February 26, 1996, 42; Kathy Rebellow and Peter Burrows, "The Fall of an American Icon," *Business Week*, February 5, 1996, 34–42; and *Hoover's Company Profile* database (Austin, TX: Reference Press, 1996) via America Online; Apple Computer Inc. 1999 Annual Report; "Apple to Postpone Software Upgrade," *New York Times*, May 16, 2000, C6; Doug Bartholomew, "What's Really Driving Apple's Recovery," *Industry Week*, March 15, 1999, 34–38; Peter Burrows, "Can Apple Take Its Game to the Next Level?" *Business Week*, December 20, 1999, 52; Don Clark, "Apple's Net Easily Tops Forecasts Again," *Wall Street Journal*, July 15, 1999, A3; Tobi Elkin and Joan Voight, "Return of the King," *Brandweek*, October 12, 1998, 41–44; Lee Gomes, "Apple Revamps Web Strategy, Operating System," *Wall Street Journal*, January 6, 2000, B8; Constance Gustke, "Apple Peels Out," *Worth*, April 2000, 51–54; David Kirkpatrick, "The Second Coming of Apple," *Fortune*, November 9, 1998, 87–92; Jerry Langton, "Opening New Doors," *Computer Dealer News*, December 17, 1999, 37; Philip Michaels, "Is Apple Going All Out Online?" *Macworld*, April 2000, 27–28; Anthony B. Perkins, "Gates vs. Jobs: The Rematch," *Wall Street Journal*, March 13, 2000, A46; "Andy Reinhardt and Steve Hamm, "Can Steve Jobs Keep His Mojo Working?" *Business Week*, August 2, 1999, 32; Brent Schendler, "Steve Jobs' Apple Gets Way Cooler," *Fortune*, January 24, 2000, 66–72; Brent Schlender, "The Three Faces of Steve," *Fortune*, November 9, 1998, 96–104; "What's Next for Apple & Microsoft," *Money*, May 2000, 76–77; Stephen H. Wildstrom, "Mac Hits Another Home Run," *Business Week*, February 28, 2000, 24.

5

IBM

International Business Machines (IBM), or "Big Blue," consistently maintained a position of leadership in the computer industry for most of the last three decades. For much of that time, experts and novices alike held the IBM name to be synonymous with the U.S. computer industry. A number of IBM products—including the System/ 360 mainframe computer, the AS/400 minicomputer, and its line of personal computers—have set industry standards. Despite a reputation for providing high-quality computers and strong customer service, increasing levels of consumer dissatisfaction and declining sales, profits, and market share forced IBM's upper echelon into turmoil early in 1993.

During the 1980s, the company's share of the world computer market fell from 36 percent to 23 percent; its share of the $50 billion personal computer market dropped from 42 percent to a mere 14 percent. By late 1992, IBM posted its first operating loss, and share prices dropped by half. During that year, the firm lost more than $5 billion. Many of IBM's major customers voiced complaints about the company's inability to keep up with computer technology, citing the firm's lack of applications software, poor integration of its different computer product lines, and unwieldy systems. The early 1990s represent a dark page in IBM's corporate story. Recognizing that Big Blue's performance had deteriorated to an alarmingly critical low, its board of directors called, in January 1993, for the replacement of Chairman John Akers and two top members of his executive team. This move was coupled with an unprecedented 55 percent reduction in the company's dividend. These moves were met with confusion and skepticism from Wall Street and the computer industry as to whether IBM's drastic attempts to regain its top position in the computing industry were too little, too late.

The future hopes of IBM were pinned on an outsider with no background in technology, Louis V. Gerstner. On April Fool's Day, 1993, he became the first outsider to hold the CEO position at IBM. Gerstner's background included positions as an executive vice president at American Express and CEO of RJR Nabisco. His mission was to restore prominence to an ailing Big Blue; the company famous for lifetime employment was in the process of slashing its workforce from 406,000 in 1986 to 219,000 in 1994. It had taken $20 billion-plus in write-offs, and its debt rating was deteriorating.

This case was prepared by Don Roy, Middle Tennessee State University, for classroom discussion rather than to illustrate either effective or ineffective handling of an administrative situation. An earlier edition of this case was prepared by O. C. Ferrell, Colorado State University.

Reorganizing Big Blue

Early in 1988, then-Chairman John Akers announced a reorganization to make the computer giant more responsive to customers' needs, allowing it to respond more competitively in the stagnating computer market. At that time, the company combined its personal computer and typewriter divisions, based on the rationale that customers of those products have similar needs. It also merged its mainframe computer operation with the less profitable midsize computer division. Akers decentralized IBM somewhat, pushing decision-making responsibilities down to six major product and marketing divisions to help reduce the bureaucracy that had been slowing down new-product development—one of the most frequent and loudly voiced complaints from dissatisfied customers. Still attempting to maintain its long-standing policy of no lay-offs, IBM asked 15,000 employees—mostly managers—to retire early, and left another 25,000 positions vacant. It retrained and moved thousands of employees to new positions within the company. Although these efforts helped improve the company's performance, IBM continued to struggle with slow, at times negligible, growth, in part because of increasingly intense competition in its mainframe and personal computer markets.

In January 1990, IBM announced another restructuring in an attempt to reduce its costs. Company executives said they would make the company more competitive by slashing costs by $1 billion and by eliminating 10,000 jobs, again through early retirements and attrition rather than layoffs. The company took a $2.3 billion pretax charge against fourth-quarter 1989 earnings to cover severance pay, consolidations, and other expenses associated with reorganizing. Akers vowed that IBM would generate "modest growth" in revenues for the first time since 1985.

Despite Akers' declaration, industry analysts continued to predict gloom for Big Blue, pointing out that IBM had repeatedly forecast turnarounds that did not materialize. Critics blamed John Akers for IBM's dismal performance, particularly for the manufacturing problems, product delays, and managerial decisions that blemished IBM's reputation and its earnings. Some argued that IBM had maintained its policy of no layoffs at the expense of shareholder value and that IBM's board of directors was reluctant to criticize executives or enact tough cost-cutting measures. They also accused IBM of clinging to its old line of mainframe computers at the expense of developing technologically sophisticated new products that could help boost the company's revenue and image. IBM's continued slow performance in an increasingly competitive and fast-paced industry seemed to lend merit to these criticisms.

IBM announced yet another restructuring late in 1991, in which it further decentralized decision-making authority and created dozens of nearly independent operations. Some divisions were given almost complete autonomy: Facilities Management, which operates customer data centers; Maintenance, which repairs and upgrades systems; Software, the world's largest software company with projected 1991 revenues of $10.6 billion; Systems Integration, which provides custom programming and networking; Personal Computers and Workstations; Printers; Storage Products, which includes the company's high-quality Rochester, Minnesota, operation; and Semiconductors.

The new IBM functioned essentially like a holding company, with control over many mostly autonomous divisions. Managers of each operation effectively became CEOs with freedom to make decisions, particularly regarding the development and marketing of products for their divisions. Their new decision-making authority should allow the company to speed up development of innovative products and allow it to be more effective against stiff global competition. With freedom, however, comes accountability and responsibility for a division's performance; if managers fail to perform adequately, they may be fired. In fact, with the 1991 restructuring, IBM abandoned its no-layoff policy, eliminating 20,000 jobs.

Additionally, in 1991, IBM announced that it had formed a joint venture with rival Apple Computer and Motorola Inc. to develop future personal computing technology. The same year, the company formed another joint venture with Siemens AG to develop and produce more advanced memory chips. More such alliances were likely because IBM executives believed that no single company can provide all the technologies, goods, and services that customers want. By the end of 1992, two former executives, Paul Rizzo and Kaspar Cassini, had been called from retirement to bolster IBM Chairman John Akers' fading position, although he vehemently denied pressure to resign. In just over a month, following the report of IBM's first quarterly operating loss of $45 million, Akers' departure became a reality.

When Lou Gerstner became CEO in 1993, he faced decisions that would decide IBM's fate and had to move quickly to address the company's mounting financial losses. Gerstner's predecessor, John Akers, was attempting to split Big Blue 13 ways and possibly divest some of the parts. That strategy was immediately dropped, and Gerstner made mainframes his priority for the company. The logic behind the emphasis on mainframes was not to sell hardware, but rather to offer customers expertise in the implementation of computer systems. Another major decision involved changing the company's organization structure. Gerstner mandated that IBM dismantle its geographic organization structure in favor of an organization structure in which every function, from development to sales, was organized along industry lines.

Changes in product offerings were made after Gerstner's arrival through divestitures and acquisitions. IBM sold its online service, Prodigy. Gerstner added brands such as Lotus, which gave IBM a major player in desktop software and groupware, and Tivoli, which aided in the ability to build corporate networks. In addition to adding new products to the IBM line, Gerstner demanded that the company accelerate product development.

IBM's Products

Analysts have argued for years that IBM suffered stagnation in responding to the changes taking place constantly within the computer industry. Particularly in high-technology industries, innovation and rapid responsiveness are essential components of the success, and oftentimes the very survival, of competing firms. Industry watchers place much of the blame for IBM's resistance to innovation on the sheer size of the organization. Particular criticisms include having too many employees, staggeringly high overhead, near-sighted reliance on its cash cow (mainframe computers), and dangerous inbreeding of management teams, resulting from the strong corporate culture, which was the company's greatest asset. For many years, mainframe computer sales made up the largest percentage of the company's sales. The multimillion-dollar mainframes link the company to its largest, most profitable customers, and they also heavily influence computer and software purchases. But as the IBM-dominated mainframe market matures, growth is slow, and competition has become fierce.

CASE EXHIBIT 5.1   PERCENT OF REVENUE, BY BUSINESS SEGMENT

	1999	1998	1997
Segment	Percent of Total Revenue	Percent of Total Revenue	Percent of Total Revenue
Hardware	42.3	43.4	46.7
Global services	36.7	35.4	32.1
Software	14.5	14.5	14.2
Global financing	3.6	3.5	3.6
Enterprise investments/other	2.9	3.2	3.4
Total	100	100	100

Source: IBM 1999 Annual Report.

CASE EXHIBIT 5.2   GROSS PROFIT MARGIN PERCENTAGE, BY BUSINESS SEGMENT

Segment	1999	1998	1997
Hardware	26.9%	31.6%	35.9%
Global services	27.6%	26.9%	26.6%
Software	82.3%	80.9%	75.1%
Global financing	53.9%	48.1%	48.4%
Enterprise investments/other	38.6%	34.3%	36.9%
Total company	36.4%	37.8%	39.0%

Source: IBM 1999 Annual Report.

The product mix of IBM is now composed of five business segments: hardware, global services, software, global financing, and enterprise investments/other. Case Exhibit 5.1 indicates progress in these business units from 1997 to 1999. The company's reliance on hardware sales has decreased in recent years as IBM positions itself as a "solutions company" rather than a marketer of computer hardware. This strategy of being a more comprehensive technology company is evident in the increase in the global services segment as IBM has taken a more active role in managing customers' computer networks. The profitability of each business segment from 1997 to 1999 is reported in Case Exhibit 5.2 in terms of gross profit margin percentage.

Hardware

Trends in the hardware segment continued to be disappointing for IBM into the late 1990s. The company experienced flat sales (sales increased 4.6 percent in 1999 after a 3.3 percent decrease in 1998). Mainframe revenue experienced modest growth, but server revenue declined in both 1999 and 1998, thus adversely impacting the hardware segment. Furthermore, IBM experienced decreased revenue from storage products, particularly high-end products. One bright spot in the hardware area has been a marked increase in original equipment manufacturer (OEM) revenue. This increase has been sparked by strong growth in hard disk drive (HDD) storage products and static random access memory (SRAM) products. Gross profit margin in the hardware segment has been negatively impacted as the company has seen a shift in revenues from higher-gross-margin server products to lower-gross-margin products such as personal computers, HDD storage products, and OEM chip technology.

To overcome some of the problems in the hardware area, IBM upgraded its server product line. The new system/390 G4 enterprise servers represent the complete conversion of mainframes to microprocessor technology. In 1999, the system/390 product line delivered a 60 percent increase in processing capacity over 1997, as measured in millions of instructions per second (MIPS). Also, the company introduced Web-enabled RS/6000 and AS/400 servers, Netfinity servers for business networking applications, and the NUMA-Q, a high-end server for complex business applications. Weak revenues for servers can be partially attributed to customers' concerns about the Year 2000 (Y2K) issue. As customers tested their systems for Y2K readiness, they were not inclined to purchase new servers until after the Y2K conversion was completed.

The market for personal computers remains a battleground for IBM. Over the years, intense competition from makers of clones of IBM's XT and AT personal computer line cut sharply into the company's market share. Savvy competitors such as Gateway and Dell Computers, among others, have won market share at IBM's expense by offering good value and strong customer support; other clone makers won customers through ultralow prices. Although IBM is fighting back with new high-quality computers, consumers have been reluctant to pay higher prices just for the IBM name.

IBM is using its rediscovered prowess in the PC market to win back major customers. It won contracts to supply PC products for such corporations as Signa, Barnes & Noble, United Parcel Service, and Home Depot. Despite the resurgence of the PC unit and an impressive list of new customers, IBM still finds itself behind Compaq and Dell in PC market share. However, the company believes its faster, simpler distribution system will enable it to bolster profit margins and increase market share.

It appears that IBM has made progress in reversing its missteps in the personal computer market. The PC unit reached a low point in 1994, when it reported a $1 billion operating loss. Inefficient operations that included a 3,400-model assortment of machines, an excessive number of available options, and excessive parts inventory contributed to IBM's poor performance. Today, the company's PC unit is much more efficient, offering fewer models and reducing available options. Streamlined product offerings have enabled IBM to reduce the number of different parts it keeps in inventory to less than one-third of 1994 levels. Also, the company has reduced inventory levels by having suppliers replenish parts on a daily basis, with 62 percent of all parts replenished daily in 1997, up from 5 percent in 1994. Finally, the PC unit has become more efficient because distributors are assembling PCs rather than IBM doing it in-house. Today, approximately one-third of the company's PCs are assembled by distributors, compared to no outside assembly in 1994. The results of this increased efficiency are evident for IBM. Sales grew 19.7 percent in 1999, and the company has been able to maintain the low profit margins PCs offer.

IBM has undergone a significant shift in its distribution strategy for personal computers. In 1998, the company decided no longer to sell PCs through retail outlets. Instead, IBM is focusing on sales through ibm.com to be competitive with Dell,

Gateway, and other manufacturers that now sell their PC products online. The company instituted a program known as "Buy Today, Ship Today," in which customers can choose from 17 models of PCs, workstations, and notebooks. Products in this program are preconfigured and can be shipped the same day they are ordered (no customization of components is possible for same-day shipment). Implementation of this online program was expected to help IBM boost the percentage of PCs sold directly to 34 percent in 2000, up from 30 percent in 1999. Despite the growth in online PC sales, IBM lags behind competitors. For example, IBM derived 14 percent of its personal systems revenue from online sales in 1999. In contrast, online sales accounted for more than 50 percent of Dell's revenue for the same period.

Global Services

Another bright spot for IBM has been the growth of its global services segment. Services revenue increased 11.3 percent in 1999, growing from revenues of about $4 billion in 1990 to $32.3 billion in 1999. Today, IBM is the market leader in global services and has the highest customer satisfaction rating in the industry. The growth in the services segment is consistent with the company's desire to become a complete information technology company and not just a hardware manufacturer. Revenues from services accounted for about 37 percent of total company revenues in 1999. Growth in this segment has come from managed operation of systems and networks. Emphasis on the services segment has come from the top levels of management, for Lou Gerstner himself occasionally speaks at conferences attended by current and prospective IBM services clients. Despite the company's downsizing activities following Gerstner's arrival in 1993, the services segment has added employees. In 2000 the company had approximately 130,000 employees in the global services unit.

Growth in the global services unit has been fueled by IBM's focus on e-business (a term IBM coined in 1997). The company is poised to take a leadership position in electronic commerce. IBM's e-business client roster is rather impressive—Ford, Charles Schwab, Prudential Insurance, and the New York Stock Exchange are among dozens of firms that have signed strategic outsourcing contracts with IBM. Also, a survey of chief information officers at 53 major corporations named IBM as one of only two companies that was best positioned to take on their Internet projects (Sun Microsystems was the other). It is estimated that 60 percent of all revenues for the entire e-commerce industry will come from services by 2003. IBM continues to add new services to support e-commerce. Among the services IBM now offers are e-business strategy and planning, e-commerce services, e-procurement for business-to-business marketers, and Web site hosting and Web infrastructure outsourcing. Revenue from e-business services grew 60 percent in 1999 to over $3 billion. Additional opportunities for the global services unit exist in such business services as supply chain management, customer relationship management, and business intelligence.

Software

IBM is growing its software business unit (systems management, business integration software, database products, and Web application servers) at a faster rate than the industry. This growth is the result of a shift in recent years from operating systems software to applications software. Consistent with its focus on e-commerce, IBM is giving emphasis to its middleware technology. *Middleware* is the layer of software between computer operating systems and Web applications. Among the applications for middleware are data management, transaction processing, systems management, and business processes, such as supply chain management.

IBM is using its middleware technology in collaboration with the global services unit to help businesses transform into e-businesses. Growth of middleware business is attributed to IBM's ability to integrate various applications, increased use of middleware on non-IBM platforms, expanded market coverage resulting from partnerships with independent software vendors, Web integrators and service providers, and a sales force of 6,600 people. IBM has invested heavily in middleware technology—$1 billion over 1998 and 1999 and another $1 billion in 2000. The market opportunity for middleware software is expected to be $1.6 billion in 2000 (of which IBM will have a 24 percent market share) and is projected to reach $9 billion by 2003.

IBM and Its Competition

IBM's newest organizational structure has somewhat improved the company's decision-making time, allowing it to respond more quickly to changes in the marketplace. While IBM's turnaround under Lou Gerstner has been impressive, the company is not growing as fast as some of its new-economy competitors. For example, in the high-growth market for high-end data storage products, EMC Corp. increased its revenues by 23.5 percent in 1999, compared with IBM's 3 percent decrease for similar products. Also, sales of personal computers have lagged behind competitors'. Dell Computer Corp. enjoyed a 38 percent increase in revenue during 1999 while IBM suffered a 13 percent decrease in PC sales. These numbers suggest that IBM may be too big and too slow to make changes to products and/or practices. Defenders of the company say it is not fair to compare Big Blue to its much smaller competitors.

Although many industry experts warn that IBM may confuse its customers by broadening its product line, the company has implemented this strategy. Knowing that in the computer industry, equipment can become obsolete in a matter of years, IBM continues to develop products and technology critical to its survival. New products the company has introduced recently include the space-saving PC NetVista, Netfinity servers, and an e-commerce software platform known as WebSphere, which allows integration of activities required in making e-commerce transactions. IBM is also cultivating a long-term approach by entering the education sector more aggressively, an arena it once left to Apple. Discounting means the education sales will not generate high profits, but company executives recognize that schools represent a reliable and growing market and that the children getting familiar with IBMs in the classroom today will be the adults who buy computers tomorrow.

With the worst of times hopefully behind it, IBM is optimistic about its future. The company has renewed its commitment in two key areas. First, it has reaffirmed its desire to be the company for mainframe computers. Second, it has reaffirmed its commitment to its customers. For years, IBM's customer service was legendary. However, as the company fell on hard times in the early 1990s, customer confidence in Big Blue fell too. With its increased emphasis on providing complete network management services to its customers, pursuing a leadership role in e-commerce, and restructuring its distribution system to be more responsive to market needs, IBM appears to be in a position to be competitive in the coming years.

Questions for Discussion

1. Characterize IBM's current situation. What are the firm's unique strengths? Weaknesses?

2. Evaluate the most recent series of changes taking place at IBM. Does the firm seem to be on the "right track" again. Why or why not?

3. Evaluate the record of Louis V. Gerstner, IBM CEO since 1993.

Sources

These facts are from "Big Blue Sees Red," *USA Today*, Oct. 20, 1992, 2B; Paul B. Carroll, "Big Blues: Hurt by a Pricing War, IBM Plans a Writeoff and Cut of 10,000 Jobs," *Wall Street Journal*, Dec. 6, 1989, A1, A8; Harris Collingwood, "IBM May Be Crowding Its Own Turf," *Business Week*, Feb. 19, 1990, 42; "Computer Makers Find Schools a Reliable Market," *The Kansas City (MO) Business Journal*, Aug. 13, 1990; John Hillkirk, "As IBM Falters, Shareholders and Critics Take Aim at Akers," *USA Today*, Dec. 6, 1989, 10B; "IBM Slashes Dividends to Stem Red Ink," *USA Today*, Jan. 27, 1993; IBM 1991 Annual Report; IBM 1997 Annual Report; Louise Kehoe, "The New Big Blue," *Electronics*, July 1990, 27–28; Carol J. Loomis, "Can John Akers Save IBM?" *Fortune*, July 15, 1991, 40–56; Sharon Machlis, "'Big Blue' Makes Push for Engineering Market," *Design News*, March 26, 1990, 186; Jim McNair, "IBM Rolls Out Next Generation," *The Miami Herald*, Sept. 6, 1990; Jeff Moad and Susan Kerr, "How Customers Help the New IBM," *Business Month*, Jan. 1990, 13; Betsy Morris and Joe McGowan, "He's Smart, He's Not Nice. He's Saving Big Blue," *Fortune*, April 14, 1997, 68; Raju Narisetti, "How IBM Turned Around Its Ailing PC Division," *Wall Street Journal*, March 12, 1998, B1, B4; Therese Poletti, "IBM Unveils System, Enters 'Super' Market," *The Commercial Appeal*, Feb. 3, 1993, B-4; Larry Reibstein, "IBM's Plan to Decentralize May Set a Trend—But Imitation Has a Price," *Wall Street Journal*, Feb. 19, 1988, 17; Frank Ruiz, "IBM Blazes Trail with New 16-Megabit Computer Chip," *The Tampa (FL) Tribune*, Feb. 14, 1990; Robert L. Scheier, "IBM Redraws its Big Blueprint," *PC Week*, Dec. 2, 1991, 1, 6; John Schneidawind, "Apple Computer Seizes IBM's PC Crown," *USA Today*, Oct. 23, 1992, 1B; John Schneidawind, "IBM Faces Dilemma in CEO Quest," *USA Today*, Jan. 27, 1993; John W. Verity, "Guess What: IBM Is Losing Out in Mainframes Too," *Business Week*, Feb 8, 1993, 106–107; John W. Verity, "A Slimmer IBM May Still be Overweight," *Business Week*, Dec. 18, 1989, 107–108; John W. Verity, "What's Ailing IBM? More Than This Year's Earnings," *Business Week*, Oct. 16, 1989, 75–86; and John W. Verity, Thane Peterson, Deidre Depke, and Evan I. Schwartz, "The New IBM," *Business Week*, Dec. 16, 1991, 112–118.

Napster: Intellectual Property and Copyright Infringement or Technological Breakthrough?

Shawn Fanning, a 17-year-old freshman of Northeastern University, left college to develop a method, utilizing advanced MP3 technology, to trade music over the Internet. MP3s provide almost perfect digital copies of music originally recorded on CDs. Napster, Fanning's company, began operations on June 1, 1999. Their downloadable MusicShare software allows computer users worldwide to send and receive high-quality digital music files among themselves for free. Napster's first round of funding came from Shawn's uncle, John Fanning, and other investors. Their first official CEO, Eileen Richardson, was hired in September 1999. A largely unknown venture capitalist from Boston, Richardson took the job during the most crucial months of Napster's development. Although she was viewed as combative and inexperienced, Napster moved forward with Richardson at the helm.

Problems Begin

Unhappy with what they viewed as copyright infringement, recording industry executives met with Napster management in late 1999 to discuss an acceptable means of distributing music over the Internet. CEO Richardson's abrasive style, however, destroyed any chance of a compromise at the time. Therefore, on December 7, 1999, the Recording Industry Association of America (RIAA) filed suit against Napster for copyright infringement, requesting damages of $100,000 each time a song was copied.

Napster's woes continued. By March 2000, some universities were banning Napster because of the congestion the technology brought to their computer systems. In addition, on April 13, 2000, the rock band Metallica filed suit against Napster for copyright infringement. The suit requested that all Metallica music be removed from the Web site. Claiming they could not physically remove the Metallica songs, Napster attempted to demonstrate concern by booting more than 300,000 members from their site for downloading Metallica songs. On May 21, 2000, Napster hired a new CEO, Hank Barry. Barry was a member of the venture capital firm Hummer Winblad,

---

This case was prepared by Dana Schubert, Robyn Smith, Jane Swoboda, and O. C. Ferrell for classroom discussion rather than to illustrate either effective or ineffective handling of an administrative situation.

which had invested $15 million in Napster. Soon after Barry's hire, Richardson left the company.

The RIAA continued its fight against Napster, filing a motion on June 13, 2000, for an injunction blocking all trading of major-label music through Napster. It was time for Napster management to think seriously about their defense. David Boies, the lawyer who had fought for the Department of Justice in the Microsoft case, was hired on June 15, 2000. To demonstrate their "good faith" efforts, Napster announced plans to work with Liquid Audio, a digital-rights technology company, in an attempt to make music downloads safe for copyright holders. This move was not enough to convince U.S. District Judge Marilyn Patel, who basically ordered Napster's demise by ruling that the company must stop allowing copyrighted material to be traded over the Internet. However, on July 28, 2000, only nine hours before Napster would have had to shut down, the Ninth U.S. Circuit Court of Appeals issued a stay, allowing them to continue operating. Napster again met in court with the Ninth U.S. Circuit Court of Appeals on October 2, 2000. As of this writing, a decision was still pending from the three-panel judge who listened to arguments from both sides. If this ruling goes in favor of Napster, a trial date for the larger copyright issues will be set.

Parties to the Controversy

In addition to Napster, this controversy affects four other parties—artists, the recording industry, retailers, and consumers. Artists have mixed feelings about Napster. Leading the opposition are Dr. Dre and Metallica, who both sued Napster as well as several universities in an attempt to remove their songs from the play list, shut down the service, and receive compensation for copyright infringement. Lars Ulrich, Metallica's drummer, said, "It is sickening to know that our art is being traded like a commodity rather than the art that it is."

Some music artists, however, have come to realize how Napster can benefit them. In 1999, Tom Petty released his song "Free Girl Now" on MP3 before the release date of his new album. The group Offspring released their first single on September 29, 2000, and proceeded with other releases until the album was officially sold on November 14, 2000. The lead singer, Dexter Holland, said, "Digital downloading was not hurting our sales. In fact, it may have been helping." In addition to releasing some of their songs, the band showed its support to Napster by giving away $1.83 million as a promotional tool to get people to download music. Other artists, such as Beck and the Beastie Boys, stated they also have seen an increase in album sales after releasing an MP3 file. Still other artists, like Chuck D are working with Napster to create deals on such items as concert tickets, T-shirts, posters, and other promotional merchandise. Although artists may have individual interactions with Napster, their contracts are enforced by the RIAA, so they remain subservient to the larger organization's fight.

The second group involved in the Napster controversy is the RIAA, which says it is fighting to protect its investment in promoting artists. The recording studios listen to aspiring artists and determine which to support. They organize the business side, which allows the musicians to concentrate on the creative development of songs. The industry is facing the concern of "dis-intermediation" and is wondering if the Internet and the changing economy will eliminate its role in the distribution chain. Music companies are trying to compete online by opening their own subscription music service provider.

CASE EXHIBIT 6.1	MUSIC FILES DOWNLOADED

	How many music files have you downloaded?	How many music files have you kept and stored?
1–10	32.2%	45.6%
11–100	26.6%	6.6%
101–250	15.3%	3.1%
250+	10.7%	2.4%
Never	15.3%	42.2%

Source: Martin Peers, "Survey Studies Napster's Spread on Campuses," *Wall Street Journal*, May 5, 2000, B8.

How does Napster affect listeners' purchasing practices and, therefore, music retailers? The effects are varied. A study by Jupiter showed that people who use Napster are 15 percent more likely to purchase music than nonusers. Another survey by Digital Media Association and Yankelovich Partners showed that of the "two-thirds of respondents who had downloaded music from an online source, 66 percent said listening to a song online had at least once prompted them to later buy a CD or cassette featuring that song." According to a survey by the Wharton School of Business, "70 percent of Napster members polled reported they have used the service to sample music before buying it." Evidence supporting these statistics varies among those most effected—record stores.

An owner of a nine-store music chain in Maine stated, "We've had absolutely no negative effect from Napster. . . . sales are actually up because Napster has brought music to the forefront. Everybody's talking about music. . . . If Napster is stealing sales from Eminem, I want it to steal from every new release. Because that was our biggest selling CD, ever." Another record store owner agreed that, "our sales are up 19 percent over last year because of all the publicity. . . . You can't open a newspaper or magazine and not see a Napster headline. We've never got so much free advertising. Music is exciting again."

Not all record store owners paint such a rosy picture when discussing the effects of Napster, however. Oliver's Records Inc. in Syracuse, New York, has virtually been wiped out by the widespread use of Napster. According to owner Charlie Robbins, the store sells approximately $37 a day in walk-in sales, down from $500 a day two years ago.

Conflicting information has surfaced about the Napster audience and their music purchasing practices. Many people believe college students are the dominant music downloaders. However, according to one study of almost 4,300 New England college students, 19.2 percent used Napster daily, 37.6 percent weekly, and 16 percent monthly, while 27.3 percent had never used the service. The same study also determined the number of times the students downloaded and stored music. As Case Exhibit 6.1 indicates, college students varied in the quantity of downloads, but overall they stored relatively few music files. In addition, a significant number of students (over 42 percent) never stored music.

Some universities struggled to accommodate Napster traffic. Napster was prohibited at Indiana University because use of their technology expanded to 50 percent of the school's traffic between the campus and the Internet between January and February 2000. Due to student demand, however, Indiana University improved their network performance in order to reinstate the service.

Contrary to popular belief, college students are not the only fans of online music sites. In fact, Media Metrix found that adults over age 50 made up 17 percent of the visitors to music sites in June 2000, increasing by 92 percent in the last year. In October 2000, Napster had 32 million registered users, marking an increase of 2 million in just one week. Many supporters increased their usage in fear of a shutdown.

Legal Aspects

Although many people are concerned with the outcome of this controversy, the only groups involved in the litigation are Napster and Napster-like music providers and the recording industry. The first two suits were against MP3.com and Napster. Both suits concern intellectual property and copyright infringement over the Internet.

MP3.com settled out of court in June 2000, agreeing to begin paying 1.5 cents each time a user stores a song and one-third of a cent each time a song is downloaded. Sony Music, Bertelsmann AG's BMG, Warner Music Group, and EMI, four of the five top music labels, agreed to pay nearly $20 million each for past copyright violations. Universal Music decided not to accept the settlement offer and has since filed suit requesting $45,000 for each of 10,000 CDs produced by Universal that were available online. This could amount to a fine of $450 million for MP3.com.

In July 2000, Scour, a Beverly Hills–based company, was sued by the RIAA and the Motion Picture Association of America (MPAA). The duo targeted Scour for their attempt to bring music, movies, and pictures to the Internet public. Scour was called "a vehicle for global piracy of copyrighted motion pictures and sound recordings." As a result of the pending lawsuit, Scour laid off fifty-two of its sixty-four employees.

Napster's Arguments and the Industry's Rebuttal

Despite lawsuits against other companies, the biggest player in the battle of piracy remains Napster. In their war with the RIAA, Napster has turned to three past rulings on copyright infringement for support in their defense: Sony Betamax, the 1992 Audio Home Recording Act, and the 1998 Digital Millennium Copyright Act.

Napster argues they should have the same protections that saved the Sony Betamax in the early 1980s. In that case, the MPAA filed a lawsuit against Sony stating that the home videotape recorder (VCR) unlocked the door for widespread film reproduction. Napster believes this supports their claim because they are a "new" technology with legitimate uses, such as promoting new bands. The lower courts found Sony, just like Napster, guilty of copyright infringement. However, the Supreme Court overruled the lower court's decision for the MPAA, stating that technology must be "merely capable of substantial noninfringing uses in order to be protected by law." Supporters argue Napster should have the same protection as Sony because they have other legitimate uses.

The opposing side of the Betamax case states that Napster technology is not unique. Another argument against Napster is that their service would not be banned from the Internet; it would just prevent them from listing unauthorized music. For these reasons, Napster opponents do not believe this ruling applies to their case.

The 1992 Audio Home Recording Act (AHRA) may apply to Napster. This act, allowing people to make copies of music for personal use, was passed in response to the development of digital audiotape recorders. This occurred prior to the Internet revolution and therefore did not consider Web transport of music. Napster enthusiasts say that this case is relevant because the music copied is for personal use, not redistribution for profit. Of the music downloaded, users listen to 92 percent on their desktops, 10 percent in portable devices, and 14 percent on home stereos. Because this act was based on digital audiotapes, not Web music, many people disagree on its relevance to the case. The Justice Department, the Patent Office, and most of the legal community agree this act does not support Napster.

The 1998 Digital Millennium Copyright Act (DMCA) refers to whether or not there is knowledge and blatant disregard of copyrighted material. The DMCA grants immunity to Internet service providers (ISPs) and says that online service providers cannot be held responsible for the actions of their customers. According to Napster, they have broad protection from copyright claims because the technology functions like a search engine rather than having direct involvement with music swapping. The main argument against Napster's seeking support from the Digital Millennium Copyright Act pertains to their "search engine" status. According to the legal community, "Napster does not take the legal steps required of search engines in dealing with copyright violations."

Intellectual Property

Intellectual-property rights losses in the United States total more than $11 billion a year from the illegal copying of computer programs, movies, compact discs, and books. The argument against intellectual property rights is not that protection is not warranted but that the protection should not go so far as to destroy competition. According to copyright experts at the University of California at Berkeley, "Intellectual-property owners are not entitled to prohibit or exercise monopoly control over new technologies that incidentally threaten their established business models. . . . Having to change business plans in response to evolving technologies is what competition is all about." Based on this argument, all developers of intellectual property, whether it be music, computer software, or written text, need to develop new methods to market and distribute their products. The other side of the controversy suggests that the creation of intellectual property will be stifled if unprotected and that copyright laws should cover the gamut of possibilities.

Dual Standards?

Napster claims to support protection of intellectual property and has tried diligently to protect their own creations. In June 2000, the rock band Offspring sold T-shirts displaying the Napster logo. Napster was not pleased with this action and requested that a cease-and-desist order be issued against Offspring. Napster reconsidered as Web sites began commenting on the hypocrisy involved in the issue. Along these same lines, Napster has also attempted to halt all independent software developers from trying to create Napster-compatible software and Web sites. To ensure this, Napster refused to share their software code and has made changes to their own software that prevent others from running with Napster. They have also blocked outside music sites from accessing their database of songs. Napster, in guarding their method of operations, has also demanded that users of their software agree that they will not "decompile, reverse engineer, or dissemble" their program. This only reinforces, according to the RIAA, that Napster is a euphemism for music piracy on a large scale.

The Future of Internet Services Such as Napster

There are other sites that offer Napster-like services, but they have not faced the same legal issues as Napster. Scour, Exchange, iMesh, and CuteMX, for example, can be used to search for audio and video images, as opposed to the sole MP3 searching done by Napster. These services allow all file types to be shared. Wrapster is a Napster spin-off that allows any file to be disguised as an MP3 and therefore transmitted via Napster. Finally, Gnutella, an AOL site, does not require a central Web site like Napster does. Instead, this site connects users directly to each other to trade wanted music files.

Despite the strong arguments for both sides, many people feel that the best solution is to develop a compromise between the recording studios, the artists, and Napster-like music providers. Bertelsmann, parent company to BMG Music, was the first in the recording industry to strike a deal with Napster. Project Thunderball, the code name for the attempt to join the two businesses, was first made public on October 31, 2000. Bertelsmann provided Napster with $50 million to expand and improve the current software, with the goal of prohibiting pirated music transfer and counting the number of times a song is downloaded in order to reimburse the artists. Suggestions include using the "MD5 hash," a digital fingerprint, and using software that monitors sound patterns to detect illegal copies. The joint venture is dependent on the development of such a system because Bertelsmann will not withdraw their lawsuit until Napster proves they can protect the artists' music. Napster and BMG will also have to develop a revenue model for future service. The most likely solution is a monthly subscription fee for users who want to download music from Napster. Bertelsmann is hoping to rally rival music producers behind the effort to use Napster-like services in order to expand the industry to include online books, films, and magazines. EMI and Sony have expressed interest in similar negotiations with Napster. However, Universal and Warner have begun work on their own digital distribution projects, therefore decreasing the likelihood of a joint venture between these companies and Napster. With the details of the current Bertelsmann arrangement not yet determined, the agreement with other labels will most likely be delayed until Napster can prove themselves.

Without a doubt, file sharing will continue to exist in both the media and entertainment industries. However, a ruling by the District Court of Appeals on February 12, 2001, made it clear that the court feels that current copyright laws apply to the Internet. In a unanimous decision by the appeals court, the original ruling by Judge Marilyn Patel that Napster was aware that users were swapping copyrighted materials was upheld. The appeals court refuted all of Napster's defense tactics in one form or another and ordered the site to stop allowing their millions of users to swap copyrighted material without a fee.

The appeals document stated that the RIAA adequately verified ownership of the copyrighted material in question. It further stated that approximately 87 percent of the music traded on Napster does belong to the RIAA. Due to a direct violation of rights of reproduction and distribution, Napster was found guilty of direct infringement of the RIAA's musical recordings. Napster insists that their service does not directly infringe copyrights because their users engage in fair use of the material. The uses they referred to are: (1) *sampling*, where temporary copies may be heard prior to purchasing; (2) *space-shifting*, which refers to a user's accessing a recording of a CD they already own; and (3) *permissive distribution* of material by artists.

The court did not agree that those who frequent Napster practice fair use, for several reasons. First, the court determined that Napster users engage in commercial use of the copyrighted material because users are able to obtain something they would normally have to pay for, and the recording is permanent. Second, the fair-use claim was refuted because of the creative nature of musical recordings. Third, because Napster users engage in "wholesale copying" of copyrighted material, the use is not fair. According to the court, space-shifting does not apply because the copyrighted material is distributed from the individual who downloads the material to other individuals. Finally, the use of Napster harms the market by reducing CD sales among college students and raising the barrier of entry into the digital-music-download market for the RIAA. This decision was supported by several studies conducted on behalf of the RIAA.

One study by Dr. E. Deborah Jay, known as the "Jay Report," randomly sampled college and university students to track the impact Napster had on their buying habits. Evidence proved a loss of sales attributable to college use of the service. Another study, by Michael Fine, CEO of Soundscan (known as the "Fine Report") determined that online file sharing resulted in a loss of album sales within college markets. Napster tried to refute these studies with one of their own, but they were unsuccessful. The judge determined that the administrator, Dr. Peter S. Fader, did not properly oversee the study or collect enough objective data. The document was not excluded, but neither were its results relied upon for findings.

Napster was also labeled as a contributor to copyright infringement by the court. It was determined that Napster knowingly contributed to the infringing conduct of their users. Napster provided the site and service for infringement. Also, Napster could block users who violate infringement laws if they desired. Finally, the court did determine that Napster should be held liable for contributory copyright infringement because they failed to remove copyrighted material from their service.

The final form of copyright infringement is termed *vicarious* copyright infringement. This applies to whether or not the system operator has the ability to supervise infringing activity and also whether or not the system operator has direct financial interest in the activity. The court decided that Napster did have financial interest in the activity of infringement. It was determined that Napster's future revenue is dependent on the number of users. As more users register, more music would be made available. Napster also had proven that they did have the ability to police their service, because they had blocked users in the past when lawsuits were filed by Metallica and Dr. Dre. They also have a reservation of rights policy on their Web site that specifically states that they have the "right to refuse service and terminate accounts in its discretion, including, but not limited to, if Napster believes that user conduct violates applicable law . . . or for any reason in Napster's sole discretion, with or without cause." Again, the court of appeals noted that Judge Patel did not fully recognize the ability of Napster to monitor their users. The appeals court suggested that the architecture of the current system did in fact limit the extent to which Napster could police the service. In other words, Napster did not have a control system to document all usage of their site. Regardless of the recognition, once again the court determined that Napster is also a vicarious infringer.

The courts also addressed the two statutes and the Sony Betamax case used by Napster. The court determined the Audio Home Recording Act was "irrelevant" because it does not cover the downloading of MP3 files or any digital audio recording device. The court refuted the argument based on the Digital Millennium Copyright Act, stating simply that it does not include contributory infringers. Finally, the court refuted Napster's argument that if Sony could not be held liable when consumers used their device to record television programs or movies for personal use, then they should not be liable for their users' behavior. The noticeable difference between the two cases is that people use videotaped movies and programs in their own home and generally do not distribute the material to millions of people, as is done with Napster. Since the court of appeals agreed with Judge Patel on all accounts, Napster was ordered to shut down once Judge Patel revised and condensed her report. Napster requested to pay royalties to the RIAA in place of the injunction, which request was also denied.

In response to the ruling, Hank Barry, CEO of Napster and Shawn Fanning, Napster's founder, released statements to the public. The two claimed they are still working on an industry-supported solution, such as a membership-based service. They acknowledged the negotiations with Bertelsmann and still believe that service will be up and running within a few months. They also agreed they do plan to make payments to the affected artists as needed. Both Barry and Fanning encouraged all users to contact their local congressional representative to let them know how much Napster means to the public.

Options for Napster at This Point

Despite the ruling, Napster may still have options. Clearly, other labels are trying to create alternative ways to deliver music online. Warner Records, for example, can now use AOL, because of a merger, to deliver online music to their already established customer base. Universal Records has set up a site of their own, called farmclub.com, where users can download music. However, neither of these efforts has proven successful, which puts Napster, with 58 million users, in the driver's seat. So what do they have to do? Napster must quickly create a business model that benefits themselves as well as the music industry. Napster proposed a $4.95-a-month fee for service when their merger with Bertelsmann was announced. Critics argue that once the music company, the music publishing house, artists, and everyone else receive their royalties, there will be nothing left. Sony Music Entertainment, Inc., and Universal have discussed a joint venture and charging $9.95 a month for it, but Napster fears this high price will encourage users to switch to other sites. The best strategy for Napster may be to charge less for basic service while charging heavier users a progressively higher fee. This would encourage users to stay with them while Napster took time to research pricing schemes. Regardless of what they choose to do, Napster needs to act fast. Software evolution, along with their marketing strategy, may be their only chance to turn a Napster death sentence into an opportunity.

On February 20, 2001, Napster offered $1 billion to the recording industry to settle the lawsuit. Under the proposal, $150 million would be paid annually for the first five years to Sony, Warner, BMG, EMI, and Universal, with $50 million allotted annually for independent labels. The proposal was not accepted by the record industry representatives, who were unwilling to settle for anything less than shutting down Napster. On March 16, 2001, the music industry was pleased as the appeals court supported all charges against Napster. The court system did stop short of closing down the business, which leaves Napster the opportunity to work on a new version of their service that would pay copyright holders. In the meantime, Napster is asking users to contact Congress in support of Napster. Judging by the 80,000 hits the Ninth Circuit Court's Web site received the day of the ruling (1,000 is normal), Napster users were listening. Go to http://www.e-businessethics.com for updates on the Napster case.

Questions for Discussion

1. Are current court rulings favoring copyright owners? Why or why not?

2. Based on the facts in the Napster case, who do you think should have control over intellectual property—the artists or the agents? What are the arguments for both sides?

3. How do intellectual property rights relate to fair competition? Can Napster's existence be defended based on the idea that other online music services would take Napster's place if they were shut down?

4. While there are many legal issues in this case, identify several ethical issues that relate to Napster's activities in serving their users' needs.

Sources

These facts are from Martin Peers, "Survey Studies Napster's Spread on Campuses," *Wall Street Journal*, May 5, 2000, B8; http://news.cnet.com, March 23, 2000; Anna Wilde Mathews, "Web Music Isn't Just for Kids," *Wall Street Journal*, September 26, 2000, B1; "Study: Napster Boosts CD Sales," from http://www.zdnet.com, July 21, 2000; "Stats Speak Kindly of Napster," from http://www.thestandard.com, July 21, 2000; "Napster: Downloading Music for Free Is Legal," from http://news.cnet.com/news, July 3, 2000; "Napster vs. the record stores," from http://www.salon.com/business/feature, August 7, 2000; Martin Peers and Lee Gomes, "Music CD Sales Suffer in Stores Near 'Wired' Colleges, Study Says," *Wall Street Journal*, June 13, 2000, A4; Ron Harris, "Heavy Metal Thunder," from http://www.abcnews.go/com (accessed September 25, 2000); "Early Birth on Web for Latest Offspring," from http://www.smh.com.au/news, September 19, 2000; "Napster Grows Up," from http://www.redherring.com/industries, March 10, 2000; Margarita Lenk, "Our Music: Can We Mutually Support the Artist and the Business?," Working Paper Series, College of Business, Colorado State University, Summer 2000; Amy Doan, "MP3.com Loses Big in Copyright Case," from http://www.forbes.com (accessed September 7, 2000); Lee Gomes, "Napster Ruling May Be Just the Overture," *Wall Street Journal*, July 28, 2000; "How VCRs May Help Napster's Legal Fight," from http://www.thestandard.com/article, July 24, 2000; Anna Wilde Mathews, "Sampling Free Music Over the Internet Often Leads to Sale," *Wall Street Journal*, June 15, 2000, A3, A12; Lee Gomes, "Napster, Fighting for Survival, to Make Case Before Appeals Panel," *Wall Street Journal*, October 2, 2000, B24; "Bigger battle brewing: Napster–RIAA court case becoming Goliath vs. Goliath," from http://www.sfgate.com, September 18, 2000; Lee Gomes, "Think Music Moguls Don't Like Sharing? Try Copying Software," *Wall Street Journal*, August 14, 2000, B1; Don Clark and Martin Peers, "Can the Record Industry Beat Free Web Music?" *Wall Street Journal*, June 20, 2000, B1; Lee Gomes, "When Its Own Assets Are Involved, Napster Is No Fan of Sharing," *Wall Street Journal*, July 26, 2000, A1, A10; "Napster Wins Reprieve; Next Move up to Recording Industry," from http://www.cnn.com (accessed August 30, 2000); Jack Ewing, "A New Net Powerhouse?" *Business Week*, November 13, 2000, 46–52; Appeal from the U.S. District Court for the Northern District of California, Marilyn Hall Patel, Chief District Judge, Presiding, argued and submitted October 2, 2000, San Francisco, CA, filed February 12, 2001; Spencer E. Ante, "Now Napster Can Get Down to Business," *BusinessWeek*, February 26, 2001, 35; and "Napster Ruling Angers Fans, Pleases Artists," from http://www.usatoday.com/life/music/2001-02-13-napster-ruling.htm, March, 17, 2001.

Microsoft and the U.S. Government

In 1975 William H. (Bill) Gates III and Paul G. Allen started Microsoft; in 1981 Microsoft incorporated. Microsoft's mission has been to create software for the personal computer in the workplace, the school, and the home. Microsoft's innovative products and marketing have made it the world's leading software provider. Some of its products include software, operating systems for server applications, client–server environments, business and consumer productivity applications, interactive media programs, and Internet platform and development tools. Microsoft is developing software and services on large computers so they can be downloaded, not only for personal desktop computers, but also for any other devices imaginable (such as handheld wireless devices). Microsoft markets online services and personal computer books and researches and develops advanced technology software products. The company's products now extend capabilities to international communications. Microsoft Office 2000 offers a MultiLanguage Pack, which allows users to deploy a single version of Office all around the world. The user can then work with a Standard English interface and switch to online help in another language. Microsoft is compatible with most personal computers (PCs), including Intel microprocessor–based and Apple computers.

Along with its innovative products and marketing, Microsoft contributes substantially to charities. Its community affairs programs rely on both corporate commitment and employee involvement to provide money, software, and volunteer support for nonprofit organizations nationwide. For example, in 1999 Microsoft employees donated to the annual giving campaign, with Microsoft matching each employee contribution up to $12,000. Some organizations that benefit from such contributions are low-income housing developments, YMCA, Easter Seals, Boys and Girls Club of America, museums, and schools. Microsoft also donated to eighteen Connected Learning Community grants totaling $270,000 in cash and $325,000 in software in 1999. Another program by Microsoft is Libraries Online, through which Microsoft provides computers, cash, and software to help link libraries to the Internet. The goal is to enable people who may not have access to computers to learn about the PC, explore the latest software, and experience the Internet. In addition, in 1999 Microsoft provided nearly $47.4 million in cash and software to 800 K–12 schools nationally to support teacher training. They also donated more than $982,000 in cash and $6,234,000 in software to universities and colleges, not including the amount contributed by employees.

This case was prepared by Robyn Smith for classroom discussion rather than to illustrate either effective or ineffective handling of an administrative situation. An earlier edition of this case was prepared by John Fraedrich, Southern Illinois University at Carbondale.

Issues Demeaning Microsoft's Reputation

Despite Microsoft's reputation for innovation and charity, the company is facing ethical and legal problems. In 1990, the Federal Trade Commission (FTC) began investigating Microsoft for possible violations of the Sherman and Clayton Antitrust Acts, which are designed to stop restraint of trade by businesses, especially monopolists. In August 1993 the FTC was deadlocked on a decision regarding possible Microsoft violations of the Sherman and Clayton Antitrust Acts. However, instead of dropping the case, the FTC handed it to the Department of Justice. At the time, Microsoft agreed to settle the lawsuit without admitting any wrongdoing. Part of the settlement provided the Justice Department with complete access to Microsoft's documents for use in subsequent investigations.

An important part of the settlement was a stipulation that would end Microsoft's practice of selling MS-DOS to original equipment manufacturers at a 60 percent discount. Those manufacturers received the discount if they agreed to pay Microsoft for every computer they sold (this is called a "per processor" agreement) as opposed to paying Microsoft for every computer they sold with MS-DOS preinstalled (which would be termed a "per copy" agreement). If an original equipment manufacturer wished to install a different operating system in some of its computers, the manufacturer would, in effect, be paying for both the Microsoft and the other operating system—that is, paying what is called "double royalties."

The argument goes that such business practices are unfair because consumers, in effect, pay Microsoft when they buy another product. Furthermore, the practices are deemed unfair because the practices make it uneconomical for an original equipment manufacturer to give up the 60 percent discount in favor of installing a less popular operating system on some of its computers. These issues focus on whether Microsoft has a monopoly in the market.

The Supreme Court has defined *monopoly power* as the "power to control prices or exclude competition." In other words, a monopolist is a company that can significantly raise the barriers to entry within the relevant market. A monopolist may engage in practices that any company, regardless of size, could legally employ; however, it cannot use its market power in such a way as to prevent competition. In essence, a company is allowed to be a monopoly, but when a monopolist acts in a way that exploits its position, the monopolist has broken the law.

Another battle that Microsoft is facing is with Apple Computer. Apple alleges that Microsoft's chief executive officer, Bill Gates, called and threatened to stop making Macintosh-compatible products if Apple did not stop the development of a program that was to compete with a similar Microsoft program. Because Microsoft is the largest producer of Macintosh-compatible programs, Apple argued that it was being forced to choose between a bad deal or extinction. Apple also alleges that Microsoft would not send it a copy of Windows 95 until Apple dropped Microsoft's name from a lawsuit. This issue may no longer be as significant for the Justice Department as it started out to be, because the two companies have now formed closer ties and are hesitant about cooperating with the federal government. In late 1998, Microsoft bought $150 million in nonvoting stock in Apple, as well as paying $100 million for access to Apple's patents.

Microsoft was also under a federal court order to surrender part of its blueprints for Windows 95 to a rival, Caldera, Inc. However, Microsoft will show only the so-called source code for Windows 95 to Caldera lawyers and experts; it is difficult to make commercial products based on the code alone. United States Magistrate Ron Boyce refused a request by Microsoft to prevent Caldera's experts from consulting on the design of any operating system software for up to eighteen months. Caldera is also suing Microsoft in federal court for designing early Windows software that allegedly was deliberately incompatible with DR-DOS, an operating system that competed directly with Microsoft's own, similar product, MS-DOS. Caldera further claims that Microsoft intentionally misled customers into believing that Windows 95 made it unnecessary for computer users to buy DR-DOS or MS-DOS. Prior versions of Windows ran explicitly as a supplement to the underlying operating system, whether consumers chose Microsoft or Caldera's operating system. However, Caldera's own witnesses admitted there was technical justification for the changes made by Microsoft to its products to make them run with Windows. Also, the problems that Caldera mentioned regarding the incompatibility between DR-DOS and Windows have been proven not to be a result of Microsoft's improvement to the software. Under federal antitrust law, a company generally cannot require customers who buy one of its products also to buy another without some benefit to the customers—a practice known as "tying." In a recent decision, the District of Columbia U.S. Court of Appeals rejected the claim of tying raised by Caldera. The appeals court specifically cited the integration of MS-DOS and Windows into Windows 95 as an example of innovation that was beneficial to consumers. Caldera's lawsuit went to trial in late 1999.

There is also a claim regarding Sun Microsystems, Inc.'s trademark and a breach-of-contract case against Microsoft. This case accuses Microsoft of deliberately trying to sabotage Sun's Java "write once, run anywhere" promise by making Windows implementations incompatible with those that run on other platforms. Specifically, the suit alleges that Microsoft's Java-compatible products omitted the Java native interface (JNI) and remote method invocation (RMI)—features that help developers write Java code. Sun claims Microsoft replaced certain parts of the Java code with Windows-specific code in a way that confuses programmers into thinking they are using pure Java.

Sun acknowledged that Microsoft has fixed some of the earlier glitches, but Sun is adding two new alleged incompatibilities to its list. One allegation concerns the addition of new keywords that are available to programmers, and the other revolves around new directives in Microsoft's Java compiler that make it dependent on Windows implementations.

In late 1998 Sun added new allegations of exclusionary conduct on the part of Microsoft and Windows 98. Sun requested an injunction that would require Microsoft either to make the Java features in the new operating system compatible with its tests or to include Sun's version of Java with every copy of Windows sold. In January of 2000, the Ninth District Court of Appeals ruled that it was software developers and consumers, not Sun, that would decide the value of Microsoft's language extensions, so Microsoft is allowed to support their development tools with their own Java enhancements. Furthermore, Sun's motion to reinstate the injunction on the basis of copyright infringement was denied. The court ruled that the compatibility test was a contractual issue, not a copyright issue.

The federal government has taken an aggressive stand, in that it believes Microsoft is practicing anticompetitive tactics, thus creating a monopolistic environment, which has substantially lessened and reduced competition in the industry. In

October 1997 the Justice Department asked a federal court to hold Microsoft in civil contempt for violating the terms of a 1995 consent decree. The decree barred Microsoft from imposing anticompetitive licensing terms on manufacturers of personal computers and asked the court to impose a $1 million-per-day fine. Microsoft argued that its Internet Explorer Web browser software was an integrated, inseparable part of Windows 95 and that it was legal to install the entire program. However, the U.S. District Court judge did not agree with the argument and issued an injunction prohibiting the company from requiring Windows 95 licensees to bundle Internet Explorer with the operating system. Microsoft filed an appeal against the injunction and asked for the petition to be heard on an expedited basis, while it supplied PC makers with an older version of Windows 95 without the Internet Explorer files or with a current version of Windows 95 stripped of all Internet Explorer files. The problem was that this product would not boot up, and Microsoft admitted that it knew about the problem beforehand. Consequently, the Justice Department asked the district court to hold Microsoft in contempt. At the same time Microsoft's stock began to drop. Possibly fearing larger stock devaluation, Microsoft agreed to provide computer vendors with the most up-to-date version of Windows 95 without the Internet Explorer desktop icon.

Microsoft's Rebuttal to the Allegations

Under the 1995 consent decree, Microsoft was unable to require companies such as Dell and Hewlett-Packard to obtain a license for the Windows operating system. In lay terms, Microsoft could not make others include Windows. However, the decree did not restrict Microsoft from integrating products, such as putting the Web browser into Windows.

In response to its detractors and the Justice Department, Microsoft has denied all of the essential allegations, claiming that it had planned to integrate its Internet Explorer technologies into the Windows operating system long before rival Netscape even existed. Microsoft also refuted the government's central accusation that the company incorporated its browser technologies into Windows only to disadvantage Netscape. Microsoft is arguing that its Internet Explorer is gaining popularity with consumers for the simple reason that it offers superior technology.

In addition, Microsoft is rejecting government allegations that the company tried to "illegally divide the browser market" with rival Netscape and that it had entered into exclusionary contracts with Internet service providers or Internet content providers. Finally, Microsoft is arguing that it did not illegally restrict the ability of computer manufacturers to alter the Windows desktop screen that users see when they turn on their computers for the first time.

Like other software products, Windows 95 and Windows 98 are subject to the protections afforded by the Federal Copyright Act of 1976, enacted in accordance with Article 1, Section 8, of the U.S. Constitution. The Copyright Act states that copyright owners have the right to license their products to third parties in an unaltered form. Microsoft has asserted a counterclaim against the state attorneys general because Microsoft believes the state attorneys general are inappropriately trying to use state antitrust laws to infringe on Microsoft's federal rights.

Microsoft on Trial

The federal government, along with twenty states, has charged Microsoft with abusing its monopoly in the computer software business. The three primary issues are: (1) bundling the Internet Explorer Web browser with the Windows 98 operating system to damage its competition, particularly Netscape Communications Inc.; (2) using cross-promotional deals with Internet providers to extend its monopoly; and (3) illegally preventing PC makers from customizing the opening screen showing Microsoft. The trial started October 19, 1998, and the government specifically accused Gates of illegal bullying, coercion, and predatory pricing to undermine Netscape because that company's products were becoming more popular than Microsoft's. Gates denied ever being concerned about Netscape's increasing share of the browser market. However, Microsoft memorandums and e-mail messages show otherwise.

In June 1995, Microsoft and Netscape executives met to discuss "ways to work together" regarding the browser market and each other's share of that market. Netscape's CEO, James Barksdale, testified that Microsoft's proposal regarding working together involved illegally dividing the market. When Netscape rejected the proposal, Microsoft supposedly used predatory pricing, along with other tactics, to "crush" the company.

History

This, along with what the government calls a lack of cooperation, led the government to step in to take action on behalf of Microsoft's competitors. The government and economists have put two long years into negotiations with Microsoft. The intended purpose of the intervention, according to the government, was to help competitors regain some market share. They are hopeful this will also decrease prices for computers and software as well as spark innovation while expanding choice and quality. Another reason the government cites for the intervention is to prevent Microsoft from punishing other companies that wish to sell operating and application systems outside of Windows, an accusation filed by many competitors throughout the legal process.

The Depositions

In August 1998, the deposition of Microsoft management began in Redmond, Washington. Bill Gates was placed under oath and testified before a camera for 30 hours. During this taping Bill Gates did not help Microsoft's case, for he refused to answer most questions during the deposition. He also caviled over the exact meaning of words such as "complete" and "ask" when used in questions throughout the deposition. Bill Gates was then questioned about the controversial e-mails sent throughout the company regarding treatment of competition. This is another allegation that Gates claimed to know nothing about, and therefore he did not have an effective argument as to the exact meaning of those e-mails. At this point it appeared that Bill Gates was not concerned about the trial ahead.

His feelings might have changed, however, in November of 1998 when Judge Thomas Penfield Jackson released his findings of facts. The document consisted of 412 paragraphs, of which only four showed any favoritism toward Microsoft. Jackson also named Jim Allchin, a computer expert, as the mastermind behind the bundling of Internet Explorer and the operating system in an attempt to destroy Netscape. It seemed there was nothing Microsoft could do at this point to eliminate its monopolistic image.

The Trial

By January of 1999, the credibility of Microsoft had been severely damaged, and it was time to begin their defense. During this time, there were several company witnesses that testified regarding the e-mails in question. However, the prosecutor was usually able to rebut his or her version of the story. The most damaging testimony by far came from Jim Allchin, a computer guru and longtime employee of the company, who was often referred to as "Microsoft's lord of Windows." His testimony was supposed to reinforce the detriment of separating the Internet browser from the operating system. Instead, the videotaped demonstration did exactly the opposite. Throughout the tape, icons on the computer screen mysteriously appeared at a moment's notice, adding yet one more serious blow to Microsoft's reputation. This led to a second settlement attempt by Microsoft, but again the two sides couldn't agree. By the end of February 1999, Microsoft had three proposals ready for the Justice Department. The meetings were still unsuccessful because both sides had opposing ideas for a solution. One remedy the government suggested was for Microsoft to place government-appointed people as active members of the Microsoft board. Microsoft saw this as the government's attempt to take control of the company. In April 2000, the government began talks of splitting the company into two divisions. Judge Jackson then appointed Judge Richard Posner, a well-respected member of the Seventh Circuit Court, to try once more to make a deal, but the gap was still too wide. Judge Jackson felt Microsoft was "untrustworthy," and some of the twenty states, also parties in the suit, opposed all negotiations. The last meeting took place on June 2, 2000; by this time all negotiations had reached a stalemate. Both the government and Microsoft had exhausted all efforts; therefore all that remained was the judge's decision.

The Ruling

On June 7, 2000, Judge Thomas Penfield Jackson ordered Microsoft Incorporated to split into two independent companies. His decision ordered one company to sell Windows and the other to sell everything else. Jackson stated several grounds for his decision, the first being simply that Microsoft would not admit to any wrongdoing. He also stated that one intention was to prevent Microsoft from insulting the government with noncompliance to the antitrust laws. Jackson said he found Microsoft to be "untrustworthy" because of past antics, including sending defective Windows software when ordered to unbundle the Internet browser from the operating system. Finally, Jackson was trying to prevent Microsoft from bullying its competitors. Despite the criticisms, Jackson provided some insight as to what he thought the breakup could do for the industry.

By splitting up Microsoft, Jackson was hoping to achieve a few objectives. First, the split was intended to respark competition among the industry. Second, dividing Microsoft in two could possibly spur some innovation that had been stifled by the size and force of the software giant. Third, this split should rejuvenate some of the "dead zones" within the industry, such as word processing, spreadsheets, databases, and e-mail. Finally, and possibly most important, lessening the power Microsoft had over the industry should renew some creativity among software engineers. Although Judge Jackson has high hopes that these things will happen, Microsoft's opinion of the outcome falls at the opposite end of the spectrum.

According to Microsoft, splitting their company in two is the equivalent of the government's imposing a "corporate death sentence." Microsoft feels there are several things this ruling will do, but none are as optimistic as Judge Jackson's vision. Unlike Jackson's idea of spurring innovation, Microsoft believes the split will do just the opposite, stifle innovation. The split would impose complexity on software development. With two businesses working separately, it would be more difficult to effectively integrate two or more programs. Also, because of the difficulty in bundling, software would be marketed separately, thus driving the prices up for consumers. Finally, Microsoft sees the split as causing a delay in product completion and introduction. An example of this is their Next Generation Windows Services, a program that integrates Windows with the Internet, whose release was delayed three weeks due to the ruling. The government and Microsoft may be the two entities directly involved in this trial, but the public will also be affected in the long run, and they too have their opinion on the case.

Microsoft has long seen itself as the symbol of the American dream to its consumers. A public opinion poll conducted by Harris Interactive, a research firm, in late April 2000 supported that notion to a certain extent. A little over half of 3,830 people surveyed agreed that Bill Gates was in fact a positive role model. The respondents were randomly selected to participate in a survey regarding the possible split of Microsoft. Of the respondents, 48 percent said they disagreed with the government's proposal to split Microsoft into two companies. However, of that 48 percent, only 60 percent said Microsoft should remain one company. In addition to the positive responses for Microsoft, there were negative ones as well. Of those surveyed, 42 percent believed that Microsoft is a monopolist and only 23 percent felt that Microsoft treated its competitors in an appropriate manner. Another survey conducted on the e-businessethics.com Web site at Colorado State University showed that 55 percent of 137 respondents felt that Microsoft was in fact guilty of deliberately trying to crush its competitors. Public opinion polls aside, where does Microsoft go from here?

The Appeal

Microsoft's appeal of Judge Jackson's ruling could delay an actual split for at least one year. The Justice Department would like to have the Supreme Court review the case next, bypassing the D.C. Circuit Court of Appeals, which already backed Microsoft in a similar case. However, the Supreme Court declined the case, so it will first go to the Circuit Court of Appeals. Until the appeals process is over, the split has been stayed, or suspended. The government-imposed restrictions are to take effect in three months; however, Microsoft can and will appeal those to the D.C. Circuit Court of Appeals for a stay as well. The D.C. Circuit Court of Appeals will consist of a three-judge panel selected randomly by a computer. Since this court errs on the conservative side, it is believed that they will support Bill Gates' claim that courts should not meddle in the high-tech industry, as ruled in 1998 when Microsoft was first accused of tying software. Even with that anticipated support, there are a few issues experts believe the higher courts will support. The most likely issue is that Microsoft did act in an anticompetitive manner. Regardless of all the speculation, in order for the appellate courts to overturn a trial judge's factual findings, they must prove the findings were clearly flawed. If Microsoft is not happy with the ruling of the three-judge panel, it may appeal to the full 11 members.

The Supreme Court currently consists of seven Republican and two Democratic appointees. Here again, the higher court is historically considered conservative. The Supreme Court Justices would most likely have relied on previous antitrust cases to make a decision. One past case involved Eastman Kodak, who would have been held liable for "tying" had there been separate markets for products and services. Judge Jackson used this as a reference in his case, citing that there are in fact two separate markets, one for browsers and one for operating systems. Another case that held the defendant liable for antitrust behavior was that of Aspen Skiing. The owner of three Colorado ski facilities was found to be hobbling a fourth facility by not letting customers buy one lift ticket for all four mountains. The accusation against Microsoft for "tying" its Internet browser to the operating system in order to crush Netscape sounds at least similar. A case that could aid Microsoft is that of a Louisiana hospital that was exonerated for supposedly tying "anesthesiology services with surgeries." The courts ruled that this was a "functionally integrated package of services." This was the same argument that Microsoft had made on its own behalf all along.

Where Does Microsoft Go from Here?

Speculation aside, the only certainty here is that this case will continue over the next one to two years, which will probably serve to "kill" the case altogether. So what does this mean for Microsoft? First of all, it means business will go on as usual. With the industry dramatically changing, Microsoft will have to change as well. They will focus on the bottom line while developing and promoting dot-net, their newest venture for the wireless world. Their odds of winning increased dramatically along with their stock, which rose from $1.44 to $62.69 the day of the Supreme Court ruling. As of this writing, the final decision is not yet available.

Questions for Discussion

1. Why has there been so much debate about the role of Bill Gates in the software industry?

2. How do the legal and ethical issues in this case relate to the marketing strategy of Microsoft?

3. Discuss Microsoft's corporate culture with regard to the issues involved. How has this culture affected the debate over antitrust issues?

Sources

These facts are from Dan Goodin, "New Microsoft Java Flaws Alleged." http://www.microsoft.com/BillGates/billgates_1/speeches/6-25win98launch.htm#bill, July 9, 1998; Lisa Picarille, "Microsoft, Sun Postpone Java Hearing," *Computer Reseller News;* http://headlines.yahoo.com/Full_Coverage/Tech/Sun_Microsoft_Lawsuit/, July 7, 1998; Malcolm Maclachlan, "Sun Attacks an Embattled Microsoft," *TechWeb*, May 14, 1998; Malcolm Maclachlan, "New Lawsuit Is Over

Java, Sun Says," *TechWeb*, May 12, 1998; Malcolm Maclachlan, "Sun Targets Microsoft: Software Maker Says Windows 98 Must Be Java Compatible," *Tech Web*; http://www.techweb.com/news/story/TWB19980512S0012, May 12, 1998; Dana Gardner, "Java Is an Unleashed Force of Nature, Says JavaOne Panel," *InfoWorld Electric*, posted March 26, 1998; Michael Moeller, "Amended Complaint: Microsoft Wants Access to 'Highly Confidential' Documents," *PC Week Online*, August 4, 1998; "Microsoft Asks Court to Limit Gates Disposition," http://dailynews.yahoo.com/headlines/politics/story.html/s=z/reuters/980805/politics/stories/microsoft_1.html; Margaret A. Jacobs, "Injunction Looms as Showdown for Microsoft," *Wall Street Journal*, May 20, 1998, B1, B6; John Harwood and David Bank, "CyberSpectacle: Senate Meets Electronic Elite," *Wall Street Journal*, March 4, 1998, B1, B13; John R. Wilke and David Bank, "Microsoft's Chief Concedes Hardball Tactics," *Wall Street Journal*, March 4, 1998, B1, B13; U.S. Justice Department and State Attorneys General, "Statement by Microsoft Corporation," http://www.microsoft.com/presspass.doj.7-28formalresponse.htm, August 3, 1998; Christopher Barr, "The Justice Department's Lawsuit Against Microsoft," http://www.cnet.com/content/voices/Barr/012698/ss01.html, July 13, 1998; "Microsoft Corporate Information. What We Do," http://www.microsoft.com/mscorp/, August 3, 1998; Dan Goodin, "New Microsoft Java Flaws Alleged," http://www.news.com/News/Item/Textonly/0,25,24007,00.html ?st.ne.ni.pfv, August 3, 1998; Tim Clark, "Go Away," http://ne2.news.com/News/Item/0,4,2076,00.html, August 7, 1996; Nick Wingfield, "Net Assault," http://ne2.news.com/News/Item/0,4,1940,00.html, July 25, 1996; Nick Wingfield and Tim Clark, "Dirty," http://ne2.news.com/News/Item/0,4,2072,00.html, August 7, 1996; "Feud Heats Up," http://ne2.news.com/SpecialFeature...d/0,6,2216_2,00.html'st.ne.ni.prev, July 13, 1998; Dan Check, "The Case Against Microsoft;" http://ourworld.compuserve.com/homepages/spazz/mspaper.htm, Spring 1996; "Microsoft Antitrust Ruling," http://www.courttv.com/legaldocs/cyberlaw/mseruling.html, July 13, 1998; Bob Trott and David Pendery, "Allchin E-Mail Adds to Microsoft's Legal Woes"; Ted Bridis, "More Accusations Hit Microsoft," *Denver Post*, October 23, 1998, sec. B; Aaron Zitner, "Feds Assail Gates," *Denver Post*, October 30, 1998, sec. C; Julie Schmit, "Tech Industry's Direction Hangs in Balance," *USA Today*, October 16, 1998, 3B; and Eun-Kyung Kim, "Microsoft Court Gets Lesson on Monopolies," *Fort Collins Coloradoan*, November 20, 1998, B2; Richard B. McKenzie, *Trust on Trial: How the Microsoft Case Is Reframing the Rules of Competition* (Cambridge, MA: Perseus), 2000; Michael J. Martinez, "Microsoft Buys Time to Retool," *Fort Collins Coloradoan*, September 27, 2000, A1, A2; Robert O'Brien, "Kodak, Lexmark Lead Decline As Profit Warnings Hurt Stocks," *Wall Street Journal*, September 27, 2000, C2; Jared Sandberg, "Microsoft's Six Fatal Errors." *Newsweek*, June 19, 2000, 23–27; Paul Davidson, "Microsoft Split Ordered; Appeal Could Go Directly to Supreme Court," *USA Today*, June 8, 2000, A1; Jon Swartz, "Microsoft Split Ordered: Will Breakup Help or Hurt Consumers?" *USA Today*, June 8, 2000, A1, A2; Patrick McMahon, "Stoic Staffers Shake Heads, Return to Work," *USA Today*, June 8, 2000, B3; Edward Iwata and John Swartz, "Bill Gates Won't Be Dethroned So Easily; Software King—and His Myth—to Survive on Iron Will, Talent," *USA Today*, June 8, 2000, B3; Paul Davidson, "Microsoft Awaits a New Hand: Executives' Expert Appeals to Judges to Be More Amenable," *USA Today*, June 8, 2000, B1, B2; Jared Sandberg, "Bring On the Chopping Block," *Newsweek*, May 8, 2000, 34–35; Rebecca Buckman, "Go Figure: In Valuing a Split Microsoft, Analysts Offer a Wide Range of Numbers." *Wall Street Journal*, May 2, 2000, C1, C3; Rebecca Buckman, "Looking Through Microsoft's Window: On the Firm's Sprawling Campus, It's Almost Business as Usual as Talk of Breakup Brews," *Wall Street Journal*, May 1, 2000, B1, B10; Geri Coleman Tucker and Will Rodger, "Facing Breakup, Gates to Take Case to People: Microsoft Says Don't Punish Success," *USA Today*, May 1, 2000, B1, B2; Don Clark and Ted Bridis, "Creating Two Behemoths? Company Bets Appeals Court Will Overturn Jackson, Making Any Remedy Moot," *Wall Street Journal*, April 28, 2000, B1, B4. Lee Gomes and Rebecca Buckman, "Creating Two Behemoths? Microsoft Split Might Not Be Much Help for Competitors and Could Harm Consumer," *Wall Street Journal*, April 28, 2000, B1; Kevin Maney, "Microsoft's Uncertain Future Rattle Investors: Justice Must Make Recommendation, Breakup Possible," *USA Today*, April 25, 2000, B1; Bill Gates and Steve Ballmer, "To Our Customers, Partners and Shareholders," *USA Today*, April 5, 2000, B7; Paul Davidson, "Expert's View May Influence Ruling," *USA Today*, February 2, 2000, B1; Paul Davidson, "Microsoft Responds to Judge's Findings," *USA Today*, January 19, 2000, B1; "Survey Results; May 2000 Final Survey Results," http://e-businessethics.com/view_results.htm, September 8, 2000; "Java Contract Lawsuit Update," http://msdn.microsoft.com/visualj/lawsuitruling.asp, September 28, 2000; "Notice Regarding Java Lawsuit Ruling; Notice to Customers," http://msdn.microsoft.com/visualj/statement.asp, September 28, 2000; "New "Microsoft Connected Learning Community Program Fact Sheet," http://www.microsoft.com/PressPass/press/1999/May99/CLCFS.asp, September 28, 2000; "International Design for Office 2000," http://www.microsoft.com/Office/ORK/2000Journ/LangPack.htm, September 28, 2000; "Survey Results," http://e-businessethics.com/view_results.htm, September 28, 2000; "Java Contract Lawsuit Update," http://msdn.microsoft.com/visualj/lawsuitruling.asp, September 28, 2000; "Notice Regarding Java Lawsuit Ruling: Notice to Customers," http://msdn.microsoft.com/visualj/statement.asp, September 28, 2000; "New "Microsoft Connected Learning Community Program Fact Sheet," http://www.microsoft.com/PressPass/press/1999/May99/CLCFS.asp, September 28, 2000; "International Design for Office 2000," http://www.microsoft.com/Office/ORK/2000Journ/LangPack.htm, September 28, 2000; "Microsoft Files Summary Judgment Motions in Caldera Lawsuit: Technological 'Tying' and Incompatibility Issues Shown to Be Without Merit," http://www.microsoft.com/PressPass/press/1999/Feb99/Calderapr.asp, September 28, 2000.

Papa John's Pizza:
A Promotional Dilemma

"They can make me change my words, but they can't make me change the spirit of what I'm about and what Papa John's is about."

John H. Schnatter, Founder and CEO, Papa John's

John Schnatter, his corporate officers, and Papa John's advertising agency were facing a unique dilemma. At the beginning of 2001, they were waiting for a court to decide whether their "Better Ingredients, Better Pizza" slogan was deceptive in nature or just puffery. Now, after an appeals court ruling that the slogan is simple puffery, they must decide whether to continue using a successful slogan that stands for the philosophy of the company. Papa John's management and industry experts are still surprised by all of the legal wrangling over a slogan. Why would Pizza Hut, the number-one company in the market, attack the then-number-four company? This sort of attack by the number-one firm is unheard of in virtually any industry.

History of the Company

Now the third-largest pizza company in the United States, Papa John's began in humble surroundings. John H. Schnatter started Papa John's in 1984 in a broom closet in his dad's Jeffersonville, Indiana, tavern. After selling his prized 1972 Z28 Camaro, John purchased $1,600 worth of used restaurant equipment. In 1985, John opened the first Papa John's restaurant next door to the tavern. At the company's launching, John's mother derided John and his brother over the beginning of such a business: "The last thing this world needs is another pizza-maker and another lawyer. Why don't you guys do something else so you'll be successful?" John's brother, Chuck, had been accepted into law school at the same time John launched his pizza kingdom.

The desire to enter the pizza market began for John several years prior to the opening of his first establishment. As a teenager, he had worked in a small sandwich shop. After watching others make and bake pizzas, John fell in love with the product. He successfully convinced the shop's owner to promote him to pizza-maker—a job he used to develop his trade and put himself through college. It was from these

---

This case was prepared by Keith C. Jones, Lynchburg College in Virginia, for classroom discussion rather than to illustrate either effective or ineffective handling of an administrative situation.

experiences that John developed the company strategy that would make him and his company successful: Make a better-tasting pizza, make it well, and please the customer. A high-quality product remains the focus of the company today.

A Record of Phenomenal Growth

Papa John's growth from a single store in 1985 to the 2,500 stores of today occurred in stages. In 1993, Schnatter took his 300-store company public with the first stock offering. A second stock offering occurred one year later when the company hit the 400-store mark. Between these two offerings, the company received $40.4 million.

Papa John's most aggressive growth period began in 1999. Schnatter planned to open 400 new stores that year, of which 365 would be franchised. The company maintains an ownership mix of at least 75 percent franchised stores and 25 percent company-owned stores. In April 1999, Papa John's acquired the 37 stores of Minnesota Pizza Company. This allowed the company to expand into a geographical area where it had no previous representation. To assist in capturing the full market in that area, the company planned to open an additional 10–12 stores over the two years following the acquisition.

Later in 1999, Papa John's announced their entrance into the European market with the purchase of Perfect Pizza Holdings Ltd. Europe has been deemed one of the biggest opportunities in the world for U.S.-based fast food restaurants. While per capita spending on fast food in Europe pales in comparison to that in the United States—$63.50 vs. $376.23 U.S. dollars—the European market is growing rapidly. This was not Papa John's first endeavor into international markets. The company already had a 23-store presence in Latin America and other international markets. Perfect Pizza's 205 units (190 franchised/15 corporate stores) became the company's largest acquisition. The plan was to slowly convert the stores to Papa John's while maintaining both the client base and the current management team.

Overall, this period of sustained growth had been very good for the company. Papa John's reported revenues of $224.8 million in 2000, an increase of 11 percent over the previous year. Corporate earnings also increased by 18 percent to $88 million. In terms of same-store comparisons, 2000 resulted in a 0.6 percent increase in sales—the thirtieth consecutive quarter of sales increases. Interestingly, company-owned stores were responsible for this growth; franchised stores reported no sales growth during 2000. Also in 2000, the company signed a deal to open 200 units in the Middle East over the next ten years. Success in the Middle Eastern market is not certain and will not be realized for some time. Papa John's growth plans for 2001 included opening 340–360 new restaurants, increasing systemwide comparable sales by 1–3 percent, and increasing earnings per share to $2.40–$2.50.

The Pizza Industry

Through its planned expansions and aggressiveness in the market, Papa John's moved up to third place in the $25 billion U.S. pizza market. Most of this growth came at the expense of Pizza Hut, whose market share had fallen by 3.2 percent from 1999 to 2000. The relative sizes of major competitors in the pizza industry are shown in Case Exhibit 8.1.

CASE EXHIBIT 8.1	MAJOR COMPETITORS IN THE PIZZA INDUSTRY

	Store Units	U.S. Sales (billions)	Top-Seven Market Share	Overall Industry Market Share
Pizza Hut	8,000	$5.0	44.0%	22.0%
Domino's Pizza	4,629	$2.6	22.5%	11.0%
Papa John's	2,254	$1.4	12.6%	7.0%
Little Caesar's	3,950	$1.2	10.6%	5.0%

Source: "Pizza Power Grab: Papa John's Seizes Third Place from Little Caesar's," *Nation's Restaurant News* 34 (June 2000), 104–108.

One of the growing competitors in the market is a company called Papa Murphy's, which specializes in the take-and-bake pizza market. With over 500 locations, sales of $250 million, and planned expansion into 200 locations, Papa Murphy's is a competitor the industry is watching closely. Why? Simply, no one would have predicted Papa John's phenomenal growth or Pizza Hut's concern over a company that it beats 3-to-1 in market share.

Beginning of the Advertising Battle

Papa John's actually fired the first shot in the advertising battle with Pizza Hut. At the time, Papa John's was the fourth-largest company in the pizza industry. In early 1997, Papa John's debuted its first national advertising campaign, in which company "founders" John Schnatter and Frank Carney of Pizza Hut starred in the ads. The main theme of the campaign was that Carney had moved to the better pizza company. Then Papa John's introduced its second national campaign, "Better Ingredients, Better Pizza." To Papa John's, this theme was more than just an advertising slogan; it was the founding motto of the company, one that appeared on pizza boxes, uniforms, neon window signs, car toppers, and all other materials carrying the Papa John's logo. In the advertising campaign, Papa John's specifically mentioned that it uses a fresher sauce and fresher dough than Pizza Hut.

Pizza Hut returned the volley in two ways. One was with its own television advertising campaign. In a limited number of markets, Pizza Hut aired an ad that incorporated a clip from Papa John's ads—the first time ever that a competitor's ad was used within a company's own advertising. The Pizza Hut advertisement attacked John Schnatter's "better ingredients" claim, pointing out that the "freshness" claim was not a true representation of the practices of Papa John's. Then Papa John's attacked Pizza Hut's strategy by producing an ad showing a Pizza Hut employee trying to hit a punching bag and missing. Apparently, it was this counterresponse by Papa John's that incited Pizza Hut to full action.

Pizza Hut placed an advertisement in Papa John's hometown market of Louisville, in the *Louisville Courier-Journal*, with the headline "Mudslinging. Cheap Shots. Misinformation. Hey John, This Is Pizza, Not Politics." In this ad, Pizza Hut pointed out some of the purported fallacies of Papa John's accusations: All tomatoes are vine ripened, and both sauces come from a concentrate process. One week later Papa John's returned the volley with an ad in the same paper in which Papa John's listed the ingredients of both Papa John's and Pizza Hut's sauces. While Papa John's sauce had fewer than ten ingredients, there were over 20 listed for Pizza Hut's sauce. This advertisement was a continuation of the claim of better ingredients, showing what makes Papa John's a better pizza.

The Court Battle

Following industry protocol, Pizza Hut started its legal battle by appealing to the National Advertising Division (NAD) of the Council of the Better Business Bureau. The NAD ruled that Papa John's advertisements were not misleading and that the company could continue to use them. Not accepting these findings, Pizza Hut filed a lawsuit in a Dallas district court. At the same time, Papa John's filed suit against Pizza Hut for its retaliatory advertisements. Papa John's claimed that Pizza Hut's use of a clip from Papa John's ad portrayed Schnatter as dishonest and misled consumers about the fresh dough and the dough-making process.

In November 1999, a federal jury handed down verdicts finding both parties guilty. The jury concluded that the advertisement aired by Papa John's was false and misleading. The jury also found Pizza Hut guilty of false and misleading actions because of their retaliatory advertisements. In early January 2000, the federal judge ruled that Papa John's owed Pizza Hut $468,000 in damages and that Papa John's had to abandon its "Better Ingredients, Better Pizza" slogan. United States Magistrate William E. Sanderson, Jr., gave Papa John's three weeks to stop using the slogan and until March 3 to discontinue it on delivery boxes and other materials. All signs were to be redesigned by April 3. Finally, Sanderson barred Papa John's from using the word "better" to describe its pizza and forbade the company from running ads in which it compared itself to Pizza Hut. At the same time, Sanderson barred Pizza Hut from airing advertisements that claimed its pizza was better than Papa John's without substantiating evidence for the claim.

The court in its finding recognized a difference between puffery through simply stating a product is best or better and that of false and misleading ads. The key point of distinction appeared to be the specific identification and incorporation of Pizza Hut and its product in the ads. Apparently, the court believed that Papa John's had overstepped practicality and had inflicted damage on Pizza Hut. Pizza Hut felt fully vindicated based on the findings of the court.

The Consumer Perspective: Is Papa John's Really Better?

One of the reasons the court found in favor of Pizza Hut was the lack of evidence to substantiate Papa John's claim. Papa John's provided the court with no appropriate evidence to prove that they had a better pizza because of better ingredients. Following the findings of the court, the National Quality Research Center at the University of Michigan included in its satisfaction index research questions pertaining to Papa John's product. In its American Customer Satisfaction Index, the research center found that Papa John's finished above the national average of all industries, ahead of even McDonald's, Wendy's, and KFC. As shown in Case Exhibit 8.2, Papa John's scored eight points above the closest pizza competitor.

Likewise, in the Twentieth Annual Restaurants and Institutions' Choice in Chains Survey, Papa John's captured the top overall rating and surpassed its closest pizza

CASE EXHIBIT 8.2 **RESULTS OF THE AMERICAN CUSTOMER SATISFACTION INDEX**

Fast Food Restaurants	Satisfaction Score
Papa John's	76
Wendy's	71
Group Average	**69**
Pizza Hut	68
Domino's Pizza	67
Burger King	66
KFC	64
Taco Bell	64
McDonald's	61

Source: The American Customer Satisfaction Index, National Quality Research Center at the University of Michigan (in partnership with The American Society for Quality), as reported in the *Wall Street Journal*, February 22, 2000. Based on 12,500 telephone surveys completed during the fourth quarter of 1999; out of a possible score of 100.

CASE EXHIBIT 8.3 **YEAR 2000 R&I CHOICE IN CHAINS RESULTS, PIZZA CATEGORY**

	Overall Score	Food Quality	Value	Service	Cleanliness
Papa John's	36	56	38	37	33
Pizza Hut	35	54	29	31	29
Domino's Pizza	32	42	33	33	27

Source: 2000 R&I Choice in Chains Survey results as reported in *Restaurants and Institutions*, March 1, 2000. Based on 2,818 mail survey responses completed during the fourth quarter of 1999. Scores represent the percentage of respondents who rated the chain "excellent" or "above average" for each respective attribute.

rivals in all areas (see Case Exhibit 8.3). This was the fourth year in a row that Papa John's had captured this title. Prior to the inclusion of Papa John's in the survey, Pizza Hut had been the recipient of this recognition. However, it lost its title the first year Papa John's was added to the survey.

Clearly, both surveys reveal that the claims made by Papa John's could have been substantiated. However, since this information was not presented to the court, the jury ruled in favor of Pizza Hut.

The Appellate Court

Papa John's was not going down without a battle. Standing on its company's founding beliefs that it had a better-quality pizza, Papa John's appealed the Dallas federal court ruling. Not only did Papa John's believe that the court's findings were inappropriate, the advertising industry was also concerned. The potential impact on the advertising industry was monumental. The findings would bring greater scrutiny of claims made in advertisements that were normally seen as simple puffery. This would require future claims to be substantiated by scientific facts or through other forms of research.

In September 2000, the appellate court handed down its ruling, with a twist. While the appellate court found that some of Papa John's ads were misleading, the court did not find the ads as being detrimental to Pizza Hut. The appellate court ruled that Pizza Hut had not established that the slogan had the tendency to deceive consumers to the point that it influenced the buying decision. Therefore, the three-judge panel ruled that Papa John's could continue to use the slogan and that it did not have to pay Pizza Hut the $468,000 in damages. This was a major relief to John Schnatter and Papa John's. Following the lower court ruling, Papa John's had estimated the cost of changing the slogan to be $5 million. To establish the current slogan it had cost Papa John's over $300 million.

Now Papa John's is waiting to see what Pizza Hut's next move will be. Pizza Hut can appeal the appellate court decision to the U.S. Supreme Court. If the Supreme Court hears the case, it could reverse the appellate court ruling and reinstate the lower court ruling. John Schnatter and his group have a decision to make: Should they continue to use their successful slogan, or should the company develop a new slogan? If the Supreme Court does not hear the case, they can continue to use the slogan they have spent years developing. If the Supreme Court hears the case, Papa John's runs the risk of losing its slogan and being forced to pay damages to Pizza Hut.

Questions for Discussion

1. Why would Pizza Hut be so concerned about Papa John's and not about Domino's Pizza?

2. Regardless of who ultimately wins the court fight, what effect has the battle had on both Papa John's and Pizza Hut?

3. Papa John's estimates that it would cost $5 million to change its slogan. This figure includes simple development and replacement costs for the logo, signs, and other materials. What are some of the intangible costs that would be associated with replacing the slogan?

4. Other than dropping its slogan and having to pay damages to Pizza Hut, what does Papa John's stand to lose if it ultimately loses the court battle?

Sources

The facts of the case are from "Papa John's Announces 2001 Growth Plans," pjweb02.com/pressrel.nsf/, December 4, 2000; "Papa John's Reports Record Third Quarter Earnings and Revenues," pjweb02.papajohns.com/presrel.nf, December 4, 2000; "Papa John's Wins Two Major National Customer Satisfaction Surveys," pjweb02.papajohns.com/Pressrel.nsf, December 4, 2000; "The Papa John's Story," www.papajohns.com/pj_story/index.htm, December 4, 2000; Carol Casper, "Uncommon Market," *Restaurant Business* 99 (February 2000), 55–58; Greg Cebrzynski, "Judge Orders Papa John's to Change Ad, Pay Fine," *Nation's Restaurant News* 34 (January 2000), 1, 65; Greg Cebrzynski, "Pizza Power Grab: Papa John's Seizes Third Place from Little Caesar's," *Nation's Restaurant News* 34 (June 2000), 104–108; J. Dee Hill, "Papa John's Seeking a New Tag After Court Fight," *Adweek* 20 (November 1999), 2; Jacqueline Kochak, "Pie Chart," *Restaurant Business* 98 (November 1999), 49, 66; Ron Ruggless, "John Schnatter: Mom Never Thought There'd Be Days Like This, But Papa John's CEO Is Rolling in Dough," *Nation's Restaurant News* 34 (January 2000), 158–160; Amy Zuber, "Pizza Hut, Papa John's Wages War over Quality," *Nation's Restaurant News* 32 (April 1998), 3, 67; Amy Zuber, "Pizza Hut-vs.-Papa John's Battle Signals Intensifying War Among Segment Leaders," *Nation's Restaurant News* 32 (June 1998), 114–120; Amy Zuber, "Papa John's Acquires Minnesota Pizza Co.," *Nation's Restaurant News* 33 (April 1999), 4, 91; Amy Zuber, "Papa John's European Expansion to Mushroom via Perfect Pizza Buy," *Nation's Restaurant News* 33 (December 1999), 8; and Amy Zuber, "Pizza Hut Weighs Appeal after Reversal of Papa John's Ad Ban," *Nation's Restaurant News* 34 (October 2000), 6–8.

Sunbeam and "Chainsaw Al"

Introduction

When John Stewart and Thomas Clark founded the Chicago Flexible Shaft Company in Dundee, Illinois, in 1897, they probably never expected the company would be facing ethical and financial dilemmas more than a century later. Like many corporations, the firm has experienced changes and faced many crises. It has acquired rival companies, added totally new product lines, changed its name, gone through bankruptcy, gone public, rebounded, restructured, relocated, and hired and fired many CEOs, including "Chainsaw Al," who contributed to its latest crisis.

Sunbeam: 100+ Years of Change

Sunbeam is a well-known and recognized designer, manufacturer, and marketer of consumer products, both nationally and internationally. Sunbeam products are considered household staple items and are known for their use in cooking, health care, and personal care. Over its 100 years of operation, Sunbeam has grown and changed according to societal needs. It operates facilities in Canada, England, Hong Kong, Mexico, the United States, and Venezuela. A few of the most recognized brand names Sunbeam markets today include: Coleman (the acquisition of The Coleman Company, Inc., was completed when it became a wholly owned subsidiary of Sunbeam Corporation on January 6, 2000), First Alert, Grillmaster, Health-O-Meter, Mixmaster, Mr. Coffee, Oster, Osterizer, Powermate, and Campingaz. On May 30, 2000, Sunbeam Corporation sold its Eastpak-branded business to VF Corporation.

The first products that the company manufactured and sold over 100 years ago were agricultural tools. In 1910 they began manufacturing electrical appliances, one of the first being a clothes iron. Sunbeam's electronic products were extremely popular even during the Great Depression. The launch of the Sunbeam Mixmaster, automatic coffee maker, and pop-up toaster were warmly received by householders throughout the country.

This case was prepared by Carol A. Rustad and Linda E. Rustad for classroom discussion rather than to illustrate either effective or ineffective handling of an administrative, ethical, or legal decision by management.

Although the name was not officially changed to Sunbeam Corporation until 1946, Stewart and Clark adopted the name Sunbeam and started using it in their advertising campaigns in 1910. The next fourteen years was a time of growth and innovation; the United States' economy was stable and businesses were booming. Sunbeam acquired a rival appliance maker, the John Oster Manufacturing Company, in 1960. That acquisition helped make Sunbeam the leading manufacturer of electric appliances.

The 1980s were a time of high inflation and high interest rates, recovery from the Vietnam War, and corporate acquisitions, mergers, closings, and restructurings—companies were doing whatever they could to continue to operate profitably. In 1981, Allegheny International, an industry conglomerate, acquired Sunbeam. Allegheny kept the Sunbeam name and added John Zink (air-pollution control devices) and Hanson Scale (bathroom scales) to the Sunbeam product line. In 1988, sales of other divisions of Allegheny International declined, and, coupled with the changing times of the 1980s, the company was forced into bankruptcy.

Investors Michael Price, Michael Steinhardt, and Paul Kazarian bought the Sunbeam division from Allegheny International's creditors in 1990. They renamed it the Sunbeam-Oster Company. Two years later, they took Sunbeam-Oster public. Kazarian was forced out of the company a year after that, and at that same time Sunbeam-Oster relocated to Florida. It also purchased the consumer products unit of DeVilbiss Health Care and, a year later, bought Rubbermaid's outdoor furniture business. In 1995, the company changed its name back to Sunbeam Corporation.

Albert Dunlap, a.k.a. "Chainsaw Al"

In June 1996 Sunbeam had more than 12,000 stock-keeping units (SKUs). SKUs are individual variations of product lines: every different style or color of a product results in an item having a different SKU. Sunbeam also had 12,000 employees as well as twenty-six factories worldwide, sixty-one warehouses, and six headquarters. That was the situation when "Chainsaw Al"—Albert Dunlap—came into the picture.

Also known as "Rambo in Pinstripes" or "The Shredder," Dunlap gained his reputation as one of the country's toughest executives because he willfully eliminated thousands of jobs. Dunlap is the antithesis of the warm-hearted capitalist. Throughout the 1980s and 1990s, Chainsaw Al became, after Bill Gates, the most highly publicized executive in the United States. He was known for his ability to restructure and turn around companies that were failing financially. Sunbeam Corporation needed help. Its earnings had been declining rapidly since December 1994, and by 1996 the stock was down 52 percent and earnings had declined by 83 percent.

Dunlap's reputation and business theory preceded him throughout the world. His operating philosophy was to make extreme cuts in all areas of operations, including massive layoffs, to streamline business. The concepts of teamwork and group dynamics seemed to be foreign to Dunlap. He operated as if people are dispensable and fired them if they cost more than he felt they were worth. Dunlap even authored a book, *Mean Business*, in which he stated that making money for shareholders is the most important goal of any business. His philosophy was deficient with regard to ethical responsibility. Shareholder wealth, at any cost, was his only goal.

In order to make money for shareholders, Dunlap created and followed four rules of business: (1) Get the right management team, (2) cut back to the lowest costs,

(3) focus on the core business, and (4) get a real strategy. In following those four rules, Dunlap helped turn around companies in seventeen states and across three continents. According to Dunlap in the Preface to his book *Mean Business*, the list of companies he has worked with, prior to accepting the position at Sunbeam, includes Sterling Pulp & Paper (1967–77), American Can (1977–82), Lily-Tulip (1983–86), Diamond International, Canenham Forest Industries (formerly Crown-Zellerbach) (1986–89), Australian National Industries (1989), Consolidated Press Holdings (1991–91), and Scott Paper Company (1994–95).

Rule One: Get the Right Management Team

In July of 1996, Michael Price and Michael Steinhardt hired Dunlap as the CEO and chairman of the board for Sunbeam Corporation. As two of the original investors who bought Sunbeam from bankrupt Allegheny International, Price and Steinhardt together own 42 percent of its stock. Prior to hiring Dunlap, they had tried, unsuccessfully, to sell Sunbeam. The failure to sell made them decide to see if Dunlap could save Sunbeam and halt the declining stock and profits. Dunlap followed his four rules in trying to turn around the Sunbeam Corporation.

By hiring Chainsaw Al, Price and Steinhardt knew full well that his reputation and operating theory would mean huge cuts in all areas of the company as well as extensive layoffs. They believed that he was the one person who could turn the company around and increase stock prices and profits. The increase in stock prices did occur, almost instantly. On July 19, 1996, the day Dunlap was named chairman and CEO of Sunbeam, the stock jumped 49 percent. The jump increased the share price from $12\frac{1}{2}$ to $18\frac{5}{8}$, adding $500 million to Sunbeam's market value. During Dunlap's tenure the stock continued to increase, reaching a record high of $52 per share in March 1998.

Dunlap's reputation and acceptance of the position at Sunbeam are what caused the initial stock increase. However, Dunlap realized that his reputation alone would not hold the stock price and that he needed to start the process of turning Sunbeam around. His initial move was to work on the first step of his four simple rules of business: Get the right management team.

His very first hire was Russ Kersh, a former employee. A contract was written over a weekend so Kersh could start the same day as Dunlap, as executive vice president of finance and administration. In his book *Mean Business*, Dunlap called the right management team his "Dream Team for Sunbeam." Only one senior executive was retained from the old management team at Sunbeam. The new management team created for the Sunbeam turnaround included Kersh and twenty-five people who had previously worked for Dunlap at various companies. Dunlap saw logic in hiring these people because they had all worked with him and had been successful in past turnarounds. Once the first step had been accomplished, Dunlap and the Dream Team for Sunbeam quickly went into action implementing the second rule: Cut back to the lowest costs.

Rule Two: Cut Back to the Lowest Costs

All of the employees at Sunbeam knew of Dunlap's reputation for ruthlessly eliminating jobs. True to his reputation, one of the first areas for cutting costs was in payroll. According to Dunlap (*Mean Business*, p. 283): "Sunbeam's employees wanted a leader and knew things had to change. Employees want stability. Restructuring actually brings stability, because the future is more clear." What people want and need, many could argue, is job security, and knowing his reputation did not make the employees feel secure.

The premise of wanting and needing security relates to psychologist Abraham Maslow's hierarchy of needs, theorizing what motivates employees to perform. The theory states that all people have five basic needs and strive to satisfy those needs in a hierarchical manner. These needs can be satisfied through various means, but each need must be met before a person will move to the next level in the hierarchy. Security needs, second in the hierarchy of needs to be satisfied, relate to protecting oneself from physical and economic harm. The employees' security needs were being threatened and economic harm was about to occur for many of the employees at Sunbeam. Then-Labor Secretary Robert Reich remarked upon hearing Dunlap's layoff plans: "There is no excuse for treating employees as if they are disposable pieces of equipment" (*Chainsaw*, p. 68).

As expected, and true to Dunlap's reputation, layoffs occurred. After less than four months as chairman and CEO of Sunbeam, Chainsaw Al announced plans to eliminate half of the 12,000 worldwide employees. Layoffs affected all levels of Sunbeam's employees. Management and clerical staff positions were cut from 1,529 to 697 and headquarters staff was cut by 60 percent, from 308 to 123 employees. It was around the same time that the share price rose to the mid-$20s and one of the original investors, Michael Steinhardt, sold his shares and divested himself of his Sunbeam connection altogether.

Another method used by Dunlap to cut back to the lowest costs was to reduce the number of SKUs, by approximately 87%—from 12,000 to 1,500. When Dunlap first took the position at Sunbeam, it had thirty-six variations of styles and colors of a clothes iron! Variation allows for differentiation, which is an acceptable strategy in business, but having thirty-six variations of a consumer product such as an iron is unnecessary and costly. Eliminating variation and duplication helps eliminate cannibalization. Companies need to differentiate themselves from the competition in areas that are not easily duplicated, or they end up competing on price alone. Dunlap pursued service as the area to differentiate Sunbeam from competitors in the appliance business.

The elimination of 10,500 SKUs enabled Dunlap to eliminate unneeded factories and warehouses, which was another cost-saving method. He eliminated eighteen factories, moving from twenty-six to eight worldwide, and reduced the number of warehouses from sixty-one to eighteen. The layoff of the thousands of employees, coupled with the reduction of SKUs, factories, and warehouses, made it possible to reduce the number of headquarters. The six headquarters located throughout the country were consolidated into one facility in Delray Beach, Florida—Dunlap's primary residence. After the cost-cutting strategies had been identified, the third step of Dunlap's four simple rules began.

Rule Three: Focus on the Core Business

The third rule was to focus on Sunbeam's core business, which first needed to be defined. Dunlap and his Dream Team for Sunbeam defined the core business as electric appliances and appliance-related businesses. Five categories surrounding the core business were identified as vital to Sunbeam's success: kitchen appliances, health and home, outdoor cooking, personal care and comfort, and professional products. All products that did not fit into one of these five categories were sold. The criterion Dunlap used to decide whether to keep or sell a product line was simple and straightforward. He firmly believed that the Sunbeam name was one that consumers fondly recall. His criterion then was the answer to the simple question: Does the Sunbeam name relate to the product, or does the product relate to Sunbeam? Only those products that clearly related to Sunbeam were kept. Identifying Sunbeam's core business and paring down to that core was the goal in implementing the third rule.

Rule Four: Get a Real Strategy

The final of Dunlap's four simple rules of business is to get a real strategy. Dunlap and his team defined Sunbeam's strategy as driving the growth of the company through core business expansion by further differentiating products, moving into new geographic areas around the globe, and introducing new products linked directly to emerging customer trends as lifestyles evolve around the world. The first step in implementing the strategy was to reengineer the electrical appliances to 220 volts so they could be used and sold internationally. Reclaiming the differentiation between the Oster and Sunbeam lines was also one of the strategies. Each was designed, packaged, and advertised to target different markets. Oster products were positioned as upscale, higher-end brands and sold through completely different retailers than the Sunbeam line, which was positioned as affordable and for the middle class. In the beginning of 1997, ten Sunbeam factory outlet stores were opened to help increase brand awareness, sales, and ultimately shareholder wealth. Dunlap made all these changes within seven months of his taking the challenge to turn around Sunbeam. The stock rose to over $48 per share, a 284 percent increase since July 1996.

The Turnaround of Sunbeam

In October 1997, just 15 months after accepting the position as chairman and CEO, Dunlap issued a press release stating the turnaround was complete. He also announced that Morgan Stanley of Stanley Dean Witter & Co. had been hired to find a buyer for Sunbeam. According to John A. Byrne in his book *Chainsaw*, "No one was the least bit interested" (p 190). He also wrote that Dunlap misled a journalist into reporting that Philips, a Dutch electronics giant, was interested in purchasing Sunbeam for the $50+ per share the stock was trading at, but Dunlap wanted $70.

Unable to get the price he wanted, Dunlap decided to invest by purchasing companies. He did this to increase the value of Sunbeam stock and to increase revenues. On March 2, 1998, Dunlap announced plans to purchase three consumer products companies. Sunbeam acquired 82 percent of Coleman (camping gear) from Ronald Perelman for $2.2 billion. Perelman received a combination of stock and cash, giving him 14 percent ownership of Sunbeam. The other two purchases were from Thomas Lee for Signature Brands (Mr. Coffee) and First Alert (smoke and gas alarms). Lee was paid $425 million in cash, in return for which Sunbeam gained 95.7 percent control of First Alert and 98.5 percent control of Signature Brands. Two days after these purchases were announced, Sunbeam's stock jumped to a record high of $52 a share.

With share prices the highest they had ever been and 1997 net income reported at $109.4 million, Sunbeam truly seemed to be turned around—at least on paper.

Dunlap publicly praised himself and his Dream Team for Sunbeam for turning around the failing company within seven months of taking over. He was so confident in the success of their mission at Sunbeam that he added an entire new chapter to his book, *Mean Business*, detailing the turnaround. The chapter, "Now There's a Bright Idea. Lesson: Everything You've Read So Far about Restructuring Works. This Chapter Proves It—Again," demonstrates, in addition to his arrogance, his confidence in his belief that Sunbeam had been turned around because of him. Dunlap stated that Kersh and a dozen other people had tried to dissuade him from taking the position at Sunbeam because they thought that not even he could save the company. Dunlap disagreed, stating that where others see the impossible, he sees opportunity.

In the same chapter, Dunlap wrote that the tremendous media attention given to the first edition of *Mean Business* provided an unofficial handbook for Sunbeam employees as well as free publicity for the company. He also mentioned that he did not need to take the position at Sunbeam or with any other company because he is rich. A whole section of the chapter recalls how the media arrived in full force to cover the promotional tour and signing of his book. Dunlap also mentioned how absolute strangers, including a Greek Orthodox cleric, praised him and his book. An additional paragraph mentioned that he was on top of the most admired CEOs in a survey of business students at U.S. colleges and universities. The concluding paragraph of the chapter summarized Dunlap's high opinion of himself. It suggested that all CEOs and boards of directors should read his book and run their companies by using him as their role model.

In between the self-praise, *Mean Business* undoubtedly explained Dunlap's philosophy well. At that time, according to his philosophy and reputation, Chainsaw Al succeeded at Sunbeam. He fired thousands of employees, shut down factories and warehouses, and streamlined the company by eliminating 10,500 SKUs and selling businesses unrelated to its core products. He even attained what he considers the most important goal of any business and made money for the shareholders. In February 1998, the board of directors was satisfied with Dunlap's leadership and signed a three-year employment contract with him that included 3.75 million shares of stock.

Questions Regarding "Chainsaw Al's" Accounting Practices

Dunlap accomplished what he set out to do at Sunbeam, but the shareholder wealth did not last, nor did the board's satisfaction. Sunbeam is again facing rough times, but not because costs are too high or because of lack of strategy. The three purchases that more than doubled Sunbeam's size and helped push its price per share to $52 quickly caused upheaval and another restructuring of Sunbeam. Soon after the purchases, rumors began emerging that they were made to disguise losses through write-offs.

Paine Webber Inc. analyst Andrew Shore had been following Sunbeam since the day Dunlap was hired. As an analyst, Shore's job was to make educated guesses about investing clients' money in stocks. Shore had been scrutinizing Sunbeam's financial statements every quarter and considered its reported levels of inventory for certain items to be high for the time of year. He noted massive increases in sales of electric blankets in the third quarter, which usually sell well in the fourth quarter. He also found it odd that sales of grills were high in the fourth quarter, an unusual time of year for grills to be sold, and noted that accounts receivable were high. On April 3, 1998, hours before Sunbeam announced a first-quarter loss of $44.6 million, Shore downgraded the stock. By the end of the day Sunbeam's stock price had fallen 25 percent.

Shore's findings were indeed cause for concern regarding the price of the stock. In fact, Dunlap had been using a "bill and hold" strategy with retailers, which boosted Sunbeam's revenue, at least on the balance sheet. A "bill and hold" strategy involves selling products for large discounts to retailers and holding them in third-party warehouses to be delivered at a later date. In essence, the strategy shifts sales from future quarters to the current one. By booking sales months prior to the actual shipment or billing, Sunbeam was able to report higher revenues in the form of accounts receivable, which inflated its quarterly earnings. In 1997, the strategy helped Dunlap boost Sunbeam's revenues by 18 percent.

A "bill and hold" strategy is not illegal and follows the General Accepted Accounting Principals (GAAP) of financial reporting. Nevertheless, shareholders felt the company had deceived them so that they would purchase Sunbeam's artificially inflated stock. Several decided to file lawsuits alleging that the company made misleading statements about its finances. A class-action lawsuit was filed on April 23, 1998, naming both Sunbeam and CEO Albert Dunlap as defendants. The lawsuit alleged that Sunbeam and Dunlap violated the Securities Exchange Act of 1934 by misrepresenting and/or omitting material information concerning the business operations, sales, and sales trends of the company. The lawsuit also charged that the price of the common stock was artificially inflated so that Sunbeam could secure hundreds of millions of dollars of debt financing to complete the mergers with Coleman, First Alert, and Signature Brands. Sunbeam's subsequent reporting of earnings significantly below the original estimate caused a huge drop in the stock. A Web site at http://defrauded.com/sunbeam.html provided information about the lawsuits and financial damage to stockholders due to the alleged deception.

Dunlap continued to run Sunbeam and the newly purchased companies as if nothing had happened. On May 11, 1998, Dunlap tried to reassure 200 major investors and Wall Street analysts that the first-quarter loss was behind them and that Sunbeam would post increased earnings in the second quarter. That same day he tried to regain public confidence and divert attention from the losses and lawsuits by announcing another 5,100 layoffs at Sunbeam and the acquired companies. The tactic did not work. The press continued to report on the "bill and hold" strategy and accounting practices Dunlap used to artificially inflate revenues and profits.

Chainsaw Al's Reputation Backfires

Dunlap called an impromptu board meeting on June 9, 1998, to address and rebut the reported charges. A partner of Sunbeam's outside auditors, Arthur Anderson LLP, assured the board that the company's 1997 numbers were in compliance with accounting standards and firmly stood by the firm's audit of Sunbeam's books. Robert J. Gluck, the controller at Sunbeam, was also present and did not counter the auditor's statement. The meeting seemed to be going well until Dunlap was asked if the company was going to make its projected second-quarter earnings. His response that "sales are soft" was not what the board expected to hear, nor was his statement that he had a document in his briefcase outlining a settlement of his contract for his departure from Sunbeam. The document was never reviewed. However, Dunlap's behavior aroused board members' suspicions, which led to an in-depth review of Dunlap's practices.

The review took place over the next four days in the form of personal phone calls and interviews between the board members and select employees—unbeknownst to Dunlap. A personal conversation with Sunbeam's executive vice president, David Fannin, revealed that the 1998 second-quarter sales were considerably below Dunlap's forecast and that the company was in crisis. Dunlap had forecast a small increase, yet the numbers that Fannin revealed showed that Sunbeam could lose as much as $60 million that quarter. Outside the boardroom and away from Dunlap, controller Robert J. Gluck revealed that they had tried to do things in accordance to GAAP, but everything had been pushed to the limit.

These revelations caused the board of directors to call their own emergency meeting. On June 13, 1998, the board of directors, Fannin, and a pair of lawyers discussed the informal findings. They agreed that their confidence in Dunlap and his ability to turnaround Sunbeam was lost. The board of directors unanimously agreed that Dunlap had to go and drafted a letter stating his immediate departure would be necessary. Chainsaw Al was told that same day, in a one-minute conference call, that he was the next person to be cut at Sunbeam.

Sunbeam Looks Forward

Once again, Sunbeam faced a need to revitalize the organization, but the challenges had a different focus this time. The company once again was looking for a CEO. The stock price had dropped as low as $10 per share. There were the shareholder lawsuits, legal action regarding Dunlap's firing, the Securities and Exchange Commission's scrutiny of Sunbeam's accounting practices, the Board of Directors Audit Committee's requirement that Sunbeam restate the audited financial statements for 1997, possibly 1996, and the first quarter of 1998, and creditors' demands for payment in full. Additionally, on August 24, 1998, Sunbeam announced that it would discontinue a quarterly dividend of $0.01 per share. Shareholder confidence was at an all-time low.

Less than two years after Dunlap was hired, Sunbeam was again announcing a new organizational structure and senior management team. Jerry W. Levin accepted the position of president and CEO. He outlined a new strategy for Sunbeam focusing on growth. The plan is to decentralize operations while maintaining centralized support and organizing into three operating groups. Four of the eight plants that were scheduled to be closed under Dunlap's management remained open to ensure consistency of supply. Sunbeam's focus is now on consumers. The company's goal is on growth through increased quality of products and customer service.

Late in 1998, in a press release, Levin outlined his strategy for revitalizing Sunbeam:

> Although we still have much to do in the short term to stabilize Sunbeam's businesses, our strategic focus is on growth. With some of the most powerful brand names in consumer durables, we will focus on our consumers. We are now conducting consumer research which should have a significant impact on our rate of new product introductions in the second half of 1999.

In contrast to the prior management's approach, we are decentralizing operations while maintaining centralized support. Our goal is to increase accountability at the business unit level, and to give our employees the tools they need to build their businesses. We are shifting Sunbeam's focus to increasing quality in products and customer service.

Regarding the shareholder lawsuits, on October 21, 1998, Sunbeam announced that it signed a memorandum of understanding to settle, subject to court approval, the class-action lawsuit brought by public shareholders of The Coleman Company, Inc. The court did approve the memorandum, and on January 6, 2000, Sunbeam completed the acquisition of the publicly held shares of Coleman. The terms of the merger allowed all public stockholders of Coleman to receive $6.44 in cash, 0.5677 of a share of Sunbeam common stock and 0.381 of a warrant to purchase one share of Sunbeam common stock for each of their shares of Coleman stock.

There were indeed legal ramifications regarding Dunlap's firing. Dunlap stated in an interview on July 9, 1998, that he intended to challenge Sunbeam's efforts to deny him severance under his contract, although both Dunlap and Sunbeam agreed not to take legal action against each other for a period of six months. Dunlap claimed that his mission was aborted prematurely and that he was fired without being given a reason three days after receiving the Board of Directors' support. On March 15, 1999, Dunlap filed an arbitration claim against Sunbeam for $5.5 million in unpaid salary, $58,000 worth of accrued vacation, and $150,000 in benefits, as well as to have his stock options repriced at $7 a share. Additionally, he sued the company for dragging their feet in reimbursing him for more than $1.4 million in legal and accounting fees racked up in defending himself in lawsuits that alleged securities fraud. The board made it clear they had no intention of paying Dunlap any more money, but a judge ruled in his favor in June of 1999 (*Chainsaw*, p. 347).

In a letter to shareholders posted at the beginning of 1999, Levin stated that Sunbeam went back to basics and intensified its focus on its powerful family of brands. He also wrote that the lending banks extended covenant relief and waivers of past defaults until April 10, 2000. The $1.7 billion credit agreement had been extended until April 14, 2000, by which date Sunbeam hoped to have a definite agreement extending the covenant relief and waivers for an additional year. Sunbeam was required to restate their audited accounting reports. It took auditors four months to unravel the accounting statements from during Dunlap's tenure, which were confirmed to be legal, though not accurate. The 1997 net income under Dunlap had been stated as $109.4 million; after the auditors were done it was restated as $38.3 million, less than any one of the former CEOs Kazarian's and Schipke's full years.

Sunbeam is moving forward. They created a new company—Thalia Products, Inc. (for Thinking and Linking Intelligent Appliances) to produce smart appliances and services and to license HLT (Home Linking Technology) to other manufacturers. At the International Housewares show in January 2000, Sunbeam and Thalia introduced nine new products. These products automatically network when plugged in and "talk" to each other to coordinate tasks, such as an alarm clock that turns on the coffee pot 10 minutes before the alarm goes off—no matter what time it is set for—and an alarm that will ring to let you know if you forgot to add the water to the coffee pot. Sunbeam announced on March 23, 2000, that its Thalia Products division had made an agreement with Microsoft Corp. to join the Universal Plug and Play (UPnP)

Forum, which will further the companies' shared objective of establishing industry-leading standards for home appliance networking.

CEO Levin still has confidence in Sunbeam's ability to recover. In a press release on May 10, 2000, the first-quarter results reported that year-on-year net sales increased 3 percent to $539 million and operating results narrowed to a loss of $3 million. Levin stated in that same press release,

> These results, though improved, are not indicative of the value we have created, and will continue to create, for Sunbeam's shareholders. Looking forward, we expect operating results to further improve as we execute our long-range strategy that focuses on consumer-oriented new products.

On February 6, 2001, Sunbeam filed for Chapter 11 bankruptcy, announcing that it had reached agreement with its secured creditors to reorganize its debts. CEO Jerry Levin said Sunbeam will be privately held by its banks when it emerges from bankruptcy, with current management having some stock options in the new company. He said he expects that the company eventually will be public again and that new-product development will allow it to overcome its current difficulties.

Shares of Sunbeam last traded at 51 cents a share. The company has suspended trading the stock and filed with the Securities and Exchange Commission on February 6, 2001 to delist it.

Questions for Discussion

1. How did pressures for financial performance contribute to an organizational culture that tried to manipulate quarterly sales and to influence investors?

2. What were Al Dunlap's contributions to financial and public relations embarrassments at Sunbeam that caused investors and the public to question Sunbeam's integrity?

3. Identify ethical irregularities that Al Dunlap's management team may have created by using a short-run focus on financial performance. What lessons could be learned from the outcome?

Sources

These facts are from Sunbeam Corporation, Hoover's Online, www.hoovers.com/premium/profiles/11414.html, September 19, 1998; Albert J. Dunlap and Bob Aldeman, "How I Save Bad Companies and Make Good Companies Great," *Mean Business*, revised edition (New York: Simon & Schuster, 1997); Matthew Schifrin, "Chainsaw Al to the Rescue," *Forbes*, August 26, 1996, www.forbes.com/forbes/082696/5805042a.htm; Patricia Sellers, "First: Sunbeam's Investors Draw Their Knives—Exit for Chainsaw?" *Fortune*, June 8, 1998, 30–31; Matthew Schifrin, "The Unkindest Cuts," *Forbes*, May 4, 1998, www.forbes.com/forbes/98/0504/6109044a.htm; Matthew Schifrin, "The Sunbeam Soap Opera: Chapter 6," *Forbes*, July 6, 1998, 44–45; John A. Byrne, "How Al Dunlap Self-Destructed," *Business Week*, July 6, 1998, 58–65; Daniel Kadlec, "Chainsaw Al Gets the Chop," Time.com, www.pathfinder.com/, September 14, 1998; The Alexander Law Firm, http://defrauded.com/sunbeam.shtml, September 13, 1998; Martha Brannigan and Ellen Joan Pollock, "Dunlap Offers Tears and a Defense," *Wall Street Journal*, July 9, 1998, B1; "Dunlap and Kersh Resign from Sunbeam Board of Directors," PR Newswire, www.prnewswire.com, September 13, 1998; "Sunbeam to Restate Financial Results," PR Newswire, www.prnewswire.com, September 13, 1998; "Sunbeam Outlines New Strategy, Organizational Structure, Senior Management Team," PR Newswire, www.prnewswire.com, September 13, 1998; John A. Byrne, "The Notorious Career of Al Dunlap in the Era of Profit-at-Any-Price," *Chainsaw* (New York: HarperCollins Publishers, Inc., 1999); Douglas Bell, "Take Me to Your Leader," *ROB Magazine*, www.robmagazine.com/archive/2000ROBfebruary/html/idea_log.html, June 10, 2000; Steve Matthews, "Sunbeam's Ex-CEO Seeks $5.25 Million in Arbitration Claim," *Bloomberg News*, March 15, 1999;

"Sunbeam Balks at Dunlap's Demand for $5.5 Million," *Naples Daily News*, March 17, 1999; "Sunbeam Signs Memorandum of Understanding to Settle Coleman Shareholder Litigation," PR Newswire, www.prnewswire.com, October 21, 1998; "Sunbeam Announces Eastpak Sale Complete," PR Newswire, www.prnewswire.com, May 30, 2000; "Sunbeam Credit Waivers Extended to April 14, 2000," www.prnewswire.com, April 11, 2000; "Letter from CEO Jerry W. Levin," Sunbeam Homepage, www.sunbeam.com, June 10, 2000; "Sunbeam Reports First-Quarter 2000 Results," Sunbeam Press Release, www.sunbeam.com, May 10, 2000; "Time for Smart Talk Is Over," Sunbeam Press Release, www.sunbeam.com, January 14, 2000; "Sunbeam Joins Microsoft in the Universal Plug and Play Forum to Establish a 'Universal' Smart Appliance Technology Standard," Sunbeam Press Release, www.sunbeam.com, March 23, 2000; "VF to Acquire Eastpak Brand," Sunbeam Press Release, www.sunbeam.com, March 20, 2000; "Sunbeam Completes Acquisition of Coleman Publicly Held Shares," Sunbeam Press Release, www.sunbeam.com, January 6, 2000; and "Sunbeam Filed for Chapter 11," http://www.sunbeam.com, February 6, 2001.

Bass Pro Shops 2000

Since 1971, John Morris' fishing tackle business has grown from an eight-foot-long display area in the back of one of his father's single-employee Brown Derby liquor stores to one of today's largest U.S. retailers of outdoor sporting goods, with 7,000 employees. Bass Pro Shops is the privately owned parent of Outdoor World, a chain of retail stores headquartered in Springfield, Missouri.

The Springfield store, with $72 million in annual sales, is a 300,000-square-foot retail operation that in some ways resembles a mall, because it includes a variety of entertainment and service offerings. The huge store, with its five aquariums and four-story waterfall crashing into a 64,000-gallon pool stocked with fish native to Missouri, is the single greatest tourist attraction in Missouri. With about half of the customers coming from outside of Missouri, over 4 million people visit Outdoor World in Springfield every year, more than visit the famous arch in St. Louis or the St. Louis Cardinals baseball team. Some people plan two- or three-day visits on their vacation schedule.

The direct marketing operation sends over 34 million Bass Pro catalogs around the world annually, featuring some 30,000 items and likely attracting many customers to the store anxious to try a product before they buy it. Outdoor World was originally intended to be a special store that would provide "red carpet" treatment for catalog customers, who could see and buy products unavailable from other retailers. Rifle, pistol, and archery ranges in the store allow customers to try out merchandise before taking it home. Although the retail store operation has taken on a life of its own, the telemarketing operation continues to sell a high volume of merchandise from Outdoor World catalogs, thus indirectly encouraging store visits.

Telemarketing and Catalog Operations

The 338 full-color pages of the 2000 Bass Pro Outdoor World Master Catalog list more than 17,000 items, and there are specialty catalogs for sportsmen's clothing and for hunting, fishing, and marine enthusiasts. About 500 operators are busy around the clock every day answering some 170 incoming WATS lines at the catalog operation. About 90 percent of orders are filled immediately and do not have to be backordered.

This case was prepared by Neil Herndon, Hofstra University, for classroom discussion rather than to illustrate either effective or ineffective handling of an administrative situation.

United Parcel Service (UPS) and the U.S. Postal Service handle 400,000 packages shipped to catalog customers monthly.

Sometimes demand for catalog items is difficult to forecast exactly. A missed projection of anticipated sales for a certain fishing lure resulted in 3,000 backorders for the item and, presumably, as many unhappy fishermen and -women. Catalogs are printed a season in advance, and there is always the danger that customers will wait too long to order. Still, the catalog is one of the most convenient ways for many customers to get needed items with minimum effort, especially since many of the items that Bass Pro offers are not available in many rural and smaller towns. But as an added service, Bass Pro now has online shopping capabilities, making it increasingly convenient for customers with Internet access to shop at home or at the office.

Tracker Marine

Bass Pro's original concept was to provide the angler with everything necessary to go fishing: rod, reel, tackle box, seating, electronic fish finders, motor, boat, and trailer. At first, Bass Pro purchased boats from other companies. Then, in 1978, the Tracker Marine subsidiary was developed to build boats. Today, Tracker Marine offers over forty models, with lines ranging from pontoon boats to aluminum boats to fiberglass bass boats. Trailers are also manufactured to fit the boats they sell. Its success is partly because it was the first company to provide the customer with a complete fishing package that included everything necessary to go fishing without assembling the individual items.

In 1998, Tracker Marine introduced Tracker recreational vehicles (RVs). This line includes fold-down, fifth-wheel, and travel trailers, as well as slide-in pickup campers and mini-motor homes. The addition of RVs to their product offerings also supports the strategy of providing a complete package in one place.

The relationship between the two Bass Pro subsidiaries continues to be symbiotic. Outdoor World is Tracker's largest boat customer, and Tracker is the largest advertiser in the Outdoor World master catalog. Outdoor World stores feature large Tracker showrooms.

Tracker Marine now sells its own boats and trailers through a network of about 250 U.S. dealers and about 25 dealers in Canada. There is also one dealer in Australia as they test the Pacific market. Tracker is expanding its Canadian dealership network and is planning to enter the European market. It may be considering other foreign markets as well. Tracker Marine executives say their expansion plans will push up volume and help Tracker keep prices competitive.

Sales Promotion

Special events are an important part of marketing at Outdoor World. The Spring Fishing Classic draws 50,000 people each of its four days to the Springfield store. Not only do factory representatives from the nation's top fishing manufacturers display and demonstrate the latest products, top fishing pros present seminars on their techniques and strategies. The Fall Hunting Classic draws a total of about 80,000 visitors to the Springfield store over its four-day run.

Bass Pro founder Johnny Morris seems to be aware of the need to keep the Outdoor World name associated with community service and positive conservation efforts. He pledges large sums of money to support conservation in areas where Bass Pro conducts business, such as the $100,000 donated for habitat and conservation work to be done near the site of a new Outdoor World store in Texas. He has also donated $10 million to support a new wildlife museum and aquarium next door to the Springfield Outdoor World store.

Bass Pro points out on in-store signs that its large displays of mounted animals were not collected for display at Outdoor World but were donated by people who no longer had space for them so that the animals could be preserved. Certain displays, such as that of two very young mounted fawns at the Springfield store, point out that their deaths were accidental.

The 400,000 packages mailed each month by the Bass Pro catalog division are shipped using environmentally friendly packing material. Coins tossed into Outdoor World fountains and aquariums in Springfield are donated to Ronald McDonald House, which benefits critically ill children and their families.

Bass Pro Shops also offers safety education and hunter education classes through its Outdoor World stores, a service likely to be greatly appreciated by parents of young hunters. It also is the sole corporate sponsor of Missouri's Operation Game Thief, intended to assist authorities in enforcing game laws and protecting game animal populations.

Bass Pro was a cosponsor of Dale Earnhardt, who before his tragic death early in 2001 was one of NASCAR's top drivers. His No. 3 Chevrolet had been adorned with a large Bass Pro logo as it rushed to the winner's circle before thousands of racing fans watching at the track and on their televisions at home. Race cars have also been displayed at new-store openings as a feature attraction, to the excitement of customers, who often have their or their family's picture taken standing beside these cars.

Retailing Developments

Bass Pro Shops' retail store activities have been centered in one store location in Springfield. However, Bass Pro began expanding its operations in March 1995 with a second store in Atlanta, Georgia, called Sportsman's Warehouse. Since then, it has opened stores under the Outdoor World banner in Gurnee, Illinois (near Chicago), Auburn Hills, Michigan (near Detroit), Grapevine, Texas (near Dallas–Fort Worth), Katy, Texas (near Houston), Dania Beach, Florida (near Fort Lauderdale), Orlando, Florida, Concord, North Carolina (near Charlotte), and Nashville, Tennessee. There is also a World Wide Sportsman store in Islamorada, Florida, operated by Bass Pro but not carrying the Outdoor World name. Preliminary retail location analysis also seems to be under way for another Outdoor World store in the Kansas City area.

At least some of the funding for this expansion is likely to come from the sale of real estate, such as that near its Fort Lauderdale, Florida, location, which Bass Pro then would lease back for store locations. Closely held Bass Pro Shops does not appear to be heading for the stock market to finance growth, but outsiders know little of its capital structure and it does not release sales and profit figures.

Typically, these new stand-alone stores are smaller than the parent store, ranging from about 125,000 to 200,000 square feet, but all are intended to give the outdoor enthusiast "the best selection of top-quality merchandise, great service, and low prices—all under one roof." They have similar decor, entertainment qualities, and merchandise, giving them much of the look and feel of the parent store. A new façade pioneered at the Gurnee store has been added to the Springfield store. It appears this new entrance will become a signature for all Outdoor World stores. Although there is some variation in store hours among the retail locations, they are typically open from seven in the morning to ten at night six days a week, with shorter hours (nine to six) on Sunday. All stores are open every day of the year except Christmas.

However, some of their water features, such as waterfalls, are smaller and less impressive than those of the Springfield store, and wildlife displays do not seem to be as well integrated into the decor. At the Grapevine store, for example, life-size mounted animals are typically displayed in rows on ledges high above the merchandise racks.

Bass Pro Shops locates its stores near family attractions. Springfield is near the country music mecca of Branson, Missouri, and the Nashville store is near Opryland and the country music capital of Nashville. Stores in the Dallas–Fort Worth, Chicago, Houston, Charlotte, and Detroit areas are located close to large shopping malls. The Fort Lauderdale store is next to the International Game Fish Association Hall of Fame, built on land donated by Bass Pro Shops President Morris. The Grapevine store is next to a wilderness-themed hotel and convention center. The Springfield store will soon have a $50 million world-class American National Fish and Wildlife Living Museum and Aquarium right next door; Morris has donated $10 million (as mentioned earlier) in cash, land, and exhibits and is seeking the balance from state and local taxes.

These new stores, like their Springfield parent, are tourist destinations. Michigan economic development and tourism officials expect the Auburn Hills store, for example, to attract customers from several surrounding states and at least one Canadian province. The State of Michigan is buying ads in the Bass Pro catalog to promote Michigan's great outdoors. The Fall Hunting Classic is also being held in the new stores, as at the Springfield parent store, to encourage visits.

The Springfield Outdoor World Store

The Springfield Outdoor World Store is departmentalized, with a wide variety of merchandise and many choices within each line. There are, for example, over 7,000 fishing lures and about 200 bows and 100 handguns available. Signs help customers find departments, merchandise lines, and clothing sizes, while promotional elements attract special attention to the merchandise. Special in-store sales are announced with flyers, and brochures provide maps to the departments and show the locations of various services.

Ducks descend over the Tracker Marine boat showroom area, while a bear and cub attract customers to the hunting department, where they may also notice the nearby merchandise designed to make hunting easier. Squirrels mounted as fencers decorate the workbench of an artist working with glass at the Wildlife Art Gallery entrance, and other mounted squirrels decorate the entrance counter to the store.

Since Outdoor World customers often spend long periods in the store, a number of auxiliary services are available. Hemingway's Blue Water Café, featuring a 29,000-gallon saltwater aquarium and decorated with mounted animal trophies and African ritual masks, provides an exotic family dining experience. Local businesspeople frequently dine here, and such notables as former President George Bush have sampled the biscuits and gravy. But Big Macs are also available at the McDonald's right across the top of the four-story waterfall from Hemingway's.

Just past McDonald's is the Tall Tales Barbershop, featuring real "fighting chairs" that anglers might use on a deep-sea fishing boat. The barbershop's location provides an excellent view of the many outdoor-clothing choices below, and customers can have strands of their freshly cut hair made into a fishing lure.

Visitors can see scuba divers hand-feeding large freshwater game fish with goldfish in one of the five in-store aquariums at Uncle Buck's 250-seat auditorium on the lower level. They can visit a trout stream, see a 96-pound alligator snapping turtle (in the hunting department), and enjoy displays of antique fishing lures, mounted trophy fish, and mounted trophy animals, including a lion, seemingly ready to leap, with claws aimed at their chest. Many visitors pose by the cavernous jaws of a 3,247-pound great white shark and have a friend document their close encounter with a picture.

It's possible to have a fishing rod or reel repaired during a visit, and hunters can try out a handgun, rifle, or bow on an indoor shooting range and even have their favorite knife sharpened. Trophy animals can be mounted at the award-winning Wildlife Creations and Taxidermy shop. Golfers can test putters on an indoor putting green and test other clubs on an in-store driving range.

Outdoor World features free useful product information brochures to help customers select the right items for their needs, ranging from baseball bats to sleeping bags, from camp foods to slalom water skies. Displays show camping equipment as it would be used, and videotapes are shown near the products they feature. Salespeople are trained not only to sell the products, but also to show their proper use and proper maintenance, which helps customers get the most from their purchases, even though they're backed by an Outdoor World 100 percent satisfaction guarantee.

Other Outdoor World Stores

The other Outdoor World retail stores, although smaller, are very similar to the parent Springfield store. The 200,000-square-foot Grapevine store, for example, has the signature Outdoor World entrance with the Bass Pro Shops logo prominently displayed. Customers are encouraged to relax in the hunting-lodge-style lobby, where leather couches and deerskin chairs surround a roaring stone fireplace. The outdoorsy interior is dominated by a two-story waterfall plunging into a 30,000-gallon aquarium and accented by a spectacular collection of big game trophies, mounted life size.

There is a millpond with fish near the snack bar, and the Big Buck Brewery and Steakhouse is ready to handle a hearty appetite. The store has casting pools, bow and gun ranges, and golf greens, just like the Springfield store. The fishing lure section features over 7,000 lures; there are some 58,000 different products on display, ranging from a $9.95 fishing cap to a $23,995 package of Tracker boat, motor, and trailer. A staff of over 300 people is trained to provide knowledgeable service. And, of course, the Outdoor World 100 percent satisfaction guarantee applies. The Grapevine store is expected to produce about $100 million in sales annually.

Bass Pro executives say that their key operating philosophy has not been to add more and more to their organization. Rather, they add what they consider to be important to the outdoor enthusiast in terms of providing a new experience or element of pleasure. The key idea for the executives seems to be the value-added notion of meeting the needs of the outdoor enthusiast, right down to location convenience, an idea at the very heart of the marketing concept.

The Competition

With three years of prior retailing experience required to be considered for employment, the opening of a new Outdoor World store is likely to attract applicants from existing outdoor sports suppliers, in part because these employees consider their employers to be in jeopardy when a category killer like Outdoor World comes to town. These smaller stores just can't match prices or selection. But it appears that even smaller stores can operate successfully in market niches.

Back Country Outfitters, a small fly-fishing shop, and Archery USA, both located in the shadow of Outdoor World's parent Springfield store, survive by selling specialized items that their larger competitor does not offer. The Grapevine Mini Center, a live bait and tackle shop, believes it will survive because many customers won't want the hassle of going to the bigger store on a regular basis. Still others believe the larger store will generate spillover traffic for their smaller shops, which they can then capture via outstanding specialized service and convert into loyal customers.

Larger competitors, like Academy Sports & Outdoors, a forty-three-store chain based in Katy, Texas, carry outdoor equipment and clothing much as Outdoor World does. However, Academy believes that its stores near Grapevine can compete with Outdoor World successfully since it is a full-line sporting goods store while Outdoor World offers little in the athletic area aside from its wide and deep line of golf equipment.

Recreational Equipment Inc. (REI), a Seattle-based chain of fifty-seven retail stores in twenty-three states, is opening a store in Troy, Michigan, competing against both Bass Pro in Auburn Hills and Gander Mountain, which has nine Michigan locations. With sales of $621 million in its tent, backpacking, and mountaineering product lines, its in-store hands-on equipment testing challenges Outdoor World in these areas. And its fifty-year-old mail-order catalog competes with the Outdoor World catalog in these product categories as well.

Similarly, forty-year-old Cabela's, a Sidney, Nebraska-based catalog giant with over 5,000 employees, sends out over 60 million catalogs to customers in all fifty states and 120 foreign countries. It has six retail stores in Nebraska, Minnesota, Wisconsin, and South Dakota. It opened its seventh retail store, a 225,000-square-footer, in Dundee, Michigan, which appears intended to compete directly with Outdoor World's nearby Auburn Hills store. Outdoor World features a forty-foot waterfall and a 30,000-gallon aquarium; Cabela's has a forty-foot indoor mountain with waterfall and a 65,000-gallon aquarium. Cabela's will also position itself as a destination store "bringing the outdoors indoors"; its Michigan location will include a hotel and an RV park.

Sports enthusiasts from as far away as Cleveland are planning bus trips to both Cabela's and Outdoor World in Michigan. Cabela's estimates it will draw as many as 6 million visitors annually, making it the most visited tourist attraction in Michigan. And it will continue to target its mail-order customers with a variety of specialty catalogs, which contain products backed by Cabela's own 100 percent satisfaction guarantee.

Founded in 1912, L. L. Bean, with eleven factory stores in New Hampshire, Maine, Delaware, Maryland, Oregon, and Virginia, is headquartered in Freeport, Maine. The flagship Freeport retail operation contains 129,000 square feet and receives 3.5 million visitors each year. Its catalog operations, based in Lewiston, Maine, also offer outdoor products that come with a 100 percent satisfaction guarantee through several specialty catalogs. Bean now has annual sales of more than $1 billion and employs about 4,000 people in its retail and catalog operations. It also has an international presence, with twenty retail stores in Japan, the first opened in 1992 in Tokyo.

Bean appears to be targeting a more upscale market with its offerings than is Bass Pro, and does not seem to be competing directly with them. The Freeport store has fewer and smaller aquariums and only a few mounted animals and is located among upscale outlets like London Fog, Ralph Lauren, and Timberland. While federal regulations prevent both Bass Pro and Bean from offering firearms through their catalogs, Outdoor World stores offer a very large selection of rifles, shotguns, and handguns, while L. L. Bean stores offer a smaller selection of only rifles and shotguns. Bass Pro executives, however, do keep an eye on L. L. Bean, especially because of Bean's tremendous emphasis on customer service. Their store has no locks on its front door, so customers come and go at all hours of the day and night, every day of the year.

The sheer size of this market may attract other competitors as well. The wholesale value of camping equipment shipped in 1999 was $1.7 billion. Hunting equipment and firearms worth $2.1 billion were shipped. Camping equipment sales were up 2.1 percent over the previous year, and sales of hunting equipment and firearms were up 1.5 percent.

Questions for Discussion

1. What is the corporate and marketing strategy at Bass Pro Shops?

2. What are the external opportunities and threats and the internal strengths and weaknesses facing Outdoor World?

3. What promotion components are emphasized at Bass Pro Shops? Why?

4. Does your SWOT analysis suggest the need for changes in Outdoor World's retailing strategy? Support your position with facts from the case.

Sources

These facts are from O. K. Carter, "Bass Pro Shop opening in Grapevine," *Fort Worth Star-Telegram*, March 19, 1999, 2; Bass Pro Shop *2000 Master Catalog*; Bass Pro Shop pamphlet "Welcome to Outdoor World Dallas–Ft. Worth, Texas"; Bass Pro Shop pamphlet "Store Map & Directory Outdoor World Grapevine, Texas"; Bass Pro pamphlet "Outdoor World Springfield, MO"; visits by the case author to Outdoor World stores in Grapevine, Texas, and Springfield, Missouri, and to the L. L. Bean Store in Freeport, Maine, May and June 2000; Jon Pepper, "Michigan version of Bass Pro Shop to Boost Tourism," *Detroit News*, April 5, 1998, C1; Rick Alm, "Tourist Attraction May Be Looking at KCK as Site," *Kansas City Star*, June 27, 2000, D21; Mark P. Couch, "TIF Panel Tries to Land Bass Pro," *Kansas City Star*, May 11, 2000, C1; Andrew Backover, "Tracking the Competition—Smaller Stores Plan to Keep an Eye on Bass Pro Shops," *Fort Worth Star-Telegram*, March 25, 1999, 1; Karen Talaski, "Outdoors Store Opens," *Detroit News*, May 19, 2000, 1; Andrew Backover, "Bass Pro Opener in Grapevine Reels in Thousands," *Fort Worth Star-Telegram*, March 26, 1999, 1; Kelly Ryan, "Grapevine's Bass Pro Shops to Open Soon," *Dallas Morning News*, February 28, 1999, 11A; Anonymous, "Tanger Acquires Bass Pro Tract," *Wall Street Journal*, November 16, 1999, A6; Mark Couch, "Bass Pro Shops Not Hooked on Bannister Area," *Kansas City Star*, July 25, 2000, D23; D'Arcy Egan, "A Hot Lure: Megastores," *The Plain Dealer* (Cleveland), September 7, 2000, 6D;

Robert Baun, "Sporting Goods Giant Takes First Colo. Store to Loveland," *Fort Collins Coloradoan*, September 4, 2000, A1, A2; Cabela's *Master Catalog Spring 2000 Edition I*; Anonymous, "Springfield's Famous Bass Pro Shops Is Expanding into Texas," *St. Louis Post-Dispatch*, February 21, 1998, 6; Gordon Dickson, "Store Angles for Easy Opener Traffic Control," *Fort Worth Star-Telegram*, March 24, 1999, 1; Anonymous, "Our History," cabelas.com, October 2000; Anonymous, "L. L. Bean Today," *llbean.com*, October 2000; Anonymous, "In the Beginning" and "The Growth of Tracker Marine," basspro.com, October, 2000.

11

New Belgium Brewery: Fat Tire Amber Ale

History of Fat Tire Ale and the New Belgium Brewery

Fat Tire Amber Ale originated when Jeff Lebesch was cruising around Belgium on his fat-tired mountain bike. As he pedaled across the country, he visited several of the local breweries, which were typically monasteries. These visits made Jeff decide to pursue his dream of opening a small brewery back home in Colorado. Shortly after the trip ended he began experimenting with brewing Belgian-style beers. After earning friend-tested approvals, Jeff decided to try to go commercial.

In 1991 the New Belgium Brewery (NBB) opened as a tiny basement operation in the home of Jeff Lebesch and Kim Jordan in Fort Collins. Their first brew was named Fat Tire Amber Ale, in memory of Jeff's bike ride. New Belgium Brewery beers developed a small but happy following and experienced rapid growth almost immediately. They soon outgrew their basement operation and moved into an old railroad depot. Finally, in 1995, they designed their present brewing facility, which is still a marvel in their industry. This brewery features two quality assurance labs, an automated brewhouse, and numerous technological innovations for which they have become a "nationally recognized paradigm of environmental efficiencies."

Company Purpose and Core Beliefs

New Belgium's dedication to quality, the environment, their employees, and their customers is expressed in their purpose for being and their shared values and beliefs about their role as a socially responsible brewer.

Company Purpose

"To operate a profitable brewery which makes our love and talent manifest." David Kemp, a longtime employee and tour connoisseur at NBB, says that this purpose gives

---

This case was prepared by Nikole Haiar for classroom discussion, rather than to illustrate either effective or ineffective handling of an administrative, ethical, or legal decision by management.

New Belgium the ability to show people what they, as a company, are like and to genuinely communicate with their customers.

Core Values and Beliefs

- Producing world-class beers
- Promoting beer culture and the responsible enjoyment of beer
- Continuous, innovative quality and efficiency improvements
- Transcending their customers' expectations
- Environmental stewardship: minimizing resource consumption, maximizing energy efficiency and recycling
- Using social, environmental, and cultural change as a business role model
- Cultivating potential: through learning, participative management, and the pursuit of opportunities
- Balancing the myriad needs of the company, the staff, and their families
- Committing themselves to authentic relationships, communications, and promises
- Having fun

Competition and Competitive Advantage

Competitors

New Belgium competes with other microbrews on-premise (in bars) and off-premise (at liquor stores) for recognition, trial, and brand loyalty. On-premise competitors are considered to be Guinness and O'Dell's 90 Shilling, while off-premise competitors are Pete's Wicked Ale and Pyramid Pale Ale. They consider their main competitor, both on- and off-premise, to be Sierra Nevada. Competition between the microbreweries is overall very friendly in nature. In fact, they often get together at events such as the Great American Beer Festival.

Competitive Advantages

New Belgium Brewery has several competitive advantages. They feel their most important, however, is their personal relationships with consumers that have been established through various events, sponsorships, and participation in festivals. In fact, they believe this is the main reason they have such a loyal following. According to David Kemp, consumers want to believe in and feel good about the products they purchase. Fat Tire accomplishes this by being socially responsible and by making a consistently good-tasting, high-quality product. Another competitive advantage is their unique packaging, which connotes nostalgia, comfort, and relaxation. Finally, with quality being so important to the long-term survival of any company, NBB employs two quality assurance labs and conducts daily tests to check for consistency in taste and overall satisfaction with each batch of brew.

Target Market

New Belgium Brewery segments their market for Fat Tire Amber Ale through values, attitudes, and lifestyles rather than demographics. According to David Kemp, this is because they have found through experience and market research that Fat Tire crosses all demographic boundaries and attracts male and female consumers of all ages (above twenty-one), professions, educational and income levels, and ethnicity.

They have found, however, that most of their consumers have similar values, attitudes, and lifestyles and participate in certain types of activities. He classifies their target market as consumers who participate in and aspire to the "typical American lifestyle." More specifically, Fat Tire drinkers tend to be environmentally considerate individuals who want to participate in socially responsible causes, enjoy good-tasting and original beer, and love the practicality and nostalgia of bicycles. They also tend to be activity based, meaning involved in or watching human-powered alternative sports like riding bikes. They tend to socialize with those who share the same interests. Their recent Tour de Fat campaign revealed an undeniable connection between bikers and their beer.

Marketing Strategy

New Belgium's current marketing formula tries to combine the quality of the product, the name and look of the product, and the way New Belgium Brewing Company shows up on the planet. The strategy currently used is called marketing the "tenderness of pleasure." New Belgium faces the possibility that the brand name Fat Tire will become a more generic term, much like happened with Kleenex, Coke, Rollerblade, and Xerox. Fat Tire has become so symbolic of the company that some customers now call New Belgium Brewery the Fat Tire Brewery.

Products Offered

Besides Fat Tire, NBB offers a wide array of permanent and seasonal ales and pilsners. Standard lines included Sunshine Wheat, Blue Paddle Pilsner, Abbey Ale, Trippel Ale, 1554 Black Ale, and of course their original Fat Tire Amber Ale, which continues to be their best-selling brew. Two types of specialty beers are also offered: seasonal and one-time-only. Seasonal ales include Frambozen and Abbey Grand Cru, which are released during Thanksgiving and Christmas. A one-time-only beer means that only one batch is produced, so their current one-time-only brew, LaFolie, a wood-aged beer, will no longer be available once the batch is gone.

Pricing for Positioning

New Belgium Brewery uses a price-for-quality pricing strategy that implies value and satisfaction to consumers. David Kemp stated that New Belgium tries to keep their brews moderately priced, at around $7 per six-pack. They feel that this price is effective in conveying their message of being special and of consistently higher quality than macrobrews, such as Budweiser and Coors, but also keeps them price competitive with other microbrews. Because consumers often associate price with quality, NBB feels this is consistent with their positioning strategy. The company positions all of its brews as high-quality beers that promote connoisseurship and enjoyment of beer, rather than a beer to be guzzled and poured through "beer bongs." To encourage and show concern for their retailers and business partners, New Belgium contracts have a noncompetitor clause, which says that they will not sell beer to consumers at the brewhouse for less than their retailers charge.

Packaging

New Belgium Brewing Company uses "good ol' days" nostalgia in their label designs. Romantic and easygoing pictures are surrounded by beautiful greenery on warm-toned backgrounds. Fat Tire specifically portrays an old-style cruiser bike, with big padded seats and a basket hanging from the handlebars, surrounded by leaves from a hops plant. All of their labels and packaging designs were created by the same watercolor artist, their next-door neighbor. Thus, packaging also plays a vital role in product positioning by emphasizing originality and good times. Every six-pack of New Belgium brews also displays the saying "In this box is our labor of love. We feel incredibly lucky to be creating something fine that enhances people's lives." New Belgium hopes this saying captures the everyday spirit of their company.

Distribution

Fat Tire, New Belgium's original ale, was initially distributed solely in Ft. Collins, Colorado, and quickly expanded throughout the rest of the state. Currently, Fat Tire can be bought at liquor stores, in bars and restaurants, and through the brewhouse. Today, Fat Tire is distributed in many western states, including Washington, Oregon, Montana, Idaho, Wyoming, Texas, New Mexico, Arizona, Kansas, Missouri, and Nebraska and is continuing to spread.

Promotions

New Belgium's most important and effective advertising comes from word of mouth. Since their beginnings, word-of-mouth advertising has benefited Fat Tire and NBB. The brewery wants the quality of the product to speak for itself, because that's the only type of marketing hype that lasts. For instance, one Telluride liquor storeowner used to offer people gas money if, when traveling through Ft. Collins, they'd stop in and pick up NBB beer. Even today, the brewery receives numerous e-mails and phone calls each day inquiring when their beers will be available in Telluride.

They also opt for alternative types of paid advertising. David Kemp said they avoid mass advertising because they believe it is ineffective and expensive and doesn't fit their image. Instead, they prefer to use small-scale, close-to-home advertising, sponsoring alternative sports events, participating in numerous festivals, and printing ads in alternative magazines. They feel these types of advertisements are more meaningful and memorable to their consumers and are more consistent with their company's core beliefs. In fact, NBB participates in fifty to seventy-five events and festivals a year in Colorado and in 115 more outside the state. New Belgium also tries to stay with their image by keeping tag lines easy and natural. For example, Fat Tire's tag is simply "Enjoy the Ride."

Market Research

Because New Belgium is so active and close with their consumers, they often combine their promotions with research. One recent example was the First Annual Tour de Fat. This festival, comprising unconventional games such as a bike push and a paperboy challenge, was held simultaneously in six different states. In each of the six cities involved they also gave away one of their popular cruiser bikes, like the one on the Fat Tire label. David Kemp explained that this was really just a way for them to get out and have fun with their customers and to see who actually attended. He also said that the number of people who came just to watch and drink beer was an unexpected delight. They had anticipated seeing mostly groups of twenty-one- to thirty-five-year-old males, but were surprised to see older couples and groups of women at the events. Even more shocking was the number of parents and children.

Another recent research campaign was a consumer-understanding project entitled "What Beer Means to Me." This project was designed and implemented by an outside marketing team who went to various bars and restaurants across Colorado and asked people of different demographic characteristics to make a collage from pictures in magazines of what Fat Tire beer meant to them. Respondents were also asked to describe the meaning of the clippings on the back. The results were different across the board, but some common threads were present in the male responses. One theme was that it was a social event. Almost all respondents showed groups of people together having a good time. A lot of the collages also depicted some type of sport, ranging from football to fishing, with little or nothing left out. Most of the female respondents also included sports, but in addition they showed groups of people (mostly women) hanging out together and laughing.

Efficiency and Innovation

Innovations permeate the New Belgium Brewery. From leading-edge environmental gadgets and high-tech industry advances to employee ownership programs and a strong belief in giving back to the community, New Belgium shows their desire to create a living, learning community.

In staying consistent with their core values and beliefs, the entire NBB staff unanimously agreed in 1998 to make their facility the first fully wind-powered brewery in America. Since the switch, New Belgium has been able to eliminate 1,800 metric tons of carbon dioxide emissions per year. New Belgium also takes pride in reducing waste through recycling and creative reuse strategies. By the end of 1999, New Belgium was able to reduce their negative impact on the environment by recycling ninety-one tons of amber glass, twenty-seven tons of cardboard, and nine tons of shrink wrap.

They also strive for cost-efficient and energy-saving alternatives. A steam condenser captures and reuses the hot water from boiling the barley and hops in the production process to start the next brew, and the steam is redirected to heat the floor tiles and de-ice their loading docks in cold weather. They also reserve their spent barley and hop grains in an on-premise silo that local farmers are invited to pick up, free of charge, to feed their pigs.

Besides these creative environmental technologies and innovations, New Belgium tries to improve communities and enhance people's lives through corporate giving, event sponsorship, and philanthropic involvement. Each year, NBB donates $1 per barrel to various cultural, social, environmental, and drug and alcohol awareness programs across the ten western states in which they distribute beer. Typical grants for individual programs range from $2,500 to $5,000.

They also maintain a community bulletin board in their facility where they post an array of community involvement activities and proposals. The community bulletin board allows tourists and employees to see the different ways they can help the community and gives people a chance to make their needs known. The New Belgium Web site, through a designated link, offers people a convenient alternative for making grant requests.

NBB also sponsors a variety of events to raise money for local nonprofit organizations. The majority of these events involve "human-powered" sports, which cause minimal damage to the natural environment. Through events, such as Tour de Fat, the brewery has raised over $15,000 for various nonprofit organizations. Over the course of one year, you can expect to see New Belgium at between 150 and 200 festivals and events, across all ten western states. For example, in November 2000, NBB also sponsored the "MS-150 Best Damn Bike Tour." This was a two-day, fully catered bike tour, in which all proceeds went to benefit over 5,000 local people with multiple sclerosis. The same year, they also sponsored the annual "Ride the Rockies" bike tour that raised money to fund local projects such as improving parks and bike trails. The efficiencies and innovations employed at New Belgium stem from their founding purpose and core beliefs.

Organizational Success

New Belgium Brewery's efforts to live up to their own high standards have resulted in numerous general marvels and awards, and a very loyal following. According to David Edgar, director of the Institute for Brewing Studies, "They've created a very positive image for their company in the beer-consuming public with smart decision-making." New Belgium's image includes a multimillion-dollar brewery and rapid growth that has even gotten the attention of the local Anheuser-Busch brewery. Their most important asset is the New Belgium image—a corporate brand that stands for quality, responsibility, and concern for society. This brewer defines itself not just as a beer company, but as a caring organization that is concerned with all stakeholders, including the community, the environment, and their employees. New Belgium's success has come not merely from selling beer, but from offering the consuming public a totally positive experience.

While some members of society may assume that a company whose major product is alcohol is not socially responsible, New Belgium has set out to prove that a company can promote responsible drinking and contribute to society. Their efforts in promoting beer culture and the connoisseurship of beer has led to the design of and exclusive rights to the shape of their "Worthy Glass," which is intended to retain foam, show off coloring, enhance the visual presentation, and most importantly release aroma. New Belgium promotes responsible appreciation of beer through their participation in and support of the culinary arts. For instance, they frequently host New Belgium Beer Dinners, in which every course of the meal is served with complimentary ale. In addition, from their Web site you can access each type of beer and what culinary flavors partner up well with each one.

New Belgium has also won several awards for the taste and high quality of their beers. Kim Jordan and Jeff Lebesch were named the 1999 recipients of the Rocky Mountain Region Entrepreneur of the Year Award for manufacturing. This year they also captured the award for best midsized brewing company of the year and best mid-sized brewmaster at the Great American Beer Festival. In addition, they took home medals for three different brews, Abbey Belgian Style Ale, Blue Paddle Pilsner, and LaFolie specialty ale. One member of the staff of the Association of Brewers commented that Fat Tire is one of the only brews he would pay for in a bar. Considering that Colorado has the second-highest number of brewers in the nation, this is high praise.

Questions for Discussion

1. How has New Belgium Brewery positioned their flagship brand, Fat Tire, against the competition?

2. What are the key elements of the NBB marketing strategy that make it successful in developing a niche market in a highly competitive industry?

3. What has NBB done to be an industry leader in their environmental and social philanthropic efforts?

Sources

These facts are from Robert Baun, "What's in a Name? Ask the Makers of Fat Tire," *Fort Collins Coloradoan*, October 8, 2000, E1, E3; Rachel Brand, "Colorado Breweries Bring Home 12 Medals in Festival," http://www.insidedenver.com/news/1008beer6.shtml, *Rocky Mountain News*, November 6, 2000; Steve Deter, "Review of Fat Tire Amber Ale," *http://www.thenet.com/review/fat.html*, November 6, 2000; David Kemp, personal interview, November 21, 2000; http://www.newbelgium.com, October 30, 2000.

12

Mattel, Inc.

Mattel, Inc., with $4.5 billion in annual revenues, is the world leader in the design, manufacture, and marketing of children's toys. The company's major toy brands include: Barbie (with more than 120 different Barbie dolls), Fisher-Price, Disney entertainment lines, Hot Wheels and Matchbox cars, Tyco Toys, Cabbage Patch Kids, and games such as Scrabble. In addition, Mattel promotes international sales by tailoring toys for specific international markets, instead of simply modifying favorites from the United States. The company's headquarters are in El Segundo, California, but Mattel also has offices in 36 countries. In fact, this company markets its products in more than 155 nations throughout the world.

Mattel's marketing reach has paid off. For example, in a 1997 poll conducted by the annual Power Brands study, Mattel had strong popularity among consumers. As many as four out of ten people said if they were shopping for toys, Mattel would be the brand they most prefer. Retailers also singled out Mattel as the number-one performer, with over six of ten mentions. This survey clearly proved that both children and adults are enthused about Mattel and its line of products.

Until early 2000, this top manufacturing company for toys had been under the managerial control of CEO Jill Barad for the preceding three years. For several years, she was one of only four female CEOs at Fortune 500 companies. The glass ceiling is still at work today, but a few women, such as Barad, have made it to the top despite doubters and increased scrutiny. Female CEOs are now at the helm of very large international firms, including Hewlett-Packard Co., Golden West Financial Corp., and Avon Products Inc. Even though top companies claim to be demolishing the glass ceiling, this just is not evident when thoroughly examining the numbers of women executives and board members.

Barad was the subject of many press articles because she was one of a few women leading Fortune 500 firms. She usually resisted being depicted as a "female executive" and preferred to focus on merit alone. However, by 1999 she was hinting that gender might have played a role in the negative publicity and scrutiny she was beginning to receive in the press. This chief executive's management style has been characterized as strict, businesslike, and people oriented. In addition, Barad was known for her personal preferences, including brightly colored suits and a lively presentation style that reportedly put off some of the conservative Wall Street establishment.

This case was prepared by Debbie Thorne and Kevin Sample for classroom discussion rather than to illustrate either effective or ineffective handling of an administrative situation.

When Barad was named chief executive in January 1997, Mattel's stock was trading for less than $30 a share. However, by March 1997, it had risen to more than $46. Before she was CEO, Barad was in charge of the Barbie product line and played a crucial role in building the sales of Barbie from $200 million in 1982 to $1.9 billion in 1997. The challenges this CEO faced increased throughout 1998 and 1999. Mattel announced in October 1998 that earnings growth for the year would be between 9 and 12 percent, rather than the 18 percent that Wall Street had anticipated. This, in turn, was due to the decline in sales to Toys "Я" Us, the retail chain that accounted for 18 percent of Mattel's revenue in 1997. Barad stated in an interview that if performance continued to deteriorate sharply, the generous rewards given to employees might have to be cut back. In other words, holiday time and overtime would be shortened. However, throughout 1999, some industry analysts said that Mattel's overall strategy was sound and that the company should rebound to outperform most stock market indexes. Other analysts and investors publicly called for her departure. While Mattel did have net sales of $5.5 billion and earnings of $182.1 million in 1999, its acquisition of The Learning Company brought more problems than anticipated. Over Barad's three-year reign as CEO the stock plummeted 60 percent.

A pretax loss of $183 million occurred due to the slowdown in sales of Mattel's CD-ROM software, inventory problems, and discounting on products. This, along with the 1999 fourth-quarter net loss of $18.4 million, led to the resignation of Jill Barad. Even amidst the problems in 1998 and 1999, many analysts believed she would stay on as CEO for another full year, partly because she was very close to the firm's board of directors. The fourth-quarter performances of Fisher-Price, Barbie, and Mattel Entertainment were all strong, but the Learning Company problems overshadowed these achievements. The board appointed Ronald M. Loeb as acting chief executive officer, and the debate on the correct person to lead Mattel through this problem still loomed. By March 2000, Mattel's stock price was below $10 a share, representing an eight-year low for a stock that once traded above $45. One frustrated analyst commented, "I'm done with Mattel."

History of Mattel

In 1945, a garage workshop housed the beginnings of Mattel. Harold Matson and Elliot Handler combined their names and their ideas to form Mattel. While picture frames were the first Mattel product, Handler soon began making dollhouse furniture out of picture frame scraps. Shortly thereafter, Matson sold out to Handler, who, along with his wife, Ruth, expanded the Mattel product line.

The company emphasis switched to toys due to the success of the dollhouse furniture. Child-sized ukuleles, a patented music box, and variations on these products were Mattel's "staple" business and the primary revenue generators in the 1950s and 1960s. The Burp Gun, an automatic cap gun, was introduced in 1955, along with a "Mouseguitar." For the first time, a company had bought advertising to market toys year-round, and this advertising was for 52 weeks on *The Mickey Mouse Club*.

The musical toy success was followed by replica rifles and guns that were prevalent on television during the 1950s. This move capitalized on the popularity of the numerous western-themed television shows of the time, such as *Gunsmoke* and *Bonanza*. At the end of the 1950s, Mattel made the move that would establish them at the forefront of the toy industry. After seeing her daughter's fascination with cutout paper dolls, Ruth suggested that a three-dimensional doll should be produced so that young girls could live out their dreams and fantasies. This doll was named "Barbie," the nickname of Ruth and Elliot Handler's daughter.

Mattel went public in 1960, and within five years they were ranked in Fortune's list of the 500 largest U.S. industrial companies. Mattel also went global during the 1960s. Favorable responses to test marketing prompted the company to grant licensing agreements in England, France, Germany, South Africa, Italy, and Mexico. Mattel's first international sales office was opened in Switzerland in 1964 as headquarters for the worldwide marketing program.

Chatty Cathy, See 'N Say, and the Thingmaker were some of Mattel's stronger product innovations in the 1960s. In 1968, Hot Wheels were introduced, and boys' imaginations were captured in the same way Barbie captured girls' imaginations. At the onset of the 1970s, Mattel was generating revenues of $300 million annually. Not only was the company very profitable, but it was now diversifying via acquisitions. These acquisitions consisted of nontoy companies, such as Barnum and Bailey Circus, Circus World, Turco, Metaframe, and even a motion picture company, Radnitz/Mattel Productions.

The Handlers left the Mattel ranks in the mid-1970s, and the new management expanded into electronics. Handheld electronic games and "Intellivision," a gaming platform, were soon released. However, Intellivision was not as successful as hoped because a plethora of cheap imitation software was produced by pirates of the technology. This forced retailers to drop the price and become disenchanted with Intellivision.

In 1984, there was once again a shift in Mattel's strategy. Their expansion into nontoy areas was continually lowering revenues, and the toy lines of Mattel were constantly increasing revenues. As a consequence, Mattel sold off or closed all nontoy parts of the company and focused on its core revenue producer, the toys. Thus, Mattel aligned its business with the core competency of toy manufacturing and marketing. This also helped launch the Masters of the Universe, or "He-Man," line of toys that really captured boys' attention with large action figures.

However, soon after the introduction of "He-Man," demand for the toy all but stopped. This failure and the failure of Intellivision caused Mattel to refocus its strategy to profitability instead of sales volume. Manufacturing plants, headquarters staff, and overhead spending were all reduced. Soon thereafter, a joint venture with Bandai, the largest Japanese toy company, was entered into. And in 1987, Mattel started a successful strategy that continues today: maximization of core brands while at the same time identifying new brands with core potential. Hot Wheels and Barbie saw many new accessory lines and add-ons accompany their products.

In 1988, Mattel revived its association with The Walt Disney Company and began to make baby products and toys based on famous Disney characters. Mattel began to see more and more success due to this strategy, and a merger with Fisher-Price in 1993 further strengthened the strategy. The acquisition of UNO, Skip-Bo, Power Wheels, and Scrabble continued to support the core brand strategy. In 1997 Mattel merged with Tyco Toys, makers of Matchbox cars, Tyco R/C, View-Master, and Magna Doodle. This merger also gave Mattel the toy license for *Sesame Street*, the popular children's educational program. The most recent merger, that with The Learning Company in 1999, made Mattel the second-largest consumer software company in the world. The Learning Company produces interactive software for computer games and activities that could be tied to Mattel's brands.

All of these mergers and acquisitions have continued to support Mattel's marketing strategy. The fervent pursuit of licenses for popular products and properties by Mattel is also aligned with the strategy. Characters for all programming on Nickelodeon, the Cabbage Patch Kids, and even Harry Potter (the character from the popular children's books by J. K. Rowling) are licenses that Mattel has acquired. The addition of the Mattel Interactive software division has also helped Mattel evolve from a children's toys producer to a family products company. This evolution has come at a cost though, considering the losses that Mattel has suffered due to the complications with low sales and problems with The Learning Company acquisition.

Customer Orientation at Mattel

Mattel's marketing concept is a management philosophy focusing on satisfying customers' needs and wants. Today this philosophy, commonly known as customer orientation, has been widely adopted by consumer goods manufacturers like Mattel. For example, Mattel has redesigned Barbie to more naturally reflect a normal athletic woman, in an attempt to meet the demands for a more realistic doll. Barbie has also taken on many different professions so as to reach a wider audience. These product modifications and extensions are designed to meet consumer and social demands while still accomplishing company objectives.

Hot Wheels now feature NASCAR logos in an attempt to meet the consumer demand for more merchandise related to this most popular watched sport. Mattel's pursuit of interactive multimedia is an attempt to adapt to the shorter span of time that young girls want Barbie and other dolls and toys. Children are turning to more interactive toys and outlets sooner than was the case in years past, and Mattel's acquisition of The Learning Company was designed to meet this demand and capitalize on it.

As another indicator of its commitment to customers, Mattel employs market research so that its strategy and tactics meet customer wants and when they want it. This is combined with research and development in an effort to release new products yearly based on these consumer needs and wants. There is even a Fisher-Price Robotic Puppy that listens and responds to the voice with lifelike actions. It is hoped that by yearly release of this and like products that meet consumer demand, Mattel will be able to make up for the shorter time that children demand the company's staple products.

Mattel's Core Products

Barbie

Open-toed shoes, a ponytail, sunglasses, earrings, and a zebra-striped bathing suit were sported by the first Barbie doll. Fashions and accessories were also available for the doll. While buyers at the annual Toy Fair in New York took no interest in the Barbie doll, little girls of the time certainly did. The intense demand seen at retail stores was insufficiently met for several years. Mattel just could not produce the Barbie dolls fast enough.

Though Barbie was introduced as a teenage fashion model, she has taken on almost every possible profession. She has also acquired numerous male and female friends and family over the years. Ken, Midge, Skipper, Christie, and others were introduced from the mid-1960s on. More recently the Barbie line has seen a disabled friend in a wheelchair, Share a Smile Becky. Popularity of the Barbie dolls is even breaking stereotypes. Retrofitted versions of Barbie dolls, on sale in select San Francisco stores, feature "Hooker" Barbie, "Trailer Trash" Barbie, and "Drag Queen" Barbie. There are also numerous other "alternative" Barbies, such as "Big Dyke" Barbie, but Mattel does not want the Barbie name to be used in these sales. Redressed and accessorized Barbies are okay with Mattel as long as no one practices trademark infringement. Altogether the Barbie line has sold more than 1 billion dolls in four decades. This makes Barbie the best-selling fashion doll in most global markets, which involves about $2 billion in worldwide sales annually. According to Associated Press, the 100 different Barbie dolls are sold on the average of two per second.

Barbie is one of Mattel's major product lines, accounting for more than 50 percent of its total sales. In the summer of 1998, the giant toy company announced it would pay $700 million to Pleasant Co., maker of the American Girls collection, a well-known line of historical dolls, books, and accessories. Roughly nine years old and sold exclusively through catalogs at the time, the American Girls dolls have a wholesome and educational image—the antithetical Barbies. This move by Mattel represents a long-term strategy to reduce reliance on traditional products and to take away the stigma surrounding the "perfect image" of Barbie. Not everyone can be skinny with a tiny little waist and full upper body like the popular doll. However, Mattel is working extensively to replace the feminist view of Barbie as a symbol of America's obsession with unattainable physical beauty. In response to criticism and the need to keep the brand strong, the company is developing a more modern version of Barbie, with a smaller chest, larger waist, and softer hairstyle.

In addition to the American Girls acquisition, Mattel's CEO at the time, Jill Barad, said that the company planned to open a new flagship Barbie store in Beverly Hills, California, and make its first serious foray into publishing and other emerging products and marketing techniques. For example, for the Christmas season of 1998, Mattel first used the Internet to market its products. Also, more Barbie CD-ROM games are being introduced.

March 1999 marked the fortieth anniversary of Barbie. It also marked a new campaign, the "Be Anything" Barbie campaign, which focused on girls being anything, from athletes to computer hacks to dreamers. This ad campaign focuses primarily on the girls. A Barbie doll is barely present in the ads, and not one of Barbie's accessories appears. The whole effort is an attempt to retain the interest of girls for another two years after the usual post-Barbie age of seven, to make things more "real" with these older girls.

Barbie is also expanding into the realm of young girls' clothing. Barbie clothes are now available for children, and Barbie herself received a makeover. Wider hips and a smaller bust line more accurately reflect a natural female body. More in-style clothes are available for the doll, and a bellybutton is now found on the doll. The Barbie line is even being expanded into computers, which are designed with a Barbie theme and include a Barbie digital camera. This is all being done in an effort to recapture more of a customer base and even to expand the market by attracting older girls to the Barbie product line.

Hot Wheels

One unexpected bright spot in Mattel's 1998 toy lineup was Hot Wheels, the thirty-year-old line of die-cast miniature cars. Hot Wheels sales were up 40 percent for the quarter that ended June 1998, easing the impact of a 15 percent drop in sales of its Barbie doll line. The boost in sales of Hot Wheels can be traced to a deal with NASCAR under which Mattel manufactures toys with the auto racing association's logo. Hot Wheels has also ventured into entertainment licensing for the first time, producing vehicles tied to films like *Armageddon*.

Looking to the future, Mattel sees other advantages in licensing the Hot Wheels name to diverse manufacturing companies, ranging from sporting goods to bedding. Heading up that effort will be Robert McCandlish, former Chicago Cubs pitcher and current director of boy's licensing for Mattel. McCandlish, who joined Mattel in 1996, is known for extending brands beyond the toy aisles to apparel, school products, collectibles, and the like. He was also responsible for overseeing the introduction of the successful NASCAR line. Moreover, Mattel is confident this new license will give Hot Wheels more adult appeal.

So far, more than seventy companies, including JEM Sportswear and Mead, have agreed to the licensing arrangements. Hot Wheels licensing deals could bring in nearly $100 million in sales, boosting the car line to annual revenue of $400 million. This would make Hot Wheels the top toy vehicle in the world, even stronger than the Matchbox line that Mattel acquired in the late 1990s.

Cabbage Patch Kids

Since the introduction of Cabbage Patch Kids in 1983, more than 80 million dolls have been purchased around the world. The dolls were unique in many respects, including their representation of many races and ethnicities through individualized facial and body features. When Mattel introduced the Cabbage Patch Kids Snacktime Kids in the fall of 1996, it expected the dolls to continue the success of the original product line.

The Snacktime Kids had moving mouths that enabled children to "feed" the doll. Unfortunately, this unique feature proved dangerous to some kids. Reports of children getting their fingers and hair caught in the dolls' mouths surfaced soon after the 1996 holiday season. By January 1997, Mattel had voluntarily pulled all Snacktime Kids from store shelves. In addition, consumers were offered a cash refund of $40 when returning the dolls. As CEO Barad indicated, "Our job is to bring joy to children's lives. If any of our products are causing concerns, we are committed to responding in a responsible manner." The U.S. Consumer Product Safety Commission applauded Mattel's effort with the Snacktime Kids situation.

International Sales

According to CEO Jill Barad, Mattel, Inc., planned to double its international sales throughout the late 1990s and early 2000, as part of a new strategy aimed at worldwide growth. In an interview at the September 1997 American International Toy Fair in New York, Barad disclosed that the strategy included producing toys for individual foreign markets rather than simply adapting the U.S. products. Thus, Mattel was using marketing research to adapt products to cultural values and customers. In addition, the company's management structure was organized to focus more aggressively on overseas sales and linked bonus incentives for employees to international growth targets.

These changes and the new strategy followed a six-month study of Mattel by Boston Consulting Group to determine key markets and product areas for growth. This study is in alignment with Mattel's customer orientation, and it identified a potential $6 billion in additional sales growth over the next five years for Mattel by increasing the size of the toy market and Mattel's market share. Two-thirds of that growth should come from Japan and Europe and less than a quarter from the United States and Latin America.

Mattel constantly pursues this growth, and they are seeing benefits. However, the traditional Barbie doll is not receiving a warm welcome in some international markets. The Malaysian Consumers' Association of Penanghas tried to ban Barbie because of her non-Asian appearance and the lack of creativity needed to play with her. The public and media outcry soon retaliated against this ban. But government agencies in other countries, such as Iran, are carrying out like practices. No matter the case, Barbie is selling very well, despite her appearance, all over the world.

Responsibility at Mattel

Like any other organization, Mattel has recognized the different responsibilities it has to various stakeholders, including customers, employees, investors, suppliers, and the community. These stakeholders have some claim, or stake, in Mattel's products, markets, and business outcomes. Mattel demonstrates a commitment to economic, legal, ethical, and philanthropic responsibilities. This section focuses on the latter two responsibilities.

Mattel's core products and business environment can present ethical issues. For example, since the company's products are designed primarily for children, it must be sensitive to societal concerns about children's rights. In addition, the international environment often complicates business transactions, especially in the area of employee rights and safety in manufacturing facilities. Different legal systems and cultural expectations about business can create ethical conflict. Finally, the use of technology may present ethical dilemmas, especially with regard to consumer privacy. Mattel has recognized these potential issues and has taken steps to strengthen its commitment to business ethics and social responsibility.

Privacy and Marketing Technology

Advances in technology have created special issues for Mattel's marketing efforts. Mattel has recognized that, because it markets to children, it has the responsibility to communicate with parents about corporate marketing strategy. The company has taken special steps to inform both children and adults about its philosophy regarding Internet-based marketing tools, like the Hot Wheels Web site. For example, the Web site for Hot Wheels contains the following statement:

> It is Mattel's intention, with each of its Web sites, to adhere to the Better Business Bureau's Children's Advertising Review Unit (CARU) guidelines, including its guidelines on Internet advertising. All Mattel marketing efforts, including this Web site, are closely scrutinized to conform to these guidelines. We encourage parents to monitor their children's online use, and to

help us protect their privacy by instructing them never to provide personal information on this site or any other without permission.

Hot Wheels Speed City is a place for kids to play and explore their imagination in an online environment. We understand your concern as a parent about Internet safety and privacy, and we would like to take this opportunity to clarify what we do and offer some suggestions on making this an entertaining experience for you and your child *(site provides several suggestions)*. If you are interested in more information about helping your child understand advertising and its impact, please visit the Better Business Bureau's Web site at http://www.bbb.org.

Thus, a key ethical issue for Mattel's products and marketing activities relates to its online marketing efforts. Since the company relies heavily on communication with children to market it products, any legislation in this area must be carefully monitored. For example, the U.S. Federal Trade Commission is developing new rules as a result of the Children's Online Privacy Protection Act of 1998. These rules require Web-based marketers to get parental permission before collecting any personally identifiable information from children (e.g., name, address, e-mail address). Further, since its Web sites are accessible to children around the world, Mattel must be cognizant of regulations in other parts of the world.

Global Manufacturing Principles

Beyond concerns about marketing to children, Mattel, Inc., is making a serious commitment to general business ethics. In late 1997, the company completed its first full ethics audit of each of its manufacturing sites and those facilities of primary contractors. The audit indicated the company was not using any child labor or forced labor, a problem that has plagued other overseas consumer products manufacturers (e.g., Nike). However, several contractors were found in violation of Mattel's standards and have been forced to change their operations or lose Mattel's significant business. In an effort to continue its strong record on human rights and related ethical standards, Mattel instituted a code of conduct called "Global Manufacturing Principles." These principles require all Mattel-owned and -contracted manufacturing facilities to, among other things, favor business partners who are committed to ethical standards that are comparable with Mattel's. Other principles relate to safety, wages, and adherence to local laws.

Mattel's auditing effort and subsequent code of conduct are not designed as a punitive force. Rather, the international company is dedicated to creating and encouraging responsible business practices. As one company consultant has noted, "Mattel is committed to improving the skill level of workers . . . (so) in turn (they) will experience increased opportunities and productivity." This statement reflects Mattel's concern for relationships with employees and business partners that extend beyond pure profit considerations. While the company will surely benefit from its code's principles, Mattel has formally acknowledged its willingness to consider multiple stakeholders' interests and benefits in its business philosophy. The company's code is a signal to potential partners, customers, and other stakeholders that Mattel is making a serious commitment to ethical values and is willing to base business decisions on them.

For example, contracts with business partners will be based on how well they meet all of Mattel's manufacturing principles. If Mattel determines that any one of its partners' manufacturing facilities or any vendor has violated these principles, it can either terminate their business relationship or require the facility to implement a corrective action plan. If corrective action is advised but not taken, Mattel will immediately terminate current production and suspend placement of future orders. Thus, a key challenge for Mattel is the certification of business partners and potential partners with respect to the manufacturing principles.

Mattel Foundation

In another effort to demonstrate a strong commitment to its stakeholders, Mattel established the Mattel Foundation. This foundation "promotes the spirit of philanthropy and community involvement among" Mattel's employees and makes charitable investments to help children in need. Mattel views philanthropy as an investment and has therefore sought out nonprofits that hold and demonstrate the same beliefs of compassionate outreach to children and financial accountability.

The work of the Mattel Foundation is funded primarily through a percentage of Mattel's pretax corporate profits. The limited resources and numerous needs has made the Foundation focus primarily on national Foundation-sponsored initiatives that address relevant children's issues. These investments are continually reviewed to ensure that the most is being made of Mattel's philanthropic activities. The 1999 goals of the Mattel Foundation were to provide for construction of the Mattel Children's Hospital at UCLS, complete the final year of Mattel's Hand in Hand initiative, sustain the Mattel Family Learning Program, and promote the spirit of giving among Mattel employees.

Conclusion

As this case has shown, while the last few years of the twentieth century challenged Mattel's executive leadership and financial standing, the company also made strong strides with respect to its ethical and social responsibilities. Today, Mattel faces many market opportunities and threats, including the rate at which children are growing up and leaving toys, the role of technology in consumer products, and purchasing power and consumer needs in global markets. While Jill Barad's career led to the outstanding success of the Barbie line, the rest of Mattel's strategy did not realize strong financial results. For a company that began with two friends making picture frames, Mattel has demonstrated marketing prowess. But the next few years will test the firm's resolve and strategy within the highly competitive, yet lucrative, toy market.

Questions for Discussion

1. Why is a company's stock price so important? What role does the CEO and the company's strategy have in this price? Discuss Jill Barad's leadership issues with regard to Mattel's strategy and subsequent financial performance.

2. Why do manufacturers of products for children seem to have special responsibilities to consumers and society? What are these responsibilities, and how well has Mattel met them? Provide evidence of Mattel's strengths and weaknesses in this area.

3. Visit Mattel's Web site, including information on its recent financial performance and new-product initiatives. What has changed since this case was written? Has Mattel continued with its core strategy, or has it taken a new direction? What recommendations do you have for Mattel with regard to its marketing strategy?

Sources

These facts are from Deborah Adamson, "Trouble in Toyland," *CBS MarketWatch*, March 8, 2000, http://cbs.marketwatch .com/; Anonymous, "Mattel, Inc. Launches Global Code of Conduct Intended to Improve Workplace, Worker's Standard of Living," *Canada NewsWire*, November 21, 1997 (for more information on Mattel's code, please contact the company at (310) 252-3524); Lisa Bannon, "Let's Play Makeover Barbie," *Wall Street Journal*, February 17, 2000, B-2; Lisa Bannon and Joann S. Lublin, "Jill Barad Abruptly Quits the Top Job at Mattel," *Wall Street Journal*, February 4, 2000, A-1; Adam Bryant, "Mattel CEO Jill Barad and a Toyshop That Doesn't Forget to Play," *New York Times*, October 11, 1998, C-8; Bill Duryea, "Barbie-holics: They're Devoted to the Doll," *St. Petersburg Times*, August 7, 1998, B-1; Kathleen Grassel, (1999), "Barbie Around the World," *New Renaissance*, 8(4) (1999), 33–88; James Heckman, "Legislation," *Marketing News*, December 7, 1998, 1, 16; Hot Wheels Web site, http://www.hotwheels.com/; Nancy J. Kim, "Barbie Gets an Image Makeover," *Puget Sound Business Journal*, March 15, 1999, 17; Mattel's corporate Web site, http://www.mattel.com, accessed February 29, 2000; Marla Matzer, "Deals on Hot Wheels," *Los Angeles Times*, July 22, 1998, D-18; Road Trip America, http://www .roadtripamerica.com/people/minna.htm, accessed March 27, 2000; Patricia Sellers, "The 50 Most Powerful Women in American Business," *Fortune*, October 12, 1998, 32–36; Pamela Sherrid, "Troubles in BarbieLand," *U.S. News & World Report*, January 17, 2000, 47–48; "The Glass Ceiling: The CEO Still Wears Wingtips," *Business Week*, November 22, 1999, 62–63; "Toymaker Mattel Bans Child Labor," *Denver Post*, November 21, 1998, A-8; U.S. Consumer Product Safety Commission, Office of Information and Public Affairs, "Mattel and U.S. Consumer Product Safety Commission Announce Voluntary Refund Program for Cabbage Patch Kids Snacktime Kids Dolls," January 6, 1997, Release #97 055; Michael White, "Barbie Will Lose Some Curves When Mattel Modernizes Icon," *Detroit News*, November 18, 1997, E-32.

The Gillette Company

The Gillette Company has established itself as the leading producer and seller of grooming products. The corporate history of Gillette will be described briefly in order to provide an overview of the strategy behind Gillette's phenomenal success. Closer attention will then be paid to the situation, as it existed at the end of 1999, and the prospects, outlook, options, and opportunities that were present then. The major focus of the case will be on corporate strategy, business segments, and product mix.

A Sharp Beginning

Founded in 1901 by King C. Gillette, the Gillette Company was one of the first great multinational organizations and a marvel of marketing effectiveness. Only four years after founding the firm in Boston, King Gillette opened a branch office in London and rapidly obtained sales and profits throughout Western Europe. About twenty years later, he said this of his safety razor:

> There is no other article for individual use so universally known or widely distributed. In my travels, I have found it in the most northern town in Norway and in the heart of the Sahara Desert.

Gillette set this goal for himself: to offer consumers high-quality shaving products that would satisfy basic grooming needs at a fair price. Having gained more than half of the entire razor and blades market, Gillette's manufacturing efficiency allowed it to implement marketing programs on a large scale, which propelled Gillette forward in profits and in market leadership. Riding this tide of good fortune, the company was able to weather the storm brought on by World War II and emerged in a very healthy condition. In 1948, Gillette set its all-time-performance record with profits per share of $6.80. Gillette has not approached this level of success since that time.

In 1955, Gillette decided to tread new waters and undertook two unrelated acquisitions. The first acquisition was the Toni Company, maker of do-it-yourself home permanent wave kits. Although this was a profitable venture initially, sales and profits soon faded. The second major acquisition was the Paper Mate pen company, which at

This case was prepared by Donald P. Roy, Middle Tennessee State University, and Brent Wren, University of Alabama-Huntsville, for classroom discussion rather than to illustrate either effective or ineffective handling of an administrative situation.

that time made only retractable, refillable ballpoint pens. It, too, was profitable, but soon Bic low-priced, disposable (nonrefillable) pens came over from France. Partly due to these two acquisitions, Gillette slowly began to lose its edge, and net profit slumped to $1.33 per share in 1964.

A Tough Lesson Learned

In 1962, Gillette's U.S. market share hovered around 70 percent while its success abroad was even better. Around this time, the English firm Wilkinson Sword introduced a stainless steel blade in the United States and began taking a substantial portion of Gillette's market share. Partly due to the time devoted to experimenting with the home permanent wave and pen businesses and partly due to the small size of the Wilkinson Sword Company, Gillette underestimated the potential impact on its core business. Also, Gillette executives were unsure how to react. Should they introduce their own stainless steel blade, or ignore the rival and hope that its market niche would remain small?

Gillette was lucky. Although it eventually introduced its own stainless steel blade, the real break came when Wilkinson was unable to exploit the niche it had created. Due to its lack of resources, Wilkinson Sword was unable to compete with the powerful Gillette machine and eventually sold much of its blade business to Gillette. However, the impact of this dilemma had already been felt. In 1965, Gillette's market share hit an all-time low of 49 percent. The lessons learned from this debacle are still with Gillette today and guide many of its decisions and actions.

The Move Toward Diversification

Attempting to resolve the crises of the early 1960s was Gillette's new CEO, Vincent Ziegler. Ziegler was aggressive, marketing oriented, and ambitious for the company, believing in diversification through the acquisition of companies in other business segments. Within the next few years, Ziegler spearheaded the acquisition of the following companies:

Braun AG (German manufacturer of small appliances)

S.T. Dupont (French maker of luxury lighters)

Eve of Roma (high-fashion perfume)

Buxton Leather goods

Welcome Wagon, Inc.

Sterilon hospital razors

Jafra Cosmetics (home sales)

Four of these acquisitions proved to be unprofitable or unsuitable and were divested, and the other three yielded low profits by Gillette's standards. Other troubles came from the French manufacturer Bic, which excelled in disposable products. Its 19-cent disposable stick pens particularly affected the Paper Mate line of refillable pens and drove Paper Mate's share of the retail ballpoint pen market from over 50 percent down to 13 percent, approximately a 75 percent drop. Gillette had retaliated quickly with its new Write Brothers line of disposable pens, which failed on the first introduction in 1972 but succeeded in building market share when reintroduced to the market in 1975 with heavy price promotions. Bic was also threatening Gillette's strengths with two other products—its disposable razors and lighters—which were being marketed very successfully in Europe and elsewhere.

The Ziegler era had its successes. Cricket disposable lighters were brought on through the Dupont firm and did well. Soft & Dri antiperspirant joined Right Guard, expanding Gillette's position in the deodorant market. However, the belief that aerosols destroy the ozone layer caused sales of spray versions of these products (along with all other brands of spray) to plummet suddenly, creating a crisis in these segments. Meanwhile, Gillette's Trac II razor was a great success, and the razor segment continued its dominance. Earnings per share rose to $2.83 in 1974 but slipped again the next year.

At this juncture, Ziegler retired from active direction of the company and sought to hire a successor. The first choice of candidate did not remain in the position very long, and Colman Mockler was then asked to step into this position, which he accepted in 1976. Under Mockler, Gillette's strategy was to cut costs dramatically and pour the money saved into ad and product development budgets. The Mockler era was one of the most successful in Gillette history, producing such memorable innovations as the Atra razor, the Good News! disposable razor, and the Daisy razor for women. With such product additions, Gillette not only held a majority of the U.S. shaving market (including the leading shaving cream), but up to 75 percent of market shares in countries around the world.

During this period, Gillette's major marketing war was in disposable lighters. When Cricket was launched in 1972, it was an instant success. Then Bic entered the U.S. market and enticed smokers to "Flick your Bic." A long-term price war ensued in which Bic succeeded in outselling the Cricket by a small margin, but Gillette was persistent.

A principal aim of the Mockler management team in the 1980s was the recovery of the company's earnings to previously established levels. Through a series of aggressive economizing measures and acquisitions, the company was able to show strong growth in earnings per share throughout the decade. Two outside acquisitions played key roles in Gillette's resurgence in the early 1980s. First, Gillette acquired the Liquid Paper Company, the leading maker of typewriter correction fluids. This gave a much needed boost to its writing instruments segment. Second, in what appeared to be a minor acquisition at the time, Gillette purchased a small maker of skin care products, Aapri.

Along with these acquisitions, the introduction of new products that were developed in the Gillette laboratories helped boost sales in the razor and blades, personal care, and writing instruments segments. First, in the razor and blades segment, Gillette introduced the Atra-Plus shaving system, which featured a refillable Atra cartridge with a lubricating strip. This overtook the Trac-II as the best-selling razor. Also, Gillette updated the Good News! line to include a disposable razor with a lubricating strip.

In the personal care segment, Gillette made several introductions, including Aapri facial care products, Dry Idea deodorant, Bare Elegance body lotion, Mink Difference hair spray, White Rain hair care products, and Silkience shampoo and moisturizers.

These additions had mixed results and left Gillette still searching for the keys to success in this business segment. In the writing instruments segment, Gillette achieved moderate success with the development of Eraser Mate erasable, disposable pens. Also, the steady sales of Paper Mate pens and Liquid Paper correction fluids helped to maintain company performance.

Despite its ability to post above-average performance during the 1980s, many analysts saw Gillette as a stagnant, lazy, sleeping giant, with earnings potential far above current realizations. The analysts based this evaluation on Gillette's considerable name recognition and market power, and its well-established marketing and production channels worldwide. In fact, Gillette's attractiveness led to an unsuccessful takeover attempt in 1986.

Business Segments and Products

Having provided the background information on Gillette's activities, we will now review the situation in the various business segments in the second half of the 1990s. This section is designed to provide an idea of the scope of operations and current product offerings, as well as strategies being pursued in each segment. Case Exhibits 13.1 and 13.2 depict the financial situation as it existed at the end of 1999. After enjoying record sales and profits in 1997, Gillette experienced a reversal in the growth to which it had been accustomed. The company pointed to economic problems in Asia, Brazil, and Russia and a decline in the value of the Euro currency as reasons for sales and profit decreases. In addition, Gillette made some strategic changes that will no doubt shape the future direction of the company. In February 1999, Alfred Zeien retired as Chairman and CEO and was replaced by Michael Hawley, a 39-year Gillette employee. Later in 1999, the company announced that it would focus on three key segments: grooming products (blades, razors, and related toiletries), portable power (alkaline and specialty batteries), and oral care (toothbrushes and plaque removers). Gillette operated two other business segments at the end of 1999 that were not considered primary businesses: Braun products and stationery products.

Grooming Products

Gillette is still the world leader in blades and razors, and this business continues to grow. The company holds dominant market share worldwide for men's blades, razors, and shaving preparations as well as women's wet shaving products and hair epilation devices. As Case Exhibits 13.1 and 13.2 illustrate, sales and profits have shown a strong upward trend over the past several years, during which annual gains in sales and profits averaged approximately 6 percent. The blades and razors segment accounts for about 30 percent of its sales and over 50 percent of the company's profits. Sales in this segment have more than doubled to almost $3.2 billion since 1989, and the outlook for this segment is promising as the shaving population increases, particularly in such locations as Asia, Eastern Europe, and Latin America, and with an increased popularity of shaving among women. The company's progress in its principal line of business reflects the outstanding market success of its technologically superior products, including the Sensor family of shaving systems and more recently the Mach3 system.

The original Sensor was introduced in early 1990 and is now sold in over 80 markets worldwide. It remains the best seller in the United States and most other major

CASE EXHIBIT 13.1	NET SALES AND OPERATING PROFIT CONTRIBUTION BY BUSINESS SEGMENT

	Blades and Razors		Toiletries		Duracell Products		Oral-B Products		Braun Products		Stationery Products	
Year	Net Sales	Segment Profit	Net Sales	Segment Profit	Net Sales	Segment Profit	Net Sales	Segment Profit	Net Sales	Segment Profit	Net Sales	Segment Profit
1999	32%	56%	11%	4%	28%	28%	6%	4%	16%	7%	7%	1%
1998	30%	50%	12%	2%	26%	26%	6%	4%	17%	13%	9%	5%
1997	29%	50%	14%	5%	25%	22%	6%	4%	17%	13%	9%	6%
1996	29%	52%	14%	4%	23%	21%	6%	3%	18%	14%	10%	6%
1995	30%	51%	14%	4%	23%	23%	5%	2%	18%	14%	10%	6%

Source: Gillette 1999 Annual Report.

CASE EXHIBIT 13.2	FINANCIAL INFORMATION BY BUSINESS SEGMENT

	Blades and Razors	Toiletries	Duracell Products	Oral-B Products	Braun Products	Stationery Products	All Other	Total
1999								
Net Sales	$3,167	$1,062	$2,726	$616	$1,583	$743	$—	$9,897
Profit from Operations	1,206	85	606	77	154	18	(41)	2,105
Identifiable Assets	3,532	696	3,310	663	1,602	1,214	769	11,786
Capital Expenditures	459	85	145	40	130	43	30	932
Depreciation	186	29	56	23	83	21	22	420
1998								
Net Sales	$3,028	$1,214	$2,576	$642	$1,740	$856	$—	$10,056
Profit from Operations	1,153	54	597	101	291	108	(515)	1,789
Identifiable Assets	3,378	771	3,288	680	1,679	1,330	776	11,902
Capital Expenditures	453	69	144	62	135	48	89	1,000
Depreciation	167	27	51	18	73	24	13	373
1997								
Net Sales	$2,881	$1,410	$2,478	$624	$1,744	$924	1	$10,062
Profit from Operations	1,186	124	526	85	304	156	(57)	2,324
Identifiable Assets	3,006	1,004	3,138	622	1,544	1,299	251	10,864
Capital Expenditures	423	88	165	45	126	40	86	973
Depreciation	111	37	58	17	77	23	7	330

Source: Gillette 1999 Annual Report.

markets. Gillette followed the Sensor with launch of the Excel in 1993. Gillette leveraged both the Sensor and Sensor Excel brand names by developing versions of these products targeted at women. The Sensor for Women system, launched in 1992, holds about one-fourth of the market share for female razor products in the United States. The Sensor Excel for women, launched in 1996, was very successful in the key markets where it was introduced. The continued success of the Sensor family of shaving systems has led to the gradual decline of the Atra and Trac II twin-blade shaving systems. These systems, key brands since the 1970s, have yielded their standing as market leaders. Despite this gradual decline, both systems continue to hold sizable share positions worldwide. The company's disposable twin-blade razors' moderate increases in sales have enabled it to maintain its position as the number-one seller in this product category worldwide. Gillette's Good News! brand has been the best-selling disposable razor in the United States each year since 1976.

In 1998, Gillette introduced a new razor with three thin blades, the Mach3, that is designed to provide a closer shave in fewer strokes with less irritation than any other razor on the market. To develop this new product, Gillette made major investments in research and development and a strong commitment to gain market share. It is the first major product launch since Gillette introduced Sensor's independently floating double blades in 1977. The Mach3 blades are mounted on tiny springs like Gillette's Sensor Excel. The Mach3 became the company's most successful new product ever. Sales of the Mach3 hit $1 billion in only 18 months. Mach3 was named winner of the American Marketing Association's Grand Edison award as the best new product of 1998. Mach3 technology has been used to develop a similar shaving system for women. The product, which is known only as "226" (Gillette guards brand names until products are introduced) was to become available in late 2000. Further efforts to build market share for women's shaving products include targeting teen shavers with a line of Sensor razors in a variety of colors in an attempt to develop lifelong customers at a young age.

Gillette is actively pursuing two main growth strategies to strengthen its global blade and razor position. The first is to upgrade the value of the blade market worldwide. In the more developed countries this means further developing its Sensor, Excel, and Mach3 brands. In developing countries, increasing blade value involves accelerating the conversion from double-edge blades to more profitable twin-blade products. The second strategy is continued geographic expansion, with the company taking such steps as creating selling organizations in Romania and the former Yugoslavia and the acquisition of blade firms in the former Soviet Union and the Czech Republic.

Toiletries products are now considered part of the grooming products business segment. At the end of 1999, the toiletries and cosmetics line includes deodorants, antiperspirants, shave preparations, and hair care products. The strategy for toiletries is to focus resources on core grooming product categories, such as deodorants/antiperspirants and shave preparations, while providing supporting products in key markets. The product lineup included Gillette Gel, Satin Care for Women gel, and Foamy shaving creams; Right Guard, Gillette Series, Soft & Dri, and Dry Idea deodorants/antiperspirants; and White Rain, Adorn, Dippity-Do, Mink Difference, Tame, The Dry Look, and Toni hair care products. Sales and profits in this category peaked in 1997; the average annual sales growth rate between 1994 and 1999 was 1.8 percent.

Intense competition and slow growth for certain products prompted Gillette to pare its product portfolio of toiletries. In 1998, Gillette sold its Jafra cosmetics line to narrow the focus of the segment to toiletries. The product line was reduced further in 2000 when Gillette's hair care brands were sold to Diamond Products Company, a private-label marketer. Remaining toiletries products include shaving preparation products and antiperspirant/deodorants.

Portable Power

With a merger between Gillette and Duracell International at the end of 1996, Gillette instantly achieved worldwide leadership in the alkaline battery business. This segment is key to Gillette's portfolio, with Duracell products generating over one-fourth of the company's sales and profits (see Case Exhibits 13.1 and 13.2). Sales of Duracell products have increased in recent years, and the prospects for growth continue to be promising. The Duracell product line includes alkaline batteries, specialty batteries such as lithium batteries used in cameras and zinc air batteries used to power hearing aids, and high-power rechargeable batteries for use in such consumer products as cellular phones and camcorders.

Gillette's strategies for sustaining growth in the Duracell segment are similar to strategies developed for its other segments. First, the company emphasizes research and development for new product introductions. For example, Duracell introduced PowerCheck AA batteries, which feature an on-battery, heat-sensitive strip that gauges remaining battery power when activated. This innovative technology was made available on AAA, C, and D batteries in 1997. Second, geographic expansion opportunities exist in this segment. In 1996, Duracell purchased Eveready South Africa, whose zinc carbon battery is the best seller in that country, and Sunpower, a leading alkaline battery brand in South Korea.

Although Gillette has enjoyed solid performances in sales and profits from each of its existing business segments, the company viewed the Duracell merger as adding a long-sought "new leg" to its portfolio. Duracell is considered to be an excellent fit with Gillette's focus on technologically driven consumer products. Also, Duracell and Gillette share numerous characteristics, including global brand franchises, common distribution channels, and geographic expansion potential. The company sees opportunities for Duracell to enjoy significant economies of scale and greater market penetration through Gillette's worldwide distribution network.

Perhaps the most attractive aspect of Duracell for Gillette is the market potential of the alkaline batteries category. Duracell has market leadership in alkaline batteries with approximately a 40 percent share. Among the reasons for this growth is the booming popularity of portable electronic products, aggressive merchandising by battery manufacturers, and constant performance improvements, especially in battery lifetime (for instance, the "run time" of a portable personal stereo powered by a pair of AA batteries had been stretched from 11–12 hours in 1984 to nearly 20 hours in 1997).

Duracell can benefit from the growing market in three ways. First, geographic expansion opportunities exist for Duracell given the fact that only one-fifth of Duracell's business is now in markets outside Europe and North America. In international markets where Duracell has not been strongly represented, there are quick, clear benefits to be gained from the linkage with Gillette's well-established marketing and distribution networks. Second, opportunities exist in both new and established markets to upgrade customers from lower-value zinc carbon batteries to better-performing, longer-lasting Duracell alkaline technology. Alkaline batteries deliver five to six times the life for two to three times the price. This upgrade opportunity is strikingly clear in the emerging countries of China, India, and Russia. These three countries account for some 30 percent of the world's consumer battery market, but less than 5 percent of batteries currently sold in these countries are alkaline. Third, Duracell's focus on improving its alkaline technology could significantly expand the capabilities of alkaline batteries, thus dramatically expanding their worldwide market. In 1998, Duracell set a new standard in quality with Duracell Ultra, a new line of AA and AAA batteries specially designed for use in powerful digital cameras, cellular phones, and remote-controlled toys. It is estimated that the Ultra has a 50 percent longer life than current alkaline batteries. The company believes that the 20 percent price differential above regular alkaline batteries will be accepted because of the extended battery life. The Ultra product line was expanded in 1999 to include C, D, and 9-volt batteries.

Ultra was the result of four years of development in which Duracell improved the performance of the alkaline design by reducing electrical resistance and reformulating the battery's chemistry. However, Duracell was not the only company tweaking batteries for high-tech products. Eastman Kodak, the fourth-place player in the battery battle, launched the Photolife AA, which claims to outlast competitors' batteries in digital cameras. Also, number two, Energizer, promoted AA and AAA batteries as superior for high-drain devices such as minidisc players and cell phones.

Gillette faces competition for Duracell alkaline batteries from two sources. One source of competition for Duracell is price-based competitors for regular alkaline batteries. Longtime competitor Rayovac has experienced a resurgence in recent years. Although Rayovac's aggressive marketing appears to have taken market share from Duracell's primary competitor, Energizer, it is possible that Duracell may be vulnerable on the basis of price. Additional price competition for alkaline batteries is coming from private-label batteries. In 1999, Wal-Mart began selling its own brand of alkaline batteries. Consumers who perceive little difference among different brands of batteries might select lower-priced batteries. A second source of competition for Duracell's alkaline batteries is rechargeable batteries. However, alkaline offers more convenience to consumers because the internal construction allows for storage of more than twice as much energy as a comparably sized rechargeable. To exploit Ultra's potential, Duracell must convince rechargeable users to switch to alkaline.

Oral Care

In a strong and well-established partnership with dental professionals, Oral-B develops and markets a broad range of superior oral care products worldwide. Led by toothbrushes, the Oral-B line also includes interdental dental products, specialty toothpastes, mouth rinses, and professional dental products. Sales and profits continue to increase for this segment (see Case Exhibits 13.1 and 13.2), and developments in product technology are largely responsible for this increase. For example, the Oral-B CrossAction toothbrush features innovative technology that is clinically proven to provide a greater level of manual plaque removal.

Oral-B's strategy for growth relies on a combination of new product development and geographic expansion. The oral care category has experienced growth due to new product development of both manual and power-assisted toothbrushes. Oral-B holds about 20 percent of the worldwide market for manual toothbrushes and a nearly 70 percent market share for power-assisted toothbrushes. Geographic expansion continues with the establishment of sales organizations in Portugal and India and the opening of a joint-venture toothbrush manufacturing plant in Vietnam. These two strategies for growth will be supported by advertising and promotion in an effort to sustain Oral-B's worldwide growth.

Braun

The Braun segment turned in a record performance in 1997, but has since struggled to contribute profits to Gillette and is no longer considered one of the company's primary business segments (see Case Exhibits 13.1 and 13.2). Gillette still values Braun's oral care and hair removal appliances. These products fit with Gillette's emphasis on grooming products and oral care. Other Braun products do not fit with Gillette's new business focus. Kitchen appliances, personal care products, and health care instruments are among Braun products that are not as attractive to Gillette as they once were. As a result, the company is contemplating selling most of the Braun line but keeping the key products (oral care and hair removal appliances).

Stationery Products

Intense competition had a major impact on Gillette's writing products and correction products businesses. This segment includes Parker, Paper Mate, and Waterman pens and Liquid Paper correction products. Despite owning some of the most valuable brands in the industry, this segment has experienced a decline in sales and profits in each the three years from 1997 to 1999 (see Case Exhibits 13.1 and 13.2). Heavy price competition squeezed profitability for disposable writing instruments, and the distribution channels for the Waterman and Parker brands, stationery and gift stores, are significantly different than Gillette's familiar distribution channels of mass merchandisers, supermarkets, and drug stores. When Gillette management redefined the company's primary businesses, the Stationery Products business no longer fit the company's focus. As a result, the Stationery Products business was sold to Newell Rubbermaid in 2000.

Toward the Future

Gillette has plans to return to its impressive performances of the early and mid-1990s. A major emphasis continues to be development of new products; 1999 was the sixth consecutive year in which at least 40 percent of Gillette's sales came from products introduced within the previous five years. Gillette management has taken steps in an attempt to improve marketing efficiency. In 1999, the company implemented a change in its organizational structure. Gillette now has a Global Business Management Group that has responsibility for all research and development, manufacturing, and strategic marketing for all Gillette brands. Also, the company split its sales and marketing efforts into two groups: Western Hemisphere (North America and Latin America) and Eastern Hemisphere (all other geographic regions). These changes followed a decision in 1998 to close fourteen factories and twelve distribution centers as well as layoff 4,700 employees worldwide. Gillette is putting its future in the hands of its three core businesses and a reorganized marketing operation in an effort to strengthen the company.

Questions for Discussion

1. What are the current conditions in each of Gillette's business segments? Is each business segment moving in the right direction? Do you see new products that should be added or old products that should be eliminated? Which products and why?

2. Identify the environmental variables (market, competition, government, technology) that have affected Gillette over its life. Which have had the greatest positive

and negative impacts? At the present time, what do you perceive to be the chief environmental forces with which Gillette must cope?

3. What actions would you recommend over the next five years? What specific marketing mix decisions would you recommend for each business segment? What is the timeframe for your actions?

Sources

These facts are from Wes Conard, "3-Blade Razor a Cut Above, Gillette Says," *The Commercial Appeal*, April 15,1998; Gillette 1997 Annual Report; "Gillette's Edge," *Business Week*, January 19, 1998, 70–77; "How Gillette Is Honing Its Edge," *Business Week*, Sept. 28, 1992, 60; Gillette Company, 1991 Annual Report; Gillette Series Marketing Support Report, Gillette Company 1992; Lawrence Ingrassia, "Gillette Ties New Toiletries to Hot Razor," *Wall Street Journal*, September 18, 1992, B1, B6; Lawrence Ingrassia, "Keeping Sharp," *Wall Street Journal*, December 10, 1992, A1, A6; Seema Nayyar, "Gillette Jumps Into Men's Toiletries," *Brandweek*, July 20, 1992, 6; Rekha Balu, "Hop Faster, Energizer Bunny: Rayovac Batteries Roll On," *Wall Street Journal*, June 15, 1999, B4; William M. Bulkeley, "Gillette Studies a Possible Sale of Braun Assets," *Wall Street Journal*, February 23, 2000, B8; Mercedes M. Cardona, "Gillette's Mach3 Captures Top Prize at Edison Awards," *Advertising Age*, March 22, 1999, 54; Christopher Cooper and Marcus Walker, "Plunging Euro Batters U.S. Firms," *Wall Street Journal*, May 30, 2000, A16; Gillette 1999 Annual Report; " Gillette Reaches Definitive Agreement to Sell Stationery Products Business," Gillette News Release, August 22, 2000; "Gillette Reaches Agreement to Sell White Rain Brand, St. Paul Manufacturing Center," Gillette News Release, March 23, 2000; Jeremy Kahn, "Gillette Loses Face," *Fortune*, November 8, 1999, 147–152; Mark Maremount, "Gillette to Unveil Women's Version of Mach3 Razor," *Wall Street Journal*, December 2, 1999, B14; Mark Maremount, "Gillette to Shut 14 of Its Plants, Lay Off 4,700," *Wall Street Journal*, September 29, 1998, A3; Mark Maremount, "Gillette's New Strategy Is to Sharpen Pitch to Women," *Wall Street Journal*, May 11, 1998, B1; The Gillette Company World Wide Web Site, http://www.gillette.com, September 18, 2000; "Wal-Mart Selling Its Own Brand of Alkaline Batteries," *Wall Street Journal*, December 10, 1999, C4–5.

USA Today: The Nation's Newspaper and the World's Online News Source

USA Today, subtitled "The Nation's Newspaper," debuted in 1982 as America's first national general-interest daily newspaper. The paper was the brainchild of Allen H. Neuharth, who until 1989 was Chairman of Gannett Co., Inc., a diversified international $5.3 billion news, information, and communications company that publishes newspapers, operates broadcast television stations, and is engaged in marketing, commercial printing, a newswire service, data services, and news programming. Gannett is currently the largest U.S. newspaper group in terms of circulation, with seventy-four daily newspapers having a combined daily paid circulation of 6.6 million and a daily readership of over 5.4 million. Gannett publications include *USA Today*, the nation's largest-selling daily newspaper, with a circulation of approximately 2.3 million, and *USA Weekend*, a weekly newspaper magazine, as well as a number of nondaily publications. Online properties have also exploded in recent years, with Gannett generating about $40 million in revenue in 1999 from Internet activities, with minimal loss.

Prelaunch Situation Analysis

In February 1980, Allen Neuharth met with "Project NN" task force members to discuss his vision for producing and marketing a unique nationally distributed daily newspaper. Satellite technology had recently solved the problem of limited geographical distribution. Neuharth was ready to take advantage of two seemingly disparate trends among the reading public—an increasingly short attention span in a generation nurtured on television rather than print, coupled with a growing hunger for more information. Neuharth believed that readers face a time crunch in a world where so much information is available but where there is so little time to absorb it. *USA Today*'s primary mission would be to provide more news about more subjects in less time. Task force members were enthusiastic about the concept.

Research suggested that *USA Today* should target primarily achievement-oriented men in professional and managerial positions, who are heavy newspaper readers and frequent travelers. Whereas the *New York Times* is targeted at the nation's intellectual

---

This case was prepared by Geoffrey Lantos, Stonehill College, for classroom discussion rather than to illustrate either effective or ineffective handling of an administrative situation. Cheryl Anne Molchan, Stonehill College, and James G. Maxham, University of Virginia, provided research assistance on earlier versions.

elite, its thinkers and policymakers, and the *Wall Street Journal* is aimed at business leaders, *USA Today* would be edited for what has been called Middle America—young, well-educated Americans who are on the move and care about what is going on.

By early 1982, a team of news, advertising, and production personnel from the staffs of Gannett's daily newspapers developed, edited, published, and tested several different prototypes. Gannett sent three different forty-page prototype versions of *USA Today* to almost 5,000 professional people. Along with each prototype, they sent readers a response card that asked what they liked best and least about the proposed paper, whether or not they would buy it, as well as whether they would give it approval. While the content of each prototype was similar, what differed were the layout and graphics. For example, one prototype included a section called "Agenda" that included comics and a calendar of meetings to be held by various professional organizations. According to marketplace feedback, readers liked the prototypes. The Gannett Board of Directors unanimously approved the paper's launch, and so, on April 20, 1982, Gannett announced that the first copies of *USA Today* would soon be available in the Washington/Baltimore area.

Product Launch

On September 15, 1982, 155,000 copies of the newspaper's first edition hit the newsstands. On page 1, founder Neuharth wrote a short summary of *USA Today*'s mission statement, explaining that he wanted to make *USA Today* enlightening and enjoyable to the public, informative to national leaders, and attractive to advertisers. The first issue sold out. A little over a month following the debut, *USA Today*'s circulation hit 362,879, double the original year-end projection. In April 1983, just seven months after its introduction, the newspaper's circulation topped the 1 million mark. The typical reader turned out to be a professional, usually a manager, about forty years old, well educated, with an income of about $60,000 a year (in 1997 dollars). He or she is often a news and sports junkie. As one company official put it, "When he wakes up in the morning his first thought is: 'What city am I in?' The local newspaper doesn't mean a thing to him."

For a newspaper, *USA Today* was truly unique. It was a paper created for the TV generation, an idea reflected in its distinctive coin box, designed to look like a television set. News was layered for easy access and quick comprehension by time-pressed readers. Among examples of this format were extensive use of briefs columns, secondary headlines, subheads, breakouts, at-a-glance boxes, and informational graphics. These techniques capture the most salient points of a story and present them in a format that readers appreciate. Gannett's research had shown that readers get most of their information from such snippets in a newspaper.

Because *USA Today* was nontraditional, the critics were all over it. In their view, it was loaded with "gimmicks"—tight, short stories; no jumps from page to page, except for the "cover story" (stories that jump to another page are one of newspaper readers' major complaints); splashy, colorful graphics everywhere; a distinctive, casual writing style; a colorful national weather map; a roundup of news items from each state, one paragraph each; summary boxes; little charts and statistics-laden sports coverage; and a focus on celebrity and sports, with more detailed sports stories than almost any other paper in the nation. There was no foreign staff and little interest in the world outside the United States. It was quickly labeled "McPaper"—junk-food journalism—the fast food of the newspaper business—due to its terse, brash writing style and its short coverage of complex issues. It was not considered serious. Even within Gannett, Neuharth met with bitter resistance from certain senior executives. "Brought new depth to the meaning of the word *shallow*," quipped John Quinn, its editor. Nevertheless, readers admired the paper for its focus on brevity and clarity—short sentences and short words.

Each issue presented four sections, labeled News, Money, Life, and Sports. The paper's motto was: "An economy of words. A wealth of information." Page 1 included a bulletin board announcing what is inside. Each issue featured a box for top sports news in the upper left corner of page 1, a box for top entertainment news in the upper right corner, and a news summary running down the left side of the page, like a table of contents. A prospective reader could grasp the top news of the world on the top of page 1 while viewing it in the coin box.

Gannett did not plan a grand nationwide debut. In order to monitor results carefully and modify the paper and its marketing as needed, Gannett implemented a regional rollout distribution strategy. Produced at facilities in Arlington, Virginia, *USA Today* was transmitted via satellite to printing plants across the country. The newspaper's marketers divided the country into 15 geographical market segments. *USA Today* was available within a 200-mile radius of these 15 major markets, making the paper accessible to 42 percent of U.S. households. Significantly, these markets contained 23 million of the 35 million adults who read two or more newspapers daily.

Gannett's focus group research indicated that many readers were bringing the paper into their homes rather than reading it on their commute or at work. Consequently, Gannett launched a home delivery subscription service in 1984. Home delivery caused problems at first, because the in-house computer technology could not handle subscription mailing lists efficiently, and the postal service did not always deliver the paper on its publication day. Nevertheless, subscriptions grew, and by 1991 nearly half of *USA Today*'s distribution was via home and office delivery.

Clearly, the paper filled a gap in the market, satisfying several unmet needs and wants. *USA Today*'s success came from listening to its readers and giving them what they wanted. The paper communicates with readers on a personal level very quickly (many of the short, fact-filled stories are under 250 words), clearly, and directly, in an upbeat and positive way. The color is riveting and gives the paper a contemporary look. The space-defying number of stories, factoids, larger-than-usual pictures, bar graphs, and charts that are squeezed onto each page never seem crowded. Instead of confusion, readers get neatness and order. The paper's dependably consistent organization enables readers to go directly to any one of *USA Today*'s major sections. It takes an average of only 25 minutes for a reader to peruse the paper.

USA Today strives to be a balanced newspaper, reporting positive stories along with negative ones and reflecting America's diversity. The editorial page always presents the main editorial, called "Our View." Directly beneath it there is usually an editorial labeled "Opposing View." This approach earned the paper a reputation for fairness. *USA Today*'s own editorial position on most major social, economic, and political issues can be described as middle-of-the-road, a position its staff believes is in tune with the general public. The newspaper's intent is to allow readers to get the information and opinions they need to form their own views, rather than pushing an overtly liberal or conservative agenda. Fair and balanced reporting appeals to readers, some of whom become very angry and look for another newspaper when they think the reporting isn't fair.

Marketing Mix Changes

Despite the media's early criticism, circulation surpassed 1.4 million by late 1985 as the paper expanded to 56 pages in length. The cover price of the paper had also increased to 50 cents, double its original price. By this time, *USA Today* had become the second-largest paper in the country, with a circulation topped only by the *Wall Street Journal*. Although Neuharth's early predictions were that *USA Today* would turn a profit within a few years of launch, that proved to be overly optimistic. It took about five years to move from the red to the black, but by 1993 profits were approximately $5 million and the following year they doubled to about $10 million.

Although *USA Today* competes more directly with news weeklies and business newspapers than with local papers, many papers, including its previous detractors, began to adopt some of *USA Today*'s style. Old-line newspapers, even the "gray lady," the *New York Times*, began adding more colorful looks, shorter, more tightly written stories, and beefed-up circulation campaigns to compete with "The Nation's Newspaper." In the face of this competition, as well as an awareness of changing reader needs, by the late 1980s it was time for *USA Today* to respond to those needs and evolve.

Product Innovation

To stay ahead of the imitative competition, *USA Today* had to continue to innovate. Long identified with short stories, infotainment, bright colors, and its weather map, Gannett's national daily decided to become a more serious newspaper with improved journalism. The shift from primarily soft news to mainly hard news began with the space shuttle Challenger disaster in 1986, when the paper played that news story big and circulation skyrocketed as a result. By 1991, editors began focusing much more sharply on hard news rather than soft features, and by 1994, under president and publisher Tom Curley, there was a massive drive to upgrade the product to be a more serious, more responsible news-oriented product.

Beginning in the late '80s, Gannett began incorporating less traditional value-added features to keep readers interested. The paper added 1-800 and 1-900 "hot-line" numbers that readers could call for expert information on financial planning, college admissions, minority business development, taxes, and other subjects. By 1989, over 3 million readers had called the hot-line numbers, with over half of them calling for up-to-the-minute information on sports, weather, stocks, and lottery numbers. Thousands of readers responded to reader-opinion polls and write-in surveys on political and current event issues. In 1991, the editorial pages were also redesigned to provide more room for guest columnists and to encourage debate. The change was popular: The volume of letters to the editor increased by over 500 percent. Gannett also initiated a high school "Academic All Star" program that it later expanded to include colleges and universities. In its continuing quest to upgrade product quality, in 2000 *USA Today* asked sources in a special survey if the paper accurately reported their data, quotes, and other newsworthy information. The yearlong survey was devised to counter growing reader complaints of declining credibility and accuracy in many daily publications.

The increasing ubiquity of the Internet in the late 1990s also resulted in some changes in content. For instance, the Money section began to focus more on technology issues and to look at business through an "e-lens," that is, a filter for the electronic revolution in the economy. For example, a stock index, the Internet 100, was added to traditional stock indexes. The Life section incorporated a daily e-world feature, covered just as aggressively as entertainment and TV.

The year 2000 saw the first major redesign in *USA Today*'s history as the paper moved from a 54-inch to a 50-inch web width. This was aimed at making the paper easier to read and cleaner in look. The slimmer pages were easier to handle, especially in tight spaces like airplanes, trains, buses, and subways, and they fit more readily into briefcases, as Gannett had learned was desirable from focus groups.

Promotional Innovation

USA Today has also innovated over the years in its promotional activities. Historically, the paper limited its promotions mostly to outdoor advertising and television. However, in the late 1980s Neuharth undertook a "BusCapade" promotion tour, traveling to all fifty states and talking with all kinds of people, including the governor of each state. Neuharth succeeded in raising public awareness of his paper, allowing *USA Today* to make money for the first time. Encouraged by his success, Neuharth forged ahead with a "JetCapade" promotion in which he and a small news team traveled to thirty countries in seven months, stimulating global demand for the paper. During a visit to the troops of Operation Desert Storm in the Persian Gulf in 1991, General Norman Schwarzkopf expressed a need for news from home. *USA Today* arranged for delivery of 18,000 copies per day. The overseas success of *USA Today* led to the publication of *USA Today International*, which is available in more than ninety countries in Western Europe, the Middle East, North Africa, and Asia.

The paper continued to drum up demand among advertisers by adding marketing enhancements. Selling space to Madison Avenue advertisers presented a challenge to *USA Today*, because those agencies weren't convinced that it would pay to advertise in the paper. Gannett's first strategy for enlisting advertisers, called the Partnership Plan, provided six months of free space to those who purchased six months of paid advertising. In 1987 *USA Today* also began to accept regional advertising across a wide variety of categories, such as regional travel, retail, tourism, and economic development. Color advertisements could arrive as late as 6 p.m. the day before publication, giving local advertisers increased flexibility. The paper also moved aggressively into "blue-chip circulation," where bulk quantities of *USA Today* are sold at discounted prices to hotels, airlines, and restaurants and are provided free of charge to customers. Today, over 500,000 copies of *USA Today* are distributed through blue-chip circulation every day.

In 1998 *USA Today* became a delivery vehicle for product samples, thanks to Maverick Media's AD/IMPAC, through which an advertiser can contract for production of product samples and associated advertising, which then may be distributed in *USA Today* either nationwide or regionally. Samples are inserted right in the centerfold. Initial customers included America Online and Prodigy, which distributed diskettes in a limited run in the Washington, D.C., area, and AT&T, which distributed samples of its One Rate calling card nationwide in May of that year. Gannett has plans to work on specific promotions for specific days, such as Alka-Seltzer on Thanksgiving Day and gambling chips when a new casino opens.

USA Today pulled off another promotional first in 1999 when they broke one of the most sacred practices of most daily newspapers and began offering display advertising space on page one, with one-inch strips across the entire width of the bottom of the front page, a position that the paper had previously used to promote itself. This front-page bottom color bar position was sold through one-year contracts for $1 million to $1.2 million each, with each advertiser taking one day a week.

Given the success of *USA Today*, advertisers are obviously quite attracted to the paper's large volume of readers. To help cope with advertiser demand, in the mid-1990s the paper implemented the necessary technology to allow advertisers to transmit advertising copy electronically twenty-four hours a day. As has been true for so many of *USA Today*'s innovations, critics were quick to criticize this move, claiming that the paper had "besmirched" its front page with advertising.

Distribution Innovation

Fast delivery has always been important to *USA Today*. By the mid-1990s the paper was earning kudos for its ability to deliver timely news, thanks to its late deadlines. For instance, in many parts of the country *USA Today* prints later sports scores than local or regional papers. In hard news, *USA Today* was able to offer more up-to-date coverage by rolling the presses over four hours earlier than the *Wall Street Journal* and almost three hours later than the *New York Times*.

To speed distribution, the paper has added print sites around the world, with the tally in 2000 being thirty-six. An innovative readership program brought *USA Today* to 160 college campuses in 1999, with more to be added in 2000. Technological advances in 1999 allowed production of *USA Today* to be totally digital. Arriving in 2000 was computer-to-plate technology that provides newsrooms with later deadlines and readers with earlier delivery times.

Spin-off Activities

A decade after *USA Today*'s launch, Gannett found itself in the enviable position of owning one of America's most successful newspapers. *USA Today* was the most widely read newspaper in the country, with daily readership of over 6.5 million. In an era when nearly all major national media were suffering declines in readership or viewing audience, *USA Today* continued to grow. Rising distribution and promotion costs, however, were beginning to make the newspaper slightly unprofitable.

To reverse this trend, *USA Today* created several spin-offs, including its first special-interest publication, *Baseball Weekly*. During its first month of operation, *Baseball Weekly*'s circulation reached 250,000 copies. Today, the *Weekly*'s circulation is roughly 425,000.

Venturing into news media, *USA Today* joined with Cable News Network to produce a football TV program, and launched SkyRadio to provide live radio on commercial airline flights. In 2000, Gannett launched a new broadcast and Internet initiative known as *USA Today Live* to provide information to Gannett television stations. *USA Today Live* produced prepackaged segments based on *USA Today* content and made them available for use by Gannett television stations in their news reports, with *USA Today* reporters also being available for live interviews.

USA Today Online

The major spin-off, however, was *USA Today Online*, which the company introduced in 1995. Five of the reasons Al Neuharth gave for starting *USA Today*, as outlined in the October 1982 Bulletin of the American Society of Newspaper Editors, were equally applicable for the paper's expansion from print to online news delivery. They are as follows.

1. *The information age:* Neuharth recognized that the "explosion of new and/or improved information sources have stimulated, rather than satisfied, the American people's appetite for still more news and information when they want it, where they want it, and how they want it." The World Wide Web led to an even greater explosion of news and information sources, creating an even bigger craving for knowledge.

2. *Satellite technology:* Neuharth observed that "along with instant global communications, the space age brought the feasibility and flexibility to deliver a daily newspaper across the United States." Likewise, the global communications network of the Internet brought the feasibility of delivering a daily online newspaper across the world.

3. *Changing lifestyles:* "America is a nation on the move—physically, geographically, intellectually, and sentimentally," noted Neuharth back in 1982, suggesting the rationale behind creating a daily national newspaper, so that anyone traveling anywhere could find some news from his or her own hometown. With the development of niche information services on the Internet, people want to be able to find deep and rich resources on very narrow geographic or lifestyle interests.

4. *Stability:* "With the excitement of mobility comes the grasp for stability." Neuharth wanted *USA Today* to provide that stability, that common look and easy access that a comfortable and familiar publication gives readers. Likewise, this became the goal of most online newspapers too.

5. *The need to know:* "This Information Age generation is looking for more—more local emphasis in the hometown newspaper, more detailed news on radio and TV, more frequent news broadcasts." This "need to know," coupled with "give me more," is the compelling reason that news organizations ventured into Web publishing. Online news allows the breadth and depth of coverage plus the frequency of updating that Neuharth saw as being of interest to news consumers.

The *USA Today* venture into online products began on April 17, 1995. The online version was seen as a natural companion to the print version of *USA Today*, given the paper's worldwide distribution. The first version was available through CompuServe's Mosaic browser and required special software, a CompuServe Network connection, and a monthly subscription of $14.95 plus $3.95 per hour. By June of 1995, they unveiled the World Wide Web version, which worked with any Web browser and Internet provider service, and it was free.

Like its print sister, the Web site (http://www.usatoday.com) is bright, upbeat, and full of nugget-sized news stories. The online version allows readers to receive up-to-the-moment news that incorporates colorful visuals and crisp audio. It provides one of the most extensive sites on the World Wide Web, featuring over 140,000 pages of up-to-the-minute news, sports, business and technology news, five-day weather forecasts, and travel information, available twenty-four hours a day, seven days a week.

The Web site's design features brightly colored buttons in the banner that invite you to go to News, Sports, Money, Life, or Weather. The left-hand column has choices of places to go: world, politics, stocks, scores, etc. Story links off the home page offer other directions to take. However, the home page, with its links to the next layers, has a cluttered, crowded look. Nonetheless, the bright blue of the banner and the clean white background of each page help the eye when trying to make choices from all the options available. At the bottom of the page is a navigation bar with links to the main sections of the Web site: Front Page, News, Sports, Money, Life, Weather, and Marketplace.

The price since migrating to the Web has been free, although Gannett leaves open the option to charge site users sometime in the future. It is primarily advertising that provides revenue streams. Ad revenues increased as new advertisers were attracted to the online format and the potentially huge worldwide reach, and by the dawn of the new millennium *USA Today* led all major publications in paid dot-com advertising. Thus, while the consumer's monetary cost is free, the intangible cost is the consumer's time and attention, which is then sold to advertisers.

Another revenue generator, launched in response to frequent reader requests for archived material, was the pay-per-view archives service (http://archives.usatoday .com) launched in 1998. The *USA Today* Archives section allows readers to do a free, unlimited search of the paper's articles that ran since April 1987. Articles may be downloaded for $1 per story, with payments handled by credit card.

Given the surge in Internet subscribers, *USA Today* made a strategic decision to link their online news with popular Internet providers' Web sites. These Internet providers agreed to incorporate *USA Today Online* as their default news source. This strategy allowed *USA Today* to increase its readership substantially while also increasing its name recognition.

Like its print cousin, *USA Today Online* has evolved to meet consumers' changing desires. In 1987 the Web site launched an online classifieds area and twenty-four marketplace partnerships, giving readers the capability to buy the goods and services of twenty-four companies found in six marketplaces: classifieds, travel, financial, technology, entertainment, and flowers and gifts. Partners in this venture include AutoWeb Homebuyer's Fair, The Monster Board, and The National Association of Realtors' Realtor.com.

In another effort at quality improvement, since its inception this Web site has studied its server logs to make decisions about editorial content, transfer and addition of staff, and even budgetary expenditures. In 1998 it adopted custom software developed by Intelligent Environments, a leading provider of Web development software and services, to create a real-time system to survey online readers. It was incorporated into the Web site as "Quick Question," an area devoted to gauging the opinions of *USA Today Online* readers on newsworthy events and issues. Not only does this survey system capture and tally votes in real time, it even recognizes if someone tries to vote more than once.

Looking Ahead

In looking at the total national newspaper market, *USA Today* has been quite successful. It has seen 17 years of continuous circulation growth. By 2000, over 5.4 million consumers were reading *USA Today* on a daily basis and approximately 2.3 million people were subscribing to the paper. This success had occurred during a time when newspaper readership overall was declining. Of all the national daily papers in the United States, only *USA Today*, the *Los Angeles Times*, and the *Denver Post* were experiencing large gains in circulation.

In 1999, advertising revenues grew 17 percent as several of the paper's largest ad categories experienced double-digit growth. Dot-com advertising added to the boom: *USA Today* led all major print publications in the share of paid dot-com advertising pages. *USA Today Online* was one of the few moneymakers on the Web. *USA Today Online* was the world's most visited Web site, according to Media Metrix, with 15 million different people per month clicking on the site by the end of 1999, a 79 percent increase over 1998. The number of domestic newspaper Web sites grew to sixty by the end of 1999, and Gannett more than doubled the products offered online to 480+, including news sites, rich classified verticals, community-oriented sites, and numerous specialty sites based on the unique characteristics of the individual markets.

At the corporate level, earnings for 1999 advanced 13 percent to approximately $886 million, fueled by strong advertising demand at all the papers and lower newsprint prices. For 2000, the corporation intended to add more products and launch the remainder of the small-market newspaper sites.

Because newspapers are often subjected to high newsprint costs, most newspaper firms, just like *USA Today*, have added online news as a means to increase readership and cut distribution expenses. Whether online news poses a major threat to *USA Today* and other newspaper firms is debatable. Some experts suggest that approximately 14 percent of readers will switch from newspaper to online news, effectively cannibalizing the readership of printed news. However, Tom Curley, the publisher of *USA Today*, said he is not worried about the Internet and the other media competitors that are pushing into traditional newspaper markets because newspapers have unique strengths that competitors can't rival. He confidently told the 1998 Coronado convention of the California Newspaper Publishers Association: "This era is about massive data transfer, and nobody is in a better position to analyze it, put it in context, and shape it than newspapers. And we still have the ability to connect with people in ways that other media can't." However, at this same meeting other speakers sounded dire warnings about the inroads the Internet and other media are making into newspaper advertising and readership. The current editor, Karen Jurgensen, is nonetheless upbeat, telling *Advertising Age*, "One question I am often asked is whether there is a future for newspapers in the era of the Internet. The answer is obvious: Of course there is. . . . If we are able to deliver a daily report that is insightful, informative, and even entertaining, then they will continue to make time for papers. And *USA Today*—and the advertisers in its pages—will continue to thrive."

But despite the enormous potential of online news, many companies have yet to turn a profit on their online ventures. In 1998, *USA Today Online* for the first time only broke even, even though it earned over $4 million from online ad revenues. Still, the Gannett Letter to Shareholders in the 1999 Gannett Annual Report viewed the Internet as an opportunity, not a threat: "The Internet is a challenge and an exciting opportunity for our community newspapers to extend their brand, generate revenue and, ultimately, profits. Our newspapers will continue to use the Internet to leverage those important local brands, and enhance the strong relationships we already enjoy with our readers and advertisers in the communities we serve. And our Web sites are attracting visitors who are not readers and are generating subscriptions for our print products."

To remain competitive, *USA Today* has moved to increase the value-added components of both its print and online versions. In the print version, in the late 1990s *USA*

Today split its Friday Life section into two separate sections: Weekend Life and Destinations & Diversions. This format change, the first major change in the history of *USA Today*, allows the paper to devote more space to weekend entertainment and travel news. This entertainment and travel focus has been mirrored in the online version of *USA Today* in its Travel Marketplace. *USA Today* in the late 1990s signed up six travel partners that will offer online travel services via the *USA Today* Web site.

In 2000, the print version planned to expand from fifty-six to sixty-four pages per issue. Despite cost pressures, the publisher sees holding the price at 50 cents as priority 1. Another priority is to continue to update both products to make sure they are breaking stories and providing a complete read that people can trust. A third priority is to push the technology so the print product can be later with sports scores and news. Adopting a value-added strategy can help *USA Today* differentiate itself from other national news providers. In the future, the key will be to ensure that both the print and online versions of *USA Today* provide readers with content they cannot find anywhere else.

Questions for Discussion

1. What opportunities in the marketing environment did Gannett seize in launching *USA Today?* How did it learn about these opportunities? How did it respond to the opportunities identified?

2. Who is *USA Today*'s competition? What are the implications for their marketing strategy?

3. What competitive growth strategies did Gannett use in introducing *USA Today* and in developing the paper over time? Were these strategies appropriate?

4. What performance standards did Gannett measure in assessing *USA Today*'s success? According to these measures, is the paper a success?

5. Evaluate *USA Today*'s decision to enter the online news market. What strategy should *USA Today Online* employ? Should the marketing strategy for the print version of *USA Today* be changed?

Sources

These facts are from "Baseball Weekly Hits Record Circulation," *PR Newswire*, April 13, 1998, 413; "Circulation Slide for Newspapers," *Editor & Publisher*, May 10, 1997, 3; R. Cook, "Gannett Hits Heights in Print but Falls Short of TV Stardom," *Campaign*, January 17, 1997, 24; R. Curtis, "Introducing Your New *USA Today*," *USA Today*, April 3, 2000, 27A; J. Duscha, "Satisfying Advertiser Position Demands Now Easier," *NewsInc*, September 13, 1999; Gannett Company, Inc., 1997 Annual Report; Gannett Company, Inc., 1999 Annual Report; Gannett Company, Inc., 1996 Form 10-K (on file with the Securities and Exchange Commission); "Giving Samples Made Easy Through *USA Today* from Shampoo to CDs," *NewInc*, June 22, 1998; K. Jurgensen, "Quick Response; Paper Chase: *USA Today* Editor Sees Shifts in How Information Is Generated and Delivered to Readers," *Advertising Age*, February 14, 2000, S6; K. Jurgensen, "*USA Today*'s New Look Designed for Readers," *USA Today*, April 3, 2000, 1A; A. M. Kerwin, "Daily Paper's Circulation Woes Persist into '97," *Advertising Age*, May 12, 1997, 26; P. Long, "After Long Career, *USA* Today Founder Al Neuharth Is Ready for More," *Knight-Ridder/Tribune Business News*, April 28, 1999; J. McCartney, "*USA Today* Grows Up," *American Journalism Review*, September 1997, 19; B. Miller, "*USA Today*, Gannett to Launch *USA Today Live*," *Television & Cable*, February 8, 2000; T. Noah, "At Least It's Free, Right?" *U.S. News & World Report*, December 2, 1996, 60; N. Paul, "McWeb Site: *USA Today Online*," *Searcher*, May 1997, 58; M. L. Stein, "Don't Sweat the Internet Says *USA Today*'s Curley," *Editor & Publisher*, August 22, 1998, 40; M. Stone, "*USA Today Online* Listens to Its Logs," *Editor & Publisher*, August 7, 1999, 66; J. Strupp, "Accuracy Is the Aim," *Editor & Publisher*, May 1, 2000, 9; J. Strupp, "*USA Today* Ads Go Page One," *Editor &*

Publisher, May 8, 1999, 40; Sullivan, "Where Are Newspapers Headed?" *Editor & Publisher*, June 28, 1997; R. Tedesco, "Internet Profit Sites Elusive," *Broadcasting & Cable*, November 17, 1997, 74; "*USA Today:* A Case Study," prepared by M. Condry, R. Dailey, F. Gasquet, M. Holladay, A. Johnson, S. Menzer, and J. Miller, University of Memphis, 1997; "*USA Today* Launches New Life Section Friday Format," *PR Newswire*, March 16, 1998, 316; "*USA Today* Launches Online Classifieds Area and 17 New Marketplace Partnerships," *Business Wire*, April 15, 1997; "*USA Today* Launches Pay-per-View Archives Service," *Business Wire*, January 5, 1998; "*USA Today Online* Launches Real Time Survey System," *Business Wire*, February 18, 1998; *USA Today* Press Kit, 1997, Gannett Company, Inc.; "*USA Today* Sells Page One Advertising Space," *PR Newswire*, May 5, 1999, 3517; and I. Wada, "*USA Today* Marketplace Signs Up Six for Online Services," *Travel Weekly*, April 28, 1997, 44.

15

Firestone's Recall of Ford Explorer Tires

The relationship between Ford and Firestone began in the early 1900s. Firestone emerged in 1900 in Akron, Ohio. In 1906, the first transaction occurred when Henry Ford bought 2,000 sets of tires from Harvey Firestone. Since that sale, both companies have become major players in their industries. Ford had record operating earnings of $7.2 billion in 1999, the most ever for any automotive company. The company spends about $7 billion annually on research and development and boasts a global portfolio of more than 5,000 patents. Ford Motor Co. consists of Ford, Volvo, Mazda, Lincoln, Mercury, Jaguar, Land Rover, and Aston Martin vehicles.

Firestone, despite growth over the past 100 years, has faced more turbulence than Ford. In 1978, Firestone recalled 14.5 million tires, the largest tire recall in history. Excess application of the adhesive that binds the rubber to the steel belts caused 500 tread separations and blowouts. Firestone paid a $500,000 fine for concealing safety problems. This recall weakened the financial position of the company and resulted in its 1988 purchase by Tokyo-based Bridgestone, Inc., for $2.6 million. The parent company was founded in 1931 by Shojiro Ishibashi and developed its name from the English translation of his family name, "stone bridge." Bridgestone successfully eased the struggling company back to profits. Firestone made up 40 percent of the parent company's 1999 consolidated sales.

Many other tire manufacturers faced recalls in the late 1900s. On March 12, 1980, Uniroyal recalled almost 2 million tires due to tread separation. B.F. Goodrich recalled a million tires on August 13, 1974, due to improper inflation and installation. Kelly Springfield faced a recall on January 28, 1976, when 300,000 tires were recalled for tread separation. General Tire recalled 187,000 on January 24, 1979, for exposed belt wire. Cooper Tire and Rubber recalled 156,266 tires on August 11, 1988, for bead flaw. More recently, on April 14, 1998, Kelly Springfield recalled over 500,000 tires for sidewall cracking. The number of recalls shows that tire failure has been an industry-wide problem for the past 25 years.

The Timeline for the Firestone Recall

In July 1998, Sam Boyden, an associate research administrator for State Farm Insurance, received a phone call from a claims handler asking him to determine if other cases of Firestone tread failure existed. He discovered twenty such cases dating back to

---

This case was prepared by Dana Schubert for classroom discussion rather than to illustrate either effective or ineffective handling of an administrative situation.

1992. Being a car fanatic, Boyden realized this was probably not a coincidence but rather a series of related accidents. He sent an e-mail to the National Highway Traffic Safety Administration (NHTSA) alerting them to his findings. They thanked him but basically ignored the message until early 2000.

In January 2000, reporter Anna Werner and two colleagues researched tread separation and accidents in Texas after an attorney mentioned the issue. Based on the results of their investigation, the television station aired a nine-minute segment. Werner also reported her findings to Joan Claybrook, former chief of the NHTSA. In the weeks that followed, many citizens called the television station to relate their own stories of Firestone tire failure on Ford Explorers. Soon, KHOU-TV began directing the flood of calls to the NHTSA.

Sean Kane also tried to alert the NHTSA to the recurrent problems. Kane, a former employee of the Center for Auto Safety, started Strategic Safety, a research group interested in product liability issues. In late July, Kane received an e-mail from a Venezuelan source that disclosed Ford's tire replacement program there. On August 1, Strategic Safety and Public Citizen issued a press release asking Ford for a vehicle recall.

Despite the flow of information from these sources, the NHTSA was slow to take action. In early March, the initial two investigators, Steve Beretzky and Rob Wahl, found twenty-two tread separation complaints that they marked for "initial evaluation." Between March and May, the number of complaints skyrocketed. On May 2, three senior NHTSA officials increased the status to "preliminary investigation." Within six days, NHTSA requested that Firestone supply production data and complaint files. Firestone submitted this data to NHTSA on July 27, and Ford was sent copies the next day.

After Ford received the data, they immediately started the analysis process. Within 18 hours, the information was crammed into Cray Supercomputers and results printed. Of the 2,498 complaints on tire failure, 81 percent involved the 15-inch P235/75R15 models. When tread separation was considered, 84 percent of some 1,699 complaints involved Ford's Explorer, Bronco, Ranger, or F-150 SUVs and trucks. Ford relayed the results to Bridgestone/Firestone, and the two companies met in Dearborn, Michigan, on August 5 to discuss the issue. At that time, the NHTSA was investigating twenty-one deaths that were possibly related. When the number of deaths being investigated jumped to forty-six three days later, Ford, Firestone, and the NHTSA met to discuss a plan of action. The next day, August 9, they issued a recall of 6.5 million tires.

The Recall

The recall included 3.8 million P235/75R15 radial ATX and ATXII and 2.7 million Wilderness AT tires from the Decatur, Illinois, plant. Bridgestone/Firestone's official recall procedure was organized by state. The recall immediately affected Arizona, California, Florida, and Texas. The greatest percentage of casualties occurred in these states. Based on NHTSA data, Florida and Texas each represented 22 percent of the complaints, followed by California at 20 percent, and Arizona at 5 percent. This first recall portion was expected to be complete by October 2000. The second phase involved Alabama, Georgia, Louisiana, Mississippi, Nevada, Oklahoma, and Tennessee and was expected to be complete by the end of 2000. Firestone announced that the recall in all remaining states would be complete by the end of 2001.

Firestone issued letters to all customers detailing the procedure for replacement. Customers affected by the recall could take their tires to Firestone retailers, Ford dealerships, or other tire retail outlets and expect a similar Bridgestone/Firestone tire or equivalent competitor's model. Ford began testing other brands on the Explorer and found thirty-four acceptable replacements. In addition to the tire cost, the replacement included mounting and balancing fees. If replacements had been purchased before the official recall, customers who provided a receipt would be issued a credit of up to $100 per tire.

Both companies developed advertisements and public statement announcements to inform consumers how to determine if their tires were included. Consumers could call a toll-free number if they had questions about tire models or eligibility. Despite Firestone's gradual plan, Ford encouraged all concerned motorists included in the recall, regardless of their location, to replace questionable tires immediately and, if necessary, save the receipts for reimbursement later. Consumers not directly included in the recall could purchase new Firestone tires based on a credit system determined by the age and wear of their current tires.

After continued investigations, the NHTSA encouraged Firestone to expand the recall to other sizes and models of tires, but Firestone declined. On September 1, the NHTSA issued a consumer advisory to warn of potential problems with other Firestone tires. These included ATXP205/75R15 tires on 1991 Chevy Blazers and ATX 31X10.50R15LT tires on 1991–94 Nissan pickups, other sizes of ATX, Firehawk ATX, ATX23 Degree, Widetrack Radial Baja, and Wilderness AT tires, originating mostly from the Decatur factory. Because these tires are not included in the official recall list, replacements are not free. The NHTSA suggested that consumers save receipts in the event that Firestone increased the breadth of the recall. Included in this advisory was a list of precautionary measures for consumers to help avoid tire failure.

Firestone's Response to the Crisis

- During the recall, Firestone faced a potential strike by the United Steelworkers of America that would have disrupted production at nine of eleven U.S. plants. Firestone successfully negotiated with union officials to avoid that potentially disruptive strike.

- Firestone began shipping tires from the parent company on August 23 and expected between 325,000 and 350,000 to arrive before September 1. Bridgestone planned to send at least one shipment per day until the recall issue was resolved.

- The Bridgestone/Firestone U.S. factories doubled the number of tire molds in use and increased production by 7,000 tires per day.

- During Senate hearings, Firestone officials accepted full responsibility and admitted the company had made "bad tires."

Ford's Response to the Crisis

- Ford increased the staff monitoring its help line from 300 to 800 employees and kept it open twenty-four hours a day.

- Ford closed three plants for three weeks to increase tire availability. The 6,000 affected workers were still paid and spent much of their time assisting in the transport of tires to dispersal outlets.

- Ford created a 500-person crisis management team to devise creative tactics to speed the recall procedure.

- Ford purchased tire molds from Firestone competitors that enabled them to produce a greater number of tires.

"The Blame Game," or Whose Fault Was It?

The timing of the discovery of tire failure and decisions to communicate with owners of Ford Explorers is a highly debated issue in this recall. The tire problem is now better understood, with statistics pointing to the same conclusions. Firestone made a public announcement accepting full responsibility for faulty tires. When Ford analyzed Firestone's data, they noticed ten times more complaints stemming from the Decatur factory, specifically involving tires made in 1994 and 1995. Questions arose about the skill of replacement workers filling in during a two-year strike known as "The War of '94–'95." Many people suggest that quality inspections were compromised as tires piled up on the factory floor and that when employees returned from the strike, old dried rubber was used in production.

Another factor under consideration is the quality of the facility. The building was constructed in 1942, used to store telecommunications for the U.S. Armed Forces for nineteen years, and then purchased by Firestone in 1962. The factory environment highly affects the quality of steel-belted tires, like those recalled. The Decatur plant, deficient in air conditioners, had higher humidity levels, which decreased the adhesive properties needed to bind rubber to steel. This effect became apparent because tires produced during the low-humidity winter months were of higher quality than those produced during the humid summer months. A second contributing factor was the age and condition of equipment used to mix raw materials and press steel together. In addition, the vulcanization process, which uses heat and pressure to unite the rubber fragments into one product, is being questioned about temperature control problems. Poor quality can result when temperatures are too hot or not hot enough.

Although many people feel that Firestone is to blame, others believe that Ford should share in the blame. The design of the Ford Explorer, along with tire pressure recommendations, have been under scrutiny to determine if these factors contributed to the rate of tire separations and rollover accidents. Ford initially recommended a tire pressure of 26 psi, for two main reasons. First, lower tire pressure negates the stiff suspension and produces a softer ride. Underinflated tires are problematic because more surface area encountering the road creates more wear and more flexible sidewalls, ultimately leading to overheated tires. Excess weight is another factor that leads to high friction and high heat. Ford Explorers are often overloaded with passengers, luggage, and other items, so investigators are trying to determine if this could be a contributing factor. The Explorer's design consists of a high center of gravity and a short wheelbase, both characteristic of high rollover frequency. Low tire pressure creates sloppy steering, or low responsiveness, which could increase the chance that a driver would roll by overcorrecting or making sudden steering maneuvers.

After learning that tread separation might be an issue, Ford requested that Firestone complete tests to determine if a problem existed involving Ford Explorers and

Firestone tires. The tests, completed in Arizona in late February and early March, involved 243 heavily worn tires from sixty-three Explorers. At that time, no problems were discovered, and both companies dropped the issue.

Regardless of what consumers believe to be the predominant cause, research is being conducted to develop more concrete evidence. Until that time, both companies and the NHTSA are taking precautions by increasing suggested acceptable pressure requirements to between twenty-six and thirty psi, advising consumers to wear seatbelts, travel lighter, reduce speeds, and limit travel in hot areas.

Legal and Financial Implications for Ford and Bridgestone/Firestone

According to then-current vehicle liability conditions, automobile manufacturers are not responsible for replacing poor-quality tires. While Ford is not directly liable for the recall costs, they are subject to private lawsuits and criminal charges for the 1,400 complaints, 250 injuries, and eighty-eight deaths within the United States. The Venezuelan government and its consumer protection agency are pursuing Ford concerning forty-six deaths involving Explorers that occurred in Venezuela.

The financial implications of the recall have been detrimental to the survival of Bridgestone/Firestone. While the company is trying to isolate the problem to involve only certain tires made in one Illinois plant, they are having a difficult time maintaining an image of overall quality. According to a Harris poll, 67 percent of 814 people responded "extremely to very likely" to the question "How likely is it that this tire recall would influence your decision to purchase a Firestone product?" An additional 18 percent responded "somewhat likely." After the recall announcement, Firestone's stock price dropped 47 percent in just one month. The estimated costs to Bridgestone are $500 million. It is yet to be determined if Firestone will recover from this substantial blow. It is unlikely that another U.S. tire manufacturer will purchase Firestone, because the market share of the combined companies would exceed the recommended limits, resulting in suspicions of monopolistic intent.

Ford has suffered less financial setback than Firestone thus far, but its image and stock price are not untouched. According to the poll just mentioned, the recall was "extremely or very likely" to influence 25 percent of the decisions to purchase a Ford product, while 22 percent said the recall was "somewhat likely" to influence the decision. Ford has tried to focus the problem on Bridgestone by saying it is a "tire issue" not a "vehicle issue." Ford's stock price dropped 18 percent in the month after the recall announcement, partially as a result of decreased consumer confidence.

The Impact on Other Companies

Many other organizations were influenced by the recall, including tire distributors nationwide. Many large tire retailers took a proactive stance and removed Firestone brands from their sales floors. Leading this movement was Sears, who made that decision before the recall was officially announced. Sears, National Tire and Battery, and other retailers fully refunded money to customers who had purchased recalled tires, and they included the mounting and balancing costs if replacements were purchased. Many small retail operations that focused strictly on Firestone tires changed their names and expanded or altered their product lines to avoid the possibility of becoming obsolete or going bankrupt.

The recall affected competing tire companies as well. Other manufacturers, such as Goodyear and Michelin, helped ease the recall effort by increasing production to reduce the tire shortage caused by consumers seeking replacements. However, many consumers speculate on possible gains to competitors through the crisis. Goodyear spent an extra $1 million on television and radio promotions, full-page newspaper ads, and banner ads on Yahoo! and AOL. They said the increases were "in specific response to the recall, but done with good taste." Michelin decided to continue with normal advertising plans, which happened to coincide with the recall news. Before the crisis, each tire company had a brand image they hoped to promote. Goodyear produced reliable tires; Michelin produced safe tires; and Firestone made high-performance tires. Now, those images are being called upon to help customers associate desired benefits with the companies that provide them.

In addition to financial and legal implications for Ford and Firestone, the problems and subsequent recall will affect the government, regulatory agencies, and other businesses. Suggestions have arisen at the organizational, industry, and national levels. These include implementing a nylon layer, or cap, to brace the tire and reduce the risks of separation and creating stricter quality inspection procedures and requirements within the individual companies. On the industry level, it has been suggested that tires pass more rigorous testing by unbiased parties. Currently, consumers can research all aspects of car quality except tires. A suggestion has been made to create consumer reports on tire durability, traction, strength, and other important traits. During the Senate hearings, Ford vowed to disclose voluntarily to the U.S. government any future overseas recalls. However, in our increasingly global economy, the government may decide to take this a step further and require all foreign recalls to be disclosed.

Questions for Discussion

1. To what extent do companies need to make a proactive effort to collect and analyze data concerning possible safety issues?

2. What mistakes did Ford, Firestone, and the NHTSA each make in early attempts to handle the tire recall crisis?

3. What are some possible ethical implications involved with accepting responsibility vs. blaming others?

4. Determine some measures that Bridgestone-Firestone could take to improve tire quality in the future.

Sources

These facts are from Stephen Power and Clare Ansberry, "Bridgestone/Firestone Says It Made 'Bad Tires,'" *Wall Street Journal*, September 13, 2000, A3, A6; Bill Vlasic, "Anatomy of a Crisis," *Fort Collins Coloradoan*, September 4, 2000, C1, C2; Devon Spurgeon, "State Farm Researcher's Sleuthing Helped Prompt Firestone Recall," *Wall Street Journal*, September 1, 2000, B1, B6; Jason Szip, "Firestone's Japanese Parent Hit Again," *Fox Market Wire* from http://foxmarketwire.com/090100/tirestrike_side2.sml, accessed September 1, 2000; Melita Marie Garza, Lauren Comander, and Patrick Cole, "Problems at Tire Plant Alleged," *Chicago Tribune*, August 20, 2000, 1, 10; Lori Grant, "More Retailers Pull 3 Firestone Tires from Stock," *USA Today*, August 7, 2000, 1B; Timothy Aeppel, "Firestone Milestone Brings on Dilemma," *Wall Street Journal*, August 18, 2000, B8; Lauren Comander, "Firestone Tires Shipped from Japan to Boost Supply," *Chicago Tribune*, August 23, 2000, 1, 2; Claudia H. Deutsch, "Where Rubber Meets the Road; Recall of Firestone Tires Is Aimed at Damage Control," *New York Times on the Web* from http://archives.nytimes.com.../fastweb?getdoc_allyears2-qpass+db365+564511+11+wAAA+Firestone%7, accessed August 21, 2000; Calvin Sims, "A Takeover with Problems for Japanese Tire

Maker," *New York Times on the Web* from http://archives.nytimes.com.../fastweb?getdoc+allyears2-qpass+db365+564535 +10_wAAA=Firestone%7, accessed August 21, 2000; David Kiley, "Bridgestone Exec Will Speak to Congress," *Fort Collins Coloradoan*, August 30, 2000, D7; James R. Healey, "What You Don't Know About Your Tires," *USA Today*, August 11, 2000, B1; Robert L. Simison, "For Ford CEO Nasser, Damage Control Is the New 'Job One,'" *Wall Street Journal*, September 11, 2000, A1, A8; Kathryn Kranhold and Erin White, "The Perils and Potential Rewards of Crisis Management for Firestone," *Wall Street Journal*, September 8, 2000, B1, B4; Robert Guy Matthews, "How the Rubber Meets the Road," *Wall Street Journal*, September 8, 2000, B1, B4; Stephen Power, "Update Needed for Tire Rules, Activists Argue," *Wall Street Journal*, September 8, 2000, B1, B4; "Consumer Advisory: Potentially Dangerous Tires," *Fox Market Wire* from http://www.foxmarketwire.com/090100/tiredeaths_list.sml, accessed September 1, 2000.

HCA—The Healthcare Company

Columbia/HCA Healthcare Corporation was one of the largest health care services companies in the United States. In 1997 the company operated 343 hospitals, 136 outpatient surgery centers, and approximately 550 home health locations and provided extensive outpatient and ancillary services in thirty-seven states, the United Kingdom, and Switzerland. With revenues of nearly $20 billion, Columbia was the seventh-largest U.S. employer. The stated mission of Columbia was "to work with our employees, affiliated physicians, and volunteers to provide a continuum of quality healthcare, cost-effectively for the people in the communities we serve." The vision for Columbia was "to work with employees and physicians to build a company that is focused on the well-being of people, that is patient-oriented, that offers the most advanced technology and information systems, that is financially sound, and that is synonymous with quality, cost-effective healthcare."

Columbia/HCA built the nation's largest chain of hospitals based on cost effectiveness and financial performance. New hospitals were acquired and health services provided throughout the nation by developing competitive advantages with internal control of costs and sales activities. The focus was bottom-line performance and new business acquisition. Although Columbia had a stated mission and value statement, quality care of patients was only a small part of that statement. Quality efforts were run by nonphysicians from sales and marketing departments. For example, the frequency of home health care visits often increased dramatically after a new unit was acquired.

A number of critics have charged that health care services and staffing often took a backseat to the focus on profits. For example, short training periods were used as opposed to training time provided by competitive hospitals. One former administrator indicated that training that typically takes six months was sometimes done in as little as two weeks in a Columbia/HCA hospital. In 1995, a Columbia women's hospital in Indianapolis decreased nursing staff to save money. The hospital was fined $25,000 for failing to keep appropriate staffing. The company reorganized and reengineered job titles and redefined duties of many staff at Columbia/HCA hospitals. For example, in one hospital, the concept of a "patient's support associate" included unlicensed personnel—housekeepers, patient-care assistants, physical therapy aides, orderlies, EKG technicians, and others—who are trained to perform some, but not all, of each other's duties. Some housekeepers, for example, received a few weeks of training in drawing

This case was prepared by O. C. Ferrell, Colorado State University, for classroom discussion rather than to illustrate either effective or ineffective handling of an administrative situation. Research assistance was provided by Rachel Smith, The University of Memphis.

blood and other skills (there is no license required to draw blood). In addition, the company was accused of patient dumping. Patient dumping involves discharging emergency room patients or transferring them to other hospitals when the patient is not in a stable condition. In 1997, officials at the Department of Health and Human Services Inspector General's office indicated that they were considering imposing fines on Columbia/HCA for an unspecified number of patient dumping cases.

Columbia/HCA aggressively recruited doctors to be co-owners in the growing business of outpatient surgical centers. Local doctors were often asked to buy stock through a limited partnership agreement. The company's hard-driving sales tactics came under scrutiny, and the outpatient surgical units were considered a conflict of interest by many critics.

The Problems Begin

In late July 1997, a hospital in Florida was named as the focal point of the biggest case of health care fraud in the health care industry. The focus of a government probe was Fawcett Memorial Hospital in Port Charlotte, Florida. An investigation resulted in the indictment of three mid-level Columbia/HCA Healthcare Corporation executives that charged them with filing false cost reports for Fawcett that resulted in losses of more than $4.4 million from government programs. Federal investigators seized hospital documents relating to its home health care services and its close relationships with doctors as well as to charges of defrauding the Federal Medicare and military healthcare programs by inflating reimbursement requests. The government declared a criminal investigation, meaning that there was evidence not only to indict individual Columbia executives but also alleging that the company was involved in systematic organizational efforts to defraud the government. The government alleged that at least part of the profit obtained by Columbia was gained by overcharging for Medicare and other federal health programs by unscrupulous executives who billed the government for nonreimbursable interest expenses. Other concerns were illegal incentives to physicians and possible overuse of home health services.

Top Columbia Officials Are Seen as Key to Problems

Federal investigators claimed that Columbia/HCA Healthcare Corporation engaged in a "systematic effort to defraud government health care programs." In a seventy-four-page document made public, federal investigators quote confidential witnesses saying that former Columbia Chief Executive Officer Richard Scott and former President David Vandewater were routinely briefed on issues relating to Medicare reimbursement claims that the government charged were fraudulent. It was also claimed that Samuel Greco, Columbia's former chief of operations, also knew of alleged fraud that resulted in the indictment of three Columbia officials affiliated with Fawcett Memorial Hospital in Port Charlotte.

In addition, confidential witnesses said that Columbia made an effort to hide internal documents from federal regulators that could have disclosed the alleged fraud and that Columbia's top executive in charge of internal audits instructed employees to soften the language used in internal financial audits critical of Columbia practices. According to the affidavit signed by FBI agent Joseph Ford, "investigation by the [Federal Bureau of Investigation] and the [Defense Criminal Investigative Service] has uncovered a systematic corporate scheme perpetrated by corporate officers and managers of Columbia's hospitals, home health agencies, and other facilities in the states of Tennessee, Florida, Georgia, Texas, and elsewhere to defraud Medicare, Medicaid, and the [Civilian Health and Medical Program of the Uniformed Services]."

Columbia officials indicted pleaded "not guilty," and defense lawyers for Columbia tried to diminish the importance of the allegations contained in the government's affidavits. Although a Columbia spokesperson said the company is cooperating with the government, other allegations included:

- Columbia officials at the Nashville headquarters transferred $800,000 in fictitious expenses to a Columbia hospital in Florida so that it could show higher costs and get higher Medicare reimbursements.

- Columbia stamped "attorney/client privilege" on audit reports to hide results.

- Officials under indictment told a coworker to steer a Medicare auditor away from sensitive cost figures or offer the auditor a job.

- Columbia had a "corporate policy" to shift hospitals' overhead costs to its home health care units so it could bill Medicare for more money.

- A former administrator alleged in a lawsuit that the hospital fired her for whistle-blowing that other executives had destroyed documents.

Developing a New Corporate Culture at Columbia/HCA

Soon after the investigation was launched, Dr. Thomas Frist, Jr., was hired as chairman and chief executive. Frist had been president of Hospital Corporation of America, which had merged with Columbia. Frist vowed to cooperate fully with the government and develop a 100-day plan to change the corporate culture. Under the Federal Sentencing Guidelines for Organizations, companies with effective due diligence compliance programs may receive reduced organizational fines if convicted of fraud. Although the requirements are that a senior executive be in charge of compliance, Columbia's general counsel had been overseeing the company's existing compliance program. In order for penalties to be reduced, an effective compliance program must be in place before misconduct occurs, and any crimes that occur after indictment for criminal activities will be even more severely punished.

After 100 days as chairman and chief executive of Columbia/HCA, Dr. Frist outlined changes that would reshape Columbia. His reforms included a new mission statement and support for the new senior executive to oversee legal compliance and quality issues. The new mission statement emphasizes a commitment to quality medical care and honesty in business practices. It makes no mention of financial performance.

"We have to take the company in a new direction," Dr. Frist said. "The days when Columbia/HCA was seen as an adversarial or in-your-face, a behind-closed-doors kind of place, is a thing of the past." The corporate culture was viewed as so unethical by some managers that they had resigned before the fraud investigation.

Columbia/HCA hired corporate ethics specialist Alan Yuspeh as senior vice president of ethics, compliance, and corporate responsibility. Yuspeh was given a staff of twelve at the corporate headquarters and was assigned to work with group, division, and facility presidents to create a "corporate culture where Columbia workers feel compelled to do what is right." Yuspeh indicated that his first initiatives would be to refine monitoring techniques, boost workers' ethics and compliance training, develop a code of conduct for employees, and create an internal mechanism for workers to report any wrongdoing. The Inspector General's Office of the Department of Health and Human Services has developed a model compliance program for hospitals. Yuspeh said he wanted to build the model ethics and compliance program for the health care industry. Because only about 5 percent of the 5,400 hospitals and medical schools in the United States have comprehensive compliance programs, the Department of Health and Human Services plans to release its suggestions for a model program.

Columbia/HCA Changes Rapidly

Immediately after announcing a new mission and vision for the company, organizational restructuring started. The company announced that it would be changing its name to create a new image as it continues to battle the federal fraud investigation. The company removed large, lighted Columbia signs with the company icon from the sites of its headquarters building and canopies over its entrances in Nashville, Tennessee. This act indicated the Columbia name had been damaged by negative publicity. Within a few weeks, 25 percent of the hospitals had dropped "Columbia" from their name. Consumers, doctors, and the general public had lost confidence in Columbia as an institution. Columbia's stock price dropped over 50 percent from its 1997 high, and new management was much more concerned about developing a compliance program than growth and profits. At a conference in Phoenix, twenty Columbia managers were asked by a show of hands how many of them had escaped taunts from friends about being a crook. No hands went up, and the discussion was not on surgery profit margins but on resolving the investigation and the importance of the intangible corporate image and values.

As of mid-1998, Columbia had not held serious settlement talks with the government concerning allegations of overbilling Medicare. A number of health care fraud experts have predicted that Columbia could pay fines as high as $1 billion to settle the allegations.

In addition, a restructuring may include the possible sale of one-third of its 340 hospitals and the spinoff or sale of thirty-three of its 148 freestanding surgery centers. Currently, the company is consolidating into eighteen divisions from thirty-six and reorganizing its core hospital business into five groups, of which three are slated for spin-off or sale. The goal is to return the company's attention to local hospitals and health care networks. It is estimated that the restructuring may take twelve to eighteen months and is unlikely to be completed until after Columbia resolves its conflict with the federal government.

The efforts to quickly change the corporate culture and become the model corporate citizen in health care are a real challenge for what was Columbia/HCA. This health care provider learned the hard way that maintaining an organizational ethical climate is the responsibility of top management.

Developing an Ethical Compliance Program

Compliance, including both ethical and legal issues, will continue to be at the forefront of organizational concerns as managers and employees face increasingly complex decisions in the twenty-first century. An organizational compliance effort establishes formal accountability and responsibility for appropriate organizational conduct. An effective program has the potential to encourage all employees to understand organizational values and ethical climate and to comply with policies and codes of conduct that create a good citizen organization. It takes into account values, ethics, and legal requirements, helping an organization develop trust and prevent misconduct.

The federal government created the United States Sentencing Commission to institutionalize ethical compliance programs and help prevent illegal activity. Its Federal Sentencing Guidelines for Organizations (FSGO), approved by Congress in 1991, broke new ground by codifying into law incentives for organizations to develop effective internal compliance programs to prevent misconduct. Of critical importance is the fact that these guidelines hold businesses accountable for the misconduct of their employees. The sentencing guidelines take a carrot-and-stick approach. Companies that lack effective ethical compliance programs can incur severe penalties if their employees violate the law. The seven recommended steps to develop an effective program include: (1) establishing codes of conduct, (2) appointing or hiring a high-level compliance manager, (3) taking care in delegation of authority, (4) instituting a training program and communication system, (5) monitoring and auditing for misconduct, (6) enforcing and providing for discipline, and (7) revising the program as needed. Many organizations are implementing integrity programs based on these seven recommendations. Alan Yuspeh, the new Columbia/HCA senior vice president of ethics, compliance, and corporate responsibility, was a leader in developing this seven-step compliance program for firms in the defense industry.

Creating an ethical workplace requires an understanding of the challenges and pressures that most employees face on a daily basis. Developing a strategic approach to compliance will provide an organization with a way to manage legal and ethical issues and to improve its relationships with employees, customers, and other constituencies. An ethics program will be effective only if it becomes a part of the core values and corporate culture that influence decisions on a daily basis. Just as quality management principles have become commonplace, the future will require that organizations also have an effective program for workplace integrity.

Health Care Provider Compliance Programs

The Office of Inspector General (OIG) and the Department of Health and Human Services (HHS) have supplied health care providers with industry-specific compliance program guidelines. Fashioned upon the framework of the Federal Sentencing Guidelines for Organizations' seven-step program previously discussed, these two agencies have embarked upon a mission to provide for various health care provider segments a more specific and targeted set of guidelines. The specific guidelines strive to assist health care providers in developing effective internal controls that promote adherence to applicable federal and state law and the program requirements of federal, state, and private health plans by expanding upon each guideline. In February 1998, a "Compliance Program Guidance for Hospitals" was released. It represents the OIG's suggestions on how a hospital can best establish internal controls and monitoring procedures to correct and prevent fraudulent activities. Based on the seven steps, these guidelines specify requirements for a minimum comprehensive compliance program.

The guidelines are only a framework for organizing a specific program that addresses risks. The seven steps are necessary but not sufficient for an effective compliance program. One of the prevailing tenets of the guidelines is that there is no one special compliance program for all providers. No prototype exists that fits all organizations. It is not a procedure but a guide for planning compliance activities. The seven basic elements of the hospital guidelines can be used by all hospitals, regardless of size, location, and structure. The OIG recognizes that all entities must internalize the guidelines, and it implores organizations to structure them to fit their unique organization. The Sentencing Guidelines acknowledge that different organizations require different kinds of compliance programs. It follows then that larger organizations will have more formal compliance programs.

According to the OIG, the adoption and implementation of voluntary compliance programs significantly advance the prevention of fraud, abuse, and waste in health care plans while furthering the fundamental mission of all hospitals—providing quality care to patients. Compliance programs guide a provider's governing body, chief executive officer, managers, employees, physicians, and other health care professionals in the management and operation of the organization. The program is especially germane in the reimbursement and payment areas, where claims and billing operations can be the source of fraud and abuse. Compliance efforts help to establish a culture within a health care provider that promotes prevention, detection, and resolution of conduct that does not conform to federal and state regulations. In the past, health care compliance endeavors have included statistical audits, medical reviews, and fraud detection. Typically the reviews were funded by the Health Care Financing Administration (HCFA) in its contracts with intermediaries such as Blue Cross/Blue Shield.

Soon after the investigation into Columbia, regional FBI officers urged hospital executives to reform their own industry, because law enforcement's interest in health care fraud was not waning. The FBI defined physician referral fees as "kickbacks" and urged executives to be upfront in any gray areas related to Medicare reimbursements. Not only has the FBI brought in former hospital administrators as agents, but it has also encouraged competing hospitals and insurance companies to blow the whistle on improper billing practices and referrals. The statement has been made that hospital administrators are the ones responsible for making sure that the health care industry operates ethically. On the other hand, if the FBI and the U.S. Attorney's office can prove "a pattern of corruption and conspiracy" in a hospital, federal law allows the government to seize the hospital's property and ban it from participating in federal health care programs. It is estimated that three out of four hospitals face scrutiny from the Department of Justice's probe of Medicare billing. To help hospitals set up compliance programs, the American Hospital Association is working with Coopers & Lybrand to offer a video, a workbook, a help line, and a Web site. The case of Columbia/HCA is ongoing but provides an incentive for other hospitals to install an ethical compliance program as suggested by the Federal Sentencing Guidelines for Organizations.

Columbia/HCA Launches Ethics and Compliance Training Program

By February 1998, Columbia released a press statement indicating it was taking a critical step in developing a companywide ethics, compliance, and corporate responsibility program. The company designated more than 500 employees as facility Ethics and Compliance Officers (ECOs). The new ECOs started with a two-day training session in Nashville. The facility ECOs will be the key links in making sure the company continues to develop a culture of ethical conduct and corporate responsibility. Local leadership for each facility will bring the overall ethics program for Columbia/HCA to its full implementation. As the compliance officer, Alan Yuspeh was focused on developing a world-class ethics and compliance program for the company. Yuspeh made a fifteen-minute videotape that was sent to managers throughout the Columbia/HCA system announcing the launch of the compliance training program and the unveiling of a code of ethics designed to communicate effectively Columbia's new emphasis on compliance, integrity, and social responsibility. Columbia's chairman and chief executive officer, Thomas F. Frist, Jr., M.D., said, "We are making a substantial investment in our ethics and compliance program in order to ensure its success," and "Instituting a values-based culture throughout this company is something our employees have told us is critical to forming our future. The ethics and compliance initiative is a key part of that effort."

Actions taken to date at Columbia/HCA include: (1) development of a Code of Conduct intended to guide employees through ethical and compliance issues in their daily work, (2) production of a videotaped training program on the code, (3) creation of numerous policies to support the code of conduct, (4) establishment of a compliance committee of the board of directors and an internal compliance committee, (5) appointment of ECOs at each facility, and (6) development of an enhanced ethics hotline for employees to report ethics and compliance problems.

The training seminars include introductions to the training program that each ECO will be expected to implement locally, as well as the code of conduct and the overall ethics and compliance program. The program also includes presentations from senior management and small-group discussions in which participants will discuss application of the new code of conduct in ethics-related scenarios.

Yuspeh has said he does not believe that the program will have to change personal values. Although the company wants individuals to bring their highest sense of personal values to work each day, the purpose of the program is to help employees understand how strictly a company defines ethical behavior. Columbia/HCA's ethical guidelines tackle basic issues like whether nurses can accept tips—they can't—and complicated topics, such as what constitutes Medicare fraud. In addition to random audits and continuing education on ethics topics, the hotline deals with employees' billing questions. The company has developed certification tests for employees who determine billing codes. A forty-minute training video was shown in April 1998 to all 285,000 employees and featured three ethical scenarios for employees to examine.

The Future

The effort to quickly change the corporate culture and become the model corporate citizen in the health care industry was a real challenge for what was Columbia/HCA. This health care provider learned the hard way that maintaining an ethical organizational climate is the responsibility of top management. The name of the health care giant was changed to HCA—The Healthcare Company. Since 1997, the company has closed or consolidated more than 100 hospitals. It is currently composed of locally managed facilities that include 196 hospitals and seventy outpatient surgery centers in twenty-four states, the United Kingdom, and Switzerland.

In August 2000, HCA became the first corporation ever to be removed from INFACT's Hall of Shame. The executive director of INFACT indicated that HCA had drastically reduced its political activity and influence. The corporation has no active federal lobbyists and has a registered lobbying presence in only twelve states. According to the director, "This response to grassroots pressure constitutes a landmark development in business ethics overall and challenges prevailing practices among for-profit health care corporations." The company continued to move toward a resolution of outstanding issues with the federal and state governments, and those issues no longer consume an undue amount of management focus. Many of the issues for which HCA was under scrutiny are the same ones facing most of the nation's hospitals and health care providers. All HCA facilities have designated Ethics and Compliance Officers and established Facility Ethics and Compliance Committees. HCA compliance programs and policies have become a model for the industry.

In December 2000, HCA announced it would pay the federal government more than $840 million in criminal fines and civil penalties in the largest governmental fraud settlement in history. In January 2001, Jack Bovender Jr. (former chief operating officer) was named CEO. Of the fraud investigation, Bovender said, "We think the major issues have been settled," although the company still has some "physician relations issues and cost report issues" to resolve in civil actions involving individual hospitals.

Questions for Discussion

1. Columbia developed competitive advantages with internal control of cost and sales activities. What was the fundamental marketing strategy mistake in developing long-term profitability?

2. Evaluate the progress made in changing corporate and marketing strategy in the "new" Columbia.

3. Evaluate the ethical compliance program that Alan Yuspeh has established at Columbia.

Sources

The OIG's Compliance Program Guidelines for Hospitals, 1998; Columbia/HCA Healthcare Corporation 1996 Annual Report to Stockholders; Kurt Eichenwald and N.R. Kleinfield, "At Columbia/HCA, Scandal Hurts," *The Commercial Appeal*, December 21, 1997, C1, C3; "Columbia/HCA Launches Ethics and Compliance Training Program," AOL News, February 12, 1998; Charles Ornstein, "Columbia/HCA Prescribes Employee Ethics Program," *Tampa Tribune*, February 20, 1998, 4; Tom Lowry, "Loss Warning Hits Columbia/HCA Stock," *USA Today*, February 9, 1998, 2B; "Columbia/HCA Changing Name and Revising Signs," *The Commercial Appeal*, November 19, 1997, B7; Kevin Drawbaugh, "Columbia to Refocus Business," *The Commercial Appeal*, November 18, 1997, B5, B10; Michael Connor, "Whistle-Blowing Got Woman Fired, Suit Says," *The Commercial Appeal*, November 6, 1997, B4, B8; Kurt Eichenwald, "Reshaping the Culture at Columbia HCA," *New York Times*, November 4, 1997, C2; Tom Lowry, "Columbia/HCA Hires Ethics Expert," *USA Today*, October 14, 1997, 4B; Lucette Lagnado, "Columbia Taps Lawyer for Ethics Post: Yuspeh Led Defense Initiative of 1980s," *Wall Street Journal*, October 14, 1997, B6; Eva M. Rodriguez and Lucette Lagnado, "Top Columbia Officials Seen Key to Fraud," *Wall Street Journal*, October 7, 1997, A3; Chris Woodyard, "FBI Alleges Systemic Fraud at Columbia," *USA Today*, October 7, 1997, 1B; Tom Lowry, "Columbia Still Woos Doctors as Business Partners," *USA Today*, October 3, 1997, 1B; Vickie Chachere, "Fraud Warning Issued," *Tampa Tribune*, September 26, 1997, 5; Kris Hundley, "In the Eye of a Storm," *Times*, September 15, 1997, 8–10; "Executive Departs Besieged Columbia," *Times*, September 12, 1997, 1; Eva M. Rodriguez, "Columbia/HCA Probe Turns to Marketing Billing," *Wall Street Journal*, August 21, 1997, A2; Joseph B. White, "Suits by Two Big Public Pension Funds Broaden the Attack on Columbia/HCA," *Wall Street Journal*, August 19, 1997, A20; Anita Sharpe, "Columbia/HCA Confirms Departures of Another 2 Executives, More Expected," *Wall Street Journal*, August 15, 1997, B5; Lucette Lagnado and Steven Lipin, "Columbia/HCA Is Object of HealthSouth Interest," *Wall Street Journal*, August 15, 1997, A3; Eva M. Rodriguez, "Columbia May Have Destroyed Data," *Wall Street Journal*, August 14, 1997, A3; Eva M. Rodriguez, "Health Giant Is Targeted in U.S. Probe," *Wall Street Journal*, August 13, 1997, A3; Greg Jaffe, Anita Sharpe, and Eva M. Rodriguez, "Columbia/HCA Turns Over Key Cost Records," *Wall Street Journal*, August 8, 1997, B3; Eva M. Rodriguez, "Florida Becomes Third State to Probe Medicaid Billings of Columbia/HCA," *Wall Street Journal*, August 6, 1997, B6; Anita Sharpe, "Bovender Joins Frist Team at Columbia/HCA," *Wall Street Journal*, August 5, 1997, A3; "Columbia/HCA Prescribes Employee Ethics Program," *Tampa Tribune*, February 20, 1998, 4; "Corporate Influence Curtailed," PRNewswire, August 2, 2000; and Duncan Mansfield, "HCA Names Bovender Chief Executive," January 8, 2001, http://biz.yahoo.com/apf/010108/hca_change_2.html (accessed January 16, 2001).

FedEx Corporation

Frederick W. Smith founded the Federal Express Corporation in 1973 with part of an $8 million inheritance. At the time, the U.S. Postal Service and United Parcel Service (UPS) provided the only means of delivering letters and packages, and they often took several days or more to get packages to their destinations. While a student at Yale in 1965, Smith wrote a paper proposing an independent overnight delivery service. Although he received a C on the paper, Smith never lost sight of his vision. He recognized that time is money and believed that many businesses would be willing to pay more to get letters, documents, and packages delivered overnight. He was right.

Federal Express began shipping packages overnight from Memphis, Tennessee, on April 17, 1973. On that first night of operations, the company handled six packages, one of which was a birthday present sent by Smith himself. Today, FedEx, as the company is now called, handles about 3.25 million packages and documents per day—a figure that gives the company more than 50 percent of the overnight delivery market and 43 percent of the express delivery market. FedEx's total revenue in 2000 was an astounding $18.25 billion, with net income of $688 million. According to the company, FedEx is not in the package and document transport business; it moves information around the globe for both private consumers and industrial customers.

Though most people are familiar with FedEx's overnight delivery services, the company is actually divided into five major service divisions:

FedEx Express®: time-definite, global express transportation

FedEx Ground®: small-package ground delivery (formerly RPS)

FedEx Logistics®: integrated logistics and supply chain solutions

FedEx Custom Critical®: expedited, door-to-door, super-critical delivery (formerly Roberts Express)

FedEx Trade Networks®: customs brokerage and trade facilitation solutions

FedEx Express and Ground provide the bulk of the company's business, offering valuable services to anyone who needs to deliver letters, documents, or packages. Whether dropped off at one of over 44,000 drop boxes or picked up by a FedEx courier, packages are taken to a local FedEx office, from where they are trucked to the nearest airport. The package is usually flown to one of the company's distribution hubs

---

This case was prepared by Michael D. Hartline, Florida State University, for classroom discussion rather than to illustrate either effective or ineffective handling of an administrative situation.

for sorting and then flown to the airport nearest its destination. The package is then trucked to another FedEx office, where a courier picks it up and hand delivers it to the correct recipient. All of this takes place overnight, with many packages being delivered before 10:30 a.m. the next day. Couriers use handheld computers to keep track of packages. FedEx confirms that more than 98 percent of its deliveries are made on time.

To accomplish this amazingly high on-time delivery rate, FedEx maintains an impressive infrastructure of equipment and processes. The company owns over 14,000 service centers and airport facilities, 600 airplanes, and 41,000 trucks and vans around the world. FedEx even has its own weather forecasting service, ensuring that most of its flights arrive within fifteen minutes of schedule. Most packages shipped within the United States are sorted at the Memphis superhub, where FedEx takes over control of the Memphis International Airport at roughly 11 p.m. each night. FedEx planes land side by side on parallel runways every minute or so for well over one hour each night. After the sorting of packages, all FedEx planes take off in time to reach their destinations. Not all packages are shipped via air. When possible, FedEx uses ground transportation to save on expenses. For international deliveries, FedEx uses a combination of direct services and independent contractors.

FedEx's services are priced using a zone system by which the distance a package must travel to reach its final destination determines the price. Typical rates for a one-pound package using various services are:

FedEx Express Services	Delivered by:	Zone Rates
First Overnight® Service	8:00 a.m. next business day	$41.25 to $48.50
Priority Overnight® Service	10:30 a.m. next business day	$16.25 to $23.50
Standard Overnight® Service	3:00 p.m. next business day	$14.00 to $18.00
2-Day Delivery®	4:30 p.m. 2nd business day	$7.25 to $10.25
Express Saver®	4:30 p.m. 3rd business day	$6.40 to $8.80

FedEx also offers FedEx SameDay® Delivery for $159 for packages up to twenty-five pounds. FedEx Ground rates vary widely by package weight and shipping zone. For an extra $3, customers can have a courier pick up their packages rather than dropping them off at a drop box. Saturday pickup is also available for $10 more. Prices vary for larger packages and international shipments.

Growing Pains

Despite its tremendous success, FedEx has had to face some difficult times in its efforts to grow and compete against strong rival firms. The overnight delivery market matured very rapidly as intense competition from the U.S. Postal Service, UPS, Emery, DHL, RPS, and electronic document delivery (that is, fax machines and e-mail) forced FedEx to search for viable means of expansion. In 1984, facing a growing threat from electronic document delivery, FedEx introduced its ZapMail service for customers who could not afford expensive fax machines. For $35, FedEx would fax up to 10 pages of text to any FedEx site around the world. The document was then hand delivered to its recipient. Soon after the service was introduced, the price of fax machines plummeted, ultimately forcing FedEx to drop ZapMail after losing over $190 million. Many analysts still argue that the overnight delivery market could eventually lose as much as 30 percent of its letter business to electronic document delivery, especially to e-mail.

After its experience with ZapMail, FedEx began to focus its resources on expanding its overseas operations, the most rapidly growing area of the overnight market. In an increasingly global economy, businesses must be able to communicate quickly with employees around the world, with partners in other nations, with other businesses, and with customers. Though FedEx had been shipping packages from the United States to Canada since 1975, its acquisition of Gelco International in 1984 enabled FedEx to expand its operations to Europe and the Far East. Political changes in foreign markets—such as the establishment of the European Economic Community and the dismantling of once-closed Eastern European markets—allowed FedEx to gain entry into large, untapped markets.

FedEx's most important strategic move into international markets was its 1988 purchase of Tiger International Inc., owner of the Flying Tiger Line airfreight service. The $880 million purchase gave FedEx valuable routes, airport facilities, and expertise in European and Asian markets that it had been struggling to enter. Such valuable assets would have taken the company years to develop on its own. The purchase also gave the company valuable landing slots in Sydney, Singapore, Bangkok, Hong Kong, Seoul, Paris, Brussels, and Tokyo. However, the purchase of Flying Tiger created some problems for FedEx. The purchase left the company with a debt of $2.1 billion. It also thrust FedEx into the heavy-freight distribution market, which was more cyclical and capital intensive than small-package distribution. In addition, many of Tiger's key customers, including UPS, were competitors of FedEx. Finally, FedEx had trouble integrating Tiger's 6,500 union employees into its own nonunion workforce. Despite the difficulties in merging the two companies, the merger was a key ingredient in making FedEx a powerful global delivery service.

By 1991, the company had taken advantage of its opportunities and was offering international service to more than 100 countries. By 1992, next-morning service was available to and from major markets, including Paris, London, Frankfurt, Milan, Brussels, Geneva, Zurich, Antwerp, Amsterdam, Hong Kong, Tokyo, Singapore, and Seoul. FedEx's Canadian operations remained strong, and the company's operations in Latin America were growing. Despite this success, however, FedEx's international operations were troublesome. This was particularly true in Europe, where the total volume of express shipments between European countries was only 150,000 packages per night. Deciding that the intra-European market lacked potential, FedEx abandoned it and closed some domestic businesses in Italy, Germany, France, and the United Kingdom. The company took a $254 million restructuring charge in the third quarter of its 1992 fiscal year to cover the closures. FedEx then restricted its European focus to shipments to and from Europe rather than within Europe. By the end of 1992, FedEx experienced a total loss of $113 million and a negative earnings per share of $2.11. Company officials pointed to several reasons for the losses. First, the company was still recovering from its purchase of Flying Tiger, which increased its fixed costs in international operations. Second, FedEx had difficulty building a global infrastructure to support its operations. Negotiating for landing rights, dealing with foreign customs regulations, and establishing information networks all proved to be very costly.

Despite the problems in Europe, FedEx was doing very well in Asia. The Asian economy was growing rapidly—seven of the top ten growth economies at the time were in Asia. Additionally, Asia's manufactured-product exports were increasing at a rate of 28 percent per year. To capitalize on this growth, FedEx introduced its "AsiaOne" network in 1995. AsiaOne is an express network that offers effective "late-day" pickups and "next-day" deliveries not only across Asia, but also between Asia and North America. This quick service is due in part to FedEx's unparalleled capability to gain Asian air-route authority. For instance, FedEx is the only U.S. all-cargo airline with aviation rights to the Chinese trade centers of Shenzhen, Shanghai, and Beijing. The AsiaOne network attempts to provide quick, reliable package delivery to, from, and within Asia, all backed by a money-back guarantee. The overall growth of the Asian market is forecast to continue for some time.

In 1997, FedEx became the only cargo carrier in Moscow allowed to fly its own aircraft and utilize its own warehousing facilities. This was a breakthrough for FedEx because the Moscow and overall Russian market is forecast to grow dramatically. This exclusive capability allows FedEx customers to receive reliable next-business-day service (by 10:30 a.m.) from Moscow to North America and Western Europe. Likewise, FedEx offers two- to three-day service between Moscow and many Asian cities. FedEx has instituted a similar plan from the United States to Argentina, because projections indicate that the South American market will grow substantially.

To maintain its impressive growth, FedEx introduced several new services in the late 1990s. On the international front, FedEx introduced its International First® service offering one- to two-day, 8:00 a.m. delivery to/from twenty European countries. They also introduced International Priority® service (one- to three-day, 10:30 a.m. delivery to 210 countries) and International Economy® service (four- to five-day delivery to twenty-nine countries). Given that firms increasingly work seven days a week, FedEx added Sunday Priority Overnight® delivery by 3:00 p.m. to selected zip codes in the fifty largest U.S. markets. All of FedEx's traditional service features were made available for the Sunday service (for example, twenty-four-hour package tracking and money-back guarantees).

More Recent Developments

The most important recent development for FedEx was its 1998 acquisition of Caliber System, a trucking company whose RPS subsidiary was second only to UPS in ground shipments. The $2.7 billion merger created a new holding company, called FDX, that owned both FedEx and Caliber System. The RPS fleet of 13,500 trucks helped FedEx grow and compete more effectively with UPS in the nonexpress, ground-delivery business. The acquisition, along with the 1997 UPS strike, allowed FedEx to steal business from UPS and increase its market share. The purchase of RPS not only made FedEx more profitable, it also made FedEx more attractive to current and potential customers. Suddenly FedEx had the ability to fulfill any customer's needs by providing one-stop shopping for express and nonexpress shipping and delivery.

Also in 1998, FedEx established FedEx Logistics as a world leader in transportation management and integrated logistics. This move included the acquisition of Viking Freight, a leading freight carrier in the western United States, and Caribbean Transportation Services, an airfreight company serving points between the United States and Puerto Rico. By 2000, the company had a broad base of transportation services at its disposal, including the acquisition of Tower Group International to create FedEx Trade Networks (a division that provides trade facilitation and customs brokerage to FedEx customers). In an effort to better leverage the FedEx brand globally, the FDX holding company was renamed FedEx Corporation in 2000.

FedEx Express executed a major coup in January 2001 when it announced two seven-year service agreements with the U.S. Postal Service. In the first agreement, FedEx Express will provide air transportation for certain postal services, including Priority Mail. The second agreement gives FedEx Express the option to place a drop box in every U.S. Post Office. FedEx did not get the exclusive rights to drop boxes, leaving the potential for UPS to negotiate with the postal service to add its own boxes in the future. These agreements are expected to generate an additional $7 billion in revenue for FedEx Express. Both FedEx and the Postal Service will operate competitively and maintain separate services in every other category.

Looking Toward the Future

In an attempt to convert its challenges into competitive advantages, FedEx is now focused on a new strategic initiative called "Project ARISE." The plan has three principles:

> *Leverage competitive differentiation*—Each company in the FedEx family is free to operate independently yet compete collectively. While all FedEx companies work together to provide solutions to customers, each company is free to focus on the distinct needs of its market.

> *Extend the strength of the FedEx brand*—Each company in the FedEx family was renamed to carry the "FedEx" brand.

> *Provide a single point of access for customers*—A new FedEx Corporate Services company was created to integrate all customer-related activities, including sales, marketing, and information technology. FedEx customers have one "touch point" to access the full range of FedEx services—one sales rep, one toll-free number, one Web site, one account number, and one invoice.

FedEx continually strives to improve its services by enhancing its distribution networks, transportation infrastructure, information technology, and employee performance. FedEx has invested heavily in information technology by installing computer terminals at customers' offices and giving away its proprietary tracking software. Today, the vast majority of FedEx customers electronically generate their own pickup and delivery requests. The company has plans to move more aggressively into e-commerce, particularly with respect to order fulfillment for business-to-business and business-to-consumer merchants. FedEx's recently introduced Home Delivery service, for example, allows customers to set delivery options at night, on Saturdays, or by appointment.

As it moves ahead, FedEx has a lot going for it. No other carrier can match FedEx's global capabilities or one-stop shopping. FedEx has an enviable corporate culture and a workforce that is second to none. Because employees are critical to the company's success, FedEx strives to hire the best people and offers them the best training and compensation in the industry. FedEx employees are loyal, highly efficient, and extremely effective in delivering good service. In fact, FedEx employees claim to have "purple blood" to match the company's official color.

Why has FedEx been so successful? Good marketing—the company recognized an untapped customer need and filled it well. FedEx is also never content to sit on its laurels as it constantly strives to improve service and offer more options to its customers. There is little doubt that Fred Smith's "C" paper has become an indispensable part of the business world.

Questions for Discussion

1. Evaluate the methods used by FedEx to grow, both domestically and internationally. Why do you think the company had problems in its global operations?

2. What are the major SWOT considerations in FedEx's attempt to continue its growth and dominance in the domestic and global overnight delivery markets?

3. Picture a world without FedEx. How would business be different? How would your life be different?

4. Comment on the service agreements with the U.S. Postal Service. Is this a big deal or just an interesting partnership? If you were a senior manager for UPS, how would you react?

Sources

These facts are from FedEx Corporation, *2000 Annual Report;* FedEx Corporation Web site, http://www.fedex.com; "FedEx Ground Opens 'Super Hub,'" *Transportation & Distribution*, November 2000, 12–13; Linda Grant, "Why FedEx Is Flying High," *Fortune*, November 10, 1997, 155; Nicole Harris, "Flying Into a Rage?," *Business Week*, April 27, 1998, 119; Michele Kayal, "FedEx Launches Sunday Service Amid Skepticism," *Journal of Commerce and Commercial*, March 11, 1998, 1A; Kristin S. Krause, "Handling the Holiday Crush," *Traffic World*, December 4, 2000, 33; Theo Mullen, "Delivery Wars Go High-Tech—FedEx Ground Sends Message with $80M Investment to Improve Package Tracking," *Internetweek*, October 23, 2000, 18; Jayne O'Donnell, "FedEx–Postal Service Alliance Delivers Goods," *USA Today Online*, January 11, 2001, http://www.usatoday.com/money/; "Post Office, FedEx to Work Together," *USA Today Online*, January 10, 2001, http://www.usatoday.com/money/; Monica Roman, "FedEx Hitches Up a New Trucker," *Business Week*, November 27, 2000, 66; Marc L. Songini, "FedEx Expects CRM System to Deliver," *Computerworld*, November 6, 2000, 10; Richard Tomkins, "The Bear and the Alligator Enter Into a Race to Deliver," *Financial Times*, March 13, 1998, 30; and Michael Weingarten and Bart Stuck, "No Substitutions?" *Telephony*, February 2, 1998, 26.

18

DoubleClick, Inc.

DoubleClick, Inc., is an information-revolution phenomenon. What started out as an outgrowth of self-proclaimed computer "geeks" and savvy advertising agency executives has grown into a high-tech heavyweight providing advertising services and information about Internet users for advertisers, Web site operators, and other companies. The nature of its business has also put DoubleClick in the center of a brewing digital storm. At the core of this controversy is the issue of a person's right to privacy on the Internet. DoubleClick, which contends that it is committed to protecting the privacy of all Internet users, views its role as important in maintaining the Internet as a free medium driven by highly targeted advertising. Consumer groups, however, see it differently, noting that DoubleClick's actions loom larger than its words regarding access to personal information. Opponents, which include Michigan Attorney General Jennifer Granholm, regard DoubleClick's business practices as little more than a "secret, cyber-wiretap." To understand how DoubleClick found itself in this uncomfortable position, it is helpful to examine the firm's history, key strategic business units, and the issue of Internet privacy.

Merge onto Silicon Alley

Like many entrepreneurs in recent years, Kevin O'Connor and Dwight Merriman, two Atlanta-based engineers, saw an opportunity to cash in on the growing popularity of the Internet. O'Connor and Merriman had observed the challenges faced by niche-driven, subscription-based content Web sites attempting to compete with America Online's growing mass audience. They reasoned that they could capitalize on this situation by creating a single network to bring together numerous online publications to create a critical mass of information. With the idea of multiple publications forming a larger online network, it became crucial to address a significant issue for each of the various publications: advertising. After substantial research, O'Connor and Merriman decided to move forward with a network concept. However, after careful research, they decided that the advertising industry, rather than the publishing industry, could be better served with such a network. Thus, they founded the DoubleClick Network in January 1996.

This case was prepared by Tracy A. Suter, Oklahoma State University, for classroom discussion rather than to illustrate either effective or ineffective handling of an administrative situation.

Although O'Connor and Merriman's engineering backgrounds helped them tremendously with the technology issues associated with their concept, their engineering experience provided little insight into the world of sophisticated advertising. To resolve this issue, the software-based start-up formally merged with a division of ad agency Poppe Tyson. O'Connor believed the marriage of nerd and Madison Avenue cultures was possible because of a common bond—the love of the Internet. However, as O'Connor admitted, "The two cultures are completely ignorant of each other's ways." The "offspring" of this union set up shop in the heart of Silicon Alley in New York City—the same location, coincidentally, where some of New York's first advertising agencies sprang up a century ago.

Like traditional advertising agencies, DoubleClick's focus is to get the right advertisement to the right person at the right time. The difference between DoubleClick and offline ad agencies is the use of technology to track Web-surfing activities more directly as opposed to older media such as magazines. A magazine publisher, for instance, can detail the number of subscribers as well as the number of issues sold at newsstands. Unfortunately, the publisher does not have a very clear picture as to which articles in a magazine issue have been read, by whom, and when. Online, however, technology developed by DoubleClick can track traffic to a given customer's Web site and identify specific articles selected. Moreover, DoubleClick can trail traffic to and from the Web site to establish a surfing portfolio of site visitors. This breadth and depth of information quickly made DoubleClick a valuable service provider to online advertisers trying to make advertising work on the Internet.

Throwing Darts

The heart of DoubleClick's technology is its DART—Dynamic Advertising Reporting and Targeting—system. DART works by reading twenty-two criteria about Web site visitors' actions, such as their cyberlocation and time of visit. This technology also leaves, often without the user's knowledge, a "cookie" on his or her computer. Cookies are simply bits of information sent to a Web browser to be saved on the user's hard drive. Cookies are helpful for Internet users because they can contain important information like login information and user preferences that make return visits to subscription-based Web sites more manageable. Cookies are also useful for Web site operators because they can include additional information such as evidence of repeat visits and advertisements viewed. The information provided by the cookie about a Web site visitor's activities and interests helps DoubleClick tailor advertisements to specific users. It should be noted, however, that cookies do not collect personally identifiable information, such as a user's name, mailing address, telephone number, or e-mail address, so individual profiles are essentially anonymous. Instead of tracking an identifiable individual, cookies track users' digital footsteps.

With the wealth of information DoubleClick can provide for its network members, customers continue to join. By the end of its first year of business, DoubleClick had secured the business of twenty-five Web sites. Today, the company places banner advertisements on more than 11,500 Web sites. As Andy Jacobson, regional vice president for sales, says, "We set a goal: sell $500,000 of advertising in a week, and we'll buy lunch for everyone in the room." With 2000 revenues of almost $507 million—an average of nearly $10 million a week—DoubleClick is buying a lot of lunches these days (see Case Exhibit 18.1). The company is buying a lot of cookies, too—the eatable

CASE EXHIBIT 18.1	DOUBLECLICK, INC., FINANCIAL PERFORMANCE (IN MILLIONS EXCEPT PER-SHARE AMOUNTS) DURING FOUR FISCAL YEARS ENDED DECEMBER 31, 2000

	2000	1999	1998	1997
Net Sales	$505.60	$258.30	$80.20	$30.60
Cost of Sales	$228.10	$90.40	$51.10	$19.70
Selling, General & Admin. Expenses	$284.40	$168.30	$47.20	$18.40
Net Income (Loss)	($156.00)	($55.80)	($18.20)	($8.40)
Earnings per Share	($1.29)	($0.51)	($0.29)	($0.20)

Source: MSN MoneyCentral, http://moneycentral.msn.com/investor/.

kind. After the company achieved the milestone of 500 million advertisements placed in one day, company executives had cookies delivered to the technical engineers who manage the DART system.

This growth and increasing volume have allowed DoubleClick to command fees of 35–50 percent of advertising expenditures compared to the 15 percent fee structure charged by more traditional offline advertising agencies. Consider as well that the DoubleClick network has the capability to add hundreds of thousands of anonymous consumer profiles per day. Thus, it becomes clear that its technological capabilities make it an increasingly attractive ad-servicing option.

Despite the phenomenal sales growth DoubleClick has achieved, executives believe there is further potential available from the DART system. In fact, the expectation is for DART technologies alone to account for 50 percent of future revenues. However, those revenue expectations are not limited just to the DoubleClick network. The company is intent on servicing clients outside of its own network and growing complementary businesses in the projected $11.3 billion (by 2003) ad-servicing business. Like traditional companies, DoubleClick has used its expanding clout to develop and acquire important worldwide subsidiaries both on- and offline.

Key Subsidiaries

Despite the prevalence of high technology today, targeting remains surprisingly low-tech. According to Jim Nail, a Forrester research analyst:

> To get advertisers to continue to pay the big premiums, DoubleClick will have to tell advertisers more than just where you are and the kind of site you visit. It might have to tell them whether you are married or single, what your income is, and whether or not you have kids. What it needs to do above all is predict, with greater accuracy, how likely you are to buy an advertised product.

To that end, DoubleClick acquired offline catalog database company Abacus Direct shortly after buying NetGravity, Inc., a direct competitor. The idea behind the Abacus acquisition was the potential to merge that company's database of personally identifiable offline buying habits with DoubleClick's database of nonpersonally identifiable online habits to provide even greater depths of information to current and future clients. The trend toward collecting more personally identifiable information continued with DoubleClick's development of Flashbase, an automation tool that allows DoubleClick clients a means of collecting personal information by running contests and sweepstakes online. Additionally, DoubleClick Web sites such as http://www.NetDeals.com and http://www.IAF.net collect personally identifiable information online. However, DoubleClick contends that it provides ways for consumers to limit communication only to prize- or deal-specific information. In other words, consumers have the ability to "opt out" of future communications not specific to the instance when and where they entered their personal data.

The Controversy

The only problem with these developments and acquisitions is that their intended use signaled a significant philosophical shift in the way DoubleClick had always done business. Specifically, it created a drastic change in the company's consumer privacy position, a fact that consumer privacy groups and the Federal Trade Commission (FTC) did not take long to notice. According to Jason Catlett of Junkbusters, an Internet privacy activist, "Thousands of sites are ratting on you, so as soon as one gives you away, you're exposed on all of them. For years, [DoubleClick] has said (their services) don't identify you personally, and now they're admitting they are going to identify you."

In the face of growing public concern, Kevin O'Connor defended the company's plans: "The merger with Abacus Direct, along with the recent closing of the Net-Gravity merger, will allow us to offer publishers and advertisers the most effective means of advertising online and offline." Kevin Ryan, DoubleClick's CEO, took it a step further: "What we continue to hear from consumers is that they'd like to be in a position to have better content, greater access for everyone in the United States, and they would love it all to be free and advertising-served." Ryan pointed out that the Internet is driven by advertising and that advertising companies need to know their substantial investments are being spent in the best way possible—that is, targeted to the right audience or individual. Without more accurate information, Ryan asserted, much of the gratis content on the Internet would no longer be free.

Initially, the merger announcements were well received as shares of DoubleClick traded as high as $179.00 per share in early December 1999. Unfortunately, the comments of O'Connor and Ryan failed to stem the stock's decline after privacy concerns were voiced by Junkbusters and others in the aftermath of the Abacus Direct merger (see Case Exhibit 18.2).

DoubleClick's posted privacy policy states that online users are given *notice* about the data collection and the *choice* not to participate or to opt out. However, Internet users must read carefully to understand that granting permission, or failing to deny permission, at even one DoubleClick- or Abacus-serviced Web site allows the company to select personal information across all sites. Consequently, the Center for Democracy and Technology (CDT), a Washington-based watchdog organization, launched a hard-line campaign against DoubleClick. The focus of the campaign centered on a "Websit" under the slogan, "I Will Not Be Targeted," where users can opt

CASE EXHIBIT 18.2	DOUBLECLICK, INC., STOCK VALUATION DURING THREE YEARS SINCE THE INITIAL PUBLIC OFFERING (SYMBOL = DCLK)

	2000	1999	1998
January	$98.81	$24.06	N/A
February	$88.81	$22.47	N/A
March	$93.63	$45.52	N/A
April	$75.88	$69.91	$10.42
May	$42.25	$48.72	$8.66
June	$38.13	$45.88	$12.42
July	$35.94	$40.50	$11.00
August	$40.69	$49.94	$5.97
September	$32.00	$59.56	$5.97
October	$16.25	$70.00	$8.25
November	$14.19	$80.03	$10.13
December	$10.38	$126.53	$11.13

Source: MSN MoneyCentral, http://moneycentral.msn.com/investor/.

out of DoubleClick's profiling activities. According to Deirdre Mulligan, CDT's staff counsel, "You may have already been doublecrossed by DoubleClick or you may be next in line. In either case, if you care about your privacy and want to surf the Web without your every move being recorded in a giant database connected to your name, its time to opt out."

The CDT campaign was just one of the challenges DoubleClick faced as public concerns about Internet privacy escalated. A California woman brought a lawsuit against DoubleClick, alleging the company had unlawfully obtained and sold her private personal information. Media critics labeled DoubleClick an online "Big Brother" that passed information about employees' Internet surfing behavior on to their employers. Attorneys general in Michigan and New York launched investigations into DoubleClick's business practices. One of the most publicized challenges was the Electronic Privacy Information Center (EPIC) complaint filed with the FTC regarding DoubleClick's profiling practices. The complaint led to a full-scale investigation of DoubleClick's business practices by the federal watchdog. EPIC and similar privacy groups prefer an opt-in mechanism as opposed to DoubleClick's current opt-out platform. EPIC Executive Director Marc Rotenberg said, "Several years ago, DoubleClick said it would not collect personally identifiable information and keep anonymous profiles. Privacy experts applauded that approach." But as a result of the Abacus merger, "DoubleClick has changed its mind and they're trying to convince users they should accept that [new] model."

DoubleClick attempted to defuse the growing controversy (and reverse the plummet of the stock price) by announcing a program to protect consumers it tracks online. The program included a major newspaper campaign, 50 million banner ads directing consumers to the privacy rights information and education site PrivacyChoices (http://www.privacychoices.org/), the appointment of a chief privacy officer, the hiring of an external accounting firm to conduct privacy audits, and the establishment of an advisory board. The board, in particular, was less than well received. Calling the board a "facade," Jeffrey Chester, executive director of the Center of Media Education, said, "This is a public relations ploy to ward off federal and state scrutiny." Chester and other privacy organizations expressed dismay that the advisory board included no true privacy advocates and worse, it included a DoubleClick customer. Moreover, that customer advocated technologies called "Web bugs" or "clear-gifs" that some consider even more intrusive than cookies. These sentiments prompted O'Connor to state, "It is clear from these discussions that I made a mistake by planning to merge names with anonymous user activity across Web sites in the absence of government and industry privacy standards."

Another attempt to regain consumer goodwill is DoubleClick's participation in the Responsible Electronic Communication Alliance (RECA) along with fifteen of the nation's leading online marketers. The purpose of the RECA is to give consumers greater choice and notice regarding their online activities. To identify companies that subscribe to the RECA's proposed standards, the alliance is developing a "seal of approval" program in the spirit of *Good Housekeeping*. According to Christopher Wolf, RECA President, "Our ultimate goal is to phase in a set of firm standards on privacy, notice, access, and choice."

A New Era

On January 22, 2001, the Federal Trade Commission announced that it had completed its investigation of DoubleClick. In a letter to the company, the commission said, "It appears to staff that DoubleClick never used or disclosed consumers' PII [personally identifiable information] for purposes other than those disclosed in its privacy policy." On news of the announcement, the company's stock price jumped 13 percent, although it remained well below the company's historic high. However, the FTC also warned that its decision "is not to be construed as a determination that a violation may not have occurred" and reserved the right to take further action. Needless to say, the privacy advocates were not happy with the announcement. EPIC, for example, contends that the FTC never addressed its allegations. CEO Kevin Ryan, however, feels DoubleClick has been vindicated: "We felt from the beginning that our privacy policy and practices are solid. We never felt there was any substantial problem with them." Although it seems that the storm has quieted for now, Internet consumers, privacy advocates, and government officials will be watching DoubleClick closely, and the issue of Internet privacy will almost certainly continue.

Even DoubleClick was not able to escape what the market terms a dot-com fallout. In early 2001, DoubleClick laid off 150 employees, approximately 7 percent of their 2001 workforce. According to an article published in *eCompany*, however, DoubleClick is expected to rise from its ashes and flourish as an e-business. Currently it has a stock price of $10.55 and a three- to five-year estimated EPS growth rate of 46.91 percent. DoubleClick has also made a change to their current business model. They have left the pay-for-performance approach and are trying an upfront fee. At present they are selling 1,000 impressions for $2.00, well below past fees in the market of $20.00 per 1,000 impressions. This switch will have a large impact on competitors, for DoubleClick's fee will depress ad rates for the entire market, and other media companies typically sell only one-quarter of their available space. The ride has been wild for DoubleClick, but if they can persevere, as suggested by *eCompany*, they will continue to change the advertising market forever.

DoubleClick should continue to monitor feedback regarding privacy policy issues. The company can be successful both internally and externally if they can find a way to regain consumer trust. Many consumers enjoy and examine advertising on the internet in order to learn about interesting products. As long as they feel their personal information is being used in an appropriate, unthreatening manner, they will continue to click through the ads. DoubleClick is on the right track with the announcement of a recent alliance with NetScore. NetScore enables the tracking of Internet use at home, work, and school as well as international Internet use. Perhaps along with this alliance, DoubleClick should change their opt-out option to an opt-in option. Allowing the customer to choose whether or not to make personal information available would probably be welcomed more than leaving the consumer with the responsibility of requesting their information not be recorded.

DoubleClick may consider reevaluating their growth strategy. The company started, as all do, small and unrecognized. They proceeded by building brand equity while simultaneously growing. Now that they have had to downsize some, they should take advantage of that by concentrating on rebuilding their name and making their service more customer friendly without trying to expand. Currently, they have a wide enough customer base to sustain the business. Once they have established a stronger reputation and a service that accommodates privacy issues, they can focus on growth.

All in all, DoubleClick is still in a position to revolutionize marketing. In early 2001, they reached a milestone by achieving the one-trillionth-ad mark. If they play their cards right, they could be the leading player in this industry.

Questions for Discussion

1. Why did DoubleClick's decision to merge Abacus Direct's database of personally identifiable offline buying habits with DoubleClick's nonpersonally identifiable online habits so upset privacy advocates and arouse the attention of federal and state officials? What other ethical issues exist in this situation?

2. How has DoubleClick taken a strategic approach to addressing these issues?

3. What else could/should DoubleClick do to address stakeholders' concerns about personal privacy protection?

Sources

These facts are from Eryn Brown, "The Silicon Alley Heart of Internet Advertising," *Fortune*, December 6, 1999, 166–167; Lynn Burke, "A DoubleClick Smokescreen?" *WiredNews*, May 23, 2000, http://www.wirednews.com/news/print/ 0,1294,36404,00.html; "Company Briefing Book," *Wall Street Journal Interactive*, http://interactive.wsj.com, accessed January 29, 2001; Tom Conroy and Rob Sheffield, "Hot Marketing Geek," *Rolling Stone*, August 20, 1998, 80; "Crisis Control: DoubleClick," *Privacy Times*, February 18, 2000, http://www.privacytimes.com/New Webstories/doubleclick_priv_2_23 .htm; "DoubleClick Accused of Double-Dealing Double-Cross," *News Bytes News Network*, February 2, 2000, http:// www.newsbytes.com; "DoubleClick Completes $1.8 Bil Abacus Direct Buyout," *News Bytes News Network*, November 30, 1999, http://www.newsbytes.com; "DoubleClick Outlines Five-step Privacy Initiative," *News Bytes News Network*, February 15, 2000, http://www.newsbytes.com; "DoubleClick Tracks Online Movements," *News Bytes News Network*, January 26, 2000, http://www.newsbytes.com (originally reported by *USA Today*, http://www.usatoday.com); Jane Hodges, "DoubleClick Takes Standalone Route for Targeting Tools," *Advertising Age*, December 16, 1996, 32; "I Will Not Be Targeted," Center for Democracy and Technology, http://www.cdt.org/action/doubleclick.shtml; Chris Oakes, "DoubleClick Plan Falls Short," *WiredNews*, February 14, 2000, www.wirednews.com/news/print/0,1294,34337,00.html; Chris O'Brien, "DoubleClick Sets Off Privacy Firestorm," *San Jose Mercury News*, February 26, 2000, http://www.mercurycenter.com/ business/top/042517.htm; "Online Marketing Coalition Announces Proposals for Internet Privacy Guidelines," *MSN*

MoneyCentral, September 25, 2000, http://news.moneycentral.msn.com/; "Privacy Choices," DoubleClick, Inc., http://www.privacychoices.org/; "Privacy Policy," DoubleClick Inc., http://www.doubleclick.net/; "Privacy Standards Proposed," *MSNBC*, September 25, 2000, www.msnbc.com/news/467212.asp; Randall Rothenberg, "An Advertising Power, but Just What Does DoubleClick Do?" *New York Times: E-Commerce Special Section*, 1999, http://www.nytimes.com/library/tech/99/09/biztech/technology/22roth.html; Allen Wan and William Spain, "FTC Ends DoubleClick Investigation," CBS MarketWatch.com, January 23, 2001, http://www.aolpf.marketwatch.com/pf/archive/20010123/news/current/dclk.asp; "DoubleClick's Reprieve," *Marketing News*, February 16, 2001, 48; "eCompany 40," *eCompany*, April 2001, 147; and "DoubleClick Rolls Out Better Method for Ad Tracking," http://news.moneycentral.msn.com/ (March 5, 2001).

19

Hewlett-Packard's Home Products Division in Europe (1996–2000)

Making money in the [home PC] business is like landing a man on the moon.[1]

—*Webb McKinney, General Manager, Home Products Division*

By November 2000, Hewlett-Packard's (HP) Home Products Division in Europe (HPD-E) had been selling HP's Pavilion line of personal computers in Europe for almost five years. During that time, HPD-E had entered and exited Germany, fought for a 13.5% and 5.2% market share in France and in the United Kingdom, respectively, and had significantly reorganized its European operations twice.[2] Some felt that the European operation had now become everything HP aspired to be. Others wondered why Europe had been so hard and whether the model of "operational excellence"[3] adopted by HPD-E to compete there was adequate for a very fast changing market.

First Lessons from Europe—1996

In September 1996, *Business Week* reported that even though "[HP] had made an impressive leap to Number 4 in the U.S. market in just 16 months, the business ha[d] barely broken even."[4] HP was nevertheless intent on sticking with home PCs and turning the business into a moneymaker. HPD's strategy was to straddle the gap between the price-conscious Packard Bell and the more technologically sophisticated Compaq Computers. Webb McKinney, HPD's general manager, was striving for 25% annual growth in sales, but, as a senior HP manager noted, "just because [the Pavilion]

Professor David J. Arnold and Caren-Isabel Knoop, Executive Director, Global Research Group, prepared this case as the basis for class discussion rather than to illustrate either effective or ineffective handling of an administrative situation. This case contains information from two supplements, Hewlett-Packard's Home Products Division in Europe (C): Lessons from Europe, HBS case no. 399–060 and Hewlett-Packard's Home Products Division in Europe (D): The Matrix Model, HBS case no. 500-063. The two supplements can be used instead of the case.

[1] Peter Burrows in "The Printer King Invades Homes PCs," *Business Week*, August 21, 1995, p. 74.

[2] Some of the data in the case has been disguised.

[3] Broadly defined as tightly matching supply and demand.

[4] Burrows, ibid., p. 74.

was successful in the United States [did] not mean that it [would] be successful elsewhere. . . . We [knew we had] to be careful to balance that business with our return on investment."[5]

The first HPD products launched in Europe were priced at parity or better with Compaq and IBM on like-for-like features. HPD's prices and features placed them at the higher end of the market. "One of the fundamental things we did not realize about the European market," McKinney recalled, "is that prices were lower than expected." In the United States the $2,000 price point had become almost standard, buying ever-more capability (processor speeds, amount of memory).[6] "We assumed that whatever technology we developed in the U.S. was fine for Europe," McKinney explained.

> Although we customized our products for Europe, they were basically assembled from a menu of technology developed in the United States. With the price points we selected, we could only expect to reach the top third of the market. In the United States these price points cover 80% of the market. In the portion of the market we reached in Europe we did well, but did not go down far enough. We basically screwed up.

In addition, while HPD's four-tiered product line changed seasonally, its German competitors' six-week product cycles enabled them to adjust price and product. Explained Fay Barrow, the HPD-E marketing manager who had taken over from Amanda Barker:

> They manage a lot of SKUs[7] and do not come to market with five products that last six months [as manufacturers such as HP and Compaq typically had]. They bring new products to market every few months. To cope, we need to have flexible manufacturing and this will require complete reengineering. We are geared to bringing a product line with a fixed number of SKUs to market in each country.

Moreover, the selling window in Europe was compressed to two weeks, particularly during rapid-turnover seasons such as Christmas. "It only takes two weeks for the entire business to collapse unless you manage inventory and price movement well," Barrow explained. "The challenge is getting the data from retail chains [that is imperative to] price accurately and responding fast to any price movements by major competitors, especially in peak selling season."

Thinking Things Through—1997

Barrow decided that to compete in Europe, HPD needed to do things differently. In January 1997, the European division undertook a major strategy review. Recalled Barrow:

---

[5] Jennifer Lien, "HP Cautious Over Home PC Push Into Asia-Pacific Market," *Business Times*, September 23, 1996, p. 12.

[6] "The Worldwide Web," *WorldTraveler*, December 1996, p. 136.

[7] Stockkeeping units.

We said, "let's take a clean sheet of paper and see whether we need a different business model in Europe than the one we have today." A different business model could be a different channel, different products, anything. We gathered everything we knew about the marketplace and consumers, country by country. That led us to explore three classic business models: operational excellence, product innovation, and customer intimacy. We evaluated the models by cross-referencing them with all of the marketplace scenarios we could imagine.

HPD decided to focus on operational excellence, broadly defined as tightly matching supply and demand. Product innovation would cost too much in R&D to enable HPD to succeed in Europe. Moreover, Barrow believed direct marketing, although successful in some European countries such as the United Kingdom, was not widely enough accepted in Europe in 1997 to warrant investment in the customer intimacy model.

HPD undertook two projects to implement operational excellence. The first was to review customer behavior in six European markets. Barrow explained, "We really did not understand the purchasing behavior of consumers." The second was to analyze those six markets through a simulation exercise. Barrow asked:

How do you compare one country against another when you are not in that country? We took the product lines we were about to launch in the U.K. and France and asked retailers what we would have to price them at today if we were going to launch them in their country in the coming summer. We also asked them how many they thought they could sell over six months, through which channels and at what margins. This gave us a notion of a price point. This way we figured out whether our current structure for manufacturing was appropriate or out of range. The aim was to simulate the revenue and profit size with the existing product lines. The financial model told us what exactly we had to do to build a profitable operation.

The evaluation revealed that some smaller countries would be too unprofitable to consider (e.g., Switzerland, in part because of its several language groups).

Next Product, Next Approach—1998

By summer 1997, the Pavilion's respective market shares in the United Kingdom and France were 2.2% and 6.4%, well below HPD-E's 15% target. Difficult market conditions and lack of experience with channels in their existing markets had forced Barrow and her team to set aside plans to enter new markets such as Spain and the Netherlands. In July 1997, HP was no. 3 in the United States, three years ahead of HPD's plan. The $300 billion PC industry was booming. HP managers felt that the secret to HP's success in the United States was not technological advantage (HP's traditional strength), but the company's brand, excellent relationships with major chains created by HP's dominant position in printers and fax machines, and "perfect" supply and demand management.

In September 1997, HPD-E launched a back-to-school product in France and the United Kingdom to address these issues. Armed with customer and market information, the division worked with retailers to set a price point for particular product specifications. The team added margins to manufacturing costs and then production cost to matched target pricing. It then tendered the work to four OEM manufacturers and suppliers in addition to HP. HP responded surprisingly well to the unusual step (for HP) of taking product to an OEM. Barrow felt this reflected an understanding that HPD was "doing what it takes to be successful in this business."

Although the initial launch was a success (earning HP the no. 3 position in France, no. 7 in the United Kingdom), "we made a few mistakes," Barrow conceded:

> We did a good job of selling to the channel, but were not good enough at managing sellout and watching our competitors as carefully as we should have. In addition, when a major competitor cut the price of its products by 17%, we were slow to react. Inventory built up in the channel extremely quickly and the technology became obsolete. We had to pay a huge price protection bill in France and the U.K.

At the same time the team had to contend with a fundamental shift caused by an aggressive low-price-point market attack by French hypermarkets. By summer 1998, hypermarkets accounted for 60% of industry sales in France. Barrow explained:

> Hypermarket chains contributed in a major way to price decline as well as volume increase. We did not really understand this channel and therefore did not know how to manage it as well as we should. We had to build the relationship and go through wholesalers to reach hypermarket chains. This is where the information bottleneck is. We started to negotiate a direct contract with them. We have also reduced the number of retail chains we sell to and built share in each retailer to match demand with supply in a perfect manner.

Twin Objectives—1999

These events led to a change in strategy for the European operation and a decision in October 1998 to temporarily forego expansion for profitability in France and the United Kingdom and build market share there through improved supply chain management ("operational excellence"). According to Barrow, expansion was on hold "until we learn to execute well in a very challenging market like France and take the learning elsewhere." HPD also reorganized its local management team and created a European P&L.

Some at HP believed that operational excellence in the traditional retail arena was precisely the wrong focus at a time when the industry was being revolutionized by direct sales. Industry analysts were also surprised by HPD's decision.[8] HPD managers nevertheless felt that the strategy would prove successful for the 1998 back-to-school season and allow HPD to gain back market share in France and the United Kingdom. Barrow summarized:

---

[8]"HP Breaks through UK 1K Barrier with Premium II PCs," *Newsbytes*, February 20, 1998.

We backed into really managing the business to profitability and not to growth. It was a total reversal. We realized that to make money in this industry we had to drive all the costs out of the system; that is, manage the entire value chain from manufacturing to the final sales at retail very tightly. This forced us to focus on every aspect of internal operation.

Didier Chenneveau, HPD-E's general manager Europe, was transferred from California to Grenoble, France, to head up the European organization as it implemented this strategy. He felt that HP had to reassess the way it was approaching the European market:

We are still following what is basically an American model, based on tackling relatively static markets one by one and focusing resources on within-market battles for dominance. The European market is too volatile for this to work. I [suggested] more of a matrix model, where we attack either regional segments or emerging business models which are better suited to our own and which offer some form of first-mover advantage.

This meant redefining HPD's business by channel rather than by country, marking a departure from the country priority matrix approach.[9] According to him, "market entry [was] not the major barrier to profitability, but maintenance of margins once in the market." He estimated that the fixed costs of entry into a new market were approximately $1 million, to cover market research, some localization of keyboard and software (particularly help files), and packaging. Margins were lower than in the United States because of more price-sensitive market conditions, higher retailer margins, and also because of structural factors such as higher sales taxes and less efficient transportation and supply chain systems. The net unit contribution to HP could be $50 to $100 lower in Europe than in the United States, depending upon the price level and distribution channel.

Two strategic options to boost profitability were considered: (1) enter the region's less developed markets to gain pioneer market share advantage; and (2) develop new marketing models. Spain provided a test case for the first option. Traditionally a specialty retail market, a number of franchised chains offered the chance for HPD to experiment with the configure-to-order model. In addition, Nordic countries (especially Sweden and Norway) and the Netherlands appeared less price-sensitive than other markets and were also apparently open to new business models such as employee purchase program and Internet sales.

The second option was using new marketing models and approaches with which HP, like other major computer brands, was experimenting (often through marketing partnerships). These included selling hardware at a reduced price in combination with a contract which generated revenues via a subscription to online services;[10] and pre-installing a portal on the PC, accessed by a single clearly labeled key, in return for a royalty from the portal owner every time the user used the key. Such new integrated

---

[9] See HBS case no. 397–001, "Hewlett-Packard Co.'s Home Products Division (A): Top Three in the Home PC Market by 1997."

[10] For example, a recent program in France offered consumers a FF2,000 discount off a PC retailing at FF4,900 in return for a two-year subscription to an Internet Service Provider (ISP) at FF124 per month. This program was offered via telephone sales.

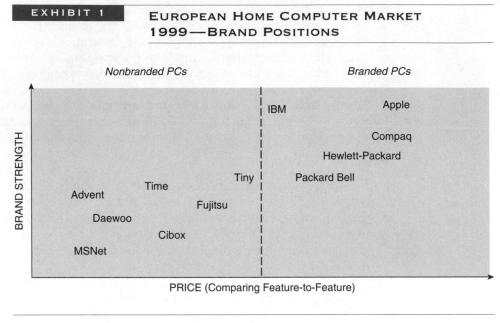

| EXHIBIT 1 | EUROPEAN HOME COMPUTER MARKET 1999—BRAND POSITIONS |

Source: HP.
Note: Vobis was not measured.

business models were in line with the strategy for HP being articulated by new CEO Carly Fiorina—putting HP at "the intersection of e-services wrapped around products, appliances, and infrastructure."[11]

By mid-1999, substantial market share gains had been achieved in France, where Pavilion was third in the market with a 12% market share. Progress in the United Kingdom had been slower, although HPD was the top-selling brand in two retailers. See Exhibit 1 for brand positions in 1999.

Getting It Right—2000

In September 2000, HPD managers felt that they "finally got it right [in Europe]." Much had changed. Emilio Ghilardi took over from Chenneveau on January 1, 2000. The concept of regional organization, which HPD-E had pioneered, was now being adopted across the company.[12] In mid-2000 HP was organized in four sectors, two product-facing organizations (all computer products and all imagining products) and two customer-facing ones (Business and Consumer). In 2000, HPD and the Pavilion were subsumed into a larger organization called Consumer Computing & Appliances, which also included the palmtop, the calculator business, personal storage appliances, CD writers, and Internet services. Ghilardi was its general manager for Europe, Middle East and Africa. The worldwide organization made product available and let regional organizations decide on the combination of technology and marketing

---

[11] Speech delivered at the COMDEX trade show, Las Vegas, November 15, 1999.

[12] HP used to manage its business as a combination of product centric businesses with people with worldwide responsibility for managing different P&Ls.

strategy local markets warranted. Regional organizations had their own P&L. Noted Ghilardi:

> The regional organization takes care of product marketing, finance, business development, etc., all the standard things you would expect a regional organization to do—local people speak the same language and have the same culture as the customers and the people in the channels. That helps. Our support group devises and implements plans to support products everywhere in Europe. It is hoped that the new organization will increase speed and accountability. Sometimes speed is more important than cost.

Ghilardi felt that it was also "sometimes more important to be quick than right" and that the new organization would correct for past mistakes:

> At the outset HPD was given total autonomy. So they focused on making the best business model for the retail market in the U.S. That made it harder to internationalize. We thought we could make worldwide business decisions centrally and that proved difficult. Counterparts do not see us as being able to move fast. The fundamental point is that in Europe the market is dominated by local players, so the answer is coming from asking yourself the following question—why should people buy an HP instead of a no-brand home PC? Technology? No. Faster machine? No. What we have inside? No. So why would a customer value HP instead of somebody else? The first is look and feel in the product sense—quality and good value for what I am buying. The second is customer care, HP is known for excellence in dealing with customers. Third, the product is optimized to give the best possible Internet experience. We want people to go through the Internet experience; in many cases we are still the first computer people buy. These are three areas we can add value that are consistent with HP values that echo with customers. People who make the rest their core competencies should do all the rest. For example, why were we doing the physical repair of breaks? The physical manufacturing? We can let other people focus on that.

On the strength of this realization, HPD was planning to relaunch in Germany on October 13 and moving into pretty much every country in Western Europe in the next 12 months. "We will be using blended channels—we will be where customers want to buy; retail is still by far the dominant place where people buy." Ghilardi was expecting to sell 150,000 to 200,000 units in Germany in the next 12 months. "We are aiming at 10% plus market share in two years in a market of 3 million units by 2002," Ghilardi explained.

European Market Structure

The European home PC market meanwhile was still growing at 15%–16% per year, though without predictable seasonality for most manufacturers. Competition remained strong and volatile across Europe (see Exhibits 2 and 3). Price points continued to fall. HPD's prices decreased in line with the overall market. "The delta in price between the branded and nonbranded PCs, or 'white boxes,' has shrunk dramatically

EXHIBIT 2					

YEAR-ON-YEAR TOP 10 UNITS FOR CONSUMER DESKTOP IN SELECTED EUROPEAN COUNTRIES

Vendor	1999, Q2	% Share	2000, Q2	% Share	Growth
WESTERN EUROPE					
Fujitsu Siemens	174,123	13.1%	239,258	14.3%	37.4%
Compaq	105,423	7.9	200,614	12.0	90.3
NEC CI	98,642	7.4	192,495	11.5	95.1
Apple	44,853	3.4	86,136	5.2	92.0
IBM	57,562	4.3	72,305	4.3	25.6
Tiny Computers/Opus	55,952	4.2	70,415	4.2	25.8
Hewlett-Packard	33,124	2.5	62,304	3.7	88.1
Dell	49,847	3.8	60,030	3.6	20.4
Vobis	95,587	7.2	57,619	3.4	−39.7
Gateway	19,575	1.5	37,480	2.2	91.5
Others	593,057	44.7	593,387	35.5	−0.1
Total	**1,327,745**	**100%**	**1,671,043**	**100%**	**25.9%**
AUSTRIA					
Fujitsu Siemens	6,487	26.9%	24,491	40.9%	277.5%
Compaq	2,069	8.6	13,728	22.9	563.5
IBM	369	1.5	5,105	8.5	1,283.5
NEC CI	374	1.6	3,249	5.4	768.7
Birg	1,893	7.8	2,400	4.0	26.8
Maxdata	0	0.0	1,650	2.8	0.0
Vobis	3,822	15.8	1,260	2.1	−67.0
Apple	758	3.1	1,082	1.8	42.7
Actebis	1,985	8.2	703	1.2	−64.6
Acer	176	0.7	590	1.0	235.2
Others	6,196	25.7	5,563	9.3	−10.2
Total	**24,129**	**100%**	**59,821**	**100%**	**147.9%**
BELGIUM					
NEC CI	6,054	24.7%	12,711	34.1%	110.0%
Compaq	3,688	15.1	9,932	26.6	169.3
Apple	1,271	5.2	3,200	8.6	151.8
Vobis	2,822	11.5	2,203	5.9	−21.9
Fujitsu Siemens	2,121	8.7	2,015	5.4	−5.0
Dell	1,333	5.4	826	2.2	−38.0
IBM	1,087	4.4	306	0.8	−71.8
Actebis	0	0.0	138	0.4	0.0
Gateway	95	0.4	100	0.3	5.3
Laser	789	3.2	97	0.3	−87.7
Others	5,210	21.3	5,748	15.4	10.3
Total	**24,470**	**100%**	**37,276**	**100%**	**52.3%**
DENMARK					
Fujitsu Siemens	2,076	8.8%	6,210	19.4%	199.1%
Compaq	4,884	20.8	4,171	13.1	−14.6
IBM	2,850	12.1	3,996	12.5	40.2
Amitech	2,617	11.2	3,485	10.9	33.2
Newtech	4,275	18.2	2,264	7.1	−47.0
Apple	1,184	5.0	1,739	5.4	46.9
Actebis	0	0.0	1,599	5.0	0.0
Dell	1,084	4.6	1,447	4.5	33.5

continued

EXHIBIT 2 **YEAR-ON-YEAR TOP 10 UNITS FOR CONSUMER DESKTOP IN SELECTED EUROPEAN COUNTRIES** (*continued*)

Vendor	1999, Q2	% Share	2000, Q2	% Share	Growth
DENMARK (continued)					
Zitech	900	3.8	1,409	4.4	56.6
NEC CI	648	2.8	1,145	3.6	76.7
Others	2,951	12.6	4,485	14.0	52.0
Total	**23,469**	**100%**	**31,950**	**100%**	**36.1%**
FINLAND					
Fujitsu Siemens	3,390	14.1%	4,522	18.0%	33.4%
IBM	1,720	7.2	3,277	13.0	90.5
Compaq	1,308	5.5	2,528	10.0	93.3
DGC	1,302	5.4	1,771	7.0	36.0
DTK	755	3.2	1,617	6.4	114.2
Oshorne	2,110	8.8	1,034	4.1	−51.0
ARC	701	2.9	870	3.5	24.1
Wings	1,116	4.7	762	3.0	−31.7
Apple	751	3.1	716	2.8	−4.7
Hewlett-Packard	1,004	4.2	706	2.8	−29.7
Others	9,811	40.9	7,364	29.3	−24.9
Total	**23,968**	**100%**	**25,167**	**100%**	**5.0%**
FRANCE					
NEC CI	21,360	11.4%	37,430	16.8%	75.2%
IBM	10,054	5.4	36,135	16.2	259.4
Hewlett-Packard	9,147	4.9	30,062	13.5	228.7
Apple	14,361	7.7	16,142	7.2	12.4
Fujitsu Siemens	10,370	5.5	15,816	7.1	52.5
Unika	10,710	5.7	9,680	4.3	−9.6
Cibox	16,965	9.0	9,294	4.2	−45.2
Compaq	6,279	3.3	7,872	3.5	25.4
Gateway	1,744	0.9	6,424	2.9	268.3
Acer	7,253	3.9	6,137	2.7	−15.4
Others	79,349	42.3	48,181	21.6	−39.3
Total	**187,592**	**100%**	**223,173**	**100%**	**19.0%**
GERMANY					
Fujitsu Siemens	93,947	25.5%	127,755	26.7%	36.0%
Compaq	15,168	4.1	93,779	19.6	518.3
Medion	16,317	4.4	26,851	5.6	64.6
Vobis	55,428	15.0	25,388	5.3	−54.2
Actebis	15,097	4.1	22,667	4.7	50.1
Peacock	0	0.0	22,609	4.7	0.0
PC Spezialist	12,062	3.3	22,456	4.7	86.2
Maxdata	0	0.0	20,168	4.2	0.0
Apple	8,877	2.4	16,155	3.4	82.0
Comtech	13,831	3.8	15,000	3.1	8.5
Others	138,028	37.4	86,262	18.0	−37.5
Total	**368,755**	**100%**	**479,090**	**100%**	**29.9%**
GREECE					
Quest	860	9.9%	2,180	18.7%	153.5%
Altec	1,080	12.4	2,115	18.2	95.8

continued

| EXHIBIT 2 | | **YEAR-ON-YEAR TOP 10 UNITS FOR CONSUMER DESKTOP IN SELECTED EUROPEAN COUNTRIES** (*continued*) | | | |

Vendor	1999, Q2	% Share	2000, Q2	% Share	Growth
GREECE (continued)					
ICE	1,320	15.2	1,890	16.2	43.2
NEC CI	188	2.2	1,180	10.1	527.7
Compaq	297	3.4	984	8.5	231.3
Toshiba	0	0.0	544	4.7	0.0
Apple	276	3.2	317	2.7	14.9
Hewlett-Packard	104	1.2	147	1.3	41.3
Fujitsu Siemens	417	4.8	132	1.1	−68.3
Dell	3	0.0	118	1.0	3,833.3
Others	4,163	47.8	2,035	17.5	−51.1
Total	**8,708**	**100%**	**11,642**	**100%**	**33.7%**
IRELAND					
NEC CI	3,016	20.1%	3,463	15.7%	14.8%
Gateway	1,822	12.1	3,125	14.2	71.5
Dell	1,974	13.1	3,066	13.9	55.3
Fujitsu Siemens	1,751	11.6	3,028	13.7	72.9
Compaq	2,443	16.3	2,832	12.8	15.9
Apple	309	2.1	969	4.4	213.6
PC Pro	0	0.0	397	1.8	0.0
Computer City	0	0.0	327	1.5	0.0
Acer	741	4.9	169	0.8	−77.2
IBM	694	4.6	134	0.6	−80.7
Others	2,282	15.2	4,563	20.7	100.0
Total	**15,032**	**100%**	**22,073**	**100%**	**46.8%**
ITALY					
Compaq	8,176	9.4%	17,429	15.8%	113.2%
CDC	20,365	23.5	16,722	15.1	−17.9
Vobis	11,259	13.0	10,978	9.9	−2.5
NEC CI	5,666	6.5	10,398	9.4	83.5
Olidata	7,837	9.1	9,391	8.5	19.8
Apple	2,743	3.2	8,565	7.8	212.2
Acer	3,367	3.9	7,321	6.6	117.4
Fujitsu Siemens	6,750	7.8	6,760	6.1	0.1
IBM	2,491	2.9	5,861	5.3	135.3
Dell	2,458	2.8	3,083	2.8	25.4
Others	15,425	17.8	13,973	12.6	−9.4
Total	**86,537**	**100%**	**110,481**	**100%**	**27.7%**
NETHERLANDS					
NEC CI	11,911	17.3%	23,776	28.6%	99.6%
Compaq	15,567	22.6	14,277	17.2	−8.3
Vobis	9,769	14.2	9,616	11.6	−1.6
Fujitsu Siemens	11,994	17.4	8,441	10.2	−29.6
Gateway	1,303	1.9	6,475	7.8	396.9
Apple	3,269	4.7	4,141	5.0	26.7
Laser	2,334	3.4	3,978	4.8	70.4
Shitec	3,075	4.5	2,836	3.4	−7.8
Acer	1,194	1.7	1,724	2.1	44.4
Dell	2,430	3.5	1,679	2.0	−30.9

continued

EXHIBIT 2	**YEAR-ON-YEAR TOP 10 UNITS FOR CONSUMER DESKTOP IN SELECTED EUROPEAN COUNTRIES** *(continued)*

Vendor	1999, Q2	% Share	2000, Q2	% Share	Growth
NETHERLANDS (continued)					
Others	5,981	8.7	6,128	7.4	2.5
Total	**68,827**	**100%**	**83,071**	**100%**	**20.7%**
NORWAY					
Fujitsu Siemens	1,831	5.9%	4,013	14.7%	119.2%
Compaq	9,376	30.2	3,586	13.1	−61.8
Actebis	965	3.1	2,533	9.3	162.5
IBM	7,124	23.0	2,154	7.9	−69.8
Dell	2,049	6.6	1,563	5.7	−23.7
NEC CI	503	1.6	1,359	5.0	170.2
Apple	916	3.0	1,251	4.6	36.6
Evercom	1,334	4.3	1,224	4.5	−8.2
Hyundai	1,925	6.2	990	3.6	−48.6
REC	906	2.9	973	3.6	7.4
Others	4,068	13.1	7,676	28.1	88.7
Total	**30,997**	**100%**	**27,322**	**100%**	**−11.9%**
PORTUGAL					
Compaq	3,746	18.7%	3,222	12.9%	−14.0%
Solbi/Citydesk	2,515	12.6	2,199	8.8	−12.6
Fujitsu Siemens	1,124	5.6	1,815	7.3	61.5
Triudus	1,107	5.5	1,705	6.8	54.0
Shine	1,346	6.7	981	3.9	−27.1
Vobis	483	2.4	919	3.7	90.3
Tsunami	315	1.6	816	3.3	159.0
Apple	111	0.6	560	2.2	404.5
Accr	20	0.1	179	0.7	795.0
Dell	624	3.1	160	0.6	−74.4
Others	8,603	43.0	12,381	49.6	43.9
Total	**19,994**	**100%**	**24,937**	**100%**	**24.7%**
SPAIN					
Fujitsu Siemens	3,021	7.5%	10,532	17.9%	248.6%
NEC CI	3,955	9.8	7,472	12.7	88.9
Hewlett-Packard	3,476	8.6	7,044	12.0	102.6
Jump	4,856	12.1	5,192	8.8	6.9
El System	0	0.0	4,846	8.2	0.0
Inves	4,564	11.3	4,736	8.1	3.8
Compaq	3,505	8.7	3,899	6.6	11.2
Apple	2,394	6.0	2,938	5.0	22.7
KM Computers	1,820	4.5	1,950	3.3	7.1
Toshiba	0	0.0	1,655	2.8	0.0
Others	12,638	31.4	8,496	14.5	−32.8
Total	**40,229**	**100%**	**58,760**	**100%**	**46.1%**
SWEDEN					
Fujitsu Siemens	2,734	7.3%	8,054	25.3%	194.6%
Dell	4,455	11.9	4,258	13.4	−4.4
Compaq	7,164	19.1	4,096	12.9	−42.8

continued

EXHIBIT 2	YEAR-ON-YEAR TOP 10 UNITS FOR CONSUMER DESKTOP IN SELECTED EUROPEAN COUNTRIES (*continued*)

Vendor	1999, Q2	% Share	2000, Q2	% Share	Growth
SWEDEN (continued)					
Apple	816	2.2	3,499	11.0	328.8
NEC CI	1,241	3.3	1,787	5.6	44.0
Network	475	1.3	1,361	4.3	186.5
Hewlett-Packard	1,693	4.5	1,139	3.6	−32.7
Acer	304	0.8	761	2.4	150.3
DGC	355	0.9	696	2.2	96.1
IBM	7,554	20.1	672	2.1	−91.1
Others	10,729	28.6	5,485	17.2	−48.9
Total	**37,520**	**100%**	**31,808**	**100%**	**−15.2%**
SWITZERLAND					
Fujitsu Siemens	7,711	17.8%	9,923	18.6%	28.7%
Vobis	10,783	24.9	6,555	12.3	−39.2
Apple	2,046	4.7	6,385	12.0	212.1
Compaq	6,257	14.5	6,124	11.5	−2.1
Maxdata	0	0.0	5,379	10.1	0.0
Mandax	2,568	5.9	2,592	4.9	0.9
Dell	2,788	6.4	2,585	4.9	−7.3
Microspot	1,136	2.6	2,483	4.7	118.6
Athena	1,660	3.8	2,066	3.9	24.5
Actebis	121	0.3	1,074	2.0	787.6
Others	8,182	18.9	8,015	15.2	−0.9
Total	**43,252**	**100%**	**53,271**	**100%**	**23.2**
UNITED KINGDOM					
NEC CI	39,444	12.2%	75,489	19.3%	91.4%
Tiny Computers/Opus	55,952	17.3	70,415	18.0	25.8
Granville/Time Computer	25,395	7.8	32,324	8.3	27.3
Dell	19,997	6.2	28,391	7.3	42.0
Hewlett-Packard	8,549	2.6	20,292	5.2	137.4
Viglen	21,844	6.7	19,348	4.9	−11.4
Apple	4,771	1.5	18,475	4.7	287.2
Gateway	11,217	3.5	17,595	4.5	56.9
Compaq	15,497	4.8	12,155	3.1	−21.6
Fujitsu Siemens	18,399	5.7	5,751	1.5	−68.7
Others	103,202	31.8	90,966	23.3	−11.9
Total	**324,267**	**100%**	**391,201**	**100%**	**20.6%**

Source: Company documents.

in the past two years," Chenneveau noted. "There are HP and competitive branded products at FF4,990,[13] along with clones and white boxes. This was unheard of two years ago" (see Table A). He continued:

The European market remains a tough one for major international brands. Compared to the United States, it's much less brand-sensitive and more

---

[13] In September 1999, US$1=FF6.4.

EXHIBIT 2

WESTERN EUROPEAN PC MARKET SHARES BY MANUFACTURERS, YEAR-END 1999

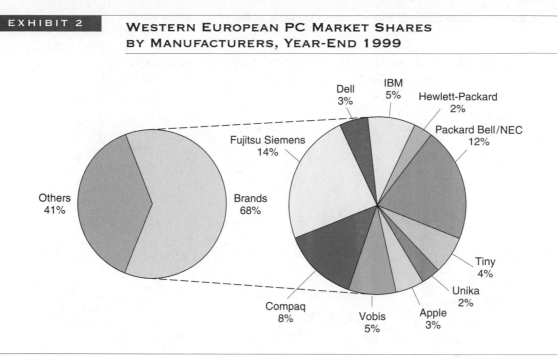

Source: Company documents.
Note: Total home PC market: 6.4 million.

EUROPE COUNTRY SHARE, YEAR-END 1999

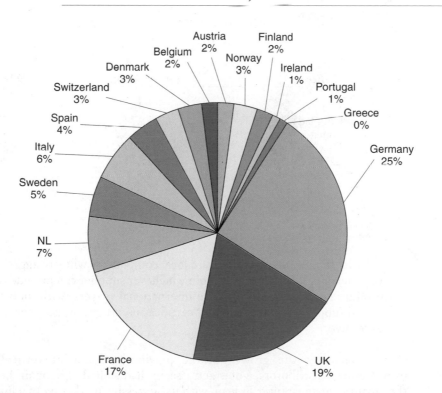

Source: Company documents.

EXHIBIT 3	HP PAVILION SALES VS. MARKET IN FRANCE, JULY 1999–AUGUST 2000

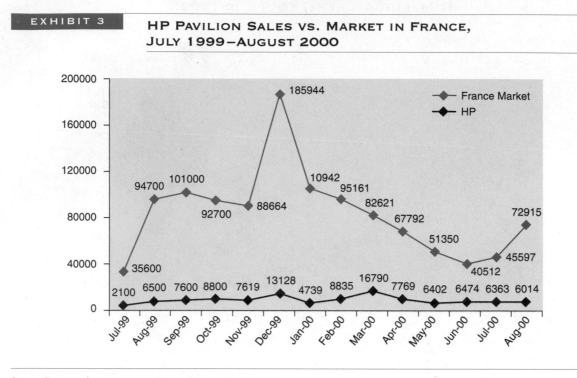

Source: Company documents.

TABLE A	HP PRICE POINT VERSUS COMPETITION IN FRANCE

France	Nov. '98–Feb. '99	Jan. '99–Apr. '99
Apple	8,780	8,506
Compaq	7,474	6,974
Fujitsu	7,268	7,319
Hewlett-Packard	7,399	5,358
IBM	7,711	8,400
Packard-Bell	7,371	7,152
Total Market	6,591	6,411

Source: Company documents.

volatile. In most markets there are local competitors who are aggressive and very flexible, sourcing locally from whichever supplier can provide the right product fastest. By contrast, the international players, with globally integrated supply chains and supplier certification programs, can seem slow and expensive.

In Germany, the growth of the previously dominant vertically integrated manufacturer/distributors, Vobis and Escom, had stalled. The main beneficiary was the Japanese manufacturer Fujitsu, with its aggressive marketing of a limited range of relatively unsophisticated and low-priced PCs ("the simple box model," as Chenneveau described it). Following Escom's bankruptcy in 1997, Vobis had lost momentum during a period when it changed ownership and outsourced many of its procurement and operational functions.[14] While still present in Germany in late 2000, Vobis, too, had run into financial difficulties.

In France, HPD had overtaken IBM for third rank in unit market share in late 1999. Chenneveau attributed this gain to operational excellence in serving major retailers and the traditional strength of the HP brand in France, long the company's largest European operational base. "We have a strong salesforce here who have good relations with the very powerful mass merchants, such as Carrefour, Auchan, and Casino," explained Chenneveau. The strength of the brand made France the best cross-selling market for HP. HPD managers reported that the Pavilion was very strong in France, present in all retails channels as well as e-channels and HP's "shopping village." In late 2000, HP was fighting it out with Packard-Bell who remained the leader in France. IBM had exited retail and Fujitsu was a shadow of its former self, having lost its entire management team in France. In FY00, the Pavilion was expected to be a $120 million business, up 195% from FY99.

In the United Kingdom, HPD was only represented in small retail chains and had been unable to win space in the dominant outlets of PC World. Tiny, a fast-growing local player, was pioneering inventory-less store formats, in which consumers looked at sample machines and placed orders for product which was later home-delivered from a central warehouse. The United Kingdom was also the fastest growing market in Europe for direct sales by telephone and the Internet (the format growing fastest in the United States).[15] It, too, had been good to the Pavilion, expecting to register a FY00 300% increase in sales (in dollar terms) on FY99, despite the strong dollar that had increased the average sales price and HPD's underestimating of the back-to-school demand.

Evolving Business Models

At the same time, a range of business models had evolved (see Exhibits 4A and 4B). *Mainstream retail* was still the dominant model, but within this channel there were a number of alternative models in operation. *Line-up* described the conventional format, in which retailers carried a range of brands in inventory. This model had proven difficult to manage in both North America and Europe, principally because of rapid product obsolescence resulting from product range relaunch every two or three months. *Deal-based* business was when retailers placed large orders for single product types with configuration or branding often exclusive to the deal. Mass merchants frequently placed such orders because of the volumes they turned over, and this model was also employed by retailers who would otherwise not sell computers, such as the Conforama furniture hypermarket chain in France. Profitability was a challenge in these types of deals, despite the volumes involved—for example, the German discount chain Aldi could place orders for 30,000 units or more which it then used as loss-leaders to generate store traffic. The emerging retail format was *configure-to-order* (CTO), in which consumers visited a store to place an order for a PC built to their own specifications. This model, which Gateway was experimenting with in the United

---

[14] In mid-1998, U.S.-based CHS Electronics acquired Vobis. Other major European computer distributors were bought by larger U.S. multinationals.

[15] HP had established its own online sales operation in the United Kingdom in 1998.

EXHIBIT 4A	CHANNEL STRUCTURE—WESTERN EUROPE, 2000

Country	-Consumer Elec -Mass Merch -Computer Shore	Direct Retail	Local Shops	Fax/Phone Catalog	Web based	Employee Purchase Programs	-Bank Promos -Education -Trade Orgs
United Kingdom	46%	9%	10%	31%	2%	2%	0%
France	54%	3%	30%	5%	3%	5%	0%
Germany	46%	44%	5%	2%	1%	2%	0%
Spain	29%	46%	18%	6%	0%	0%	1%
Italy	48%	25%	22%	4%	0%	1%	0%
Nordics	47%	6%	10%	10%	2%	25%	0%
Netherlands	37%	25%	7%	9%	1%	21%	0%
Switzerland	45%	25%	20%	8%	1%	1%	0%

Source: Company documents.

EXHIBIT 4B	CHANNEL MARGINS—WESTERN EUROPE, 2000

	Traditional Retail	Direct Retail	Kiosk order mgt	Fax/Phone Catalog	Web based	Corporate deals	Tax Advantage deals	Local Dealers
United Kingdom	28%	\	\	\	8%	8%	\	20%
France	22%	\	\	\	8%	8%	\	15%
Germany	20%	\	10%	\	8%	\	\	15%
Spain	18%	\	10%	\	10%	\	\	15%
Italy	20%	\	10%	\	\	8%	\	15%
Nordics	25%	\	\	\	\	\	7%	20%
Netherlands	25%	\	\	\	\	\	7%	20%
Switzerland	18%	\	\	\	\	8%	\	15%

Source: Company documents.

States, was proving successful in the United Kingdom for Tiny and Time Computer. Gateway had also opened up stores in France and the United Kingdom, but Chenneveau noted that the jury was still out about their success. It could deliver gross margins of up to 15%, compared with the 5% typical of line-up retail. In 2000, HPD ran a couple of experiments of kiosks within retail that did not prove to be as successful as expected. Average selling prices were up but unit sales were low and the experiments stopped. By contrast to these models, the *specialty retail* model relied on the economics of low-volume and high-margin business. Service in these outlets was personalized, with knowledgeable staff advising customers on the right computer for their needs, and even in some cases assembling the machine before delivery and installing it in the customer's home. This model was followed by both "mom-'n'-pop" outlets serving first-time buyers, and highly sophisticated boutique stores serving computer aficionados.

Direct sales offered three additional variants. *Internet sales*, relatively rare in Europe compared to North America, showed signs of growth particularly in the United Kingdom and Nordic countries. This model was also more profitable than retail (except retail CTO) because of the higher prevailing prices, a situation Chenneveau attributed to the fact that consumers typically undertook less brand comparison than when shopping in a retail environment. By contrast, *"direct direct,"* which consisted of telephone or catalog direct mail, was an established business model but one which showed little growth; HP was not represented in this channel in Europe. In 2000, HP opened HP.com e-stores in Germany and France in addition to the United Kingdom and Sweden.

Finally, an *employee purchase program* (EPP) model had emerged in certain high-tax countries, notably Sweden, where home computers were increasingly purchased through the consumer's employer to benefit from significantly more favorable tax treatment. EPP opportunities had been fueled by the publicity around some major deals with U.S. corporations, such as Ford. Ford's European competitors as well as large European MNCs were eager to replicate the formula. HP had won a lion share of this business worldwide and was at the forefront in Europe either implementing the European portion of worldwide deals (Ford, Intel, etc.) or in discussions with European MNCs.

In three years, HPD managers forecast, retail would still represent over 70% of the market, direct sales might be 15% in some countries, and EPP was increasingly popular and might reach 15% of sales in some countries. And within retail, Ghilardi noted, "the big boys are gaining momentum."

Lessons for 2001

In November 2000, despite the division's economics (see Exhibits 5 and 6), Chenneveau remained convinced that operational excellence was "the strategic way [for HPD] to win" in Europe:

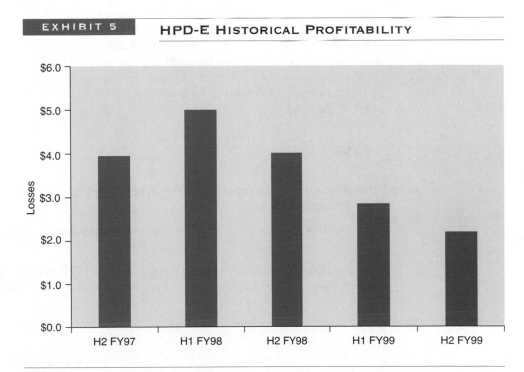

| EXHIBIT 5 | HPD-E HISTORICAL PROFITABILITY |

Source: Company documents.

| EXHIBIT 6 | **HPD-E BREAKEVEN** |

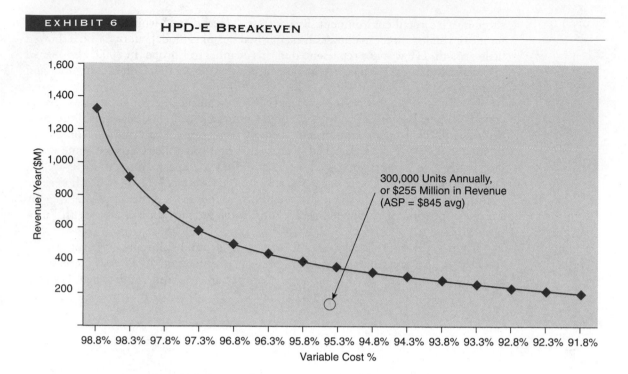

Source: Company documents.

Right products at the right place at the right time is key. Inventory anywhere in the supply chain is evil. Suppliers price negotiation is crucial, a few dollars can make or break profitability. You cannot run your European consumer PC business from Palo Alto or from Austin. Beyond-the-box revenue (add-ons, e-services, etc.) are essential to improve profitability of an otherwise commoditized PC business. Despite all the talk of convergence with TV or handheld, PC's remain the platform of choice for consumer personal computing needs.

Questions for Discussion

1. What were some of the lessons that HP learned from its entry into the European home products market?

2. Evaluate HP's reaction to a significantly lower market share than its 15 percent market share target.

3. Evaluate the strategic options that HP considered in 1999: (1) enter the region's less developed markets to gain pioneer market share advantage; and (2) develop new business models.

Kentucky Fried Chicken and the Global Fast Food Industry

Kentucky Fried Chicken Corporation (KFC) was the world's largest chicken restaurant chain and third-largest fast food chain in 2000. KFC held more than 55 percent of the U.S. market in terms of sales and operated more than 10,800 restaurants in eighty-five countries. KFC was one of the first fast food chains to go international in the late 1950s and was one of the world's most recognizable brands. KFC's early international strategy was to grow its company and franchise restaurant base throughout the world. By early 2000, however, KFC had refocused its international strategy on several high-growth markets, including Canada, Australia, the United Kingdom, China, Korea, Thailand, Puerto Rico, and Mexico. KFC planned to base much of its growth in these markets on company-owned restaurants, which gave KFC greater control over product quality, service, and restaurant cleanliness. In other international markets, KFC planned to grow primarily through franchises, which were operated by local businesspeople, who understood the local market better than KFC. Franchises enabled KFC to expand more rapidly into smaller countries that could only support a small number of restaurants. KFC planned to expand its company-owned restaurants more aggressively into other major international markets in Europe and Latin America in the future. Latin America was an appealing area for investment because of the size of its markets, its common language and culture, and its geographical proximity to the United States. Mexico was of particular interest because of the North American Free Trade Agreement (NAFTA), a free trade zone between Canada, the United States, and Mexico that went into effect in 1994. However, other fast food chains, such as McDonald's, Burger King, and Wendy's, were rapidly expanding into other countries in Latin America, such as Venezuela, Brazil, Argentina, and Chile. KFC's task in Latin America was to select the proper countries for future investment and to devise an appropriate strategy for penetrating the Latin American market.

Company History

In 1952, fast food franchising was still in its infancy when Harland Sanders began his travels across the United States to speak with prospective franchisees about his "Colonel Sanders Recipe Kentucky Fried Chicken." By 1960, "Colonel" Sanders had

This case was prepared by Jeffrey A. Krug, University of Illinois at Urbana–Champaign, for classroom discussion rather than to illustrate either effective or ineffective handling of an administrative situation.

granted KFC franchises to more than 200 take-home retail outlets and restaurants across the United States. He had also established a number of franchises in Canada. By 1963, the number of KFC franchises had risen to more than 300 and revenues topped $500 million. The Colonel celebrated his seventy-fourth birthday the following year and was eager to lessen the load of running the day-to-day operations of his business. Thus, he looked for potential buyers and sold his business to two Louisville business-men—Jack Massey and John Young Brown Jr.—for $2 million. The Colonel stayed on as a public relations man and goodwill ambassador for the company. During the next five years, Massey and Brown concentrated on growing KFC's franchise system across the United States. In 1966, they took KFC public and the company was listed on the New York Stock Exchange. By the late 1960s, a strong foothold had been established in the United States, and Massey and Brown turned their attention to international markets. In 1969, a joint venture was signed with Mitsuoishi Shoji Kaisha, Ltd., in Ja-pan and the rights to operate franchises in England were acquired. Subsidiaries were later established in Hong Kong, South Africa, Australia, New Zealand, and Mexico. By 1971, KFC had established 2,450 franchises and 600 company-owned restaurants in forty-eight countries.

Heublein, Inc.

In 1971, KFC entered into negotiations with Heublein, Inc., to discuss a possible merger. The decision to pursue a merger was partially driven by Brown's desire to pursue other interests, including a political career (Brown was elected Governor of Kentucky in 1977). Several months later, Heublein acquired KFC. Heublein was in the business of producing vodka, mixed cocktails, dry gin, cordials, beer, and other alco-holic beverages; however, it had little experience in the restaurant business. Conflicts quickly erupted between Colonel Sanders and Heublein management. In particular, Colonel Sanders became increasingly distraught over quality control issues and restau-rant cleanliness. By 1977, new restaurant openings had slowed to only twenty a year, few restaurants were being remodeled, and service quality had declined. To combat these problems, Heublein sent in a new management team to redirect KFC's strategy. A "back-to-the-basics" strategy was implemented, and new restaurant construction was halted until existing restaurants could be upgraded and operating problems elim-inated. A program for remodeling existing restaurants was implemented, an emphasis was placed on cleanliness and service, marginal products were eliminated, and product consistency was reestablished. This strategy enabled KFC to gain better control of its operations, and it was soon again aggressively building new restaurants.

R.J. Reynolds Industries, Inc.

In 1982, R.J. Reynolds Industries, Inc. (RJR), acquired Heublein and merged it into a wholly owned subsidiary. The acquisition of Heublein was part of RJR's corporate strategy of diversifying into unrelated businesses, such as energy, transportation, food, and restaurants, to reduce its dependence on the tobacco industry. Tobacco had driven RJR's sales since its founding in North Carolina in 1875; however, sales of cigarettes and tobacco products, while profitable, were declining because of reduced consump-tion in the United States. Reduced consumption was primarily the result of an in-creased awareness among Americans of the negative health consequences of smoking.

RJR, however, had little more experience in the restaurant business than did Heublein when it acquired KFC eleven years earlier. In contrast to Heublein, which tried to actively manage KFC using its own managers, RJR allowed KFC to operate autonomously with little interference. RJR believed that KFC's executives were better qualified to operate the business than their own managers; therefore, KFC's top management team was left largely intact. By doing so, RJR avoided many of the operating problems that plagued Heublein during its ownership of KFC.

In 1985, RJR acquired Nabisco Corporation for $4.9 billion. The acquisition of Nabisco was an attempt to redefine RJR as a world leader in the consumer foods industry. Nabisco sold a variety of well-known cookies, crackers, and other grocery products, including Oreo cookies, Ritz crackers, Planters peanuts, Lifesavers, and Milk-Bone dog biscuits. RJR subsequently divested many of its nonconsumer food businesses. It sold KFC to PepsiCo, Inc., one year later.

PepsiCo, Inc.

Corporate Strategy PepsiCo, Inc., was formed in 1965 with the merger of the Pepsi-Cola Co. and Frito-Lay, Inc. The merger created one of the largest consumer products companies in the United States. Pepsi-Cola's traditional business was the sale of soft drink concentrates to licensed independent and company-owned bottlers that manufactured, sold, and distributed Pepsi-Cola soft drinks. Pepsi-Cola's best-known trademarks were Pepsi-Cola, Diet Pepsi, and Mountain Dew. Frito-Lay manufactured and sold a variety of leading snack foods that included Lay's Potato Chips, Doritos Tortilla Chips, Tostitos Tortilla Chips, and Ruffles Potato Chips. Soon after the merger, PepsiCo initiated an aggressive acquisition program, buying a number of companies in areas unrelated to its major businesses, such as North American Van Lines, Wilson Sporting Goods, and Lee Way Motor Freight. However, PepsiCo lacked the management skills required to operate these businesses, and performance failed to live up to expectations. In 1984, chairman and chief executive officer Don Kendall restructured PepsiCo's operations. Businesses that did not support PepsiCo's consumer product orientation (including North American Van Lines, Wilson Sporting Goods, and Lee Way Motor Freight) were divested. PepsiCo's foreign bottling operations were then sold to local businesspeople who better understood their country's culture and business practices. Last, PepsiCo was organized into three divisions: soft drinks, snack foods, and restaurants.

Restaurant Business and Acquisition of KFC PepsiCo believed that the restaurant business complemented its consumer product orientation. The marketing of fast food followed many of the same patterns as the marketing of soft drinks and snack foods. Pepsi-Cola soft drinks and fast food products could be marketed together in the same television and radio segments, thereby providing higher returns for each advertising dollar. Restaurant chains also provided an additional outlet for the sale of Pepsi soft drinks. Thus, PepsiCo believed it could take advantage of numerous synergies by operating the three businesses under the same corporate umbrella. PepsiCo also believed that its management skills could be transferred among the three businesses. This practice was compatible with PepsiCo's policy of frequently moving managers among its business units as a means of developing future executives. PepsiCo first entered the restaurant business in 1977, when it acquired Pizza Hut. Taco Bell was acquired one year later. To complete its diversification into the restaurant industry, PepsiCo acquired KFC in 1986. The acquisition of KFC gave PepsiCo the leading market share in the chicken (KFC), pizza (Pizza Hut), and Mexican food (Taco Bell) segments of the fast food industry.

Management   Following its acquisition of KFC, PepsiCo initiated sweeping changes. It announced that the franchise contract would be changed to give PepsiCo greater control over KFC franchisees and to make it easier to close poorly performing restaurants. Staff at KFC were reduced in order to cut costs, and many KFC managers were replaced with PepsiCo managers. Soon after the acquisition, KFC's new personnel manager, who had just relocated from PepsiCo's New York headquarters, was overheard in the KFC cafeteria saying, "There will be no more home-grown tomatoes in this organization."

Rumors spread quickly among KFC employees about their opportunities for advancement within KFC and PepsiCo. Harsh comments by PepsiCo managers about KFC, its people, and its traditions, several restructurings that led to layoffs throughout KFC, the replacement of KFC managers with PepsiCo managers, and conflicts between KFC and PepsiCo's corporate cultures created a morale problem within KFC. KFC's culture was built largely on Colonel Sander's laid-back approach to management. Employees enjoyed good job security and stability. A strong loyalty had been created among KFC employees over the years as a result of the Colonel's efforts to provide for his employees' benefits, pension, and other nonincome needs. In addition, the southern environment in Louisville resulted in a friendly, relaxed atmosphere at KFC's corporate offices. This corporate culture was left essentially unchanged during the Heublein and RJR years.

In contrast to KFC, PepsiCo's culture was characterized by a much stronger emphasis on performance. Top performers expected to move up through the ranks quickly. PepsiCo used its KFC, Pizza Hut, Taco Bell, Frito-Lay, and Pepsi-Cola divisions as training grounds for its executives, rotating its best managers through the five divisions on average every two years. This practice created immense pressure on managers to demonstrate their management skills within short periods in order to maximize their potential for promotion. This practice also reinforced the feelings of KFC managers that they had few opportunities for promotion within the new company. One PepsiCo manager commented, "You may have performed well last year, but if you don't perform well this year, you're gone, and there are 100 ambitious guys with Ivy League MBAs at PepsiCo's headquarters in New York who would love to have your job." An unwanted effect of this performance-driven culture was that employee loyalty was often lost and turnover was higher than in other companies.

Kyle Craig, president of KFC's U.S. operations, commented on KFC's relationship with its corporate parent:

> The KFC culture is an interesting one because it was dominated by a lot of KFC folks, many of whom have been around since the days of the Colonel. Many of those people were very intimidated by the PepsiCo culture, which is a very high-performance, high-accountability, highly driven culture. People were concerned about whether they would succeed in the new culture. Like many companies, we have had a couple of downsizings, which further made people nervous. Today, there are fewer old KFC people around, and I think to some degree people have seen that the PepsiCo culture can

drive some pretty positive results. I also think the PepsiCo people who have worked with KFC have modified their cultural values somewhat, and they can see that there were a lot of benefits in the old KFC culture.

PepsiCo pushes their companies to perform strongly, but whenever there is a slip in performance, it increases the culture gap between PepsiCo and KFC. I have been involved in two downsizings over which I have been the chief architect. They have been probably the two most gut-wrenching experiences of my career. Because you know you're dealing with people's lives and their families, these changes can be emotional if you care about the people in your organization. However, I do fundamentally believe that your first obligation is to the entire organization.

A second problem for PepsiCo was its poor relationship with KFC franchisees. A month after becoming president and chief executive officer in 1989, John Cranor addressed KFC's franchisees in Louisville in order to explain the details of the new franchise contract. This was the first contract change in thirteen years. It gave PepsiCo greater power to take over weak franchises, relocate restaurants, and make changes in existing restaurants. In addition, restaurants would no longer be protected from competition from new KFC units and PepsiCo would have the right to raise royalty fees on existing restaurants as contracts came up for renewal. After Cranor finished his address, there was an uproar among the attending franchisees who jumped to their feet to protest the changes. KFC's franchise association later sued PepsiCo over the new contract. The contract remained unresolved until 1996, when the most objectionable parts of the contract were removed by KFC's new president and CEO, David Novak. A new contract was ratified by KFC's franchisees in 1997.

PepsiCo's Divestiture of KFC, Pizza Hut, and Taco Bell   PepsiCo's strategy of diversifying into three distinct but related markets—soft drinks, snack foods, and fast food restaurants—created one of the world's largest consumer product companies and a portfolio of some of the world's most recognizable brands. Between 1990 and 1996, PepsiCo's sales grew at an annual rate of more than 10 percent, surpassing $31 billion in 1996. PepsiCo's growth, however, masked troubles in its fast food businesses. Operating margins (profit after tax as a percent of sales) at Pepsi-Cola and Frito-Lay averaged 12 and 17 percent, respectively, between 1990 and 1996. During the same period, margins at KFC, Pizza Hut, and Taco Bell fell from an average of more than 8 percent in 1990 to a little more than 4 percent in 1996. Declining margins in the fast food chains reflected increasing maturity in the U.S. fast food industry, more intense competition, and the aging of KFC and Pizza Hut's restaurant bases. As a result, PepsiCo's restaurant chains absorbed nearly one-half of PepsiCo's annual capital spending during the 1990s, but they generated less than one-third of PepsiCo's cash flows. This meant that cash had to be diverted from PepsiCo's soft drink and snack food businesses to its restaurant businesses. This reduced PepsiCo's corporate return on assets, made it more difficult to compete effectively with Coca-Cola, and hurt its stock price. In 1997, PepsiCo decided to spin off its restaurant businesses into a new company called Tricon Global Restaurants, Inc. The new company would be based in KFC's headquarters in Louisville, Kentucky (see Case Exhibit 20.1).

PepsiCo's objective was to reposition itself as a beverage and snack food company, strengthen its balance sheet, and create more consistent earnings growth. PepsiCo received a one-time distribution from Tricon of $4.7 billion, $3.7 billion of which was

---

CASE EXHIBIT 20.1   TRICON GLOBAL RESTAURANTS, INC.—
ORGANIZATIONAL CHART (2000)

Tricon Global Restaurants, Inc.
Corporate Offices
Louisville, Kentucky
Andrall E. Pearson, Chairman of the Board
David C. Novak, Chief Executive Officer

KFC USA
Louisville, Kentucky
Terry D. Davenport, Chief Concept Officer
Charles E. Rawley, Chief Operating Officer

Pizza Hut USA
Dallas, Texas
Michael S. Rawlings, President & CCO
Michael A. Miles, Chief Operating Office

Taco Bell USA
Irvine, California
Peter C. Waller, President & CCO
Robert T. Nilsen, Chief Operating Officer

Tricon Restaurants International
Dallas, Texas
Peter Bassi, President

---

used to pay off short-term debt. The balance was earmarked for stock repurchases. In 1998, PepsiCo acquired Tropicana Products, which controlled more than 40 percent of the U.S. chilled orange juice market. Because of the divestiture of KFC, Pizza Hut, and Taco Bell, PepsiCo sales fell by $11.3 billion and assets fell by $7.0 billion between 1997 and 1999. Profitability, however, soared. Operating margins rose from 11 per cent in 1997 to 14 percent in 1999 and ROA rose from 11 percent in 1997 to 16 percent in 1999. By focusing on high cash flow market leaders, PepsiCo raised profitability while decreasing its asset base.

Fast Food Industry

According to the National Restaurant Association (NRA), food service sales increased by 5.4 percent to $358 billion in 1999. More than 800,000 restaurants and food outlets made up the U.S. restaurant industry, which employed 11 million people. Sales were highest in the full-service, sit-down sector, which grew 7 percent to $121 billion. Fast food sales grew at a slower rate, rising about 5 percent to $110 billion. Fast food sales surpassed the full-service sector during the mid-1990s; however, maturation of the fast food sector and rising incomes among many Americans helped full-service restaurants again overtake fast food as the largest sector in the restaurant industry. The full-service and fast food segments were expected to make up about 65 percent of total food service industry sales in 2000.

Major Fast Food Segments

Eight major segments made up the fast food segment of the restaurant industry: sandwich chains, pizza chains, family restaurants, grill buffet chains, dinner houses, chicken chains, nondinner concepts, and other chains. Sales data for the leading restaurant chains in each segment are shown in Case Exhibit 20.2. Most striking is the dominance

CASE EXHIBIT 20.2

TOP 50 U.S. FAST FOOD RESTAURANTS (RANKED BY 1999 SALES, IN MILLIONS OF DOLLARS)

Rank	Sandwich Chains	Sales	Share
1	McDonald's	19,006	35.0%
2	Burger King	8,659	16.0
3	Wendy's	5,250	9.7
4	Taco Bell	5,200	9.6
7	Subway	3,200	5.9
10	Arby's	2,260	4.2
11	Dairy Queen	2,145	4.0
12	Hardee's	2,139	3.9
18	Sonic Drive-In	1,589	2.9
20	Jack in the Box	1,510	2.8
32	Carl's Jr.	887	1.6
46	Whataburger	503	0.9
	Other Chains	1,890	3.5
	TOTAL SEGMENT	54,238	100.0%

Rank	Pizza Chains	Sales	Share
5	Pizza Hut	5,000	44.0%
8	Domino's	2,560	22.5
21	Papa John's	1,426	12.6
23	Little Caesars	1,200	10.6
50	Sbarro	466	4.1
	Other Chains	703	6.2
	TOTAL SEGMENT	11,355	100.0%

Rank	Family Restaurants	Sales	Share
13	Denny's	2,079	22.7%
24	Cracker Barrel	1,163	12.7
26	IHOP	1,077	11.8
33	Shoney's	869	9.5
35	Perkins	790	8.6
36	Bob Evans	727	8.0
40	Friendly's	671	7.3
42	Waffle House	620	6.8
	Other Chains	1,144	12.6
	TOTAL SEGMENT	9,140	100.0%

Rank	Grill Buffet Chains	Sales	Share
31	Golden Coral	899	32.3%
39	Ryan's	704	25.3
45	Ponderosa	560	20.1
	Other Chains	621	22.3
	TOTAL SEGMENT	2,784	100.0%

Rank	Dinner Houses	Sales	Share
9	Applebee's	2,305	14.9%
15	Red Lobster	2,005	13.0
16	Outback Steakhouse	1,729	11.2
17	Olive Garden	1,610	10.4
19	Chili's Grill & Bar	1,555	10.1
22	T.G.I. Friday's	1,364	8.8
30	Ruby Tuesday	920	5.9
49	Lone Star Steakhouse	468	3.0
	Other Chains	3,520	22.7
	TOTAL SEGMENT	15,476	100.0%

Rank	Chicken Chains	Sales	Share
6	KFC	4,378	55.2%
28	Popeyes	986	12.7
29	Chick-fil-A	946	12.1
34	Boston Market	855	11.0
38	Church's	705	9.0
	TOTAL SEGMENT	7,870	100.0%

Rank	Other Dinner Chains	Sales	Share
37	Long John Silver's	716	15.7%
41	Walt Disney Co.	666	14.7
43	Old Country Buffet	589	13.0
47	Luby's Cafeteria	502	11.0
48	Captain D's Seafood	499	11.0
	Other Chains	1,574	34.6
	TOTAL SEGMENT	4,546	100.0%

Rank	Nondinner Chains	Sales	Share
14	Dunkin' Donuts	2,007	42.9%
25	7-Eleven	1,117	23.8
27	Starbucks	987	21.1
44	Baskin-Robbins	573	12.2
	TOTAL SEGMENT	4,684	100.0%

Source: *Nation's Restaurant News.*

of McDonald's, which had sales of more than $19 billion in 1999. McDonald's accounted for 15 percent of the sales of the nation's top 100 restaurant chains. To put McDonald's dominance into perspective, the second-largest chain—Burger King—held less than 7 percent of the market.

Sandwich chains made up the largest segment of the fast food market. McDonald's controlled 35 percent of the sandwich segment, while Burger King ran a distant second with a 16 percent market share. Despite continued success by some chains, such as McDonald's, Carl's Jr., Jack in the Box, Wendy's, and White Castle, other chains, such as Hardee's, Burger King, Taco Bell, and Checker's were struggling. McDonald's generated the greatest per store sales of about $1.5 million per year. The average U.S. chain generated $800,000 in sales per store. Per-store sales at Burger King remained flat and Hardee's per-store sales declined by 10 percent. Franchisees at Burger King complained of leadership problems within the corporate parent (London-based Diageo PLC), an impending increase in royalties and franchise fees, and poor advertising. Hardee's corporate parent (CKE Enterprises), which also owned Carl's Jr. and Taco Bueno, planned to franchise many of its company-owned Hardee's restaurants and to allow the system to shrink as low-performing units were closed. It also planned to refocus Hardee's strategy in the southeastern part of the United States, where brand loyalty remained strong.

Dinner houses made up the second-largest and fastest-growing fast food segment. Sales of dinner houses increased by more than 13 percent during the year, surpassing the average increase of 6 percent among all fast food chains. Much of the growth in dinner houses came from new-unit construction, a marked contrast with other fast food chains, which had already slowed U.S. construction because of market saturation. Much of the new-unit construction took place in new suburban markets and small towns. Applebee's and Red Lobster dominated the dinner house segment. Each chain generated more than $2 billion in sales in 1999. The fastest-growing dinner houses, however, were chains generating less than $500 million in sales, such as On the Border, The Cheesecake Factory, O'Charley's, Romano's Macaroni Grill, and Hooters. Each of these chains increased sales by more than 20 percent.

Increased growth among dinner houses came at the expense of slower growth among sandwich chains, pizza chains, grill buffet chains, and family restaurants. Too many restaurants chasing the same customers were responsible for much of the slower growth in these other fast food categories. However, sales growth within each segment differed from one chain to another. In the family segment, for example, Friendly's and Shoney's were forced to shut down restaurants because of declining profits, but Steak 'n Shake and Cracker Barrel expanded their restaurant base by more than 10 percent. Within the pizza segment, Pizza Hut and Little Caesar's closed underperforming restaurants, but Papa John's and Chuck E. Cheese's continued to aggressively grow their U.S. restaurant bases. The hardest-hit segment was grill buffet chains, which generated the lowest increase in sales of less than 4 percent. Dinner houses, because of their more upscale atmosphere and higher-ticket items, were better positioned to take advantage of the aging and wealthier U.S. population, which increasingly demanded higher-quality food in more upscale settings. Even dinner houses, however, faced the prospect of market saturation and increased competition in the near future.

Chicken Segment

KFC continued to dominate the chicken segment with sales of $4.4 billion in 1999 (see Case Exhibit 20.3). Its nearest competitor, Popeyes, ran a distant second with sales of $1.0 billion. KFC's leadership in the U.S. market was so extensive that it had fewer opportunities to expand its U.S. restaurant base, which was growing at only about 1 percent per year. Despite its dominance, KFC was slowly losing market share as other

CASE EXHIBIT 20.3   **TOP U.S. CHICKEN CHAINS**

	1994	1995	1996	1997	1998	1999	Growth Rate
Sales ($Millions)							
KFC	3,587	3,740	3,935	4,002	4,171	4,378	4%
Popeyes	614	660	677	720	843	986	10%
Chick-fil-A	451	502	570	643	767	946	16%
Boston Market	371	754	1,100	1,197	929	855	18%
Church's	465	501	526	574	620	705	9%
Total	5,488	6,157	6,808	7,136	7,330	7,870	7%
U.S. Restaurants							
KFC	5,081	5,103	5,078	5,092	5,105	5,231	1%
Popeyes	853	889	894	945	1,066	1,165	6%
Chick-fil-A	534	825	717	749	812	897	11%
Boston Market	534	829	1,087	1,166	889	858	10%
Church's	937	953	989	1,070	1,105	1,178	5%
Total	7,939	8,599	8,765	9,022	8,977	9,329	3%
Sales per Unit ($ 000s)							
KFC	706	733	775	786	817	837	3%
Popeyes	720	742	757	762	790	847	3%
Chick-fil-A	845	608	795	859	945	1,055	5%
Boston Market	695	910	1,012	1,027	1,045	997	7%
Church's	496	526	532	536	561	598	4%
Average	691	716	777	791	816	844	4%

Source: Tricon Global Restaurants, Inc., *1999 Annual Report*; Chick-fil-A, corporate headquarters, Atlanta; Boston Chicken, Inc., *1999 Annual Report*; *Nation's Restaurant News*, 2000.

chicken chains increased sales at a faster rate. KFC's share of chicken segment sales fell from 71 percent in 1989 to less than 56 percent in 1999, a ten-year drop of 15 percent. During the same period, Chick-fil-A and Boston Market increased their combined market share by 17 percent (see Case Exhibit 20.4). In the early 1990s, many industry analysts predicted that Boston Market would challenge KFC for market leadership. Boston Market was a new restaurant chain that emphasized roasted rather than fried chicken. It successfully created the image of an upscale deli offering healthy, "home-style" alternatives to fried chicken and other fast food. In order to distinguish itself from more traditional fast food concepts, it refused to construct drive-thrus, and it established most of its units outside of shopping malls rather than at major city intersections.

On the surface, it appeared that Boston Market and Chick-fil-A's market share gains were achieved primarily by taking customers away from KFC. Another look at the data, however, reveals that KFC's sales grew at a stable rate over the last ten years. Boston Market, rather than drawing customers away from KFC, appealed primarily to consumers who did not regularly frequent KFC and wanted healthy, nonfried chicken alternatives. Boston Market was able to expand the chicken segment beyond its traditional emphasis on fried chicken by offering nonfried chicken products that appealed to this new consumer group. After aggressively growing its restaurant base through

CASE EXHIBIT 20.4

TOP U.S. CHICKEN CHAINS—MARKET SHARE (%, BASED ON ANNUAL SALES)

	KFC	Popeyes	Chick-fil-A	Boston Market	Church's	Total
1989	70.8	12.0	6.2	0.0	11.0	100.0
1990	71.3	12.3	6.6	0.0	9.8	100.0
1991	72.7	11.4	7.0	0.0	8.9	100.0
1992	71.5	11.4	7.5	0.9	8.7	100.0
1993	68.7	11.4	8.0	3.0	8.9	100.0
1994	65.4	11.2	8.2	6.7	8.5	100.0
1995	60.7	10.7	8.2	12.3	8.1	100.0
1996	57.8	9.9	8.4	16.2	7.7	100.0
1997	56.1	10.1	9.0	16.8	8.0	100.0
1998	56.9	11.5	10.5	12.7	8.4	100.0
1999	55.6	12.5	12.0	10.9	9.0	100.0
5-Year Change (%)	−9.8	1.3	3.8	4.2	0.5	0.0
10-Year Change (%)	−15.2	0.5	5.8	10.9	−2.0	0.0

1997, however, Boston Market fell on hard times, and it was unable to handle mounting debt problems. It soon entered bankruptcy proceedings. McDonald's acquired Boston Market in 2000. It had acquired Denver-based Chipotle Mexican Grill in 1998 and Columbus, Ohio-based Donatos Pizza in 1999. McDonald's hoped the acquisitions would help it expand its U.S. restaurant base, since fewer opportunities existed to expand the McDonald's concept. Chick-fil-A's success came primarily from its aggressive shopping mall strategy that leveraged the trend toward large food courts in shopping malls. Despite gains by Boston Market and Chick-fil-A, KFC's customer base remained loyal to the KFC brand because of its unique taste. KFC has also continued to dominate the dinner and takeout segments of the industry.

Popeyes replaced Boston Market as the second-largest chicken chain in 1999. Popeyes and Church's had traditionally followed similar strategies—to compete head-on with other "fried chicken" chains. Popeyes, however, was in the process of shifting its focus to Cajun fast food, after it successfully launched its Louisiana Legends One-Pot Cajun Meals of jambalaya, gumbo, shrimp, and crawfish etouffee. Church's was determined to distinguish itself by placing a heavier emphasis on its "made-from-scratch," Southern image. In 1999, it broadened its menu to include buffalo chicken wings, macaroni and cheese, beans and rice, and collard greens. Chick-fil-A focused on pressure-cooked and char-grilled skinless chicken breast sandwiches, which it had traditionally sold to customers in sit-down restaurants in shopping malls. As more malls added food courts, however, malls became less enthusiastic about allocating separate store space to restaurants. Therefore, Chick-fil-A began to open smaller units in shopping mall food courts, hospitals, and colleges as a way of complementing its existing sit-down restaurants in shopping malls. It also began to open freestanding units in selected locations.

Demographic Trends

A number of demographic and societal trends influenced the demand for food eaten outside of the home. During the last two decades, rising incomes, greater affluence among a greater percentage of American households, higher divorce rates, and the fact that people married later in life contributed to the rising number of single households and the demand for fast food. More than 50 percent of women worked outside of the home, a dramatic increase since 1970. This number was expected to rise to 65 percent by 2010. Double-income households contributed to rising household incomes and increased the number of times families ate out. Less time to prepare meals inside the home added to this trend. Countering these trends, however, was a slower growth in the U.S. population and an overpopulation of fast food chains that increased consumer alternatives and intensified competition.

Baby-boomers thirty-five to fifty years of age constituted the largest consumer group for fast food restaurants. Generation X'ers (ages twenty-five to thirty-four) and the "Mature" category (ages fifty-one to sixty-four) made up the second- and third-largest groups. As consumers aged, they became less enamored with fast food and were more likely to trade up to more expensive restaurants, such as dinner houses and full-service restaurants. Sales of many Mexican restaurants, which were extremely popular during the 1980s, began to slow as Japanese, Indian, and Vietnamese restaurants became more fashionable. Ethnic foods in general were rising in popularity as U.S. immigrants, who constituted 10 percent of the U.S. population in 2000, looked for establishments that sold their native foods.

The greatest concern for fast food operators was the shortage of employees in the sixteen to twenty-four age category. Most Americans in this category had never experienced a recession or economic downturn. During the 1970s, Americans experienced double-digit inflation, high interest rates, and high unemployment, as well as two major oil crises that resulted in gas shortages. The U.S. economy began to expand again during the early 1980s and continued to expand almost unabated through 2000. Unemployment was at its lowest point in more than two decades, and many high school and college graduates, especially those in business and engineering, enjoyed a robust job market that made it more difficult for fast food operators to find capable employees.

Labor costs made up about 30 percent of the fast food chain's total costs, second only to food and beverage costs. Intense competition, however, made it difficult for restaurants to increase prices sufficiently to cover the increased cost of labor. Consumers made decisions about where to eat partially based on price. Therefore, profit margins were squeezed. In order to reduce costs, restaurants eliminated low-margin food items, increased portion sizes, and improved product value to offset price increases. Restaurants also attempted to increase consumer traffic through discounting, by accepting coupons from competitors, by offering two-for-one specials, and by making limited-time offerings.

Costs could also be lowered and operations made more efficient by increasing the use of technology. According to the National Restaurant Association, most restaurant operators viewed computers as their number-one tool for improving efficiencies. Computers could be used to improve labor scheduling, accounting, payroll, sales analysis, and inventory control. Most restaurant chains were also using point-of-sale systems that recorded the selected menu items and gave the cashier a breakdown of food items and the ticket price. These systems decreased serving times and increased cashier accuracy. Other chains, like McDonald's and Carl's Jr., converted to new food preparation systems that allowed them to prepare food more accurately and to prepare a great variety of sandwiches using the same process.

Higher costs and poor availability of prime real estate was another trend that negatively affected profitability. A plot of land suitable for a normal-size freestanding restaurant cost between $1.5 million and $2.5 million. Leasing was a less costly alternative to buying. Nevertheless, market saturation decreased per-store sales as newer units cannibalized sales from existing units. As a result, most food chains began to expand their U.S. restaurant bases into alternative distribution channels in hospitals, airports, colleges, highway rest areas, gas stations, shopping mall food courts, and large retail stores or by dual branding with other fast food concepts.

While the news media touted the benefits of low-fat diets during the 1970s and 1980s, consumer demand for beef began to increase again during the 1990s. The U.S. Department of Agriculture estimated that Americans ate an average of sixty-four pounds of red meat each year. The growing demand for steak and prime rib helped fuel the growth in dinner houses that continued into 2000. According to the NRA, other food items that were growing in popularity included chicken, hot and spicy foods, smoothies, wraps and pitas, salads, and espresso and specialty coffees. Starbucks, the Seattle-based coffee retailer, capitalized on the popularity of specialty coffees by aggressively expanding its coffee shop concept into shopping malls, commercial buildings, and bookstores, such as Barnes & Noble. Starbucks increased its store base by 28 percent in 1999, the greatest increase of any major restaurant chain.

International Fast Food Market

As the U.S. market matured, many restaurants expanded into international markets as a strategy for growing sales. Foreign markets were attractive because of their large customer bases and comparatively little competition. McDonald's, for example, operated forty-six restaurants for every 1 million U.S. residents. Outside of the United States, it operated only one restaurant for every 3 million residents. McDonald's, KFC, Burger King, and Pizza Hut were the earliest and most aggressive chains to expand abroad, beginning in the late 1950s. By 2000, at least thirty-five chains had expanded into at least one foreign country. McDonald's operated the largest number of restaurants (more than 12,000 U.S. units and 14,000 foreign units) in the most countries (119). In comparison, Tricon Global Restaurants operated more than 20,000 U.S. and close to 30,000 non-U.S. KFC, Pizza Hut, and Taco Bell restaurants in eighty-five countries. Because of their early expansion abroad, McDonald's, KFC, Burger King, and Pizza Hut had all developed strong brand names and managerial expertise operating in international markets. This made them formidable competitors for fast food chains investing abroad for the first time.

Case Exhibit 20.5 lists the world's thirty-five largest restaurant chains in 2000. The global fast food industry had a distinctly American flavor. Twenty-eight chains (80 percent of the total) were headquartered in the United States. The U.S. chains had the advantage of a large domestic market and ready acceptance by the American consumer. European firms had less success developing the fast food concept because Europeans were more inclined to frequent more mid-scale restaurants, where they spent several hours enjoying multicourse meals in a formal setting. KFC had trouble breaking into the German market during the 1970s and 1980s because Germans were not accustomed to buying take-out or ordering food over the counter. McDonald's had greater success penetrating the German market because it made a number of changes to its menu and operating procedures to appeal to German tastes. German beer, for example, was served in all of McDonald's restaurants in Germany. In France, McDonald's used a different sauce on its Big Mac sandwich that appealed to the French palate. KFC had more success in Asia and Latin America, where chicken was a traditional dish.

CASE EXHIBIT 20.5

THE WORLD'S 35 LARGEST FAST FOOD CHAINS (2000)[a]

	Franchise	Operational Headquarters	Parent Country	No. of Countries
1.	McDonald's	Oakbrook, Illinois	U.S.A.	119
2.	Pizza Hut	Dallas, Texas	U.S.A.	88
3.	KFC	Louisville, Kentucky	U.S.A.	85
4.	Subway Sandwiches	Milford, Connecticut	U.S.A.	73
5.	TCBY	Little Rock, Arkansas	U.S.A.	68
6.	Domino's Pizza	Ann Arbor, Michigan	U.S.A.	64
7.	Burger King	Miami, Florida	U.K.	58
8.	T.G.I. Friday's	Dallas, Texas	U.S.A.	53
9.	Baskin-Robbins	Glendale, California	U.S.A.	52
10.	Dunkin' Donuts	Randolph, Massachusetts	U.S.A.	41
11.	Wendy's	Dublin, Ohio	U.S.A.	29
12.	Sizzler	Los Angeles, California	U.S.A.	22
13.	A&W Restaurants	Livonia, Michigan	U.S.A.	21
14.	Popeyes	Atlanta, Georgia	U.S.A.	21
15.	Chili's Grill & Bar	Dallas, Texas	U.S.A.	20
16.	Little Caesar's Pizza	Detroit, Michigan	U.S.A.	19
17.	Dairy Queen	Edina, Minnesota	U.S.A.	18
18.	Taco Bell	Irvine, California	U.S.A.	15
19.	Carl's Jr.	Anaheim, California	U.S.A.	15
20.	Outback Steakhouse	Tampa, Florida	U.S.A.	13
21.	Hardee's	Rocky Mt., North Carolina	U.S.A.	11
22.	Applebee's	Overland Park, Kansas	U.S.A.	10
23.	Arby's	Ft. Lauderdale, Florida	U.S.A.	10
24.	Church's Chicken	Atlanta, Georgia	U.S.A.	9
25.	PizzaExpress	London, England	U.K.	9
26.	Denny's	Spartansburg, South Carolina	U.S.A.	6
27.	Mos Burger	Tokyo	Japan	5
28.	Taco Time	Eugene, Oregon	U.S.A.	5
29.	Yoshinoya	Tokyo	Japan	5
30.	Loterria	Tokyo	Japan	4
31.	Orange Julius	Edina, Minnesota	U.S.A.	4
32.	Quick Restaurants	Brussels	Belgium	4
33.	Skylark	Tokyo	Japan	4
34.	IHOP	Glendale, California	U.S.A.	3
35.	Red Lobster	Orlando, Florida	U.S.A.	3

[a] Case writer research.

Aside from cultural factors, international business carried risks not present in the domestic market. Long distances between headquarters and foreign franchises made it more difficult to control the quality of individual restaurants. Large distances also caused servicing and support problems. Transportation and other resource costs were higher than in the domestic market. In addition, time, cultural, and language differences increased communication and operational problems. As a result, most restaurant chains limited expansion to their domestic market as long as they were able to achieve corporate profit and growth objectives. As companies gained greater expertise abroad, they turned to profitable international markets as a means of expanding restaurant bases and increasing sales, profits, and market share. Worldwide demand for fast food was expected to grow rapidly during the next two decades, because rising per capita incomes worldwide made eating out more affordable for greater numbers of consumers. In addition, the development of the Internet was quickly breaking down communication and language barriers. Greater numbers of children were growing up with computers in their homes and schools. As a result, teenagers in Germany, Brazil, Japan, and the United States were equally likely to be able to converse about the Internet. The Internet also exposed more teenagers to the same companies and products, which enabled firms to more quickly develop global brands and a worldwide consumer base.

Kentucky Fried Chicken Corporation

Marketing Strategy

Many of KFC's problems during the 1980s and 1990s surrounded its limited menu and inability to quickly bring new products to market. The popularity of its Original Recipe Chicken allowed KFC to expand through the 1980s without significant competition from other chicken chains. As a result, new product introductions were not a critical part of KFC's overall business strategy. KFC suffered one of its most serious setbacks in 1989 as it prepared to introduce a chicken sandwich to its menu. KFC was still experimenting with the chicken sandwich concept when McDonald's test-marketed its McChicken sandwich in the Louisville market. Shortly after, McDonald's rolled out the McChicken sandwich nationally. By beating KFC to the market, McDonald's developed strong consumer awareness for its sandwich. This significantly increased KFC's cost of developing awareness for its own sandwich, which KFC introduced several months later. KFC eventually withdrew the sandwich because of low sales. Today, about 95 percent of chicken sandwiches are sold through traditional hamburger chains.

By the late 1990s, KFC had refocused its strategy. The cornerstone of its new strategy was to increase sales in individual KFC restaurants by introducing a variety of new products and menu items that appealed to a greater number of customers. After extensive testing, KFC settled on three types of chicken: Original Recipe (pressure cooked), Extra Crispy (fried), and Tender Roast (roasted). It also rolled out a buffet that included some thirty dinner, salad, and dessert items. The buffet was particularly successful in rural locations and suburbs. It was less successful in urban locations because of space considerations. KFC then introduced its Colonel's Crispy Strips and five new chicken sandwiches to appeal to customers who preferred non-chicken-on-the-bone products. KFC estimated that its Crispy Strips and chicken sandwiches accounted for $250,000 (30 percent) of KFC per-restaurant sales, which averaged $837,000 a year. One of the problems with these items, however, was that they cannibalized sales of its chicken items; they were less expensive and easier to handle. The latter was especially appealing to drive-thru customers.

Overcapacity in the U.S. market made it more difficult to justify the construction of new free-standing restaurants. Fewer sites were available for new construction, and those sites, because of their increased cost, drove profit margins down. KFC initiated a three-pronged distribution strategy that helped beef up sales. First, it focused on building smaller restaurants in nontraditional outlets, such as airports, shopping malls, universities, and hospitals. It also experimented with units that offered drive-thru and carryout service only, snack shops in cafeterias, scaled-down outlets for supermarkets, and mobile units that could be transported to outdoor concerts and fairs. Second, KFC continued to experiment with home delivery, which was already firmly established in the Louisville, Las Vegas, and Los Angeles markets. Third, KFC established "2-n-1" units that sold both KFC and Taco Bell products (KFC/Taco Bell Express) or KFC and Pizza Hut products (KFC/Pizza Hut Express). By early 2000, Tricon Global Restaurants was operating 700 multibranded restaurants that simultaneously sold products from two of the three chains. It was also testing "3-n-1" units that sold all three brands.

Refranchising Strategy

When Colonel Sanders began to expand the Kentucky Fried Chicken system in the late 1950s, he established KFC as a system of independent franchisees. This strategy helped the Colonel to minimize his involvement in the operations of individual restaurants and to concentrate on the things he enjoyed the most—cooking, product development, and public relations. The franchise system resulted in a fiercely loyal and independent group of KFC franchises. When PepsiCo acquired KFC in 1986, a primary objective was to integrate KFC's operations into the PepsiCo system to take advantage of operational, financial, and marketing synergies. This strategy, however, led to greater interference by PepsiCo management in franchise menu offerings, financing, marketing, and operations. This interference was met by resistance from KFC franchises. PepsiCo attempted to decrease these problems by expanding KFC's restaurant base through company-owned restaurants rather than through franchising. It also used its strong cash flows to buy back unprofitable franchises. Many of these restaurants were converted into company-owned restaurants. By 1993, company-owned restaurants accounted for 40 percent of KFC's worldwide system. When PepsiCo spun off its restaurants into Tricon Global Restaurants in 1994, Tricon's new top management team began to sell company-owned restaurants back to franchises they believed knew the business better than they. By 2000, company-owned restaurants had fallen to about 27 percent of the total KFC system.

International Operations

KFC's early experiences operating abroad put it in a strong position to take advantage of the growing trend toward international expansion. By 2000, more than 50 percent of KFC's restaurants were located outside of the United States. Historically, franchises made up a large portion of KFC's international restaurant base, because franchises were owned and operated by local entrepreneurs who had a deeper understanding of local language, culture, customs, law, financial markets, and marketing characteristics. Franchising was also a good strategy for establishing a presence in smaller countries, like Grenada, Bermuda, and Suriname, which could support only a single restaurant. The costs of operating company-owned restaurants were prohibitively high in these smaller markets. Of the 5,595 KFC restaurants located outside of the United States in 1999, 69 percent were franchised, while 21 percent were company-owned and 10 percent were licensed restaurants or joint ventures. In larger markets, such as Mexico, China, Canada, Australia, Puerto Rico, Korea, Thailand, and the United Kingdom, there was a stronger emphasis on building company-owned restaurants. By coordinating purchasing, recruiting and training, financing, and advertising, fixed costs could be

| CASE EXHIBIT 20.6 | LATIN AMERICA RESTAURANT COUNT— MCDONALD'S, BURGER KING, KFC, AND WENDY'S | | | |

	McDonald's	Burger King	KFC	Wendy's
Mexico	170	108	157	7
Puerto Rico	121	148	67	30
Caribbean Islands	59	57	91	23
Central America	80	85	26	26
Subtotal	430	398	341	86
% Total	24%	80%	78%	60%
Colombia	21	0	19	3
Ecuador	7	12	18	0
Peru	10	10	17	0
Venezuela	83	13	6	33
Other Andean	6	7	0	0
Andean Region	127	42	60	36
% Total	7%	9%	14%	25%
Argentina	205	25	0	21
Brazil	921	0	8	0
Chile	61	25	29	0
Paraguay + Uruguay	32	5	0	0
Southern Cone	1,219	55	37	21
% Total	69%	11%	8%	15%
LATIN AMERICA	1,776	495	438	143
% TOTAL	100%	100%	100%	100%

Restaurant data obtained from corporate offices at McDonald's Corp. (as of December 1999), Burger King Corp. (as of June 30, 2000), Tricon Global Restaurants, Inc. (as of June 30, 2000), and Wendy's International (as of May 15, 2000).

spread over a larger number of restaurants. Increased bargaining power also enabled KFC to negotiate lower prices from suppliers. KFC was also better able to control product and service quality.

Latin American Strategy

KFC operated 438 restaurants in Latin America in 2000 (see Case Exhibit 20.6). Its primary presence was in Mexico, Puerto Rico, and the Caribbean. KFC established subsidiaries in Mexico and Puerto Rico beginning in the late 1960s and expanded through company-owned restaurants. Franchises were used to penetrate other countries in the Caribbean whose market size prevented KFC from profitably operating company-owned restaurants. Subsidiaries were later established in the Virgin Islands, Venezuela, and Brazil. KFC had planned to expand into these regions using company-owned restaurants. The Venezuelan subsidiary, however, was later closed because of the high costs of operating the small subsidiary. KFC had opened eight restaurants in Brazil but decided to close them in 1999 because it lacked the cash flow needed to support an expansion program in that market. Franchises were opened in other markets that had good growth potential, such as Chile, Ecuador, Peru, and Colombia.

KFC's early entry into Latin America gave it a leadership position over McDonald's in Mexico and the Caribbean. It also had an edge in Ecuador and Peru. KFC's Latin America strategy represented a classic internationalization strategy. It first expanded into Mexico and Puerto Rico because of their geographic proximity, as well as political and economic ties, to the United States. From these regions, KFC expanded its franchise system throughout the Caribbean, gradually moving away from its U.S. base as its experience in Latin America grew. Only after it had established a leadership position in Mexico and the Caribbean did it venture into South America. McDonald's pursued a different strategy. It was late to expand into the region. Despite a rapid restaurant construction program in Mexico during the 1990s, McDonald's still lagged behind KFC. Therefore, McDonald's initiated a first-mover strategy in Brazil and Argentina, large markets where KFC had no presence. By early 2000, more than 63 percent of McDonald's restaurants in Latin America were located in the two countries. Wendy's pursued a slightly different strategy. It first expanded into Puerto Rico, the Caribbean Islands, and Central America because of their geographical proximity to the United States. The shorter distance to the United States made these restaurants easier to manage. Wendy's late entry into Latin America, however, made it more difficult to penetrate the Mexican market, where KFC, McDonald's, and Burger King had already established a strong presence. Wendy's announced plans to build 100 Wendy's restaurants in Mexico by 2010; however, its primary objective was to establish strong positions in Venezuela and Argentina, where most U.S. fast food chains had not yet been established.

Country Risk Assessment in Latin America

Latin America comprises some 50 countries, island nations, and principalities that were settled primarily by the Spanish, Portuguese, French, Dutch, and British during the 1500s and 1600s. Spanish is spoken in most countries, the most notable exception being Brazil, whose official language is Portuguese. Catholicism is the predominant religion, though Methodist missionaries successfully exported Protestantism into many regions of Latin America in the 1800s, most notably on the coast of Brazil. Despite commonalities in language, religion, and history, however, political and economic policies often differ significantly from one country to another. Historically, frequent changes in governments and economic instability increased the uncertainty of doing business in the region.

Most U.S. and Canadian companies were beginning to realize, however, that they could not overlook the region. Geographic proximity made communications and travel easier and quicker between countries, and the North American Free Trade Agreement (NAFTA) had eliminated tariffs on goods shipped between Canada, Mexico, and the United States. A customs union agreement signed in 1991 (Mercosur) between Argentina, Paraguay, Uruguay, and Brazil eliminated tariffs on trade among those four countries. Many countries, such as Chile and Argentina, had also established free trade policies that were beginning to stimulate growth. These factors made Latin America an attractive location for investment. The primary task for companies investing in the region was to accurately assess the different risks of doing business in Latin America and to select the proper countries for investment.

Miller (1992) developed a framework for analyzing country risk that was a useful tool for analyzing the attractiveness of a country for future investment. He argued that firms must examine country, industry, and firm factors in order to fully assess country risk. *Country factors* addressed the risks associated with changes in the country's political and economic environment that potentially affected the firm's ability to conduct business. They included the following:

1. Political risk (e.g., war, revolution, changes in government, price controls, tariffs and other trade restrictions, appropriation of assets, government regulations, and restrictions on the repatriation of profits)

2. Economic risk (e.g., inflation, high interest rates, foreign exchange rate volatility, balance of trade movements, social unrest, riots, and terrorism)

3. Natural risk (e.g., rainfall, hurricanes, earthquakes, and volcanic activity)

Industry factors addressed changes in the structure of the industry that inhibited the firm's ability to successfully compete in its industry. They included the following:

1. Supplier risk (e.g., changes in quality, shifts in supply, and changes in supplier power)

2. Product market risk (e.g., changes in consumer tastes and availability of substitute products)

3. Competitive risk (e.g., rivalry among competitors, new market entrants, and new product innovations)

Firm factors examined the firm's ability to control its internal operations. They included the following:

1. Labor risk (e.g., labor unrest, absenteeism, employee turnover, and labor strikes)

2. Supplier risk (e.g., raw material shortages and unpredictable price changes)

3. Trade secret risk (e.g., protection of trade secrets and intangible assets)

4. Credit risk (e.g., problems collecting receivables)

5. Behavioral risk (e.g., control over franchise operations, product quality and consistency, service quality, and restaurant cleanliness)

Many U.S. companies believed that Mexico was an attractive country for investment. Its population of 103 million was more than one-third as large as the U.S. population and represented a large market for U.S. goods and services. In comparison, Canada's population of 31 million was only one-third as large as Mexico's. Mexico's close proximity to the United States meant that transportation costs between the United States and Mexico were significantly lower than to Europe or Asia. This increased the competitiveness of U.S. goods in comparison with European and Asian goods, which had to be transported to Mexico across the Atlantic or Pacific Ocean at significantly greater cost. The United States was in fact Mexico's largest trading partner. More than 80 percent of Mexico's total trade was with the United States. Many U.S. firms also invested in Mexico to take advantage of lower wage rates. By producing goods in Mexico, U.S. goods could be shipped back to the United States for sale or shipped to third markets at lower cost.

Despite the advantages of doing business in Mexico, Mexico accounted for only about 20 percent of the United States' total trade. Beginning in the early 1900s, the percentage of total U.S. exports going to Latin America has declined as exports to other regions of the world, such as Canada and Asia, have increased. The growth in economic wealth and consumer demand in Canada and Asia has generally outpaced that in Mexico for most of the last century. However, the volume of trade between the United States and Mexico has increased significantly since the North American Free Trade Agreement went into effect in 1994.

A commonly held perception among many Americans was that Japan was the United States' largest trading partner. In reality, Canada was the United States' largest trading partner by a wide margin. Canada bought more than 22 percent ($154 million) of all U.S. exports in 1998; Japan bought less than 9 percent ($58 billion). Canada accounted for about 19 percent of all goods imported into the United States ($178 billion); Japan accounted for 13 percent ($125 billion). The perception that Japan was the largest U.S. trading partner resulted primarily from extensive media coverage of the long-running U.S. trade deficit with Japan. Less known to many Americans was the fact that the United States was running a balance of trade deficit with China that almost equaled the deficit with Japan. China was positioned to become the United States' largest trading partner in Asia within the next few years.

The lack of U.S. investment in and trade with Mexico during the twentieth century was mainly the result of Mexico's long history of restricting foreign trade and investment. The Institutional Revolutionary Party (PRI), which came to power in Mexico during the 1920s, had a history of promoting protectionist economic policies to shield Mexico's economy from foreign competition. Many industries were government owned or controlled, and many Mexican companies focused on producing goods for the domestic market without much attention to building exports. High tariffs and other trade barriers restricted imports into Mexico, and foreign ownership of assets in Mexico was largely prohibited or heavily restricted.

A dictatorial and entrenched government bureaucracy, corrupt labor unions, and a long tradition of anti-Americanism among government officials and intellectuals also reduced the motivation of U.S. firms to invest in Mexico. The nationalization of Mexico's banks in 1982 led to higher real interest rates and lower investor confidence. This forced the Mexican government to battle high inflation, high interest rates, labor unrest, and lower consumer purchasing power during the early to mid-1980s. Investor confidence in Mexico, however, improved after 1988, when Carlos Salinas de Gortari was elected president. Salinas embarked on an ambitious restructuring of the Mexican economy. He initiated policies to strengthen the free market components of the economy, lowered top marginal tax rates, and eliminated many restrictions on foreign investment.

The privatization of government-owned companies came to symbolize the restructuring of Mexico's economy. In 1990, legislation was passed to privatize all government-run banks. By the end of 1992, more than 800 of 1,200 government-owned companies had been sold, including Mexicana and AeroMexico, the two largest airline companies in Mexico, and Mexico's eighteen major banks. More than 350 companies, however, remained under government ownership. These represented a significant portion of the assets owned by the state at the start of 1988. Therefore, the sale of government-owned companies in terms of asset value was still modest. A large percentage of the remaining government-owned assets was controlled by government-run companies in certain strategic industries, such as steel, electricity, and petroleum. These industries had long been protected by government ownership. However, President Salinas opened up the electricity sector to independent power producers in 1993, and Petroleos Mexicanos (Pemex), the state-run petrochemical monopoly, initiated a program to sell off many of its nonstrategic assets to private and foreign buyers.

North American Free Trade Agreement (NAFTA)

Prior to 1989, Mexico levied high tariffs on most imported goods. In addition, many other goods were subjected to quotas, licensing requirements, and other nontariff trade barriers. In 1986, Mexico joined the General Agreement on Tariffs and Trade (GATT), a world trade organization designed to eliminate barriers to trade among member nations. As a member of GATT, Mexico was required to apply its system of tariffs to all member nations equally. Mexico subsequently dropped tariff rates on a variety of imported goods. In addition, import license requirements were dropped for all but 300 imported items. During President Salinas' administration, tariffs were reduced from an average of 100 percent on most items to an average of 11 percent.

On January 1, 1994, the North American Free Trade Agreement (NAFTA) went into effect. The passage of NAFTA created a trading bloc with a larger population and gross domestic product than the European Union. All tariffs on goods traded between the United States, Canada, and Mexico were eventually phased out. NAFTA was expected to benefit Mexican exporters, since reduced tariffs made their goods more competitive compared to goods exported to the United States from other countries. In 1995, one year after NAFTA went into effect, Mexico posted its first surplus balance of trade in six years. A large part of this surplus was attributed to greater exports to the United States.

Despite its supporters, NAFTA was strongly opposed by farmers and unskilled workers. The day after NAFTA went into effect, rebels rioted in the southern Mexican province of Chiapas, on the Guatemalan border. After four days of fighting, Mexican troops drove the rebels out of several towns the rebels had earlier seized. Around 150 people—mostly rebels—were killed. Later in the year, thirty to forty masked men attacked a McDonald's restaurant in the tourist section of Mexico City. The men threw cash registers to the floor, smashed windows, overturned tables, and spray-painted "No to Fascism" and "Yankee Go Home" on the walls. Such protests continued through 2000, when Mexican farmers dumped gallons of spoiled milk in the streets to protest low tariffs on imported farm products. Farmers also protested the Mexican's government's practice of allowing imports of milk powder, corn, and wheat from the United States and Canada above the quotas established as part of the NAFTA agreement. The continued opposition of Mexican farmers, unskilled workers, and nationalists posed a constant threat to the stability of the NAFTA agreement.

Another problem was Mexico's failure to reduce restrictions on U.S. and Canadian investment in a timely fashion. Many U.S. firms experienced problems getting required approvals for new ventures from the Mexican government. A good example was United Parcel Service (UPS), which sought government approval to use large trucks for deliveries in Mexico. Approvals were delayed, forcing UPS to use smaller trucks. This put UPS at a competitive disadvantage vis-à-vis Mexican companies. In many cases, UPS was forced to subcontract delivery work to Mexican companies that were allowed to use larger, more cost-efficient trucks. Other U.S. companies, such as Bell Atlantic and TRW, faced similar problems. TRW, which signed a joint-venture agreement with a Mexican partner, had to wait fifteen months longer than expected before the Mexican government released rules on how it could receive credit data from banks. TRW claimed that the Mexican government had slowed the approval process to placate several large Mexican banks.

Foreign Exchange and the Mexican Peso Crisis of 1995

Between 1982 and 1991, a two-tiered exchange rate system was in force in Mexico. The system consisted of a controlled rate and a free market rate. A controlled rate was used for imports, foreign debt payments, and conversion of export proceeds. An estimated 70 percent of all foreign transactions were covered by the controlled rate. A free market rate was used for other transactions. In 1989, President Salinas instituted a policy of allowing the peso to depreciate by one peso per day against the dollar. In 1991, the controlled rate was abolished and replaced with an official free rate. The peso was thereafter allowed to depreciate by 0.20 pesos per day against the dollar. When Ernesto Zedillo became Mexico's president in December 1994, one of his objectives was to continue the stability of prices, wages, and exchange rates achieved by ex-president Carlos Salinas during his tenure as president. This stability, however, was achieved primarily on the basis of price, wage, and foreign exchange controls. While giving the appearance of stability, an overvalued peso continued to encourage imports that exacerbated Mexico's balance of trade deficit. At the same time, Mexican exports became less competitive on world markets.

Anticipating a devaluation of the peso, investors began to move capital into U.S. dollar investments. On December 19, 1994, Zedillo announced that the peso would be allowed to depreciate by an additional 15 percent per year against the dollar. The maximum allowable depreciation at the time was 4 percent per year. Within two days, continued pressure on the peso forced Zedillo to allow the peso to float freely against the dollar. By mid-January 1995, the peso had lost 35 percent of its value against the dollar and the Mexican stock market plunged 20 percent. By the end of the year, the peso had depreciated from 3.1 pesos per dollar to 7.6 pesos per dollar. In order to thwart a possible default by Mexico, the U.S. government, International Monetary Fund, and World Bank pledged $25 billion in emergency loans. Shortly thereafter, Zedillo announced an emergency economic package called the "pacto" that included reduced government spending, increased sales of government-run businesses, and a freeze on wage increases.

By 2000, there were signs that Mexico's economy had stabilized. Gross domestic product was increasing at an average annual rate of 24 percent and unemployment was low, at slightly more than 2 percent (see Case Exhibit 20.7). Interest rates and inflation were also low by historical standards (respectively 24 and 17 percent in 1999), far below their highs of 61 and 35 percent in 1995. Interest rates and inflation were, however, still considerably higher than in the United States. Higher relative interest rates and inflation put continued pressure on the peso to depreciate against the dollar. This led to higher import prices and contributed to inflation.

A number of social concerns also plagued President Zedillo's government. These included a lack of success in controlling organized crime surrounding the drug trade, high-profile political murders (e.g., the murder of a Roman Catholic Cardinal at the Guadalajara airport in 1993), and a high poverty rate, particularly in southern Mexico.

CASE EXHIBIT 20.7	MEXICO—SELECTED ECONOMIC DATA (ANNUAL GROWTH RATES)						
	1994	**1995**	**1996**	**1997**	**1998**	**1999**	**Annual Growth Rate**
Population (millions)	93	91	97	96	100	102	2%
Gross Domestic Product	13%	29%	36%	27%	19%	21%	24%
Money Supply (M1)	4%	5%	43%	33%	19%	26%	22%
Inflation (CPI)	7%	35%	34%	21%	16%	17%	22%
Money Market Rate	17%	61%	34%	22%	27%	24%	31%
Peso Devaluation Against $US	71%	44%	3%	3%	22%	−4%	23%
Unemployment Rate	3.6%	4.7%	3.7%	2.6%	2.3%	n/a	

Source: International Monetary Fund, *International Financial Statistics*, 2000.

These social problems, and voters' disenchantment over allegations of continued political corruption, led to strong opposition to the ruling PRI. In 2000, the PRI lost its first presidential election in five decades when Vincente Fox, leader of the opposition National Action Party, was elected president. Fox took office on December 1, 2000.

Risks and Opportunities

KFC faced a variety of risks and opportunities in Mexico. It had eliminated all of its franchises in Mexico and operated only company-owned restaurants that enabled it to better control quality, service, and restaurant cleanliness. Company-owned restaurants, however, required more capital than franchises. This meant that KFC would not be able to expand as quickly as it could using a franchised restaurant base. KFC still had the largest number of restaurants in Mexico of any fast food chain. However, McDonald's was growing its restaurant base rapidly and was beating KFC in terms of sales. KFC's other major competitors included Burger King and El Pollo Loco ("The Crazy Chicken"). Wendy's had also announced plans to open 100 restaurants in Mexico by 2010, though Wendy's emphasis in Latin America continued to be in Venezuela and Argentina. Another threat came from Habib's, Brazil's second-largest fast food chain, which opened its first restaurant in Mexico in 2000. Habib's served traditional Middle Eastern dishes, such as falafel, hummus, kafka, and tabbouleh, at prices below those of KFC and McDonald's. It planned to open 400 units in Mexico between 2000 and 2005.

Another concern was the long-term value of the peso, which had depreciated at an average annual rate of 23 percent against the U.S. dollar since NAFTA went into effect. This translation risk lowered Tricon Global's reported profits when peso profits were translated into dollars. It also damaged Tricon Global's stock price. From an operational point of view, however, KFC's Mexico operations were largely insulated from currency fluctuations because it supplied most of its needs using Mexican sources. KFC purchased chicken primarily from Tyson Foods, which operated two chicken processing plants in Mexico. Tyson was also the primary supplier of chicken to McDonald's, Burger King, Applebee's, and Wal-Mart in Mexico.

KFC faced difficult decisions surrounding the design and implementation of an effective Latin American strategy over the next twenty years. It wanted to sustain its leadership position in Mexico and the Caribbean, but it also hoped to strengthen its position in other regions in South America. Limited resources and cash flow, however, limited KFC's ability to aggressively expand in all countries simultaneously. What should KFC's Latin American strategy be? KFC's strategy in 2000 focused on sustaining its position in Mexico and the Caribbean but postponed plans to expand into other large markets, like Venezuela, Brazil, and Argentina. This strategy carried significant risk, since McDonald's and Wendy's were already building first-mover advantages there. A second strategy was to invest more capital in these large markets to challenge existing competitors, but such a strategy might risk KFC's leadership position in Mexico and the Caribbean. Another strategy was to focus on building a franchise base throughout Latin America, in order to build KFC's brand image and prevent competitors from establishing first-mover advantages. This strategy, however, was less effective in building a significant market share in individual countries, since market leadership often required a country subsidiary that actively managed both franchised and company-owned restaurants and took advantage of synergies in purchasing, operations, and advertising. A country subsidiary could be justified only if KFC had a large restaurant base in the targeted country. KFC's Latin American strategy required considerable analysis and thought about how to most efficiently use its resources. It also required an in-depth analysis of country risk and selection of the right country portfolio.

Sources

General References

Direction of Trade Statistics, International Monetary Fund, Washington, DC.

International Financial Statistics, International Monetary Fund, Washington, DC.

Miller, Kent D., "A Framework for Integrated Risk Management in International Business," *Journal of International Business Studies*, 23(2), 311–331, 1992.

Standard & Poor's Industry Surveys, Standard & Poor's Corporation, New York.

Quickservice Restaurant Trends, National Restaurant Association, Washington, DC.

Periodicals

FIU Hospitality Review, FIU Hospitality Review, Inc., Miami, FL.

IFMA Word, International Foodservice Manufacturers Association, Chicago, IL.

Independent Restaurant, EIP, Madison, WI.

Journal of Nutrition in Recipe & Menu Development, Food Product Press, Binghamton, NY.

Nation's Restaurant News, Lebhar-Friedman, Inc., New York (http://www.nrn.com).

Restaurant Business, Bill Communications Inc., New York (http://www.restaurant.biz.com).

Restaurants & Institutions, Cahners Publishing Co., New York (http://www.restaurantsandinstitutions.com).

Restaurants USA, National Restaurant Association, Washington, DC (http://www.restaurant.org).

Associations

National Restaurant Association, 1200 17th St. NW, Washington, DC 20036-3097, (202) 331-5900, http://www.restaurant.org.

International Franchise Association, 1350 New York Ave. NW, Suite 900, Washington, DC 20005-4709, (202) 628-8000, http://www.franchise.org.

Books

Dave's Way: A New Approach to Old-Fashioned Success, by R. David Thomas (founder of Wendy's), Berkley Publishing Group, New York, 1992.

Golden Arches East: McDonald's in East Asia, by James L. Watson (ed.), Stanford University Press, Palo Alto, CA, 1998.

Grinding It Out: The Making of McDonald's, by Ray Kroc (founder of McDonald's) and Robert Anderson, St. Martins, New York, 1990.

I'd Like the World to Buy a Coke: The Life and Leadership of Roberto Goizueta, by David Greising, John Wiley & Sons, New York, 1999.

It's Easier to Succeed than to Fail, by S. Truett Cathy (founder of Chick-fil-A), Oliver-Nelson Books, Nashville, TN, 1989.

Kentucky Fried Chicken Japan Ltd.: International Competitive Benchmarks and Financial Gap Analysis, by Icon Group Ltd., London, 2000.

Kentucky Fried Chicken Japan Ltd.: Labor Productivity Benchmarks and International Gap Analysis, by Icon Group Ltd., London, 2000.

McDonaldization Revisited, by Mark Alfino, John S. Caputo, and Robin Wynyard (eds.), Greenwood Publishing Group, Westport, CT, 1998.

McDonald's Behind the Arches, by John F. Love, Bantam Books, New York, 1986, 1995, 1999.

Selling 'Em by the Sack: White Castle and the Creation of American Food, by David Gerard Hogan, New York University Press, New York, 1999.

Taco Titan: The Glen Bell Story, by Debra Lee Baldwin, Summit Publishing Group, Denver, Colorado, 1999.

The Globalization Reader, by Frank Lechner and John Boli (eds.), Blackwell Publishing, Malden, MA, 2000.

The McDonald's Thesis: Explorations and Extensions, by George Ritzer, Sage Publications, Newbury Park, CA, 1998.

The McDonaldization of Society: An Investigation into the Changing Character of Contemporary Social Life, by George Ritzer, Pine Forge Press, Little Rock, AR, 1995.

Web Pages

Boston Market Corporation (http://www.bostonmarket.com).

Burger King Corporation (http://www.burgerking.com).

Chick-fil-A (http://www.chickfila.com).

Church's Chicken (http://www.churchs.com).

McDonald's Corporation (http://www.mcdonalds.com).

Popeyes Chicken & Biscuits (http://www.popeyes.com).

Tricon Global Restaurants, Inc. (http://www.triconglobal.com).

Wendy's International Incorporated (http://www.wendys.com).

Marketing Plan Worksheets

These worksheets are designed to assist you in writing a formal marketing plan. Worksheets are a useful planning tool because they help to ensure that important information is not omitted from the marketing plan. Answering the questions on these worksheets will enable you to:

1. Organize and structure the data and information you collect during the situation analysis.

2. Use this information to better understand a firm's strengths and weaknesses and to recognize the opportunities and threats that exist in the marketing environment.

3. Develop goals and objectives that capitalize on strengths.

4. Develop a marketing strategy that creates competitive advantages.

5. Outline a plan for implementing the marketing strategy.

By downloading these worksheets in electronic format, you will be able to change the outline or add additional information that is relevant to your situation. Remember that there is no one best way to organize a marketing plan. Our outline was designed to serve as a starting point and to be flexible enough to accommodate the unique characteristics of your situation. If you need additional help in putting together your marketing plan, refer to Appendix B, where you will find sample marketing plans.

As you complete the worksheets, it might be useful to refer back to the text of the chapters. In completing the situation analysis section, be sure to be as comprehensive as possible. The viability of your SWOT analysis depends on how well you have identified all of the relevant environmental issues. Likewise, as you complete the SWOT analysis, you should be honest about the firm's characteristics. Do not depend on strengths that the firm really does not possess. Being honest also goes for your listing of weaknesses.

I. Executive Summary

The executive summary is a synopsis of the overall marketing plan. The executive summary is easier to write if you do it last, after you have written the entire marketing plan.

II. Situation Analysis

A. The External Environment

Competitive pressures

Identify the firm's major competitors (brand, product, generic, and total budget).

Identify the characteristics of the firm's major competitors:
Size
Growth
Profitability
Target markets
Products
Key strengths and weaknesses
Key marketing capabilities (production, distribution, promotion, pricing)

List any potential (future) competitors not identified in the preceding.

Economic growth and stability

Identify the general economic conditions of the country, region, state, and local area in which the firm operates.

Explain the economic climate with respect to customers:
Inflation
Consumer confidence
Purchasing patterns (buying power)
Business-to-business economic conditions

Political, legal, and regulatory issues

Identify any political activities that affect the firm or the industry:
Changes in elected officials (domestic or foreign)
Industry (lobbying) groups
Consumer groups

Identify any changes in international, federal, state, or local laws and regulations that affect the marketing activities of the firm or the industry:
Recent court decisions
Recent rulings of federal, state, local, and self-regulatory agencies
Changes in global trade agreements or trade law

Changes in technology

Identify ways that changing technology has affected the firm's customers:
Searching for product information
Place and timing of purchase (order) decisions
Comparison shopping

Identify ways that changing technology has affected the way the firm or the industry operates:
    Manufacturing
    Distribution
    Promotion
    Customer relationship management
    Partnerships and alliances

Identify current technologies that the firm is not using to the fullest potential.

Identify future technologies that may increase the risk of product obsolescence.

Sociocultural Trends

Identify changes in society's demographics and values that will affect the firm or the industry (if this becomes too broad, focus on the firm's target customers).

Explain the changes that shifting demographics and values will have on the firm's:
    Products (features, benefits, branding)
    Pricing (value)
    Distribution (convenience, efficiency)
    Promotion (message content, delivery, feedback)
    People (human resource issues)

Identify any problems or opportunities that may be created by changes in the cultural diversity of the firm's customers and employees.

Identify any environmental issues (pollution, recycling, energy conservation) that the firm or industry is facing.

Identify the ethical and social responsibility issues that the firm or industry is facing.

B. The Customer Environment

Who are the firm's current and potential customers?

Describe the important identifying characteristics of the firm's current and potential customers:
    Demographic
    Geographic
    Psychographic
    Product usage

Identify the important players in the purchase process for the firm's products:
    Purchasers (actual act of purchase)
    Users (actual product user)
    Influencers (influence the decision, make recommendations)
    Financial responsibility (who pays the bill?)

What do customers do with the firm's products?

Purchase
  Purchase quantities and combinations
  Purchase of complementary products
  Purchase situations
Consumption
  Characteristics of heavy users
  Characteristics of light users
  Consumption of complementary products
  Consumption situations
Disposition
  Issues related to the creation of waste (garbage)
  Issues related to recycling

Where do customers purchase the firm's products?

Identify the outlets (intermediaries) where the firm's products are purchased:
  Store-based retailers
  Electronic retailers (Internet, television)
  Catalog retailers
  Vending
  Wholesale outlets
  Direct from the firm

Identify any trends in purchase patterns across these outlets (e.g., how e-commerce has changed the way the firm's products are purchased).

When do customers purchase the firm's products?

Under the firm's control
  Promotional events (communication and price changes)
  Customer service (hours of operation, delivery)
Not under the firm's control
  Seasonal patterns
  Physical/social surroundings
  Time perceptions
  Competitive actions

Why (and how) do customers select the firm's products?

Describe the basic benefits provided by the firm's products relative to competing products.

Describe the degree to which customers' needs are being fulfilled by the firm's products relative to competing products.

Describe how customers' needs are expected to change in the future.

Describe the relative importance of transactional (short, one-time) vs. relational (long-term, ongoing) exchange processes when customers make a purchase.

Why do potential customers not purchase the firm's products?

Identify the basic needs of noncustomers that are not being met by the firm's products.

Identify the features, benefits, and advantages of competing products that cause noncustomers to choose them over the firm's products.

Identify problems with the firm's distribution, promotion, or pricing that cause noncustomers to look elsewhere.

C. Internal (Organizational) Environment

Review of marketing goals and objectives

Identify the firm's current marketing goals and objectives.

State whether these goals and objectives are:

Consistent with the firm's mission
Consistent with recent changes in the marketing or customer environment
Leading to expected performance outcomes (sales volume, market share, profitability, awareness, brand preference)

Review of current marketing performance

Describe the firm's current performance compared to other firms in the industry. Is the performance of the industry as a whole improving or declining? Why?

If the firm's performance is declining, what is the most likely cause (e.g., environmental changes, flawed strategy, poor implementation)?

Review of current and anticipated organizational resources

Describe the current state of the firm's organizational resources (e.g., financial, capital, human, experience, relationships with key suppliers or customers).

How are the levels of these resources likely to change in the future?

If resource levels are expected to change:

How can the firm leverage additional resources to meet customer needs better than competitors?

How can the firm compensate for future constraints on its resources?

Review of current and anticipated cultural and structural issues

In terms of marketing strategy development and implementation, describe the positive and negative aspects of the current and anticipated culture of the firm. Examples could include:

The firm's overall customer orientation (or lack thereof)
The firm's emphasis on short-term vs. long-term planning
Willingness of the culture to embrace change

Internal politics and power struggles
The overall position and importance of the marketing function
Changes in key executive positions
General employee satisfaction and morale

III. SWOT Analysis

A. Strengths

Strength 1: _____

How does this strength enable the firm to meet customers' needs?
Does this strength make the firm different from (better than) its
competitors?

Strength 2: _____

How does this strength enable the firm to meet customers' needs?
Does this strength make the firm different from (better than) its
competitors?

(Repeat as needed to develop a complete list of strengths.)

B. Weaknesses

Weakness 1: _____

How does this weakness prevent the firm from meeting customers'
needs?
Does this weakness make the firm different from (worse than) its
competitors?

Weakness 2: _____

How does this weakness prevent the firm from meeting customers'
needs?
Does this weakness make the firm different from (worse than) its
competitors?

(Repeat as needed to develop a complete list of weaknesses.)

C. Opportunities

Opportunity 1: _____

How is this opportunity related to serving customers' needs?
How can the firm capitalize on this opportunity in the short term and
the long term?

Opportunity 2: _____

How is this opportunity related to serving customers' needs?
How can the firm capitalize on this opportunity in the short term and
the long term?

(Repeat as needed to develop a complete list of opportunities.)

D. Threats

Threat 1: _____

How is this threat related to serving customers' needs?
How can the firm prevent this threat from limiting its capabilities in the short term and the long term?

Threat 2: _____

How is this threat related to serving customers' needs?
How can the firm prevent this threat from limiting its capabilities in the short term and the long term?

(Repeat as needed to develop a complete list of threats.)

E. The SWOT Matrix

Strengths:	*Opportunities:*
•	•
•	•
•	•
•	•
Weaknesses:	*Threats:*
•	•
•	•
•	•
•	•

F. Matching, Converting, Minimizing, and Avoiding Strategies

Describe ways that the firm can match its strengths to its opportunities to create capabilities in serving customers' needs.

Can the firm convert its weaknesses into strengths or its threats into opportunities? If not, how can the firm minimize or avoid its weaknesses and threats?

Does the firm possess any major liabilities (unconverted weaknesses that match unconverted threats) or limitations (unconverted weaknesses or threats that match opportunities)? If so, are these liabilities or limitations obvious to customers?

Can the firm do anything about its liabilities or limitations, especially those that affect the firm's ability to serve customers' needs?

IV. Marketing Goals and Objectives

A. Marketing Goal A: _____

Objective A1: _____

Specific and measurable outcome:
Timeframe:
Responsible unit/person:

Objective A2: _____

> Specific and measurable outcome:
> Timeframe:
> Responsible unit/person:

B. Marketing Goal B: _____

Objective B1: _____

> Specific and measurable outcome:
> Timeframe:
> Responsible unit/person:

Objective B2: _____

> Specific and measurable outcome:
> Timeframe:
> Responsible unit/person:

(Repeat as needed to develop a complete list of goals and objectives.)

V. Marketing Strategies

A. Primary Target Market and Marketing Mix

Primary target market: _____

> This target's primary need:
> Identifying characteristics (demographics, geography, psychographics):
> Purchasing/shopping habits and preferences:
> Consumption/disposition characteristics:

Product: _____

> Major features and benefits:
> Sustainable competitive advantage:
> Differentiation/positioning strategy:
> Brand name and packaging:
> Customer service strategy:
> Complementary products:

Pricing: _____

> Pricing objectives:
> Description of per unit costs:
> Discount/markdown policy:

Distribution: _____

> General supply chain strategy:
> Intermediaries and channels to be used:
> Elements of customer convenience:

Promotion: _____

> General IMC strategy:
> IMC objectives and budget:

Elements of the advertising/publicity strategy:
Elements of the personal selling strategy:
Elements of trade sales promotion (push) strategy:
Elements of consumer sales promotion (pull) strategy:
Elements of the sponsorship strategy:

B. Secondary Target Market and Marketing Mix

Secondary target market: _____

This target's primary need:
Identifying characteristics (demographics, geography, psychographics):
Purchasing/shopping habits and preferences:
Consumption/disposition characteristics:

Product: _____

Major features and benefits:
Sustainable competitive advantage:
Differentiation/positioning strategy:
Brand name and packaging:
Customer service strategy:
Complementary products:

Pricing: _____

Pricing objectives:
Description of per unit costs:
Discount/markdown policy:

Distribution: _____

General supply chain strategy:
Intermediaries and channels to be used:
Elements of customer convenience:

Promotion: _____

General IMC strategy:
IMC objectives and budget:
Elements of the advertising/publicity strategy:
Elements of the personal selling strategy:
Elements of trade sales promotion (push) strategy:
Elements of consumer sales promotion (pull) strategy:
Elements of the sponsorship strategy:

VI. Marketing Implementation

A. Structural Issues

Describe your overall approach to implementing the marketing strategy.

Describe any changes to the firm's structure needed to implement the marketing strategy (e.g., add/delete positions, change lines of authority, change reporting relationships).

Describe your internal marketing activities in the following areas:

Employee training
Employee buy-in and motivation to implement the marketing strategy
Overcoming resistance to change
Internal communication and promotion of the marketing strategy
Coordination with other functional areas

Will customer-contact employees and managers be empowered to make decisions? If yes, how will the organization ensure that empowered employees make the right decisions?

B. Tactical Marketing Activities

Specific Tactical Activities	Person Responsible	Required Budget	Completion Date
Product activities 1. 2. 3.			
Pricing activities 1. 2. 3.			
Distribution activities 1. 2. 3.			
IMC activities 1. 2. 3.			

VII. Evaluation and Control
A. Formal Marketing Control

Describe the types and levels of formal control mechanisms that should be used to ensure the implementation of the marketing plan.

Input control mechanisms

Employee recruitment and selection procedures:
Employee training programs:
Employee manpower allocations:
Financial resources:
Capital outlays:
Research and development expenditures:
Other:

Process control mechanisms

Employee evaluation and compensation systems:
Employee authority and empowerment:
Internal communication programs:

Lines of authority/structure (organizational chart):
Management commitment to the marketing plan:
Management commitment to employees:

Output control mechanisms (performance standards)

Product performance standards:
Potential corrective actions that can be taken if actual product performance does not match these standards:

Price performance standards:
Potential corrective actions that can be taken if actual pricing performance does not match these standards:

Distribution performance standards:
Potential corrective actions that can be taken if actual distribution performance does not match these standards:

IMC performance standards:
Potential corrective actions that can be taken if actual IMC performance does not match these standards:

Output control mechanisms (marketing audits)

Explain how marketing activities will be monitored.

What are the specific profit- and time-based measures that will be used to monitor marketing activities?

Describe the marketing audit to be performed, including the person responsible for conducting the audit.

B. Informal Marketing Control

Describe the types and levels of informal control mechanisms that should be used to ensure the implementation of the marketing plan.

Employee self-control

Are employees satisfied with their jobs at a level that is sufficient for implementing the marketing plan? If not, how can employee job satisfaction be increased?

Are employees committed to the organization at a level that is sufficient for implementing the marketing plan? If not, how can employee commitment be increased?

Are employees committed to the marketing plan at a level that is sufficient for its implementation? If not, how can employee commitment to the plan be increased?

Employee social control

Do employees share the firm's values in a manner that enhances the implementation of the marketing plan? If not, how can the firm better instill its values among employees?

Describe the social and behavioral norms that exist within the organization and in work groups that are either beneficial or detrimental to implementation.

Employee cultural control

Is the organizational culture appropriate for the marketing plan? If not, what type of culture would be more appropriate?

Though cultural change is a slow process, what steps can be taken to change the firm's culture to become more conducive to implementing the marketing strategy?

Two Marketing Plan Examples

Marketing Plan for the Nissan Xterra

Executive Summary

Synopsis   This marketing plan was developed for the recently introduced Nissan Xterra. Even though the Xterra has been a huge success, it was discovered that an ample target market lies within young adults from Generations X and Y. This target market was identified through extensive research about the type of consumer that the Xterra attracted and the different needs of each generation. Understanding the consumers within this generation is crucial when trying to advertise a product. By gaining consumer understanding and awareness, the Nissan Xterra will be even more successful within this market.

Our plan is designed to keep Nissan Xterra one step ahead of competitors by increasing market share and continuing product quality. This plan discusses the goals and objectives that can be implemented to create success for the Xterra. We have compiled a list of ideas that will increase the value of the Xterra within the target market without increasing the price. If Nissan continues to promote quality and innovation within the Xterra, it will continue as one of the leading SUVs for many years to come.

Through the promotional campaign we have devised and the new theme we have created, Nissan Xterra will become a market leader in the mid-SUV market. Increasing consumer appreciation and awareness is the primary aim of this campaign strategy. The end result should be an increase in the number of consumers who purchase the Xterra, which increases market share and ultimately creates a positive future with many opportunities.

Major Aspects of the Marketing Plan

Goals and Objectives   With so many different types of SUVs being offered, the perceived value of the SUV is how consumers decide to purchase (or not to purchase) your SUV. If Nissan can maintain a strong value proposition with customers and staying ahead of the competition, consumers will purchase an Xterra over another SUV. We also feel that Nissan should continue to satisfy the Xterra's current customers. By having satisfied customers, profits will increase. These are the broad goals for the Xterra. The following objectives stem from these goals:

1. To increase by 25 percent the number of customers who repurchase by the year 2005.

2. To increase market share 3 percent by the year 2003.

3. To have 90 percent of current owners perceive Xterra as a strong value.

This marketing plan was prepared by Kim Branner, Melanie Holmes, Mike Murray, Phillip Noble, and Jeff Witt of Mississippi State University under the supervision of Dr. Debbie Thorne. This marketing plan is intended for classroom discussion rather than to illustrate either effective or ineffective marketing planning.

Marketing Strategy To accomplish our objectives, we must gain an understanding of the consumers within Generation X. The strategy is focused on the ideas of convenience, consumer needs, and consumer awareness. The strategy is implemented through:

1. A consumer convenience campaign, which consists of improving the Nissan Web site to offer a purchase and financing option

2. A consumer awareness campaign, which consists of local TV and radio advertisements

3. A model-year-end campaign, which consists of low APR financing and cash rebates

These campaigns will not only help increase Xterra's market share, but also create loyalty with current consumers.

Situation Analysis

To effectively design a marketing plan for the Xterra, an analysis of the marketing environment is essential. Through this situation analysis, the marketing devices best suited for the Xterra will be identified. This analysis will explore not only the external environment (such as competition and economic, political, legal, and technical conditions), but also the customer and internal environments.

Competition The Xterra's major competitors in the transportation category were analyzed within the four categories of competition. The following chart gives three examples of competition that the Xterra faces within each category.

Brand Competition[1]	Product Competition	Generic Competition	Total Budget Competition
Toyota RAV4	Minivans	Rental cars	Home remodeling
Jeep Cherokee	Cars	Motorcycles	Family vacations
Isuzu Rodeo	Trucks	Bicycles	Debt reduction

Each competitor was evaluated on several key factors, such as the types of vehicle offered, the effectiveness, and the overall presence in the market. As a basis for comparison, an evaluation of the Xterra is offered as well.

Nissan Xterra
- Features and specifications
  Small four-door SUV (2- and 4-wheel drive)
  Smaller than the Pathfinder and based on the Nissan Frontier
  Made for on- and off-pavement travel
  Length = 178 in./width = 70 in.
  Weight = 4,315 lb
  Engine: 2.4-liter V4 (143 hp) or 3.3-liter V6 (170 hp)

- Availability
    Dealerships are located throughout the United States
    Nontraditional channels such as the Internet
    Future availability from previous owners and used-car dealers

- Promotion
    National and local dealer advertisements, car magazines, and *Consumer Reports*
    Word-of-mouth advertising through current owners
    Awards: "Sports Utility of the Year"

- Summary: The Xterra made a huge impact on the SUV market during the 2000 model year. With a very reasonable sticker price and a sporty look, the Xterra has become very popular with Generation X. Since it is a new vehicle, the reliability and availability will increase over time. If Nissan continues to be innovative, then over time the company can continue to update the Xterra.

Toyota RAV4

- Features and specifications
    Small four-door SUV (2- and 4-wheel drive)
    Made for driving on pavement
    Drives more like a car than a truck
    Length = 163 in./width = 67 in.
    Weight = 3,000 lb
    Engine: 2.0-liter V4 (127 hp)

- Availability
    Dealerships are located throughout the United States
    Nontraditional channels such as the Internet
    Used-car dealers and previous owners

- Promotion
    National and local dealer advertisements, car magazines, and *Consumer Reports*
    Word-of-mouth advertising through current and previous owners
    Consumer Reports recommends the RAV4

- Summary: The RAV4 is a significant competitor for Nissan. It is a similar, Japanese-made vehicle. The RAV4 has been on the market since 1996 but has not had the impact of the Xterra. This is mainly because the RAV4 lacks the horsepower and the sporty look of the Xterra. The RAV4 is also built on a car platform, whereas the Xterra is built on a truck platform. Over time, Toyota and Nissan will continue to compete within the same markets.

Isuzu Rodeo

- Features and specifications
    Medium, four-door SUV (2- and 4-wheel drive)
    Made for on- and off-pavement travel
    Length = 177 in./width = 70 in.
    Weight = 3,935 lb
    Engine: 2.2-liter V4 (130 hp) or 3.2-liter V6 (205 hp)

- Availability
    Dealerships are located throughout the United States
    Nontraditional channels such as the Internet
    Used-car dealers and previous owners

- Promotion
    National and local dealer advertisements, car magazines, and *Consumer Reports*
    Word-of-mouth advertising through current and previous owners

- Summary: The Rodeo is another strong competitor for the Xterra. Isuzu came out with the current body style in 1998, and it has been just as popular as the old one. This sporty SUV also competes against the Xterra with similar body styles and engines. One difference is that the Rodeo offers upscale models with leather, CD changers, and a sunroof. This is one step up from the Xterra and is more comparable to the Nissan Pathfinder.

Other Major Expenditures   Since an automobile represents a large expenditure, any other type of major consumer expenditure must also be considered in the analysis of competitors.

- Features and specifications
    Home remodeling and family vacations are viable competitors for the consumer's dollar. The choice is heavily dependent on family needs and preferences.
    Using available funds for debt reduction also depends on family needs and is a matter of personal choice.

- Availability
    Home remodeling is not always a choice; sometimes it is a necessity.
    Family vacations are taken on average about once a year.

- Promotion
    Home remodeling is promoted within a local market area.
    Travel agencies and vacations are promoted heavily in both local and national arenas.
    Discounts are also widely available.

- Summary: Customers have many alternative uses for their dollars other than purchasing an SUV. This is especially true because many consumers purchase an SUV as a second vehicle.

Economic Conditions   Nissan is a global firm and is very dependent on the status of countries' economies throughout the world. Nissan North America is concerned mainly with the United States, Canada, and Mexico. Over the past few years, American automakers have seen a steady 2–3 percent growth in sales, but future growth requires increased cost effectiveness. Many manufacturers are now outsourcing the manufacturing of parts. Cost cutting has helped automakers' bottom lines, but an increase of the dollar against foreign currency has made foreign cars more affordable in the United States.

The economy has been in a state of growth for quite a few years. In response to this growth, consumers are buying bigger cars, including SUVs. SUV sales have sky-rocketed from fewer than 7 percent of car and truck sales in 1990 to 18 percent in 2000. In 1995, there were 35 different SUV models sold in North America. By 2005, it is predicted there will be 70 different models.

Political, Legal, and Technological Conditions   The political, legal, and techno-logical environments are very important to car manufacturers. In the political envi-ronment, governmental actions can affect the economy and consumers' willingness to buy an SUV. However, governmental actions of late have been very good for the econ-omy as well as the SUV market. The federal government has also mandated the pro-duction of low-emission vehicles. However, this has not affected the SUV market to date.

In the legal environment, consumers are concerned about two main problems with SUVs. First, SUVs typically are heavier than cars, which have been lightened over the years to meet strict fuel-economy standards. A heavier vehicle prevails in a colli-sion. This is a concern for every car owner. Second, SUVs tend to be stiffer than cars, and the frame and the engine mounts are often higher than in a car. Consequently, car passengers are more likely to be injured in side-impact collisions with SUVs. Manu-facturers are just now starting to address this problem.

Technological advances have changed the way that vehicles are manufactured—today's vehicles are more aerodynamic, safer for the environment, and more user friendly than ever before. Improved technology has also led to increased cost efficien-cies in production, a benefit that helps somewhat to stabilize retail prices. Technology has also changed the way vehicles are purchased. Thanks to the Internet, potential cus-tomers can now conduct any and all research before visiting a dealer.

Sociocultural Factors   Social trends greatly influence the purchase of automobiles. Currently, SUVs are very popular, and interest shows no signs of waning. But there is always the chance that Generation Y will reject SUVs, much like Generation X re-jected the station wagon. Likewise, American consumers are extremely time con-scious, so it is not surprising that online car shopping is growing in popularity. Another important social trend is the disappearance of the "American vs. Japanese" label placed on many vehicles. In today's global economy, many American vehicles are assembled in foreign countries. Even Nissan manufactures vehicles in the United States to help decrease costs.

The Customer Environment

Who Are They?   The Nissan Xterra is a new-generation mid-range SUV. Like the vehicle itself, the target market for the Xterra is also a new generation of buyers, or what could be termed "upscale Generation Xers." This vehicle appeals to the younger generation that is looking for a sporty and practical alternative to the minivan but can-not yet afford the luxurious, but a more expensive, full-size SUV. This mid-range SUV is attractive to young families, college students, and yuppies alike. While a fully equipped Xterra is not cheap, it is affordable for young, middle- to upper-middle-class couples just starting their families. Young women are expected to buy a significant por-tion of these vehicles as they become trendier.

What Do They Do with Our Product? The Xterra is an excellent all-purpose vehicle that can serve several functions equally well. It can be used for travel, delivery service, or everyday commuting or just to shuttle the kids around town. Many features of the Xterra play a key role in the purchasing process and satisfaction of the customer. The Xterra is stylish, practical, and, in some cases, luxurious. The Xterra is larger than most of its competition, so it delivers a lot of bang for the buck. Since it is built on a truck platform, it can handle fairly heavy loads if necessary. The value of the Xterra is enhanced not only by its size, but also by the number of available options, such as 4WD and a powerful V6 engine. Dealer add-on and aftermarket accessories are readily available for customization if desired.

Where Do They Buy? Since the Xterra is a relatively new vehicle, it is available primarily only through new-vehicle dealerships. Used Xterras will soon become more readily available through other sources, including individual sales, as owners begin the natural upgrade cycle. The Internet is also becoming a popular shopping alternative for both new and used vehicles.

Why and How Do They Buy? The majority of automobile purchases are due either to an immediate transportation need or merely to a desire for change. Nissan has conducted an extensive advertising campaign to raise public awareness of the features, availability, and uniqueness of the Xterra. Its relatively low cost makes it affordable for a very large segment of potential buyers. Family life cycles, such as the stages of active children, play a very important role in the type of vehicle purchased. The Xterra offers a very stylish and practical alternative to the traditional station wagon or minivan design, and its features and functionality will surely create a desire to own one.

Why Do Potential Customers Not Buy? Nissan has long been known for delivering a quality product. Since the Xterra is built on the popular truck platform, there should be little concern about its reliability, even though it is a new vehicle. Nissan is also offering the Xterra as an affordable alternative to the popular, but expensive, full-size Nissan Pathfinder. This should create an attitude among the younger generation that the Xterra is designed specifically for them. Of course, some customers will choose not to buy an Xterra simply because they are not aware of its existence, they do not like Nissan, or they do not want an SUV. Others may choose not to buy the Xterra because they are loyal to other brands.

Will Current Customers Buy Again? Since it has been so heavily advertised, awareness should not be a problem with the Xterra. Specific styling features will likely be the most significant factor on Xterra purchasing decisions because of consumer attitudes toward the vehicle's image. The customer environment surrounding the Xterra will be an exciting one for Nissan to manage because of the wider market the Xterra has opened.

Nissan's Internal Environment The internal environment of Nissan is very important to the success of Nissan in the United States. The company has focused on three major elements within its internal environment: investing in America, developing communities, and building relationships. Nissan has implemented these factors all over the United States on its way to success.

Nissan is a contributor to all communities in which it does business. Nissan is dedicated to creating a positive economic impact in communities across the United States. The company employs over 73,000 Americans through its Nissan/Infiniti retailer network. Another positive impact Nissan has on American cities is its sponsorship of sporting and cultural events across the country. They are also active in supporting local charities and other good causes. These relationships help form a positive image for Nissan in the American eye.

Commitment to building relationships across the United States through its dealerships and suppliers is also a priority. Nissan believes that in order for its North American operation to remain a success, it must maintain its strong network of suppliers. The company purchases from over 400 U.S.-based suppliers, annually spending well over $4.2 billion. This strong network of suppliers helps to keep prices for parts low so that Nissan can continue to offer the same quality automobile for the same reasonable price (the Xterra currently costs between $17,599 and $24,799).

SWOT Analysis

The environmental analysis revealed many market issues that could potentially be beneficial or harmful to the Xterra. By creating the SWOT analysis, we have identified the internal strengths and weaknesses and the external opportunities and threats.

Strengths
- Innovative design
- Quality of the Nissan name
- Good product image
- Good management at Nissan
- Recent increase in sales
- Increased customer service
- Increased market share
- Highly supported through positive advertisements

Weaknesses
- Similarity of the Xterra to other SUVs creates low customer switching costs.
- No reliability or dependability data is available due to the newness of the Xterra.
- The Xterra is available only through Nissan dealerships.

Opportunities
- Consumer interest in Web-based information is expanding.
- Consumers enjoy innovative, high-tech designs.
- The economy is strong.

- More women are purchasing SUVs.

- Roughly 27 million Generation Y consumers are of driving age.[2]

Threats
- Many strong competitors with similar products

- Growing consumer interest in environmentally friendly cars

- Increasing government regulation

- Changing consumer tastes (trendy products)

- Many American firms building smaller SUVs

Goals and Objectives

	Marketing Goal 1 To maintain a strong value proposition with customers	**Marketing Goal 2** To become the market leader in the midsize SUV category
Objective 1 To increase by 25 percent the number of customers who purchase by the year 2005	X	X
Objective 2 To increase market share 3 percent by the year 2003	X	X
Objective 3 To have 90 percent of current owners perceive the Xterra as a strong value	X	

The results of the situation and SWOT analyses point to two marketing goals and three objectives. These goals and objectives have been established to help Nissan become a bigger and better automobile manufacturer.

Goal 1: To maintain a strong value proposition with customers. A strong characteristic of Nissan is that it has always been a top-quality vehicle for an affordable price. By continuing with this strong value proposition through product innovation and low pricing, the brand image of Nissan will continue to be that of affordable quality, and this will strengthen the Nissan name and image.

Goal 2: To become the market leader in the midsize SUV category. A goal for everyone is to be a leader. Nissan is on its way to becoming that leader by offering a top-quality vehicle—*Motor Trend's* SUV of the Year—at a very affordable price with exceptional quality and performance.

Objective 1: To increase by 25 percent the number of customers who repurchase by the year 2005. Increasing the number of customers who repurchase would be a definite step in creating loyalty among customers and keeping brand image high.

Objective 2: To increase market share 3 percent by the year 2003. The SUV market is very saturated. A 3 percent increase would be a huge step in becoming the frontrunner in the SUV category.

Objective 3: To have 90 percent of current owners perceive the Xterra as a strong value. Having satisfied customers is a high priority. By keeping current customers happy, the chances for repurchase increase.

Marketing Strategy

Target Customer Profile   By evaluating key aspects of the marketing environment, we have identified the target market for the Xterra as males and females ages 18–30. The Xterra appeals to the younger generation since many Generation Xers are looking for a sporty SUV at a realistic price. It is very hard to target Generations Xers because they do not trust advertisements or like to be considered a target market. The Xterra subtly targets this market by having "terra for the land it crosses and X for the generation that it intends to target."[3]

Younger consumers have opted for the SUV over the minivan, just like their predecessors opted for the minivan rather than the station wagon. One difference, though, is how this generation uses the SUV. SUV owners range from single high school and college students to parents with small children to middle-aged couples who need another vehicle. The SUV offers this generation the size and comfort of the minivan with a sporty look. So, while many mothers do not like driving a minivan, they enjoy driving a sporty SUV. This also applies to teenagers, who would much rather be seen driving an SUV than the family van.[4]

Marketing Mix Elements   The marketing strategy we have created for Nissan has two distinct purposes. The first purpose is to generate a stronger value proposition in the public's mind. We feel this is one of the most important goals that Nissan can accomplish. The best way to begin this process is by starting a new slogan and intensifying ad campaigns. The second purpose of the marketing strategy is to become the market leader, as evidenced by increases in sales and market share. Nissan must strive to increase by 25 percent the number of customers who repurchase within a five-year turnaround. There are several options that will make this idea a reality. Maintaining the current pricing strategy will generate repurchase, offering a lower annual percentage rate (APR) to customers who trade in their old Xterra, and sending birthday cards to consumers that own Xterras. During key times of the year, Nissan can offer a lower APR and give larger rebates to future consumers, offer great promotions, such as giveaways for test drives, and increase community involvement with local dealers.

Product Modification and Product Quality   Nissan is known for being an innovator within the automobile industry. The Xterra represented a highly innovative step into the midsize SUV market. Nissan has to continue with product modifications and quality since the SUV market is so saturated with different models. The best way to keep the pool of SUV adopters growing faster than the number of defectors is to consistently upgrade and offer new products.[5] Since the Xterra was a huge success for Nissan, customers' wants and needs must be recognized through increased quality and continued product modifications.

Maintain Price   Since the Xterra is seen as such good quality for a great price, we do not want to increase the price of the Xterra. Over the years, the price will rise in line with inflation. However, the goal should be to keep the Xterra within its current price range in the SUV market.

Offer a Purchasing and Financing Option   The number of consumers who use the Internet on a daily basis is increasing. Just about everything you could imagine is offered on the Internet, and many automobile manufacturers are offering a "build your own" option. Saturn.com, for example, has a Web site link where you can build your own Saturn. Since the target market for the Xterra is Generation X, this is an option that Nissan should add to their Web site. In addition, the Nissan Web site should include a purchase and financing option. This increases the convenience for the customer, and all Nissan has to do is ship the personally designed Xterra to the nearest dealership.

Offer an Employee Seminar   Car salespeople are the direct link to customers. These salespeople should understand everything there is to know about the products being offered and new products being designed. Once a year, Nissan should offer an employee seminar where all salespeople and managers can come together to learn about Nissan as a whole and about the company's overall goals and objectives.

New Slogan   Through the years, Nissan has used several different slogans. To this day, Nissan has yet to find a slogan that markedly increases their market share or image. Nissan's current slogan is "Driven." This is an average slogan that should be used only until Nissan can implement a stronger, more recognizable slogan. The slogan we propose is "Drive the Best!" This implies quality and performance at the same time. No matter what slogan Nissan chooses, they need to find one that works and sticks with it.

Increased Advertising (TV and Radio)   October and November are the prime months for automobile sales. During these months, Nissan should increase television advertising in order to attract new customers. This will also help in selling the current model year and making room for the new models. If Nissan could have local rather than national commercials, they could be much more personal with customers. A personal relationship is always a strong attribute that any and all companies need. To further this, Nissan should have radio commercials enticing people to come out and test drive a variety of vehicles. Radio advertising allows the firm to make customers aware of the products available in the area without their having to call or go out of the way. Our overall theme of "Drive the Best" could be modified to "Come Test Drive the Best" to help the theme stick in consumers' minds.

Community Involvement   Local dealers need to be more involved in community activities. This would provide Nissan with a very positive image to the people in the area. Community involvement would also establish the business within the area. For example, Nissan could sponsor area golf tournaments and have an Xterra giveaway for a hole-in-one. They could also sponsor drug awareness week in high schools and recreation centers. In larger cities, Nissan could display their affordable SUV in malls. This has become a very popular and effective method of marketing.

Consumer and Competition Reactions   Due to the saturated SUV market, no one determining factor will have a major impact on sales or market share. Competition will follow a good lead if they notice a change in sales through similar activities. Consumers, however, will remember Nissan as the pioneer in the marketing strategy. Increased traffic in the parking lot will lead to stronger sales, and Nissan must find a way to make this possible. Where there is one car dealership, there are normally five. We need customers to come to the Nissan dealership before visiting the others. As long as Nissan can become the pioneer in an industry, other businesses will not be as likely to catch up on this competitive advantage.

Objectives and Strategy Matrix

Target Market Profile: Generation Xers—Males and Females, ages 18–30

	Objective 1: Increase repurchase by 25 percent	**Objective 2:** Increase market share by 3 percent	**Objective 3:** At least 90 percent of current owners see the Xterra as a strong value
Product			
• Continue product modifications to match customers' needs and wants	X	X	
• Increase production quality			X
Pricing			
• Maintain current pricing range of $17,000–$24,000	X	X	X
Distribution			
• Enhance the Web site to include a "Build your own Xterra" option, as well as purchase and finance options		X	
• Offer an employee educational seminar on an annual basis		X	
Promotion			
• Offer a $500 cash rebate and low-APR financing on year-end models		X	
• Offer a lower APR rate to customers who repurchase the Xterra	X		
• Change the advertising slogan to "Drive the Best!"		X	X
• Increase community involvement	X	X	
• Increase TV and radio advertising	X	X	

Marketing Implementation

The purpose of marketing implementation is to pinpoint how to execute the marketing strategies that have been created. This implementation illustrates the routes that need to be taken in order to properly execute the marketing strategies for Nissan.

Implementation and Control Matrix

January 1, 2002, through December 31, 2003	Timeframe	Control Measures
Product Product modifications	October 2002 to October 2003	Survey current owners annually about their likes and dislikes
Pricing Maintain Price	January through December 2002	Determine if market share is increasing via the purchase of a monthly market share report
Distribution Improve Web site	January 2002	Measure number of hits
Offer employee educational seminar	Once a year	Survey retail salespeople on their perceptions of the company
Promotion Rebate	April through June 2002	Measure rebate usage in May 2002
Low APR	October through November 2002	Measure APR usage immediately
Slogan: "Drive the Best!"	January 2002	Surveys to measure popularity
Community involvement	January through December 2002	Survey dealers to assess changes in customer traffic in showrooms
TV and radio advertising	October through November 2002	Survey dealers to assess changes in customer traffic in showrooms

Customer Recognition   A new slogan should help to give Nissan a boost within the industry. Consumers will view the slogan as the vehicle sits on the lot. Advertising on television and on the radio will also help in making customers more aware of the Xterra. The community involvement we plan to participate in will also increase local awareness of the product.

Customer Appreciation   Once a customer has bought a Nissan, he or she should never switch brands. The quality checks on the vehicle will help in making better-quality vehicles. These features all entice customer retention. We will also show appreciation with birthday cards. Each owner will receive a birthday card on that day of the year. This makes business much more personal as well. A final way to implement customer appreciation is through surveys. Owners will be asked to fill out surveys in order for us to make the best product possible. We want to meet our customers' needs.

Maintain Value Proposition   Nissan has always been a high-quality vehicle at an affordable price. With the SUV category becoming saturated, Nissan must continue to offer "affordable quality" while at the same time proceeding with product innovation. By continuing to sell this vehicle, Nissan should strive to maintain the "SUV of the Year" title. Nissan recognized that the affordable, attractive Xterra was needed and took advantage of the situation. This has already given Nissan a competitive advantage over its rivals.

Conclusion

Nissan Xterra speaks for itself: "terra for the land it crosses and X for the generation that it intends to target." It is a product designed with the ideals of Generation X in mind. Our plan is designed to capitalize on this aspect of the market. Since the SUV market is becoming saturated with different models, Nissan has to stick in consumers' minds as the SUV to purchase. Most consumers want a new car approximately every four years, so the Xterra has to keep up with today's market. If Nissan can continue to cultivate strong brand recognition, long-term customer relationships, and overall customer satisfaction, they will remain a strong competitor within the SUV market for many years to come.

Marketing Plan for the Apple iBook

Executive Summary

Synopsis   The following marketing plan has been created for one of Apple computers latest, most innovative products, the iBook. Extensive research discovered that the target market for this product is students. This was derived through an analysis of the product's features and the help of the Apple Web site. Determining the target market was important in deciding the best ways to promote the Apple iBook and reach maximum success with this product.

Our plan has been designed to explain and implement new goals and objectives that will help to create even more success for the Apple iBook. We completed our research and thought up new and innovative ways to increase the presence and value of the Apple iBook. With the increasing demand for computers and new technology, the iBook will be the biggest success in the laptop industry. If Apple works with the goals and objectives stated in this plan, they will remain ahead of the competition for years ahead.

With up-to-date technology and promotional techniques to be discussed later in this plan, the Apple iBook and its value will be appreciated nationwide, especially on college campuses. Increased distribution, awareness, and value are the primary intentions for this marketing plan. The end result for the Apple iBook will be a positive one, increasing laptop awareness and value while paving the way for new technologies that hold abundant opportunities.

"Say Hello to the iBook!"   Apple Computer has been around for many years, and they have provided numerous different products. However, one of their newest

This marketing plan was prepared by Andrea Allen, Andy Anderson, Garry Boyd, Charley Jones, Courtney Kellogg, and Anna Trousdale of Mississippi State University under the supervision of Dr. Debbie Thorne and is intended for classroom discussion rather than to illustrate either effective or ineffective marketing planning.

products is the Apple iBook laptop computer. It currently comes in many colors to offer a customer some choice of customization. A few new directives in marketing, as proposed in the following marketing plan, may allow the iBook to eventually meet the goal of being the highest-quality laptop within the industry. We hope to maintain the pricing strategies; however, we want to instill a sense of value and satisfaction with every iBook sale. We plan to ensure that every customer feels that he or she is getting the best value for his or her money by providing excellent customer service, helpful technical support, one of the best graphically intensive interfaces, and an upbeat, fun computer. With all this in mind, we invite you to say hello to the iBook.

Situation Analysis

It is very important to establish an effective situation analysis. Our group came up with the one that utilizes case studies and knowledge of the product. A full analysis of the external environment, the customer environment, and the internal/organizational environment will allow for an effective and comprehensive situation analysis. The external environment is very important to the planning process because it includes an analysis of all the competitors of Apple and assists in setting the strategy that Apple can use to compete better. The customer environment is important because it is vital for a company to realize who its customers are. This analysis will go deeper and discuss the customers who use Apple's products and will help the company to better understand their target market. The internal/organizational environment is important for understanding how the company is operated. The product we are going to focus on is the iBook.

External Environment There are many factors to consider when assessing the external environment: competitive forces, economic growth and stability, political trends, legal and regulatory factors, changes in technology, and cultural trends. These different elements drive what would be successful business if they are well defined and evaluated by the company. The competitive forces include an analysis of the firms in direct and indirect competition with Apple. The economic growth and stability section indicates how the flow of money affects the market, the company, and the industry. The political trends regard what the government is doing with Apple. The legal and regulatory factors take a look at whether or not Apple is following the rules or whether they need to change anything to comply with the regulations. The changes in technology examine how such changes might affect Apple computers. The cultural trends include an examination of the values and beliefs that influence computer usage as well as other industry issues.

Competitive Forces Four forces of competition will be discussed in this section: total budget, generic, product class, and product brand. The *total budget* consists of non-computer competitor products that grab customer attention. The *generic* competitors are simply all computers, and they are very substantial. The *product class* would be computers versus laptop computers, which are similar but different. The *product brand* would be the three main companies competing with Apple for the laptop computer market.

	Compaq	**Dell**	**Gateway**
Similarities	Well known	Good reputation	Good customer service
Differences	IBM compatible	IBM compatible	IBM compatible
Competitive edge	Has been #1 in notebooks for so long	Very good brand equity	Very good brand equity
Deficiencies	Standard look	Standard look	Standard look
Positioning	#1	#2	#3
Pricing	Student offers	More business to business	More family oriented
Promotion	Student coupons	Buy in bulk	Offer easier methods of payment
Placement/ distribution	Internet, television, telephone	Internet, television, telephone	Internet, television, telephone

Although many computer companies compete with Apple, there are three main ones that have given Apple the most direct competition: Gateway, Dell, and Compaq.

Gateway has a rather impressive line of notebook computers of a highly competitive price and quality. They have many similarities to the iBook: They are widely known, have a good reputation, and are in high demand. They are widely known because Gateway does a very good job with advertising. They have a good reputation because both Apple and Gateway strive for quality in the products they produce. There are also some differences. Gateway has a standard look, whereas Apple comes in a variety of colors. Gateway laptops are also IBM compatible, giving them an advantage over Apple. Their brand equity is very high, they concentrate on customer service, which is top of the line in the computer business, and have very competitive prices. Their promotion strategies are equal to Apple's, as is their placement.

Dell has a very competitive notebook computer that competes with Apple's iBook. They are similar because they have a good reputation and easy-to-use software. The differences with the Apple are those of Gateway: They have a standard look, whereas Apple comes in many colors. They are IBM compatible; Apple is not. They also have similar edges on the Apple iBook as Gateway: They have great brand equity and superior customer service. Their promotion strategies are similar: They use magazines, television, and the Internet. Their placement in stores is similar, as well as their Internet site.

The next competitor is the Compaq notebook computer. Like Apple, their name is very well known. The differences are that they are IBM compatible and traditionally colored. The competitive edge that they have over the Apple is that they are going after a new look in the notebook computer line. Their promotion strategies are similar to Apple's. Their placement is also very similar in that they use computer stores and their Web site.

Economic Growth and Stability In our current economy, many products in the luxury category are positively affected by the amount of consumer spending. The current low unemployment rate in the United States (Apple's primary market) is an important factor for Apple computers because consumers are more likely to buy computers with more money to spend. The country's increased wealth has also led to an increase in the number of users who might not otherwise buy computers. Apple needs to take advantage of the current economic climate.

Political Trends   Political trends will not necessarily affect the computer industry unless they affect the economy. With Microsoft being declared a monopoly, Apple has a unique opportunity to move up in the market. It is important to take advantage of current trends and to anticipate possible changes. The government has been very good to the computer industry and hopefully this will continue. The government also decides the tax situation, which could impact computer businesses and sales.

Changes in Technology and Cultural Trends   These two we grouped together because of the way Apple has decided to market their product. In the computer industry, how technology changes, and the culture accepts the change, is very important. Apple has decided to use their innovation in computers in a colorful way. By using well-known actors and interesting color schemes, Apple is trying to grab an audience that might otherwise get turned off by the computer. Technology is what drives the computer industry, and how the public accepts the change determines how culture is also involved with the changes in technology. For instance, Apple has developed a computer that will help more people get involved with the Internet.

Customer Environment   The target market for the iBook can be segmented into three major categories: students, professionals, and graphic designers. These three groups use the product to make their jobs easier. They can use it to make graphic art or make three-dimensional models for engineers. They can also access the Internet using the product. Playing games on this computer is also a huge plus, because of the great graphics. The complementary products would be printers, scanners, and Internet service providers. Consumers can buy Apple products online, at local computer stores, at office supply stores, or through the company. They buy when they want a product of high quality. This is a product people do not have to have, but it is a very useful product to own. They buy it when they have the money to buy the iBook computer. Payment methods are also very simple. Customers can charge to the company over the Internet, establish a payment plan, or use many other different methods. It involves a level of high decision making. There are four main reasons why customers might not buy:

- They are not aware of what Apple has to offer.
- They do not want an Apple and would prefer an IBM-compatible unit.
- The Apple is too expensive.
- They do not like Apple's style or software.

Internal Environment   The internal environment of the Apple company is more focused on marketing and quality than on distribution. This has hurt Apple in many ways, but it was hurt the most when talking about public image. IBM's explosive introduction in the 1980s has forced Apple to restructure its way of thinking. When thinking about computers, most people would list IBM as the major computer base for all computers. Apple has a more of relaxed way of operating and is more idea driven. This has enabled them to utilize the skills of their own employees and to use a hands-on marketing approach. They consider themselves the "hip ones" of the computer industry. This gives their employees a better environment in which to develop and create good ideas.

SWOT Analysis

The SWOT analysis for any company is very important because it reveals its strengths, weaknesses, opportunities, and threats. Apple possesses several strengths, such as brand equity and product quality. Apple does have its weaknesses, too, such as limited software, and they are sometimes viewed as unreliable. Apple's rapid market growth and their increasing number of sellers are both good opportunities for Apple. Like any company, Apple does face a few threats: Gateway's and Dell's low prices, as well as new substitutes and competitors. Apple will be examined both internally and externally by the following SWOT analysis.

SWOT Analysis for the Apple iBook

Strengths	Weaknesses	Opportunities	Threats
• Strong brand image • Good market image • Good product quality • Brand equity • High quality graphics	• Limited software initially • Problems getting and keeping management • Sometimes viewed as unreliable	• Rapid market growth • Capitalize on Microsoft problems • Branching into wireless networking • Increasing number of Apple sellers	• New substitutes and competitors • Gateway's low prices • Dell's low prices • IBM and their constant ability to grow into different parts of the market

Marketing Goals and Objectives

After carefully examining Apple's situation and SWOT analyses, we developed marketing goals and objectives that will help Apple succeed in the laptop industry. These goals and objectives will help Apple keep current customers while also attracting new customers.

Goal 1: To offer the highest-quality and most innovative laptop in the industry. Determining which laptop computer to buy is a very important and well-researched purchasing decision for most consumers. By offering the highest-quality and most innovative laptop in the industry at a competitive price, the iBook from Apple will be the logical computer for these consumers to buy.

Objective 1: To introduce at least one new product modification every three months for the next three years. Accomplishing this objective will keep the iBook up to date with, or even ahead of, the rapidly changing computer market. It will also show potential customers that the iBook is the most innovative computer offered.

Goal 2: To offer the best customer service and tech support in the laptop industry. Offering the best customer service will allow Apple to keep their current customers happy and also gain new customers through referrals and reputation.

Objective 2: To have at least 95 percent of current Apple customers rate customer service and tech support satisfactory by January 1, 2002. This objective will give Apple feedback on how their current customers feel about Apple's overall customer service and how it can be improved in order to offer the best customer service and tech support possible.

Objective 3: To have at least 97 percent of current Apple iBook customers make another major computer purchase from Apple within the next five years. This is a very important objective for Apple to accomplish because no profit is made on the first sell to a customer. It is when you have customers who buy from your company a second time that you can make a profit. It also means that customers were satisfied with your product and prefer it to competing products. This means that customer loyalty to your product has been established, and now it needs to be maintained.

Alignment of Goals and Objectives

	Marketing Goal 1 To offer the highest-quality and most innovative laptop in the industry	**Marketing Goal 2** To offer the best customer service and tech support in the laptop industry
Objective 1 To introduce at least one new product modification every three months for the next three years	X	
Objective 2 To have 95 percent of current Apple customers rate customer service and tech support satisfactory by January 1, 2002	X	X
Objective 3 To have 97 percent of current Apple iBook customers make another major computer purchase from Apple within the next five years.	X	X

Marketing Strategy

The marketing strategy is the basic guide for the implementation of the marketing mix. The strategy explains the activities planned and the tools used in the areas of the marketing mix to meet the established marketing goals and objectives. It also explains the target market and profiles the product's average consumers.

Target Market   Identifying the target market for the iBook is essential to marketing it effectively. The target market determines where and how the product is advertised. According to Apple, the iBook's target markets are (in order of priority to Apple) students, educators, designers, scientists, engineers, businesspeople, and lay consumers.

Apple has always been committed to providing top-grade computers intended for education. Apple computers are easy to use and are not intimidating for unskilled computer users. This is one of the reasons that students and educators are at the top of the target market list. Apple's easy-to-use system also makes it a good choice for designers, engineers, businesspeople, and the general public.

Marketing Mix Elements   We have constructed a marketing strategy that is intended to both draw in new customers as well as keep the existing customers coming back to Apple. We hope that this strategy will open up new markets and broaden existing ones. The marketing mix strategy is a clever and strategic combination of advertising, rebates, pricing strategies, new offerings, and innovative distribution.

Product

Software modifications: In order to keep the Apple iBook at the cutting edge of computer technology, we plan to offer software modifications every three months. This is often enough to keep the iBook current, yet it is not so often that the consumer could not keep up with the changes.

Color-coordinated printers and Zip drives: We plan to offer color-coordinated printers and Zip drives to match the existing iBook colors by October of 2001. This will broaden the iBook product line and increase sales. This should please existing iBook customers as well as attract new customers to the Apple line. With the introduction of the matching printers and Zip drives, the customer can have a complete computer set that is the same color and looks nice together.

Pricing

Maintain current price: We plan to maintain the current price and resist rising computer costs. This shows that Apple is committed to offering the best laptop in the computer industry at an affordable price.

Offer affordable upgrades: Affordable upgrades will be offered for sale every three months. This will keep consumers' iBooks current and up to date with competing laptop and notebook computers. We plan to offer these upgrades at the lowest price possible in order to increase sales and keep customers at the cutting edge of technology.

Distribution

Maintain sales in current stores: The iBook computers will continue to be offered in the existing locations, such as Office Depot and Office Max. This will help to make loyal customers. By continuing to offer iBooks in the existing locations, we can have repeat sales and make loyal customers out of existing customers. We hope to maintain sales in these current store locations with the marketing strategy.

Increase presence in college bookstores: We plan to increase presence in college bookstores by August 1, 2001, and again by January 1, 2002. These dates were chosen because they are aligned with the beginning of semesters in most universities. These are peak times for computer sales because students are getting ready for the upcoming semester. Presence in college bookstores is important due to the significance of students in the target market.

Promotion

Affinity program: In order to promote the iBook, we plan to set up an affinity program with an Internet service provider from August 2001 through September 2001 and again from January 2002 through February 2002. This affinity program will enable Apple to offer Internet service at a discounted rate and add more value to the consumer's purchase.

Student rebates: In an effort to encourage more students to purchase iBooks, we plan to give rebates with student purchases. The rebates of $150 will be offered between the dates of August 2001 and October 2001 and between January 2002 and March 2002.

Advertising: In order to promote the iBook in the media, we will have television and magazine advertising. The advertisements will focus mainly on the cost/value relationship. We will also have a few advertisements that focus on the ease of use and after-sale support of the iBooks. The main focus of the advertisements will be on cost in order to coincide with the pricing and rebates described earlier. We will advertise primarily on CNN and the College Television Network, with some advertising on other cable channels. We will also advertise in such magazines as *People* and *Newsweek*. These channels and magazines were chosen due to their frequent viewing by our target audience.

Objectives and Strategy Alignment   The target market profile (one customer segment) is students (ages 16–28), secondary education level to college level.

	Objective 1 95 percent of customers rate customer service and tech support satisfactory by January 1, 2002	**Objective 2** Introduce a new product every three months for the next three years	**Objective 3** 97 percent of current customers make another major Apple purchase in the next five years
Product			
Software modifications	X		
Color-coordinated printers and Zip drives to match computers	X		
Pricing			
Maintain current price	X	X	
Offer affordable upgrades	X		
Distribution			
Maintain sales in current stores	X	X	
Increase presence in college bookstores	X	X	
Promotion			
Affinity programs with ISP— offer connection at a discount rate	X	X	
Student rebates	X	X	
Advertising	X	X	

Key Customer and Competitor Reactions By modifying our product with software updates, we hope to retain the customers we already have, and we also hope to gain their loyalty to the Apple product line. Such loyalty should increase the odds that our customers will purchase the peripheral devices we plan to offer along with our iBook. Devices such as Zip drives and printers that are manufactured in the colors of the iBook will be available to the general public. We also hope that offering products in matching colors will continue to be a strength that many competitors have not realized.

We also plan to maintain our current pricing with the iBooks. The price is affordable for our target market of students. We understand that students do not always have a lot of money to spend, and we hope that by offering our upgrades at an affordable price, customer loyalty will be strengthened. Our current competitors offer several different computers within the same price range, but it is often hard to buy affordable upgrades for their computer systems. Our affordable upgrade program may be a competitive advantage that many of the competitors may not be willing to develop.

Our distribution channels will be extended to help us gain a further competitive advantage within our selected target market. For instance, we plan to maintain our presence in many college bookstores nationwide. If we can offer our product at the places that students frequent, our chances of recognition can be increased substantially. This distribution channel will also allow the students to have access to the upgrades, programs, and peripheral devices we plan to promote. This presence in a college bookstore is a channel that some competitors may not be willing to reproduce; therefore, it could be our chance for success within this target market.

We plan to also enhance the promotional part of the marketing mix. By offering customers the chance to purchase an iBook and receive a discount rate with an Internet service provider, we think that our affinity program will succeed within this specific target market. We also think this could be a sustainable competitive advantage if we are able to ensure that we are the only company that has a contract with a specific ISP. We could basically try to counteract competition by entering into an affinity program with an ISP. We also want to offer student rebates for computer purchases. This will help with building a good rapport with our desired target market. Rebates are a tactic that any competitor may use; however, we feel that by getting the customer to submit their rebate form and following up periodically on the sale we can increase our customer loyalty and also come closer to meeting our goal of providing the best customer service and tech support within the laptop industry.

Marketing Implementation

"Employees are ultimately responsible for implementing marketing activities." This can be seen throughout most organizations, including Apple Computers. Gaining employee cooperation, trust, and commitment is key to marketing implementation. This implementation portion of the marketing plan will demonstrate the marketing strategies stated earlier. The number-one goal is to show Apple Computer executives how to implement the marketing strategies, which will be discussed in this portion of the marketing plan. Successful implementation requires that employees know the specific activities for which they are responsible and the timetable for completing each activity. Soon after this plan is finished, a meeting will be called of all top line managers. This meeting will explain the changes to take place and how to implement them. During this meeting all managers will be told the importance of motivating and empowering other employees to achieve these goals. By the end of the meeting "roles" will have been assigned and a timeline will have been discussed. Employees will have six months to a year to complete all assignments explained. These assignments will help put Apple Computer on the road to achieving even greater success than in the past.

Modifications of Software for the iBook   This program has been designed to keep customer computers up to date. Every three months, software modifications will be offered to all customers, at a very affordable price. Computer technicians will upgrade these computers at a price slightly above the software price. The modifications will help apple achieve the highest, most innovative quality in the laptop industry, which is one of our goals for Apple Computer.

Printers and Zip Drives to Match the Color of the iBook   These fun colors are new and innovative and designed to specifically match the colors currently being sold. This will help in the industry to show Apple's creative side and how computers can match room decor and "keep up with the changing times." Our main users of the colorful iBooks are students. These colors can be used to attract them to our products. These colorful, hip items will help Apple achieve the objective of being the most innovative in the industry.

Maintain Current Price   By keeping the Apple iBook price competitive, Apple will have a strong presence in the laptop industry. The main users targeted are students, who need to be able to afford the product. While maintaining price, quality can be shown as well, with the pitch "Quality keeps going up while price remains the same." This area will be monitored closely so as to remain competitive. This change will help Apple to meet the objective of offering the best product at the lowest price possible.

Student Rebates and Affinity Programs   Offering student rebates is a good way to keep the Apple iBook affordable. Rebates are a good promotional tool for Apple, as well as a way to thank customers for purchasing Apple products. We plan to offer $150 in rebates to our customers. Affinity programs are also a great way to show customer appreciation and keep customers coming back. Through these programs apple can build long-term relationships with customers and generate positive word of mouth from satisfied customers to help recruit new customers.

Implementation and Control Matrix

May 2001 through May 2002	Timeframe	People and Resources Involved	Control Measure
Product			
1. Modifications of software	Every three months	Computer technicians R&D team	Monitor R&D
2. Printers and Zip drives to match color of computer	Introduce by October 2001	VP Marketing & Sales R&D team	Monitor store sales and distribution channels

May 2001 through May 2002	Timeframe	People and Resources Involved	Control Measure
Pricing			
1. Maintain current price	Constant	CFO and R&D team	N/A
2. Offer affordable upgrades	Every three months	VP Marketing & Sales Computer technicians	Monitor number of upgrades sold every three months
Distribution			
1. Maintain sales in current stores	Constant	VP Marketing & Sales Distribution Mgr.	Monitor sales, get sales reports
2. Increase presence in college bookstores	By August 1, 2001 and January 1, 2002	VP Marketing & Sales Distribution Mgr.	Monitor distribution channels, receive sales reports from stores
Promotion			
1. Student rebates	August 2001 to January 2002	Promotion Director CFO	Monitor rebates redeemed
2. Affinity programs with ISPs and offer connection at a discounted rate	August–September 2001 and January–February 2002	Computer technicians Promotion Director CFO	Monitor those customers who participate in program
3. Advertising	May 2001 to May 2002	VP Marketing & Sales	Monitor awareness and sales

Marketing Plan Timeframe: May 2001–May 2002

Strategic Element	1	2	3	4	5	6	7	8	9	10	11	12
Student Rebates	▓	▓					▓	▓				
Affinity Programs	▓	▓					▓	▓				
Increase Presence in College Bookstores	▓						▓					
Printers/Zip Drives in Matching Colors	▓	▓	▓	▓	▓	▓	▓	▓	▓	▓	▓	▓
Offer Upgrades	▓	▓	▓	▓	▓	▓	▓	▓	▓	▓	▓	▓
Software Modifications	▓	▓	▓	▓	▓	▓	▓	▓	▓	▓	▓	▓
Maintain Price	▓	▓	▓	▓	▓	▓	▓	▓	▓	▓	▓	▓
Maintain Sales	▓	▓	▓	▓	▓	▓	▓	▓	▓	▓	▓	▓
Advertising	▓	▓	▓	▓	▓	▓	▓	▓	▓	▓	▓	▓

Evaluation and Control

As with any organization, strict evaluation and control methods are the key to success for the business. By monitoring and assessing the financial workings of Apple as well as controlling and evaluating the marketing techniques, the iBook may be well on its way to a more successful future. The current financial environment within Apple as well as methods of evaluation for the marketing techniques are described in the following sections.

Financial Assessment   At the end of Apple Computer's first quarter for fiscal year 2000, which ended January 1, 2000, the company recorded a net income of $183 million. They also recorded a substantial $2.34 billion in sales, up 37 percent from last year. There were 1,377,000 Apple computer systems sold during the quarter; the iBook accounted for 235,000 of this total. The total number of systems sold helped increase the unit growth to 46 percent, which is above the industry average. Apple's financial backing is at a high currently. They ended this quarter with a growth in revenues, profits, and units, which was almost 2.5 times higher than the industry average, according to Steven Jobs, Apple's CEO. "Apple also continues to deliver the best asset management in the industry, ending the quarter with less than one day of inventory."

Marketing Control   The high performance of the company at this time is a trait we would like to build upon and substantially affect with our new iBook promotional efforts. A continuing rise in revenues and sales will also parallel a continuing growth in market share. Directed efforts at enhancing the distribution channel and extending the line will positively affect the sales of the iBook. Our introduction of affordable upgrades and new software will also impact sales in a positive way. Our objective of a 97 percent retention and repurchase rate will also be met.

Our organizational culture is consistent with our proposed marketing plan; therefore, we hope that synergy will exist. The organizational atmosphere of Apple is a nurturing one, and our marketing plan is built with that in mind. Our goal of providing the best customer service and tech support within the laptop industry is attainable, given sound financial backing and the 9,527 Apple employees working to achieve it. It can contribute to a substantial competitive advantage.

There are several different control mechanisms that Apple will either incorporate or build upon to ensure we obtain our objectives and meet our goal. For instance, to ensure that our products are arriving when they are supposed to, both on the market and in the stores, the research and development office as well as the distribution and production channels will be highly monitored. Our customer service can also be monitored with several output control mechanisms. Marketing audits will be conducted to ensure that the marketing plan is working. For instance, close monitoring of the market should provide significant information on the sales of our systems. Redemption rates of the rebates will provide information on just how well our promotional efforts have worked. The ISPs will provide useful feedback on how many of our customers log on to the Internet using the affinity program we have established. Close monitoring of all the processes, from conception to customer usage, will help us establish just how successful the iBook promotional efforts have been.

Conclusion

The Apple iBook offers the latest in computer technology at a price lower than or equal to those of our competitors. The Apple iBook also has the competitive advantages of a user-friendly interface and excellent follow-up technical support and customer service. The iBook is especially geared toward students, professionals, and designers. These groups are specifically targeted due to the perfect fit the iBook offers them. The iBook is a cutting-edge laptop computer that can be bought in various colors and with matching hardware. It also offers the latest in computer technology at a value that is unmatched by any in the industry.

Sources

Apple Computers financial data, *CCBN Investor Relations Website* (http://www.ccbn.com).
Apple Computers Web site (http://www.apple.com).
Hoover's Web site (http://www.hoovers.com).
Marketing Strategy Web site (http://www.harcourtcollege.com/marketing/ferrell).

Chapter 1

1. Skip Wollenberg, "Carmaker Hopes to Rejuvenate Image with New Ad Campaign," *Marketing News*, December 6, 1999, 29.
2. The Federal Express mission and vision statements are from the 1999 FDX Annual Report.
3. Sigma Marketing's mission statement can be found at http://www.sigmamktg.com.
4. Lexmark 1999 Annual Report.
5. Amazon.com Annual Report, 1999.
6. Southwest Airlines' mission statement is available at http://www.iflyswa.com.
7. "Johnson & Johnson Reincarnates a Brand," *Sales and Marketing Management*, January 16, 1984, 63; and Elyse Tanouye, "Johnson & Johnson Stays Fit by Shuffling Its Mix of Businesses," *Wall Street Journal*, December 22, 1992, A1, A4.
8. Information on Enron's business strategy can be found at http://www.enron.com.
9. Howard Sutton, *The Marketing Plan in the 1990s* (New York: The Conference Board, 1990).
10. Sutton, 9.
11. Cindy Claycomb, Richard Germain, and Cornelia Droge, "The Effects of Formal Strategic Marketing Planning on the Industrial Firm's Configuration, Structure, Exchange Patterns, and Performance," *Industrial Marketing Management* 29 (May 2000), 219–234.
12. Sutton, 16.
13. Sutton, 17.
14. Bernard J. Jaworski and Ajay K. Kohli, "Market Orientation: Antecedents and Consequences," *Journal of Marketing* 57 (July 1993), 53–70.
15. Jaworski and Kohli, "Market Orientation: Antecedents and Consequences," and Stanley F. Slater and John C. Narver, "Market Orientation and the Learning Organization," *Journal of Marketing* 59 (July 1995), 63–74.
16. Keki R. Bhote, *Next Operation as Customer (NOAC): How to Improve Quality, Cost, and Cycle Time in Service Operations* (New York: American Management Association, 1991), 102–104.

Chapter 2

1. Miller, Scott and Jeffrey Ball, "The Pressure On Daimler Ratchets Up," *Wall Street Journal*, December 4, 2000, A19.
2. Cynthia Graber, "No Dumping: State Bans Techno-Trash, Donated Old Computers, TVs Add Up," *Boston Globe*, March 31, 2000, A1.
3. Michael Levy and Barton A. Weitz, *Retailing Management*, 3rd edition (Boston: Irwin/McGraw-Hill, 1998), 108–109.
4. Susan G. Strother, "Doing Business the Old-Fashioned Way: Barter in United States Totals $1.5 Billion Annually," *Roanoke Times & World News*, August 7, 1999, A7.
5. Eric Martineau, "No-charge Web Access Gains," *Tulsa World*, January 19, 2000, 3.
6. Dave Carpenter, "Gatorade Has Competition on the Run," *The Los Angeles Times*, May 30, 2000, 3.
7. Deogun, Nikhil, "PepsiCo to Buy Quaker for $13.4 Billion in Stock," *Wall Street Journal*, December 4, 2000, A3.
8. Gary Burtless, "Growing American Inequality: Sources and Remedies," *The Brookings Review*, Winter 1999, 31–35.
9. Mike Duff, "Old Navy: The Master of Downmarket Apparel Dollars," *DSN Retailing Today*, May 8, 2000, 89–90.
10. "Credit Cads?," *Boston Globe*, June 18, 2000, E6.
11. Jennifer Loven, "EPA Can't Explain High Gas Prices, Lawmakers Fume Over Industry 'Profit-Taking,'" *New Orleans Times-Picayune*, June 16, 2000, A08.

451

12. Jonathan Rauch, "Forget About China—Can Trade Be Saved From the WTO?," *National Journal*, May 13, 2000, 1495–1496.

13. Administration on Aging Web site: http://www.aoa.dhhs.gov

14. "What If?," *American Demographics*, December 1997.

15. Chip Walker and Elissa Moses, "The Age of Self-Navigation," *American Demographics*, September 1996.

16. Walker and Moses, *American Demographics*, 1996.

17. Efraim Turban, Jae Lee, David King, and H. Michael Chung, *Electronic Commerce: A Managerial Perspective*. (Upper Saddle River, NJ: Prentice Hall, 2000), 403.

18. "Study: Intranet Spending Reaches $10.9 Billion," *Internet News* (http://www.internetnews.com), July 19, 1999.

Chapter 3

1. Nigel Piercy, *Market-Led Strategic Change* (Oxford, UK: Butterworth-Heineman Ltd., 1992), 257.

2. Deborah Dougherty and Sarah M. Corse, "What Does It Take to Take Advantage of Product Innovation?," *Marketing Science Institute Working Paper Series*, Report No. 96–109, (Cambridge, MA: Marketing Science Institute, 1996).

3. Mary C. Gilly and Mary Wolfinbarger, "Advertising's Second Audience," *Journal of Marketing* 62 (January 1998), 69–88.

4. Shelby D. Hunt, *A General Theory of Competition* (Thousand Oaks, CA: Sage Publications, 2000), 67–68.

5. Kathleen Kerwin, "GM: It's Time to Face the Future," *Business Week*, July 27, 1998, 28.

6. Alex Taylor, "GM Tries to Woo Skeptics with Food and Chardonnay," *Fortune*, July 24, 2000, 52.

7. "Business and Finance," *Wall Street Journal*, June 18, 1999, A1; Joe Miller, "Wait Until Next Year: Deal Dodges Tough Issues," *Automotive News*, August 3, 1998, 46.

8. Louis E. Boone and David L. Kurtz, *Contemporary Marketing*, 10th edition (Fort Worth, TX: Harcourt College Publishers, 2001), 188.

9. Boone and Kurtz, 414.

10. Dina El-Boghdady, "Chrysler Recalls 2.5M Minivans," *Detroit News*, August 17, 1999, A1; "Chrysler Leads U.S. Safety Recalls," *Financial Post*, October 8, 1998, 22.

11. *Consumer Reports Annual Auto Issue*, April 2000.

12. Earle Eldridge, "Minivan Buyers Just Can't Get Enough of Honda Odyssey," *USA Today*, April 24, 2000, 1B.

13. These facts are from Patti Bond, "CEO Says Ace's Dealer Cooperative Must Improve or Fail to Big Boxes," *Atlanta Journal and Constitution*, April 8, 2000, G3; Jennifer Goldblatt, "Hard Times. TruServ Hardware Cooperative Struggles to Recover from Recent Merger," *Virginian-Pilot*, July 23, 2000, D1.

14. Patricia Wen, "Fit to Be Tied: Office Casual-Dress Policies Sparking a Backlash," *Boston Globe*, July 28, 2000, A1.

15. Louise Lee, "Can Levi's Be Cool Again?," *Business Week*, March 13, 2000, 144–148.

16. George Stalk, Philip Evans, and Lawrence E. Shulman, "Competing on Capabilities: The New Rules of Corporate Strategy," *Harvard Business Review*, 70 (March–April 1992), 57–69.

17. Michael Treacy and Fred Wiersema, *The Discipline of Market Leaders* (Reading, MA: Addison-Wesley Publishing, 1995).

18. http://www.airborne.com.

19. Fast facts from http://www.homedepot.com.

Chapter 4

1. Wayne Clark, "Finding the Training Ground," *Black Enterprise*, 30 (September 1999), 144–150.

2. Judy Strauss and Raymond Frost, *E-Marketing*, 2nd edition (Upper Saddle River, NJ: Prentice Hall, 2001).

3. Strauss and Frost, 243–244.

4. Karl-Heinz Sebastian and Ralph Niederdrenk, "Strategic Purchasing Will Turn Buyer–Seller Confrontation into Cooperation," *Marketing News*, September 15, 1997, 4.

5. Greg Farrell, "Will Dealers Stand by Firestone? Some Profess Loyalty While Others Hesitate," *USA Today*, October 16, 2000, 4B.

6. This quote taken from http://www.fordvehicles.com/cars/windstar/.

7. Taken from the "About Sears" section at http://www.sears.com.

8. These facts are from Avital Louria Hahn, "Barnes&Noble.com Gearing Up to Pose a Threat to Amazon," *The Investment Dealer's Digest*, September 25, 2000, 1; and Randall E. Stross, "Why Barnes & Noble May Crush Amazon," *Fortune*, September 29, 1997, 248–250.

Chapter 5

1. Judy Strauss and Raymond Frost, *E-Marketing*, 2nd edition (Upper Saddle River, NJ: Prentice Hall, 2001), 285–286.

2. Strauss and Frost, 283–284.

3. Strauss and Frost, 282.

4. This material is adapted from Valarie A. Zeithaml, A. Parasuraman, and Leonard L. Berry, *Delivering Quality Service* (New York: The Free Press, 1990).

5. Strauss and Frost, 287.

6. Linda Rosencrance, "FTC Warns Online Retailers to Fulfill Shipping Promises," *Computerworld*, November 27, 2000, 7.

7. Valarie A. Zeithaml, "Consumer Perceptions of Price, Quality, and Value: A Means–End Model and Synthesis of Evidence," *Journal of Marketing* 52 (July 1988), 2–22.

8. Bernard J. Mullin, Stephen Hardy, and William A. Sutton, *Sports Marketing*, 2nd edition (Champaign, IL: Human Kinetics, 2001), 14.

9. Charles W. Lamb, Jr., Joseph F. Hair, Jr., and Carl McDaniel, *Marketing*, 3rd edition (Cincinnati, OH: South-Western College Publishing, 1996), 265.

10. Adapted from Strauss and Frost, 294–295.

11. Susan Fournier and David Glen Mick, "Rediscovering Satisfaction," *Journal of Marketing* 63 (October 1999), 5–23.

Chapter 6

1. "Harley-Davidson Owners Can Protect Their Bikes with Motorola CreataLink 2XT Two-Way Data Transceiver." Retrieved March 5, 2001, from the World Wide Web: http://www.newproductnews.com/npn_detail.tpl?command=search&skudata+5391&db=Products.db&News_Categories=Product.

2. Peter Elstrom, "This Cat Keeps on Purring," *Business Week*, January 20, 1997, 82, 84.

3. Sue Zesiger, "It's a Car. It's a 4X4. It's a Benz." *Fortune*, September 29, 1997, 310–311.

4. Joan O'C. Hamilton, "Brighter Days at Clorox," *Business Week*, June 16, 1997, 62, 65.

5. Almar LaTour, "Want to Find Your Teenage Daughter? New Mobile-Phone Service Will Do It." *Wall Street Journal*, August 31, 2000, B9.

6. New Products Management for the 1980s (New York: Booz, Allen & Hamilton, 1982), 14.

7. Anthony Bianco, with William C. Symonds, "Gulfstream's Pilot," *Business Week*, April 14, 1997, 64–76.

8. Christopher P. Power, Kathleen Kerwin, Ronald Grover, Keith Alexander, and Robert D. Hof, "Flops: Too Many New Products Fail," *Adweek's Marketing Week*, November 5, 1990, 20, 24.

9. Ron Lieber, "Boing," *Fast Company*, November 2000, 346–354.

10. Richard C. Morals, "Eau de Toilette Training," *Forbes*, October 30, 2000, 60.

11. Peter Burrows, with Geoffrey Smith and Steven V. Brull, "HP Pictures the Future," *Business Week*, July 7, 1997, 100–109.

12. Joan O'C. Hamilton, "Brighter Days at Clorox," *Business Week*, June 16, 1997, 62, 65.

13. "Chrysler's Eagle Faces Extinction," *Marketing News*, July 21, 1997, 12.

14. Nicole Harris, "Home Depot: Beyond Do-It-Yourselfers," *Business Week*, June 30, 1997, 86–88.

15. Louise I. Driben, "The Service Edge," *Sales and Marketing Management*, June 1993, 80–84.

16. Christopher H. Lovelock, *Services Marketing*, 2nd edition (Englewood Cliffs, NJ: Prentice-Hall, 1991), 248–249.

17. J. Paul Peter and James H. Donnelly, Jr., *A Preface to Marketing Management*, 6th edition (Burr Ridge, IL: Richard D. Irwin, 1994), 225.

18. "The World's Greatest Brands," *Interbrand*, 1998.

19. Jennifer Gilbert, "When Brands Get Burned," *Business2.com*, January 23, 2001, 62.

Chapter 7

1. Charles Slack, "Spies Help Web Sellers Track Their Rivals," *Investors Business Daily*, October 23, 2000; RivalWatch Web site: RivalWatch.com; Cheryl Rosen, "Online Service Keeps an Eye on the Competition," Informationweek.com, October 16, 2000; and "Corporate Espionage: The Latest Net Snoop Keeps Tabs on Competitors," *Business2.0*, November 28, 2000.

2. The discussion in this section is based on Michael H. Shenkman, *Value and Strategy: Competing Successfully in the Nineties* (New York: Quorum Books, 1992); and Valarie A. Zeithaml, "Consumer Perceptions of Price, Quality, and Value: A Means–End Model and Synthesis of Evidence," *Journal of Marketing* 52 (July 1988), 2–22.

3. Peter Coy, "A Revolution in Pricing? Not Quite," *Business Week*, November 20, 2000, 48–49, with commentary by Timothy J. Mullandy, 49.

Chapter 8

1. Marcia Jedd, "Returns Happen," *Inbound Logistics*, February 2000, 22–30; and in the same issue, "Old-Fashioned Service with a Modern Twist," 26; and The Return Store Web site at http://www.thereturnstore.com.

2. Leslie H. Harps, "The Haves and the Have Nots," Supply Chain Best Practices for the New Millennium," *Inbound Logistics*, January 2000, 75–94.

3. Leslie H. Harps. "CEOs in the Know," *Inbound Logistics*, June 1999, 30–34.

4. Harps, "The Haves and the Have Nots."

5. Harps, "CEOs in the Know."

6. Lisa Harrington, "How to Join the Supply Chain Revolution," *Inbound Logistics*, November 1995, 21.

7. Robert Dawson, *Secrets of Power Negotiation*, 2nd edition (Franklin Lakes, NJ: Career Press, 1999).

8. *Category Management Report*, © 1995 by the Joint Industry Project on Efficient Consumer Response.

9. *Category Management Report*.

10. Michael Levy and Barton A. Weitz, *Retailing Management*, 2nd edition (Chicago: Richard D. Irwin, 1995), 48.

11. Leslie H. Harps, "EuroLogistics," *Inbound Logistics*, August 2000, 44–53.

12. Deborah C. Ruriana, "The WorldSpy Mission," *Inbound Logistics*, May 1999, 48–51.

13. Todd Carter, "Choosing and E-Fulfillment Services Provider," *Inbound Logistics*, July 2000, 73.

14. Jedd, "Returns Happen"; and Harps, "EuroLogistics."

15. Press Release from the Alliance Against Counterfeiting and Piracy, "New Cross-Industry Alliance Calls for Government to Combat Counterfeiting and Piracy," July 8, 1999.

16. Bert Rosenbloom, *Marketing Channels: A Management View* (Hinsdale, IL: Dryden, 1991), 103.

Chapter 9

1. Pat Wechsler, "A Curiously Strong Campaign: How Leo Burnett Turned an Obscure Breath Mint into a Fad," *Business Week*, April 21, 1997, 134.

2. Terence A. Shimp, Advertising and Promotion: Supplemental Aspects of Integrated Marketing Communications, 5th edition (Fort Worth, TX: Dryden Press, 2000), 17–22.

3. Robert Johnson, "Ad-Packed TVs May Soon Be Boarding City Buses," *Wall Street Journal*, February 21, 2001, B1, B2.

4. "Ad Spending Doesn't Equal Brand Awareness," http://cyberatlas.internet.com/markets/advertising June 29, 2000 (accessed February 27, 2001).

5. Theresa Howard, "John Hancock Ads Reflect Real Life," *USA Today*, December 11, 2000.

6. Lisa Guberniack, "Hancock Ad Raises Alarm in Adoption Community," *Wall Street Journal*, September 14, 2000, B1.

7. "How to Tackle the High Cost of Super Bowl Advertising," http://www.superbowlspot.com/pitch.html, January 19, 2001.

8. Beth Snyder Bulik and June Hodges, "Dot.com Hits and Bombs, *Business2.0*, January 9, 2001, 60.

9. http://www.pets.com, accessed January 19, 2001.

10. Xueming Luo, "Measuring Advertising Spending Inefficiency: A Comparison of Data Envelopment Analysis and Stochastic Frontier." 2001 AMA Winter Educators' Conference: Marketing Theory and Applications (Ram Krishnan and Madhu Viswanathan, editors), 4–5.

11. "The Stadium Effect." Study conducted by Business Week Online, reported in *Business Week*, February 2, 2001, 12.

12. Ben & Jerry's Homemade, Inc. News Release, http://lib.benjerry.com, February 22, 1999.

13. Gregory Hiesler, "The Radical: Carly Fiorina's Bold Management Experiment at HP," *BusinessWeek*, February 19, 2001, 70–80.

14. William C. Moncrief, Emin Babakus, David W. Cravens, and Mark W. Johnston, "Gender Differences in Sales Organizations." *Journal of Business Research* 49(3) (September 2000), 245–257.

15. Laurel Wentz, "Global Village," *Advertising Age*, June 1, 2000, 8.

Chapter 10

1. Orville C. Walker, Jr., and Robert W. Ruekert, "Marketing's Role in the Implementation of Business Strategies: A Critical Review and Conceptual Framework," *Journal of Marketing* 51 (July 1987), 15–33.

2. Frank V. Cespedes, *Organizing and Implementing the Marketing Effort* (Reading, MA: Addison-Wesley, 1991), 19.

3. Robert Howard, "Values Make the Company: An Interview with Robert Haas," *Harvard Business Review* 68 (September–October 1990), 132–144.

4. Michael D. Hartline, James G. Maxham, III, and Daryl O. McKee, "Corridors of Influence in the Dissemination of Customer-Oriented Strategy to Customer-Contact Service Employees," *Journal of Marketing* 64 (April 2000), 35–50.

5. Hartline, Maxham, and McKee.

6. Cespedes, 622–623.

7. Robert W. Ruekert, Orville C. Walker, Jr., and Kenneth J. Roering, "The Organization of Marketing Activities: A Contingency Theory of Structure and Performance," *Journal of Marketing* 49 (Winter 1985), 13–25.

8. Hartline, Maxham, and McKee.

9. Michael Hammer and James Champy, *Reengineering the Corporation: A Manifesto for Business Revolution* (New York: Harper Business, 1993), 35.

10. Myron Glassman and Bruce McAfee, "Integrating the Personnel and Marketing Functions: The Challenge of the 1990s," *Business Horizons* 35 (May–June 1992), 52–59.

11. Michael D. Hartline and O. C. Ferrell, "Service Quality Implementation: The Effects of Organizational Socialization and Managerial Actions on Customer-Contact Employee Behaviors," *Marketing Science Institute Working Paper Series*, Report No. 93–122, (Cambridge, MA: Marketing Science Institute, 1993).

12. Michael Levy and Barton A. Weitz, *Retailing Management* 4th edition (Boston: McGraw-Hill, 2001), 113–120.

13. Richard L. Oliver and Erin Anderson, "An Empirical Test of the Consequences of Behavior- and Outcome-Based Sales Control Systems," *Journal of Marketing* 58 (October 1994), 53–67.

14. Hartline, Maxham, and McKee.

15. FedEx Corporation, http://www.fedex.com.

16. Jeanne M. Plas, *Person-Centered Leadership: An American Approach to Participatory Management* (Thousand Oaks, CA: Sage Publications, 1996).

17. The material in this section has been adapted from L. J. Bourgeois III and David R. Brodwin, "Strategic Implementation: Five Approaches to an Elusive Phenomenon," *Strategic Management Journal* 5 (1984), 241–264; and Steven W. Floyd and Bill Wooldridge, "Managing Strategic Consensus: The Foundation of Effective Implementation," *Academy of Management Executive* 6 (November 1992), 27–39.

18. Cliff Edwards, "'Campaign 55' Flop Shows Growing Power of Franchises," *Marketing News*, July 7, 1997, 9.

19. Bourgeois and Brodwin.

20. Hartline, Maxham, and McKee.

21. Nigel F. Piercy, *Market-Led Strategic Change* (Stoneham, MA: Butterworth-Heinemann, 1992).

22. Piercy.

23. Glassman and McAfee.

24. Howard.

25. Hartline and Ferrell, "Service Quality Implementation."

26. This section is based on material from Hartline, Maxham, and McKee; and Bernard J. Jaworski, "Toward a Theory of Marketing Control: Environmental Context, Control Types, and Consequences," *Journal of Marketing* 52 (July 1988), 23–39.

27. Michael D. Hartline and O. C. Ferrell, "The Management of Customer-Contact Service Employees: An Empirical Investigation," *Journal of Marketing* 60 (October 1996), 52–70.

28. Hartline and Ferrell, "The Management of Customer-Contact Service Employees."

29. Hartline and Ferrell, "The Management of Customer-Contact Service Employees"; and Brian P. Niehoff, Cathy A. Enz, and Richard A. Grover, "The Impact of Top-Management Actions on Employee Attitudes and Perceptions," *Group & Organization Studies* 15 (September 1990), 337–352.

30. Ben M. Enis and Stephen J. Garfein, "The Computer-Driven Marketing Audit," *Journal of Management Inquiry* (December 1992), 306–318; and Philip Kotler, William Gregor, and William Rodgers, "The Marketing Audit Comes of Age," *Sloan Management Review* 30 (Winter 1989), 49–62.

31. Jaworski.

32. Jaworski.

33. Hartline, Maxham, and McKee.

34. Hartline and Ferrell, "Service Quality Implementation."

Appendix B

1. "New Car Preview," *Consumer Reports*, April 2000.

2. Nancy Shepherdson, "New Kids on the Lot," *American Demographics*, January 2000.

3. 2000 Nissan Xterra, *Edmund's Review*, http://www.edmunds.com.

4. David Kiley, "A New Set of Wheels," *American Demographics*, August 1999.

5. William J. Cook, "Size Doesn't Matter," *U.S. News & World Report*, April 19, 1999, 51.